THE PALACES OF
CRETE

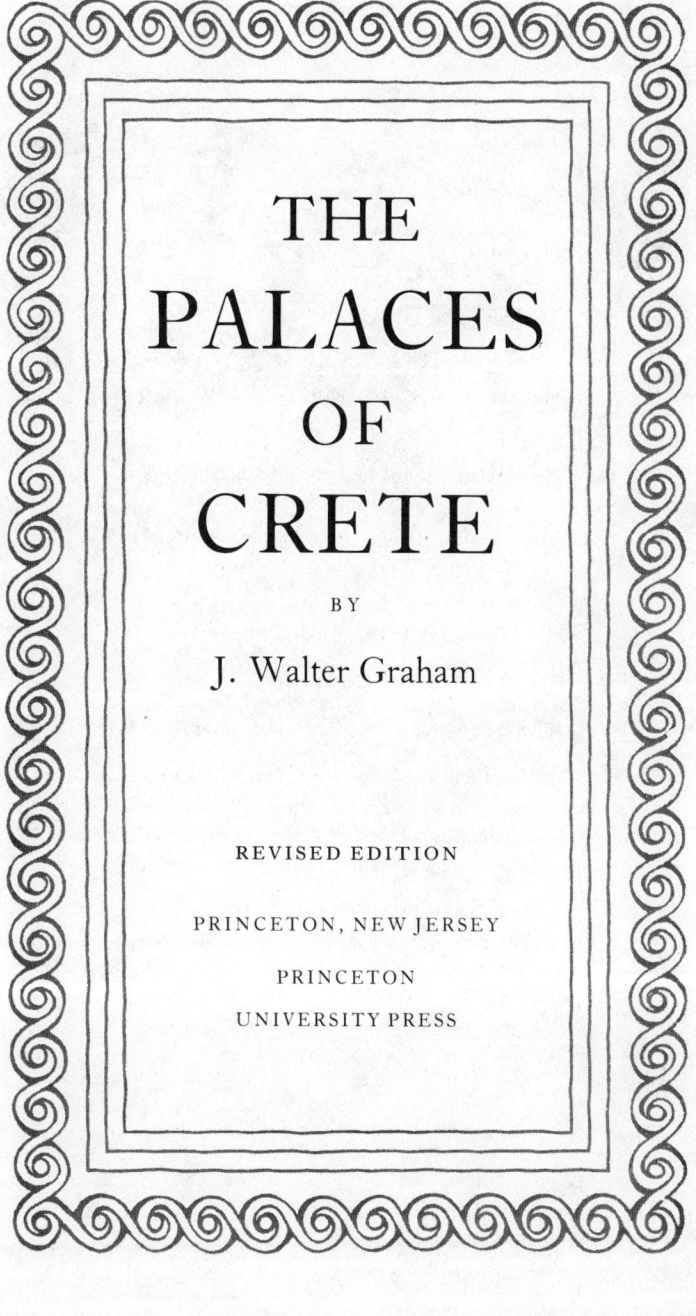

THE
PALACES
OF
CRETE

BY

J. Walter Graham

REVISED EDITION

PRINCETON, NEW JERSEY

PRINCETON
UNIVERSITY PRESS

Published by Princeton University Press, 41 William Street,
Princeton, New Jersey 08540

In the United Kingdom: Princeton University Press,
Guildford, Surrey

Copyright © 1962, 1969, 1987 by Princeton University Press

First Princeton Paperback printing, with revisions, 1987

LCC 85-43376

ISBN 0-691-03585-7   ISBN 0-691-00216-9 (pbk.)

Printed in the United States of America by
Princeton University Press, Princeton, New Jersey

PREFACE

THE STORY OF Minoan Crete is as new as the twentieth century. Much of importance doubtless remains to be discovered, and much that archaeologists have unearthed they have as yet failed to publish fully in scientific reports. It is not surprising therefore that students of Minoan architecture have hesitated to attempt to present a comprehensive account of the dwellings of the Bronze Age Cretans.

Yet the attempt cannot be postponed indefinitely. And surely the efforts of two generations of such outstanding scholars as Evans, Pernier, Hazzidakis, Chapouthier, Mrs. Hawes, and their successors, should make it possible, by a careful comparison of similar features wherever they occur, to determine with considerable clarity what is truly typical in Minoan architecture. Likewise by combining every clue which the large number of excavated ruins now makes available, we may endeavor to go a little further in reconstructing in imagination even those important parts of the palaces of which there exist little or no actual remains; but we must constantly remember that for the stability even of "castles in the air," firm foundations are an essential requirement.

In this volume, which it is hoped will prove of interest to the layman and prospective visitor to Crete, as well as to the scholar, footnotes and other scholarly paraphernalia have been kept to a minimum. This has been facilitated by publishing the more complex problems in a series of fully detailed and documented discussions in the *American Journal of Archaeology* (which I have been permitted to draw upon freely) between 1956 and 1961 (see Bibliography), and to these the specialist reader is referred for further information.

The viewpoint of the study is architectural. The first chapter is intended as an introduction for the general reader, and whatever the individual specialist may think of the views of the chronology and history of the Minoan civilization there outlined (a very controversial subject at the moment), these have very little bearing on the conclusions reached in the following chapters. It is on the form of the houses and palaces presented in their final, pre-destruction, phase that I have concentrated; we are not, I think, ready at present to attempt to trace the evolution of Minoan architecture and to relate it closely to the political or social history of the period.[1] Nor are we yet in a position, I believe, to assess the influence of foreign architectures on the development of the Cretan palace, in spite of the confident assertions recently made by several distinguished archaeologists.

With but one or two exceptions all the photographs reproduced in this volume were taken by the author during visits to the island in 1955 and 1959. These trips were made possible by grants from the American Philosophical Society and the University of Toronto, together with a senior fellowship awarded by the Canada Council; to these institutions I express my sincere thanks.

The many individuals to whom I am grateful for assistance in various ways include Professors John L. Caskey and Henry Robinson, the former and the present director of the American School of Classical Studies at Athens, Eugene Vanderpool of the same institution, Nikolaos Platon, the ephor of Cretan Antiquities, and Stylianos Alexiou, now the ephor for Western Crete; and many others connected with the Cretan Antiquities Service, especially Emmanuelis Phigetakis of Siteia, Alexandros Venetikos at Phaistos, Manolis Katsoulis at Mallia, and Eleutherios Synadinakis at Arkhanes. Officials of the British, French, and Italian Schools have also been most helpful, particularly Misses Luisa Banti and Carla Gerra, and Messrs. Hood, Piet de Jong,

---

[1] Ludwika Press has shown what can be done along this line in two articles cited under his name in the Bibliography.

Levi, Courbin, Daux, Demargne, and Dessenne; and I am grateful for the permission to photograph and to measure freely at the various sites controlled by these Schools, and to draw on their published plans and illustrations for publication. My indebtedness for particular figures is listed at the end of the book, but I am especially glad to be able to reproduce, I believe for the first time, though unfortunately not in the original colors, two of the excellent restorations recently done by Piet de Jong in cooperation with Platon, and now exhibited in the Herakleion Museum (Figs. 44, 45). I am also greatly indebted to the interest of Prof. Hugo-Brunt of the Division of Town-Planning in the University of Toronto, which led him to make for me the axonometric restoration of the Palace of Phaistos, Fig. 55. Miss Frances Brittain, of the staff of the Royal Ontario Museum, has taken great pains in doing the final versions of three of the restored drawings: the perspective of the Palace of Mallia (Fig. 58), that of House Da at Mallia (Fig. 21), and the west entrance of the Palace of Phaistos (Fig. 48). I am likewise grateful to my wife, my daughter Margaret, and my son Robertson for their assistance during the six pleasant weeks we toured the far corners of Crete in our "Volvo" station-wagon in the spring of 1959, and especially to my wife for her criticisms and helpfulness at all stages of my work. The Princeton University Press and particularly Miss Harriet Anderson have always been most encouraging, and Mrs. E. B. Smith, through whose capable hands have passed first the *AJA* articles, and afterwards, as copy editor, the text of this book, has suggested many improvements in the style. To include all these in my thanks is not to incriminate them for the shortcomings that remain.

Prof. Spyridon Marinatos' recent book, *Crete and Mycenae,* with its magnificent plates by Prof. Max Hirmer, only became available to me in the last stages of my work. Most of the translations from Homer are from Lang, Leaf, and Myers' *Iliad,* and Butcher and Lang's *Odyssey*; a few (so marked) are from Rieu's translation in the Pelican Series.

L. R. Palmer's *Mycenaeans and Minoans,* so important for the history and chronology of the Late Bronze Age, appeared when my book was already in proof (Nov. 1961), and I have made no changes in the text of Chapter I. His views, which are based on first-hand knowledge only in the philological field (though he has been careful to consult archaeological authority), do not alter my conviction (1) that there is no significant relationship between the supposedly Luvian palace at Beycesultan and the Minoan palaces, and (2) that architecturally the Palace of Minos remained essentially Minoan (not Mycenaean) down to its last days. Whether there is any valid evidence for the presence of Greeks at Knossos in the half century before 1400—an idea largely (but not wholly) based on the assumption that the Linear B tablets found there were LM II—should be carefully reconsidered (see Chapter I, note 16); I agree with Prof. Palmer that historically it would be much simpler to suppose that the Greeks first invaded Crete about 1400 B.C.

For reasons largely of economy, references within the book are made by chapter and section rather than by page; more exact references can usually be found by consulting the full index. Except for a few well-Anglicized forms like Athens and Mycenae, Greek names have been transliterated directly; the *delta* of modern place-names has, however, been represented by "dh" (pronounced like "th" in "there").

It should be noted, especially by those who use the book at the sites, that detailed descriptions of special rooms or architectural features (such as the "Grand Staircase" at Knossos) may appear in chapters other than those presenting the general description of the building (Chs. II, III). Such descriptions can be located through the Index.

J.W.G.

University of Toronto

ADDENDUM TO THE PREFACE

WHILE the original edition of *The Palaces of Crete* was still in the press, a new palace was discovered by the then Director of Cretan Antiquities, Nikolaos Platon, at the extreme east end of the island near a tiny hamlet called Kato Zakro, in an area considered most unlikely for a palace in view of the very limited amount of arable land in that part of the island (below, p. 4).

The excavations, conducted with great care and skill, are still in progress, and apparently a considerable area of the palace remains to be uncovered. The palace was destroyed, according to Platon (*Ancient Crete*, p. 167), about 1450 B.C. as a result of the cataclysmic eruption of Thera (below, p. 11); and the destruction evidently came so rapidly that the inhabitants abandoned almost everything in their haste to escape, and never returned to reclaim their lost possessions. Platon has consequently discovered vast amounts of stone and clay vessels as well as many other objects of fine quality in various parts of the ruins, and these often provide valuable clues as to the original function of the rooms in which they were found. Some of the finest of these treasures have been put on display by Alexiou in one of the galleries of the great museum at Herakleion, and photos in color and in black and white have now been published in Platon's recent book, *Crete*, and in an even more recent volume, *Ancient Crete*, to which Platon has contributed a valuable chapter about Kato Zakro (see bibliography, p. 250, under Alexiou).

From the standpoint of the present volume it is the architecture of the new palace that offers the most interest, particularly because it affords an opportunity to check some of the theories put forward in the original edition of this book on the basis of the evidence then available at Knossos, Phaistos, Mallia, and Gournia.

Until Platon has finished the excavation and publication of the palace at Kato Zakro, any description must be very incomplete and entirely provisional. But certain features are already clear, as its excavator has pointed out. In size, the new palace, when fully excavated, will probably be comparable to the palaces at Phaistos and Mallia (*Anc. Crete*, p. 164). The general layout would also appear to be very similar, for it is built around the four sides of a large oblong central court whose long axis lies a little more northeast to southwest than the fairly strictly north-south oriented courts of the other palaces. Similar also is the concentration of the main public rooms in the large block of rooms to the west (or southwest) of the court, but different is their location on the ground-floor level, just off the court, rather than in the Piano Nobile. This promises to be a very useful point of difference for it means that these important public halls will be, in comparison with the vanished halls of the Piano Nobile of the other palaces, well preserved both in form and in contents. Whether there was any important series of rooms on the upper storey to the west of the court at Zakro seems at present uncertain; we can only await Platon's further investigations.

One of these ground-floor rooms at Zakro (xxix) at the southwest corner of the court, Platon has identified, on the strength of finding in it a number of wine jars and jugs, as a dining-room (*Anc. Crete*, p. 166 and plan p. 165). But the real Banquet Hall seems to have been situated, just as at Phaistos and Mallia, in the storey above a large ground-floor room (xxxii) at the northwest corner of the central court. The identification is suggested by the resemblance of xxxii to the similarly situated ground-floor rooms at Phaistos and Mallia in size and shape and in the rough bases which indicate the presence of two rows of (wooden?) pillars, three in each row, directly above which in the upper storey the presence of two rows of three columns each may fairly be postulated. The similarity with Mallia is especially close because, in each instance, access to the Banquet Hall was gained by way of a two-flight stairway leading up from the rear of a portico on the north side of the central court. But it is the nature of the contents of room xxxii and of the small rooms under and around the stairway that clinches the identification. In one corner of xxxii was found "an enormous cooking-pot still standing in the ashes of the fireplace," while "two small adjoining rooms were full of cooking-pots and kitchen utensils" (*Anc. Crete*, pp. 166f).

Even more recently, the publication of the palace at Pylos on the Greek mainland, destroyed about 1200 B.C., has permitted the identification of a remarkably similar Banquet Hall. Its resemblance in plan to the one at Mallia is particularly close, while the discovery of masses of crockery and miscellaneous pieces of cooking apparatus in the adjacent rooms parallels the evidence of Kato Zakro. This new evidence has led me slightly to modify the suggested plan of the Banquet Halls in the second storey at Phaistos and Mallia, as explained in *AJA* 71 (1967), pp. 353-360.

Another new suggestion put forward in the original edition of *The Palaces of Crete* that has been confirmed by the evidence of the new palace, is the use of a foot as the unit of linear measurement, a foot with the approximate value of 30.36 cm. (below, pp. 222-229) and possibly divided into twelve parts (*Second International Cretological Conference* I, pp. 157-165). At Phaistos and Mallia the central courts were both interpreted as having been laid out to be 170 Minoan feet long by 80 feet wide, but, especially in the former, there were slight uncertainties about these measurements, and the number 170 may also have seemed a somewhat odd choice. But about the Kato Zakro central court there can be no doubt whatever since it can be closely measured between well-preserved wall faces. The east to west dimension varies, according to my measurements (which Platon kindly allowed me to make), from 12.03 m. near the south end to 12.15 m. at the north end. Forty Minoan feet would be 12.14 m. The north to south length, also on my own measurement, is approximately 30.30 m.; 30.36 m. would be the theoretical value for 100 Minoan feet. Surely then the determination can no longer be in doubt and the result is of very considerable significance for our understanding of the way in which the palaces were planned (below, pp. 222-229). So long as there existed any reasonable doubt regarding the unit of measurement used by the Minoan architects, my theories of palace-planning in terms of round numbers of feet could not fail to appear somewhat problematical; the new evidence puts the theory on a far sounder footing. It will be difficult, in the future, to maintain that the palaces of Crete were haphazard labyrinths; in fact such a view will run counter to the clear evidence of the ruins themselves.

In a recent article the present director of Cretan antiquities, Stylianos Alexiou (*Kret. Chron.* 17, 1963, pp. 339-351) identifies certain tall vertical architectural members seen on several stone vases, mural paintings, etc., and what I spoke of as an "odd form of capital" (below, p. 196), as masts or banner poles held in place against the walls by rectangular cleats or "tie-blocks" as I have suggested terming them in English. Alexiou's interpretation has much to recommend it and I have therefore suggested in an unpublished article a modification of my restoration of the north end of the central court at Phaistos (Fig. 50). Instead of two ranges of half columns on either side of the central doorway I would now propose to restore two banner poles held firmly against the wall, probably at the level of the bottom of the third storey, by a pair of large cleats or tie-blocks. Alexiou's idea about the banner poles was suggested by the form of the New Kingdom Egyptian temple pylons, and the general resemblance of the façade at Phaistos, if so restored, to such a pylon is obvious.

Finally, I should like to mention that the very competent young American architect-archaeologist, Joseph W. Shaw, who has worked with the University of Chicago expedition at Cenchraeae on the isthmus of Corinth and with Platon at Kato Zakro, for whom he has drawn the plans of that palace during several campaigns, has undertaken to study the materials and techniques used in Minoan architecture as the subject of a doctoral dissertation at the University of Pennsylvania. Such a study is badly needed, and Mr. Shaw seems admirably qualified for the task.

University of Toronto   J.W.G.
October 1968

PREFACE TO 1987 EDITION

THE CONTINUED DEMAND for *Palaces of Crete* that has led to the preparation of this new edition (first edition, 1962) indicates a lively interest in these structures which mark the beginnings of monumental European architecture. Unfortunately even though nearly twenty years have passed the time still does not seem ripe to attempt to trace the chronological development of Minoan architecture inasmuch as what little is left of the early stages of the palaces still lies hidden beneath their later remains, and what has been brought to light is still woefully insufficient to produce a comprehensive and unambiguous account. To date, the most ambitious attempt to investigate the earlier phases of the palaces is that of the veteran Italian archaeologist, Professor Doro Levi; but even at Phaistos only a small part of the original building or buildings could be revealed and published.

I shall attempt, then, to describe the palaces as they appeared in the final and most splendid period of their existence, i.e. about 1700-1450 B.C., basing the account on the actual remains but not hesitating to endeavor to conjure up those parts of the buildings that formed part of the now missing upper storeys, especially if they seem to represent significant aspects of the palace functionally or architecturally.

So many new archaeological discoveries have been made, or older ones published during the last two decades, that many sections of this book might be the better for a complete rewriting. Since that has not been possible, we hope that the usefulness of the book may be recovered by incorporating in the text numerous major or minor corrections or amplifications; by bringing the Bibliography up to date; by revising the Analytical Index to include the new additions; and by improving and increasing the number of illlustrations to represent the recent discoveries. Where additions could not be introduced without disturbing the pagination, the material has been put in six Addenda at the end of the text.

One very important aspect of Minoan architecture and building which I have treated in a single chapter (VIII), has now been properly studied and published by my colleague, Professor J. W.

Shaw, in his *Minoan Architecture: Materials and Techniques*, Rome, 1973 (*Annuario della Scuola Archeologica di Atene* 33, 1971), abbreviated to *M. and T.* In a recent article (see Select Bibliography, 1980) Shaw has discussed the interesting topic of the orientation of the palaces. He suggests that the east-west axis might be the controlling factor in the planning of the palaces rather than the north-south. The most important piece of evidence favoring his view is offered by the remains of a four-legged table-altar(?) located in the exact center of the Central Court at Mallia, since an east-west line extended westward through this altar would exactly bisect the interval between two cult pillars—each bearing common Minoan cult symbols, especially the double-ax—on the long axis of a cult room that corresponds closely in its position with the East and West Pillar Crypts at Knossos.

My acknowledgments and thanks expressed in the Preface to the first edition still stand. In recent years I have profited particularly by discussions with Nikolaos Platon, Stylianos Alexiou, Sinclair Hood, Joseph Shaw, and my wife, with whom I have made many enjoyable journeys in the lovely island of Crete "in the midst of the wine-dark sea." I am particularly grateful to Mrs. Giuliana Bianco for her skill and patience in redrawing several of my figures (Figs. 3, 6, 50, 58, 87-88, 159). My thanks are also due to J. W. Shaw for his plan of the Northwest Entrance at Knossos (Fig. 158) and to Sinclair Hood and the British School for permission to use it.

Anyone using the book, especially at the sites, should bear it in mind that individual features at particular sites, such as the Grand Staircase at Knossos (Chapter II, Section 1), may be further described in the section dealing specifically with such features, in this instance with staircases in general (Chapter X, Section 1); the index should be consulted to bring together such related material. It is hardly necessary to point out that Chapter I is intended as an introduction for the general reader.

Toronto   J.W.G.

CONTENTS

CONTENTS

CONTENTS

THE PALACES OF
CRETE

THE LAND, THE PEOPLE, AND THE HISTORY OF MINOAN CRETE

There is a land called Crete in the midst of the wine-dark sea, a fair land and a rich, begirt with water, and therein are many men innumerable, and ninety cities.—(ODYSSEY, 19, 172-174)

SUCH was Crete when Homer sang, nearly three thousand years ago, when the island was still heavily forested with cypress, and when the fertile earth still supported a teeming population.

But even by Homer's day the memory had already grown dim of a time, little more than half a millennium earlier, when Crete had enjoyed a prosperity eclipsing anything in the Aegean area, and could boast a civilization rivaling that of its contemporary, New Kingdom Egypt. Today, the forests have vanished through most of the island, the fertility of the valleys has diminished, and the ninety "cities" have mostly shrunk to small towns.[1] Yet the island is still beautiful. Along its hundreds of miles of rocky shores and gleaming sand beaches the clear blue waters of the Mediterranean still break in white surf, and never is one far from sight or sound of the sea (Figs. 35, 63), for the island is nowhere more than thirty-six miles (58 km.) in width (Fig. 1).

Rugged mountains stretch almost continuously from east to west the entire 160 miles (250 km.) of its length, and allow no room even for a road along much of the nearly harborless south coast. The White Mountains in the west (Fig. 34), traversed by spectacular gorges, leave scant space for man except for a

---

[1] Paul Faure, "La Crète aux cent villes," *Kret. Chron.*, 13 (1959), pp. 171-217.

few small plains along the north coast where the present capital, Khanea, is located; and somewhere in its neighborhood, still undiscovered, lay the important Minoan city of Kydonia with its palace. The range of Ida reaches heights of over 8000 feet (2500 m.) in the center of the island (Fig. 51); but since Crete is wider here, room is left for a considerable plain on the north, where lies Herakleion (Fig. 36), the largest city, with a population of about 40,000, and for a much larger and more fertile valley in the south, the Messara (Fig. 46). It is no accident that in Minoan times Crete's greatest cities, Knossos and Phaistos, were situated in these two plains. East of Ida the range of Dikte, over 7000 feet (2150 m.), encloses the high plain of Lasithi, possibly the site, at Plati, of a Minoan palace (Fig. 30); today it is famous for its potatoes and for the ten thousand windmills that pump water to the thirsty fields in summer. In a coastal plain to the north lies the third largest known palace, that of Mallia (Fig. 56). Across the low isthmus of Hierapetra the mountains stage one final grand upheaval before they slip down steeply into the sea at the east end of the island. The coastal road from Hagios Nikolaos on the Gulf of Mirabello, at the north end of the isthmus, to Siteia near the northeast tip of the island, is one of the most spectacular in Crete. Far below, for much of the way, the two tiny islets of Mochlos and Pseira, where the American archaeologist Seager dug early in the century, rise from a sea of unbelievable blues and greens. Even in the very rugged eastern end of the island an important palace was discovered in the 1960s by Nikolaos Platon at the harborage of Kato Zakros.[2]

In addition to abundant timber—especially the cypress, highly valued in ancient days for building ships and palaces—the mountains furnished plenty of limestone of good quality and, while little of the fine marble for which the mainland of Greece is famous was available, gypsum quarries supplied a

[2] Wroncka, *BCH*, 83 (1959), p. 538. A bibliography of Cretan geography is given by Philippson, *Die griechischen Landschaften, IV, Das aegäische Meer und seine Inseln* (Frankfurt am Main, 1959), pp. 353-354; but unfortunately no account of Cretan geography is given in this otherwise comprehensive survey of Greece.

handsome and easily worked stone particularly prized for decorative purposes (Fig. 125).

On the highest mountains snow lingers through much of the year (Fig. 51), but in general it is rarely very cold in winter; the latitude, 35° north, is about that of Memphis, Tennessee. In summer the sun's blazing heat, felt especially on the south side facing Africa, is usually relieved by tempering breezes from the surrounding sea. In the west there is a fair annual rainfall, but this tapers off badly toward the east and, thanks to the progressive deforestation, there is little running water during the long summer months. Spring is the botanist's paradise; even the rocky hillsides are carpeted with an amazing variety of wildflowers, many of them of diminutive size.

Though less than half the size of Lake Ontario (Fig. 1, inset) and but two-thirds that of the state of Connecticut, Crete is much the largest of the hundreds of islands that compose the Aegean archipelago, and as the nearest considerable land-mass of Europe to the ancient civilizations of Egypt and the Near East—a half-way house, as it were, between three continents—it is not surprising that it cradled the first European civilization. This historical fact is mirrored mythologically in the quaint tale of the princess of Phoenicia, bearing the significant name of Europa, who was ferried in miraculous fashion from her Asiatic homeland on the back of a handsome white bull—Zeus in bovine disguise according to Greek legend—to Crete, where she became by courtesy of the god the mother of three famous Cretan dynasts, Minos, Rhadamanthys, and Sarpedon.[3]

As early as the Neolithic Period the island was inhabited by a scattered population living partly in caves, but also concentrated at Knossos in one of the largest Neolithic settlements in the eastern Mediterranean area. Little is known of the origins of these first settlers, but the associations suggested by the pottery and other artifacts are with Anatolia and possibly Egypt rather than with the Greek mainland; considerable reinforcements seem to have arrived perhaps from the same areas about

[3] Marinatos, *RA*, 34 (1949), pp. 5-18.

the beginning of the Bronze Age, that is sometime after 3000 B.C. A recent study of place-names suggests that a considerable element in the Cretan population may have been related to the Luvians who, in the Middle and Late Bronze Ages, were established in Asia Minor southwest of the Hittites. Luvian-speaking Beycesultan has recently been partially excavated by British archaeologists led by Seton Lloyd (Fig. 1, inset).[4]

Cultural development through the third millennium (3000-2000 B.C.) was "accelerando" and the population increased and spread throughout the island in this Early Bronze or Early "Minoan" period. Sir Arthur Evans, who more than anyone else is responsible for the recovery of this forgotten civilization, devised a system of chronology into which to fit his discoveries which is still generally followed, though many have grave doubts about certain details such as the date of the beginning of Early Minoan. Here in round numbers, adequate for our purposes, is the scheme, named of course from the famous legendary king of Knossos:

Early Minoan (E.M.)	3000-2000 B.C.
Middle Minoan (M.M.)	2000-1600 B.C.
Late Minoan (L.M.)	1600-1200 B.C.

These three divisions correspond roughly to, and in fact were suggested by, Old Kingdom, Middle Kingdom, and New Kingdom Egypt, and the tentative dates are largely dependent upon lists of pharaohs and their regnal years as recorded by the Egyptians.

Little is yet known of the architecture of Crete during the Early Minoan period (Fig. 33), still less of its history, government, and religion, matters which the material remains unearthed by the archaeologist can only dimly and very imperfectly illumine.[5] The consistent improvement of pottery in quality,

[4] Mellaart, *AJA*, 62 (1958), pp. 9-33; cf. Palmer, *Mycenaeans and Minoans* (London, 1961), chap. VII, 3.

[5] On 3rd millennium architecture see K. Branigan, *Foundations of Palatial Crete* (New York, 1970), *Tombs of Mesara* (London, 1970); also P. Warren, *Myrtos: An Early Bronze Age Settlement in Crete* (London, 1972).

shape, and decoration throughout the period, however, is an index of the general cultural progress. Quantities of handsome vessels in a variety of shapes were made from beautifully veined and colored stones—a craft long practised by the Egyptians; and gold jewelry and ornaments found in E.M. graves exhibit remarkably advanced craftsmanship both in design and execution.

The significant but unspectacular developments of this "prepalatial" period may be compared to the heat which builds up unseen within a great stack of hay until it explodes spontaneously into a brilliant burst of flame. About 2000 B.C. such a "cultural explosion"—not without parallel in the history of other civilizations—occurred. At the very beginning of the Middle Minoan period fairly large and substantial palaces spring into being, and a system of writing appears. No doubt the latter was triggered by developments in Egypt where an intricate system had been in use for a millennium; yet the Cretan shows little resemblance in the form of the characters to the Egyptian and develops quite on its own into a reasonably efficient syllabic method of writing known to the archaeologist as Linear A.

But nothing, so far as the available archaeological record goes, is so eloquent of the new progress as pottery. The most significant variety is called Kamares Ware, named from a cave sanctuary on the south slopes of Mt. Ida facing Phaistos (Fig. 51), where quantities of this pottery were dedicated. The love of color and movement, so characteristic of Cretan art, is brilliantly illustrated. A common shape is a bridge-spouted, two-handled jar with a strongly swelling profile, painted in white, red, and orange against a black background (Fig. 153, A). Though resembling vegetable or animal forms, often in swirling patterns which suggest the vitality of nature, the designs are strongly formalized and excellently suited to the shape of the vase. This happy union of nature and convention is typical of Cretan art at its best, though at times the feeling becomes much more informal, and architecture is always predominantly informal.

Our knowledge of the history of the Middle Minoan period is almost as meager as that of the preceding period. Of material and artistic progress and of the growth of population there can be no doubt, and the brilliant development of the palaces and the mansions of the rich by the end of the age bears witness to a level of civilization reached by the aristocracy comparable to that found in contemporary Egypt and Mesopotamia. Such finds as Kamares pottery discovered in association with the monuments of Middle Kingdom pharaohs, a statue of an Egyptian merchant[5a] of the twelfth or thirteenth dynasty found in the Palace of Minos, a Babylonian sealstone about the time of Hammurabi in a Cretan tomb, and objects of Cretan style in the Shaft Graves of Mycenae around 1600 B.C., show that Crete was in contact with her neighbors on all sides, and incidentally provide badly needed clues for dating the development of Minoan civilization.

Cretan ships were probably responsible for most of the transferal of such goods as these to and from Crete. The scarcity of identifiable fortifications or of other signs of martial activity on the island is usually interpreted, especially in the following period (L.M.), as meaning that Crete possessed a fleet of warships with which she fended off her enemies; yet this picture of Crete as the first Mediterranean sea power, supported though it is by ancient Greek historians, is far from proven.[6] In any case it may be doubted whether Egypt or any other of the Near Eastern nations during the period 2000 to 1400 B.C. ever had the power, the opportunity, and the incentive to mount an organized naval expedition against an island so well removed from their shores as Crete.

[5a] Hardly an official, as Evans thought; see Ward, *Orientalia*, 30 (1961), pp. 28-29. On the date of the statue see Pendlebury in *Studies presented to D. M. Robinson* (ed. G. E. Mylonas, St. Louis, 1951), I, p. 189.

[6] Starr, "The Myth of the Minoan Thalassocracy," *Historia*, 3 (1954-1955), pp. 282-291, and *Origins of Greek Civilization* (New York, 1961), p. 38. However, Lionel Casson holds to the traditional view, largely on the grounds of the lack of fortifications, *The Ancient Mariners* (New York, 1959), p. 31; he also reviews the general question of Cretan relations with her neighbors (pp. 21-24). Also R. J. Buck, "The Minoan Thalassocracy Re-examined," *Historia*, 11 (1962), pp. 129-137. That battle-fleets were possible in early Late Minoan is shown by the new Theran miniature fresco.

But another growing power was closer at hand. On a clear day the mountains of western Crete can actually be seen from the southeastern tip of the Greek mainland (Fig. 1, inset), and since about 2000 B.C. the dominant element of the mainland population had been a Greek speaking people. Their descendants, the Greeks of the Classical period (first millennium B.C.), however brilliant they may have been, can scarcely be accused of having been a peaceful folk. Nor were their Bronze Age ancestors, from the first bands who conquered new homes with fire and sword at the beginning of the Middle Bronze Age to those who toward the end of the Late Bronze (thirteenth century B.C.) sacked and burned the citadel of Troy.

It is therefore not an unlikely hypothesis that a destruction of the Palace of Minos which occurred toward the end of the M.M. period, that is sometime in the early seventeenth century, was due to a piratical, sea-borne raid by the "Mycenaean" Greeks of the mainland, or, since Crete was subject to periodic devastating earthquakes, that the Greek raiders followed in the track of a severe quake which had left the Cretan cities temporarily defenceless. On this hypothesis some of the masses of gold and other treasure found by Schliemann in the royal Shaft Graves inside the citadel of Mycenae, the leading city of the mainland, would represent part of the loot. Indeed a recent ingenious theory, for which there is some evidence at the Egyptian end, goes further and suggests that the temporary shift in the balance of power between Crete and the Greek mainland was partly responsible for the expulsion of the Asiatic Hyksos from Lower Egypt where they had ruled for a century, and for the consequent founding of a new Egyptian dynasty (the eighteenth) initiating the New Kingdom. According to this theory the Hyksos had been favored by Crete (the lid of an Egyptian alabaster vessel bearing the cartouche of the Hyksos king Khyan was discovered in the ruins of the Palace of Minos), whereas the native Egyptians were now aided by the Greeks who, like the Classical Greeks a millennium later, served as mercenaries

9

in the Egyptian army. This would also help to explain the numerous traces of Egyptian (as well as Cretan) influence in the Mycenaean Shaft Grave burials.[7]

The last and the most brilliant, if not the most prosperous, phase of the Minoan civilization is that of the Late Minoan period, about 1600-1200 B.C. Extensive excavations, thousands of inscribed tablets, and numerous traditions preserved by the Classical Greeks, combine to throw a flood of light (comparatively speaking) on this period. In spite of this it is impossible at the present time even to outline with any confidence the history of the final glory, decline, and fall of the Minoan civilization, for recent happenings have thrown all the ideas about this period that seemed to be safely established back into the melting pot for reinterpretation. The following sketch, therefore, is offered with the full realization that much of it may shortly be contradicted by evidence not yet available to the writer.

Expressive of the level of refinement and culture attained in the first century of the Late Minoan period, following the rebuilding of the palaces on lines more splendid than before and the appearance of many handsome new mansions throughout the island,[8] are the beautiful naturalistic pottery styles known as the Floral (L.M. Ia) and the Marine (L.M. Ib). A magnificent example of the latter is the Octopus Vase discovered in the ruins of the modest little town of Gournia (Fig. 153, B): the Cretan potter with his Midas touch has transformed the repulsive creature of the deep into a thing of beauty, into a living pattern whose eight tentacles surround and confine the globular vase as naturally as its skin envelopes an orange. A Mycenaean Greek rendering of the same subject already displays the Classical Greek preference for symmetry and geometric form (Fig. 153, C). Both representations are beautiful, but in quite different ways.

---

[7] Cf. Schachermeyr, *Archiv Orientální*, 17² (1949), pp. 331-350.

[8] Marinatos suggests that many of these mansions, often spaced 7 to 10 miles apart, were centers of local administration, *C. and M.*, pp. 18, 66.

For all its brilliance this first phase of the new epoch was also, for most of the important centers except Knossos, virtually their final stage as well. That these flourishing cities and towns were suddenly destroyed is clear from their remains, but the cause of such a general catastrophe is less obvious. The eminent Greek archaeologist and explorer of many Cretan sites, the late Professor Spyridon Marinatos, put forward the attractive hypothesis that it was the result of a violent explosion on the island of Thera (modern Santorini) in the Aegean Sea directly north of Crete.[9] The evidence for a cataclysmic eruption in which the major part of the island disappeared in one or more gigantic blasts is clear from the excavations on Thera made by the Germans in the 1890's, and has been dated to approximately 1500 B.C. Like the catastrophic eruption of Krakatoa in the Dutch East Indies in 1883 tremendous "tidal waves" must have been generated, which Marinatos believes would have been far greater in the case of the eruption of Thera. The entire north coast of Crete, hardly more than seventy miles away, was exposed to the full force of these titanic waves.

In the Villa at Amnisos, only a few yards from the sea (Fig. 76), massive blocks of the stone foundations were found by Marinatos to have been shifted out of place, and quantities of volcanic pumice, carried in by the flood, mantled the ruins. The waves must have traveled far inland over the lower parts of the island, overwhelming many other sites including Mallia, Gournia, Nirou Khani, and Palaikastro.

Such a terrific onslaught of nature would have at least temporarily crippled the social, economic, and political life of Crete. How many tens of thousands of its inhabitants may have perished we shall never know. Since coastal communities would have been the hardest hit we may suppose that for a time Cretan contacts with its neighbors were abruptly severed. Is this the long sought origin of the Lost Island of Atlantis? According to the tale told by the Egyptians a millennium later to the

[9] *Antiquity*, 13 (1939), pp. 425-439; *C. and M.*, pp. 20, 22; *Kret. Chron.*, 4 (1950), pp. 195-213.

Greek sage, Solon, Atlantis, though a large, populous, and powerful island, in the course of a single dreadful day and night and after a series of calamitous earthquakes and inundations, disappeared forever beneath the sea.[10]

But what of the fact that other Cretan sites, surely high above the reach of the ravaging waves, were also destroyed at a perhaps slightly later date or dates, including Sklavokambos, Tylissos, and Hagia Triadha. Even the great palace at Phaistos, on its hilltop site, was destroyed sometime in the fifteenth century and never rebuilt. Was this due to the earthquakes which often follow such eruptions? Or was it the result of the Mycenaean Greeks' seizing the opportunity to invade the island when Cretan defences were down, especially if, as ancient tradition claims,[6] she depended on a navy for her protection.

The Palace of Minos, too, three miles from the sea and enclosed by high hills, seems to have been seriously damaged somewhat later still, about the year 1400 B.C.[11] Perhaps the damage to the palace at this time was not nearly so extensive, however, as its excavators have thought, and Sir Arthur Evans himself was constrained to admit that the building had been reoccupied to some extent, though in his opinion this was but a degenerate "squatter" occupation. Professor L. R. Palmer of Oxford University has lately challenged this opinion.[12] He suggests that the palace was inhabited throughout the closing centuries of the Bronze Age by a dynasty of Mycenaean Greek rulers who adapted the Minoan system of writing to suit (rather badly) their own language, and continued to keep administrative

[10] The above account was written about 1960; for a more recent comprehensive survey of the problems of Atlantis, Thera, and the destruction of Crete see J. V. Luce, *The End of Atlantis* (1969).

[11] The relative dating of the destruction of the various sites is a much disputed point; see Levi, *Boll. d'Arte*, 44 (1959), pp. 253-264.

[12] Orally, in the public press, and in multigraphed statements circulated privately; a definitive expression of his views will perhaps not be published until certain manuscript notebooks of Sir Arthur Evans and possibly others, relative to the excavations at Knossos, are published; cf. Hood, *Antiquity*, 35 (1961), pp. 80-81, for a contrary view and for bibliography. See now Palmer, *Mycenaeans and Minoans*, especially chap. VI.

records as the native Cretan kings had done before them—a practice which spread to the Greek rulers of the mainland.

Signs of the inevitable change in spirit at Knossos, due to the installation of this foreign and warlike Mycenaean dynasty, did not go entirely unobserved by Evans and others, though they interpreted them differently. Pendlebury referred to the L.M. II "Palace Style" pottery, conspicuous for its grandiose character and pompous monumentality, as the "pottery of empire";[13] significantly, this pottery has rarely been found in Crete except at Knossos, though it is common on the Greek mainland. Evans noticed similar changes in the wall paintings of the L.M. II period, illustrated for example in the stiff, symmetrical composition of the Griffin Fresco in the Knossos Throne Room (Fig. 130), which has since been found at Pylos on the mainland. "As compared with the great artistic traditions, such as characterized the preceding Palace stage . . . ," he remarks, "the new work takes a severely regulated shape. Lost is the free spirit that had given birth to the finely modelled forms of the athletes in the East Hall groups and to the charging bull of the North Portico. Vanished is the power of individual characterization and of instantaneous portraiture that we recognize in the lively Miniature groups of the Court Ladies. Departed, too, is the strong sympathy with wild Nature. . . . A sacral and conventional style now prevails . . . grandiose conceptions . . . the wholesale adoption . . . of the processional scheme. . . ."[14] The aesthetic feeling in the murals and pottery is indeed so distinct that a close student of the development of Cretan pottery styles, Arne Furumark, commented on the "colossal change in mentality that had taken place during one or two generations."[15]

Recognized also was a *volte-face* in the previous peaceful character of the Minoan civilization. The appearance of "warrior tombs," of military elements in the wall paintings, of clay tablets recording military equipment, all sound a new militaristic note

[13] *A. of C.*, p. 208.
[14] *Knossos*, IV, p. 880.
[15] *Op. Arch.*, 6 (1950), p. 258.

which Evans sought to explain as due to a sudden wave of imperialism infecting the Lords of Knossos: the appearance of a new and aggressive dynasty which proceeded to conquer and destroy the other Minoan palaces and to develop a great maritime empire.[16]

The Greek historian, Thucydides, writing in the fifth century B.C., remarked that the navy of Minos was the first to control the seas.[17] But Thucydides is likely to have been wrong, unless we interpret this as meaning a Greek "Minos." At any rate the navy that dominated the East Mediterranean in the Late Bronze Age was surely that of the Mycenaean confederacy; and the discovery, thanks to Ventris' brilliant decipherment of "Linear B" in 1952,[18] that thousands of the tablets found at Knossos were written in Mycenaean Greek, makes it certain that the "new and aggressive dynasty" was not native Cretan but composed of invaders from the mainland—a conclusion diametrically opposed to Evans' tenaciously held conviction that the mainland had been colonized and ruled by the Minoans.

The picture, then, which seems to be emerging of Crete in the latter part of the Late Minoan period is that it was dominated by Greek-speaking rulers ruling from a single center, namely Knossos; and that there occurred a gradual spread of Mycenaean Greek influence throughout the island, accompanied by a weakening of the native Cretan culture. The loss of population from the tidal catastrophe of 1500 seems to have been more than made good.

It is not surprising, therefore, that when Agamemnon summoned his vassal kings to join him in the war against Troy,

[16] *Knossos*, IV, pp. 884-888. However, some of the signs of change I have mentioned above should perhaps be attributed to the LM III rather than to the LM II period; and if Palmer (*Mycenaeans and Minoans*, especially pp. 210-215) is correct the seizure of Knossos by the Greeks from the mainland occurred about 1400 (marked by a partial destruction of the palace) rather than about 1450. According to Palmer (p. 214), agreeing with Furumark, the "peaceful and fruitful coexistence (of Crete and the mainland) degenerated (about 1450) into rivalry and conflict, resulting in the victory of the mainland *c*. 1400" (the parentheses are mine). The more military aspect of Knossos during this half century could then be due to an attempt to prepare to meet the threat from the mainland.

[17] I, 4.   [18] Ventris and Chadwick, *JHS*, 73 (1953), pp. 84-103.

sometime after the middle of the thirteenth century, Homer represents Idomeneus, "grandson of Minos," as joining him: "And of the Cretans Idomeneus the famous spearman was leader, even of them that possessed Knossos and Gortys of the great walls, Lyktos and Miletos and chalky Lykastos and Phaistos and Rhytion, stablished cities all; and of all others that dwelt in Crete of the hundred cities. . . . With these followed eighty black ships."[19]

Not many years after the return of the Greek leaders from Troy, that is about 1200 B.C., Knossos shared the fate of Mycenae, Tiryns, Pylos, and many another "stablished city": to be sacked and burned by the invading Dorian Greeks. But the blaze that destroyed the palaces at Knossos and Pylos also baked thousands of the clay tablets containing the records of royal administration, and so they were preserved for the archaeologist to find and painfully but eagerly decipher more than three thousand years later.

If this interpretation of Cretan history from about 1600-1200 B.C. proves to be near the truth it naturally follows that the architectural stage presented by the ruins of the Palace of Minos is not exactly comparable to that presented by the other palaces, since these were destroyed some two centuries earlier. Indeed we might expect to observe certain Mycenaean Greek architectural features in the ruins at Knossos, and something of a case could perhaps be made out in favor of such a view. Details which, in the present state of our knowledge (or ignorance), are common to Knossos and the mainland palaces, but are elsewhere unknown in Crete, include fluted column shafts and the triglyph half-rosette frieze (Fig. 136, A,B), as well as mural decorations such as the Shield Fresco, and the Griffin Fresco which "guards" the throne both at Knossos and Pylos. Some would even add the Knossos Throne Room plan as a whole. Surely, however, its resemblance to the Mycenaean "megaron" is very slight,[20] in spite of the fact that if the Mycenaean dynasts

[19] *Iliad*, 2, 645-652.
[20] Reusch in *Minoica*, pp. 334-358; but cf. Blegen, *ibid.*, p. 66.

of Knossos did any extensive remodeling or repairing of the Palace of Minos, as a result of a destruction about 1400, we might well expect them to have introduced the megaron, so indispensable a feature of their own palaces (Fig. 150).[21] Its conspicuous absence reassures us, in my opinion, that we are right in treating the Palace of Minos as essentially a Minoan palace; and I find it highly unlikely that even such features as the fluting of columns or the carving of the triglyph half-rosette frieze were introduced into Crete from Mycenaean architecture.

If we can accept the hypothesis of an occupation of Crete by Mycenaean Greeks for a period of more than two centuries during the Late Bronze Age this will have to be considered as a factor of considerable significance in the development of western civilization. Contact with Crete had undoubtedly been largely responsible for the first beginnings of culture amongst the rude Greek-speaking folk who began to enter the peninsula of Greece sometime about 2000 B.C., and for the development of a rudimentary civilization there by the end of the Middle Bronze Age, the time of the famous Shaft Graves of Mycenae. But the infinitely closer contacts arising from a prolonged residence of Mycenaeans of the ruling class in Crete itself would result in a far more intensive and extensive transference of Cretan ways of life to the less cultured Greeks. The more obvious effects of this would appear in architecture, wall painting, pottery, gem engraving, etc., and, we should add, in the art of writing. But in the less directly provable fields of thought and behavior, the influence is also likely to have been great: in religion and law, for example, and probably in oral (and written?) literature—how much may the Homeric epic owe to a succession of nameless Minoan predecessors?[22]

Something of the rich Minoan heritage perhaps continued to affect the development of Greek culture down to early Classical times; but eventually Crete became little more than a back-

---

[21] See Mylonas, *Ancient Mycenae*, pp. 51-59.

[22] Severyns, *Grèce et Proche-Orient avant Homère*, Brussels, 1960, pp. 99-100, 171, 204. On the date of the coming of the Greeks see Palmer, *Mycenaeans and Minoans*, chap. VII; he would put it about 1600 B.C.

water of Hellenism, though some of the "true" Cretans (the "Eteocretans") lived on in the eastern part of the island and continued to speak a non-Greek tongue. Through the Roman and later periods Crete in general shared the fate of the Greek mainland, though it was not until 1896 and after many bloody revolts that it was freed from foreign domination; in 1912 it finally became part of the modern Greek nation.

Today Greek archaeologists from both the mainland and from Crete itself are busily engaged in recovering the long and varied history of the island. British, French, and Italian excavators have resumed the investigations interrupted by the last war, and the magnificent treasures of Minoan art are worthily displayed in a new museum at Herakleion under the capable direction of Nikolaos Platon.

We have spoken of the land and the history of Crete, but what sort of people were the Minoan Cretans who dwelt in the palaces and houses we shall visit in the following pages? Perhaps this is a question which should not be asked in a book which seeks to maintain an architectural point of view and does not pretend to be a social study. Perhaps it is a question which should not be asked at all since the Minoans cannot speak directly to us through a written literature—if they produced one—and since even the Greeks of Pericles' day knew of the Minoan civilization only what a meager stream of oral tradition had passed on to them, for the art of writing was lost in the "Dark Ages" that separated the Bronze Age culture from the Classical. Yet to rebuild in imagination these homes of 3500 years ago, only to leave them desolate and deserted, seems so unsatisfying that we can scarcely do other than grasp at whatever clues may be available.

A Greek historian of the time of Julius Caesar, Diodorus Siculus, repeats the tradition that the days of Minos coincided with the Golden Age of Cronus, father of the sky-god Zeus (the Roman Jupiter) who, it was said, was born in Crete. And since Diodorus remarks that "all the subjects of the rule of

Cronus lived a life of blessedness, in the unhindered enjoyment of every pleasure," this has given rise to an impression that the Minoans were an enervated and decadent race of hedonists.[23] Yet their "life of pleasure" (a modern would consider it simple indeed) is pictured by Diodorus as a reward of virtue: "because of the exceptional obedience to laws no injustice was committed by any one at any time."[24] Surely the tradition is not to be interpreted as meaning that the Cretans because of their virtue were privileged henceforth to lead a life of depravity!

The law-abiding character of the Cretans is also attested by the tradition that Minos "established not a few laws for the Cretans, claiming (Moses-like) that he had received them from his father Zeus when conversing with him in a certain cave."[25] The probity of Minos and of his brother Rhadamanthys (king of Phaistos?)[26] was posthumously recognized by making them perpetual judges in the Greek afterworld. It is also significant that the earliest known Classical Greek law code (ca. 500 B.C.) was found at Gortyn, a site where a large Minoan farmhouse has recently been excavated.

It should also be set down to the credit of the Minoans that, in the words of Sir Arthur Evans, their ever valiant and doughty champion, "from the beginning to the end of Minoan Art (there is) ... not one single example ... of any subject of an indecorous nature."[27]

Whether or not the Cretans were a highly religious people is difficult to decide on material evidence alone. On the one hand the entire absence of temples and of statues of gods is strikingly at variance with the situation in contemporary Egypt and Mesopotamia; on the other hand we seem scarcely able to move in the Palace of Minos, at least under the guidance of Sir Arthur, without running into small shrines or small representations of deities or their symbols: lustral chambers, pillar crypts, columnar shrines, temple repositories, incurved altars, sacral horns, double-axes, libation tables, baetylic stones, sacral

---

[23] 5, 66, 6.   [24] *loc. cit.*   [25] Diod. Sic. 5, 78, 3.
[26] See note 3, above.   [27] *Knossos*, II, p. 279.

knots, etc., not to mention representations of sacred birds, trees, bulls, and snakes. Religious scenes are common on gems and other forms of Minoan art (Figs. 100, 101). Possibly the fact that the Cretans built no great temples and carved no large statues of their deities merely indicates that they stood in no immoderate awe of the supernatural.

We have already referred to the fact that the Cretans seem to have been a remarkably peaceful people. The apparently exceptional change in spirit that took place in Late Minoan II or III merely proves the rule for, as we have seen, the military, imperialist character which Evans thought had led to a forceful conquest of the Greek mainland, was on the contrary apparently due to the Mycenaean invaders' having established themselves at Knossos.

This peaceful character is as strange in the world of the Bronze Age Egyptians, Babylonians, Assyrians, Mycenaean Greeks, Hittites, and, we may add, Hebrews, as in the world of the Classical Greeks and Romans, or in the distracted world of today—so strange indeed that it has encouraged the charge that the Minoans were decadent and enervated. Alas for more such "decadence"! Perhaps it was due in part to the isolated position of Crete and to the lack of any excessive pressure of population, but more I think to the homogeneity of the Minoan people. No doubt they came ultimately from a variety of racial stocks, but the continuity of the archaeological strata from earliest times suggests that the bulk of the population had lived on the island long enough to have become essentially homogeneous in language and in customs;[27a] one important illustration of this is the remarkable similarity in architectural forms throughout Crete but especially among the three major palaces. The peaceful co-existence of the two kingdoms of Phaistos and Knossos, hardly over twenty-five miles (40 km.) apart as the crow flies, may be compared to the century and a half of peaceful

[27a] A striking illustration of the close interconnections between the different Minoan centers is the finding of impressions from identical seal-stones at Sklavo-kambos, H. Triadha, Gournia, and Zakros (see Fig. 1), *DMG*, p. 110.

relations that have, for the same reasons, prevailed between Canada and its neighbor to the south.[28]

It is often possible to judge something of the character of an individual or of a people from their dress. The typical Cretan costume of the court class, an elaborately patterned short kilt for the men (Fig. 131, B), and a long elaborately flounced garment for the women which covered the legs entirely but left the breasts bare (Fig. 43), presents a rather odd medley of primitive and sophisticated elements, and this is probably also true of their general outlook, religious and social. They were obviously a brilliant, gifted people living in a physically beautiful and stimulating environment, but the transition from a condition of simple peasantry to a relatively complex urban society, at least in the upper levels of the social scale, was rapid and recent. The transformation was naturally not complete.

The considerable degree of urbane elegance reached by this society is revealed in their domestic architecture. From the spacious and commodious design of the living quarters of the palaces and better houses, often adorned with alabaster veneering and plaster walls painted with scenes from nature or court ceremonial (Figs. 131-134), provided with bathrooms and toilets and with ingenious devices to secure adequate lighting and ventilation, and looking out through columned porticoes upon terraced and beautiful landscapes, it is clear that the Cretans aimed at comfortable living. The great suites of state reception halls and banquet halls, which must be left largely to our imagination to picture, for they were on the lost upper floors,

[28] Yet A. W. Lawrence writes, "It is incredible that there can have been three separate independent states so close together in central Crete"; he suggests that Phaistos was the winter residence for the dynasty that reigned at Knossos in summer. (*Gk. Arch.*, pp. 24-25). To me it seems more incredible that the same dynasty should have possessed two or even three palaces, so similar in plan "that their functions must have been almost identical" (Lawrence). What a biennial moving day that must have been when the whole court transferred itself bag and baggage across the 2000 foot pass of Mt. Ida from Knossos to Phaistos and vice versa!—and when did they trek to Mallia? On the other hand the H. Triadha villa, so near Phaistos and surely of royal character, is a distinctly different type of structure and might well have served as a pleasant occasional retreat from the official residence.

would tell the same story. But this can hardly be called luxuriant debauchery.

They were not a soft, lazy people, however much they may contrast with the vigorous and bellicose Mycenaean Greeks. Fat bellies, as common in Egyptian officialdom, to judge from their art, as in America today, are rarely seen in Cretan art. Characteristically the Cretans are shown with shoulders carried far back, with slim limbs, and a waist so small that some suspect the Minoans of practising artificial constriction (Fig. 131, B). Boxing, dancing, acrobatics, and bull-leaping we know from direct representations were popular, while the traditions of the great athletic festivals of Classical Greek times perhaps point to Crete as their ultimate place of origin. Many think that Homer has the Cretans in mind when he draws his delightful picture of the mythical Phaeacians in the *Odyssey*. They boast that they "excel all men in boxing, and wrestling, and leaping, and speed of foot," though it is true that after viewing Odysseus' prowess they tone down their claims somewhat, "for we are no perfect boxers, nor wrestlers, but speedy runners, and the best of seamen; and dear to us ever is the banquet, and the harp, and the dance, and changes of raiment, and the warm bath, and love, and sleep."[29]

Finally it may be noted that women played an important part in Cretan society. Goddesses seem to have had the dominant role in Cretan religion, and their ministrants were as predominantly priestesses (Figs. 100, 101); female likewise were the sacred dancers. Even in the dangerous bull games lady toreadors took part, while in the audience women mingled with the men, and the special "boxes" were reserved for ladies of the court (Fig. 133). The elaborate costumes of the female aristocracy likewise indicate the importance of women (Figs. 100, 101, 131, A). The assured place which they held in Mycenaean society, to judge from the Homeric epics, probably owed much to the example of the polished culture of the Minoan courts.

[29] *Odyssey*, 8, 102-103, 246-249.

A strong hint of this is found in one of the scenes on the famous Shield of Achilles, as described in the *Iliad*, which is actually placed at Knossos itself: "Also did the glorious lame god (Hephaistos) devise a dancing-place like unto that which once in wide Knossos Daidalos wrought for Ariadne of the lovely tresses. There were youths dancing and maidens of costly wooing, their hands upon one another's wrists. Fine linen the maidens had on, and the youths well-woven doublets faintly glistening with oil. Fair wreaths had the maidens, and the youths daggers of gold hanging from silver baldrics. And now would they run round with deft feet exceeding lightly . . . and now anon they would run in lines to meet each other. And a great company stood round the lovely dance in joy; and among them a divine minstrel was making music on his lyre (Fig. 100), and through the midst of them, leading the measure, two tumblers whirled."[30]

[30] *Iliad*, 18, 590-606.

CHAPTER II

THE MAJOR PALACES

1. THE PALACE OF MINOS AT KNOSSOS

The mighty city of Knossos wherein Minos ruled in nine-year periods, he who held converse with mighty Zeus.—(ODYSSEY, 19, 178-179)

AT ATHENS with its wealth of remains of Classical Greece the traveler can board a plane and in less than two hours find himself a thousand years further back in time at the court of King Minos. To fly to the island of Daedalus and Icarus has a certain appropriateness. It also affords splendid panoramas of sea and islands en route, and for many miles the view to the south embraces the whole length of the island of Crete with the three great mountain masses of Dikte, Ida, and the White Mountains standing out high above all else.

A more intimate and leisurely first look at Crete is provided by a comfortable Greek steamer which will bring one in the early morning light, after an overnight trip from Athens, to Soudha Bay near the west end of the island (Fig. 1). Then, after several hours sail along the north coast, the harborage of Retimo is reached, and toward noon the northern slopes of Mt. Ida loom in the distance. Bare hills dip steeply down into a sea of indigo blue through which the ship ploughs a wake of white foam; and shortly before Herakleion is reached the isolated mountain of Iuktas, conspicuous also from Knossos, takes on the profile of a gigantic recumbent human face—according to the Classical Greeks, that of Zeus himself.

23

Gliding into the harbor through a narrow gap in the break-water, the ship berths beside Venetian walls from which the Lion of St. Mark still looks down. Though hard hit in World War II Herakleion is now rebuilt and well supplied with hotels both large and small. At water-front restaurants one can eat to the music of the pounding surf, or on the main square enjoy a meal in the open beside a quaint old Venetian fountain appropriately carved with Nereids and other beings of the sea.

The chief attraction of Herakleion to most visitors is the newly built, well lighted, and attractively arranged Archaeological Museum with its fabulous treasures of Minoan art. An Historical Museum also provides interesting displays representing the Venetian, Turkish, and modern periods, while extensive Venetian fortifications are still to be seen.

The site of the Minoan city of Knossos, whose population in its heyday might be more conservatively estimated at about half the 80,000 generously accorded it by Sir Arthur Evans,[1] lies some three miles (5 km.) inland, and can be reached in a few minutes by car or public bus. The palace was far from spectacularly situated on a low hill which slopes off fairly steeply on the east and south to the small stream known as the Kairetos. For even a glimpse of the sea or of Mt. Ida one must climb one of the bare hills that now rise bleakly on all sides (Fig. 36). A scattering of small houses, a guardroom and pavilion for visitors, a grove of pine trees that have grown up since the excavations and through which the winds blow gratefully in the summer heat: that is all (Fig. 37).

Inevitably one wonders why such a site should have been thickly populated from Neolithic times. However, there is a considerable amount of good agricultural land in the vicinity (better watered in antiquity); also it enjoyed a position conveniently near the bay at the mouth of the Kairetos which supplied the best outlet for central Crete on the Aegean side, and

---

[1] *Knossos*, II, pp. 563-564; cf. Faure, *Kret. Chron.*, 13 (1959), p. 210, who estimates 30,000.

commanded the cross-island road which ran from this port to Phaistos in the Messara plain and on to the southern beaches that looked toward distant Africa.

It is certain, at any rate, that Homer's "mighty city" was the outstanding city of Crete in Minoan times. To the Greeks its semi-mythical founder and ruler, Minos, was the son of their principal deity, Zeus, and enjoyed his confidence. Indeed most of the familiar mythical tales associated with Crete center about Knossos: Glaukos who was drowned in a jar of honey (one of his father's giant "pithoi"?—Fig. 93); Daedalus, builder of the Labyrinth to house the Minotaur and father of Icarus who flew too near the sun; and Theseus, the Athenian hero, who slew the Minotaur with the help of Minos' daughter, "Ariadne of the lovely tresses."

No wonder then that the name of Knossos is well known, and that many visitors are content to see its legend-haunted ruins and look no farther. Sir Arthur Evans, who spent the last forty years of his life and a large fortune in excavating, preserving, and sumptuously publishing the site, has contributed no little to its fame through his own colorful career, which lack of space prevents us from recounting here.[2] Since Sir Arthur throve on controversy it is not surprising that much of what he wrote and did here has provoked dissension. The present study will not infrequently disagree with his pronouncements. The four-volume (in six), three thousand page publication, *The Palace of Minos at Knossos*, is both magnificent and exasperating; it is at once an encyclopedia covering the whole range of Minoan Antiquities, and at the same time if often omits details essential to the understanding of the Palace of Minos itself. It provides no plan of the building adequate for serious study,[3] and the architectural description is distributed throughout the six books in a fashion which without the Ariadne's clew furnished

---

[2] See the recent biography by his half-sister, Joan Evans, *Time and Chance* (London, 1943); also her autobiography, *Prelude and Fugue* (1965).

[3] But an excellent plan has now (1981) been published by S. Hood.

by a seventh *Index Volume* would leave the user almost as lost in labyrinthine meanderings as the youths and maidens of the ancient tale.

Much of the criticism has been leveled at his restorations or, as he preferred to term them, "reconstitutions." They have been called unnecessary, ugly, and downright wrong, and occasionally perhaps they are all three. Yet after considerable study both of the actual ruins and of Evans' writings I cannot help but agree on the whole with the judgment of Georg Karo,[4] the distinguished former director of the German Archaeological Institute, of whom Nilsson says, "no living scholar knows the course of excavations in Crete so well."[5] Karo caustically comments that many of the most vocal critics are "unencumbered by knowledge of the facts," and that he himself is perhaps the only living scholar who knows what brain-racking (*Kopfzerbrechung*) each new phase of the excavations brought because of the extremely perishable nature of the remains. Without restoration, he declares, the site would be little today but a heap of ruins. "If one will examine the immense remains carefully to see how many restorations were essential and mandatory he will find surprisingly little that was unnecessary." Certainly it cannot be doubted that the restorations add much to the interest of the ordinary visitor; if he is occasionally misled this will be outweighed by what he is helped to comprehend correctly. Unrestored buildings are often, in their way, quite as misleading as over-restored.

However, to return to an examination of the site. The general map shows that crowding around the palace itself were many large mansions or villas, the abode, we may suppose, of Minos' prime officials. These we must visit later. The finest of them vied with the palace itself in splendor though they were far

[4] *Greifen am Thron*, especially pp. 18, 24-26; Platon agrees with Karo, in a review of his book, *Kret. Chron.*, 13 (1959), p. 233. Marinatos, *C. and M.*, p. 126, and Levi, *PdP*, 71 (1960), pp. 112-114, express similar views. Evans explained and defended his reconstitutions in *Antiquaries Journal*, 7 (1927), pp. 258-267.

[5] In a review of Karo's book, *AJA*, 64 (1960), p. 198.

outranked in size, for the Palace of Minos in its final period sprawled over an area of three-and-a-half acres (Fig. 2).[6]

And sprawl it did, for the Cretan palace was not laid out within definite exterior limits, rectangular or square, like a Classical Greek temple. Instead it grew, or was planned, from the inside out, rather like a tree (Ch. XIII, 1). The "heart" was the great Central Court around which the different units of the building centered and which formed the focus of the system of circulation and intercommunication (Ch. IV).

It is not quite accurate to say, however, that the palace *faced* on the Central Court, or at least that it faced exclusively inward like the Classical Greek house, since in three of the major palaces (and Gournia too) the west exterior façade was given special architectural treatment and fronted on a broad area paved with slabs of stone. At Knossos slightly raised walks or "causeways" crossed this West Court in various directions, one leading directly to the West Porch (Figs. 2, 128). The lower part of the wall of the west façade was massively constructed of a high course of smoothly dressed blocks of stone, the orthostates ("standers"), resting on a low sill course, the euthynteria ("leveling" course). As in the other palaces this west wall is not straight but advances and retreats in a curious series of bays and projections the reason for which we will perhaps discover later (Ch. XIII, 3); in addition the wall is interrupted at intervals by shallow breaks or recesses that are peculiarly characteristic of the west palace façades (see pp. 162-164; Fig. 155).

North of the West Court lies a small flagged area flanked by banks of low steps on the east and south and enclosing a kind of elevated "box" at the junction (Fig. 41). The "Theatral Area," as Evans dubbed it, was evidently designed for some kind of spectacle or performance, though hardly of a dramatic nature

---

[6] This estimate is based on the use of a grid over Evans' plan of the palace. The "over six acres" mentioned by Evans, and often repeated, includes a generous amount of the nearby courts and houses (*Knossos*, I, p. 206). My estimate for Mallia is 1.8 acres, and for Phaistos, 1.6 acres, though part of the last palace on the east and south has disappeared down the hill.

as the name might suggest. Inevitably one thinks of Homer's description of the "dancing-place that in wide Knossos Daedalus wrought for Ariadne of the lovely tresses."[7]

The ordinary visitor to the site, whether he uses a plan or not, can scarcely fail to find the layout of the building bewildering. This is in part due to the numerous alterations and modifications that were introduced in the course of the successive partial rebuildings which followed severe earthquakes or other forces of destruction. But a more adequate explanation is that most of what we see merely constitutes the service rooms: storage rooms, workrooms, small cult rooms, etc. Many of the more important rooms, with the exception of the main floor of the residential quarters, were located in the upper storeys, an arrangement also found in the other palaces. In fact it is from the Palace of Minos that we get our word "labyrinth," for like some other words with this ending that we still use, such as hyacinth, plinth, and turpentine (from *terebinthos*), it is a Cretan word in origin. The "labrys," that is, double-axe, occurs innumerable times carved on the stone blocks of the palace walls, or on sacred pillars, or represented on objects found within the palace; recently too the cult title, "Our Lady of the Labyrinth," has been read on a tablet from the palace.[8] The palace, then, was the Labyrinth itself, the "House of the Double-Axe," where the Minotaur was housed, in other words where, in the Central Court, the bull games were performed (Ch. IV). After the destruction of the building the term gradually came to be understood as referring to the "labyrinthine" character of the ruins, and with this new meaning the word passed on to the Greeks and Romans.

A magnificent entranceway in the form of a stepped and columned portico led up from the river-crossing to the southwest corner of the palace in its earlier days, but before the Late Minoan period this had disappeared and the palace seems to have had but two main entrances, a northern and a western.

[7] *Iliad*, 18, 590-592.
[8] *DMG*, p. 310, no. 205.

The north entry was reached, as at Mallia (Fig. 6), by a well-paved road from the west; passing a large pillared hall of uncertain use[9] (Fig. 40) it continued south as a narrow passage sloping sharply upward to the north end of the Central Court. The west entry was clearly the ceremonial one. Causeways from the north and from the west led the visitor into the West Court where rose the impressive façade whose upper storey housed the main reception rooms of the palace (Fig. 128 and Ch. vi, 1). The great stone orthostates that form the base of the walls are still smoke-blackened from the furious fire that destroyed this part of the building. At the southeast corner of the court a columned porch, once decorated with scenes from the bull ring, led past a guardroom into the narrow "Corridor of the Procession" which, when excavated, retained traces of brightly painted rows of processional figures. In Egypt such figures would represent foreigners bringing tribute to Pharaoh and kneeling humbly at his feet; here they seem to be Minoan subjects of Minos bringing presents or offerings to him, or possibly to "Our Lady of the Labyrinth." We can imagine the colorful procession passing along the narrow corridor which, after turning twice at right angles, reached the foot of a broad staircase (entirely restored) leading up to the Piano Nobile, where the king was waiting to receive it. On the restored west wall of the formal porch or "South Propylon" preceding the stairs several of these processional figures, including the best preserved, the famous "Cupbearer" (Figs. 42, 131, B), have been replaced in replica.

The floor of some of the great public halls of the Piano Nobile has been restored, partly as a protective measure for the rooms below (Fig. 116); and although the plan is conjectural in detail it is clear that these upper halls were spacious and that they were handsomely decorated with wall paintings of which

[9] "It is improbable that the north hypostyle hall served as an agora (so Karo on p. 30) or as a custom's house (so Evans); rather it would have been a waiting-room for those coming by the harbor road," writes Platon in a review of Karo, *Greifen am Thron, Kret. Chron.*, 13 (1959), p. 238. Its form and size were largely determined by the Banquet Hall above (see p. 127 and Fig. 156.)

scanty fragments were found in the fill. We shall have something to say of their plan at a later point (Ch. vi, 1).

On the ground floor, beneath the western series of rooms of the Piano Nobile a long row of storage magazines opens off a common corridor running north to south, parallel to the Central Court (Fig. 93). Huge clay jars (pithoi), perhaps once numbering over four hundred and capable of holding, altogether, some 65,000 American gallons (over 246,000 liters) of olive oil, line their walls. The wealth of the Cretan kings is further tantalizingly suggested by the shreds of gold found in rows of sub-floor pits (see Ch. VII, 1 and **Addendum 1**).

Between the Corridor of the Magazines and the Central Court, and south of another monumental stairway leading from the court to the Piano Nobile, lies a group of small rooms used for religious purposes. Their front on the Central Court apparently took the form of a "Tripartite Columnar Shrine" whose appearance may be conjectured from a detail of the so-called Grandstand Fresco (Figs. 44, 133). Two of the inner rooms have stone pillars marked twenty-nine times with the sacred symbol of the *labrys* or double-axe, and in another room are large cists for the storage of sacred apparatus or sacerdotal treasure (Ch. VII, 2). In fact in excavating these a wealth of objects in clay, faïence, and crystal was discovered: two-handled jars, decorative pieces, snake-goddess figurines, libation tables, shells, and two beautiful relief plaques, one representing a goat suckling its kids, the other a cow with its calf.

North of these cult rooms and the stairway to the Piano Nobile lies a group of rooms including the famous "Throne Room," where a formal stone chair was found by the excavators in its original position against the north wall (Fig. 130). To preserve the room the upper walls were rebuilt and the whole roofed over with a clerestory chamber above, whose walls are now hung with reproductions of restored Minoan wall paintings from this palace and elsewhere. From the Central Court four openings between piers lead (Figs. 37, 44), by way of a broad flight of four steps, down to an anteroom with low benches of stone against the walls, and in a gap between them a wooden replica of the throne in the inner room. In the center of the anteroom now stands a shallow stone basin, found nearby, perhaps intended for ablutions.

The walls of the main room are painted with restored scenes of griffins, one pair of which heraldically guards the throne, and are lined with stone benches as in the outer room. The "oldest throne in Europe" is a handsome piece of furniture with a high back of undulating outline, a comfortably hollowed seat, and an arched design of legs and cross-braces which plainly betrays its origin in a wooden chair (Fig. 139, D). Gypsum flagging frames a red-painted plaster panel in the center of the floor, and the remains of a number of decorated clay jars found here conjured up for the excavators a dramatic scene of Minos and his councillors performing some religious ceremony in this room just before the final catastrophe, perhaps with a view to averting the impending danger.[9a]

In any event the presence of a "lustral chamber," that is a stone-lined pit reached by a short flight of steps directly opposite the throne, does indicate that the room was used for certain ritual purposes (Ch. v, 3). That this low-ceilinged "basement" chamber constituted *the* Throne Room of the palace is most unlikely[10]; the important ceremonial rooms were surely in the upper storeys (Ch. vi, 1). In fact the view that Minos here performed certain ritual acts depends on the hypothesis that he was a priest-king; but Helga Reusch is probably nearer the truth in her recent suggestion that this "throne"—better, "cathedral chair"—was intended not for a king but for a high priestess who, sitting here amid her ministrants, represented the epiphany or divine apparition of the Minoan Goddess—the "Lady of the Labyrinth(?)."[11]

[9a] Pendlebury in *Studies presented to D. M. Robinson*, I, p. 195.
[10] Hugh Plommer also says of it, "surely not the only throne room," *Ancient and Classical Architecture*, p. 77.
[11] *Minoica*, pp. 334-358 (another gem showing the goddess guarded by two griffins has recently been found by Platon, *Praktika*, 1959, pl. 110c); Platon likewise considers it a cult room, *Kret. Chron.*, 5 (1951), pp. 392-394.

Miss Reusch has also made it clear that this complex of rooms, though not closely paralleled elsewhere in Crete, is essentially Minoan in nearly all details. The resemblance to the Mycenaean megaron in the position of the throne, to which some have called attention,[12] is confined to this feature alone; and even this point is weakened by its identification as a cathedra for the priestess.

The northeast quarter of the palace, that is the section lying north of the heavy east-west wall on the axis of the east side of the Central Court, was largely occupied, on the ground floor, by storerooms and by the royal workshops. Remains of unfinished products and of the raw materials used by the potters, lapidaries, metal workers, and so forth, were found in this area. The conspicuous rectangular block of heavy walls in the southern part of this quarter, with its west end facing on the Central Court, indicated to Evans that in the storey above there was a Great East Hall; and this view is strengthened by the finding of fragments of fine mural paintings and reliefs which had fallen into the rooms beneath. The discovery of bronze locks of hair, apparently from a colossal statue, further suggested to the excavator that the room had been a sanctuary for the Mother Goddess.[13]

The best preserved part of the Palace of Minos is the southeast quarter, termed by Evans the "Domestic Quarter," that is, the residence of the royal family (Fig. 10). In this area the hill sloped off rapidly to the east and south, and in the later history of the palace a great cutting or vertical scarp was made to a depth of nearly thirty feet (9 m.), providing space for the construction, below the level of the Central Court, of two storeys served by a handsome and ingeniously built stone stairway known as the "Grand Staircase" (Fig. 38). Thanks to the fact that this portion of the palace seems not to have collapsed

[12] Blegen in *Minoica*, p. 66; the use at Pylos of griffins on either side of the throne does not prove that the room at Knossos was a throne room—for one thing the theme may have been imitated without comprehension of its religious meaning. On the dating of the Throne Room see Palmer, *Mycenaeans and Minoans*, chap. VI, 5.

[13] *Knossos*, III, pp. 497-525.

till long after the ruin of the rest of the building, sufficient time elapsed for a great mass of debris from the floors above the level of the Central Court to fall into the lowest storeys, and thus to help maintain much of the walls and even much of the Grand Staircase in nearly their original positions. Evans' careful excavation, followed by a skilful replacement of the decayed wooden columns and of the flooring over the lowest storey, enables us to get an almost uncanny but essentially accurate impression of an entire suite of rooms much as they appeared in 1500 B.C. A detailed description will be given in connection with an account of similar suites in the other palaces (Ch. v, 1). For the present it will be enough to say that the lowest storey contained a great hall, the "Hall of the Double-Axes" (double-axe signs were cut on the walls of the light-well) opening on broad terraces (Figs. 39, 45); a smaller and more private chamber, the "Queen's Hall," with private bathroom, and a series of small rooms, reached by a long passage, including a toilet (Figs. 43, 81). The floors, walls, and ceilings of the halls were beautifully decorated with alabaster veneering or with painted designs and representations. South of the Residential Quarter a complex of small rooms including two bathrooms may have been designed for the reception of guests (Ch. v, 5).

The north, east, and south sides of the Central Court are too poorly preserved to determine whether they resembled the porticoed courts at Mallia and Phaistos. The west side, however, was certainly similar to the west side of the Phaistos Central Court, and the restored drawing in Fig. 44 probably gives a fairly correct impression: from right to left, the series of piers framing the doorways into the Throne Room; the broad stairway to the Piano Nobile with its intermediate column; the Tripartite Sanctuary; and a pillared portico perhaps continuing to the south end of the court. In the upper storeys open galleries probably formed a front for the halls of the Piano Nobile.

But before we attempt to ascend to these upper halls let us leave Knossos for the time being and cross the island to the plain of the Messara.

2. THE PALACE OF PHAISTOS

The amenities and excellencies of its design, with the advantage of a superb situation, admittedly make Phaistos the most attractive of the Cretan Palaces, if not one of the finest architectural achievements of the Bronze Age in the Near East. (SINCLAIR HOOD, *Director of the British School of Archaeology at Athens*)[14]

ALTHOUGH the drive from Herakleion to Phaistos is only thirty-five miles (56 km.) it takes considerably longer by car than might be expected, partly because the road winds up to a pass some 2000 feet (600 m.) above sea level and then zigzags down again with fine panoramas of the fertile Messara valley. The picturesquely situated citadel of Prinias, an important archaic Greek site, can be seen en route, and a stop is usually made at Gortyn, capital of Crete in the Roman period. Here a large Minoan farmhouse has recently been excavated by the Italian School of Archaeology, which has also been excavating at Phaistos and Hagia Triadha since 1900, the year in which Evans began at Knossos.

Leaving the main road, which continues on past H. Triadha to the south coast, we cross the Geropotamos, a small but constantly flowing stream, and wind up the steep motor road to the top of the ridge at the eastern end of which lies Phaistos, and at the western, H. Triadha. A small tourist pavilion just above the palace welcomes the many daily visitors to Phaistos and finds space for the few who wish to stay overnight.

If the visitor, instead of driving, walks up the hill from the main road a question will present itself rather forcibly: why did the Minoans build their palace on the top of this ridge more than two hundred feet (70 m.) above the plain? It is not likely that it was for defence, for although the edge of the hill on the north, east, and south of the palace drops off steeply, it continues to rise toward the west, reaching a height of nearly four

[14] *Gnomon*, 26 (1954), p. 375.

hundred feet (120 m.) above the palace in an eminence known as the Acropolis, and there are no traces of fortifications facing in this direction along the unprotected west front of the palace.

A possible explanation is that it was considered to be more healthful on the hill. Or it may be that the psychological value of setting the king's house above those of his "subjects" (literally "those placed beneath") was fully appreciated. But it is difficult to avoid the impression that the magnificence of the view exercised not a little influence on the rulers of Phaistos in selecting this site for their royal residence.

Forty miles (64 km.) to the east the bold profile of Mt. Dikte, best seen with the "rosy-fingered Dawn" behind it, marks the landward end of the valley. To the west one may catch a glimpse from the Central Court of the Bay of Messara; to the south a long ridge (Asterousia Mts.) shuts off the valley from the coast (Fig. 46). But it is to the north that the eye is drawn again and again. Here the long sheltering range of Ida throws up a 6000-foot truncated cone (Fig. 51) topped by double peaks that earn it its modern name, the Saddle of Digenis. From dawn to dusk the deeply creviced hills fluctuate in an ever-changing pattern of light and shade, and the cloud masses that float over, and sometimes partly envelop, the rugged slopes are never alike two days in succession.

At night there are no urban lights to dim the brilliance of the sky, and standing among the shadowy ruins one starred night we looked down into the valley to discover, as it seemed, another starry heaven beneath us. Had some great flood, we wondered momentarily, converted the whole plain from hill to hill into a vast, still mirror? No, for these "stars" were moving uncertainly about and blinking in and out in most erratic fashion. They were, we presently realized, but the torches of nearby villagers gathering succulent snails for tomorrow's dinner.

A fine, almost bird's-eye, view of the palace may be gained from the roof of the Pavilion (Fig. 46). The ground plan is well preserved except along the south end and the southern half of the east side of the Central Court, where whatever rooms there may have been have disappeared over the eroded edge of the hill (Fig. 4).[15]

Along the west side of the palace are two courts (not shown) connected by a stone staircase (Fig. 138). The lower, West Court, during the existence of the penultimate palace—and it is in this stage that the excavators have left it (Fig. 49)—had a flagged surface, and was bounded on the north by a long flight of steps terminating at the top in a blank retaining wall supporting the south side of the Upper Court. The West Court with its flight of steps, or seats, is referred to as a "Theatral Area." But when the last palace was built the level of the West Court was raised about four feet (1.30 m.), just high enough to cover the orthostates of the older palace façade (now visible in the middle of the court, Fig. 49) and all but four of the flight of northern steps, and was then surfaced with cement (Fig. 55); the court was also enlarged by moving the west face of the new building eastward about twenty-four feet (7.20 m.). In both stages the main entrance to the Central Court lay in the middle of its west side, and in the last palace the broad passage, 7, was controlled by double doors at both ends. The Central Court could also be reached at ground level by at least two other entrances: 41, in the center of the north end; and 62, at the northeast corner (Fig. 4).

North of the Central Court, and connected with it by Corridor 41, was a smaller paved court, 48; and at a higher level to the west of this was still another court enclosed by porticoes on all sides. This Peristyle Court, 74, with four columns on each side (Fig. 126), finds its only Minoan parallel, on a monumental scale, in the Little Palace at Knossos (Fig. 13).

But the Central Court, which is similar in size, proportions, and orientation to that at Knossos, is of course the principal court. The surface was paved in a fairly regular fashion with flagstones, and along probably the whole of both the long east and west sides ran continuous porticoes, possibly with galleries

[15] Marinatos suggests that parts of the palace were never finished, *C. and M.*, pp. 60, 134.

along the east, if not also along the west, at the second storey level (Fig. 55). On the east, where a considerable stretch is preserved, the portico was fronted by an alternating succession of square pillars and round columns, a scheme popular in Minoan architecture.

On the west side of the Central Court near its northern end a central oval column of large size flanked by two pillars on either side—all rising, it would seem, to a height of two storeys (Fig. 50)—forms the imposing façade of Room 25, the largest room on the ground floor of the palace, about 31 by 28 ft. (9½ by 8½ m.). The importance of the room is further emphasized by the two oval column bases on its east-west axis, by the floor laid in a particularly careful pattern of gypsum slabs, and by the walls lined with a wainscotting of gypsum veneer surmounted by painted plaster and furnished with niches let into the walls on three sides. Surely the room served some function more important than merely to act as an anteroom to a series of magazines (27-38), though that is the view taken by the official Italian publication of the building; a suggestion of what that function may have been will be made later (Ch. IV).[16]

Along the north end of the Central Court occurs one of the most carefully designed schemes for which there is evidence in Minoan architecture (Fig. 51). Set almost precisely on the axis of the court, the broad doorway to Corridor 41 is flanked on either side by a pair of semi-circular bases (Fig. 53); next, symmetrically spaced to right and left, by a deep niche decorated with a distinctive pattern to be discussed in another connection (p. 79), and finally, and again symmetrically on either side, by a shallow recess of a type otherwise met only along the main (west) façades of the palaces (Fig. 122). As shown in Fig. 145 the position of the individual elements was fixed by a predetermined plan based on whole numbers of Minoan feet, though the placing of each point was not always precisely adhered to in the actual process of building. A reconstruction of the façade is presented in Fig. 50 where,

---

[16] It is called a "vestibolo," *Festòs*, II, pp. 67, 79; note that there was at least another opening into the area of the magazines via Room 31 from Corridor 7, *Festòs*, II, pp. 44, 90.

on the semi-circular bases on which I originally thought of restoring half-columns in the manner of the later tholoi at Mycenae, I would now propose to place two flagpoles such as were used to adorn the pylons of Egyptian New Kingdom temples. This restoration is encouraged by Alexiou's belief that a steatite rhyton from Zakro represents flagpoles decorating the façade of a Minoan Peak Sanctuary.[17]

The imposing character of this façade, the discovery of fragments of painted wall decoration fallen from above into the rooms behind, and the broad stairway, 42-43, guarded by a sentry box in Corridor 41 (see Ch. iv), is ample evidence that the rectangular block measuring some 75 by 50 ft. (ca. 23 by 15 m.) and lying between the Central Court and Court 48, contained rooms of outstanding importance (Fig. 89). The position of bases in the walls of the ground floor rooms 58-61 and 91-92, points to a large "East Hall" on the second floor, about 30 by 47 ft. (ca. 9 by 14½ m.), containing two rows of four columns each; while the narrowness of the partition walls separating Rooms 44-46 indicates a single large "West Hall" in the second storey, about 15 by 30 ft. (ca. 4½ by 9 m.), which is narrow enough to be roofed without internal supports. For various reasons it is clear that the area over Corridor 41 was unroofed except near its south end. A third storey above the level of the Central Court, originally postulated, should, I think, be eliminated in favor of a flat roof at the second-storey level sheltered by a light canopy of reeds (see Fig. 50; AJA, 83 (1979), pp. 64-69). It will be suggested later that the dining halls of the palace were located in this block of rooms north of the Central Court, probably in the second-storey East Hall.[18] The small rooms on the ground floor would be suitable for the storage and preparation of food, and it is a fact that the excavators did discover quantities of pottery in a cupboard under the stairway 42-43, and that there are stone-lined niches in the walls

---

[17] AJA, 74 (1970), pp. 231-239; Kret. Chron., 17 (1963), pp. 339-351; cf. J. W. Shaw, AJA, 82 (1978), pp. 438f., note 18.
[18] For a full discussion see AJA, 65 (1961), pp. 165-172.

of 45 and 46 (Fig. 99), similar to niches found recently in early stages of the Phaistos palace with pottery still in place in them as if on a pantry shelf.[19]

The rooms beneath the East Hall were in easy communication by way of Corridor 58 with the northeast quarter of the palace which, as at Knossos and Mallia, would seem to have been the service quarter (Fig. 4). This quarter was provided with a direct outside entrance, 53, a small room with doorways on the north, east, and west, and with benches against the walls. A few yards north of 53 a steep stairway descends to a loosely planned building which includes a number of storerooms, some of them "stock-piled" with domestic pottery. From this building the fields are easily reached by a gentle slope where the hill runs out in a long point toward the northeast.[20] All of this would suggest an obvious route for bringing the daily food supplies into the palace.

Court 90, with the remains of an oven or furnace in the middle, must have been designed for the use of the staff, and the series of rooms marked 54-55, for storage. Rooms 88 and 89 would also have been used for storage; the former, below ground level and entered by steps down, was considered by Pernier as a rather mysterious room possibly used for religious purposes (on the analogy of the "lustral chambers"), but it would seem more likely that it was simply a kind of "cold cellar."[21] North of 88 were several cisterns. Finally 49, which was almost certainly an unroofed area with a single door opening off another court, 48, can be reasonably explained in this general context as a pen for animals awaiting conversion into meat for the royal table or to provide a fresh supply of milk.[22]

The principal royal Residential Quarter was located at the north end of the palace, and reached by a long stairway descend-

[19] *Annuario*, 30-32 (1952-54), p. 457, figs. 94, 95; *Festòs*, II, fig. 156, shows pottery in the niche in Room 46.

[20] *Festòs*, II, p. 455.

[21] *Festòs*, II, pp. 203-208, 586; Banti rejects the religious hypothesis but leaves the purpose of the room unexplained.

[22] The responsibility for most of the ideas suggested in this paragraph is mine; the Italian publication presents the facts and avoids conjecture.

ing from the Peristyle Court (74). This court, together with the very large room, 93, opening on it through a six-bayed pier-and-door partition, should quite possibly be considered as forming a part of the private rather than of the public apartments of the palace, as some would regard them. Room 93 and the porticoes of Peristyle 74 were paved with gypsum flagstones, those of the former being of a unique rhomboidal shape; at least the west wall of 93 was gypsum faced and contained a niche like those in Room 25.

As at Knossos the Residential Quarter was built on an artificially leveled terrace at the edge of the hill, and much of it is quite well preserved. Since it enjoyed a northern exposure with a superb panorama of the range of Ida, it was probably used as the summer residence of the royal family. A smaller but similar suite east of the Central Court (63-64) would then have served as living quarters in colder weather. Both have a Main Hall (77-79 and 63), a Queen's Hall (81 and 63b), a bathroom off the latter (83 and 63d), and a porticoed terrace (85 and 64); they will be described in more detail later (Ch. v).

West of the Central Court Rooms 23 and 24 (Fig. 96), with wide openings on the west portico and furnished with gypsum benches, may have been used merely as comfortable and convenient "sitting rooms," like the Classical Greek "exedra," but it is quite possible that they were used for some cult purpose. Behind them and reached by a long corridor, 12-13, from the passage, 7, two suites of rooms each with a private bath (17, 18, 19 and 16, 20, 21) and with a "living room" shared in common (15), may have been Guest Apartments (Ch. v, 5).[23] Rooms 27-37 opening on either side of Corridor 26 must have served for storage or other service purposes, though they may have played a special role at the time of the bull games (Ch. iv).

The most conspicuous architectural feature of the Phaistos palace was the magnificent entranceway north of the Magazine

---

[23] I would agree with Miss Banti (*Festòs*, II, pp. 452-455) that there was no circuitous southwest entry to the palace similar to that at Knossos (Corridor of the Procession); the wall west of the guest rooms, shown in lighter hatching on the plan (Fig. 4), is only a retaining wall.

Block. It consisted of a splendid stairway, forty-five feet (over 13½ m.) broad with deep, low risers, which ascended to an imposing propylon in the form of a double porch, the outer opening of which (67) was supported by a massive central column of oval shape, while the inner (69) consisted of two large portals (without doors) on either side of a broad pier (Figs. 49, 137, 138). At the rear of these porticoes three oval columns supported the front of a very large light-well (69A). A door at the southeast corner of 69A connects by means of a stairway with Room 25 and the Central Court, and in the other direction with Peristyle 74.

From 69 three steps through a doorway ascend into Room 70 whose cement floor is about 7½ ft. (2.30 m.) above that of the magazines, 27-38; 70 may have been merely a guardroom, or it may have formed an anteroom to a suite of public rooms at this level (Ch. VI, 1). Another rather wider doorway at the opposite end of 69 opens on a broad two-flight stairway, 72-73, which led, we believe, via a corridor over 68-69, to a grand suite of State Apartments covering the entire area of the Magazine Block.[24]

Even in plan the great square block, about a hundred feet (30 m.) to a side, which includes the Grand Propylon and Magazine complex, is impressive. What a magnificently unified and harmoniously proportioned architectural composition the combination of monumental entranceway and massive three-storeyed block containing the State Reception Halls must have presented is faintly suggested by our restoration of it as seen from the West Court (Fig. 48)—a splendid setting for the pomp and pageantry of a Minoan court. Did it serve as the Minoan equivalent of the "Window of Appearances"—suggested, it may be, by the well-known Egyptian practice where the pharaoh appeared on an elevated balcony for the admiration of his subjects?[24a] One thinks of today's balcony at Buckingham Palace!

[24] For full discussion see *AJA*, 60 (1956), pp. 151-157.
[24a] For details see *AJA*, 74 (1970), pp. 235f.

3. THE PALACE OF MALLIA

LESS THAN 25 miles (40 km) to the east of Herakleion is the third of the great palaces of Crete.

It is true that Mallia lacks the antique fame and the mythological glamor of Knossos; indeed even its ancient name is uncertain. It also falls short of Phaistos in beauty of location, though in this respect it excels Knossos since it has a view of the sea, which, with an excellent beach, is but a few minutes walk from the palace (Fig. 56); in addition the site, though low-lying, has a fine background of towering hills, part of the Dikte range (Fig. 57). The fertile fields of the surrounding plain are watered by scores of white-sailed windmills.

It is also true that the Palace of Mallia is considerably smaller than that at Knossos, being about 1.8 acres (nearly 8000 sq. m.) or about the size of the Palace of Phaistos (Fig. 7); it is also less sumptuously decorated than its sister palaces. Yet the Mallia palace enjoys the distinction of having its ground plan virtually intact; only one small building was later built on the site (Fig. 6). It was discovered by the Greek archaeologist Hazzidakis who commenced its excavation in 1915, but since 1922 the site has been excavated by the French School which has at last published its final account of the palace and has recently brought out a splendid stateplan of its remains.[25]

The Central Court, which is almost identical with that at Phaistos in dimensions and orientation, is of special interest for its excellent preservation, particularly of the porticoes on the north and east, which supply valuable clues for solving the problem of where the bull games were staged (Ch. IV). The court also resembles the one at Phaistos in having a broad portico along its eastern side, consisting of alternating piers and columns spaced with great regularity. But it excels Phaistos in one particular: across the north end of the court there was also a portico of columns set on white stone bases (Fig. 57). Except between the last two columns at the west end, where there was

[25] Pelon, O., *Le palais*, V, Paris.

an opening with double doors, the spaces between the columns seem to have been closed either with low screen walls or some kind of balustrade.

To the west of the Central Court a block of magazines and service rooms is served by a "Corridor of the Magazines" running north to south as at Knossos.[25a] These magazines are grouped into two distinct blocks, and in each of these, as in the group of magazines 6 to 16 at Knossos, the partition walls are thickened at the center into piers to receive the weight of columns in the halls of the Piano Nobile overhead.

Between the Corridor of the Magazines and the Central Court and facing on it for about the northern two-thirds of its length is a rectangular group of rooms, vi and vii (Figs. 5, 6), some or all of which probably were connected with the religious activities of the palace. The position is similar to that of the Tripartite Shrine and associated rooms in the Palace of Minos. In the center of the northern section, vi 1 opens on the court for its entire width of fourteen feet (over 4 m.), and a flight of four steps ascends on either side of a pier to the floor of the room where a low base appears to have been intended for an altar or table of offerings. Behind this a narrow stairway of four steps between two columns descends again to a series of rooms used, it seems, for storing the cult paraphernalia, for in vi 2 was discovered a cache of several evidently highly prized objects now in the Herakleion Museum: a bronze bracelet, a bronze dagger, a great bronze sword with a crystal hilt, and a votive hatchet in the form of a panther.[26] In the middle of the southern group of rooms is a large Pillar Crypt, vii 4, with a flagged floor and two stone pillars marked with double-axes, stars, and a trident (Figs. 95, 98). Sections vi and vii connect via a short passage at the foot of a stone stairway 10 ft. 5 in. (3.20 m.) wide and with nine steps still in position. The plan of this area west of the Central Court is so similar to that of the same area in the Palace

[25a] Reached from the West Court by a passage north of Mag. 8.
[26] *Mallia*, I, p. 21; *Mon. Piot*, 28 (1925-1926), pp. 1-18.

of Minos—especially in the position of the elevated shrine room, in the pillar room (two rooms at Knossos), in the groups of magazines on the west façade, in the Corridor of the Magazines, and in the broad stairway just mentioned—that it would seem that we should expect still further analogies to Knossos, that, for example, the stairway would have led up to a series of shrines above vi and vii, and also would have opened on the corridor above the Corridor of the Magazines, which in turn provided access to the two great halls referred to above as well as in Ch. VI, 1, pp. 114-125.

Farther south along the west side of the Central Court is what appears to be another somewhat wider flight of four steps ca. 25 feet (7½ m.) long. No clear supporting walls are to be seen, however, on which further steps might have rested, and it seems better to assume, with Marinatos,[27] that they formed a small "theatral area," i.e. a viewing platform commanding performances in the court.

Beyond this platform, at the southwest corner of the court, is the principal entrance to the palace, carefully flagged and measuring ca. 18 by 50 feet (5½ by 15 m.).[28] Another broad passage (10 feet) opens into the court near its southeast corner, and there are four service entries, one of them into the Corridor of the Magazines.[29]

The Palace of Mallia is especially remarkable for the large number of storage rooms and small workrooms in all parts of the building, which give it almost the agrarian character of a great country villa. In addition, at the southwest corner of the palace are two rows of circular granaries (Figs. 58, 62 and Ch. VII, 1). Exactly what the irregular clusters of rooms to the southeast and southwest of the Central Court were used for is not clear except that a group of rooms, xviii, with an entry only from outside the palace was used for cult purposes.[30]

To the east of the Central Court is an interestingly designed and

[27] *C. and M.*, p. 137 and fig. 58.

[28] No evidence for paving south of the palace has yet been found.

[29] Some have claimed that this is a magazine, not a passage, but careful examination at the site has convinced me this is wrong; Pelon agrees (*Malia*, 5, p. 56²).

[30] *Mallia*, 4, pp. 9-13, 69.

well preserved complex of magazines (xi 1-7), now enclosed to protect them, which will be described later (Ch. VII, 1, and Figs. 57, 91). Another group of three storage rooms, xii, lies to the south of these, and still another distinct group of six at the extreme north end of the palace (xxvii), with other storage or workrooms to the south. The North Service Court, as we would call it, had short, roughly-paved porticoes on the north, east, and south, and here we can picture the domestic staff busily receiving, sorting, or preparing food supplies for the royal household.

Between the Central Court and the North Service Court are to be seen the remains of three stairways and a very large room containing six square bases in two rows, preceded by a long room with a single base (Figs. 59, 87).[31] The evidence points to the existence of a large, second storey room (which we may call the "Northeast Hall") with two rows of columns, accessible from two stairways. In size, form, and position its resemblance to the "East Hall" we have restored in the second storey north of the Central Court at Phaistos (Ch. II, 2) is so close as to suggest that both rooms were used for the same purpose, and both will be further discussed in Chapter VI, 2, "The Banquet Hall."

Another feature which links the Palace of Mallia with the other two great palaces is the presence of a royal Residential Quarter, although it was long before this was recognized.[32] Located in the northwest corner of the building (iii) it resembles in position, and to a remarkable degree in arrangement, the principal Residential Quarter at Phaistos. It includes a Main or Men's Hall (iii 7) with a light-well at its south end, a Queen's Hall (iii 1) with attached bathroom (iii 4) and probably a toilet (iii 2). Both Halls opened on a columned portico with a view toward the sea. Stairs at iii b led to upper rooms. On some of the walls are remains of painted and incised plaster, but there is no evidence of alabaster veneering; the bases for the pier-and-door partitions were not of stone

---

[31] The room with the six bases has been much discussed, and supposed Egyptian analogies have caused it to be referred to as the Hypostyle Hall, Joly, *BCH*, 52 (1928), pp. 324-346; *Mallia*, II, pp. 1-5; Charbonneaux rejected these analogies, *BCH* 54 (1930), pp. 352-356. The third stairway led to the roof; see *AJA*, 83 (1979), pp. 64-69.

[32] By Platon, *Kret. Chron.*, I (1947), pp. 635-636.

but apparently of wood, as were three bases, recently discovered, for a double doorway into iii 7 from iv 6 (Fig. 11).

Thus the atmosphere at Mallia is much more modest than at Knossos or Phaistos, almost rustic in tone compared with their urban splendor. Yet the palace displays the same solidly constructed west façade with vigorously projecting and receding blocks of rooms further enlivened with shallow recesses (Fig. 58) and reared on a solid base of stone orthostates and projecting sill course.

West of the west façade of the palace are the remains of a broad, flagged West Court, crossed, as at Knossos and Phaistos, by raised walkways. Stone-paved streets radiate from the palace, at least on the north and east sides, and some of the houses reached from these streets we will visit later (Ch. III, 13-17).

Finally we note a peculiar feature, unique to Mallia and occurring several times along the east side of the palace, at CDEFG and J. It consists of a space, formed by an extension of the foundations, filled in solidly with clay, stone, or potsherds. Their purpose was surely to form a buttress at a weak point, such as a reentrant angle, FGJ, or to take the thrust of a stairway, CDE. See *AJA*, 83 (1979), p. 69.

***

A fourth major palace was excavated at Kato Zakro by Platon in the 1960s. See **Addendum 2**.

CHAPTER III

MINOR PALACES, VILLAS,
AND HOUSES

1. THE PALACE OF GOURNIA

IN ADDITION to the four major palaces there are several smaller and incompletely preserved or incompletely excavated structures which may have been minor palaces. The best known of these, excavated by an expedition from the University of Pennsylvania in 1901-1904, is at a site today called Gournia, easily reached by road from the small town of Hagios Nikolaos (Fig. 1).

Gournia lies on the Gulf of Mirabello at the northern end of the seven-mile (11 km.) Hierapetra Isthmus, and today it is but a few minutes' drive over a fine level road, dominated by a magnificent mass of hills on the east, to Hierapetra on the south coast, the site of a small but interesting local museum. Cross-island traffic along this route must have been heavy in ancient times.

The American expedition led by three intrepid women archae-ologists proceeded to uncover the little town systematically. Scores of small, irregularly planned houses were crowded together along narrow winding streets which clambered up the slopes of a small hill (Figs. 8, 63). Though excavated in the early years of this century the site is still in a surprisingly good state of preservation and provides the visitor to Crete with his best opportunity to sense what conditions of everyday life were for the ordinary Minoan. A surprising variety of the tools and objects of daily living were found in the houses, and provided the basis for an account which still makes interesting reading though the excavator wrote it in the first decade of Minoan archaeology.

On the top of the hill on which the town was built, and commanding a fine prospect over the gulf, were discovered the poorly preserved remains of a structure which in certain features resembles the major palaces, though it covers an area of less than a third of an acre, or about one-tenth that of the Palace of Minos (Fig. 9).

The resemblance is clearest along the west façade. This fronts on a passage paved with cobblestones which widens out toward its northern end in a diminutive piazza or "West Court." Part of the base of the wall of this west façade and around the corner on the south end of the palace is built of dressed limestone blocks of considerable size set on a low plinth, a style of masonry which, as we have seen, is characteristic of the west façades of the major palaces. The similarity is heightened by the fact that just south of the main west entrance, which is marked by a well dressed stone threshold, there occurs one of those recesses (twelve Minoan feet long) which are so typical of the west palace façades. Moreover portions of the façade alternately project and recede as in the larger palaces (though on a very modest scale), and one section measures sixty Minoan feet, a figure repeated at Phaistos and Mallia (Ch. XIII, 1).

A further point of likeness is the occurrence of a number of magazines of the usual elongated shape which are distributed in not too distinct groups along the west front, while above these, as the excavator conjectured, would have been the State Apartments reached by stairs of which there are slight traces just south of the west entrance.

The higher terraces to the east and north have been so denuded as to provide little further information about the plan of the building. Three long magazines (24) were surely covered by a single large room in the upper storey, and in the adjacent magazine (23) twelve clay jars were found in their original position around the walls. A small, cement-floored room (28) at the north end of the palace has been identified as a bathroom, though it does not have the familiar descending steps, this may provide a clue to the position of the Residential Quarter. Near the southeast corner of the palace is a small, open-fronted room with a low bench around its walls; in both these respects it resembles Rooms 23 and 24 west of the Central Court at Phaistos. This room faces west on what is surely a small court[1] bounded along its west side by a row of alternating pillars and columns, a common Minoan scheme (Ch. xi, 1).

The small court just mentioned is of course very unlike the great central courts of Knossos, Phaistos, and Mallia; but immediately adjacent to the palace, on the south, is a large, open, cement-floored area called on the plan of the site a "Public Court." Though a little narrower and perhaps a little shorter than the courts of the three major palaces, it is similar in proportions and orientation, and this suggests that it too may have been designed with the bull games in mind (see Chapter iv). At its northern end is a low flight of steps forming an angle, quite reminiscent of the "Theatral Areas" at Knossos and Phaistos. Just south of this, opening along the west side of the court, is a short pillared portico with small rooms behind it which form a southward extension of the palace. Again we are reminded of the Tripartite Columnar Shrine at Knossos, Room 25 at Phaistos, and Room vi 1 at Mallia. Fragments of stone "sacral horns" were found nearby, likewise a large flat block of stone pierced transversely with a hole. The possible meaning of this will be discussed later, page 142.

2. THE VILLA OF HAGIA TRIADHA

A forty minute walk along the northern foot of the ridge, on whose opposite extremities the two palaces of H. Triadha and Phaistos stand, leads through groves of citrus and gnarled old olive trees seen against the snowy peaks of Ida to one of

---

[1] The excavator felt uncertain on the point (*Gournia*, p. 26); but the spans would have been long (minimum 6.65 m. from east to west), and there is a capacious drain through the south stylobate (16 cm. wide by 17 cm. deep).

the loveliest Minoan sites in Crete. The oddly inappropriate name, "Holy Trinity," comes from a chapel and hamlet which once existed nearby.

It is commonly supposed that H. Triadha formed a sort of seasonal residence for the rulers of Phaistos. Its situation not only afforded a magnificent view of Ida (Fig. 65) but of the whole sand-fringed Bay of Messara with the mountains of western Crete in the background. Gypsum veneering was lavishly used throughout the palace, and the frescoes, so strangely absent at Phaistos, rank among the finest discovered in Crete. In addition to a hoard of nineteen bronze ingots together weighing over 1100 lbs. (over 500 kgs.), choice objects of Minoan art were discovered in the ruins, including steatite (soapstone) vases with scenes carved with the utmost skill and liveliness in low relief, one showing a festive procession of harvesters, another a presentation of sacrificial bulls' hides,[2] and a third, scenes of boxing and the bull game.[3]

The Villa was excavated by the Italian School of Archaeology in the first decade of the 20th century, but not until 1980 did its definitive publication, accompanied by a detailed plan of the building and its surroundings, appear.

In plan the structure was roughly L-shaped: the vertical stroke running west to east, the horizontal, from north to south. Within the L was a partly flagged, court-like area occupying the crest of the ridge into whose slopes the ground-floor rooms of the Villa were terraced (Fig. 66).

Occupying most of the southern extremity of the building was a series of small rooms served by a common corridor (Fig. 164); the excavators suggest that these were used by the servants. A number of storerooms containing large clay jars are located in the middle of the north wing, and to the east of these is a suite of interconnecting Minoan Halls with many pier-and-door

[2] So Forsdyke, *Journal of the Warburg and Courtauld Institutes*, 15 (1952), pp. 13-19. Platon calls it the presentation of the spoils of the hunt, review of Karo, *Greifen am Thron, Kret. Chron.*, 13 (1959), p. 239.
[3] All three are well illustrated in Matz, *Kreta, Mykene, Troja*, Stuttgart, 1957, pls. 66, 67, 69.

partitions of the familiar pattern (Ch. v, 2). These rooms were well decorated with gypsum floors and walls lined with alabaster veneering; they were also liberally supplied with gypsum benches, and with windows and light-wells.[4] A substantial stairway led to obviously important rooms on the upper floor or floors. Clearly this constituted an important residential part of the palace but its exact purpose seems unknown.

A handsome suite of rooms in the northwest corner of the palace evidently formed the main Residential Quarter (Fig. 165). Its plan is similar to that of the major palaces and will be described in more detail later (Ch. v). The Men's Hall with connecting rooms (3, 12, 4) is as fine as anything at Knossos (Fig. 151), while one of the rooms (14) in the women's section (Fig. 68) contained the Cat and Bird Fresco and other beautiful mural paintings (Fig. 134). From the colonnaded court (11) the view is unsurpassed.

Although in many features the Villa of H. Triadha does resemble the major palaces it has no Central Court; its façades on the north and west, though built of ashlar masonry, lack the typical recesses; and there is no clear indication of a series of royal reception halls on the Piano Nobile. It seems reasonable then to regard it as a pleasure palace for the rulers of Phaistos, a Trianon to its Versailles, rather than as the administrative center of a separate realm.

3. THE LITTLE PALACE AT KNOSSOS

Some two hundred and fifty yards (230 m.) northwest of the Palace of Minos, and reached from it by way of the Minoan paved road running west from the North Entrance, Sir Arthur Evans excavated the remains of a building which he called the Little Palace (Figs. 3, 36, c).[5] Though it was far smaller than the great palaces, measuring only about one-fifth of an acre

---

[4] The *Enciclopedia Italiana*, *s.v.* Hagia Triada, says that the rooms were "decorate con affreschi, bagni, gabinetti"; I have been unable to see anything of these at the site.
[5] *Knossos*, II, pp. 513-544; *Handbook*, pp. 57-62.

(about 800 sq. m.), yet it contained a suite of connecting rooms which can help us gain some idea of the splendor of the vanished State Apartments in the Piano Nobile of the palaces at Knossos and Phaistos (Fig. 13).

The Main Hall at the north end of this suite is paved with gypsum and divided into two halves by a pier-and-door partition of four bays; another of six bays runs the whole length of the room and opens on a narrow columned portico or veranda which seems to have opened in turn on a terrace with a broad view to the east (Fig. 64). On the south the Hall opened through another four-bayed partition into a spacious square peristyle with three columns on each side; the only comparable peristyle known in Minoan architecture is the one in the Palace of Phaistos (74). Three steps extending the full width of the peristyle led down to an entrance hall, but the details of the actual approach have been lost.

In addition the Little Palace contained three Pillar Crypt rooms, a lavatory off the Main Hall, a "Lustral Chamber" of considerable architectural interest (Ch. v, 3), and a broad two-flight stairway to the second storey. There is, however, no clearly defined "women's quarter." The lower part of the outer walls was built of fine dressed masonry still standing on the west to a height of eight courses. See **Addendum 3**.

4. THE ROYAL VILLA, KNOSSOS

The "Royal Villa" was apparently reached by a short paved road running northeast from the palace (Fig. 3).[6] Built on an artificial terrace created by scarping back the hill, the Villa enjoyed a protected position and a pleasant view to the eastward over the valley (Fig. 36, b). Although of outstanding quality it was not particularly large, measuring only about sixty feet from north to south by about thirty-two, as preserved, from east to west (ca. 18 by 10 m.). The plan, except for the oblique

[6] *Knossos*, II, pp. 396-413; *Handbook*, pp. 62-64.

line of the northeast corner, is fairly compact and rectangular with only slight jogs on the west and south (Fig. 14); if restored correctly, an entrance on the ground floor level opened into the light-well of the Hall (C).

As the name implies this was no ordinary house. It will be noticed that even on the ground floor there are no storerooms. The entire east-west axis is occupied by the Hall, with the usual pier-and-door partition and two-columned light-well. The lower part of the walls was adorned with panels of gypsum veneer preserved to a height of over six feet (2 m.), and the floor of the main (inner) part of the Hall was surfaced with gypsum slabs laid in the usual system of a broad border about a central rectangle. Access to this part of the Hall could also be gained by a double door on the south near the foot of a stairway in the southwest corner of the house. But the most interesting feature of the room is the heavy stone balustrade, 32 in. (81 cm.) high at its west end, supporting columns on either side of an opening through which three steps led up to a narrow area behind the balustrade, 15 in. (38 cm.) higher than the floor of the Hall (Fig. 74). A handsome pedestaled lamp of purple stone was found standing on the steps, and in a niche on the axis of the room the remains of a formal stone seat were discovered in position.

Immediately adjacent to the balustrade a door opens to the north into a Pillar Crypt, almost as large as the main part of the Hall from which it is entered, and the finest and best preserved of cult rooms of this type (Ch. VII, 2). Its walls were of gypsum blocks in regularly coursed masonry, and the ceiling was supported by a system of huge split tree trunks resting on a central gypsum pillar and lodged in sockets in the masonry at the top of the walls (Fig. 97). In the gypsum floor were sunk a channel and two basins, evidently intended to catch liquid offerings poured before the sacred pillar.

It seems clear that the whole complex served some important

function of a religious nature, or at least with religious overtones. It is tempting to imagine that Minos, who "ruled wholly in accordance with law and paid the greatest heed to justice,"[7] sat in judgment on the recessed seat, accompanied by his advisers, on the dais behind the balustrade. Here he was able to communicate, unobserved, with his clerks or officials on the floor above through the open well which, as Evans has shown, existed over the area beyond the balustrade; they in turn could communicate with the functionaries in the Pillar Crypt by means of a stairway at the west end of the room. The whole arrangement is pregnant with suggestive possibilities of awesome religious or political ceremonies, or of downright chicanery designed to impress the lay audience in the Hall.

The southeast corner of the Villa was occupied by what appears to be a private suite of rooms: a paved Hall (E) with a closet (F) and a bath (?) opening off it (G), and a light-well or little court (H). Was it intended for guest rooms, women's quarters, or as rest rooms for His Worship during recesses in the session?

The second storey seems to have had a Hall above, and similar in plan to, the one (C) on the ground floor, and there was no doubt an entrance from the terrace on the west.

The form of the stairway in the southwest corner of the house is unique. The first flight, from the ground floor, runs up to a wide landing from which a second flight ascends to the second storey at each end, on either side of the well of the first flight (Fig. 73). The upper flight to the east, with a door at its head, served the Upper Hall and adjoining rooms; the western one seems to have continued on up to a third storey. Again the arrangement whereby the second floor rooms could be secured against intrusion, while leaving the stairway to the first and third storeys free, is suggestive of the special purposes this edifice appears to have served.

[7] Diod. Sic., 5, 79, 2.

5. THE SOUTH HOUSE, KNOSSOS

Evans calls the South House the "best normal idea of a good burgher dwelling of the beginning of the New Era (L.M.) either at Knossos or elsewhere."[8] It was built on a scarped terrace encroaching on part of the early southwest approach to the palace (Fig. 3), and faced south over the ravine in the direction of the "Caravanserai." Slightly larger than the Royal Villa (62 by 38 ft.; 19 by 11½ m.) it was a little more regular in outline though not without the usual jogs corresponding to the arrangement of the rooms (Fig. 15).

Thanks to the slope of the hill remains of three storeys are preserved and have been supplemented by restoration (Fig. 71). The rear (north) wall stands to a height of eight courses of massive masonry (Fig. 72).

The lowest storey consists of a long narrow storeroom with three stone pillars on the axis, and a smaller room opening off it in which was found a number of bronze tools, including three saws and two double-axes. The peculiar way in which the doors of these rooms were secured will be described later (Ch. ix, 3). Platon considers these rooms shrines.

Twelve steps lead up from the basement to the main floor where is found the usual Hall with light-well, pier-and-door partitions, and gypsum-faced walls and floor, the center of the main part being occupied by a "mosaiko" pavement (Fig. 72); in the east wall was a window placed, when first built, in a bay. Other rooms include a lavatory (?), a toilet with drain through the wall, and a bathroom. In its original form the bathroom floor was at a lower level reached by a short flight of steps, and the walls seem to have been decorated with paintings of birds and flowers. In the northwest corner of the house a Pillar Crypt contained a single pillar flanked by a base for a double-axe and a stand for sacral objects (horns?). As in the Royal Villa

---

[8] *Knossos*, II, pp. 373-390 (quotation, p. 389); *Handbook*, pp. 65-66.

adjacent stairs led to a room above, from which appears to have fallen a "silver service," consisting of a pitcher and three bowls, one decorated with spirals. Whether for ceremonial or for household use they give evidence of the affluence of the owner of the South House.

6. THE HOUSE OF THE CHANCEL SCREEN, KNOSSOS

The House of the Chancel Screen, built at the southeast corner of the palace (Fig. 3), was about the size of the Royal Villa, about 55 by 42 ft. (17 by 13 m.), and was also generally rectangular with the usual jogs (Fig. 16).[9] On the ground floor, which alone is preserved, are three magazines (9, 12, 13), a Pillar Crypt with a single pillar (10), a bathroom (6) perhaps forming part of the Private Apartments, and an important complex of rooms in the northeast angle of the house.

This complex consists of a Hall (2) with pier-and-door partitions on three sides and the main house entrance on the fourth. This connects through a four-bayed partition on the north side with another large Hall whose floor was paved with irregular flagging, and which was lighted not from a light-well but, according to the excavator, by a large window in the east wall. On the opposite side of the room is a balustrade similar to the one in the Royal Villa. Beyond an opening in the center of this balustrade, framed by columns, two shallow steps lead up to a higher floor level. In the center of the rear wall of the balustraded area, which was much deeper than in the Royal Villa, traces were found of a raised dais supposedly for a formal seat. Here again, then, we seem to have some kind of formal audience chamber; but it will be noted that the Pillar Crypt is not in this instance so intimately associated.

7. THE SOUTHEAST HOUSE, KNOSSOS

The Southeast House lies next to the House of the Chancel Screen at the southeast corner of the palace (Fig. 3).[10] The

[9] *Knossos*, II, pp. 391-395; *Handbook*, p. 64.
[10] *Knossos*, I, pp. 425-430; *Handbook*, pp. 64-65.

Main Hall, K 1, in the southwest corner, has gypsum-faced walls and a floor of clay surrounded on the inner sides with a narrow, slightly raised border paved with gypsum (Fig. 17). The Hall opens east through a three-bayed pier-and-door partition on a small flagged court, about 8 by 6½ ft. (2½ by 2 m.), with three columns about an angle (Fig. 80), similar to one in House A at Tylissos (Fig. 19).

Room H 1, opening off the north portico of this court, presents a puzzle. Its walls on three sides are built of fine limestone masonry—unusual for interior walls—nine courses being preserved in one place, and faced with gypsum veneer. The fourth (east) side was also "faced" with the same thin gypsum "veneering," but without a solid backing of any kind, only a narrow space, G 1, with a door adjoining the one into H 1.

The Pillar Crypt, C 1, will be discussed later (Ch. VII, 2). Against the base of the single pillar, which was marked with three double-axe signs, was found a stone base for a double-axe, and nearby a "sacral knot" in ivory.

At the northwest corner of the house is a two-flight stairway with the ten gypsum steps of the first flight and two of the second in position; the total height of the stairway, and therefore of the first storey, must have been approximately 8½ ft. (2.60 m.). Remains of plaster painted with lilies were found in the narrow passage from the stairs, A 1.

8. THE HOUSE OF THE FRESCOES, KNOSSOS

The House of the Frescoes lies to the northwest of the palace and south of the "Royal Road" running west from its North Entrance (Fig. 3).[11] It was a small and simple house and much disturbed by later building. Little can be said of the individual rooms (Fig. 18). The principal room, H, in the southeast corner had a floor with a plaster border and an ironstone center; its walls bore remains of an interesting zoned decoration (Fig. 129, A).

The chief interest of the house, however, lies in the frescoes,

---

[11] *Knossos*, II, pp. 431-467; *Handbook*, p. 57.

which were found not on the walls nor even fallen from them, but neatly and evidently deliberately stacked in E, as if awaiting the archaeologist, in fragile sheets of stucco little more than an eighth of an inch (4 mm.) thick. As many as thirty-four layers could be counted, and the whole formed a pile some twelve feet long by five feet wide. "Eighty-four trays (2 × 2 ft.)," writes Evans, "were finally filled with the fragments, and the process of extraction and removal, mainly carried out by four expert workmen specially trained in this work, took over five weeks."[12] Among the fine paintings thus rescued were the Blue Monkeys and the Blue Bird Fresco.

9. THE HOUSE AT NIROU KHANI

One of the finest houses, if it really was a private house, outside of Knossos, was excavated in 1918-1919 by Xanthoudides at Nirou Khani, about eight miles (13 km.) east of Herakleion and only a few yards from the sea at a point where traces of Minoan harbor works have been found (Fig. 31).[13]

Like the Knossian villas the base of the outer walls in conspicuous positions is built of coursed and dressed masonry; there are remains of wall paintings; and a Hall of normal form (2a, 2) had a carefully paved gypsum floor and walls dadoed with gypsum panels (Fig. 75). Two other rooms, 5 and 12, have floors with a central rectangle of ironstone flagging within a border of gypsum, and 12 has a gypsum bench around the walls on two sides. A stone stairway (10, 10a), and remains of stone jamb bases and of gypsum flooring fallen from above indicate that there was a second storey of importance. The small room, 9, and the narrow passage, 8, leading to it, were both floored with gypsum flagging, and both were lighted by small windows in the exterior walls. Other features worthy of mention include a light-well providing light to Room 12, and, through a window, to Corridor 11; a large paved court to the east and

[12] *Knossos*, II, pp. 445-446.
[13] *Ephemeris*, 1922, pp. 1-25; *Knossos*, II, pp. 279-285.

a smaller paved area to the south, several storage rooms in the house itself (15-18), a number of magazines with pithoi (24, 25, 31), and a series of rectangular grain-bins (26-30) in a walled courtyard to the north.

The possibility that it may have been something other than a private dwelling is suggested mainly by the contents of certain rooms. Room 18 contained some forty to fifty clay altars neatly stacked in piles, and others were found in 16 and 17; in Room 14 were four large stone lamps; and in 7 were discovered four very big double-axes of thin bronze, one about four feet (1.20 m.) wide, intended obviously for ritual use. One fragment of wall painting bears a representation of a sacral knot; in the court to the east there were remains of sacral horns and a niche evidently designed to receive them, and nearby a kind of altar.

The Greek excavator and Evans have suggested that the building was the headquarters of a High Priest, indeed a kind of central bureau for the dissemination of the Faith. Architecturally, however, there is little or nothing to distinguish it as anything but a private house. Very unusual, if not unique, is the use of the smaller part of the Hall (2) as a sort of porch with two columns facing on to an open court rather than on to a lightwell. This superficially megaron-like scheme may have occurred also in the Royal Villa and in House Za at Mallia, but these are probably to be restored as true light-wells. The group of small rooms, 3-10, opening off the Hall may have formed the private living quarters, though there is no distinct bathroom (see Ch. v).

10. HOUSES AT TYLISSOS

In the heart of a little town, still known by its perhaps four thousand year old name of Tylissos, lie the remains of three very interesting Minoan buildings. Tylissos is reached today from Herakleion (7½ m. or 12 km.) by a winding road which continues on through picturesque valleys to the northern foothills of Mount Ida, which form a magnificent background for the Minoan ruins.

Their excavation by Hazzidakis (1909-1913) was occasioned by the accidental discovery of three huge bronze cauldrons (Fig. 142, G). Platon has recently made a restudy of the buildings, accompanied by further excavation, conservation, and restoration; he has generously allowed me to mention some of his findings, but for the revised plans we must await his publication.[14]

Two of the buildings, A and C, were no doubt houses, though A is so large that it is sometimes referred to as a Little Palace; much of their walls is built of excellently dressed and coursed masonry (Fig. 78). The other building, B, is a remarkably regular rectangular structure, but it has no clear features of Minoan domestic architecture, and may have been simply a storehouse for A.

11. HOUSE A, TYLISSOS

Largest of the houses at Tylissos, House A has a maximum length of about 115 ft. (35 m.) and a width varying from 54 to 60 ft. (16½ to 18 m.). It falls into two distinct halves, each fairly rectangular in outline, and each containing two sets of stairways; the northern half, on the ground floor, is the service quarter, while the southern contained the living quarters of the family (Fig. 19).

The most important complex of rooms includes the Hall, 6, which is paved irregularly with flagstones interrupted by two slightly raised rectangular platforms of unknown use. At the west end of the room is a slight variation of the plaster-floored light-well; the small extra portico on its north side was apparently intended to provide a covered passage from the Hall into the important room, 3. Other small rooms open off the Hall, including a possible toilet, 7, with a drain in the southwest corner, and a bathroom, 11, which, like the one in the South

[14] The new plans (by Piet de Jong) are now hung in the Herakleion Museum.

House at Knossos, was changed from a room with steps leading to a lower floor level to one with a floor level even with that of the Hall.

A group of small rooms, 12-14, with a corridor, A, is entered by a single door from the Hall. This is strongly reminiscent of the arrangement of the women's quarters in the residential area of the palaces, and the resemblance is strengthened by the private stairway to the upper rooms.

Room 3 with a central pillar was the Pillar Crypt; a pyramidal stand for a double-axe was found in it, and two smaller rooms, 4 and 5, opening off it seem to have been associated "treasuries." In 5 was discovered a bronze ingot like those from H. Triadha, and in 4 the three bronze cauldrons mentioned above.

In the northern half of the house a deep L-shaped portico, 15, faced on a small paved court into which the main entrance opened by way of a narrow corridor (not shown on our plan). The two large rooms, 16 and 17, north of this, contained many big storage jars. On their axes were two pillars each, and the finding of painted fragments of stucco in 17 suggests that there were two large and important rooms over them in the second storey, or more probably a single very large hall with two rows of three columns each. In its plan such a room would have resembled the banquet halls (as we have identified them) in the palaces (Ch. VI, 2); like the one in the palace at Mallia it would also have been accessible from two stairways. The stair adjacent to the west, located conveniently near the storerooms and a series of small rooms where food could have been prepared, would be used by household servants; the long stairway reached from the portico opposite the main entrance, and leading directly to the southwest corner of the room, would be used by guests.

12. HOUSE C, TYLISSOS

House C at Tylissos is considerably smaller than House A, but is better preserved; indeed many of its walls are intact almost to the second storey. Some remains at a high level, including two column bases and a cistern at the northeast corner, belong to a rebuilding of the house in the L.M. III period.

The house has the characteristic irregular outline with the various groups of rooms forming projecting wings (Fig. 20). Four quarters or groups of rooms may be distinguished: cult rooms, 2-3, in the southeast—one with a central pillar; a complex of storage rooms, 8-10, in the west; the living quarters, 12-15, in the north; and a central group, 4-6, of unknown use. To serve these rooms there was an extensive and remarkably preserved system of corridors, A to D, repeated no doubt on the second floor, which was reached by three sets of stairways.

The Main Hall of the Residential Quarter, 15, had a flagged floor and the usual pier-and-door partition (Fig. 77). A remarkably deep light-well opened on the east end of the Hall through the regular two-columned portico; on its south side a well preserved and now fully restored window, over eight feet (2½ m.) wide and divided into three openings, supplied light to Room 14. From the main part of the Hall a door opens into the more private quarters. The first room, 12, as Platon has discovered, in its original form contained a bathroom of the usual type with steps down to a lower level; later, however, like the one in House A, it was remodeled. Room 14 would presumably be the Women's Hall. A long corridor, D, secured by a door, led to a flight of stairs no doubt serving the bedrooms, and, at its far end, to a room, 13, with a toilet provided with a drain through the outer wall (Fig. 79).

A single large Hall presumably covered the area over Magazines 8-10, and four of the bases of a pier-and-door partition are preserved in position on the north-south wall between 8 and 9-10. The arrangement bears an obvious resemblance to the great public halls over the west magazines in the Minoan palaces.

13. HOUSES AT MALLIA

At Mallia, as well as at Knossos and Phaistos, the palace was surrounded by districts of houses, such as Quarter D to the west of the palace. Excavations have been made in various of these residential areas, but the only one which has been linked up directly with the palace itself is that currently being excavated to the east of the palace and known as Quarter Z (Fig. 24).

An irregular and not yet fully defined area along the east side of the palace forms a large cobble-paved "East Court," and through this, beginning at the southeast entry of the Central Court, runs a fairly straight, narrow street paved partly with cobblestones, partly with a line of stone flagging. On this street lie Houses Za and Zb, about 120 ft. (nearly 40 m.) east of the palace on the north side, and over 220 ft. (nearly 70 m.) on the south side, respectively.

Like the palace itself the houses at Mallia are of simpler quality than those at Knossos. Most have rubble foundations, floors flagged (at best) with irregular slabs of schist, and pillar bases of roughly rectangular blocks of stone. However they share many characteristics with the better houses at other sites, and two of them, Da and Za, provide very clear and typical examples of the upper-class Minoan house.[15]

14. HOUSE Da, MALLIA

Particularly well preserved is the ground plan of House Da (Fig. 22). Its indented outline reveals very distinctly the typical Minoan way of building houses, or palaces, in a series of "agglutinative" units corresponding to the arrangement of the rooms.

The entrance from the west opened into a probably unroofed vestibule, 1, with flagged floor and a doorway at the left giving access to a double storage room found filled with large jars. A double doorway at the end of the vestibule opened into a flagged corridor, 2, and so directly into the Main Hall, 5, entered through a four-bayed partition. Another four-bayed pier-and-door partition divided the Hall unequally into two parts, both

[15] Houses Za and Da are published in *Mallia, Maisons,* 1; Zb, House E, and a general discussion of the street and area to the east of the palace, in *Mallia, Maisons,* II.

roughly flagged. The usual light-well at the end of the smaller part had a single central column and a drain through the wall at the northwest corner. A flagged corridor continues north from just outside the entrance of the Hall to a door controlling access to the private apartments. These consisted of a large flagged room, 6; a bathroom, 7, with the usual sunken floor; and a smaller room with a thin partition shielding the entrance to the toilet in the corner (Fig. 114), a toilet which has the distinction of being the best preserved one in Crete (Ch. v, 4). Another corridor, 4, leads directly into the private apartments through a double door.

The rooms in the south end of the house seem to have been used for work and storage. Near the entrance to the Hall a stairway with the unusual feature of "winders" at the bottom suggests that there was an upper storey of some importance.

To preserve the remains of this interesting house the excavators have rebuilt the walls in rubble and roofed it over at the level of the first storey. Our Fig. 21 attempts to restore the original appearance of the house with the aid of the "Town Mosaic" from Knossos (Fig. 103).

15. HOUSE Zₐ, MALLIA

House Za has a remarkably regular rectangular outline for a Minoan building and measures about 80 by 57 ft. (24½ by 17½ m.). The part of the house used for living purposes was limited, at least on the ground floor, to about one-third of the total area, and was sharply separated from the rest, used for storage and work purposes, by a straight line of wall broken only by a single doorway (Fig. 25). This door, which seems to have been the only entrance to the living quarters, was reached by a long corridor, 2, from a roughly flagged vestibule housing a two-flight stairway, 15, to the upper floor.

The door at the end of 2 opened at right angles into a second corridor, 4, from which one passed directly into the Main Hall, 12. The walls of the Hall were stuccoed and the floors of both parts, on either side of the usual pier-and-door partition, were roughly flagged. At the west end of the room opened a plaster-floored, single-columned light-well; its walls should be shown on the restored plan (Fig. 25).[16]

Close to the entrance to the Hall a doorway opened into the private apartments, while just outside this door, and therefore conveniently located with respect to both the Hall and the Women's Quarters, was placed the usual bathroom, 11, with sunken floor. The principal room, 5, of the Women's Quarters was a kind of small edition of the Main Hall, with flagged floor and transverse pillar partition, and apparently a small light-well, 8, beyond; this is particularly surprising since the pillar partition and light-well do not otherwise seem to occur in the Women's Hall outside of the Palace of Minos itself. Reached from the far corner of the apartment was a narrow doorway to the toilet which projected entirely beyond the walls of the house in an extravagance of hygienic enthusiasm.

In addition to the entrance into the main part of the house an adjacent entrance into 21 retains in place a fine stone threshold with the door-pivot holes and mortises for the upright posts of the jambs (Fig. 110 and Ch. ix, 3). Room 24, apparently reached from this by a double doorway with three rough jamb bases in position, has certain features of interest (Fig. 26). In the center of the western part of the room is a round column base, and in line with this in the north wall is a flat block intended, it would seem, for a post; evidently a transverse beam to support the ceiling ran from the north to the south walls. Around the sides of the room against the foundations of the walls was set a low rubble wall; this was surely not part of the foundations, as treated in the restored plan, but a low bench of a type found not infrequently elsewhere. This bench is interrupted at the northeast corner of the room, but certainly not for a window, as proposed; a window in a corner with its sill at the floor level would be strange indeed, and there is no support for

[16] Part of the plaster floor of the light-well is actually preserved.

such a restoration in the appearance of the outer foundation wall at this point. The resemblance of the arrangement to that in the "Throne Room" at Knossos suggests to me that a wooden seat or "thronos" was placed in the gap between the benches. Whoever sat here was well placed to see all those sitting on the benches as well as to command the doorway. But the nature of the meetings or ceremonies that took place in this chamber is not explained by any objects found in it.

16. HOUSE Zʙ, MALLIA

House Zb is more irregular than the preceding houses and inferior in quality, but not without architectural features of interest.

As in Za there was a two-flight stairway opening off the vestibule, *a*, in the northeast corner of the house (Fig. 27). The entrance corridor turns into a central room whose roof was supported by a single column. Were it not for the column base and for the rarity of courts in Minoan house architecture the manner in which the other rooms revolve about and open off this central room would suggest that it was an open court;[16a] possibly, like the central hall of the Egyptian houses at Amarna (ca. 1375 B.C.), there was a clerestory above this room providing light and air to the surrounding rooms.

The space under the stairs, i, was used as a cupboard for the best pottery; vi, xv, and perhaps other rooms, served for storage; the presence of ashes in xii, unless they fell from an upper storey, may indicate that it was a kitchen.

The main living room or Hall, vii, served apparently by a private entry on the south, *b*, opened directly, without the usual portico-like section, through a pillar partition on a light-well. The excavators termed iii a weaving room since loomweights were found in it, but it is hard to see where there would have been space for a loom to be set up. The small, flagged room, ix,

[16a] Cf. Weinberg, *AJA*, 65 (1961), p. 318; he suggests that the irregular south half of the house was a later addition.

opening off the Hall, is called a bathroom; but the very large drain at floor level in the southwest corner suggests that it was really a toilet.

A few other points of disagreement with the restored plan may be mentioned. Along the east side of the south entrance, *b*, runs a low rubble bench, not shown on the plan; such benches are found at the entrance to House B at Palaikastro (Fig. 29), and in Room 53, the northeast entry at Phaistos (Fig. 4). In spite of the difference in levels it does seem that there was a doorway to xii from the southeast corner of xvii, and that xii connected in turn with xiv through a door at the west end of the wall dividing them. The proposed window in ii at a low level and directly on the street is most unlikely; though the sill is a little high for the threshold of a door this is not an unreasonable precaution against surface water running into the house from a flooded street.

17. HOUSE E, THE "LITTLE PALACE," MALLIA

It is not surprising that the excavators at Mallia have been tempted to refer to a large building, accidentally discovered about a hundred yards south of the palace in 1931, as a "Little Palace," for its area (so far as it can be defined) is nearly twice that of the Little Palace at Knossos, while the workmanship of certain features rivals that of the Mallia palace.

Nevertheless the plan is so unorthodox that the French archaeologists were still vainly attempting to make sense of its maze of irregular rooms a quarter of a century later. The official publication has now appeared and is a model of conscientious thoroughness, yet it asks almost more questions than it answers. Some of the confusion is due to the incorporation of elements of an earlier house (M.M. I), and to a late rehabilitation of parts of the building after a partial destruction. In Fig. 23 we present a "regularized" plan, based on a tracing from the excellent French "excavated condition" plan, in the hope of making it more intelligible. See now Pelon, *BCH*, 90 (1967), pp. 494-512.

The main entrance "sidles" in from the street on the north, much in the manner of the north entrance of the palace, to a paved vestibule, i.[16b] From this a corridor, ii, leads into a large flagged court, ii *bis*. Northwest of this a smaller court, v, has an L-shaped colonnade with four fine column bases in position. West of v only workrooms and storerooms seem to have existed, the clearest being a row of six rooms opening on a corridor, xlvii-xli. In the southwestern area of the house is a small impluvium-like court, xiv, with piers perhaps on all sides.

The south-central part of the house presumably contained the living quarters since ix is a bathroom of the usual type. In its west wall are two niches, not known elsewhere in a bathroom; a fine stone lamp (Fig. 140, G) and a fragment of an offering table were found in the room. The large room, viii, off which it opens, has none of the characteristic features of a "Minoan Hall," but the remains of plaster painted with plant designs found there has earned it the name of "Salle aux Fresques."

A number of other minor features of interest occur, but nothing that seems to throw further light on the nature of the building. No evidence was obtained for the existence of a stairway to a second storey.[16c]

18. THE VILLA OF THE LILIES, AMNISOS

Amnisos: one jar of honey to Eleuthia. (LINEAR B TABLET from Knossos)[17]

Amnisos is remembered in later tradition, and under its correct Minoan name, as a harborage for Knossos. Odysseus mentions it as the site of a cave where Eilithyia was worshiped,[18]

[16b] Seton Lloyd appears to have found a similar entrance in his palace at Beycesultan in Asia Minor, and he notes the Mallia parallel (it also appears in the palace and in House Db), *Anatolian Studies*, 6 (1956), p. 121. It is also common in the Amarna houses; cf. e.g. W. S. Smith, *Art and Architecture of Ancient Egypt*, fig. 70.

[16c] Weinberg suggests that there was a stairway in the vestibule, i, *AJA*, 65 (1961), p. 319; but I am inclined to suppose that this formed a passage to Court v, and that there may have been a stairway in ii, leading to a portico along the north side of Court ii *bis*.

[17] *DMG*, p. 310, no. 206.

[18] *Odyssey*, 19, 188.

a Cretan deity whose name has recently been read on a Linear B tablet from Knossos, and who survived into Greek times as a goddess of childbirth. The cave, containing stalagmites—one manifestation of the Cretan pillar cult—was explored as early as 1884, and its entrance is now marked by a fig tree high up on a hillside some distance back from the sea and within a few yards of a modern motor road.

A few yards from the sea a fine Minoan mansion was excavated and published by Marinatos in 1932.[19] Recently it has been further studied and restored by Platon, but since his findings and a revised plan have not yet appeared we can only describe it in a general way and illustrate it with a photograph taken in 1959 (Fig. 76).

The quality of the house is indicated by the massive outer walls built of huge dressed limestone orthostates marked with tridents and a star. Some of these blocks, in spite of their size, had been toppled out of position by a quake, or more probably by a tidal wave (Ch. 1), which destroyed the house around 1500 B.C. Graceful wall paintings of lilies have given the villa its modern name; and a large Hall in the northeast corner had a six-bayed pier-and-door partition with gypsum bases opening north on a flagged terrace with a fine view of the sea and the island of Dia. The rest of the Residential Quarter is badly destroyed, but Platon has succeeded in identifying a short flight of steps leading down to a bathroom. That there was a second storey is proved by the remains of a stairway.

19. HOUSE B, PALAIKASTRO

Excavations made by the British School at Palaikastro on the east coast from 1902 to 1906 revealed part of a small town with narrow, winding streets and a considerable number of small houses (Fig. 28). Few yield intelligible plans, and the site was completely ruined during the last war.[20]

[19] *Praktika*, 1932, pp. 76-94; cf. *BCH*, 57 (1933), pp. 292-295.
[20] *BSA*, 8 (1901-1902), pp. 306-316; 9 (1902-1903), pp. 277-296; 10 (1903-1904), pp. 192-226; 11 (1904-1905), pp. 272-290.

In the center of House B is a large rectangular room with an impluvium-like court having a column at each of the four corners; since there was no drain it may have been covered by a clerestory (Fig. 29). Two other houses at this site have similar courts, termed "megarons" by the excavators, and we have noticed a similar arrangement in House E at Mallia.

The smaller room, 2, off the court, with a stepped bathroom of the usual type, would apparently constitute the "Women's Quarters." The so-called bathroom, 15, in another part of the house, was perhaps a toilet. There are also remains of stairs leading to a second storey. One other feature of interest is the row of alternating pillar and column bases in front of the entrance (Fig. 28).

20. HOUSE AT SKLAVOKAMBOS

Some six miles (9-10 km.) west of Tylissos the remains of a large house were accidentally found by road builders in the 1930's, and much of the northern part was destroyed before archaeologists could be summoned to excavate the rest;[21] it was further damaged during the war. The site, impressive in its lonely isolation, lies near a small stream at the foot of a high rocky hill, with the nearest settlement, Gonies, visible on a hillside some distance to the west.

The southern half of the house was used for storage and service and had a separate entrance (Fig. 32). In the center is a small court, 15, with four pillars, resembling those at Palaikastro and Mallia E. Traces of a hearth were found in the portico and two rooms opening on the west side of the court seem to have been used in the preparation of food.

The main part of the house was entered by a double door near the southeast corner, 1. The largest room, 4, was badly destroyed; it opened through three bays on a narrow corridor, 5, at the west end of which was a group of three rooms. One of these, 12, was used for storage, and three jars were found in 11, which however seems to have served principally as a con-

[21] *Ephemeris*, 1939-1941, pp. 69-96.

necting link with a broad, pillared veranda facing the north and a fine view. Beneath the stairway, 6-7, was a toilet with a drain through the outside wall. Of the other rooms little is known.

21. PLATI, LASITHI PLAIN

In the plain of Lasithi near the cave sanctuary of Psychro in east-central Crete a one month campaign was conducted by the British School in May 1913.[22] A number of rather nondescript rooms were excavated around three sides of an open area; best preserved are those along the southwest side, at A on the plan (Fig. 30). Two periods of construction were distinguished: L.M. I and L.M. II. At the close of the excavation the remains were refilled (only a few blocks are visible today), and the report left it an open question whether part of a regularly planned Minoan town with a number of houses about an open area had been discovered, or whether the remains were those of a single unidentified building about a central court.

Our plan presents a redrawing of the published excavation plan with some simplification and omission of walls that do not belong to the main period of occupation. It will be seen that the various rooms appear to belong together in a unified complex rather than to be parts of separate houses, and, except for the orientation, which is more east-west than north-south, the plan bears a remarkable resemblance to the central court scheme of the major palaces. In particular it will be noted that though rather narrower than the courts of such palaces as Mallia—a little over 50 ft. (16 m.) instead of 80 ft. (over 24 m.)—it is, as preserved, about as long. Further, the pillared front at A, with the complex of rooms (13, 15, 17-20) behind it, is definitely reminiscent in form and position of the Tripartite Shrine at Knossos, Room 25 at Phaistos, Suite vi at Mallia, and a pillared portico at Gournia (Ch. vii, 2).

If not part of a palace, possibly we have here a court for the bull games surrounded by the suite of rooms needed to accommodate the bulls, performers, officials of the games, etc., and for the associated religious ceremonies.

[22] *BSA*, 20 (1913-1914), pp. 1-13.

22. OTHER SITES

Houses of the Minoan period have been excavated at many other sites, but because of poor preservation, architectural insignificance, or incomplete excavation or publication, they would not repay description here, though some may be referred to later for particular details. Among these we may mention Knossos itself, Mallia, Phaistos, Prasa and Katsamba near Herakleion, Kefala (southwest of Mt. Dikte), Pseira, Siteia, Zou (near Siteia), and Zakros in east Crete, and Apodhoulou and Monasteraki in south central Crete (Fig. 1).[23] The Italian School has likewise excavated (1958) a large farmhouse near Gortyn, whose lower floor was almost entirely given up to store- and cult-rooms; no stairs were found, though it presumably had a second storey.[24]

In addition, remains of three large buildings, identified as "palaces," have been found southwest of Knossos: at Arkhanes, Vathypetro, and Kanli Kastelli. Evans suggested that the first was a summer palace for the lords of Knossos; the other two are candidates for the site of Lykastos, mentioned by Homer as one of the seven important cities of Crete.[25] Vathypetro was perhaps never completed. It has a marvelous view over the valley toward Kanli Kastelli, and is the most fully excavated; but Marinatos plans further excavation before publication.[26] Its most unusual feature is a grape or olive press (Fig. 94). Kydonia in west Crete, mentioned by Diodorus Siculus along with Knossos and Phaistos, has possibly been found within the last few years by Swedish and Greek archaeologists, but excavations are in a preliminary stage.[27]

[23] See recent numbers of *Ergon* and *Deltion*; also Stefan Sinos, *Die vorklassischen Hausformen in der Ägäis* (Mainz am Rhein, 1971), chapter III.

[24] Levi, "La Villa rurale minoica di Gortina," *Bollettino d'Arte*, 44 (1959), pp. 237-268; Sinos, *op.cit.*, p. 159, fig. 137.

[25] *Iliad*, 2, 646-648.

[26] Marinatos, *C. and M.*, pp. 66, 68.

[27] Diod. Sic., 5, 78, 2; C. Davaras, *Guide to Cretan Antiquities* (Park Ridge, New Jersey, 1976), *s.v.* Kydonia.

See also **Addendum 4**, Archanes Model.

THE CENTRAL COURT AND THE BULL GAMES

THE IMPORTANCE of the central court is clear from a glance at the plan of any of the major palaces (Fig. 7). At Mallia, where an estimate can be made most accurately, it occupies, together with its porticoes, nearly a fifth of the total area (Fig. 6). Indeed the Cretan architects, at least at Phaistos and Mallia, seem to have laid out the court first and then to have employed two of its adjacent sides as base lines to develop outwards the various quarters of the palace (Ch. XIII, 1).

Perhaps there is no need to look far for an explanation of the existence of these large courts. Besides serving as the organizing nucleus of the plan, at once dividing and uniting the parts of the palace, they must also have formed, like the court of the Classical Greek house, the focus of much of the daily activities of normal palace life. The porticoes and galleries, which constituted an integral part of the court, provided a pleasant retreat from rain, wind, or the blaze of the summer sun. Palace domestics and artisans would have found the court a pleasant spot for some of their tasks, although at Phaistos and Mallia there were special service courts and areas, and the children of the royal household and their friends had ample space for their endless games.

Again as in the Hellenic house many of the rooms and groups of rooms faced on the central court and derived their light and air from it or from its porticoes. Nevertheless, since it was not shut in by contiguous structures as was the Greek town house, nor confined within high fortification walls like the Mesopo

73

tamian palace at Mari (Fig. 148), the Minoan palace was not entirely "introverted": the royal residential apartments looked outward through columned porticoes, and the great state halls in the Piano Nobile had large windows opening upon the west courts. Moreover a central court is not a characteristic, let alone invariable, feature of even the larger Minoan houses, suggesting that the inner court was not an indispensable and inevitable feature of Minoan domestic architecture. The more restricted "light-well" was perhaps more congenial to the Cretan climate.

It is probable, also, that entertainments such as boxing, a popular Cretan sport, and dancing, perhaps always a religious rite, took place in the central court, whose west side was lined by various shrines. Of course the "Theatral Areas" and the west courts must likewise have been the scene of various ceremonies, as in fact the "causeways" in the fresco of the "Sacred Grove and the Dance" indicate.[1]

However the central courts have certain peculiarities which seem to call for some explanation beyond what we have so far suggested.[2] For instance, it is a strange fact that the "central" court at Gournia lies actually outside the limits of the palace (Fig. 8), as if it were not so much a necessary and integral part of the palace structure itself as a large open area which provided for some form of activity associated with palatial or civic life. There may even have been, at times, a "central court" without a palace at all, a possibility we have mentioned at Plati (Ch. III, 21, and Fig. 30).

The Central Courts of the major palaces are similar in various respects. Mallia, Phaistos, and Knossos are quite alike in size, the first two especially so (80 by 170 M.ft.). Zakro is smaller (40 by 100 M.ft.) but similarly proportioned. Phaistos and Mallia had porticoes with alternating pillars and columns on their long east

---

[1] *Knossos*, III, pl. 18; Evans takes the "causeways" to be low isodomic walls, and so Karo (*Greifen am Thron*, p. 50), but cf. Platon, *Kret. Chron.*, 13 (1959), p. 239.

[2] For a fuller discussion, with references, of the use of the central courts for the bull games see my article in *AJA*, 61 (1957), pp. 255-262.

sides. All four were oriented more or less north-south on their long axis. Two had flagged floors: Knossos and Phaistos. This all suggests some degree of standardization, like a football field or a tennis court.[3]

In several ways the Minoan central courts resemble the long narrow public plazas or forums of early Italian towns with their surrounding porticoes and galleries. These were so designed, the Augustan architect Vitruvius tells us, not only to serve the traffic and commerce of everyday life, but also to double as a place for staging the favorite public entertainment of the time, gladiatorial exhibitions.[4]

If we take a cue from this and ask what was the favorite spectacle of the Minoan Cretans there can be no doubt of the answer. Over and over again in their wall paintings, their gems, and their minor arts, we see represented the famous bull games (Fig. 102). At least in origin these shows were no doubt of a religious nature, a form of sacred ceremonial, designed to please or to appease the gods; in actual practice they may have tended, like our Christmas celebration, to become more and more secularized. They were not bull *fights*, as they are sometimes carelessly called, for no weapons were involved, and the animals were apparently not injured in any way—unless it may be that they were sacrificed at the conclusion (Fig. 101). The performances were a test of skill and agility. Cretan youths, and girls too, no doubt after lengthy preliminary training, pitted their dexterity, strength, and courage against powerful bulls in a thrilling display of skilful manoeuvers which culminated in (the favorite moment for the artists to select for their representations) an almost incredible tour de force: the acrobat faced the charging animal head-on, deftly seized its horns and, as it angrily tossed back its head, used the impetus thus gained to perform a full somersault over the bull's back, and so alight on the floor of the arena behind. If the performer

[3] Conspicuously on the axis of the Central Courts at Phaistos and Knossos are the "holy mountains" Ida and Iuktas, respectively (Fig. 51, and *Knossos*, IV, fig. 7, and suppl. plate 56).

[4] 5, I, 1-2.

were killed—ritually immolated in effect to the Minoan goddess —perhaps he could look forward to the assured enjoyment of some Minoan Elysium.

Representations of the bull games sometimes hint at an architectural background, and Evans himself was of the opinion that the "Grandstand Fresco," as he called it, depicted a large crowd of Cretan men and women watching these sports in a setting of columns and a tricolumnar shrine (Fig. 133). He also fancied that this signified some kind of amphitheater with tiers of seats rising amid a grandiose architectural framework: a special arena somewhere outside the limits of the palace. But no traces of any such structure have ever been detected at the three major sites, and it is in fact plain that no specialized form of sports auditorium on such an elaborate architectural scale existed before the amphitheaters of Roman times (but see now pp. 81-83).

Although the porticoes and galleries and (at Knossos) the Tripartite Shrine embedded in them irresistibly suggest themselves as the source of inspiration for the background architecture of the "Grandstand Fresco," it is sufficiently evident why Sir Arthur could not conceive of this rough-and-tumble sport taking place in the central court of the palace. For at Knossos he could see no sign of precautions taken to prevent a careering bull from penetrating into the surrounding porticoes or passages, with dire results both to the palace and to the spectators. But the boundaries of the Knossos court are very badly preserved, and the search must be extended beyond the Palace of Minos.

At Phaistos there are clear traces of doors to protect all the openings on the Central Court, although it is difficult to see their usefulness in the ordinary régime of palace life. The most extraordinary and significant instance is the façade of the large hall, 25, near the northwest corner of the court, which is composed of two great pillars on either side of an oval central column (Fig. 50). At some time after its original construction the intervals between the pairs of pillars were walled up, probably, we may imagine, for only four or five feet above the floor level; and doors were then set up to close the remaining space between the pillars and the column. The Italian publication comments on this astonishing architectural practice of closing a door against a column, but does not offer any explanation.[5]

An even more peculiar situation is found at Mallia, where the surroundings of the court are very well preserved (Fig. 6). On the west side of the court access to a flight of steps some 10½ ft. (3.20 m.) broad, leading to important rooms in the second storey, was controlled by a set of double doors. The French excavators remark on the strangeness of this feature, but do not attempt to explain it.[6] Along the north end of the same court runs a columned portico with another odd arrangement: a distinct threshold, and therefore a doorway, between the two columns at the west end (Fig. 57). This can only mean that passage between the other columns was not left free; what form the barrier between these columns took is not known, but one might conjecture a mud brick wall four or five feet high. On the east side of the court there is a well-preserved portico about 110 ft. (ca. 33½ m.) long, made up of alternating pillars and columns, a common Minoan arrangement. On the upper surface of the stone sill between each pillar and column are three circular cuttings, plainly sockets for the tenons of vertical posts some 9 in. (22 cm.) in diameter, capped no doubt by a horizontal railing.[6a] Such a balustrade in an upper gallery would be quite understandable as a means of protection against a fall, but here portico and court are practically on the same level. Nor can it be explained as a barrier to keep humans from entering the portico from the court (even if any reason were apparent for so doing), for the spacing of the posts is wide enough to allow even an adult to squeeze between them, and probably one could also have climbed over the railing. It seems difficult, then, to explain this barrier except as designed to prevent some large domestic animal from getting into the portico from the court.[7] But the palace court was certainly not the place for

[5] *Festòs*, II, pp. 71f.   [6] *Mallia*, I, p. 32.   [6a] *M. and T.*, p. 161.
[7] There is a possible trace of a barrier in the similar portico on the east side of the Central Court at Phaistos, as I noticed in 1959: the top surface (1.20 m. above

stabling cattle, while the horse was still very rare in Minoan Crete.

Thus the rooms and porticoes surrounding the central court were in fact protected, which removes the objections felt by Evans and others to the otherwise obvious suggestion that the central court was also the bull ring. Since the animals were not goaded to fury by the tortures to which they are subjected in the Spanish arena the doors and railings indicated by the remains would no doubt have formed an adequate barrier. On a fragment of a mural painting from Knossos a Minoan lady is shown standing behind a fence similar to that suggested by the remains of the east portico at Mallia, while beside her enough remains to indicate a crowd of male spectators, as in the Grandstand Fresco (Figs. 133, 136, C).

A well-known gem which Evans described as "the finest combination of powerful execution with minute detail to be found, perhaps, in the whole range of the Minoan gem-engraver's Art" represents a bull with its forelegs up on a large rectangular object decorated by a series of latticed lines which follow the four sides and the diagonals of the rectangle; above the rectangle, at the upper left, a man in the usual Minoan toreador's costume is leaping head first on to the animal's head (Fig. 54).[8] The common but hardly possible explanation of this scene is that it shows a man capturing a bull which he has surprised drinking from a tank. Surely no bull would drink in such a fashion nor would a Minoan artist have so represented him!

On the diamond-cut-diamond principle we propose to solve this riddle by conjuring up a second. In the northwest corner of the Phaistos court is a construction which the official publication leaves as an "enigma" (Fig. 52). It consists of a carefully built platform of dressed masonry about 8 ft. 3 in. (2.50 m.) long by 2 ft. 8 in. (0.80 m.) wide by 3 ft. 8 in. (1.12 m.) high,

---

the stylobate) of the top block of the northernmost base shows, in the center of its south edge, the traces of a cutting 4½ cm. wide by 4 cm. deep.

[8] *Knossos*, III, p. 185, fig. 129. In the latest publication of the seal V.E.G. Kenna interprets the scene in the usual way without further comment (*Cretan Seals*, Oxford, 1960, p. 118, pl. 8, no. 202).

which narrows at its east end and drops down to a height of 2 ft. (0.60 m.). This gives it a step-like appearance, and in fact the upper edge of both the lower and the upper stone block at the east end is worn as if from frequent stepping up and down upon the platform. Yet as a flight of steps it makes no sense, for there are no openings at or near this level in the well preserved wall behind it. Can we suppose that one of the doubtless numerous manoeuvers which were devised to lend variety and interest to the bull games was one in which the acrobat, cornered, whether intentionally or not, in this blind angle of the court, quickly stepped up on this platform and, at the right moment, as the bull perhaps succeeded in getting his forefeet on the narrow end of the first step, bounded upon its back and thence to the ground behind the bull, safe from his apparent impasse (Fig. 50). In early Spanish bull baiting, it is interesting to note, vaulting over the bull from a chair or table was a recognized manoeuver.

That there is a significant correspondence between the scene on the gem just described and the platform in the Central Court at Phaistos is indicated by the fact that the distinctive pattern on the rectangular object on the gem (which represents, in our view, the stone leaping-platform) occurs nowhere else in Cretan art except painted at a large scale on the rear face of the two deep niches which, symmetrically set on either side of the great central doorway, are a very conspicuous feature of the impressive façade which formed the north end of the Central Court (Fig. 50), and on a similar niche just within the same doorway.[9] One of these niches is in fact but a few feet away from the stone platform in the northwest corner of the court (Fig. 53); small wonder that the gem-engraver associated the pattern and the platform in his mind! Indeed it is quite possible that the pattern had some symbolical connection, presumably religious, with the bull games.[10]

[9] Fragments of plaster apparently with a similar design were also found in the fill under Stairway 76, evidently from the ruins of an earlier palace, *Festòs*, II, p. 62.

[10] Cf. *Knossos*, I, pp. 375-376.

It is tempting to suppose that it is not merely coincidence that the main north-south axis of the Central Court of Phaistos, the scene of the bull games (Fig. 50), points directly toward the sacred cave of Kamares, much frequented from Early Minoan times, on the south slope of Mount Ida (Fig. 51). And surely the double-peaked crest of that mountain must have suggested to the Minoans, as it does to us, their sacred symbol the sacral horns, which are commonly supposed to have their origin in a conventionalization of the horns of a bull.[11]

It may also be due to some connection with the bull games that toward the north end of the west side of the court in each of the major palaces, and perhaps also at Gournia, Plati, and Vathypetro, there is a room where religious rites may have been performed. At Knossos this is the "Tripartite Columnar Shrine"; at Mallia, a large room with an altar (vi 1); and at Phaistos, Room 25 with its imposing façade of piers and central column (Fig. 50). Was the bull sacrificed here at the end of the performance?[12] Or was it the scene of certain preparatory rituals? One further conjecture: were some of the rooms facing on Corridor 26, which connects with the rear of Room 25 at Phaistos, temporary stalls for the bulls while awaiting the performances (Fig. 4)? They must have been kept somewhere nearby, and where else more suitably? This might also explain the curious ramp down into Room vi 12 at Mallia, one of the rooms behind the room with the altar (Fig. 6).[13]

The above account of the uses of the palace central courts has been reprinted almost verbatim from the first edition of the *PoC*, but recent excavations have made it necessary to reconsider one point, namely the correctness of the statement on p. 76 (supra) that "no specialized form of sports auditorium . . . with tiers of seats rising amid a grandiose architectural framework . . . has

[11] Nilsson, *MMR*[2], pp. 185-186.

[12] Forsdyke interprets the scenes on the Chieftain Cup found at H. Triadha, as the presentation of the hides of sacrificed bulls to Minos, *Journal of the Warburg and Courtauld Institutes*, 15 (1952), pp. 13-19; Evans says that "the bull of sacrifice, in fact, is a bull of the arena" (*Knossos*, IV, p. 44). And see further discussion Ch. VII, 2 (end).

[13] *Mallia*, I, p. 24, fig. 3, pl. 15, 2.

ever been detected" (in Crete). This may still, I think, be accepted as generally true in spite of the fact that northwest of the palace at Mallia and, possibly, at Knossos structures have recently been found that might qualify as rather modest examples of arenas in which the bull-games were held.

The first of these was excavated between 1957 and 1962 by two experienced excavators, Henri and Micheline van Effenterre, for the French School of Archaeology (Fig. 160).[14] The center of the area is a large open court, 130 M.ft. east to west and 100 M.ft. north to south, or sufficiently close to these figures to indicate that the court was laid out at a specified size. Originally it seems to have been enclosed on all four sides by a clay embankment nowhere preserved thicker than two meters nor higher than one meter; its inner face was lined with thin slabs of stone, and three short, narrow stairs are preserved, showing that the embankment was meant to be mounted. Access to the court was gained by two broad openings near the northeast and the southeast corners. Beyond the embankment on three sides were rooms, mostly small, except for those in the southwest corner marked "crypte" and "magasins"; the north side was bordered by a street.

The van Effenterres suggest that the court might at times have served for athletic performances or even for the bull-games, but they are of the opinion that its principal use was as an "agora" for political gatherings of the local citizenry, while the carefully constructed "crypte" would have been reserved for some such body as a "Council of Elders" or the "Members of the Board." All this is possible, but rather futile to propose in view of our crass ignorance of the organization of the Minoan state, and it is especially difficult to comprehend the *raison d'être* of the surrounding embankment in the scheme of things or, for that matter, of the vast court.

Platon also argues against the van Effenterres' political interpretation of the "agora" and the "crypte" and instead he argues

---

[14] Henri and Micheline van Effenterre, *Fouilles exécutées à Mallia, le centre politique, I, l'Agora* (Paris, 1969), and Marie-Claire Amouretti, *II, La crypte hypostyle* (Paris, 1970), both in *Études Crétoises* series, nos. 17, 18.

that it was the locus of the bull-games.[15] His detailed argument is first concerned with refuting my view that the games were held in the central courts of the palaces. I think I have adequately answered his objections in an article in a volume presented to Doro Levi.[16]

As for Platon's arguments in favor of the agora as the site of the bull-games, I would agree thoroughly. Its chalky clay (*asprochoma*) surface would provide excellent footing for man and beast; but it is important to note that the surface of the Central Court of the Mallia palace is similar, if not identical, and that the surface of the earlier palace court at Zakro is also the same;[17] the clay embankments would be an excellent "container" for the bulls; and the dimensions of the court would also be suitable for the purpose, but note that, though somewhat differently proportioned, the area of court and agora are virtually identical (ca. 13,000 sq. ft.). If, then, Platon's intepretation of the "agora" as an arena for the bull-games and other athletic performances is satisfactory it is certainly *not* satisfactory with regard to the provision of space for spectators. Wall paintings like the Grandstand Fresco indicate the great crowds that attended these fiestas. How many would be able to make their way along the at-most six-foot-wide embankment to find a precarious place to stand, and to see something of what was happening in the arena? On the other hand there would have been abundant room around a central court in the porticoes, galleries, windows, and on the flat roofs for even a very large crowd.

But if our conclusions so far seem to be very contradictory there is, I think, a simple way out of the dilemma. It lies in the answer to the question: where did the prospective performers in the bull-games acquire their astonishing skill? Such precisely timed maneuvers could only have been the result of long and intensive training with—at first—co-operative animals.[18] But the Central

[15] N. Platon, "On the Problem of the Site of the Cretan Bullfights," in *KERNOS, in Honor of Prof. George Bakalakes* (Thessalonike, 1972), pp. 143-145 (in Greek).

[16] J. W. Graham, "A New Arena at Mallia," in *Antichità Cretesi*, I, pp. 65-73 (Università di Catania, 1973).

[17] *M. and T.*, p. 226.

[18] See the graphic reconstruction by Mary Renault, *The King Must Die* (Pantheon Press, 1958).

Court, where the whole life of the palace—domestic, religious, commercial, administrative—was concentrated, could not be the answer. Surely at Mallia it was the structure excavated by the van Effenterres. The surrounding rooms could have housed the trainees and served a multitude of other purposes; the games-officials would have had their headquarters in the "crypte." The system of embankments served primarily, of course, to contain the bulls, but their upper surfaces could easily have accommodated the comparatively small number of trainers and superintendents, performers awaiting their turn, and the usual idlers and habitués.

To the northwest of the Palace of Minos and just south of the Royal Road, British excavators in the early 1970s uncovered the remains of a large building of L.M. II or III date. One of them writes: "this platform may have been the podium of a grandstand for spectators watching the ceremonial use of the Royal Road or, perhaps, something more vigorous such as the bull-sports taking place in the open ground to the south."[19] Obviously much more extensive and intensive investigations are needed in order to produce reliable conclusions. At the moment it seems difficult to understand how the hypothetical grandstand could face both north and south.

[19] *JHS, Archaeological Reports for 1972-73*, pp. 27f.

CHAPTER V

THE RESIDENTIAL QUARTERS OF THE ROYAL FAMILY

1. GENERAL DESCRIPTION

NOWADAYS one is likely to think of a "palace" only as the dwelling place of the royal family. Webster, for example, defines it as "the official residence of a sovereign." But, as we have already seen, the Minoan palace was much more than that; the part used for the royal apartments occupied, in fact, but a small fraction of the total area of the palace. Yet they are of especial interest for several reasons. They give us an intimate glimpse into the life of the royal family—ever a subject of peculiarly engrossing concern to the "commoner"; they are often particularly well preserved compared with other parts of the palace; and they are amongst the most carefully built and decorated suites of palatial chambers.[1]

As the best preserved of all (even without the "reconstitutions") it is inevitable that we should visit first the royal apartments in the Palace of Minos, or as Evans called them, the "Domestic Quarter."[2] We prefer to avoid this term in order to prevent any misunderstanding that it was intended for the "domestics."

The Residential Quarter of the palace at Knossos was situated, as in the other palaces, well away from the principal entrances, in the *penetralia* of the building, east of the Central Court and just south of its mid point (Fig. 12). Here the

---

[1] For a fuller treatment of the palace residential quarters see *AJA*, 63 (1959), pp. 47-52.

[2] *Knossos*, I, pp. 325-359; III, pp. 282-390.

ground sloped off rapidly toward the east, and in a later phase of the construction of the palace a broad flat terrace for these rooms was created by cutting a great vertical scarp running along the eastern edge of the court and reaching a depth of nearly thirty feet (9 m.) below its flagged surface. This allowed sufficient space for two storeys below the court, and above it there must have existed one more storey, but probably not two as I once believed (*AJA*, 83 [1979]), p. 65.

When this part of the Palace of Minos was destroyed the collapse of the upper storeys preceded that of the lower, filling them with debris almost to their ceilings; perhaps not until the slow decay of their woodwork did the lower piers and columns finally give way. The result was that when Evans dug into this part of the building it was a dramatic, almost eerie, experience. Approaching from the north, he found himself tunneling through a doorway to a landing from which stairs both ascended and descended. This was, of course, the "Grand Staircase," as he named it, the walls of which, starting at the level of the Central Court (though originally it went still higher), he supported and consolidated wherever necessary with remarkable skill (Fig. 38). In later years he went much further, rebuilding many of the piers and columns, heightening the remains of the walls, and constructing ceilings over the first storey rooms, employing, instead of the original wood and stone, modern structural steel and concrete. It is the fashion now to criticize him severely for this, and undoubtedly his reconstructions here involve some uncertainties and even errors; the new materials are somewhat disturbing, and at times it is difficult to be certain what is new and what is old. Yet if he had done nothing, much of what he uncovered would have been later destroyed by the weather and by the destructive earthquakes to which Crete is still subject.

At any rate it is an unforgettable experience for the modern visitor to descend from the Central Court to the "Hall of the Colonnades" at the foot of the Grand Staircase, where he finds four massive columns of the typical Minoan form, with bulging convex capitals and shafts that taper downward instead of upward (Fig. 136, F). These columns (of course restored) flank two sides of a small unroofed court about 11½ by 18½ ft. (3.50 by 5.65 m.), forming as Evans called it, a light-well or light area. The stairway forms a third side, and a wall, with windows on a smaller stairway, the fourth.

From the Hall of the Colonnades one passes through a doorway in its northeast corner into a long corridor illuminated by two openings from another light-well on the right. A few feet farther a door opens into the most impressive room preserved (or reconstituted) in the palace. Evans dubbed it, with his ear for the picturesque name, the Hall of the Double-Axes, from the numerous double-axe symbols cut in the walls of the light-well (Fig. 39). More simply, and to bring it into line with the similar rooms in the other palaces, we may term it the Men's Hall, for such it must have been, though this is not meant to exclude the probability that women also used the room.[3]

Measuring about 26 by 40 ft. (ca. 8 by 12 m.) the hall was floored with fine gypsum flagging laid in a regular pattern of blocks; the walls were plastered above a high dado of gypsum veneer, and perhaps hung, along the line of a painted spiral band, with a series of large "figure-of-eight" shields consisting of layers of bullhide stretched over a wooden frame. The inner half of the room, lighted through a two-columned portico from a light-well at its west end, was divided from the eastern half by a row of five rectangular piers, restored on the stone bases

[3] Evans also called it the "Hall of State Receptions" (*Knossos*, I, p. 329), but this was surely the main room of the private suite; there was ample provision for public rooms elsewhere in the palace. He also referred to it in *Knossos*, III, p. 481, as the Piano Nobile, but this is hardly a proper use of the term. The sign now in the room calls it in Greek the Μέγαρον τοῦ Βασιλέως, and in English the "King's Room." Marinatos (*C. and M.*, p. 126) also writes of the suites I (with most others) identify as residential quarters, "these elegant rooms, which are found in the best positions in all the palaces, must have been reception rooms rather than private apartments. At Phaistos and Mallia they lie at the northwest corner of the palace to face the cooling winds during the long and scorching summer months." The position is "best," I agree, for the living quarters, but the magnificent west façades and the position of the formal entranceways combine with other evidence (Ch. VI, 1) to indicate that the reception halls were placed along the west fronts of the palaces on the upper floors.

which were found in their original positions (Fig. 45). In each of the four openings between the five piers there once existed, as the pivot holes prove, a set of double doors which when open folded back flush into a panel in the face of each pier; when all the doors were closed it created a kind of temporary partition separating the two halves of the room. This pier-and-door partition, as we have called it, was a very popular feature of Cretan palace and house architecture, its purpose being perhaps partly to gain greater privacy for one part of the room, but probably it was chiefly a device to adapt the room to the extremes of Cretan weather (see Ch. v, 2). In the Hall of the Double-Axes there is another similar partition at the east end of the room and again along the east end of the south side, both of which open on an L-shaped veranda. Thus in pleasant weather all the doors could be left open for both air and view, while in bad weather as many doors could be closed as desirable, and the chill further tempered by portable charcoal braziers (Fig. 140, E, F). Above the doorways there was perhaps a series of "transoms" which may have been filled with waxed parchment to enable some light to filter through when the doors were closed (Figs. 45, 151).

The columned portico opened on what was probably a garden terrace, bounded on east and south by a low retaining wall and commanding a view over the valley beyond.[4]

From the southwest corner of the Men's Hall a narrow passage, turning at right angles and guarded by doors at both ends (Fig. 12), leads into a smaller but well decorated hall. This formed, as Evans recognized, the main room of a more private suite; it may therefore be called the Queen's Hall or Women's Hall (Fig. 43).[5] The floor of the room was flagged

[4] Evans would restore here a wall to the full height of the first storey (*Knossos*, III, p. 328), and it is in fact partly rebuilt; but there seems to be no evidence for more than a low parapet, or, as Dinsmoor (*Arch. Anc. Gr.*, p 9) says, "little more than a garden wall."

[5] Evans called it the "Queen's Megaron." But "megaron" should be reserved for the distinctive main room of the Mycenaean palace (Fig. 150), which bears no resemblance whatever to this room. This and the attached rooms were no doubt not exclusively used by the women (and so Lawrence, *Gk. Arch.*, p. 39); but

with gypsum, the walls beautifully painted in bright colors with scenes of marine life and figures of dancing girls, and the ceiling was decorated with an intricate spiral pattern. On two sides were light-wells with high stone sills forming convenient seats. From the northeast corner of the room the ladies could pass by means of a winding corridor, closable at several points by doors, into the area of the garden terrace and verandas to the east and south of the Men's Hall. One can hardly avoid seeing in this arrangement a nice respect for the privacy of the fair sex, as well as a due appreciation of their society.

Opening immediately off the Queen's Hall and lighted from it by a window is a small bathroom; the remains of a clay tub were found nearby (Fig. 81). South of this room another passage leads to still more private rooms, the general nature of which is indicated by the presence of a remarkably well designed toilet connecting with an extensive system of palace drains (Ch. v, 4).

A narrow stairway led directly from the Queen's Hall to rooms above, used perhaps as sleeping rooms, no doubt for both men and women. This upper floor was also accessible by another stairway that could be reached either from the inner rooms of the lower floor, or by a door opening off the southeast corner of the Hall of the Colonnades at the foot of the Grand Staircase.

The fact that the royal suites in the other palaces bear a remarkable resemblance to the one in the Palace of Minos makes it clear that the excellent planning of the residential apartments is not the result of chance, nor is it likely to be due to the happy inspiration of a single architect. Rather it seems the result of the combined and traditional experience of generations of island architects working wherever their services were from time to time required. If true, this has considerable bearing on our understanding of the relationship of the architecture of

since they must have been used particularly by the women we may, for the sake of convenience, continue to employ the terms "Queen's" or "Women's Hall," or "Apartments."

the palaces in general, and so it will be worthwhile to examine the private apartments of the other palaces with some attention.

Next, then, we turn to Phaistos. The principal royal suite—for there seem to have been two in this palace—is located well away from the public part of the palace and set on a terrace scarped out of the edge of the hill at the northern end of the building (Fig. 4).[6] The single approach to it was, as at Knossos, by way of a long stairway, descending however not from the Central Court but from the northeast corner of the Peristyle Court (Fig. 10).

At the foot of the stairs a doorway opens to the left (north) into a large room, 77-79, which is remarkably like the Hall of the Double-Axes—clearly the Men's Hall (Fig. 47, at right). The entrance, as is normal in this type of room, is placed near the end of one long side. The floor is covered with a fine gypsum flagging laid in a regular pattern, the joints between the slabs being filled with red plaster (Fig. 127); the walls were wainscotted with the same material. Gypsum is indeed used with prodigality in the Phaistos palace for there were quarries providing a fine grade of gypsum, i.e. alabaster, in the neighborhood of H. Triadha and Gortyn. These are again being utilized in the work of restoration (Fig. 125).

The arrangement of the light-well with its two columns at one end of the room (the right on entering), and the four-bayed partition dividing the room into two parts, is virtually identical with that in the Men's Hall at Knossos. Along the whole north side of the room a similar pier-and-door partition opens on a colonnaded portico, and there was, we would like to think, a terraced garden beyond.

The Queen's Hall, 81, is reached from the Men's Hall by way of a narrow corridor, 80, secured with doors at both ends, exactly as in the sister palace (Fig. 82). The floor and wall dado were done in alabaster veneering, and the plastered upper walls seem to have borne painted designs. As at Knossos the

[6] *Festòs,* II, pp. 254-304.

bathroom, 83, opens off the main room, but is here, as regularly elsewhere, at a lower level and reached by several steps; both steps and walls are lined with gypsum (Fig. 82). Another door led from the Queen's Hall to more private rooms, 82, incompletely preserved but retaining traces of a toilet arrangement. Still another door opened on to the veranda and terrace on which the Men's Hall also opened—again as at Knossos.

In addition this Residential Quarter included an extra room, 50, located south of the access stairway (Fig. 47). It was likewise lavishly decorated with alabaster floor and wainscotting, and part of the room had a gypsum bench around the walls. The position of the light-well is unusual, not at one end of the room but in the center, and apparently confined to the square space within the area enclosed by the four columns. A narrow stairway provided communication with the rooms in the storey above.

Anyone who has experienced the summer heat at Phaistos will understand why a northern exposure was selected for the main residential suite; but this exposure enjoyed the additional advantage of providing a magnificent panorama of the range of Ida (Fig. 51). At Knossos the pleasantest available view was also chosen.

A more modest but better protected suite was built to the east of the Central Court, 63-64 (Fig. 4).[7] Here we can recognize most of the elements familiar from the preceding examples: the Men's Hall, 63, with a small plaster-floored light-well with drain to the northeast but no columns, a pier-and-door partition across the middle and another opening on an L-shaped veranda, 64, with high polychrome bases set in a stylobate; also a Queen's Hall, 63b, entered by a simple doorway from the light-well and equipped with the usual bathroom, d, and with more private rooms, ce, beyond—the drain from e suggests the position of a toilet. The most interesting feature is the natural rock terrace, perhaps left for the picturesque effect, on which the

[7] *Festòs*, II, pp. 155-191.

veranda opens; along its southeast side several steps lead down to a lower terrace. With the help of the wall paintings from the palaces it is easy to picture here an attractive flower garden along the edge of the steep slope to the valley; the view must have been even more delightful in antiquity when the opposite hills were clothed with trees.

At Mallia the Residential Quarter is built in the northwest corner of the palace, well away from the principal entrances (Fig. 6).[8] In keeping with the palace as a whole it is less well decorated than the otherwise similar suites at Phaistos and Knossos, though there are remains of painted walls and floors. The Men's Hall, iii 7, is very like the Hall of the Double-Axes in plan, while the arrangement of the Queen's Hall, iii 1, is extraordinarily close to the corresponding room in the North Residential Quarter at Phaistos, 81: four doorways connect with the Men's Hall (via the usual corridor with doors at each end); with the bathroom, iii 4; with more private rooms, iii 2 (drains indicate the position of a toilet); and with the veranda on which the Men's Hall opens through a pier-and-door partition. There was also a private stairway at III b to the upper rooms. Beyond the long columned portico on the north there seems to have been an open area, probably a garden with a view over the bay a short distance away (Figs. 11, 58).

The Villa at H. Triadha also had a fine residential suite set in an artificially leveled terrace at the northwest corner of the building;[9] they were reached from the upper level by a flight of steps lighted by a light-well at the bottom (Fig. 165). Here once again we find the L-shaped veranda opening on a terrace with a magnificent view toward Ida to the north (Fig. 65) and toward the valley and gulf to the west. Behind an unusually long pier-and-door partition is a Hall, 3, about 20 by 30 ft. (6 by 9 m.) in size, with a floor of regular gypsum flagging (Fig. 151). Combined with a space beyond a four-bayed parti-

---

[8] The Mallia Residential Quarter was first recognized by Platon, *Kret. Chron.*, I (1947), pp. 635-636; *Mallia, Maisons*, I, p. 105.
[9] *Guida*, pp. 30-32.

tion, 12, this evidently formed the Men's Hall. At the east end is the usual two-columned light-well, which however has two more columns through which to supply light in the opposite direction to Room 4 (Fig. 69). This room has a gypsum floor and paneled walls, as well as a stone bench around the walls; a smaller room off it has a low gypsum platform in one corner on which a bed may have been placed (Ch. XII, 1).

The vista of alternating light and shade created by the succession of rooms, light-wells, and porticoes from the east end of Room 4 to the west end of Room 3, a distance of nearly 75 ft. (23 m.) must have formed an architectural composition rivaled only by the suite of rooms in the Little Palace at Knossos. We have attempted to suggest the effect as seen from the west end of Room 3 in Fig. 151, bottom.

Through large openings in the walls the light-well also supplied light on the south to the stairway, and on the north, to 13, the Queen's Hall (Figs. 68, 70). What rooms there may have been beyond the pier-and-door partition on the north side of this Hall is unknown, nor is it clear what the area, 14, within a thin adobe brick partition east of 13, was used for, but fragments of the fine mural painting representing a cat stalking a bird were found here (Fig. 134). At the northeast corner stairs led down through a door, still complete with lintel (Fig. 154), to a small room with tiny columned court or light-well in the center and steps to rooms in the upper floor. No bathroom has been found in the preserved remains.

In the Little Palace at Knossos a suite of rooms along the east side (Figs. 13, 64) supposedly would constitute, on a sumptuous scale, the main living rooms of this aristocratic residence. The Men's Hall with its lavish provision of pier-and-door partitions, opens on a peristyle court. Immediately adjacent to this suite of rooms we again find a bathroom (it became a shrine in the last period of occupation) with several other adjoining rooms, but there is no clear "Queen's Hall."

Some other less pretentious dwellings present closer analogies to the residential quarter of the palaces. Perhaps the clearest instance is House Da at Mallia (Fig. 22). Room 3, with its floor paved with irregular flagstones, a four-bayed transverse partition, and a single-columned light-well, is the Men's Hall; adjacent to it and reached by either Corridor 4 or 5, is the Women's Hall, 6. It also has a flagged floor and off it opens the usual sunken bathroom, 7; a smaller space beyond 6, enclosed with a thin brick partition, has a toilet in one corner.

House Za at Mallia is similar in its layout (Fig. 25): 12, the Men's Hall; 5, the Women's Hall, with a transverse partition and a toilet at the far end; the bathroom, 11, is entered not directly from 5 but from a small passage, 4, between 5 and 12.

Other possible or probable examples may be seen in the Royal Villa E, F, G, H (Fig. 14); the House of the Chancel Screen, 4, 5, 6 (Fig. 16); House B at Palaikastro, 2, 3, 6 (Fig. 29); Nirou Khani 5 (the Women's Hall), 3, 6, 7, 8, 9, all reached by a corridor, 4, with doors at each end, from the Men's Hall, 2a, and with stairs, 10, to the second storey (Fig. 31); Tylissos A with Men's Hall, 6, and bathroom, 11, off it, and three rooms and stairs reached from Corridor A (Fig. 19); and Tylissos C with Men's Hall, 15, and a suite of rooms, 12 (bath), 14, 13, and stairs (Fig. 20).

It is evident that the living quarters in the Minoan palaces follow the general pattern of contemporary Cretan houses of the well-to-do classes, though of course on a larger and more luxurious scale—or should we say that the houses ape the palaces in this respect? One is left with the impression that the design of the royal apartments was based on long experience and on a fine understanding of, and regard for, the needs of the two sexes in their domestic relationships. It is noteworthy that the lowest floor of the private apartments—and this was probably the most important one—was located, even in the palaces, at the ground level, not in the Piano Nobile as was the case with the principal public apartments. Surely this was done so that the royal family could enjoy the pleasure of the open porticoes and terraced gardens. The Minoan would not have cared to live in a modern skyscraper apartment!

2. THE MINOAN HALL

Most of the larger excavated houses of Minoan Crete possess one room which is outstanding for its size, decoration, and certain other fairly constant characteristics, which may perhaps be best designated by the term "Minoan Hall," the "Sala Minoica" of the Italian excavators. Unless we need to be particularly specific, however, "Hall" alone (with a capital H) will be sufficiently clear.

In some ways it would be convenient to have a more distinctive term, one that could be used internationally, and Evans and others have employed the word "megaron," or "Cretan megaron" (*mègaron à la crétoise*).[10] However, not only has megaron (big room) a Greek, and specifically Homeric, flavor, but it has already been appropriated (and probably correctly) for the large and dominating rectangular room with a central hearth surrounded by four columns and preceded by one or two shallow porches (Fig. 150), characteristic of Mycenaean palatial architecture, and occurring also in domestic architecture in a simpler form. On the other hand, it is perhaps well to be satisfied with a rather vague and general word, for the room we propose to discuss in this section, as we shall see, varies considerably in form, and no doubt also in function.

The mainland palace normally had but one dominating megaron, but the Cretan palace usually contained several Halls on the ground floor, and quite possibly still more in the upper storeys. The residential quarters naturally afford the best preserved specimens, and we have already met a good many in our study of that part of the palace. Let us, however, select one for examination in more detail.

A very normal example is the "Men's Hall" of the North Residential Quarter at Phaistos (Fig. 10).[11] The whole complex,

[10] It has sometimes been called a "Pillar Hall" (*Pfeilersaal*), but this risks confusion with other types of rooms containing pillars, such as the "Pillar Crypt," or such a room as ix 2, north of the Central Court at Mallia. *Salle à portes* (*Türensaal*) has also been proposed.

[11] *Festòs*, II, pp. 281-291.

as we may call it, is about 44 ft. long by 22 ft. wide (13 by
6½ m.), a simple relationship of 2:1 frequently approximated
in these rooms. Backed up against an exterior wall at one end of
the Hall is a light-well, about 22 by 9 ft. (6½ by 2¾ m.),
which transmitted light and air to the Hall through a portico
of two columns. The Hall itself is divided into two unequal
parts by a transverse pier-and-door partition with four bays; by
closing the doors in these openings the Hall could be quickly
converted into virtually two rooms. The larger and more important part was, as invariably, the one farther from the light-
well (see below); it measured in this case about 19 ft. (nearly
6 m.) long against about 11 ft. (3½ m.) for the other part of
the room. Both parts were paved with large slabs of gypsum,
but the paving of the larger part was more carefully executed,
consisting of two concentric rectangles enclosing a single central
slab of large size (Figs. 127, 136, N). The walls of the entire
room, as well as of the end of the light-well, had a dado of
gypsum veneer preserved to a maximum height of about 3 ft.
(1 m.) but perhaps originally ca. 6 ft. high; above this the
plastered wall was decorated with geometric and plant designs
in bright colors; the fragments were too few to permit a restoration of the whole scheme.

Except in the finest houses the walls of the Hall were usually
merely plastered and the floor laid with irregular flagstones.
Nor were the columned porticoes opening on garden terraces,
found in the Men's Halls of the palaces, a feature of ordinary
domestic architecture, although an example occurs in the Villa
of the Lilies at Amnisos (Fig. 76), and another in the Little
Palace at Knossos (Fig. 13).

The area of the main part of the Halls varies greatly. The
largest by far is in the Residential Quarter at H. Triadha (Fig.
151), which measures nearly 30 by 20 ft. (ca. 9 by 6 m.) or
nearly 600 sq. ft. (54 sq. m.). Next in size are the Halls in
the Little Palace at Knossos, the Phaistos North Residential
Quarter, and the Hall of the Double-Axes, all about 385 sq. ft.

(ca. 36 sq. m.). Smallest is the one in the South House at Knossos, about 10½ feet square or some 110 sq. ft. (10½ sq. m.).

As we have already noticed, there is almost invariably a light-well or similar source of light and air at one end of the Hall complex, and the room itself is also nearly always divided into two unequal parts by a transverse pier-and-door partition. It is an odd fact that, whereas one might expect the larger and more important part of the room to be located next the light-well, the reverse is true. And since there are some seventeen instances in which this peculiar dichotomy occurs, some explanation is required.

Why was the main part of the room *not* put next the light-well, where it would certainly benefit by the more direct reception of light and air? The answer must be that rain, wind, and cold could also enter without hindrance between the columns, with possible unpleasant or harmful effects to both occupants and furnishings. Indeed the purpose of the transverse pier-and-door partition was to exclude the unpleasant elements at times emanating from the light-well.

But when the doors of the partition were all closed what, we may ask, can have been the use of the smaller part of the room next the light-well, especially when, as so frequently, there was no entrance into it save from the main part of the room? Would it not have been more practical simply to have substituted the pier-and-door partition for the columns along the light-well, thus avoiding the waste of a considerable amount of space? That this solution was in fact rarely adopted—there is one instance in House Zb at Mallia (Fig. 27)—indicates that it would have been for some reason undesirable. Perhaps the effects of the weather, especially rain, on the valuable wooden doors, may have been thought a serious objection; but we may suspect that a more important reason was that it greatly increased the usefulness of the pier-and-door partition. For example, during a heavy but warm rainstorm, some or all of the doors could remain wide open without danger that the water might splash into the main part of the room, and thus there would be little or no reduction in the amount of light and air entering the room. For the same reason the outer pier-and-door partitions in the palace residential quarters were always placed within a protecting colonnade.

Actually this involves the same principle that operated in the Mycenaean megaron where the main room was sheltered from the weather by a porch. This porch often had two columns, like the Cretan light-well, and in the palaces it was often doubled for extra protection. The main room was further protected by a door or, in the palace at Tiryns, by three double doors in a row between heavy piers (Fig. 150). The Tiryns scheme was surely inspired by the Minoan pier-and-door partition.

The Main Hall of the palace residential quarters regularly opened, as we have said, on a colonnade or colonnades which in turn faced on terraces and gardens. With such a bountiful provision of light and air why, we may ask, was it still felt necessary to provide a light-well at the *inner* end of the room beyond the transverse pier-and-door partition? Two frequently occurring situations may furnish an adequate explanation: on a cold and windy day when it would be necessary to close the pier-and-door partitions opening on to the colonnades, the transverse partition could still be left open since the light-well would be much less exposed to the wind; on the other hand, in hot weather the cross ventilation and updraught of the light-well acting like a flue would have greatly increased the comfort of the inhabitants. In fact the term "light-well" is properly too restricted in meaning, while "ventilation shaft" is open to the same objection; "light and air shaft" would be more expressive, though rather cumbersome for ordinary usage.

While most of the Minoan Halls can be classified, as regards form and function, along the lines we have followed so far, there are some interesting variations and exceptions, for example the tripartite complex of rooms, 50, south of the stairway leading down to the North Residential Quarter at Phaistos, and supposedly forming part of it (Figs. 11, 47).[12] In this the light-well, instead of being at one end, is interposed between the main and the smaller parts of the room (the "Sala" and the "Portico," as the Italian publication calls them) and supplies light to them both through two-columned openings on each face. There is thus no pier-and-door partition at all. A some-what similar situation occurs in the Main Hall of the Residential Quarter at H. Triadha, though here there is also a pier-and-door partition (Figs. 11, 151).

At Nirou Khani the Main Hall is normal in most respects except that where we expect a light-well the two-columned portico opens directly on a stone-paved court (Figs. 31, 75). In fact the portico here is a "porch" in the English sense of the word, an "entrance"—the main entrance of the house. Super-ficially it bears a remarkable resemblance to the megaron at Tiryns, to which it has been compared. But it differs in several essential respects: unlike the Tiryns megaron it has doors from its inner corners leading to other parts of the house, while it lacks the Tirynthian hearth with four surrounding columns and the place for a throne.

Hall-like rooms were sometimes used for special purposes and were then furnished with special architectural features which alter their usual character. The Royal Villa at Knossos, with its balustraded dais and niche on the axis of the Hall for a formal seat (Fig. 74), has already been described (Ch. III, 4). Two similar arrangements occur in other houses—if they were really residences—in the vicinity of the Palace of Minos: the House of the Chancel Screen (Fig. 16), and the House of the High Priest.[13]

Finally, there is a unique agglomeration of no less than three Halls communicating with each other through pier-and-door partitions in the northeast corner of the Villa of H. Triadha (Fig. 164). All three have transverse pier-and-door partitions

[12] *Festòs*, II, pp. 258-268.
[13] *Knossos*, II, pp. 391-395; IV, pp. 202-215.

of two or three bays, two have light-wells and the third a window; some or all have gypsum-faced walls and floors. A broad stairway communicates with upper rooms and the general purpose is considered to be residential. For further details we must await the publication.

3. BATHROOMS OR LUSTRAL CHAMBERS?

One of the most disputed, yet least adequately discussed, questions in Minoan archaeology is the one which forms the title of this section. Everyone has an opinion on the matter, but who has taken the trouble to debate the pros and cons in detail? Certainly not Sir Arthur Evans anywhere in the length and breadth of *The Palace of Minos at Knossos*. He tells us what are bathrooms and what are lustral chambers, but exactly what, in his mind, distinguishes them he leaves to be inferred. Nilsson does devote two pages in his last edition of the *Minoan-Mycenaean Religion* (1950) to the question whether these rooms were used for cult purposes, but the treatment falls far short of his usual thoroughness.[14]

Of the many other scholars who have declared themselves in one camp or the other on the identity of these rooms R. W. Hutchinson has expressed himself (in 1950) at greater length than most. They cannot, he declared, be bathrooms because they have no drains or piping, and because they are lined with "gypsum which dissolves in running water. . . . The one certainty about 'lustral areas' is that they had some ceremonial significance. Their character and significant positions proves this. . . . In general they are rare and possibly confined to houses inhabited by princes of the royal line."[15]

The lack of a drain and the solubility of gypsum we shall discuss later. The meaning of "their character and significant positions" is not self-evident; but to this also we will return. As for rarity, at least eighteen of the familiar type with steps

---

[14] Nilsson, *MMR²*, pp. 92-94. "Bathrooms or Lustral Chambers?" was presented at the Meeting of the Archaeological Institute of America, Dec. 28-30, 1960, *AJA*, 65 (1961), p. 189.

[15] *Town Planning Review*, 21 (1950), p. 209.

down from an adjoining room are known, ten of these in private houses. "Princes of the royal line" must have been as common in Crete as "Kentucky colonels," and Minos as fertile as Ramses II.

Let us say a word now about the *probabilities* of the case in favor of the bathroom interpretation. First: In a southern climate bathing is a relief and a pleasure, whatever be the prevalent hygienic philosophy—so let us have no comparisons with modern Eskimos or with, say, King Henry VIII.

Second: Bathrooms are usually the easiest room to identify in the ruins of an ancient house, either by bathtubs (sometimes built in), or by special waterproofing of floor or walls, or both; position and size are also often clues.

Third: Bathrooms are common in ancient houses excavated elsewhere—Olynthos, of course, in the Classical Greek period, but they are found in the Bronze Age too. At Amarna in New Kingdom Egypt (ca. 1375 B.C.) the bathroom "was invariably a small room with a bath-slab of limestone fitted into one corner, and often two upright slabs to protect the walls from being splashed . . . the water ran off into a vase cemented into the floor . . . (or) across the floor and out through a hole in the wall."[16] In this simple shower bath a slave would pour water over his master. In the palace at Mari on the Euphrates, about 1700 B.C. (Fig. 148), there were numerous bathrooms with clay tubs and often a "Turkish" toilet conveniently alongside, and even the luxury of a small fireplace in the corner with a flue to carry off the smoke.[17] At Pylos in the Peloponnesus a fine bathroom has been discovered with clay tub in place,[18] and others have been recognized at Mycenae and Tiryns; surely if the Mycenaean Greeks had bathrooms it would be perverse to deny this amenity to their cultural mentors the Minoan Cretans who, tradition asserts, lived in the lap of luxury.[19]

We will describe briefly a typical, well preserved example of

[16] Peet and Woolley, *City of Akhenaten*, I, pp. 45-46.
[17] *Mari*, II, pp. 202-205, Room 7.
[18] *Archaeology*, 13 (1960), pp. 53-54.
[19] Diodorus Siculus, 5, 66, 6.

the disputed type of Minoan room, in the North Residential Quarter at Phaistos (Fig. 4).[20] A seven-stepped stairway in two short runs descends three feet from the Queen's Hall to the "bathroom"—as we shall call it for the present, without intending to prejudge the case (Fig. 82). The floor, lower walls, steps, and parapet along the steps and between the bathroom and the main room, were all faced with gypsum; the walls were lined with thin sheets of gypsum veneering of the fine quality known as alabaster (in the modern sense of the word). On the end of the parapet once stood a short marble column. The dimensions of the sunken floor of the basin are about 7 by 7½ ft. (2.20 by 2.32 m.).[21]

Other bathrooms are fairly constantly about this size, but the quality of the decoration varies widely. The upper plaster wall in the bathroom of the Residential Quarter at Knossos is painted with a spiral band, and one in the South House with birds and flowers; in simpler rooms the floor was sometimes of plaster or merely of clay. In a wall of the bathroom of House E at Mallia were two niches, in one of which a fine stone lamp found in the room was no doubt placed.

It is commonly believed that the Queen's Hall or Women's Hall is regularly a kind of private sitting room reached by a corridor with a door at either end from the larger "Men's Hall," which at Knossos has been called the "Hall of the Double-Axes." A similar relationship of bathroom, Women's Hall, and Men's Hall occurs in the East Residential Quarter at Phaistos and in the Residential Quarter at Mallia, as well as in some of the private houses. Surely the position, which Hutchinson says proves that these rooms had a ceremonial function, very obviously in these cases at least, suggests instead a domestic function.[22] The toilet, also, is often in a similar position, off the

[20] *Festòs*, II, pp. 299-303.

[21] The floor was surfaced with seven slabs not four, as stated in *Festòs*, II, p. 299.

[22] Hutchinson must have been thinking of a few exceptional instances which we discuss below; Platon, on the other hand, notes that they are found particularly in the principal living apartments, review of Karo, *Greifen am Thron*, *Kret. Chron.*, 13 (1959), p. 238.

Queen's Hall—in both cases at Phaistos, at Knossos, at Mallia, and in some of the houses; should we therefore reinterpret these toilets as some form of chthonic shrine?

Yet Evans, and many others, persist in identifying the type of room we have just described as lustral chambers, not as bathrooms: as being used purely for cult, not for domestic, purposes. Evans however did recognize three rooms at Knossos as bathrooms, and these seem to have been generally accepted. What then are the qualifying characteristics? Here, briefly, is a description of the three.

No. 1 was a small room about 6½ feet square (2 m.) in the southeast part of the Palace of Minos, with gypsum-faced walls and floor; the floor was not lower than outside the room, hence there were no steps or parapet.[23] Remains of a clay bathtub were found in the room (Fig. 140, C). It was not in a residential quarter, at least one of the usual type.

No. 2 in the South House at Knossos was a small room first built in M.M. IIIb with steps down to its floor and a parapet (Fig. 15); in L.M. Ia it was remodeled by bringing the floor up to the outside level, eliminating the steps but retaining the parapet.[24] The floor and lower walls were gypsum faced; no tub remains were found.

No. 3 is off the Queen's Hall at Knossos (Figs. 12, 81).[25] This room in position, size, character of floor and walls, parapet and column, is essentially indistinguishable from the room already described at Phaistos, and from the one at Mallia. The one point of difference is that the floor was not at a lower level and that there were consequently no steps. Remains of a clay tub were found just outside the door of the room.

Thus it is clear that for Evans the difference between "bathrooms" and "lustral chambers" did not consist in position, size, the use of gypsum for floors and walls, the existence of a parapet, the presence of a drain, or the finding of remains of a tub (for none was found in the South House). The sole point of

[23] *Knossos*, I, pp. 579-580.
[24] *Knossos*, II, pp. 378-380.
[25] *Knossos*, III, pp. 381-386.

distinction is in the level of the floor and the consequent presence or absence of steps.

Sir Arthur's viewpoint likewise involves the assumption that a room which started out as a lustral chamber (in the South House) later became an ordinary bathroom. In fact, as a result of recent investigations by Platon it must be assumed that this also happened twice in the houses at Tylissos; and a careful investigation, I suspect, might show that the same was true of the bathroom off the Queen's Hall in the Palace of Minos. Otherwise why the parapet? Was it not also a vestigial remnant as at Tylissos House A, and in the South House at Knossos? We should have to suppose, as Evans did, that in their later days the Minoans began putting cleanliness before godliness.[26] There is however no other indication of this hypothetical decline in religiosity.

The common "proofs" adduced today by scholars who favor the lustral chamber as against the bathroom theory are, nevertheless, not the level of the floor of the room but the lack of drains and the use of gypsum—particularly the latter. How then can the same scholars accept the three rooms identified as bathrooms by Sir Arthur Evans?[27] Yet they appear to do so.

In any case neither of the objections they urge is a valid one. Drains are not necessary, merely convenient.[28] More of the Olynthian bathrooms lacked them than possessed them. And to have installed drains and maintained them in working order in the low-floored type of Minoan room would have been extremely difficult. A little water splashed from a tub could easily be sponged up; how many modern bathroom floors possess a drain? As for the tubs themselves we, accustomed to pipes which supply and evacuate the water, must not expect such conveniences in the "good old days." The built-in tubs at Olynthos had no drains; they must have been emptied rather laboriously by dip-

---

[26] *Knossos*, II, pp. 379-380; and so Pendlebury, *Handbook*, p. 44.

[27] Platon also calls attention to this anomaly in his review of Karo (p. 238), "no drain exists even in the Queen's Bathroom at Knossos."

[28] Karo writes in 1959 (*Greifen am Thron*, p. 8), "the sunken space shows no drain; it therefore cannot have been a bath." *Non sequitur.*

ping and sponging. In Crete, however, the tubs had handles or ledges for easy carrying, and so could be taken out of the room for filling or emptying.

As for the solubility of gypsum, the objection is really ridiculous. When I mentioned the problem recently to a well-known geologist he laughed and remarked that in that case one should not keep water in glass containers. Gypsum is soluble—yes—but . . . there are several "buts." For one thing, varieties differ widely. Certain types of gypsum may, some have said, "melt like sugar." Omitting the rhetorical exaggeration we may admit that some gypsum bases lying out in the weather at Knossos for half a century have been "honeycombed" by the rain (Fig. 117). Other varieties, as Evans himself observed, have "an almost unlimited power of resisting the elements."[29] Gypsum blocks are much used in exterior walls, in the great orthostates on the west façade at Knossos, for example; and gypsum was actually used for the floor of the foot basin in the "Caravanserai" at Knossos, in which water stood or flowed constantly.[30] It is also a simple physical principle that the rate of solution is directly related to the area of exposure, so that we may feel sure that the finely smoothed vertical wall surfaces of the alabaster veneering of the bathroom would resist any normal splashing practically indefinitely. And if by any unlikely contingency the floor slabs needed replacing after several decades of use the Minoan housewife must have felt that the advantages of having a "tiled" bathroom were quite sufficient to justify an occasional renewal.

Actually this objection is a legacy from the early days of Minoan excavation when it was first suggested by Evans that these rooms were partially filled with standing water to serve as tanks for fish for the royal table, or—a later suggestion—for bathing; when they got too fetid they could be bailed out.[31] But many evidently still fail to recognize that the problem has been completely altered by the realization that the bathing was done

[29] *Knossos*, III, p. 288. [30] *Knossos*, II, p. 119.
[31] *BSA*, 6 (1899-1900), pp. 38-39; 7 (1900-1901), p. 63.

in a tub.[32] It is perhaps strange that no remains of bathtubs seem so far to have been found in bathrooms of the low-floor type; but Minoan bathtubs, not being built in, were too portable and too valuable to leave in the ruins; they could be used not only to bathe the living but to bury the dead. Large numbers of such tubs have been found in L.M. III cemeteries.

It may be urged however that there is another plausible reason to suspect a religious rather than a utilitarian explanation of these rooms. The considerable additional labor needed to excavate them several feet deeper than the general level is, some may think, easier to explain if religiously motivated, and various explanations along these lines have been proposed: that it was done in order to get closer to the Powers of the Underworld that cause the dreaded earthquakes; or to provide congenial pits for the sacred snakes familiar in Minoan cult; or to imitate the popular natural cave sanctuaries.

On the other hand if we ask whether it is possible that the Cretans could have had any good practical reasons for making the floor of a *bathroom* lower than that of the surrounding rooms I think that the exercise of a little sympathetic imagination can discover several; in fact in this we may have still another illustration of the Minoan experience in urbane living. The problem which the Cretan solved with the simple means at his disposal was to build the bathroom in such a way that it could be lighted from the larger room from which it was entered[33] without running the risk of water seeping into, or being splashed into, the Queen's or Women's Hall to the discomfort of its occupants and the possible damage to its furnishings. At the same time the lower level of the bathroom would shield the bather from cold draughts, and, in combination with a parapet

[32] Even Pendlebury says of the north "lustral area" that "it can never have been filled with water—the gypsum paving and wall-slabs would not have stood it," *Handbook*, p. 44.

[33] He could have enclosed the room entirely and depended on artificial illumination, and lamps have indeed often been found in these rooms, but this would not have been a congenial solution to the Cretan, especially in view of the ineffectiveness of Minoan lamps (Ch. XII, 1); artificial daylight is a modern development.

and possibly adjustable hangings between the two rooms, provide a certain amount of privacy. Yet if we may judge from the bathing habits of the Homeric heroes such complete privacy as we prefer today may not have been considered necessary; indeed the Homeric hero was sometimes assisted in his ablutions by a favored daughter of his host.

Nevertheless, in spite of the evidence we have so far presented, which consistently permits or favors the interpretation of these rooms as bathrooms, there exists some evidence of a contrary nature that we have not yet touched on. For instance, we have not spoken of the famous "lustral chamber" off the so-called Throne Room at Knossos.[34] This room actually differs little in most physical characteristics from those we have discussed, except that on the parapet between the two rooms are several columns. But there *is* one significant difference: its location off a room which was surely used not for domestic, but almost certainly for cult, purposes. The recent thesis that a priestess, not a priest-king, sat on the throne, would not, if true, essentially alter the situation (see above, p. 31).[35]

A second room described as a lustral chamber by Evans is located at the north end of the palace, far from the Residential Quarter.[36] Its basin, larger and much deeper than usual, was reached by sixteen gypsum steps. There is the usual high gypsum dado with colored plaster above, while on the stair parapet stood three columns, with three more on the parapet dividing the two rooms. Vessels which Sir Arthur believed were of a ritual character were found within the basin, and he conjectured that the chamber was used for ceremonial washing before proceeding further within the palace to appear before the king, an idea, though often repeated, for which there is no clear evidence either here or elsewhere, though it remains within the realms of possibility. It is also possible, as I suggest elsewhere (Ch. v,

[34] *Knossos*, IV, pp. 907-908.
[35] Platon's recent study also upholds the cult character of the room, *Kret. Chron.*, 5 (1951), pp. 392-394.
[36] *Knossos*, III, pp. 8-12.

5), that the room formed part of an elaborate suite for the entertainment of distinguished visitors.

A third room with steps down to a gypsum-lined basin opens off what perhaps should be regarded as part of a suite of grand reception halls in the Little Palace at Knossos rather than as a residential quarter.[37] In most respects the room is of normal type except for a row of four convex-fluted columns on two sides of the sunken area. In the final period of the building's existence the space between the wooden columns was roughly walled up and, as the numerous ritual objects found in it clearly show, the room was used as a shrine. Did this continue an earlier practice?

But religious associations are not completely absent even in simpler examples of this type of room. For instance in the newly published and rather enigmatic House E at Mallia a broken libation table was found in the bathroom;[38] and in the bathroom of the East Residential Quarter at Phaistos there came to light a pair of stone sacral horns, a rhyton of fine quality, a terracotta bull's head rhyton, and nine small bronze double-axes.[39]

How are we to explain this apparent anomaly: that an essentially identical room form should have been used both for cult ceremonies and for domestic bathing?[40] The answer I think must lie simply in the similar physical process involved; the washing away or cleansing of sin is not a figure of speech in the ancient Near East but an actual effective process. Thus the household room could be at once "bathroom" and "lustral chamber." In taking a bath one cleansed both the body and the soul.

[37] *Knossos*, II, pp. 519-525.   [38] *Mallia, Maisons*, II, p. 136, no. 12.

[39] *Festòs*, II, pp. 171-178; but Miss Banti disbelieves in the ritual character of the room, p. 584 and notes; on the other hand Hood in reviewing *Festòs*, II, in *Gnomon*, 26 (1954), p. 376, declares that these objects "do surely indicate some sort of cult."

[40] "Many of the rooms characterized as lustral basins were in fact baths, since they are found especially in the principal living apartments; the form of the similar installations used for lustral purposes evolved directly from the bathrooms," Platon in a review of Karo, *Greifen am Thron, Kret. Chron.* 13 (1959), p. 238; and Hood in his review of *Festòs*, II (*loc. cit.*) says that the " 'Lustral basins' must have been used for anointings or washings whether ritual or not."

And so, as frequently happens when there has been a long and sharp division of opinion among competent scholars the basic trouble is with the formulation of the problem. The question should not have been whether these rooms were "bathrooms *or* lustral chambers," for they were both at once, though the relative emphasis doubtless varied in the individual instances. For supplementary considerations see **Addendum 6**.

4. THE TOILET

One of the peculiar hallmarks of western culture frequently used by the traveler as a handy touchstone with which to condemn as backward the "less fortunate" countries he visits is the modern sanitary convenience. He may succeed in avoiding the art galleries, theaters, and literature of the country in which he is traveling, but unless he keeps very close to base, i.e. the luxury hotel in which he resides, he can scarcely fail to come into contact with this homely object in its native form. It is only natural, then, that the kinds of toilets used by the nations of the past should likewise fascinate the average tourist, and there are many who will comment reverently on that small dark room in the Palace of Minos when they have quite forgotten the treasures of art in the Herakleion Museum.

And perhaps the ancient Minoan and the modern American would find this subject more mutually intelligible than many others. For the Cretan did seem to take a considerable interest in physical comfort, and it is perhaps a significant contrast that although something over a hundred houses have been excavated at the Classical Greek site of Olynthos there is remarkably little sign of provision for toilets,[41] whereas some half dozen can be identified among the score of comparable houses of Minoan Crete so far brought to light.

In several of the Minoan houses the toilet is quite clearly located in the private living quarters, and usually in as well removed a position as possible; in House Za at Mallia it projects entirely beyond the general line of the house walls. In most cases the evidence for the identification of the toilet is

[41] *Olynthus*, VIII, pp. 205-206.

little more than the existence of a large and carefully built drain at floor level passing through an exterior wall (Fig. 79). But occasionally there are traces of some sort of provision for a seat.

Toilets may be recognized in all three major palaces. At Mallia Room iii 2, next to the Queen's Hall, which has two drains through its outer west wall, is probably a toilet. And again 63e, off the Queen's Hall of the East Residential Quarter at Phaistos, has nothing to show but a careful drain in the solid rock on which the exterior wall is bedded. The toilet connected with the North Residential Quarter is more interesting. Located as far as possible from the main living room it is reached by a short corridor from a door in the southwest corner of the Queen's Hall.[42] About five feet wide by perhaps twelve long (1½ by 3½ m.), the room is paved with large square slabs of gypsum and divided from the corridor to the east by a thin adobe brick partition. In the northwest corner is a somewhat higher gypsum slab with a rectangular gap about 5 by 10 in. (ca. 13 by 25 cm.) in the middle of one end, opening into a fair-sized drain that continued northward to the edge of the hill. Presumably over the hole in the floor a wooden seat was built against the now missing north wall of the room.

The most elaborate Minoan toilet known is the water-closet in the Residential Quarter of the Palace of Minos (Fig. 12).[43] It consists literally of a "closet" about 7 ft. 3 in. long by 3 ft. 8 in. wide (2.20 by 1.11 m.), provided with a door and set against one wall of a larger room reached by a long corridor from the Queen's Hall. Like the Minoan bathrooms its floor and walls were faced with gypsum for easier cleaning as well as for appearance. Along the rear wall is a slot about 14 in. (35 cm.) wide over a drain which forms part of an extensive system of drains serving both toilets and light-wells in this part of the palace; a short branch of the drain has another opening outside the threshold of the closet to receive slops or water swept from the floor of the larger room. In the face of one of

42 *Festòs*, II, pp. 296-299.
43 *Knossos*, I, pp. 228-230.

the gypsum slabs on the south wall and at a distance of about 22 in. (55 cm.) from the east or rear wall is a vertical slot evidently designed to receive one end of the vertical facing of a wooden seat; the top surface of the seat would have been nearly two feet (60 cm.) above the floor. Below the opening is a curious projection from the rear wall which "may have been used for the attachment of a balance flap to shut off the escape of sewer gas."[44] Some confirmation of this conjecture of Evans is perhaps provided by the discovery in the sub-stairs toilet in a house at Sklavokambos of two clay objects which seem to have been used to plug the drain holes and thus prevent the backing up of odors.

One of the houses near the palace at Mallia, Da, contains a toilet seat in practically perfect condition, since it was made of stone, not of wood like the one in the Palace of Minos (Fig. 114).[45] The seat measures about 27 in. wide by 18 in. from front to back (ca. 68 by 46 cm.), and its surface is some 14-15 in. (35-38 cm.) above the floor. It is built directly against an outside wall through which passes a capacious drain. Like the example at Knossos it was evidently intended as a seat rather than as a stand, resembling therefore the Egyptian toilet more closely than the "Turkish" type found in the palaces at Mari and at Alalakh.[46]

At certain times of the year the drains in the Palace of Minos may have been adequately flushed out by the rain that fell into the light-wells; but in general we must imagine that water was poured into the toilets to flush them, and Evans observed that there was sufficient space at one end of the seat at Knossos for a large pitcher. He concludes with evident satisfaction, "As an anticipation of scientific methods of sanitation, the system of which we have here the record has been attained by few nations even at the present day."[47]

[44] *Knossos*, I, p. 228, note 2.
[45] *Mallia, Maisons*, I, p. 45, "un curieux massif fait de pierres et de terre: foyer ou latrines"; Tiré and van Effenterre, *Guide*, p. 62, opt for latrine.
[46] *Mari*, II, p. 203; *Alalakh*, pp. 123-124.
[47] *Knossos*, I, p. 230.

5. THE GUEST ROOMS

God forbid that you should go to your ship and turn your backs on my house as though it belonged to some threadbare pauper and there weren't plenty of blankets and rugs in the place for host and guests to sleep between in comfort! Indeed, I have good bedding for all; and I swear that the son of my friend Odysseus shall not lie down to sleep on his ship's deck so long as I am alive or sons survive me here to entertain all visitors that come to my door.—(Nestor urging Telemachos to stay for the night at his palace at Pylos, ODYSSEY, 3, 346-355, Rieu translation)

Aristocratic travelers in Bronze Age Greece were too few to encourage the development of hostelries adequate to accommodate them, but they could expect a hospitable welcome in the palaces of friendly monarchs. A suite of rooms near the main entrance and adjacent to the Central Court of the palace at Mycenae has recently been tentatively suggested as a guest suite.[48] The evidence is better, perhaps, for a group of rooms near the entrance of the newly excavated palace at Pylos, also on the Greek mainland.[49] The Pylos suite includes a good-sized room with painted cement floor and walls and a central hearth, two smaller rooms, probably sleeping room and toilet, and, at least conveniently near if not for its exclusive use, a bathroom. The location near the palace entrance was no doubt felt to be convenient for the guest, as well as safer for the host than bedding a stranger too near the quarters of the royal family.

In the north palace at Amarna (about 1375 B.C.) two structures which are virtually large houses, within the boundary walls of the palace, are usually supposed to have served as residences for some of the pharaoh's personal staff (Fig. 149, center right); but one might guess that they were used, at least at times, to accommodate important visitors to the court. At any rate the large homes in the vicinity of this palace, which

---

[48] Mylonas, *Anc. Myc.*, p. 49.   [49] *Archaeology*, 13 (1960), p. 53.

must have housed members of the imperial aristocracy, contained suites of rooms which the excavators have very reasonably supposed were for the use of guests. In House T. 36. 11, e.g., this suite includes a columned hall or living room adjacent to the central living room of the house; off this hall and completely separate from the rest of the house, runs a corridor serving a row of several small rooms which would certainly appear to have been bedrooms.[50]

The excavator of the great palace at Mari on the Euphrates (2000-1700 B.C.) has recently suggested that a suite of rooms, including a bathroom, court, and kitchen, near the main palace entrance, was used for the reception of distinguished guests (Fig. 148, at 160).[51] One might suggest further that a series of single rooms with attached bathrooms around Court 15 was also used for guests of lesser importance, though the publication prefers to believe that it was used by certain court officials (Fig. 148, below 106).[52]

Minoan Crete is not likely to have lagged behind Egypt or Mari in the amenities of civilized life, while one would expect her to have been well ahead of mainland Greece in this regard. I propose to recognize two such suites of guest chambers in the southwestern quarter of the Palace of Phaistos (Fig. 4). A long corridor, 12-13, opening off the main passage, 7, from the West Court to the Central Court, provides convenient and private access. A kind of anteroom, 15, serves both suites, each of which consists of two rooms and bath—sitting room, bedroom, bath? —namely 17, 18, and 19, to the north, and 16, 20, and 21, to the south.[53] Just south of these rooms are the remains of a pier-and-door partition running east to west; perhaps there was a broad veranda to the south of this for the enjoyment of the guests.

---

[50] W. S. Smith, *Art and Arch. in Anc. Eg.*, fig. 64; Frankfort and Pendlebury, *The City of Akhenaten*, II, pl. 12; E. B. Smith, *Eg. Arch.*, pl. 67.

[51] *Mari*, II, pp. 20-33.   [52] *Mari*, II, pp. 192-205.

[53] *Festòs*, II, pp. 122-130. The idea was previously suggested by Hawes, *Crete, The Forerunner of Greece* (1911), p. 81; and by G. Glotz, *Aegean Civilization* (1925), p. 124, "where staff, and perhaps guests, were lodged."

At Knossos it is possible that the "lustral chamber" near the north entrance of the palace formed part of a fine suite of guest chambers.[54] Perhaps the fragment of an alabaster jar inscribed with the name of the Hyksos king Khyan found here was the relic of the visit of some high Egyptian official to the court of King Minos. Likewise in the southeast quarter at Knossos there are two suites of rooms, a good deal altered, it seems, in the L.M. III period, each with a bath, and each accessible from a southeast entrance. Evans himself remarked that the area had a decidedly domestic appearance and might have been the residence of a priestly functionary.[55]

Since the only recognizable bathroom in the Palace of Mallia is in the Residential Quarter no clue of this nature is available to help in identifying guest suites. In view of the modest character of the palace perhaps there were none. The suggestion that I made in 1962 that two suites of rooms opening directly on the exterior of the palace just west of the south entrance (xviii 1-7) has been disproved by further excavation which shows that they were in fact cult rooms of some kind.[56]

Two of the finest private houses excavated at Knossos also have small suites of rooms including bathrooms, on the ground floor near the main entrance, which could with some plausibility be identified as guest suites, namely the Royal Villa, E-H (Fig. 14), and the House of the Chancel Screen, 4-6 (Fig. 16), although we have preferred to suggest that they formed part of the "women's quarters" of these houses. There would seem to be no possibility of setting up a hard and fast distinction in all cases between these two types of suites, and it is conceivable that the East Residential Quarter at Phaistos was used, or at least could be used at times, as a reception suite for guests of distinction.

[54] *Knossos*, I, pp. 405-422; III, pp. 8-12.
[55] *Knossos*, I, p. 576.
[56] *Mallia*, 4, pp. 10f.; St. Alexiou, *A Guide to the Minoan Palaces* (Herakleion, 1966), p. 111.

CHAPTER VI

PUBLIC APARTMENTS

1. RECEPTION HALLS

To ANYONE familiar with the Bronze Age palaces of the Greek mainland the title of this chapter may seem rather pretentious. In the Mycenaean Greek palaces almost the only really large and well decorated room is the "megaron" or "big room," a room about 30 by 40 ft. (ca. 9 by 12 m.) preceded by a narrow anteroom and a two-columned portico facing on a small court (Fig. 150). Wall paintings and floor designs gave a rather splendid effect, but so much of the central area of the room was occupied by a hearth (13 ft. or 4 m. in diameter at Pylos), and by four columns, that the king's throne was crowded against the center of a side wall in a position more conducive to the royal comfort in cold weather than convenient for the reception of a foreign embassy.[1]

When Nausicaä tells Odysseus what he will see in the great room of her father's palace at Phaeacia she paints a very domestic scene indeed: "When thou art within the shadow of the halls and of the court, pass quickly through the great chamber (megaron), till thou comest to my mother, who sits at the hearth in the light of the fire, weaving yarn of sea-purple stain, a wonder to behold. Her chair is leaned against a pillar, and her maidens sit behind her. And there my father's throne leans close to hers, wherein he sits and drinks his wine, like an immortal."[2]

The megaron, therefore, ordinarily formed part of the private quarters of the Homeric palace, though it could be pressed into

---

[1] *Archaeology*, 13 (1960), pp. 46-54.   [2] *Odyssey*, 6, 303-309.

service as a place to receive and entertain visitors of distinction. No rooms specifically reserved for this latter purpose can be definitely identified in the mainland palaces, though there was a separate Banquet Hall at Pylos, Rooms 64-65.

These palaces, however, were much smaller and more modest structures than those in Crete, and were hemmed in by great fortification walls. For analogies we should look rather to Egypt and the Near East, and there we find a very different picture.

Egyptian palaces of the eighteenth dynasty, such as that of Amenhotpe III at Thebes (Malkata), have large columned rooms identified as state reception halls,[3] while the South Palace at Amarna (ca. 1375 B.C.) has a colossal battery of hypostyle halls culminating in one around 225 ft. wide by over 400 ft. long (ca. 70 by 120 m.) and containing well over 500 columns.[4] In the Middle Bronze palace at Mari on the Euphrates the reception halls are smaller than the Egyptian, but the principal hall, 65, must have been in its way as impressive for it was over 30 ft. high, 85 ft. long, and 40 ft. wide (9 by 26 by 12 m.), without the use of a single supporting column (Fig. 148).[5]

It should not be surprising, therefore, if the Minoan Cretans built themselves rooms of considerable size and architectural pretensions as formal reception halls. Nevertheless, since very few rooms outstanding for size or quality of decoration are actually preserved in the ruins of their palaces, except in the Residential Quarters and in the newly found palace at Kato Zakro, why, it may be asked, should we suspect that important public or state apartments did exist in the vanished upper storeys; and even if they did, how can we hope to learn anything about them?[6] Reasonable questions indeed—yet the case is not really

---

[3] W. S. Smith, *Art and Arch. of Anc. Eg.*, fig. 55.

[4] *Ibid.*, fig. 66.

[5] *Mari*, II, p. 143.

[6] The publication of the last Palace of Phaistos has very little to say about second storey rooms; their existence, to some extent, is admitted, but their importance is minimized (see especially *Festòs*, II, pp. 327-336). Both Banti (*Festòs*, II, p. 330) and Lawrence are very suspicious of the proposed restorations by Evans of the Piano Nobile at Knossos between the Central and West Courts, and the latter claims that "the plan above ground level is conjectural in almost every

as hopeless as it might seem; a certain amount of evidence does exist.

In the first place analogies may be found in many times and places, including the *palazzi* of Renaissance Italy, for the practice of putting the important public rooms in the storey above the ground floor. This storey was referred to in Italy as the *Piano Nobile*, or principal floor, a term Evans adopted for the corresponding feature of the Palace of Minos. The main rooms may also have been located on the second floor of Cretan houses, at least in the more crowded urban districts, as is suggested by the houses of the "Town Mosaic," many of which have windows only in the second and third storeys (Fig. 103), and by the actual remains of houses along the narrow alleys at Gournia.[7] The better houses, however, at Mallia, Knossos, Tylissos, etc., certainly had important living rooms (lighted by light-wells, not by windows) on the ground floor, as in the Arkhanes model, though possibly on the floor above as well.

Second: in all three major palaces there are broad flights of stone steps, far broader than would be necessary for ordinary daily use—in other words clearly designed for splendor of effect —leading up toward a second storey above the area of the palace west of the Central Court (Fig. 7). At Mallia nine steps of a broad stairway still remain in position west of the Central Court. At Knossos, also, there is a broad flight leading up from the court (restored from slight remains), and perhaps another from the South Propylaeum, which was connected with the West Court by the Corridor of the Procession. At Phaistos the system of stairways begins at the West Court (pp. 66, 71-73).

Third: fragments of plaster from elaborate figure compositions found in the storage rooms west of the Central Court at

---

detail" (*Gk. Arch.*, p. 36). Yet there is some evidence, and scholarly caution does not justify ignoring it completely.

[7] Weinberg, in a review of *Mallia, Maisons*, I in *AJA* 59 (1955), pp. 340-341, remarks that above the very irregular ground floor rooms of some rather large houses excavated at that site there must have existed larger and finer rooms. Putting the main living floor one storey above the ground is certainly a common practice in modern Greece; cf. Travlos, Πολεοδομικὴ Ἐξέλεξις τῶν Ἀθηνῶν. (Athens, 1960), p. 226.

Knossos must have fallen from important rooms above. Evans also found in this area stone door and pillar bases clearly derived from the same source; in fact they sometimes seem to have subsided merely a foot or two from their original positions and therefore provide valuable clues for the restoration of the plan of the missing rooms.[8]

Fourth: particularly at Knossos and Mallia the long narrow storage rooms along the west façade are grouped in more or less square "blocks" composed of from three to six magazines each, the outer walls of the blocks being usually distinctly thicker than those dividing the individual magazines (Fig. 83). This is not explained by the character or function of the magazines themselves; and it suggests that only the heavy boundary walls of the blocks supported walls in the storey above, and therefore that one large room in the Piano Nobile occupied the area of each "block" of the ground floor. This general principle was long ago proposed and has been widely accepted; in details there may be differences of opinion. That it provides the correct explanation for at least one block at Knossos, and for two at Mallia, is rendered a virtual certainty by the symmetrically placed rectangular enlargements of the dividing walls at two places in each block: clearly to provide a firm underpinning for pillars or columns to support the long transverse ceiling beams of the large rooms above (Fig. 116).

Fifth: to anticipate the results of a later section (Ch. ix, 1), the broad shallow recesses, which are a characteristic feature of the west façades of the palaces, indicate the location of windows in the rooms of the Piano Nobile, and therefore sometimes provide further clues regarding their form.

Utilizing these various clues, a tentative restoration of the plans of the rooms of the Piano Nobile along the west front of the palaces at Knossos, Mallia, and Phaistos is presented in Figs. 86, 159, 84.[9] The form of some of the rooms is not

[8] *Knossos*, I, pp. 442, 526; II, pp. 350-352, 716-718, 817-818, etc.
[9] For further details see *AJA*, 64 (1960), pp. 329-333, "Windows, Recesses, and the Piano Nobile in the Minoan Palaces."

clearly indicated by the available evidence and should be regarded as quite conjectural; this is particularly true at Phaistos.

The restoration of the three central rooms at Knossos given here agrees with Evans' restoration only for the middle room, whose two columns are vouched for by the two bases in the lower storey, as already mentioned (Figs. 85, 86, 116). As for the "Southwest Hall" over Magazines 3 to 5, Evans at first restored this as a single room in the Piano Nobile; the evidence he adduced in favor of his final version is certainly not decisive, while the position of the window as indicated by the recess supports the single-room restoration.[10] See **Addendum 1**.

The large room over Magazines 11 to 16 presents more of a problem. MacKenzie, Evans' right-hand man during the early years at Knossos, treated the area over 11-16 as a single room;[11] but Evans, in his final publication, broke this block up into several rooms entirely on the basis of a hypothetical Northwest Entrance which he conjured up out of fragments of decorative stonework of a type sometimes used above doorways (Fig. 136, B, Ch. xi, 2).[12] If, on the other hand, we restore a single large room over 11-16, as MacKenzie did, the recess in its exterior west wall will be centrally located on the axis of the proposed Northwest Hall and indicates the position of a broad set of windows. In Evans' restoration this recess comes directly opposite a partition wall. A further important piece of evidence turned up during my visit to the site in 1959. Against the north face of the partition between Magazines 14 and 15 lies a large dressed limestone block certainly in its original position, and this is so obviously analogous to the enlargements in the walls between Magazines 7, 8 and 8, 9 that it strongly suggests that on the block stood a wooden pillar to buttress the wall beneath a column in the room above (Figs. 115, 158). No corresponding strengthening of the wall between 12 and 13 is visible, but this wall is considerably thicker than that between 14 and

---

[10] See note 17 in article mentioned in preceding note.
[11] *BSA*, 11 (1904-1905), p. 217.
[12] *Knossos*, II, p. 590.

15. This indicates that only two columns should be restored in the hall above (p. 156).

On the basis of this restoration we get three great halls over Magazines 3 to 16: the Southwest Hall, the Central Hall, and the Northwest Hall. The largest of these, the Northwest Hall, about 57 by 51 ft. (ca. 17½ by 15½ m.), would, appropriately for the bigger palace, be a little larger than the great Central Hall at Mallia, which was about 52 ft. square (ca. 16 m.) and whose existence is clearly attested by the two enlargements in the magazine walls already mentioned.

This process of "building castles in the air" involves us in complex but intriguing problems at Phaistos. The main problem is how to restore the upper floors over the great one hundred foot square including the Grand Propylon and the Magazines. The exterior walls of this block are so thick and so solidly and handsomely constructed, with massive facing blocks of finely dressed limestone, that they must have risen at least one and probably two storeys above the ground floor. Moreover the analogy of the position of the block to that of the rooms of the Piano Nobile at Knossos and Mallia strongly suggests that the state reception rooms were located in the upper storeys. Yet in the final publication of the palace recently published by the Italian excavators the view is put forward that the space above the Magazine Block was occupied not by public rooms but by a loft for the storage of grain.[13] Even on general grounds this would be highly suspicious, particularly in view of the regular Minoan practice of systematically assigning different parts of the building to specific functions (Ch. XIII, 3).

In a first study of the problem I attempted a solution which would not run counter to the peculiar conclusions reached by the Italian archaeologists. They could hardly be expected to advance a theory so derogatory to the dignity of their own palace

---

[13] *Festòs*, II, p. 330; however others have taken the obvious view that there were important rooms of a public nature here, notably Charbonneaux, *BCH*, 54 (1930), pp. 364-366, and so even the Italian *Guida* (1947), p. 52, written by Pernier and Banti.

without feeling that they had the strongest of reasons to do so;[14] and indeed the evidence of the excavations did clearly indicate that a large mass of grain had fallen from somewhere above the ground level. I was also influenced in the solution I proposed by the conviction that the ceiling above the magazines would have to be somewhat higher than the level of the floor of Room 70; but after a further prolonged visit to the site in 1959 I became convinced that the floor level of 70 could have extended over the whole area west of Room 25, as indeed the excavators maintain, without creating an abnormally low basement storage cellar. As for the presence of the grain, various explanations are possible; the simplest is that it represents an emergency measure, an emergency which in fact brought an end to the last palace. A pile of grain was also found by the excavators in the north portico of the Central Court at Mallia; but surely it was not normally stored there.[15] And grain was also found in an unlikely place in an Assyrian palace destroyed in the first millennium.[16]

The formal approach to the state apartments of the Phaistos palace was, without a doubt, the Grand Propylon. This consists first of a magnificent flight of steps in the best tradition of Minoan stair-building (Ch. x, 1); there is nothing to equal them elsewhere in Crete (Figs. 49, 137, 138). At the head of these steps is a deep landing and a broad portal over thirty feet (ca. 9 m.) wide, framed by projecting wall-heads at either end and supported by a very large oval column in the center. Beyond the porch, 68, was a cross-wall with a pair of large doorways opening into a vestibule, 69, illuminated by a light-well, 69A, fronted by three oval columns.

In spite of all this magnificent sequence of stairs, portals, and columns, none of the three exits from 69-69A displays either in its dimensions or in its position the architectural dignity for which the grandeur of the approach prepares us (Figs. 4, 48).

[14] *AJA*, 60 (1956), pp. 151-157.
[15] *Mallia*, I, p. 36.
[16] Conrad Preusser, *Die Paläste in Assur*, Berlin, 1955, pp. 19, 21.

It is not surprising, therefore, that some scholars, unable to accept the view that this complex was designed primarily as an approach, have tried to see in 69-69A a great hall where the king sat in state to receive important visitors.[17] For such a purpose, however, 69 and 69A are poorly arranged and proportioned, as well as quite un-Minoan in room form, and the floors and walls though well preserved show no sign of any place for a formal seat or thronos. The Italian excavators are surely correct in identifying 69A as a light-well.[18] Moreover, even if (and I think it a very large "if") on certain occasions the king did sit here in state, these rooms could not have taken the place of state apartments on the scale for which there is evidence at Knossos and Mallia.

Nor should anyone familiar with the vagaries of Minoan architecture (see Ch. XIII, 3) find it difficult to believe that any of the three doorways above mentioned could have formed the entrance to such apartments. Let us explore them in turn.

First, the door at the rear right corner of 69A. This opens directly on a landing from which a stairway descends to the important hall 25, and to the Central Court, while another ascends to Peristyle 74 and the large room with a pier-and-door partition, 93. Clearly, then, this doorway was an important one.

Second, the door at the south end of 69 and up three shallow steps into Room 70 with a stone bench along its west wall. This may have served as a guardroom for the control of the Grand Propylon, but must also have acted as an anteroom to the floor over Magazines 32-37 since there is no other route by which it could have been reached.[19] The plan of this area over the magazines should probably be restored as a great hall extend-

---

[17] So Platon (oral communication), and Dörpfeld, whose views were strongly opposed by MacKenzie, *Ath. Mitt.*, 30 (1905), pp. 257-297; *BSA*, 11 (1904-1905), pp. 181-223.

[18] It is drained, as light-well floors regularly are; Platon objects (orally) that the abundant light coming from the west would make such a light-well superfluous, but it would be useful in lighting rooms in the upper floors of the Central Court—See *AJA*, 65 (1961), p. 167.

[19] The objections I mentioned in *AJA*, 60 (1956), pp. 152-153 are largely met by accepting the lower floor level over the magazines.

ing west from the rear of Room 25 to the west end of the building, with two rows of columns over the reinforced stone heads of the partition walls, and perhaps a pier-and-door partition on the line of heavy wall between Magazines 36, 30 and 37, 31.[20] Such a hall would surely have been suitable for important state functions.

But there is still another door, the widest of the three, that opens at the other end of 69 on a fine broad flight of steps, 71, ascending west to a broad landing, 72, from which a second flight would continue to the second storey. The probable height of the first storey, based on reasonable calculations for the height of the stairway and for the height of the columns would be in the neighborhood of sixteen to seventeen feet (ca. 5 m.). From the head of the second flight one could pass, no doubt, east to the gallery above Peristyle 74, but in all likelihood also to a portico above 68-69, which would have provided an excellent vantage point for viewing visitors or processions passing up the stairs of the Propylon (Fig. 48). A doorway in the south end of this portico would provide a convenient entrance into another hall directly above the one entered from Room 70, but extending, possibly, the one-hundred-foot distance from the West to the Central Courts, as I represented it in 1970 (*AJA*, 74 [1970], p. 236, Fig. 31); but I now think it more likely that it extended only some seventy feet and left the roof over Room 25 free for viewing spectacles in the Central Court, as shown in our Fig. 50.

A general restoration of the Magazine-Propylon Block based on these results, and incorporating large windows for the two storeys of the Piano Nobile set in the pair of symmetrical recesses of the west façade, achieves a pleasingly harmonious and well proportioned effect which perhaps represents the high-water mark in Minoan architectural design (Fig. 48 and compare Fig. 50).

That the principal public rooms of the Cretan palaces were usually above the ground floor seems well established. But the

[20] Cf. Charbonneaux, *BCH*, 54 (1930), pp. 352-366.

question *why* may very properly be raised. Some of our answers might well surprise the Cretan architect—if only because to him it was a well established tradition which he perhaps rarely, if ever, stopped to question.

From the negative point of view one might be tempted to reply that the "ground floor" was in effect the "basement," and was consequently given over largely to storage and service areas. To have stored heavy materials on the upper floors would have involved extra labor, and required stronger floors and walls. A considerable part of the ground floor was also given over to small shrines; especially in the case of the "pillar rooms," contact with Mother Earth was perhaps desirable. The main floor of the residential quarters was also apparently always put on the ground floor close to their terraced gardens.

But there must have been more positive reasons than mere lack of space on the ground floor to explain the preference for utilizing the second storey for the main public rooms. There may have been such practical considerations involved as the desire to protect valuable furnishings from dampness, or to avoid possible damage from occasional floods to the wall and floor decorations, which could not be moved out of harm's way. Perhaps, too, flies and mosquitoes were less troublesome at the higher level. (Cf Herodotos, II, p. 95: towers for sleeping.)

Another important reason, I suggest, was that rooms on the upper floors could be equipped with numerous large windows providing abundant circulation of air and fine views over the surrounding countryside (Ch. IX, 2). At the same time privacy was secured by putting the windows sufficiently high above the ground to prevent the unauthorized multitude from viewing important official functions. Unglazed windows on the ground floor would offer a constant opportunity for prowlers.

Considerations of pomp and circumstance are also undoubtedly involved. Locating the state reception halls on the upper floors permitted the architect to design a splendid approach to the royal presence; the impressive effect, psychological as well as aesthetic, of a broad flight of steps ascending to the Piano Nobile, so skilfully employed in the Renaissance *palazzo*, no doubt did not escape the Minoan designers. The association in the human mind between royalty or divinity and a physically superior position is embedded in our very language: we are *elevated* to a peerage; we *raise up* our eyes unto the Lord.

The constant west orientation of the main suite of public halls likewise calls for some explanation. If it is not merely dependent upon the general orientation of the palace as a whole, or simply the result of following the pattern set by Knossos where the lie of the land favored such an orientation, it may be due to a desire to receive the benefit of the prevailing winds or to enjoy the maximum hours of daylight in the late afternoons and early evenings when most court functions would naturally be held. Artificial illumination in Minoan times must have been more attractive than effective.

Rooms used for public purposes were not necessarily restricted, however, to the series of rooms immediately facing on the west court. In fact Evans restored, no doubt correctly in principle though wrongly in detail, the plan of other large rooms, including the "Central Tri-Columnar Hall," between the north-south corridor serving the western rooms and the Central Court,[21] and it is possible that important rooms existed in this same position at Mallia. There may also have been large rooms in the upper storeys on other sides of the central court. At Knossos Evans considered that the plan of the basement rooms, and the masses of fine plaster relief fragments found fallen into them, on the east side of the Central Court, indicated the presence of "the most important of all the reception halls in the Palace area," which he termed the "Great East Hall."[22]

A special form of public room which it will be convenient to discuss separately is the banquet or dining hall, and to this we shall now turn.

[21] *Knossos*, II, plan C.   [22] *Knossos*, I, pp. 360-384; III, pp. 481-496.

2. THE BANQUET HALL

The tomb-paintings of New Kingdom Egypt picture elegant dinner parties, and in some palaces long narrow rooms with two rows of columns have been identified hypothetically as banquet halls.[23] It is a reasonable guess, then, that the grand reception halls of the Minoans were matched by equally splendid banquet halls, which would also probably be on the upper floors. But how can we gain any clearer idea of the location and general appearance of these vanished rooms?[24]

As in the case of the reception halls we might expect some clues to be provided in the surviving remains of the ground floors. We could look, then, for indications of a large room in the second storey, well removed from the reception halls to avoid the odor of food, the heat of cooking, and the clatter of preparation and clean-up; the presence on the ground floor, beneath or near such a hall, of rooms suitable for the storage and preparation of food; the remains of large masses of pottery both coarse and fine; and adequate provision of stairways to the upper room.

Where better to commence our search than in the Palace of Mallia, whose ground-plan is well preserved and reasonably legible (Fig. 6). The entire area east of its Central Court is occupied by magazines, while west of it are more magazines and cult rooms. South and southwest we find only small, nondescript rooms and no signs of adequate stairways. The northwest is occupied by the Residential Quarter, and the extreme north by another row of storage rooms.

Our search is thus quickly reduced to the area just north of the Central Court (Fig. 88) and fronting on it by a fine, columned portico.[25] Near the west end of this portico, a door opens into a long narrow room, ix 1, with a single central pillar base (Fig. 59). This seems to have served merely as an anteroom to a larger room, ix 2, the Northeast Hall as we may call it; this measures 30

---

[23] E. B. Smith, *Egyptian Architecture*, pp. 218f.; Winlock, *Bull. Metr. Mus.*, 7 (1912), pp. 184-188.

[24] For a more detailed account see *AJA*, 65 (1961), pp. 165-172.

[25] For what follows see *Mallia*, II, pp. 2-5, 19-24; III, 15-17, 50-52.

M.ft. square and has six high stone bases in two rows like the Egyptian rooms mentioned above. A broad stone stairway, ix ab, must have led to an upper gallery over the north portico, and from it one could have reached the Upper Northeast Hall and its anteroom.

This appears not to have been the only stairway to have served the Upper Northeast Hall, for there is a second one over xxii 1, 3. The first was surely used by the guests; the second, by the staff.[26] Directly at the foot of the service stairway was the "North Service Court," as it may be called, surrounded by magazines and small rooms well suited for storing and preparing food. No hearths have been reported but spit supports (Fig. 141, M) were found in xxi 2, also grain mills and remains of grain in jars; quantities of pottery were also discovered in the "corner cupboards" in xxv 2 and xxvii 6, as well as in xxi 2,[27] xxii 1, 2, xxv 3, and xxvii 2-5.

At Phaistos, north of the Central Court a number of bases and reinforced points in the walls of rooms 58-61 and 91-92 indicate the existence of a "Northeast Hall" in the second storey with two rows of four columns each (Fig. 87). Its resemblance to the complex we have just examined at Mallia in position, size, plan, stairways, finds of pottery, and service rooms is very clear. Here, then, we must have a second Banquet Hall complex.

In the Palace of Minos the "Teloneion" or "Customs House," as Evans thought it might have been because of its position at the north entrance of the building, provides a third example of a long narrow room with two rows of five pillars each.[28] If we assume that here, too, above the so-called Teloneion, we have still another banquet hall, the principal points of difference between this room and those at Mallia and Phaistos would be its greater size—appropriately for Knossos—and its not being directly on the Central Court; but, as shown in Fig. 158, it could have been conveniently reached from the north end of the court by a virtually level cor-

---

[26] In fact there was a third stairway over xxi 2 and xxii 2, which must have commenced at the second storey and continued to the roof, *AJA*, 83 (1979), p. 68.

[27] *REA*, 43 (1941), pp. 12-14.

[28] *Knossos*, III, p. 165 and fig. 106.

ridor. In Mackenzie's Daybook of 1901, moreover, we read of masses of pottery found in this area, especially of "immense quantities" of discarded fragments in a gap just south of the "Teloneion" where Evans would see a "Warder's" post, and masses of whole pots carefully arranged by categories were uncovered in the separate rooms of the nearby Northeast Magazines.[29]

Welcome confirmation of these rooms as banquet halls, with ancillary service rooms, came shortly after the appearance of *PoC* (1962). In the course of excavating his newly found palace at Kato Zakro, Platon discovered, at the north end of the Central Court, a room (XXXII) very similar in size and position to the room with six pillars at Mallia, and adjoining it a portico with a stairway ascending (no doubt) to an upper gallery.[30] The Zakro room (XXXII) Platon immediately identified as a kitchen, principally on the basis of a hearth with a tripod cooking pot found in one corner together with masses of meat bones and, in the adjacent rooms, quantities of pottery and a variety of cooking utensils. The identity of the room above XXXII as a banquet hall seems guaranteed.

With four banquet halls satisfactorily identified in the Cretan palaces, it has become possible to recognize a number of others, with considerable plausibility, in other structures. These include Villa A at Tylissos, over 16-17, with two stairways (Fig. 19); and a villa at Sklavokambos above 15 (Fig 22)—suggested by J. W. Shaw. An interesting example with accompanying service rooms and three stairways (two for service) may be seen in the Little Palace at Knossos in the form of an annex attached to the main building (containing reception halls) by a short "bridge" (Fig. 13).[31] See **Addendum 2**.

Even farther separated from the Reception Hall (the "megaron") is the large frescoed room with an anteroom (65, 64) excavated by Carl Blegen at Pylos on the mainland;[32] the plans of both are very like ix 1, 2 at Mallia, but, as characteristically for the

[29] *Knossos*, I, pp. 568-571.
[30] N. Platon, *Zakros* (New York, 1971), pp. 203-209, 255.
[31] *AJA*, 79 (1975), pp. 141-144.
[32] C. W. Blegen and M. Rawson, *Palace of Nestor at Pylos*, I (Princeton, 1966), pp. 247-259.

mainland megarons, they are located at the ground level. Masses of pottery, including numerous tripod cooking pots and braziers, were found in adjoining rooms, while across a small court, quantities of pottery were excavated that, like the pottery found in the Northeast Magazines at Knossos, had evidently been stored in separate categories on wooden shelving.

Thus the mainland banquet halls seem to have been influenced by the Minoan just as the Minoan appears to have been influenced by the Egyptian. Cretan envoys to Egypt may well have been entertained in such rooms, and Minos have paid Pharaoh the compliment of imitation.

CHAPTER VII

OTHER ROOMS

1. STOREROOMS AND WORKROOMS

Telemachus descended into the spacious, high-roofed room of his father, where piled up lay gold and bronze and clothing in chests, and abundant odorous oil, and there stood jars of wine old and sweet holding unmixed divine drink, ranged in order against the wall . . . closed were the double doors of closely-fitted boards.—(ODYSSEY, 2, 337-345)

TANGIBLE evidence of the wealth of the Minoan princes is furnished by the rows of magazines in the palace "basements." Almost a third of the ground floor area in the Palace of Mallia (excluding courts) was occupied by storerooms (Fig. 6).

Information available about Cretan storerooms is relatively abundant, due to their having normally been placed on the ground floor. This was done, among other reasons, to avoid unnecessary lifting, as well as to obviate the need to build stronger walls and floors in the upper storeys in order to sustain the greater weight.

A favored position for the palace storerooms was along the west façade immediately beneath the great halls of the state apartments on the Piano Nobile. At Knossos, Mallia, and Gournia they consist of a series of long narrow rooms—over twenty at Knossos—served by a long north-south corridor. At Mallia there is also a row of seven such magazines east of the Central Court, which are of special interest and will be described in detail below. Other storerooms belong to a shorter, broader type, for example those in the Magazine Block at Phaistos (27-37), and those west of Court 90 (54-55), and at

Mallia a row (xxvii 1-6) at the north end of the palace, and three more (xii 1-3) east of the Central Court.

As for the private houses, storerooms of various sizes and shapes can be identified in most of them, but it is difficult to generalize about their position except to say that they were usually well separated from the residential part of the house. In House Da at Mallia (Fig. 22) two magazines filled with storage vessels were found immediately off the entrance passage; in shape and plan they resemble the East Magazines in the palace at the same site. House Za at Mallia is clearly divided on the ground floor into two parts, one residential, the other for service, each with its own entrance; the three magazines, 26-28, at the rear of the service half were found filled with a great mass of badly shattered pottery vessels (Fig. 25). In the service half of House A at Tylissos two large rooms, 16-17, with two central pillars each, contained numerous big jars or "pithoi" ranged along the walls (Fig. 19). In the southeast corner of 16 is a bin-like structure about 29 inches north to south, 37 inches east to west, and 48 inches high (74 by 94 by 122 cm.), smooth on the outside (toward the room), rough on the interior, and with a large opening, 18 by 21 inches (46 by 53 cm.), through the south wall at floor level. Could it have been a grain bin for current use with a slot for withdrawal?[1]

The commonest type of magazine, in the palaces as in the houses, is that used for the storing of pithoi. At Vathypetro these seem to have alternated with smaller jars set on wooden shelves. The West Magazines at Knossos, which vary from about 35 to 60 ft. in length (ca. 10½ to 18½ m.) and from 5 to 8 ft. in width (1½ to 2½ m.), could have held from thirty to forty jars apiece, ranged in single or double rows along the walls (Fig. 93). Estimating some 155 gallons (ca. 586 liters) as the capacity of an average jar, and the maximum number of jars at about 420, the total maximum capacity of the magazines might amount to over 65,000 American gallons (over 246,000

---

[1] *Tylissos*, pp. 21-23; the height is there given as 2 m.; perhaps it was better preserved at that time.

liters).[2] The contents were probably entirely olive oil, according to Evans, a commodity which was used by the ancients in tremendous amounts since it served as a food, as a soap substitute, and as fuel for their lamps. Pithoi were also used to store other substances, however, such as grain, beans, peas, and lentils.

A vivid picture of the efficient way in which the royal estates were managed is given by the arrangement of the compact rectangular block of magazines east of the Central Court at Mallia (Fig. 91).[3] A single doorway from the east portico controls a corridor which turns at a right angle to serve six identical magazines (one was later shortened by a cross-wall), each about 21 ft. long by 7 ft. wide (ca. 6.35 by 2.10 m.). Along both walls of every magazine is a low platform of cement about 2½ ft. (76 cm.) wide, which provided room for fourteen large and fourteen smaller jars, approximately 158 jars in all. Together with a score of jars in the long corridor and a single row in the entrance corridor, the total capacity of the block was about 190 jars, amounting possibly to some five or six thousand gallons (ca. 23,000 liters). Remains in the jars indicate that the larger ones contained wheat and lentils; the smaller, some liquid, probably oil. Particular pains were taken to avoid wastage of oil through spilling. Each platform was scored with fourteen transverse furrows carefully set at regular intervals with two different spacings for the two sizes of jars; these open into channels running along beside the platforms and emptying into a clay jar, embedded to the level of its rim in the cement floor, at the end of each magazine. Further equipment consists of a huge trough at the northeast corner of the long corridor, with two steps up to it; in the southeast corner is a great jar protected by a row of upright slabs. Beside the latter was a block of stone where, the excavators suggest, an overseer could have sat and kept his tally as the porters carried in their oil-filled amphoras to pour into

[2] Evans' figures were falsified by his mistaking the length of the radius of a jar for its diameter and compounding this error by a mathematical mistake in calculation; cf. van Effenterre, *Études crètoises* XII, p. 42, and *Gnomon* 36 (1964), p. 622.

[3] *Mallia*, III, pp. 1-5.

the jars. To judge by the inscribed tablets found in the palaces the records were kept in scrupulous detail.

Settling basins for oil seem to have been identified recently at Gortyn in a large farm villa, and oil separator jars have been found at several sites (Fig. 143, H).[4] An interesting feature, not yet noted in Crete, has been observed lately in a magazine at Mycenae, namely provision for heating one of the jars; this is said to be normal practice in present-day Tuscany to prevent the oil from congealing in cold weather.[5]

The size of these huge jars, which run up to seven feet (over 2 m.) or more in height, is a tribute to the skill of the Minoan potter (Fig. 92). But it was evidently something of a trial for the "shorties" of the day, for in Magazine 33 at Phaistos was found a terracotta stool about 16½ in. (42 cm.) high, with hand-holes for portability, to be used as a stand by one desiring to reach the contents of a tall pithos (Fig. 143, G). The potters, proud of the gigantic offspring of their craft, decorated them with loving care: rows of small handles, curving ropework in imitation of the actual ropes used in handling the jars, lines of impressed circles, "medallions," and even plant motives in relief were methodically planned and neatly executed in parallel zones of ornament. The Cretan pithos is a handsome piece of architecture.[6]

Another form of storage, common in the Palace of Minos but strangely enough not found elsewhere in Crete, is the sub-floor chest or "cist" (Fig. 93).[7] Even at Knossos they seem to have been predominantly a Middle Minoan III feature, after which many were abandoned. The Long Corridor of the West Magazines was closed off at this time by a block at one end and a door at the other and ninety-three cists were constructed beneath the floors of the magazines and of the corridor itself. Though differing somewhat in size, all those in the magazines and seven in the corridor were of the same type and built with surprising

---

[4] *REA*, 43 (1941), p. 12; *Mallia*, III, p. 48, fig. 24.

[5] *BSA*, 48 (1953), p. 12; but Palmer now explains the heating as a step in the process of making unguents, *Mycenaeans and Minoans*, p. 108.

[6] *Knossos*, IV, pp. 633-648, for examples.   [7] *Knossos*, I, pp. 448-462.

care. A typical specimen from the corridor measures about 3 ft. long by 1 ft. 4 in. wide by 3 ft. 8 in. deep (ca. 92 by 40 by 112 cm.); the walls consisted of four gypsum slabs, the two end ones being mortised into the side pieces and all four mortised into a slab of limestone forming the bottom of the cist. All this was set rather loosely within walls of dressed stone and the intervening space packed firmly with red earth, the apparent intention being to help insulate the cists from dampness. They were likewise lined with sheets of lead, and of course covered by removable stone lids. Chests so carefully protected were evidently intended to shelter the treasure of kings, and, in spite of repeated plunderings through the ages, fragments of crystal, faïence, gold foil, and wooden boxes with bronze hinges were found in them by the excavators.

Four groups, each with five cists, in the Long Corridor are different in construction and more capacious. An average specimen measures about 3 ft. 3 in. long by 2 ft. 6 in. wide by 5 ft. 3 in. deep (99 by 77 by 160 cm.); the walls and bottom were of limestone and the whole was packed around with red earth. The cist was lined, however, with fine white plaster rather than with lead, suggesting that it was made to contain a liquid, which Evans supposes was oil. He further notes that a depression cut in the bottom of each cist would have served to catch sediment, so that the oil may first have been put in them and later skimmed off and stored in pithoi. The average capacity of these cists would be about 320 American gallons, amounting to perhaps 6400 gallons (over 24,000 liters) for the whole series.

Isolated rooms in various parts of the palaces and houses supplement though certainly do not complete the picture we have so far obtained of how the Minoans stored their property. For example, a room just behind the "Tripartite Shrine" on the west of the Central Court at Knossos was found to have two deep cists in the floor containing remains of a wealth of temple treasures; the larger measures 6 ft. 4 in. by 4 ft. 9 in. by over 5 ft. deep (195 by 145 by over 150 cm.).[8] Another cache, evi-

---

[8] *Knossos*, I, pp. 463ff.; the measurements are mine.

dently of a sacred nature, from two small rooms in House A at Tylissos, next to a Pillar Crypt, consisted of a bronze talent and three tremendous bronze cauldrons (Fig. 142, G). Nineteen other talents or metal ingots were discovered in a small room (7) in the Villa at H. Triadha; each weighed close to 64 lbs. (29 kg.), evidently the standard weight of a talent.[9] In one of the rooms (7) at Nirou Khani four very large bronze double-axes were discovered, while in another (18) quantities of stone altar tables were found neatly stacked (Fig. 31). It has been suggested that this building was a center for the distribution of Minoan cult apparatus. In one of its outer courtyards a series of storerooms had been built against one of the walls. Some contained large jars of the usual kind; more interesting is a space enclosed between heavy sidewalls and divided into five small bins (26-30) by thin partitions of adobe brick, which had been used for storing grain. Finally, in the northeast quarter of the Palace of Phaistos a long narrow room (88) was excavated several feet below the adjacent floor levels and reached by a short stairway; possibly it was a "cold-cellar" for keeping such foods as milk, cheese, or meat (see Ch. ii, 2).

Pottery was of course often stored in ordinary magazines, as in House Za at Mallia. In the Palace of Mallia, however, large quantities were kept in two "cupboards," of which only rubble foundations remain, in Rooms xxv 2 and xxvii 6, in the northeast service quarter. At Phaistos pottery was kept in what must have been a cupboard beneath the stairs north of the Central Court;[10] and in the nearby rooms, 45 and 46, small stone-lined cupboards, built into the walls (Fig. 99) were evidently used for pottery.

A group of eight circular structures about fifteen feet ($4\frac{1}{2}$ m.) in diameter and arranged in two lines of four each was excavated at the southwest corner of the Palace of Mallia (Figs. 58, 62). What remains of each is built of rough stone, lined on the interior with plaster, and surely is to be completed

[9] *Guida*, p. 33, fig. 45; Matz, *KMT*, pl. 74.
[10] *Mallia, Maisons*, ii, p. 10 and note 5 for other examples of understair cupboards.

in the form of a dome, supported on a central pillar of which the stump is preserved in most instances. The excavators have referred to them as cisterns, but the fact that they were built above ground renders this highly unlikely; their correct interpretation is surely indicated by their resemblance to contemporary Egyptian granaries.[11]

Also requiring careful storage were the clay tablets commonly used in Crete and Mycenaean Greece, as in the Near East, for keeping records (Fig. 147). "After writing, the tablets were dried (not baked) and then generally filed away in boxes of gypsum or wood, or in wicker baskets, and stacked on shelves in rooms set aside for the purpose."[12]

In the Palace of Nestor at Pylos there was a special "archive room," with an annex, opening off the main entrance, a "location very convenient for the supervision of incoming and outgoing goods and personnel";[13] and in the palace at Mari on the Euphrates some 20,000 tablets were found in a single small room (115 in Fig. 148) with two deep wall niches adjacent to the main court.[14] At Knossos, however, the tablets have been found for the most part at widely scattered points throughout the palace and its vicinity; often they seem to have fallen from upstairs rooms, and nowhere did the excavators find a room which had been definitely set aside for the exclusive storage of tablets.[15]

[11] In a letter of Aug. 19, 1960, M. Georges Daux writes, "Quant aux pseudo-citernes, il s'agit bien entendu de silos à grain, comme vous le pensez." However M. Demargne (letter of Sept. 17, 1960) writes that he prefers to abide by Chapouthier's idea that they were cisterns, and that this is retained in the ms. for the forthcoming fascicle (*Mallia*, IV). Marinatos still refers to them as cisterns, *C. and M.*, p. 64. Lawrence argues with good reason that the "hypogeum" at the south end of the early palace at Knossos (*Knossos*, I, fig. 74) was a huge granary (*Gk. Arch.*, p. 298, note 3); Karo, however, calls it a cistern (*Greifen am Thron*, p. 32), while Matz thinks it may have been designed for the sacred snakes (*KMT*, p. 50). Hood also has recently referred to the Mallia structures as granaries, *Dawn of Civilization* (ed. Piggott, London, 1961), p. 223.

[12] *DMG*, p. 114.   [13] *DMG*, p. 117.   [14] *Mari*, II, pp. 80-81.

[15] *DMG*, pp. 114-117; the only deposit found *in situ* in the palace was under a small flight of stairs in a small room at the southwest corner of the Central Court. The accuracy of the find-records of tablets in the Palace of Minos has, however, recently been challenged; see Palmer, *Mycenaeans and Minoans*, especially Ch. VI. 4; Hood, *Antiquity*, 35 (1961), pp. 80-81.

Nevertheless the tablets at Knossos were occasionally found in groups of related content, and at least once they were discovered along with the type of object listed on them.[16] In the basement of a badly preserved building to the northwest of the palace termed the "Armory" or "Arsenal," there was found, fallen from an upper floor, a great quantity of bronze arrowheads, with remains of the wooden shafts, in two groups ten feet apart. They were embedded in the débris of two wooden chests with bronze loop handles which had been carefully sealed. A broken clay tablet from the same deposit lists two lots of arrows: 6010 and 2630, a total of 8640.

The newly, and still very imperfectly, deciphered Linear B tablets give some further indication of the range of objects stored in the palace magazines, although it is often far from clear that the tablets are in any sense actual inventories of the royal property. Classes of commodities mentioned include foodstuffs, textiles, furniture, pottery and metal vessels, and military equipment (see Ch. xii, 1). Tablets referring to the last item are particularly numerous and mention is made of arrows, spears, swords, horses, and chariots. Over four hundred chariots in various states of completeness are mentioned in the known Knossos tablets, often with considerable supplementary information, for example: "Three horse-(chariots without wheels) inlaid with ivory (fully) assembled, equipped with bridles with *cheek-straps* (decorated with) ivory (and) horn *bits*."[17] (The italicized words are regarded as uncertain).

Not much definite information about workrooms is available. A grape and an olive press was found in a room at Vathypetro (Fig. 94), but otherwise remarkably little specialized equipment (except religious) has been found, that can be distinctly associated with particular types of rooms. It seems clear that the northeast quarter of all three major palaces was used largely by the domestic staff, and evidence of the activity of potters, lapidaries, etc. has been observed at Knossos. Perhaps the best example is at Mallia, where there is a small court with

[16] *Knossos*, IV, pp. 836-837.   [17] *DMG*, p. 366, no. 265.

surrounding porticoes and nearby storage and workrooms, concerned primarily, if our identification of the Banquet Hall is correct (Ch. VI, 2), with the preparation and storage of food. Two hearths were found in a portico of the court of the house at Sklavokambos (Fig. 32), but fixed hearths seem rarely to have been used. Many years ago Hazzidakis remarked on their peculiar scarcity and on the difficulty of identifying kitchens in Minoan houses or palaces; his expectation that time would bring the solution[18] has now been realized in the Zakro palace.

Many objects which might be serviceable in identifying the use of particular types of rooms have not in fact proved helpful because their use is undeterminable or undetermined, because they have been found in rooms of unspecific function such as courts or storerooms, because their finding place is unknown or unreported, or because they have not been mentioned in published reports. Excavators who have a wealth of showy material to publish are prone to neglect the drab but often very informative objects of everyday life.[19]

2. CULT ROOMS

One does not need to read the entire three thousand pages of *The Palace of Minos at Knossos* to receive the impression that the building was a labyrinth of cult rooms from one end to the other; or, as the Master of Minoan Archaeology characteristically phrased it, "The cumulative results of the exploration of the great building at Knossos have served more and more to bring out the fact that it was interpenetrated with religious elements."[20] Yet Nilsson, that most careful and conscientious student of Minoan religion, discounts much of this; and Miss Banti, the writer of the major portion of the volume which so meticulously describes the last Palace of Phaistos, is of the opinion that this palace, otherwise so like its sister palace at

[18] *Tylissos*, p. 58. For the service area at Phaistos see Ch. II, 2, above, and *AJA*, 65 (1961), pp. 167f.

[19] Chapouthier studied some objects of this nature in *REA*, 43 (1941), pp. 5-15, "La vaisselle commune et la vie de tous les jours à l'époque minoenne." See Ch. XII, 1, below.

[20] *Knossos*, I, p. 4.

Knossos, contains no cult rooms at all.[21] Surely the truth must lie somewhere between these extreme views.

A careful re-evaluation of the whole problem, bringing together all the available evidence, not only from the form and position of the rooms but from the objects found in them, is being made by Platon, the Ephor of Cretan Antiquities.[22] These studies have only begun to appear, but he has already succeeded in establishing the religious nature of a large number of rooms of a type interesting to us because of its distinctive architectural character. A description of a few of the best preserved will bring out the typical features.

Most of the examples listed in Platon's first article belong to the type of room frequently mentioned on previous pages as the "Pillar Crypt," together with associated rooms. We shall begin with the complex of rooms in the northern half of the Southeast House (Fig. 17).[23] The central room, C 1, the Pillar Crypt, measures about 10 by 12 ft. (3.15 by 3.65 m.), and the single pillar in the middle is preserved to a height of just over 6 ft. (nearly 2 m.); on three of the blocks of the pillar double-axe symbols are lightly incised.[24] At its foot a stone base of a type known to have been used for setting up a double-axe (Fig. 100) was found in place, while a rough foundation running from this to the north wall supported a number of bases for vessels probably intended for food and drink offerings. In the west wall of the room was a deep niche, but there were no windows, and light was evidently supplied by a handsome pedestaled lamp carved from a purple stone. At the northeast corner opens D 1, a narrow room doubtless used for storage of cult apparatus, and at the southeast corner another room B 1, in which was discovered a curious plaster stand evidently for ritual usage. B 1 communicated by a narrow passage, controlled by doors at both ends, with a stairway which must have led, as is known from other examples, to a Columnar Shrine whose single

[21] *Festòs*, II, p. 582.
[22] *Kret. Chron.*, 8 (1954), pp. 428-483. [23] *Knossos*, I, pp. 427-430.
[24] The publication mentions only one double-axe sign, but two on the north side and one on the east are visible.

column would be placed directly above the pillar of the Pillar Crypt. From this upper room had fallen a sacral knot made of ivory, and fragments of wall paintings including representations of lilies.

In the northwest corner of the South House (Figs. 15, 71), a Pillar Crypt, about 13 by 18 ft. (ca. 4 by 5½ m.), has a central pillar preserved to a height of about six feet (nearly 2 m.).[25] Close to one face of the pillar was a pyramidal base for a double-axe, and near the opposite face another base, with three holes perhaps intended for the sacral horns with a double-axe in the center. An adjacent stairway led to an Upper Columnar Shrine with a stone bench still in position against a wall. From the upper shrine had fallen a set of five silver vessels probably for ceremonial use. Off the Pillar Crypt opens a storeroom.

The Pillar Crypt in the Royal Villa has already been described since it is so closely associated with the Main Hall and its balustraded area (Ch. III, 4, and Figs. 14, 97).[26] The crypt resembles those in the two preceding examples in its single central pillar and stairway to a Columnar Shrine. But it differs in the provision of a rectangular channel surrounding the pillar and deepening into two basins on opposite sides of it; presumably this was designed to catch liquid offerings (cf. Fig. 100) poured before the pillar—"Jacob . . . took the stone . . . and set it up for a pillar, and poured oil upon the top of it" (Genesis 28: 18). The floor was made of gypsum slabs and the walls of coursed blocks of gypsum; no cult objects were found.

A large Pillar Crypt, about 13 by 27 ft. (4 by 8.20 m.), west of the Central Court in the Palace of Mallia, contains two pillars on the long axis (Figs. 6, 95).[27] One pillar is marked with two double-axes and a star (Fig. 98), the other with a trident and a star, and a wall block also with a star. The floor was paved with flagstones in a regular scheme. Three of the West Magazines, which are walled off from the rest, are easily accessible from this room.

[25] *Knossos*, II, pp. 386-387.   [26] Ch. III, 4; *Knossos*, II, pp. 406-408.
[27] *Mallia*, I, pp. 27-28.

Finally let us examine the rectangular complex of rooms occupying the center of the west side of the Central Court in the Palace of Minos (Fig. 2).[28] Two small connecting Pillar Crypts, each about 11 by 16 ft. (nearly 3½ by 5 m.), set end to end, contain a single pillar each, preserved, it seems, to its full height of 5 ft. 9 in. (1.75 m.). Each is made up of four blocks of limestone and all four faces of each block, except the west face of the east pillar and the top surface of the west pillar, were inscribed, according to Evans (some are difficult to see now), with double-axe signs, twenty-nine in all. Adjacent to the eastern pillar are two shallow, stone-lined basins evidently intended for the same purpose as those in the Royal Villa. Associated with these Pillar Crypts are several storage rooms, in the floor of one of which were two shallow stone-lined cists found empty; beneath these two earlier cists, much larger and deeper than those above (Ch. vii, 1), were discovered, and in and above them a mass of fragmentary objects of a ritual character, including snake-goddess figurines, a marble cross, quantities of painted shells, faïence plaques with a cow suckling its calf and a goat its kids, etc. (Ch. ii, 1).[29]

Easily accessible from the West Pillar Crypt was the Corridor of the Magazines, and it is possibly significant that the head of the partitions of the two nearest magazines (4 and 5) were marked with double-axe symbols which, as we have seen, were so generously distributed over the two pillars. To the east of the East Crypt was a larger anteroom, variously referred to as the "Room of the Stone Seat," because of a stone bench along its north wall, or as the "Room of the Column Bases," from the two round stone bases found in it, fallen from the Columnar Shrine above, which could be reached by a small stairway to the south. Just north of the steps that led up from the anteroom to the Central Court, on the line of foundations marking the west border of the court, Evans noticed faint traces of a series of four columns which he ingeniously, and perhaps correctly, in-

---

[28] *Knossos*, I, pp. 425, 441-442.   [29] *Knossos*, I, pp. 463-523.

terpreted as marking the position of a "Tripartite Columnar Shrine," whose appearance in elevation is possibly represented, with variations, by the columnar shrine seen in the Grandstand Fresco (Figs. 44, 133). The actual remains, reversing the arrangement in the mural, allow for two columns in the wings and only one in the center, where Evans supposes the shrine or cella of the goddess was located. In a narrow area behind the right wing of the Tripartite Shrine was discovered a mass of sealings representing the goddess standing on a mountain guarded by two lions, with a worshipper in front and a shrine with columns and sacral horns behind.[30]

Thus, including the "Throne Room" complex at the north, which was perhaps used exclusively for ritual purposes (Chs. II, 1 and v, 3), most if not all of the west side of the Central Court at Knossos (except for the stairs to the Piano Nobile), was occupied by a series of shrines. At Mallia the situation seems to have been similar: a complex of cult rooms at the north (vi), already described (Ch. II, 3); the Pillar Crypt, vii 4, in the center; and an area with a round table of offerings south of the stepped platform near the south end of the court (Figs. 6, 61, 95). At Phaistos Rooms 23 and 24 in the center west of the Central Court seem to have been cult rooms, and possibly the ruined rooms to the south of these were also (Figs. 4, 96). By analogy of position, then, Room 25 might likewise be expected to have a religious destination and, though no cult objects or features of a definitely religious nature seem to be associated with the room, its façade, composed of a very large central column flanked by massive piers, is not at all inappropriate (Fig. 50). Certainly with its handsome alabaster walls and floor, its niches and interior columns, it was no ordinary room, no mere anteroom to the magazines as the Italian publication describes it. I have already suggested, without, I admit, any specific proof, that it had certain functions in connection with the ritual of the bull games, and that some of the magazines behind it were used to stable the bulls at the time of the games (Ch. IV).[31]

[30] *Knossos*, II, pp. 796-810.   [31] *AJA*, 61 (1957), p. 261.

The position of Room 25 and the form of its façade bear a general resemblance, already remarked on (Ch. IV), to an open-fronted and pillared room at Mallia (VI 1), at Gournia (near the north end of the west side of the "Public Court"), at Plati (at "A"), perhaps at Vathypetro, and at Knossos (the "Tri-partite Shrine" or possibly the "Throne Room" complex); compare Figs. 2, 6, 8, 9, and 30. In view of the many archi-tectural analogies between the various palaces, this resemblance is not likely to be altogether coincidental. Is it not possible that all these rooms were in some way connected with the bull games, if these, as I believe, were put on in the central court? Let us add one further possibly significant circumstance: im-mediately north of the pillared portico at Gournia, mentioned above, p. 40, lies a huge flat stone some 9 by 7 ft. in length and width and about 8-10 in. thick (ca. 2.75 by 2.15 by 0.23 m.), pierced obliquely by a large hole from top to bottom.[32] Can this have been an altar stone on which the bull was sacrificed after the ritual games (cf. Fig. 101)?[33]

[32] This block is not described in the publication.

[33] Nearby was found a pair of stone sacral horns (E. B. Hawes, *Gournia*, p. 48), now in the University Museum, Philadelphia, MS 4171.

CHAPTER VIII

BUILDING MATERIALS AND FORMS

1. MATERIALS

THE BUILDING materials available to the Cretans of the second millennium B.C. were those in general use throughout the Bronze and Iron Ages until in the Roman imperial period the development of structural concrete and of window glass revolutionized the art of architecture. The use by the Minoans of stone, wood, lime mortar, clay, and reeds will be discussed in that order.

STONE. Gypsum, hydrous sulphate of calcium ($CaSO_4.2H_2O$), is very easy to work since it is so soft that, especially when fresh from the quarry, it can be scratched with the finger nail. When very pure it is snow-white, but it is generally clouded or veined by iron or other impurities, which may however increase its beauty. Coarser varieties of the mineral are used today for "plaster of Paris" by driving off 75% of the water content; it was commonly used by the Egyptians for ordinary plaster, but not by the Cretans, who preferred lime plaster. Thin cleavage plates can be employed, like mica, as a substitute for window glass; but no instances of its use for this purpose in the Bronze Age seem to have been observed.

Gypsum was extensively used at Knossos, where "inexhaustible" quarries occur on the neighboring hill of "Gypsadhes," for wall blocks, pillars, step treads, floor flagging, column and pier bases, etc. Except for outside wall blocks, where the exposed surface was vertical and was often shielded by a thin coat of stucco, gypsum was restricted largely to uses where it was protected from the weather because of its slight solubility in water.

The visitor to Knossos will see some gypsum bases honey-combed by the weather after half a century's exposure (Fig. 117); but some varieties are very resistant to water, as we have already noted in speaking of palace bathrooms (Ch. v, 3).

A fine-grained, marble-like variety of gypsum, capable of producing a very smooth, lustrous surface, is known today as alabaster, and was greatly prized by the Minoans for facing floors and walls in halls, bathrooms, and other important rooms. With bronze saws five feet or more long, they were able to saw this soft stone into sheets over six feet (2 m.) square and often little more than an inch (2½ cm.) in thickness (Fig. 125). Although the Egyptians from Early Dynastic times had used "ancient alabaster," a form of calcite closely related to marble, in slabs for lining passages and rooms, the Cretans were the first, so far as I can discover, to use stone essentially as a thin veneer to conceal a wall of inferior material. This very practical and economical method of achieving a fine effect with a minimum consumption of high quality stone was apparently not commonly used again until Imperial Rome learned to build its tremendous structures by combining the strength and economy of brick and concrete with the beauty of a thin revetment of marble or other fine stone.

Alabaster veneer was used with particular prodigality at Phaistos and H. Triadha. Near the latter an ancient quarry for alabaster of fine quality has been discovered and this (Fig. 125), as well as one near Gortyn, is being used by the Italian archaeologists in the work of repairing and restoring the two palaces. So lavish was its use—even occasionally for magazines —that the rulers of Phaistos and H. Triadha almost literally "dwelt in marble halls."

Limestone was the most widely used stone in Minoan buildings. It usually took the place of gypsum whenever there would be direct exposure to the weather. Outside stairways and pavements, for instance, were always made of limestone; the central courts at Knossos and Phaistos were paved with rectangular slabs of this stone. Carefully dressed blocks were extensively employed for pillars and pillar bases, column bases, door and window facings, walls, etc.

Numerous grades and varieties of limestone were in use. A very hard type of a gray-blue color, known as ironstone (*sidheropetra*), was common at Knossos in the earlier period for pavements (*mosaiko*), and in the later period it was frequently employed for the central panel of a floor with a border of gypsum. It was also much used in the form of large rough blocks at the base of the outside walls of the houses at Mallia. On the other hand a soft, poor quality of white limestone, known as *kouskouras*, was also commonly employed at Knossos and elsewhere. Marble, which is a fine crystalline form of limestone, is comparatively rare in Crete.

Sandstone, in a soft, brown, very friable variety (*ammoudha*) was used extensively in the Palace of Mallia for exterior, and for some interior, walls. Obviously its use was dictated by the fact it was easily worked and locally available; traces of ancient quarries have been found close to the modern beach. The use of a building stone so inferior in quality is in keeping with the modest character of this palace.

Other stones such as schist (slate), marble, and breccia, had a more limited architectural usage, the first for flagstone paving, the other two for column bases.

WOOD. Since well preserved remains are rare we must depend largely upon inference, conjecture, and analogy for a study of the use of wood in Minoan architecture. More will be said in the next section on construction.

Considerable carbonized remains of wooden columns have been discovered at Knossos and Mallia, one shaft in the Palace of Minos being preserved to a length of over eight feet ($2\frac{1}{2}$ m.).[1] This and the remains of other heavy timbers used in the construction of the Grand Staircase were found to be of cypress wood, and, although today Crete is badly deforested and the cypress has almost disappeared from the island, in ancient times it was evidently abundant, for Pliny says that Crete was the

[1] *Knossos*, III, p. 321.

native home of the cypress,[2] and it "supplied materials for the temples and cult-statues of Mainland Greece."[3]

Wood was in common use for columns (which were never made of stone), ceiling and roof beams, flooring in the upper storeys, stairs (especially the upper flights), door and window frames and the doors themselves, and in the form of long timbers to strengthen adobe brick and stone walls. Empty beam-sockets in the upper part of masonry walls, such as the Pillar Crypts of the Royal Villa and the Temple Tomb at Knossos, also furnish evidence regarding the size of the timbers used and the form of the construction (see next section for details).

LIME MORTAR, PLASTER, STUCCO, CEMENT. Minoan builders did not use a gypsum mortar, as the Egyptians did, but a lime mortar, composed of slaked lime, sand, and an aggregate of pebbles, potsherds, or the like. There is now apparently conclusive evidence that they also knew how to make a true cement by adding an element resembling the Roman "pozzolana," namely the Greek "Santorin earth" from the island of Thera (modern Santorini).[4] In this book the terms "plaster" or "stucco" (a finer form of plaster) are used for wall facings, and "cement" for floor surfaces; but in view of the impossibility now of determining in each case whether it was composed of plain lime mortar or of true cement, these terms are not intended to be understood as necessarily accurate.

A fine smooth stucco excellent for wall paintings was ob-

---

[2] *Nat. Hist.*, 16, 141; Evans claims that "the material of the columns, as tested by expert examination of charred specimens, seems in all cases to have been cypress, which also supplied the massive beams and framework" (*Knossos*, I, p. 344); yet Marinatos asserts that the carbonized remains of ancient columns in the Palace of Minos are fir (*C. and M.*, p. 12).

[3] Evans (*loc.cit.*); he cites Hehn, *Kulturpflanzen*, pp. 244ff.

[4] The Gournia publication states that a cement was used at that site which contained "Santorin-earth" (*Gournia*, p. 21); no analysis or other proof, however, is given. Doro Levi also refers to the use of a true cement at Phaistos, *Nuova Antologia*, 467 (1956), p. 230, and cf. *PdP*, 71 (1960), p. 113; by letter he reports that several analyses of mortars from Phaistos and elsewhere have been made, and that a member of the Italian School has nearly completed "a comprehensive study on the Minoan architecture and building techniques," to be published in the *Annuario*. See also *Festòs*, II, pp. 347, 422.

tainable from limestone quarries, producing a very pure chalk lime, within a couple of miles of the Palace of Minos. Rough walls of adobe or rubble were often faced with stucco or thick plaster which, thanks to the cohesive force of the plaster, had a considerable structural as well as decorative value. Even the massive dressed masonry of the palace façades was surfaced with a thin layer of stucco, not however to conceal the joints for they were deliberately emphasized by incised lines (Fig. 121); the purpose of the stucco coat was perhaps rather for color since it was sometimes, at least, painted red. Red stucco was also employed to fill the joints between the gypsum flagstones of floors like that in the Main Hall of the North Residential Quarter at Phaistos in order to emphasize the pattern (Fig. 127). Cement or plaster floors were regularly used for light-wells, sometimes for open courts like the large West Court in the period of the last palace at Phaistos, or for rooms where liquids might be spilt, as in the East Magazines at Mallia (Ch. VII, 1). Stone or clay receptacles such as the sub-floor cists in the West Magazines at Knossos could be made tight with a thin coating of stucco, while thicker plaster was used to line the early "keeps" (cisterns?) northwest of the Central Court at Knossos, and the granaries at Mallia (Fig. 62).

None of the uses of stucco or plaster mentioned so far can be regarded as at all unusual. But at Phaistos one quite remarkable use of true cement (*calcestruzzo*) has been brought very forcefully to the excavators' attention: a very coarse concrete, often two to three or more feet thick, was used to cover over and seal in part of the ruins of earlier stages of the palace and thus provide a firm and relatively even surface on which to rebuild.[5] This process, it has recently been discovered, was repeated no fewer than three times, presumably after catastrophic earthquake shocks had destroyed the earlier palaces. While this has made the archaeologist's task a difficult and expensive one, the labor expended in cutting through and removing these masses of

[5] *Festòs*, II, pp. 10, 422.

concrete has been amply rewarded by the remarkable preservation of the lower portion of the ground floor rooms and their contents, belonging to palaces built as early as the beginning of the second millennium.

CLAY. Clay was used principally for the making of sun-dried or adobe bricks, of which the walls of ordinary buildings and much of the upper walls even of palaces were composed; at Phaistos, however, the excavators claim, the walls were generally of stone or rubble, while adobe is not known to have been used except for thin partitions.[6] The bricks were rarely, if ever, baked in an oven, although the conflagrations in which many buildings perished have often produced this effect.[7] Both straw and seaweed have been reported used with the clay as a binder, and the bricks generally measure about 18 to 24 in. long by 14 to 16 in. wide by 4 to 5 in. thick (46-61 by 35-40 by 10-13 cm.).

Clay was employed as a cohesive element between courses of adobe brick and in walls of rubble stone; it was also used between courses of dressed masonry.[8] Clay mixed with straw was used to face rough walls, sometimes itself serving as a backing for stucco. A special kind of impermeable, bluish-black clay was laid in a thick coat over the roof to prevent leakage, as indeed it still is, under the name of *lepidha*, in present-day Crete.

Water pipes were made of terracotta, as in the Near East (Fig. 139, A); but terracotta tiles do not seem to have been known, since the roofs were universally flat.

[6] *Festòs*, II, p. 421.   [7] *Festòs*, I, p. 228.

[8] The use of clay between courses of masonry was regarded by Evans as a mark of earlier date, but Levi's recent excavations and further studies at Phaistos have cast doubt on this and many other chronological criteria of an architectural nature used by Sir Arthur. Levi writes in *PdP*, 71 (1960), p. 107, "Certain technical criteria which used to be regarded as characteristic of the second palace today should be abandoned: such as the pavements and the alabaster dadoes of the walls, the wall surfaces, the pavements in regular oblongs of rectangular slabs in comparison with the polygonal 'kalderim' pavements, these latter for the most part of limestone, the painted stuccoes of walls and pavements, the shapes and heights of the column bases of hard stone; nor is it possible, on the basis of the difference in technique between courses of limestone blocks separated by a layer of clay and structure in blocks with a framing of wooden beams, observable throughout the constructions at Knossos and Phaistos, to establish the point of separation between the first and the second palace."

REEDS. Reeds were used abundantly in the river valleys of Egypt and Mesopotamia for purposes of building; even today large structures are built entirely of reeds near the mouth of the Tigris-Euphrates.[9] Considerable use was probably also made of reeds in Crete though definite evidence is slight. No doubt the commonest architectural purpose served by reeds in palaces or large houses was that reported from Gournia, namely as a backing for plaster ceilings.[10]

2. CONSTRUCTION

In the present section we are primarily concerned not with the form and material of such features as doors, windows, stairs, or columns, but with the actual structure of the houses and palaces: with pillars and columns as supporting members, with ceilings and roofs, and with walls and foundations.

Traditional Minoan construction paid little heed to the strength of foundations. Even the imposing walls of the west façade of the palaces at Knossos and Mallia were merely bedded on a few layers of small irregular stones or simply on tamped earth, and, given the characteristic lightness of the upper walls, this was adequate under normal conditions. But Crete was subject to violent earthquakes, and they exacted a heavy toll. The Palace of Phaistos was leveled time after time and though, as we have seen in the preceding section, the ruins were sealed in with a heavy layer of concrete to create a stable base over part of the area, yet it was not until the final rebuilding that adequate measures were taken. The builders now began to construct foundations of heavy blocks of limestone considerably broader than the walls they were to support, and to extend these downward, on the west and south sides of the palace where an artificial terrace had been built on the fill, to a depth of some six to eleven feet (2 to 3½ m.); even the foundations of the interior walls were sunk, where necessary, to a comparable depth.[11] At Tylissos, also, some of the exterior house walls built

[9] *Ill. Lon. News,* 226 (Jan. 19, 1955), p. 317.
[10] *Gournia,* p. 28. [11] *Festòs,* II, pp. 425-428.

in the later period were supported on a rubble foundation carried down to bedrock.[12] That the construction of sound foundations, when felt to be needed, was well understood even at an early date, however, is illustrated by the heavy underpinning, running down ten feet (3 m.) or more to hardpan, which was provided for the individual columns of the stepped portico, erected according to Evans in M.M. Ia, mounting the steep slope below the Palace of Minos at its southwest corner.[13]

The construction of the walls varies almost infinitely, being dependent on such factors as the availability of materials, the resources and technical knowledge of the builders, the type of building, the height and weight of the superstructure, the degree of exposure to the weather, the danger from earthquakes, the position of the wall—whether interior or exterior, façade or rear, on a slope or on level ground, and so on—and often enough, it would seem, on the caprice of the builder. To give a reasonably brief and intelligible account of Minoan wall construction is correspondingly difficult.

As we have seen in the preceding section walls were constructed of a variety of materials, two or more often being combined in the same wall. Wood was probably never used alone, but was very commonly introduced into walls of adobe brick, rubble, or dressed masonry. The purpose of this "half-timber" construction was to provide a sort of semi-rigid framing which would unite and compact the other materials yet permit the wall to retain sufficient elasticity to absorb and resist the shock of earthquakes, so common in this region. It is a method of construction which has been widely used throughout the Aegean area from at least the third millennium B.C. to the present day (Fig. 124).

In the houses at Tylissos, for example, the regular practice was to run a short horizontal beam transversely through the thickness of the wall near the floor level, and on each end of this to support a vertical post flush with the wall surface on

[12] *Tylissos,* p. 48.
[13] *Knossos,* II, pp. 144-145.

each side; presumably one or more such transverse beams at higher levels would help to brace the posts firmly together.[14] In the rubble wall on the south side of Room 3 at H. Triadha a series of three sockets spaced about 4½ ft. (1.35 m.) apart on centers and about 7 in. (18 cm.) square, in the north face of the wall, correspond to three similar sockets opposite these on the south face (Fig. 67). Pairs of vertical posts rested directly on flat pieces of gypsum at the bottom of each socket, and must have been joined at intervals through the adobe wall above by transverse wooden bars.[15] Good examples of horizontal beams set flush into the wall faces, along with vertical posts and transverse tiebeams, can be seen in the ashlar masonry walls in the Hall of the Double-Axes and in the adjacent east-west corridor at Knossos.[16]

The upper parts of the walls, both exterior and interior, in all types of buildings, must have been normally built of adobe brick.[17] In ordinary houses the stonework was limited to a mere base or foundation of rough stone (rubble) leveled with clay on the top surface to receive the mud bricks; the outer face of the exterior walls of the houses east of the palace at Mallia is built of large boulders, a sort of rustic imitation of the palace orthostates. Occasionally interior walls, intended as light partitions and not to be continued beyond the first storey at most, were constructed of bricks laid on edge without any stone foundation at all. Examples of such walls, some only 4 to 5 in. thick, can be found in a storeroom for ritual double-axes (7) and in a series of grain bins (26-30) at Nirou Khani, in a bathroom (63d) and a toilet (82) at Phaistos, and in a number of small rooms at the southeast corner of the palace at Mallia.

Rubble masonry, ranging from small rough fieldstones compacted with clay to larger blocks with flattish surfaces due to natural cleavage, was also much used, either alone or in con-

[14] *Tylissos*, pp. 49-50.
[15] *Festòs*, II, p. 434.   [16] *Knossos*, I, pp. 347ff., figs. 250ff.
[17] The excavators believe that the walls of the Phaistos palace were entirely rubble, not mud brick, *Festòs*, II, p. 421.

junction with other materials. Sometimes it might serve, as already mentioned, as a foundation for adobe brick, or it might be continued up at least through the first storey; this is particularly common throughout the Palace of Phaistos and at H. Triadha (Fig. 67).

Masonry of dressed stone was used for strength, resistance, and appearance. Along the base of the principal (west) façade of the palaces, and occasionally elsewhere, as on the north façade of the Central Court at Phaistos (Fig. 122), a course of massive orthostates of dressed stone was regular. It was usually two feet or more high, and the individual blocks, sometimes exceeding six feet in length by three to four feet thick, might weigh several tons; they rested on a low projecting plinth or "euthynteria" (leveling course).

Yet these orthostate blocks, and the same is true of wall blocks of dressed stone in general, were finished smooth only on the front, top, and bottom surfaces, and not more than the front half of the ends. The rear was left quite rough since it was normal practice to complete the thickness of the wall with rubble masonry. A variation is seen in the orthostate course of the west façade of the Palace of Minos, where the walls are six feet thick (nearly 2 m.), and are completed with a series of upright blocks of the same height as the orthostates on the outer face (Fig. 118); the two faces were united by a series of transverse cross-bars of wood set in dovetailed mortises cut in their top surfaces, and the irregular space between the blocks was filled with rubble.

In a few of the finest houses part of the exterior walls was constructed of dressed stone laid in fairly regular coursing, for example in the Little Palace, Royal Villa, South House, and Southeast House at Knossos, and also at Tylissos (Fig. 78). The rear wall of the South House is built of quite massive blocks preserved, in the lee of the cutting for the artificial terrace on which it stands, to a height of eight courses (Fig. 72). The rear wall of the Southeast House is composed of an odd mixture of stones (Fig. 80): the lowest course is limestone, the next three gypsum, and the upper two preserved are limestone again. Normal wall courses of this type are usually from 1 to 1½ ft. high (30 to 45 cm.).

Interior walls were also sometimes built of dressed stone masonry, particularly where the wall was exposed to the weather, as in the unroofed passage which led up to the Central Court from the North Entrance at Knossos, in the small court (48) at Phaistos, and in the light-well of House A at Tylissos. A good illustration occurs in the Residential Quarter at H. Triadha where the north and south walls at the ends of the light-well east of Room 12 are of dressed masonry, but as soon as these walls pass beyond the limits of the light-well they abruptly relapse into ordinary rubble construction (Fig. 70).

Sometimes it would seem that the interior walls were faced with dressed stone just for the sake of appearance, as in the Pillar Crypt of the Royal Villa (Fig. 97), and perhaps this is also the reason for its use in the rooms of the Residential Quarter of the Palace of Minos. Since the stonework in the latter case would have been concealed behind alabaster paneling or plaster, however, perhaps the true explanation for its employment here was to give greater strength to walls which had to support at least two and probably three upper storeys.

A thin bedding of clay was sometimes used between the wall courses; but mortar was not used, as in modern masonry, to hold the blocks together.

A thorough examination of the remains could probably provide us with a fuller picture of the technical processes involved in preparing and laying Minoan masonry. Stone quarries have been observed in several places and the usual method of getting out the blocks seems to have been to bore rows of round holes, some 6 in. deep and 6 to 9 in. in diameter, into which posts were driven and soaked with water; the resulting expansion of the wood split away the blocks along prepared lines of fracture.[18]

[18] *Knossos*, II, p. 233; Chapouthier, *Les écritures minoennes au palais de Mallia*, pp. 87-88, Figs. 32-33.

Large numbers of bronze chisels, saws, and double-axes have been found, especially at H. Triadha. Pernier has noted the abundant traces of the strokes of the double-axe on the faces of the west orthostates of the "Primo Palazzo" at Phaistos; he would even see the origin of the term "labyrinth," applied to the Palace of Minos, in the fact that the palaces were, so to speak, the creation of the double-axe (*labrys*), which first made possible the production of dressed stone masonry and so the appearance of monumental architecture in Crete.[19] Bronze saws, some of them more than five feet ($1\frac{1}{2}$ m.) in length, must have been employed in cutting the great sheets of gypsum used particularly for paneling the interior walls.[20] Saw-strokes an inch or so wide (ca. 2 cm.) are apparent everywhere on the stones at Phaistos, both on surfaces that would be concealed by other blocks and, much more lightly, on important visible surfaces such as the orthostates at the north end of the Central Court (Figs. 120, 122). Small round holes have sometimes been observed on the sides of blocks; these have been explained as lifting-holes, but certainly the common method of moving large blocks of stone during the Bronze Age was to slide them into place by means of temporary ramps.[21]

While speaking of stone masonry we may mention one rather mystifying feature, the so-called mason's marks.[22] In the early period of the palaces these are often very large and deeply cut —a "thunderbolt" at Phaistos reaches a length of 28 in. (72 cm.);[23] later they become smaller and shallower, though rarely as tiny as a "star" in the west recess north of the Central Court at Phaistos, which measures barely $1\frac{3}{8}$ in. (3.5 cm.) in width (Fig. 119).[24] The signs, which appear on walls, pillars, etc., of both palaces and private houses (Fig. 78), include the double-axe (particularly common at Knossos), the trident (frequent at Phaistos), stars, crosses, branches, thunderbolts, and many less

---

[19] *Festòs*, I, p. 441, Fig. 77.   [20] *Knossos*, II, p. 632.   [21] *Mallia*, III, p. 20.
[22] *Festòs*, I, pp. 399-415; II, pp. 423-424; *Knossos, Index Volume*, pp. 98-99; Chapouthier, *op.cit.*, pp. 75-95; *M. and T.*, pp. 109-111; J. Sakellarakis, in *Europa* (ed. W. C. Brice), pp. 277-288.
[23] *Festòs*, I, p. 400, no. 2b.   [24] *Festòs*, II, p. 60, fig. 24.

easily describable forms. They sometimes concentrate in a particular part of a palace, for example tridents near the "sea gate" (North Entrance) at Knossos,[25] and since some appear to have been cut at the quarry it is frequently claimed that they were truly mason's marks, cut by the quarryman for the guidance of those who were to use them. But the twenty-nine double-axes cut on the eight blocks of the two pillars in the Pillar Crypts west of the Central Court at Knossos must have had a religious or magical significance. The problem is however far too complex to discuss here in detail, especially since it appears to offer little hope of providing information useful to the student of Minoan architecture.

The thickness of Minoan walls depends on a number of factors most of which cannot be closely calculated. In general, exterior walls are thicker than interior. At Sklavokambos, for example, the outer walls are usually about 3 to 4 ft. thick (rather over a meter), while the partition walls are only about $1\frac{1}{2}$ to $2\frac{1}{2}$ ft. (45 to 75 cm.); but extreme examples may vary from 8 ft. ($2\frac{1}{2}$ m.) in parts of the west façade at Knossos, to 4 in. (10 cm.) for minor adobe partitions. Walls intended to be continued in the upper storeys are generally thicker than those limited to the ground floor; we have already noticed the difference in thickness between the walls of the two-storey block north of the Central Court at Mallia (Fig. 88) and the three-storey Magazine Block at Phaistos (Fig. 84).

The frequent practice of facing all types of walls with a layer of stucco or plaster, sometimes painted, has been mentioned in the preceding section; the cohesive force of thick plaster would add considerable strength to a wall of loose rubble.

Pillars and columns were extensively employed as supporting members in Minoan architecture. Columns, except very short ones, were made of wood, not of stone; this may be due largely to the fact that it is far easier to make a round column out of a tree trunk than to shape it out of stone. Fragments of the

[25] *Knossos*, I, p. 394.

carbonized cypress-wood column shafts have frequently been found, one at Knossos having a length, as preserved, of more than 8 ft. (2½ m.). The capitals were doubtless made of separate blocks of wood. The lower diameter of three of the largest Minoan columns known at Phaistos seems to have measured between 3½ and 4 ft., giving a bearing of around 11 sq. ft. (ca. 1 sq. m.). Occasionally the base was mortised to receive a tenon on the lower end of the column, and in the court of House E at Mallia the central area of the bases was left rough, apparently also with the purpose of preventing the wood column from slipping on the stone base.

Columns rather than pillars were used in locations where appearance and not merely support was considered important. Columns are therefore regular in light-wells and porticoes of the residential quarters, in the porticoes of the central courts (often combined with pillars), in peristyle courts, on stairway parapets, and in formal entranceways. At Phaistos the great oval column of the Grand Propylon (67) supports the center of a free span of 32 ft. (9.75 m.); a round column divides the wide opening of 75 on the Peristyle Court, 74; and a pair of columns is placed on the axis of the large hall, 25, west of the Central Court, with an area of over 750 sq. ft. (72 sq. m.). This last example, the use of columns within a room, is not common in Minoan architecture on the ground floor;[26] but on the upper floors pairs of columns made possible the great halls, with areas of nearly 3000 sq. ft. (270 sq. m.) in some instances, along the west façades (Ch. VI, 1) and two rows, of two to five columns each, supported the ceilings of the banquet halls (Ch. VI, 2), which at Phaistos and Mallia had an area of about 1200 sq. ft. (115 sq. m.), and at Knossos of nearly 2600 sq. ft. (240 sq. m.). Columns will be further discussed in the section on architectural decoration (Ch. XI, 1).

Pillars, that is vertical supports of rectangular cross-section, were not infrequently made of stone. In Minoan architecture

[26] There seems to have been a single column in the center of the central room of House Zb at Mallia (see Ch. III, 16).

the pillar was usually, if not always, a plain straight-sided shaft without decoration of any sort, and purely utilitarian in function. Neither decorative nor strictly utilitarian, however, are those pillars used in the "Pillar Crypts," for these rooms were rarely so large as to require any sort of interior support.[27] The pillars must therefore have been added purely for religious reasons (Fig. 95), and their religious character is confirmed by the sacred symbols frequently cut on their blocks (Fig. 98); twenty-nine double-axes are incised on the two pillars in the pair of Pillar Crypts in the Palace of Minos (Ch. II, 1).

Examples of purely functional pillars of stone are the seven in ix 1, 2, north of the Central Court at Mallia, which in addition to supporting their own ceiling no doubt took the weight of corresponding columns in the room above (Figs. 59, 88); the single one in the Corridor of the Magazines (26) at Phaistos; and the "built-in" piers in the west magazines at Knossos and Mallia, used solely to carry columns in the halls of the Piano Nobile (Fig. 116). Similarly four piers in Magazines 16 and 17 in House A at Tylissos were not needed because of the size of these rooms, but presumably to support columns in a large hall overhead (Ch. III, 11, and Fig. 19). Stone piers were also used in long porticoes, alternating with columns, especially in the central courts; and as angle piers in two-sided porticoes in the residential quarters.

Stone pillars frequently had a mortise on their upper surface for securing in position the horizontal beams that rested on them —often a useful indication that the pillar is complete in its present condition.

The numerous instances where a rectangular stone base is preserved, but no trace of any pillar remains, indicate that they were not always of stone. However they were not made entirely of wood, as we might expect, except perhaps very small ones,

---

[27] These cult pillars were functional to the extent that they did commonly support, it is generally believed, a column in the room overhead (cf. Fig. 71), but the presence of the column was also dictated by religious rather than by functional considerations (Ch. VII, 2).

but rather of vertical wooden posts with the spaces between filled in with clay or rubble. Commonly these posts were erected on the corners of a thick block of wood secured to the stone base by tenons and mortises. On the large stone base in the center of the doorway between 68 and 69 in the Grand Propylon at Phaistos masses of the clay packing were found in place, and the imprint of a nest of vertical posts each with a cross-section about 4 in. (10 cm.) square.[28]

A similar technique was often used to reinforce wall angles. A rectangular, or triangular, block of stone was built into the corner with mortises for securing a horizontal block of wood; on this probably rested three posts, one at the corner, and one at a short interval on either side, the spaces being packed with rubble.[29] The method of strengthening the ends of walls at door openings will be discussed in connection with doors (Ch. IX, 3).

A word should be added in regard to the structural purpose of the pier-and-door partitions characteristic of the Minoan Halls (Ch. v, 2). In several instances where the width of the Hall was unusually great the presence of the partition made it possible to run shorter ceiling beams parallel with the length of the room, and support them midway on this partition. For example, the Hall of the Double-Axes is about 26 ft. (8 m.) wide (Fig. 12), but this long span could be reduced to 18 or 19 ft. (5½ m.) by running the beams from the ends of the room to the transverse partition. However the width of the Hall is frequently no more, and sometimes even less, than the length of the main part of the Hall; this would indicate that the primary purpose of the pier-and-door partition was not to reduce the free span of the ceiling beams, but rather, as we have seen (Ch. v, 2), to control the "weather" within the room.

---

[28] *Festòs*, II, pp. 313, 317, 335, 436, and fig. 197.
[29] *Festòs*, II, pp. 434-435; *Tylissos*, p. 51. The southwest corner of ix 1 (north of the Central Court) at Mallia was reinforced by a pillar set on a stone base, not in the wall but in the corner of the room.

Remains of wood, usually cypress, used for horizontal beams supporting the floors and ceilings have been found in the area of the Grand Staircase at Knossos and elsewhere, and the empty beam-sockets in masonry walls are to be seen in some excavated buildings.

One of the most interesting examples of this is the Pillar Crypt of the Royal Villa (Fig. 97). The sockets in the top course of the walls show that the main ceiling beam consisted of a huge tree trunk which had been sawn in two and still retained its original taper from a width of about 28 in. (71 cm.) at one end to about 22 in. (56 cm.) at the other. Its free span between the wall faces amounted to about 13 ft. 9 in. (4.20 m.), but it received support at its center from a heavy gypsum pillar which was apparently needed for cult reasons. Three sockets in each of the other two walls show that three smaller beams, also retaining much of their original shape in cross-section, spanned the 13 ft. (4 m.) distance which represents the width of the room, and were socketed into the top face of the great transverse beam at their centers.[30]

The ceiling of a basement room in the "Temple Tomb" at Knossos (Fig. 113, C), with two large gypsum pillars on the east-west axis, was supported on ponderous cypress beams about 1 ft. 8 in. square (40 cm.) in section resting on the pillars and in sockets in the north and south walls; the length of the beams was between 18 and 19 ft. (ca. 5.60 m.). Eight smaller transverse beams, about 20 ft. long (6.10 m.), rested on these two beams and in sockets in the top wall course.[31]

The heavy character of these floor girders suggests the splendid resources in timber upon which the Minoan architect could draw, but he was surely accustomed to spanning far greater spaces with horizontal beams. In five of the Halls with pier-and-door partitions the minimum span is over 16 ft. (5 m.), and in one instance, Room 3 at H. Triadha (Figs. 11, 151), it

[30] *Knossos*, II, p. 408.
[31] *Knossos*, IV, pp. 968-970.

reaches a length of almost 20 ft. (6 m.). Wide spans are also common in the great public rooms of the Piano Nobile. The longest for which there is practically certain evidence are the spans from the east and west walls to the central pair of columns in the Central Hall at Mallia (Fig. 159), which was in the vicinity of 23 ft. (7 m.); in the Northwest Hall of the Palace of Minos, according to the restoration proposed above (Fig. 85), the span would be slightly greater still, about 25 ft. (ca. 7½ m.).[32] Yet this falls 13 ft. (4 m.) short of the span which the excavator of the somewhat earlier palace at Mari on the Euphrates believes the Throne Room (65) must have had (Fig. 148).[33]

The corbel principle, used in masonry spans at least early in the third millennium in both Egypt and the Near East, was certainly familiar in the Late Minoan period to the Cretan architects who employed it in the stonework of large underground tombs (Fig. 136, M), and apparently also in the great viaduct south of the Palace of Minos. Corbeled doorways, vaults, and superb domes are common in Mycenaean Greek architecture at a slightly later date (Fig. 135).[34] Yet for the use of corbeling in Minoan palaces or houses, where dressed stone masonry was rarely if ever carried as high as the door lintels, there is at present no evidence. As for the true arch, long employed on a modest scale for underground structures in Egypt and the Near East, there is no certain evidence whatever either in Minoan or in Mycenaean Greek architecture.[35]

Except for a slight slope for drainage the roofs of both Minoan palaces and houses seem to have been uniformly flat. All the available evidence points to this conclusion: the lack of roof tiles in the ruins, the shape of the ground plan with its multitude of projecting elements (Ch. XIII, 3), representations such as the

[32] Yet *Mallia, Maisons*, II, p. 12, note 2, refers to the "faible longueur des bois de l'île."

[33] *Mari*, II, p. 143.   [34] *Archaeology*, 13 (1960), pp. 46-54.

[35] In *Festòs*, II, pp. 447-450, two small rough arches are described; the first (fig. 278) is possibly Hellenistic rather than Minoan; the second (fig. 279) may be Minoan, but is merely rough corbeling; cf. *M. and T.*, pp. 220, 222.

Town Mosaic (Fig. 103) and mural paintings, and actual remains of roofs, if recognized correctly, found in the fill.

The method of constructing the roof and making it watertight was probably much the same then as now. The modern procedure has been described by a native Cretan archaeologist as follows: "Throughout Crete in order to roof the houses, after having set the beams of the framework in place, a bed of thatch is strewn—brushwood or the foliage of the oleander. . . . On top of this a coat of earth two or three inches thick is laid . . . , and above this again a coat of impermeable clay called *lepidha*, which is tamped down again and again."[36]

[36] Xanthoudides, quoted in *Tylissos*, p. 54; *M. and T.*, pp. 220, 222.

CHAPTER IX

WINDOWS AND DOORS

1. THE MEANING OF THE RECESSES

A STUDY of the shallow recesses which are such a distinctive feature of the outer walls of the Minoan palaces presents some interesting problems and leads to certain important conclusions, one of a very unexpected nature.

A striking feature of these recesses is that they are so absolutely limited to palaces that we might fancy them a kind of hallmark of the residence of kings, a prerogative of royal authority. They occur only in the palaces at Knossos, Phaistos, Mallia, and Gournia in Crete, but we may add that a typical recess has lately been discovered in the fine stone façade of the Palace of Nestor at Pylos on the Greek mainland.[1] A further peculiarity is that the recesses occur, with one exception, only on the west, or principal, façade of the Cretan palaces. The exception is the very carefully designed façade at the north end of the Central Court of the Palace of Phaistos, where a symmetrical pair of recesses occurs on either side of the axial doorway (Figs. 50, 51, 122).

In their present state the recesses start at the ground level and continue upward only as high as the stone masonry is preserved; but there is no reason to doubt that they originally extended to the top or near the top of the building in the structure of the adobe brick or rubble wall. The length of the recesses varies from less than eight to about twenty feet (2¼ to 6 m.); in depth they measure fairly constantly about five to seven inches

---

[1] *AJA*, 59 (1955), pl. 28, fig. 15; cf. C. W. Blegen, *Pylos*, I, p. 52.

(12 to 18 cm.). In the plinth course the recess frequently extends a few inches wider at each end.

Agreement is quite general on one point: that the purpose of the recesses must be purely aesthetic—to relieve the monotony of the large wall surfaces. In ultimate origin they probably go back to the paneled façades, common in Egyptian and Mesopotamian architecture from early times, which seem to have developed in imitation of construction in other materials such as reeds where, to form the walls of simple buildings, sheets of reed matting were stretched between upright posts made of reeds tied in compact bundles.

It has often been suggested or assumed, for reasons obviously both aesthetic and structural, that if there were windows in the palace façades they would be located in the recesses. But Pendlebury, long Evans' principal assistant at Knossos and author of the standard handbook on Cretan archaeology (1939), came to doubt that windows could really have been located in the recesses. This opinion was the result of his failure to take adequate account of the evidence from Phaistos and Mallia, for he claimed, on the basis of what he saw at Knossos, that the recesses never bore any relation to a room behind, as they should of course have done if they contained windows. In fact he carried this argument to its logical conclusion by declaring that, in view of the recesses in the façade, it seems necessary to suppose that the main reception halls in the Piano Nobile did not have windows at all: "outside windows seem to have been avoided wherever possible." Light, he claimed, must have been furnished by clerestories and light-wells.[2] The Phaistos excavator, Miss Banti, evidently agrees with these conclusions for she states that "the idea has now been abandoned that (the recesses) indicate windows in the upper storey."[3]

But surely this conclusion is needlessly perverse. As in the problem of the location of the bull games and the existence of the Piano Nobile at Phaistos, the obvious and reasonable solu-

[2] *A. of C.*, p. 186.   [3] *Festòs*, II, p. 431.

tion has been rejected because of what superficially seemed to be insurmountable objections.[4]

But the objections are far from being insurmountable. For at Phaistos and Mallia the recesses *are* carefully related to the rooms behind them (Figs. 86, 159). Even at Knossos the southernmost recess is fairly closely centered on the room behind, although it is considerably displaced from the center of its façade unit (owing to the additional wall thickness at the south end). The recess to the north of this has a unique and unexplainable jogged form, but there are various possible solutions permitting the use of windows here, so it cannot be used as an argument one way or the other. The northernmost recess would actually be very closely centered on the single great hall which I feel should be restored here (Ch. vi, 1, Fig. 85).

In favor of the theory that windows were placed in the recesses there is a piece of negative evidence which gains considerable force from the fact that there are a score of available examples: in no case does a recess occur at a point where there is good reason to believe that there would have been a partition wall directly behind it in the upper storey. In one of the very few instances where walls abut against the rear of a recess on the ground floor, namely in the Magazine Block at Phaistos, these walls were almost certainly replaced by rows of columns on the floors above (Figs. 83, 84).

A detailed investigation of the recesses has also led to interesting conclusions regarding the unit of length used by the Cretan builders, but it will be better to return to this in a later section (Ch. xiii, 1).

2. LIGHTING AND VENTILATION

It is difficult today, in our northern climate, fully to appreciate the lighting problems of the ancient Mediterranean architect. Without window glass it was hardly possible for him to admit

[4] For further details and illustrations see "Windows, Recesses, and the Piano Nobile," *AJA*, 64 (1960), pp. 329-333.

light without also admitting air, but fortunately the generally mild climate prevented this from being a severe hardship.

The idea of windows without glass is to us almost paradoxical. Yet the Classical Greeks, for example, had numerous windows in their houses and controlled the amount of light and air with wooden shutters.[5] Whether the Minoans used shutters is not clear, but windows were certainly common, at least in the upper storeys, to judge by the "Town Mosaic" (Fig. 103), which represents the façades of a number of two- and three-storey town houses. Many of the windows on these façades seem to be divided into "panes," as many as six to a window, and some are colored red. It has been suggested that some material like an oiled parchment was used, which would at least be translucent though not transparent. Fragments of wall paintings from Crete and from Mycenaean Greece also show windows, and women looking out of them.[6]

Interior windows were probably fairly common. A number of examples of openings to transmit light from light-wells are known; there are, for example, five in the Residential Quarter of the Palace of Minos (Fig. 12). At Tylissos, in House C, a window over eight feet (2½ m.) wide, divided into three openings, lights a large room from the light-well of the Hall (Fig. 77), and in House A a window over five feet (ca. 1½ m.) wide also opens from a light-well (Fig. 19). The light-well in the Residential Quarter at H. Triadha has windows about five feet (1.49 m.) long and with sills over five feet (1.65 m.) above the floor, to light the stairs to the south and the Queen's Hall to the north (Figs. 165, 70, 151). Light is borrowed from the porticoes of Peristyle Court 74 at Phaistos to light the stairway, 71, through two large openings.

Evans believed that there was evidence for a series of openings ("transoms") above the doors of the pier-and-door partition in the Hall of the Double-Axes (Fig. 45),[7] and this prob-

---

[5] *Olynthus*, VIII, pp. 264-266.

[6] *Knossos*, I, p. 444, fig. 320; II, p. 602, fig. 375.

[7] *Knossos*, III, pp. 341-342; the transoms would admit some light when all the doors were closed.

ably was in general true of the pier-and-door partitions (Fig. 151). It must also be emphasized that the function of these rows of doors was to provide and control the admission of light and air rather than to furnish so needlessly many entrances or exits; they were in fact essentially shuttered windows, and by their use "infinite gradations might indeed be secured in regulating both temperature and ventilation."[8]

Exterior windows on the ground floor, for reasons of safety and privacy, were no doubt in general avoided. Yet some examples are definitely known and there may have been many more; the walls are rarely high enough to be sure. The rear walls of the South House at Knossos, of which eight courses remain in position, reveal the location of three windows: one into the Main Hall, one into a lavatory, and one opening on a stairway (Figs. 15, 72). Two windows are still to be seen in the northeastern quarter of the Villa of H. Triadha, and the French excavators believe there was one in the east wall of the palace at Mallia in room-group x. Outside windows have also been reported in the Little Palace, the House of the Frescoes, and the House of the Chancel Screen at Knossos, and in Houses Za and Zb at Mallia, but the last two are in my opinion doubtful.

Storerooms on the ground floor may have been ventilated and dimly illuminated by narrow slit-windows resembling those on some ivories recently found at Knossos.[9]

The position of windows in the second storeys of the west fronts of the palaces is indicated, we believe, by the recesses discussed above (Ch. IX, 1); and it is possible that the great halls in the upper storeys also received light from clerestory windows as suggested in our restoration of the Palace of Mallia (Fig. 58). And one of the principal considerations, as we have said (Ch. VI, 1), for putting the important reception rooms of the palace above the ground floor, may have been the desire to light them adequately by means of windows.

[8] *Knossos*, III, p. 340.
[9] *Ill. Lon. News*, 229 (Feb. 22, 1958), p. 301, fig. 11; also Edward Bacon, *Digging for History*, London, 1960, pl. 19. Vents of this type are suggested in our restorations, Figs. 48, 58.

However the usefulness of windows without glass is limited, and Minoan architects learned to depend for much of their lighting on open courts and airshafts of various forms and sizes. The large dimensions of the palace central courts may have been dictated by their use as an arena for the bull games; but there can be no doubt that many of the inner rooms received most of their light and air directly from the court or indirectly through the long porticoes that opened upon it.

The Knossos palace possessed but one court. Mallia had a second very much smaller one with short porticoes on two sides, on which a number of storerooms and workrooms opened. Phaistos had two smaller courts within the walls of the palace: one, 48, served partly for communication, but mostly, it would seem, as a source of light for two of the large rooms in the upper storey of the block north of the Central Court, and for some of the upper rooms of the North Residential Quarter; the other, 74, had porticoes on all four sides, with a very large hall, 93, which perhaps formed part of the living apartments of the royal family, opening on the north portico (Fig. 4).

The court was not, however, an indispensable element of domestic architecture as it was in Classical Greece, for example, for it is rarely found except in the largest houses, such as the Little Palace at Knossos, House A at Tylissos, and House E at Mallia. To some extent even the ground floor rooms of Cretan houses may have depended on windows for light and air; but for the Main Hall these were normally supplied, or supplemented, by a vertical airshaft, generally known as a light-well.[10] The light-well, in its usual form, extended across one end of the Hall on which it opened for its entire length of some 15 to 20 ft. (4½ to 6 m.), support for the lintel being provided by one or usually by two columns. The area between the columns and the back wall, some 6 to 10 ft. (2 to 3 m.) broad, was often floored with cement and regularly furnished with a drain. The shaft extended up through however many

---

[10] The distinction between a court and a light-well is a matter of size, and so must to a certain extent be arbitrary.

storeys the house, or palace, may have had, and is usually regarded as having been completely open at the top. But it is also possible that the opening was roofed over at the top and space left for wide openings at the sides, amounting to a kind of clerestory arrangement (Fig. 21); perhaps this explains the curious "penthouse" projecting above many of the roofs of the house façades in the Town Mosaic (Fig. 103 at right).[11] However, it is probable that these "penthouses" or "attics," as Evans called them, more frequently represent stairheads, designed for the protection of stairways leading up to the roofs of houses or of palaces. A good example of such stairheads is to be seen in the fascinating house model discovered in 1970 at Arkhanes by Angeliki Lembesi and dated to the M.M. III period.[12]

It is sometimes supposed that light-wells were developed to solve the problem of lighting the inner rooms in large buildings like the palaces, yet, although they were in fact useful for this purpose, it is true that commonly in Minoan houses not only the room which is lighted by the light-well, but also the light-well itself, is adjacent to an outside wall. Why was light and air not provided simply by windows in this wall? The answer must lie partly in the inadequacy of the unglazed window. The light-well, while ensuring privacy and security, provided light without the full blaze of the sun, and air without the full blast of the wind. It was admirably suited to the Cretan climate.

Instead of the usual form described above, the light-well sometimes appears as a tiny court with columns or pillars on two, or on all four, sides. The type with a column at each of the four corners of the opening (like a "tetrastyle atrium") is to be seen in Room 50 of the North Residential Quarter at Phaistos, and in House B and two other houses at Palaikastro; the other type is represented by House A at Tylissos, the South-

[11] Matz expressed the same opinion, *Crete and Early Greece* (London, 1962), p. 108, and cf. Evans, *BSA*, 7 (1900-1901), p. 24. Marinatos, however, suggested that, on Egyptian analogies, the "attics" may represent "summer bedrooms" (*C. and M.*, p. 48).

[12] Lembesi, *ArchEph*, 1976, pp. 12-43. A. W. Lawrence also suggests that the "attics" were stairheads, *Greek Architecture*[3], p. 28.

east House at Knossos, the Queen's Apartments at H. Triadha, and the great halls (XXVIII) at Zakro—each of these with three columns about an angle—and by the Hall of the Colonnades, i.e. the light-well beside the Grand Staircase at Knossos, which has four columns. House E at Mallia possibly had eight pillars about a small court (xiv).

In the palaces light-wells occur almost exclusively in the residential quarters; does this mean that the scheme originated in domestic rather than in palatial architecture? No less than five light-wells are to be found in this quarter at Knossos, since its two lowest storeys had been constructed in a great cutting which extended to a level of nearly thirty feet (9 m.) below that of the Central Court, thus severely restricting its available light (Fig. 12). The bottom of the light-well beside the Grand Staircase measured about 11 by 18 ft. (3½ by 5½ m.) and lighted not only these stairs but a smaller set to the south. A second light-well served the Hall of the Double-Axes and, through a window, the Lower East-West Corridor. The Queen's Hall was equipped with light-wells on both east and south sides, the former also lighting a narrow flight of stairs through another window. The fifth light-well in this quarter, immediately south of the Grand Staircase, had two windows but no columns, and lighted and ventilated the secluded rooms amongst which was the "water-closet" already described (Ch. v, 4).

We have left the largest light-well in Minoan architecture for final mention. It forms the rear of the Grand Propylon at Phaistos (69A), and measures about 45 ft. long by 19 wide (ca. 13½ by nearly 6 m.), or some 855 sq. ft. (over 80 sq. m.) in area. The next largest light-well, at the south end of the South Propylaeum at Knossos, as restored by Evans, would amount to about 310 sq. ft. (nearly 30 sq. m.), while that at the west end of the Hall of the Double-Axes, which with three others ranks next in size, amounts to only about 225 sq. ft. (over 20 sq. m.).

Although 69A forms a passage from the Grand Propylon, by way of a small door in its right rear corner, to a double flight of steps leading to the Central Court in one direction and to Peristyle 74 in the other, yet it is clearly also a light-well, for its floor is surfaced with cement and there is a drain near the southwest corner (Ch. XI, 4). In keeping with its superior size it is fronted by three large oval columns.

Nevertheless, in spite of its evident importance, one may wonder why there was any need of a light-well in this position at all. The stairway, 66, and the landing, 67, were surely open to the sky as well as for forty-five feet along the front. This would certainly have furnished ample light to the two shallow vestibules 68 and 69, and to the area 69A itself, for almost the whole width of the opening between 67 and 68 was left free of any obstruction, and the two doorways in the wall between 68 and 69 are each eight feet (2½ m.) wide and were never closed by doors. The real reason for the existence of this light-well, it would seem, was to supply light to some room or rooms at a higher level than the ground floor, possibly to the rooms to the east in the Banquet-Hall block to the north of the Central Court.[13]

We have spoken in this section only of natural illumination; something will be said later of the large stone lamps with which the palaces were well supplied (Ch. XII, 1). But even state functions must have been conducted largely during the daylight hours. The Minoan Cretan surely slept far more of the dark hours than does twentieth century man, with his ability to turn night into day by means of the electric light.

3. DOORS AND LOCKS

The excavator of the palace at Mari on the Euphrates was fortunate in discovering the carbonized remains of a large wooden door, which in burning had retained its original size and form to a remarkable degree.[14] No such windfall has oc-

[13] *AJA*, 65 (1961), p. 167.
[14] *Mari*, II, pp. 268-270, figs. 322-323.

curred in Crete. However, one of the doors on the house façades of the Town Mosaic, though at a very small scale, does seem to represent a door composed of a number of overlapping vertical planks quite like the batten door at Mari (Fig. 136, D).

A wide variety of uses, sizes, and forms of doorways is indicated by the remains of the Cretan houses and palaces. As a means of protection when the Central Court was in use as a bull ring, doors were used at Mallia even to close off a broad flight of stairs to the second storey, and at Phaistos, for the same reason, a large pair of doors closed against a column (Ch. IV); both these instances are decidedly unusual. The most distinctive use of doors in Cretan architecture is their employment in "batteries" in the ubiquitous pier-and-door partitions (Figs. 45, 151), where they function essentially as shuttered windows for as doors their number is quite superfluous (Ch. IX, 2). In the Main Hall (77, 79) of the North Residential Quarter at Phaistos and in the one at H. Triadha (3, 12) there were no fewer than ten sets of such double doors (Fig. 151), while the corresponding Halls at Knossos and Mallia contained eleven.

In regard to the position of doorways it has often been noted as a distinctive feature of Minoan planning that in large rooms the door is placed not on the axis but generally near the end of a long side. This may be true of the informal residential quarters of the palaces, but there is no compelling reason to suppose that it holds good for the formal public halls in the Piano Nobile as well. The windows seem to have been axially placed in these rooms (Ch. IX, 1); the doors, we may suspect, were also. The axial doorway at the north end of the Central Court at Phaistos is an instructive example (Fig. 50).

Small metal hinges were in use in the ancient world from early times for boxes and chests, but the regular system for doors was a vertical wooden pivot, one end of which revolved in a hollow in the threshold, the other in a hole in the lintel. This was the common, if not invariable, method used in Crete; but it must be admitted that in some instances there is no trace of the pivot holes we should expect to find in the stone threshold.[15] The Minoan pivot holes commonly measure 2 to 4 in. (5 to 10 cm.) in diameter, and are rarely more than 1 in. (3 cm.) deep, sometimes less than ¼ in. (1 cm.). One at Mallia seems to show two stages of use (Fig. 107). Big doors like those at the foot of the ten foot (3.20 m.) broad stairway west of the Mallia Central Court had pivot holes nearly 6 in. (15 cm.) in diameter, though still very shallow.

The bottom end of the pivot, which bore the whole weight of the door, was sometimes shod with a "shoe" of bronze, as in Classical Greek times. Bronze Age specimens have been found at Alalakh in Syria (Fig. 104, C),[16] and at Mycenae in mainland Greece.[17] Only two seem to have been preserved in Crete, both for large heavy doors: the Mallia doors just mentioned, and those from the Central Court to Room 25 at Phaistos (Fig. 104, A, B).

Minoan doorways vary in width from 2 ft. (60 cm.) or even less to 6 ft. or more, but ordinarily measure from 3 to 4 ft. (90 to 120 cm.). It is not often that the height of a doorway is preserved or can be estimated. Two doorways in the basement of the South House measure about 5 ft. 3 in. (160 cm.); one in the Residential Quarter at H. Triadha (Fig. 154), 6 ft. (1.85 m.); and others in the palace and Royal Villa at Knossos, about 6½ ft. (2 m.).[18] Formal doorways like that on the axis of the Phaistos Central Court (Fig. 50) may have been considerably higher; the width of the Phaistos doorway, over 6 ft., suggests that its height may have been as great as the height of the first storey would allow, i.e. around 10 ft. (over 3 m.).

---

[15] *Mallia, Maisons*, II, p. 9, note 2, when no pivot holes are found "it must be supposed then, as J. Hazzidakis does with regard to Tylissos, that the doors turned on hinges fixed in the doorjamb"; the reference is to *Tylissos*, p. 55. But Miss Banti writes (*Festòs*, II, p. 590, note 289), "I do not believe possible the hypothesis of Hazzidakis, of bronze hinges which would have disappeared without leaving any trace."

[16] *Alalakh*, p. 118, fig. 48.   [17] Mylonas, *Anc. Myc.*, p. 53.

[18] The door of the "Tomb of the Tripod-Hearth" measures 1.90 m. high and tapers from 0.72 at the bottom to 0.51 m. at the top, and the two doors of the niches in the forehall of the "Isopata Royal Tomb" measure 2.03 and 2.05 m. high (*Archaeologia*, 9 [1905], p. 425, fig. 32, and pls. 96, 97).

Double doors were very common. There were two advantages: by reducing the width and therefore the weight of the door the wear on the pivots and their sockets was diminished; and in the pier-and-door partitions there was room to close the leaf neatly back into the face of the jamb (Figs. 106, 151).

Let us examine some typical examples of doorways commencing with one at the southeast corner of Room 22 near the southwest corner of the Central Court at Phaistos (Fig. 105).[19] The threshold, which was of gypsum instead of the limestone more usual for thresholds at this site, was laid at approximately the same level as the flagged floor of the room; this was common practice, though sometimes the threshold was a little higher. The L-shaped jamb bases, of limestone instead of the gypsum more frequently used for jamb bases at Phaistos, rested on the ends of the threshold and rise 3 to 4 in. (8 to 10 cm.) above it. The gaps for the pivot sockets, measuring roughly 3 in. square (one is 8 by 7 cm., the other 9 by 6 cm.), are so placed behind projecting "tongues" that the pivots would have been concealed and protected by the wooden doorposts or jambs.

In Corridor 62 at the northeast corner of the Central Court at Phaistos a single pivot hole shows that there was only one leaf, over 4 ft. (1.30 m.) long (Fig. 111). The projecting tongue on the south jamb base, which rests on the threshold and is 7 in. (18 cm.) high,[20] marks the lower end of a rebate against which the door closed.

The north door of the Queen's Hall (81) in the North Residential Quarter at Phaistos had a double door each leaf of which was about 20 in. (50 cm.) long (Fig. 109). A bolt hole in the threshold shows that the left-hand leaf (on entering the room) was the "sleeping" leaf ordinarily kept closed.[21] Such bolt holes have also been reported from Knossos.

Evidence preserved at Phaistos shows that the usual method

[19] *Festòs*, II, p. 143. In this and the following examples the details and drawings are from my notes made at the sites.

[20] Contrary to the statement in *Festòs*, II, p. 438, "Gli stipiti laterali non posano mai sulla soglia."

[21] *Festòs*, II, p. 283.

of constructing the doorjambs was to cover the stone base with a flat block or "cushion" of wood about 4 in. (10 cm.) thick, and to erect on this a number of vertical posts some 6 to 8 in. (15 to 20 cm.) thick.[22] The same method of construction was employed at Mallia where, however, separate doorjamb bases were rare in the palace, and the woodwork consequently rested directly on the threshold. A well preserved example is illustrated in Fig. 108. The threshold consists of a heavy block of "ironstone" with two pivot holes and clear traces of the circular scoring caused by the dragging of one of the leaves of the double door; indeed the pivot hole on this side shows signs of readjustment (Fig. 107), perhaps intended to correct this defect. In the wall-heads on either side are gaps for the vertical posts, one at each corner, and one in the center. Probably the two corner posts were provided with projecting rebates, corresponding to the tongues on the stone jamb bases, to protect the pivots, as shown in the restored plan (Fig. 108).

A final example of a well preserved threshold in a private house, Za at Mallia, may be illustrated (Fig. 110).[23] On the main body of the threshold two small pivot holes show clear traces of wear on the edges. At the ends the block of ironstone was cut down about a quarter of an inch (1 cm.) along a straight line, and the rectangular area, about 12 by 20 in. (30 by 50 cm.), used for the setting of the doorposts. Two matched sets of holes appear on this area. The two smaller holes being very shallow were probably abandoned as too small and too near the edge; the larger pair, 2 in. (5 cm.) in diameter and 1¼ in. (3 cm.) deep, have sharp unworn edges and were evidently not pivot holes but mortises to receive round tenons on the underside of the doorjamb blocks and keep them from shifting. Such care for the stability of the jambs is uncommon, but can be paralleled for example in a pair of bases at H. Triadha (Fig. 123). The distance of the pivot holes from the doorposts suggests some such framing as shown in the plan (Fig. 110).

[22] *Festòs*, II, pp. 440-441.   [23] *Mallia, Maisons*, I, pp. 65-66, figs. 6, 7.

Rarely the whole doorframe was made of stone (Fig. 154). Examples such as the two doorways in the basement rooms of the South House and the inner doorway of the Temple Tomb at Knossos, make it perfectly clear that the projecting tongue of the characteristic stone jamb bases is but the lower end of the vertical rebate against which the door closed or which sheltered the pivot.

Two of the doors just mentioned provide somewhat enigmatic information on methods of door closure.[24] Both are very similar in detail. In both the left-hand side (on entering) was the hinge side, though no pivot hole is to be seen. On the right-hand jamb both are rebated, and just far enough beyond the edge of the rebate to allow for the thickness of the wooden door (1 to 2 in.; 2½ to 5 cm.) is a deep rectangular cutting (Fig. 113, B); there can be no doubt that this formed a socket for a horizontal bolt in the form of a wooden bar. Another inch or two beyond the cutting a hole about ⅜ in. (1 cm.) in diameter pierces the stone obliquely and penetrates the side of the cutting. This was certainly designed to receive a metal pin to be inserted into a corresponding hole in the side of the bar when it had been thrust into its socket (Fig. 112, A, B). Several bronze pins of appropriate dimensions have been found, including one in the Temple Tomb and one in the South House.

But what was the purpose of the pin? Sir Arthur Evans' answer was that it was inserted "into the wooden bar so as to prevent its withdrawal."[25] Quite so. But withdrawal by whom? Certainly not, as Evans assumed, by someone *inside* the door, since all he need do in order to be able to withdraw the bolt was to remove the pin again. On the other hand, if it was possible for someone to move the bolt from the *outside* of the door by means of such a simple device as a knob fixed in the bar and protruding through a long narrow horizontal slot in the door (Fig. 112, C, D),[25a] then the insertion of the pin

[24] *Knossos*, II, pp. 382-384; IV, pp. 993-995.
[25] *Knossos*, II, p. 382; cf. III, p. 13.
[25a] The model shown in Fig. 112 was made to prove the feasibility of such a

would have a purpose. In fact it would lock the door and prevent its being opened from the outside, and this could be useful even in a storeroom, when someone was working inside.

This same door was likewise provided with a hole for the pin running obliquely through the stone jamb from the *outside* of the door into the same bolt-socket (Fig. 112, C, D). Thus it would have been possible to come out the door, shut it, push the bolt home, and by inserting the pin prevent anyone *inside* from releasing the bolt.

The arrangement served, as Evans remarked, as a "primitive lock," a lock in which the "key" must be left inserted. The "key" could therefore be effective only against an attempt to open the door by someone on the opposite side. It would serve a useful purpose in the residential quarter, for example, where a person could lock it from the inside, the private side, to prevent intrusion. To secure a storeroom door from the outside the time-honored system of "sealing" the door must still have been relied on; sealing did not prevent a door from being opened, but it did prevent it from being opened without detection.

Whatever its efficiency as a lock the locking pin was evidently merely an added refinement, an "optional feature"; essentially the device was a *latch*. It was operated, if our deductions are correct, by pushing the bolt into position by means of a knob from either side of the door, and released in similar fashion; the modern latch is usually controlled by a revolving knob. The need for the Minoans to invent some practical form of latch is clear when we consider the ubiquitous pier-and-door partitions. The ingenious system of weather control, made possible by their use (Ch. ix, 2), depended on being able to close some or all of the doors as desired; moreover the closure must be such as to prevent the doors being opened by air currents yet be readily controllable from either side for passage. A bolt

---

latch. I have since learned that this type of latch was in actual use in pioneer days in Canada, and I have seen it employed for both outside and inside doors (for rustic effect) in a summer hotel in Ontario.

operated in the way we have described was a simple answer to the requirements, and was as suitable for double as for single doors.[26]

Let us return to Sir Arthur and the puzzles he created for himself by his failure to see that the existence of the locking pin pointed inevitably to the conclusion that the bar could be operated from both sides of the door. His belief that the "locks" (essentially "latches") could only be worked from the side of the door on which the bolt was placed made it in fact impossible for him to understand the bolt on the *inside* of the door leading to the sepulchral chamber of the Temple Tomb (Fig. 113, C) for, as his workmen sagely observed, "the dead could not lock themselves in!"[27] As a way out of the dilemma he momentarily suggested the possibility of a trapdoor and ladder exit to the room above, but discarded this explanation in favor of a side exit by way of a flight of stairs. Unfortunately Evans appears to have forgotten that the stairs in question ascended not from the room behind the door with the bolt, but from the room in front of it. Sir Arthur had evidently become confused, quite understandably, because the stairway was indeed behind a doorway, but it was an outer doorway, not the one leading to the sepulchral chamber. That he undoubtedly was confused about these two doorways is shown by his further statement that both had the same sort of locking device, for in reality the outer one was not rebated and possibly contained no doors at all; in any case the cuttings on the jambs of the two doorways are of quite a different nature.

Viewed however essentially as a *latch*, which could be operated from the outside as well as from the inside, the "Mystery of the Tomb Door" seems solved. As for the locking pin on the inside of the door we grant that it is unlikely that the corpse availed itself of the device to prevent intrusion upon its eternal slumber, but it may have been useful for the tomb officials to

---

[26] Only one door in a series would *need* to have a bolt that could be opened from either side; the rest could be closed by simple horizontal bars or by vertical bolts.

[27] *Knossos*, IV, p. 993.

be able to guard against casual intruders when preparing and furnishing the burial chambers before the interment. Or it may be that the simple process of boring the small hole for the pin was done by some workman accustomed to do so as a matter of normal building practice and not specifically instructed to omit this detail in a burial chamber. Modern workmen have been known to commit comparable lapses. At any rate no provision for a locking pin was made on the outside of the door; in other words it was considered unnecessary to lock the dead man in. As a measure of precaution against robbers the latch control on the outside of the door could have been removed after the final closing of the tomb chamber, and a crossbar wedged in the jamb-cuttings visible on the rebates on either side of the doorway would have completely concealed the horizontal slot in the face of the door. Quite possibly a guard was mounted in the entrance portico.

Finally let us return to the South House, for not all the puzzles have been solved by the hypothesis of a latch controlled from either side of the door.[28] We have suggested that the ability to lock the door into Room A (Figs. 112, 113, A) from the inside would have been useful when someone was working within. Yet it must be admitted that it seems natural to suppose that, since the room probably was used to store valuable property, it would also have been useful to be able to have the door locked when no one was in it. But, as we have seen, this had to be done from the inside, and therefore the person locking the door had no available exit from A except into Room B. This small room, however, had no door other than that into A, and a further complication is introduced by the fact that, as can be seen from cuttings in the jambs, there was a bar set slantwise on the inside face of the door from A to B. Sir Arthur's explanation was that the person who locked the door at the foot of the stairs into A then passed into B, barred its door from the inside, and left by way of a ladder and trap-door in the ceiling. Thus both rooms were secured from intrusion, and the importance of this

[28] *Knossos*, II, p. 384.

is underlined by the discovery in B of a valuable collection of bronze saws, axes, and knives, "sacerdotal treasure," Evans called it.

Sir Arthur's solution may seem somewhat arbitrary, and there is of course no positive evidence in favor of the trap-door; but what are the alternatives? I see two possible explanations of the bar on the inside of the door into B. The first is that the room was used for some purpose, probably of a cult nature, which made it desirable to be able to prevent anyone entering B from A;[29] yet the small size and plain character of B renders this suggestion implausible. The second alternative is that the slanting bar on the inside of the door was controlled from the outside (from A) on the same principle as outlined above but with a slot in the door in the shape of a "7"; this solution, however, also appears unsatisfactory since, to mention but one objection, a simple bolt on the side of the door next Room A would have served the same purpose.

We return then to the trap-door proposed by Sir Arthur as the least objectionable explanation of the enigma. The existence of trap-doors in Minoan architecture need scarcely be doubted since other excavators have been led to suppose their presence in order to explain how cellar rooms without openings in their well preserved walls were made accessible.[30]

[29] *Kret. Chron.*, 8 (1954), p. 441, no. 12.
[30] *Gournia*, p. 21.

CHAPTER X

STAIRS AND STOREYS

· 1. STAIRWAYS

Aesthetically as well as practically the designers of the Minoan palaces and finer houses displayed a remarkable appreciation of the possibilities of stair architecture, although we need not go so far as to claim, with Rodenwaldt, that "the motif of stairs and staircases could be made the center of a system of Cretan architectural aesthetics."[1]

Outside stairways, though often intended to be impressively monumental, were very simple in construction. The steps, usually made of a resistant stone such as limestone, were simply bedded firmly on a natural or artificial sloping mass of rock or rubble. Shallow risers and deep treads, each with a downward slope, were normal in Cretan stair building, and these features were often particularly prominent in outside stairways, sometimes to such an extent that they resemble stepped ramps (Fig. 138). Such stairs as the set to the east of the H. Triadha Villa may have been designed for the passage of animals as well as of humans.

The exterior flights of steps which make up the "Theatral Areas" northwest of the Palace of Minos (Fig. 41) and at the north end of the West Court at Phaistos are bleachers for watching a performance of some sort rather than true stairways; in fact the one at Phaistos terminates at the top in a blank wall (Fig. 49).[2] The height of the steps in the latter is about 9 in. (23 cm.), possibly high enough for sitting; but those at Knossos,

[1] *Gnomon*, 11 (1935), p. 331.
[2] *Festòs*, 1, pp. 185-190.

less than 5 in. (12 cm.), must have been designed only for standing (Fig. 41).[3]

A typical outside stairway, 6, connects the West Court with the Upper Court at Phaistos (Fig. 138). The steps are about 12 ft. (3½ m.) wide with treads varying from 21 to 24 in. (53 to 61 cm.) and risers 4 to 5½ in. (10 to 14 cm.) high.[4]

Most monumental of all Minoan stairways—and an outside staircase in the sense that it was open to the sky, though it lay within the palace façade—is the one (66) which formed the approach to the Phaistos Grand Propylon and the State Apartments (Figs. 48, 49, 137, 138).[5] The twelve limestone steps which compose it have sloping treads only 5 in. (13 cm.) high and some 28 in. (71 cm.) deep, and a width of no less than 45 ft. (13.70 m.). Clearly this magnificent stairway, unrivaled in the Bronze Age, was calculated to impress the visitor with the splendor of the monarch of Phaistos. Even Knossos had nothing comparable.

But this stairway exhibits an architectural subtlety which emphasizes the remarkable aesthetic sensitivity of the Cretans, namely the distinct "crowning" or upward curvature of each step toward the center (Fig. 137). This would appear to have been intended, as in the case of the well known convexity of the steps of the Parthenon and other Greek buildings, which it anticipates by over a thousand years, to produce a certain feeling of elasticity and life, as well as to offset any tendency for the long horizontal lines to appear to sag in the middle due to an optical illusion. There appear to be no other instances of such "refinements" (as they are known) in the monuments of Minoan architecture available to us.

Interior stairways may be built, like exterior ones, simply of blocks of stone laid on a solid base, for short runs like the familiar bathroom steps (Fig. 82), and occasionally even from one storey to another when these lie on different terraces, like

---

[3] *Knossos*, II, pp. 578-587.
[4] *Festòs*, I, pp. 190-191 (stairway "XXXI"); II, pp. 27-35 (stairway "6").
[5] *Festòs*, II, pp. 306-311.

Stairway 39 leading from the Central Court to Peristyle Court 74 at Phaistos.

Normally it was not practical to build a solid base to support the whole length of a stairway from one storey to another, though often the lower part was so constructed. Nor was it usually practical to build such stairways all in one run. The two-flight stairway was normal, occasionally with the two flights built at right angles to each other against adjacent sides of a room, as in Za and Zb at Mallia;[6] but far more commonly the two flights are built parallel to one another and connected by a landing. The two types may be spoken of as the L and the U types respectively. In the U type the second flight seems normally to have been approximately the same length as the first. But there is one exception of some interest: the builders of Stairway 42/43, north of the Central Court at Phaistos, took care, even to the extent of inserting two extra steps at the turn, to attain the second floor level with a very brief second flight, terminating just short of the window whose position is indicated by the recess in the west half of the north façade of the court (Figs. 50, 89).[7] The reason for doing so was surely in order that the window might be available as another vantage point from which to watch events in the Central Court, such as the bull games.

In both the L and the U type of stairway the inside of each flight was built against a regular partition wall, while the outside was supported by a special wall. Sometimes this wall may have been only high enough to carry the outer edge of the stair, though this is not provable from the remains in any known instance; usually or always it may have extended as a solid wall to the ceiling, as in the L-shaped stairway running up from Room 50 at Phaistos, especially when it carried a stairway directly overhead in the upper storey. A solid wall, however, would have created a very dark stairway, and it may be that it

[6] For the use of stairs in a vestibule, as in Zb, *Mallia, Maisons*, II, p. 10, note 3, compares *Gournia*, p. 21, and Palaikastro, *BSA*, 9 (1902-1903), p. 292, Block D, and p. 295, Block E, 36.

[7] *Festòs*, II, pp. 244-245.

was usually pierced with openings; in the Grand Staircase of the Residential Quarter at Knossos the builders boldly substituted freestanding columns for such a wall (Fig. 38).

For some distance above the solid base the steps were sometimes continued in stone; but probably they were usually of wood. How these upper steps were supported is rarely clear, but those in 42/43 at Phaistos rested on sloping beams, the sockets for which were visible in the walls, and this has also been reported at Amnisos. Whether these beams resembled our modern "stringers" is not clear.

The space under the stairs, where not occupied by a solid base, was often utilized—for a toilet at Sklavokambos (Fig. 32), and under 42/43 at Phaistos as a closet where a mass of domestic pottery was found (Fig. 4).

The nature and position of stairways often provide useful clues regarding the character and extent, and even the plan, of the upper storeys of Minoan palaces and houses. For example, as we have seen, the two sets of stairs north of the Central Court at Mallia furnish some evidence for the position of the Banquet Hall (Ch. VI, 2).

We close with a description of a few of the better preserved and more interesting palace stairways.

A typical bathroom stair is that in the North Residential Quarter at Phaistos (Fig. 82).[8] Each of its seven steps is composed of a single block of gypsum a little over 3 ft. long by 16 to 21 in. wide by about 5 to 6 in. high (100 by 40-53 by 13-15 cm.); and the landing between the upper five and the lower two steps is also a single block of gypsum. A gypsum parapet beside the steps supported a column at the end.

The stairway in the northeast quarter of the Palace of Mallia (xxii 3, 1) is a typical example of the U type (Fig. 60).[9] Eight stone steps, each about 6 ft. 6 in. long, with treads averaging 17 in. deep and nearly 6 in. high (200 by 44 by 14 cm.), remain in position on a solid base composed of rubble at the

[8] *Festòs*, II, pp. 299-301.
[9] *Mallia*, II, p. 21.

bottom and clay or mud brick above. The first run, and presumably the second also, contained approximately fifteen steps, giving a total height for the stairway of around 14½ ft. (4.40 m.).

An interesting variation in stairway arrangement occurs in the Royal Villa at Knossos.[10] From the ground floor a narrow flight of stairs ascends to a landing from which two flights of similar width proceed upward, one on either side of the stair-wall over the first flight (Fig. 73). One of these upper stairways opened into the second storey rooms; the other continued via a flight over the stairwell, directly to the third storey (Ch. III, 4).

Lastly the Grand Staircase leading down to the Residential Quarter in the southeast area of the Palace of Minos (Figs. 12, 38).[11] As a feat of engineering it is a remarkable achievement for the age; Evans referred to it as "the most daring exhibition of Minoan architectural enterprise."[12] Its excellent preservation, plus bold restoration, adds much to its interest. It was discovered in the process of excavating through a doorway from the north which opened upon the landing at the level of the second storey. In dramatic fashion, and at considerable risk, in view of the delicately balanced masses of tottering masonry above, Evans proceeded to tunnel downward following two long flights which were supported on a solid ramp. Later he straightened up and resupported the upper parts of the walls, replacing the wooden beams and columns with stone, steel, and concrete disguised so as to simulate the original appearance. Even the third flight and part of the fourth (connecting the second and third storeys), which consisted of gypsum steps resting on cypress beams whose charred remains were often distinctly visible, were found nearly in their original positions and were maintained there until they too could be resupported. Evidence was also discovered of two

---

[10] *Knossos*, II, pp. 398-399.

[11] *Knossos*, I, pp. 325-326; 337-342; III, pp. 301, 481-482, Plan D; but certain promised revised drawings seem never to have been published, III, p. 482, note 2.

[12] *Knossos*, I, p. 337.

higher flights leading to a storey above the level of the Central Court, and it is possible, though unlikely, that there was one more storey.

The stairway was built on the U plan, and the supporting wall along the outside edge was carried up only a little above the level of the steps to form a continuous stepped parapet; on the top surface of the parapet a series of circular holes were sunk to receive columns used to support the edge of the flight of stairs immediately above. Thus the stairs were abundantly lighted by the adjacent light-well.

Today the descent from the Central Court down the four long flights with the short intermediate flights at the turns—fifty-five steps in all—to the Hall of the Colonnades at the bottom of the light-well is an impressive experience. It is easy to sympathize with the fantasy of Sir Arthur who was tempted, one warm moonlight night when he was sleeping nearby during a bout of fever, to look down the well of the staircase: "the whole place," he writes in that monumental prose epic *The Palace of Minos at Knossos*, "seemed to awake awhile to life and movement. Such was the force of the illusion that the Priest-King with his plumed lily crown, great ladies, tightly girdled, flounced and corseted, long-stoled priests, and, after them, a retinue of elegant but sinewy youths—as if the Cup-bearer and his fellows had stepped down from the walls—passed and re-passed on the flights below."[13]

2. HEIGHT AND NUMBER OF STOREYS

From a ruinous ground plan and a few unprepossessing fragments of stone an archaeologist dealing with the Classical Greek period can frequently deduce with almost complete assurance what the building he has excavated looked like when newly built. This is because of the symmetry and regularity which prevailed in public buildings in that period, and because of the standardized system of proportions regulating the dimensions of columns and superstructure.

[13] *Knossos*, III, p. 301.

The restoration of Minoan buildings is, unfortunately, quite a different matter. Yet how very vague must our conception of the Cretan palaces and houses be unless we can form some idea of their appearance in elevation! Luckily we are not entirely without clues. Occasionally, for example when built against a sloping hillside, actual traces of the upper storeys may be preserved. Thus we may be sure that the Royal Villa and the South House (Fig. 71) at Knossos had at least three storeys, while the Residential Quarter of the Palace of Minos had two storeys below the Central Court and one, possibly two, above.

A valuable and unexpected source of information is provided by the discovery in the Palace of Minos of a number of fragmentary little pieces of faïence showing what are evidently the street fronts of urban houses (Fig. 103). These characteristically have a door at the street level and two rows of windows in what must be the second and third storeys.

The thickness of the walls in the palaces and houses may provide some indication of their height, but so many factors enter into this that its value is limited. One quite obvious example of a significant difference in the wall thickness is offered by the groups of magazines on the west front at Knossos and also at Mallia where most of the single-storey-high partition-walls are much thinner than the enclosing walls, which must run up at least two storeys in height.

The most useful clues for the restoration of the upper floors of the palaces are those provided by remains of stairways. For example at Mallia stairways indicate that there was a second storey to the north of the Central Court and west of the Corridor of the Magazines, but probably none over the small irregular rooms at the southeast corner of the palace. Other instances of this kind have been mentioned frequently in our descriptions of the various palaces and houses.

The height of the ground floor storey is occasionally indicated by remains of the floor above preserved at or near its original level, as in the Residential Quarter of the Palace of Minos—

a little over 13 ft. (4 m.); the Royal Villa—about 10 ft. (3 m.); and the South House—nearly 9 ft. (2.60 m.). At Phaistos the floor level of the rooms of the second storey of the North Residential Quarter is probably given by the adjacent Peristyle Court 74; the height of Room 50 should then be a little over 11 ft. (3.39 m.), and that of 77-79 about 12½ ft. (3.82 m.). For similar reasons the height of the ground floor rooms immediately north of the Central Court in the same palace was apparently about 11 ft. (3.35 m.).[14]

Sometimes the stairway to the second floor is preserved complete, or at least sufficiently to be able to calculate its original height. The floor-to-floor height of the main storey of the Little Palace at Knossos is thus given as 13 ft. (3.95 m.). At Mallia north of the Central Court are two stairways serving the Upper Northeast Hall, each of two flights and each with several of the first steps preserved (Fig. 88). The height of the first flight in both can be calculated at over 7 ft. (2.20 m.), and since the plan suggests that the second flight was of similar length, the total height of the first storey may have amounted to over 14 ft. (ca. 4.40 m.).

At Tylissos the northeast stairway in House C had a first flight of nearly 5 ft. (1½ m.); the second was probably similar, amounting in all to about 9 ft. 9 in. (3 m.). A stairway in the southwest corner having ten risers of 6 in. (15 cm.) each in the first flight yields similar results. In a room in the southeast corner of the same house is a stone pillar approximately 6 ft. (1.80 m.) high with mortises on the top face, suggesting that on it rested the wood timbering of the ceiling. How much should be allowed for the thickness of the timbering and of the flooring? The answer may be approximately supplied by the Pillar Crypt of the Royal Villa where the pillar is 6 ft. 6 in. (2 m.) and the known first floor height is about 10 ft., a difference of 3 ft. 6 in. Applying this to House C we get 6 ft. plus

---

[14] The figures for Phaistos are derived from the levels marked on plate 2, *Festòs, Tavole.* Most of the other heights given in this section have been either measured or checked by the writer.

3 ft. 6 in. = 9 ft. 6 in. or very nearly the 9 ft. 9 in. indicated by the stairways. Tylissos A, whose Pillar Crypt pillar was about the same height as that in House C, should have had a first storey height similar to that of the other house. In Houses Za and Zb at Mallia the maximum (and probable) run of the stairs was some 21 to 23 ft. (6½ to 7 m.), which, with treads and risers suitable to such houses (being of wood the steps are not preserved), would yield a floor-to-floor height of around 9 ft. (2.70 m.).

We may conclude, then, that the height of the first storey of the usual better-class Minoan house and that of the service rooms on the ground floor of the palaces might amount to about 9 to 10 ft. (2.75 to 3 m.); and that the better rooms in the palaces and outstanding mansions were often between 12 and 14 ft. (nearly 3½ to 4½ m.).

Where it was desired to obtain an impressive architectural effect, however, as in the Propylon and Room 25 of the Palace of Phaistos, much greater heights were reached, in these cases perhaps 16 to 23 ft. (5 to 7 m.). No direct estimate of the height of the State Reception Halls in the Piano Nobile is possible, but the fact that the Central Hall in the Palace of Mallia would have an area nearly three times that of the Hall of the Double-Axes indicates a great difference in scale between these public rooms designed to accommodate large crowds and even the finest private rooms of the residential quarters; that their ceilings were also much loftier is therefore not an unreasonable conclusion.[15]

As for the total height of the palaces, a recent reconsideration of the problem[16] has caused me to alter my previous opinion, one held by most scholars and originating with Evans, namely that above the storey of the magazines, along the west side of the palace at Knossos, there existed two storeys composing the Piano Nobile. Not only would this mean the apparently redundant reduplication of the series of great halls, but it would also greatly aggravate the

[15] *AJA*, 60 (1956), pp. 156-157.   [16] *AJA*, 83 (1979), pp. 64-69.

problem of support, already, one would think, nearing a critical point in these vast halls whose ceilings were upheld by no more than two columns. This theory of a third storey was developed some twenty years after the excavations, solely on the basis of what appeared to be the remains of a stairway ascending above the level of the second storey. I would accept the evidence for a stairway at this point as probable, but believe that it should be differently explained: not as leading to a third storey but as leading to the roof— useful, inter alia, as a vantage point from which to watch events taking place in either the West Court or the Central Court.

Thus the only part of the palace at Knossos which we may feel sure was built three storeys high was in the Residential Quarter where two of the storeys were supported against an artificial scarp. Similarly, at Phaistos, the lowest of the three storeys south of the Grand Staircase was also built against a scarp. At Mallia no one has ever seriously suggested the existence of three storeys in any part of the palace though I have recently pointed out that there is clear evidence that, just north of the Banquet Hall in the second storey, a stairway continued upward. But we may feel sure it was to the roof.

If it be objected that several of the house façades of the Town Mosaic show three storeys the answer, I believe, is that the ordinary house-builder had a limited amount of land at his disposal, whereas the architect of a palace could afford to sprawl over several acres. To build higher than necessary was to invite the worse damage from the frequent earthquakes.

Considering the large area the palaces covered and their flat roofs, the general effect must have been low and spreading. The proportions represented in our restoration of the Palace of Mallia (Fig. 58) are in accurate perspective and are based on the conclusions outlined in this section.

CHAPTER XI

DECORATIVE FEATURES

1. COLUMNS AND PORTICOES

THE MINOAN CRETANS anticipated the Classical Greeks in many of the forms and uses of the column, although in palace architecture it never became the principal decorative feature of the exterior that it was in the Greek temple and many other public buildings. The structural uses of the column have been discussed in a previous section (Ch. VIII, 2); its place as an element of architectural decoration will be considered here.

One area in which the Minoans showed themselves sensitive to the possibilities of the column is in the formal entranceway, where, treated monumentally, it could add greatly to the impressiveness of the approach, as the Mycenaeans and the later Greeks were also well aware. The outstanding example in Cretan architecture is the single massive column at the head of the Grand Stairway which formed the principal entry to the Palace of Phaistos (Fig. 48). The portal in the center of which this column stood was thirty-two feet (9.75 m.) wide, and the column itself measured perhaps fifteen feet (4½ m.) high.

A somewhat similar arrangement is found at Knossos where, on the stairway leading up to the Piano Nobile from the Central Court, we find two columns placed in the center of the stairs one behind the other (Fig. 44). A single great column also stood in the center of the front of the West Porch, the main approach to the Palace of Minos, which is about thirty-seven feet (11.25 m.) in width (Figs. 2, 128). Still another monumental treatment is the façade of Room 25 on the Central Court at

Phaistos, with a large central column between four massive piers (Fig. 50). On a smaller scale is the entrance to the rather enigmatic building at Nirou Khani, where we have a two-columned porch which contrives to resemble at the same time a typical Minoan light-well and the entrance to a Mycenaean megaron (Figs. 31, 75, 150).

The porticoes and peristyles of classic architecture likewise occur in Minoan, though with less prominence. We have already spoken of the porticoes, usually L-shaped, of the residential quarters (Ch. v, 1). They faced outward to command the finest view afforded by the particular site; H. Triadha is the outstanding example (Fig. 165). A long apparently continuous portico with a good view ran along the east side of the magnificent suite of rooms in the Little Palace at Knossos (Figs. 13, 64). The longest colonnade preserved is the one with eleven columns across the north end of the Central Court at Mallia (Figs. 6, 57). An even longer portico, nearly 110 ft. (ca. 34 m.) in length, extends along the entire east side of the court of the same palace, but here the columns alternate with square piers. The east side of the court at Phaistos is treated in similar fashion. This alternation of pillars and columns is a distinctively Minoan scheme, occurring at Phaistos, H. Triadha, Mallia, Gournia, and Palaikastro, but not at Knossos nor at Kato Zakro. The most remarkable instance is in a building at H. Triadha, which was built at a slightly later period (L.M. III) than that to which we have in general limited this survey.[1] This building bears a peculiar resemblance to a Greek "stoa": a long series of small rooms (shops?) at the rear all open on a portico nearly 150 ft. long (about 46 m.), fronted by an alternating series of eight pillars and nine columns.

Above the porticoes of the central courts of the palaces were, it is often supposed, colonnaded galleries, and they may also have existed above the porticoes commonly associated with the residential quarters, but both cases are quite uncertain.

---

[1] *Guida*, pp. 37-38; Lawrence, *Gk. Arch.*, p. 51 and fig. 32.

Two instances are known of the complete interior peristyle, that is with porticoes on all four sides of a court.[2] The smaller is located in the Little Palace at Knossos (Figs. 13, 64), with three columns to a side (eight in all), surrounding a flagged court about twelve by thirteen feet (ca. 4 m. square). The Peristyle Court at Phaistos (74) has four columns to a side, and enclosed an area about twenty-five feet (nearly 8 m.) square. In each case a large hall faced south on the peristyle through the usual pier-and-door partition.

Columns add a decorative note to the standard Cretan light-wells, which occur almost entirely in the residential quarters. Light-wells with columns on two sides, or even on all four sides, are occasionally found (Figs. 17, 19, 29).

Another common use of columns is on the parapets of stairways. A single column is common in the ordinary bathrooms, at the end of the parapet between the stairs and the main room (Figs. 81, 82); its function here would seem to be purely decorative, but in larger bathrooms or "lustral chambers," where a series of columns stands on the parapet between the two rooms, as in the "Throne Room" at Knossos, these columns must have also helped to shorten the free span of the ceiling beams. Certainly the columns along the parapet of the Grand Staircase in the Palace of Minos were functional as well as decorative (Fig. 38). A single column on a parapet in the North Residential Quarter at Phaistos at the foot of the stairway opposite Room 50 allowed light to reach the stairway (Fig. 47).

The semi-circular bases at the sides of the central door of the north façade of the Central Court at Phaistos may have supported half-columns (as now restored, Figs. 51, 53), like those on the façades of the Treasury of Atreus at Mycenae. But it is more likely that they supported a pair of flagstaffs (Fig. 50) as I suggested in a recent article (*AJA*, 74 [1970], pp. 231-239).

---

[2] Except for tiny courts or light-wells with a single pier at each corner (see Ch. IX, 2), and for a curious arrangement of pillars and columns in an early building northeast of the Palace of Phaistos, *Festòs*, I, figs. 209, 214, 215.

The form of the commonest type of Cretan column is familiar from Evans' restorations in the Palace of Minos (Figs. 39, 42, 44). Their general accuracy is assured by the representations on mural paintings (Fig. 133), and by the stone example in high relief preserved on the Lion Gate at Mycenae (Fig. 135). Columns were made of wood, never—so far as we know—of stone; their capitals consisted of a rounded bulging member topped by a square block, both resembling, in fact probably the architectural ancestors of, the echinus and abacus of the Greek Doric capital; the shafts tapered downward (Fig. 136, F). There can be no doubt of the downward taper, strange as it may seem to eyes accustomed to classical columns, for it is visible (and measurable) in the stone column of the Lion Gate relief,[3] in Minoan wall paintings, and in the carbonized remains of, and impressions left by, actual columns. Some have criticized Evans' restored columns as having too sharp a taper,[4] but those in the Hall of the Colonnades, for example, have a considerably slighter taper than that of the Lion Gate, which amounts to only one in thirty-six.

It is not likely that we shall be able to discover a logical explanation of this downward taper, to us a topsy-turvy way of doing things. Some have suggested that it arose out of a practice of setting tree trunks used as supports upside down in order to prevent the sprouting of new roots; another scarcely more likely theory is that the foot of the column would be less exposed to water dripping from the capital. At any rate it does provide the column with a slightly larger surface on which to rest the entablature, while leaving slightly more free space at floor level.

To judge from wall paintings the wooden shafts and capitals were both painted, one black and the other red (Fig. 136, E); the foot of the shaft might also be in a contrasting color, perhaps a substitute for polychrome stone bases.

[3] Dinsmoor, *Arch. Anc. Gr.*, p. 23 and note 3; Evans accepted Durm's claim that there was no taper, *Knossos*, I, p. 343, note 3.
[4] Lawrence, *Gk. Arch.*, p. 39, note 7.

Another unique feature of the Cretan columns is that frequently they were not round in cross-section but oval. For example, the two bases in the South Propylaeum at Knossos (Fig. 42), and all seven columns in the Magazine-Propylon Block at Phaistos were oval; but in only one case is the difference between the major and the minor axis (to judge from the oval bases on which they rested) greater than ten per cent. In every instance at Phaistos the major axis is parallel to the architrave, thus providing a greater bearing surface; but this is not true at Knossos.

It is obvious from the varying size of the column bases that the lower diameter, and so persumably the height, of the columns varied widely. From a few examples at Knossos where it seemed possible to estimate the height of the column fairly closely from the height of the room, Evans concluded that the column height was normally about five times its lower diameter. Nevertheless the proportions suggested by pictures of columns in mural paintings are much slenderer (Fig. 133), and, in one case at Phaistos where a fairly accurate and reliable estimate could be arrived at, the proportion was actually 1:8.[5] Indeed there must have been a considerable variation in proportions, as can be inferred from the difference in size between the oval base between 67 and 68 of the Grand Propylon at Phaistos, 4 ft. 8 in. by 4 ft. 4 in. (1.42 by 1.32 m.), and that of the three bases in front of the light-well in the same complex (69A)— 3 ft. 10 in. by 3 ft. 8 in. (1.17 by 1.12 m.) for two, and 3 ft. 3 in. by 3 ft. (0.99 by 0.91 m.) for the third—inasmuch as the height of all four columns which stood on these bases must have been approximately the same. The proportions of the column at the head of the stairs, about 4:1, were doubtless intentionally stockier than those of the other columns, which were about 5:1 or 5½:1, because of the much wider span it had to support (Fig. 48). It would not be in keeping with the spirit of Cretan architecture, which seems to delight in wilful

[5] *Festòs*, II, pp. 473-474.

irregularity, to expect Minoan columns to adhere to any rigidly fixed principles of proportion (Ch. xiii, 3); but we can at least expect that the architects would vary the size of the columns to suit the needs of the particular situation.

Like the Doric column, the Minoan column had no molded base. In fact it was often socketed into a shallow circular depression in the stone sill upon which it rested, as in the columns of the Grand Staircase (Fig. 38). Where the column was directly exposed to the weather it was commonly set for protection on a circular block of stone which might be socketed into a hole in the sill or be part of the sill itself. Sometimes this block was fairly high, a foot and a half or more, and often made of a polychrome stone (Fig. 80); usually it was lower, as little as a couple of inches, tapering slightly upward, and made of gypsum or limestone.

The shaft of the column was perhaps left plain and smooth as a rule, as Evans restored them. Yet he admitted that "there are strong indications that the originals were, in some cases at least, fluted,"[6] for in the area of the Residential Quarter he found a carbonized fragment of a wooden column, though of smaller diameter than those actually used there, with apparently twenty-four flutes or channels. Elsewhere in the palace clay impressions of two columns with twenty-eight concave flutes were discovered, and impressions of the small columns of the Little Palace "Lustral Area" indicate that they had probably fifteen convex flutes. From the Mycenaean mainland (but from no other sites in Crete) comes further evidence of fluted columns. Some of the small ivory columns recently found at Mycenae (probably decorative pieces from furniture) are fluted (Fig. 136, G, H), and so are the half-columns of the façade of the "Tomb of Clytemnestra" at the same site.[7] Yet the column of the Lion Gate is unfluted (Fig. 135). In the palace at Pylos distinct and complete impressions of concave fluting were left at several places in the cement floor in which the bottoms of the

---

[6] *Knossos*, I, p. 344.
[7] Mylonas, *Anc. Myc.*, fig. 30.

columns were embedded; in one case there were thirty-two flutes, in another forty-four, and in two others sixty.[8]

Spiral fluting has been found on the shafts of Cretan lampstands, and is represented on columns, evidently intended to be of full size, on Minoan sealings (Fig. 136, J). The half-columns of the façade of the "Treasury of Atreus" at Mycenae present an even more elaborate example, with a shaft of green stone carved with zigzags and spirals (Fig. 136, I), and it is highly likely that in this and the other examples noted the mainland was following the traditions of Minoan architecture.

We have already spoken of the "echinus" and "abacus" of the normal Cretan column. Some wall paintings show more elaborate forms with additional convex and concave moldings. In the "Treasury of Atreus" the echinus is carved with zigzags and spirals similar to those on the shaft (Fig. 136, I), and there is a leaf pattern on the concave molding below the echinus. That there may have been other elaborate forms of capitals is suggested by the capitals of some lampstands which show palm tree and other vegetable forms, clearly patterned after the contemporary Egyptian models (Fig. 140, J).

A peculiar rectangular block on a tall shaft that appears on the Boxer Vase and the Grandstand Fresco has generally been taken to be a capital (Fig. 136, K, L). However a similar "capital" on a newly found steatite rhyton from Zakro representing a Peak Sanctuary has been explained by Alexiou on the basis of Egyptian temple pylons as a large cleat or tie-block used to hold a tall, upward-tapering mast to the face of the sanctuary façade.[9] I have further suggested that a similar pair of banner-poles with tie-blocks stood on the pair of semi-circular bases flanking the central door in the north façade of the Central Court at Phaistos (Fig. 50).[9a] If this suggestion is correct, there may be a significant parallel between the association of bull-leaping and tie-blocks with banner-poles on

[8] *AJA*, 57 (1953), p. 60; 58 (1954), p. 29; 59 (1955), p. 32; 60 (1956), p. 99.

[9] *KretChron*, 17 (1963), pp. 339-351.

[9a] *AJA*, 74 (1970), pp. 231-234.

the Boxer Vase and the similar association in the Central Court at Phaistos.

It seems possible, then, that the tie-blocks came to have some symbolic meaning outside of their essentially functional purpose, and it is interesting that Sir Arthur Evans with his usual sagacity, though much puzzled by the "capitals," as he called them, concluded that "they were in some sense structural elements, with a certain symbolical, religious value as well.[9b] And Federico Halbherr even went so far as to say that these "capitals" might refer "to the porticoes of the courts or theatral areas (choroi) within which the games took place."[9c]

2. ARCHITECTURAL DETAIL

Much of the charm of a Classical Greek building such as the Erechtheum of the Athenian Acropolis is due to the beauty of its carved decorative detail. Minoan architectural ornament was evidently much more limited, but fragments have been found at Knossos (none elsewhere in Crete) which, in excellence of carving and beauty of design, scarcely yield to the best Greek examples.[10] Yet none of these pieces has been found in its original position.

Fortunately the slightly later mainland Greek or "Mycenaean" architecture offers some help, for in its decoration it closely imitated Cretan architecture. This may be illustrated by the close resemblance between a fragment of the "triglyph half-rosette frieze" found near the northwest angle of the Palace of Minos and another from the façade of the "Tomb of Clytemnestra" at Mycenae (Fig. 136, A, B). The greater width of the rectangular element in the later frieze is a significant change, for it is clearly moving in the direction of the Classical Greek triglyph, whose form was influenced by the Mycenaean frieze.[11]

[9b] *Knossos*, I, 688-690; III, pp. 62-65; IV, pp. 20f.

[9c] *R. Accad. dei Lincei*, XIV (1905), p. 369.

[10] More fragments have recently been discovered; see *JHS*, "Archaeology in Greece, 1956," p. 21, figs. 18-19.

[11] On this much discussed question see Bowen, *BSA*, 45 (1950), pp 113-125, who, in my opinion, makes the derivation certain. A simpler form of "triglyph-

Remains of a similar half-rosette frieze were found in another Mycenaean tomb, the "Treasury of Atreus," and belonged to its façade, the design of which can be approximately recovered.[12] In this the frieze formed a horizontal band running across the doorway above the top of the columns, much like the later Doric frieze. Below it ran other carved stone patterns in the form of a continuous spiral and a series of round disks, representing in wooden construction the ends of logs laid horizontally to support floors or ceilings.

Fragments of the half-rosette frieze discovered in the ruins of the Northwest Entrance of the palace at Mycenae must have been used in similar fashion.[13] But remains of the same design were found in place at the base of the walls of the main rooms, the megarons, both at Mycenae and Tiryns, showing that the frieze could also be used as a low dado, a use also paralleled by the Classical Doric frieze which is often employed around the bottom of Greek altars.[14]

Since some frieze fragments of this type were discovered at Knossos in the vicinity of one or two entrances to the palace,[15] it was natural, and perhaps correct, for Evans to suppose that they had been used as at Mycenae over doorways. But the proposal to restore a "Northwest Entrance" to the palace, of which there exists no clear architectural remains, merely on the basis of finding similar fragments in the area, cannot be regarded as convincing, especially when it disagrees with other evidence (Ch. VI, 1).[16]

The "log-ends," which appear in low relief on the façades of the Mycenaean tombs and above the column of the relief over the Lion Gate at Mycenae (Fig. 135), are also to be seen on

---

metope" arrangement is frequently found decorating the face of stone benches (see Figs. 43, 69). In Room 23 at Phaistos, e.g., the projecting member is marked with three groups of shallow vertical grooves, distinctly triglyph-like in appearance; the broader, recessed "metope" is marked with two sets of horizontal grooves (*Festòs*, II, pp. 148-149 and fig. 88).

[12] See the new restoration by Marinatos, *C. and M.*, fig. 25, and *Archaeology*, 13 (1960), p. 51, fig. 10.

[13] Mylonas, *Anc. Myc.*, p. 61.   [14] *Ibid.*, p. 52.

[15] *Knossos*, II, figs. 83, 436.   [16] *Knossos*, II, pp. 590-591.

the housefronts from the "Town Mosaic" found at Knossos (Fig. 103), and in various representations of architectural detail in the "Grandstand Fresco" and other Cretan paintings, where they appear in alternating colors (Figs. 101, 133, 136, E). These paintings also represent other designs, especially a kind of checker pattern,[17] and rows of "sacral horns" serving as a cornice for structures like the Tripartite Columnar Shrine. A simple "stepped" form of cornice for ordinary architecture is perhaps indicated by a block found in the Palace of Minos, and has been commonly used for this purpose in restorations (Fig. 44).[18]

Another feature, for which we must allow in attempting to imagine the appearance of Minoan palaces and houses, is color. Outside of the traces of red-painted stucco observed on wall blocks of the west façade at Phaistos, the evidence is largely limited to the wall paintings, whose accuracy in detail is of course uncertain. However we can feel sure that columns and decorative details were brightly painted in contrasting colors, a tradition which was perhaps transmitted to Classical Greece, and that the exterior of Cretan palaces was nearly as gay as the brilliantly painted halls within.

3. WALL DECORATION

The wall paintings of Minoan Crete undoubtedly have a more direct appeal to most people today than any other form of Cretan art. They delight us for their gaiety and charm, their color and animation, their love of nature. Yet many of the paintings reproduced time and again are a pitiful jigsaw of tiny fragments none too certainly coaxed into juxtaposition, and eked out with the twentieth century imagination of the artist-restorer. Are these idyllic little scenes of birds and flowers but subordinate elements in large scenes in which man played the predominant part? Where is this Minoan officer (?) and his squad (?) of Ne-

[17] *Knossos*, II, p. 600. Still valuable is Fyfe, "Painted plaster decoration at Knossos, with special reference to the architectural spheres," *Journal of the Royal Institute of British Architects*, 10 (1903), pp. 107-131, with two color plates.
[18] *Knossos*, II, pp. 814f.; but see *M. and T.*, p. 105, note 4.

groes hastening at the double, and why? Who are the (headless) "Ladies in Blue" with their sensitively drawn hands? These are but a few of the questions which the paintings arouse, and leave unanswered.[19]

Since the viewpoint of this book is architectural we are less interested in the aesthetic aspect of the paintings (which in any event has so often been treated), or even in their composition, than in such problems as this: what rooms in the palaces and houses were adorned with figure scenes, and was there any appropriateness of scene to room? How were the paintings fitted into the scheme of the wall as a whole? What sort of wall decoration was used in rooms of lesser importance? But we shall have to be content with rather meager answers to these questions; more often than not the fragments have been tediously collected from the loose fill where frequently they have fallen from the upstairs rooms, or, in the case of more modest forms of mural decoration, the archaeologist may not have bothered to note carefully or report fully on what he has found, engrossed as he is with more spectacular discoveries.

Nevertheless we can feel reasonably sure that most of the rubble or adobe walls in the palaces and better houses were plastered, and in the more important rooms the plaster was at least given a fine finish coat of stucco and painted in some plain color. When we are specifically told that throughout the house at Vathypetro plaster fragments painted in bright colors were found in abundance, we should consider this to have been the rule rather than the exception.

A simple elaboration on the plain painted wall was to paint it in a series of horizontal bands in contrasting colors (Fig. 151). Lines lightly incised in the stucco might be used as guide lines in painting the different colors; combinations of horizontal and vertical lines might give a structural effect suggesting a wall built, for example, of squared blocks at the base either with a smooth wall above, or with narrow bands to suggest wooden tie

[19] *Knossos*, II, pls. 11 and 13; I, fig. 397.

beams throughout the rubble or adobe structure (Ch. VIII, 2). The wall structure might be further imitated by painting bands or blocks to represent the veining of stone or the graining of wood. The lower part of the walls of the finer rooms, particularly at Knossos, Phaistos, and H. Triadha, was often lined with a dado about 4 to 6 ft. high of alabaster veneering about an inch (2½ cm.) thick and sometimes cut in panels over 6 ft. (ca. 2 m.) square (Figs. 69, 81). Above this the stucco might be treated in any way from plain color to elaborate figure designs.

The following are typical examples, proceeding from simple to more complex forms.

Walls painted with a few colored bands, and with or without incised lines, are mentioned not infrequently in the excavation reports, but precise details are rarely given and there is usually little remaining on the walls today. In the bathroom of the Mallia Residential Quarter the excavators found white stucco on the walls with a red band defined by incised lines, and on the alcove east of the bathroom in the North Residential Quarter at Phaistos three brown bands were seen on a yellowish background. Two rooms in the building at Nirou Khani (12, and the "Room of the Lamps") are said to have had colored bands; and in the small room, xxiv 1, in the palace at Mallia, there was a plain "baseboard" 16 in. (40 cm.) high, then a red band 3 in. (7.4 cm.) high, and 7 in. (18 cm.) above that four more incised lines close together.[20]

Three examples with more numerous painted bands are illustrated in Fig. 129. In the first, A, the stucco is preserved to a height of 32½ in. (82 cm.) in one corner of a room in the House of the Frescoes; here we have a low "baseboard" surmounted by a high dado divided into three white bands by two red lines; above the dado is a narrow band painted with red graining on yellow to imitate a beam of wood, followed by another narrow band painted with white on black in imitation of

[20] *Mallia*, II, pl. 4, 2.

stone. The walls at the foot of the stairway, 71, leading to the upper state reception halls at Phaistos, have a dado nearly 3 ft. high (87 cm.) with a 10 in. (26 cm.) band of red above, edged by narrow fillets of white and red (B). Two broad zones of gray in Magazine 12 at Knossos (C) are bordered at the top by narrow bands of red.

In a corridor of the Knossos Residential Quarter, above a black baseboard, the veining of alabaster veneering is imitated in a dado at least 4 ft. (over 120 cm.) high, divided by red lines into panels about 3 ft. (nearly 1 m.) wide; the walls above the dado seem to have been decorated with an intricate labyrinth or meander pattern.[21] In the Hall of the Double-Axes, above the top edge of the alabaster veneering, a continuous spiral band is painted on the plaster, and along this band was perhaps hung a series of great figure-of-eight shields (Fig. 45). This in turn gave rise to merely painting shields against a spiral band in the porticoes of the Grand Staircase.[22]

What is known of the arrangement of figure scenes with relation to the walls of the room? Only one reasonably complete example has been recovered, the so-called Throne Room on the ground floor of the Palace of Minos (Fig. 130). On the north wall a pair of griffins guards the throne; on the west a similar pair confronts the doorway to a small cult room; the east and south sides of the room are occupied by the entrance and by the "Lustral Chamber," respectively. The griffin frieze, some 3½ ft. (over 1 m.) high, was limited above by colored bands, probably at the level of the lintels; below, a dado nearly 2 ft. high (60 cm.) was painted in imitation of veined stonework.[23]

The symmetrical arrangement of the figures certainly cannot be typical of Minoan mural decoration, but the tripartite scheme of dado, main frieze, and upper part, was probably a very common one, for it corresponds with the structure of the wall.

[21] *Knossos*, I, pp. 356-357.
[22] *Knossos*, III, pp. 301-308, 343-345.
[23] *Knossos*, IV, pp. 908-913.

The top border of the figure scene follows the line of the horizontal timbering which forms the lintel of doors and windows, while the bottom border follows that of the sill of any windows or wall openings.[24]

Another example of the tripartite division occurs in the West Porch at Knossos, where a scene of bull grappling surmounted a 16 inch (40 cm.) dado of panels painted to imitate stone veneering, and was probably separated from the ceiling by a series of colored bands or some other simple decorative treatment.[25] Certain technical peculiarities of some of the frescoes found stacked in the House of the Frescoes (see below) indicate that they were similarly arranged on the wall.

Sometimes the figure scenes were set not above a high dado but on a low baseboard, in which case the scene occupied a much larger surface of the wall. This seems to have been true of the Cat and Bird mural in the Residential Quarter at H. Triadha (Fig. 134). The lifesize figures on both walls of the Corridor of the Procession and other parts of the approach to the Piano Nobile at Knossos were arranged in two registers (Figs. 42, 131, B), the feet of the lower row of figures being appropriately only a little above floor level.[26]

Narrow, border-like friezes are also known. Around the walls of the dining pavilion (?) of the "Caravanserai" at Knossos, just below the ceiling, ran a frieze, less than a foot high, representing a row of partridges interspersed with hoopoes. Below this, painted on the white walls on three sides of the room, was a series of brownish-yellow pilasters with red bases and blue capitals.[27] A more famous frieze of this type is the Flying Fish Fresco found on the island of Melos in the Aegean, but probably shipped there, ready painted, from Crete (Fig. 132). It was about 9 in. (23 cm.) high and at least 4 ft. (120 cm.) long, and was found in a small room along with fragments of two other murals at a larger scale, one also a seascape, the other with human beings, including two men; this might indicate that

---

[24] *Knossos*, II, p. 460.   [25] *Knossos*, II, pp. 674-676.
[26] *Knossos*, II, p. 720.   [27] *Knossos*, II, pp. 109-116.

the Flying Fish frieze formed a high border above the main scene or scenes.[28]

The most elaborate forms of mural decoration, that is figure scenes, occur principally in the residential quarters and in the important public rooms of the palaces. Fragments of fine frescoes were found at Knossos below the rooms of the Piano Nobile west of the Central Court, and below the "Great East Hall" east of the court; figures were also painted, as we have seen, on the walls of the Corridor of the Procession and of the "Throne Room" west of the Central Court. At Knossos and H. Triadha much finer murals were found in the Queen's Hall, that is in the more private part of the residential quarter, than in the Main Hall itself. The palaces at Phaistos and Mallia have produced extremely little in the way of mural paintings either with figures or with designs, but, especially for the former palace, this must be largely the accident of destruction or preservation.[29]

Mural paintings were by no means confined to the palaces. Remains have been found at Knossos in the South House, the Southeast House, the High Priest's House, and the House of the Frescoes; also in houses at Nirou Khani, Tylissos, and even in the little hamlet on the tiny island of Pseira. In the House of the Frescoes, besides fragments found on the walls, a neatly stacked "hoard" of plaster fragments, in a pile measuring about 12 by 5 ft. (3.65 by 1.50 m.) and at least thirty-four layers deep, was found on the floor of one of the rooms. This included the Bluebird Mural, the Blue Monkeys, the Fountain, and others representing myrtle branches, crocuses, etc.[30] So slight were the remains of painted scenes in some of these houses that the fact that none was discovered in such sumptuous dwellings as the Little Palace and the Royal Villa can have no significance.

Finally, a few words about the relation of the subject matter

[28] *Phylakopi*, chap. III.

[29] However Miss Banti sees differences in decorative principles between Knossos and Phaistos which would account for such discrepancies, *Festòs*, II, pp. 484-485. It may also be due in part to chronological differences between the palaces.

[30] *Knossos*, II, pp. 444-460.

of the figure scenes to the rooms they were intended to decorate. In many cases there clearly was a significant relationship. For example, the heraldic griffins "guarding" the throne of the "Throne Room" evidently had a meaning and a purpose, no doubt a religious one. The figures bringing gifts to the Mother Goddess (?) in the Corridor of the Procession reflect some ceremonial procession that must have threaded its way thus into the "Labyrinth." The shields of the porticoes of the Grand Staircase would appear to represent the martial character of the last lords of Knossos, the invader kings from the Mycenaean mainland. (This is as near as the murals ever get to scenes of war.) Suitable to the rooms occupied especially by the women are the representations of a dancing girl and a seascape of dolphins at Knossos (Fig. 43), and the delightful scenes of a leaping deer, a cat stalking a bird (Fig. 134), and a lady kneeling in a bed of flowers, at H. Triadha.[31] Or we may think of the partridges in the "Caravanserai" dining pavilion (?); or the scene of the bull games in the portico at the north end of the Central Court at Knossos.

Scenes too of ladies in elaborate court dress, some sitting in "box seats" watching the bull games (?), taking part in a solemn dance amid an olive grove, or sitting on folding stools exchanging a "loving cup," clearly have a general appropriateness to the ceremonies and festivities of court life, whatever their particular meaning in the great public halls they once adorned.[32]

Of the treatment of ceilings in Cretan architecture little is known except that the Queen's Hall in the Palace of Minos was decorated with a magnificent spiral design (Fig. 43). The occurrence of similar ceilings in contemporary Egyptian tombs, and in a beautifully carved stone example on the ceiling of the side chamber of the Mycenaean tholos tomb at Orchomenos indicates their widespread popularity.

[31] *Guida*, p. 31; *Knossos*, II, fig. 201; Matz, *KMT*, pls. 48-49.
[32] *Knossos*, III, figs. 29-32, pl. 18; IV, pl. 31.

4. PAVEMENTS

A considerable variety of materials and decorative schemes were employed by the Cretans for the floors of the rooms in their palaces and houses. Cheapest and commonest was the floor of hard-packed earth, at least for the ground floors, and perhaps also for the upper storeys, for there it could be supported on a thick bedding of poles or reeds laid on the joists.

Plaster or cement floors were used for special purposes. It was the common surfacing for light-wells and small courts, for it resisted the water and could easily be sloped to a drain. In the seven magazines to the east of the Central Court at Mallia the cement floor with inset basins and a network of channels in the cement saved from loss any of the precious oil that might be spilt (Fig. 91).

Stone of various kinds was used for surfacing floors, both inside and out; slate or limestone might be employed for either, gypsum only where protected by a roof. The great central courts at Knossos and Phaistos were laid with rectangular slabs of limestone (Figs. 44, 51), and more irregular flagging was used for the outer courts of the palaces and elsewhere (Figs. 49, 128). Flagging in limestone or schist occurs also in the Main Halls and other rooms of Houses Da and Za at Mallia, and in the rooms of the Residential Quarter and the large Pillar Crypt (vii 4) of the palace at the same site. Even rooms in upper storeys sometimes had flagged floors, among them the room we have identified as a Banquet Hall north of the Central Court at Mallia. The irregular joints between the flagging were carefully filled with plaster, sometimes colored red, an attractive example being the Main Hall of House C at Tylissos (Fig. 77).

A particularly fine grade of a very hard gray-blue limestone with attractive effects of graining, called "ironstone" (*sidheropetra*) was often used in irregularly shaped blocks for flagging floors. Evans dubbed it "mosaiko." Frequently it occurs between the older *kalderim* (rough limestone) flooring and the later gypsum floor of the Palace of Minos, for it was a popular style in the middle period of the palaces; it was rarely used in later times for entire floors, though it does appear in the Hall (3a) of the House of the Chancel Screen at Knossos.[32a]

The popular flooring in the late palace period, for those who could afford it, was fine white gypsum or alabaster laid in smooth rectangular slabs about 2 in. (5 cm.) thick (Fig. 64). Possibly the coldness of such a floor in winter, especially to bare feet, was relieved by mats. In the Palace of Phaistos floors paved with regular slabs of gypsum were used throughout the North and East Residential Quarters, in the large halls 93 and 25, in important smaller rooms such as 23 and 24, and even occasionally in magazines (33 and 88).

In some of the finest rooms striking effects were obtained by laying the large rectangular slabs of alabaster in regular patterns enhanced by broad joints filled with red plaster (Fig. 151). The pattern commonly consists of a series of slabs of uniform width around the walls of the rooms, followed by a rectangle framing one or more large slabs which form the center of the floor. The Main Hall, 79, of the North Residential Quarter at Phaistos is a handsome example (recently carefully restored) of this type of floor (Figs. 127, 136, N); but it may also be seen in the adjoining Queen's Hall, 81, in the Royal Villa at Knossos, and in the building at Nirou Khani (Fig. 31). In both parts of the Hall of the Double-Axes the series of slabs around the walls enclosed three long stripes of which the center is the broadest (Figs. 12, 39); the smaller part of the Main Hall at Phaistos, 77, and the large room, 25, opening on the west side of the Central Court of the same palace, are interesting variations on this theme. The pattern of the last is particularly intricate, and each of the two large transverse blocks supports one of the oval columns on the axis of the room. A unique scheme, of which only a fragment is complete, is the rhomboidal arrangement of the gypsum slabs of the floor of another large

---

[32a] This is based on Evans' conclusions, but Levi claims that this chronological sequence is not reliable; see Ch. VIII, note 8.

room at Phaistos, 93, which faces south on the Peristyle Court (Fig. 126).

A combination of a gypsum border with an ironstone center was also popular and made a very handsome floor. It is seen in the anteroom to the "Throne Room" at Knossos, in the Main Hall of the South House, in two rooms at Nirou Khani (5, 12), and in the Entrance Hall, Peristyle, and both inner and outer parts of the Main Hall of the Little Palace at Knossos. Sometimes the center was filled in with rough flagging which was then concealed with painted plaster, as in the "Throne Room" itself. Evans' restoration of this room with red plaster and white gypsum floor and the brightly colored Griffin Mural on the walls, appears as the frontispiece of volume IV ii of *The Palace of Minos* (Fig. 130).

The surface of the Minoan cement floor was sometimes studded with smooth water-worn pebbles of different colors, set in place before the cement hardened, as in the Room of the Lamps at Nirou Khani (14). Apparently the Minoans never took the further step of combining the pebbles into patterns or figure designs as was done in the Classical Greek period.[33]

Cement floors were sometimes decorated with color, for example a band of reddish-orange about 2 in. (5 cm.) wide in the vestibule to Stairway 71 at Phaistos, and red and blue spots on the floor of a room in the Residential Quarter at Mallia. A recently discovered floor in an early stage of the Phaistos palace was also painted in simple designs.[34] The most elaborately painted floor yet found in Crete is that of a small shrine of the L.M. III period (the shrine had predecessors) at H. Triadha, which represents octopuses, dolphins, and other fish, swimming on a white background decorated with blue lines to suggest waves.[35]

---

[33] Recent excavations at Gordion have brought to light pebble mosaics of the eighth century B.C., *Archaeology*, 9 (1956), p. 264; *Ill. Lon. News*, 229 (Nov. 17, 1956), p. 859, fig. 11.

[34] Levi, *Nuova Antologia*, 467 (1956), p. 227.

[35] It is now on display in the Herakleion Museum; a sketch of the design is given in Nilsson, *MMR²*, p. 98, fig. 23; and see Banti, *Culti di H. Triada*, p. 32, fig. 18.

On the Mycenaean mainland the floors of important rooms were often marked off by incised lines into large squares painted with a variety of patterns of lines, and at times with octopuses and dolphins.[36] Since these motives are so typically Cretan and since so many of the Mycenaean decorative schemes originated in Crete one might suspect that this type of floor also had its prototype there, but so far no exact parallels have been found. Wall dadoes painted with squares imitating marbling and very similar to the patterns on the mainland plaster floors have been found, however, in the West Porch at Knossos, and similar fragments found in the South Propylon nearby are presumed to come from a dado and not from a floor. The connecting link therefore is still missing.[37]

Floors may sometimes have been made of wood. This has been suggested, for example, for the floor of a room in a recently excavated house at Mallia (Hagia Varvara).[38]

Several fine reception halls west of the Central Court of the palace at Kato Zakro were decorated with floors laid out in patterns created by narrow frames of red-painted stucco. What the material composing the part of the floors within the framing consisted of is at present a mystery, but it is clear that the effect would have been very attractive.[39]

---

[36] Wace, *Mycenae*, pl. 90c; *Tiryns*, II, pl. 19.

[37] *Knossos*, II, pp. 674-676, 686, note 1.

[38] *BCH*, 90 (1966), p. 560, fig. 4 and note 1.

[39] *Zakros*, pp. 156f. A similar floor was found at Palaikastro, *BSA*, 11 (1904-05), p. 278, fig. 9. See also Shaw, *M. and T.*, p. 217 and note 4.

CHAPTER XII

FURNISHINGS AND EQUIPMENT

1. FURNITURE AND FURNISHINGS

Telemachos led the way home for his travel-worn friend and brought him to the great house, where they threw down their cloaks on settles or chairs, stepped into the polished baths and washed. When the maid-servants had finished bathing them and rubbing them with oil, they gave them tunics and threw warm mantles round their shoulders, and the two left their baths and sat down on chairs. A maid came with water in a fine golden jug and poured it out over a silver basin so that they might rinse their hands. She drew up a wooden table and the staid housekeeper brought some bread and set it by them, together with a choice of dainties, helping them liberally to all she could offer. Telemachos' mother sat opposite them by a pillar of the hall, reclining in an easy-chair and spinning the delicate thread on her distaff, while they fell to on the good fare laid before them. (Odysseus returns to his palace in Ithaca with his son Telemachos, Odyssey, 17, 84-98, Rieu translation.)

WOULD there were some Minoan epic preserved to which we could turn to put flesh on the bare architectural bones we have so far described as vividly as this passage calls up a picture of the Mycenaean heroes and the furnishings of their palaces! Poetry failing us, what assistance can archaeology provide to fill these empty alabaster halls?

Distressingly little in some respects! The furniture itself, which was largely of wood, textiles, or other perishable materials, has vanished utterly. Wall paintings, which show us the people and their costumes, rarely depict their furnishings; and no Minoan equivalent of Tutankhamen's tomb, crammed with royal possessions, if such ever existed, has yet been discovered.

Comparing Crete with the rest of the Aegean area Marinatos remarks that "the furnishing was always rich, particularly in clay utensils; and there were many complicated devices for cooking and heating. In Gournia, Palaikastro and Chamaizi figurines, bronze gear and all sorts of implements have been excavated on a scale which cannot be matched outside Crete. Clearly the living standards of the islanders must have been much higher than they were anywhere else."[1] It is safe to say, however, that a modern would feel that even a Minoan palace was very scantily furnished. So much of the equipment of a present day house of quite modest pretensions would be entirely missing: the pianos, radios, television sets, overstuffed chairs and chesterfields, the clocks, bookcases, and writing-desks, the refrigerators, ranges, and furnaces.

Even tables were probably few and usually small. They do however appear in considerable numbers among lists of furniture on Linear B tablets from the Greek mainland,[2] so that we may surely attribute them also to the people from whom the Mycenaeans derived their civilization. But there is little to show what form these tables took except for a scene on the H. Triadha sarcophagus, which pictures a bull trussed for sacrifice, lying on a large and heavily built table with ponderous turned legs (Fig. 101, 139, E).

Mats and cushions we may suppose were used plentifully, and they may have been used to sit on or recline on as we see guests doing at Egyptian dinner parties. However Egyptians are also frequently represented as seated on chairs at social functions, and we need hardly doubt that the Cretans were also fairly well supplied with seats of various kinds. Instead of, or in addition to, movable seats, some rooms were provided with benches of stone or plastered rubble along the walls, for example the little room, 53, at the northeast entry at Phaistos, the large

[1] *C. and M.*, p. 28.
[2] *DMG*, p. 339, no. 239; p. 341, no. 240; p. 342, no. 241.

Hall, 50, in the Residential Quarter of the same palace (Fig. 47), in Room 4 of the Residential Quarter at H. Triadha (Fig. 69), and again in the Queen's Hall at Knossos. They were also frequent in rooms where religious rites were performed, whether as seats or as shelves for the deposit of cult objects, such as Rooms 23 and 24 on the west side of the Central Court at Phaistos (Fig. 96), in the "Throne Room" and its anteroom at Knossos (Fig. 130), and perhaps in Room 24 of House Za at Mallia (Fig. 26).

One type of wooden chair has fortunately been preserved to us by being translated into stone in the famous throne of the "Throne Room" (Fig. 139, D). Evans, reversing the process, had replicas of this reproduced in wood and placed in the anteroom of the "Throne Room" and in the Hall of the Double-Axes.[3] Most Minoan chairs must have been less formal than this. A gold ring in Minoan style found at Tiryns (Fig. 139, H) shows a cross-legged chair with tall back as the seat for a goddess. This chair could probably be folded, and folding stools (well-known in Egypt) are clearly represented in the "Camp-Stool Fresco" from Knossos (Fig. 139, G). The flexible seat has been rendered more comfortable in this last example with a coverlet thrown over it, and the juncture of the legs is bound with a cord whose ends (mistaken by Evans for a glove)[4] hang down as they do on the Tiryns ring. Other simple forms of stools occur on rings, gems, and seal impressions, while Knossos has yielded two stone specimens of a seat only about 5 in. (13 cm.) high, shaped to fit the human form like the seat of the stone throne itself (Fig. 139, F).

The stone block on which it rested served the throne of the "Throne Room" as a footstool, but separate footstools did exist, as we learn from Linear B tablets,[5] where the ideogram shows a surprising resemblance to the footstool on the Tiryns ring (Fig. 139, H and I).

[3] *Knossos*, IV, pp. 915-919.
[4] The correction was made by Platon, *Kret. Chron.*, 5 (1951), p. 406.
[5] *DMG*, p. 345, nos. 245-246.

Egyptian tables, thrones, chairs, and footstools were often elaborately decorated with inlay in ivory, ebony, and various metals, as we know from actual specimens. The Linear B tablets indicate that the Minoan-Mycenaean culture kept pace. We read, for instance (italicized words are considered uncertain): "two tables of *yew*, of *encircled* type, *containing* box-wood, nine-*footers*, decorated with *running spirals*, inlaid with *silver*," and "one *ebony* chair with golden *back* decorated with birds; and a footstool inlaid with ivory *pomegranates*."[6]

Ivory pieces, including tiny columns, evidently preserved from wooden furniture which has otherwise disappeared, have recently been found at Mycenae (Fig. 136, G, H); and it has been suggested that two examples, strangely reminiscent of Ionic capitals, once decorated footstools (Fig. 139, B, C); both are of appropriate size, 14 in. (36 cm.) long.[7]

Beds appear to be mentioned once in the extant Linear B tablets ("demnia," as in Homer).[8] The fact that they were familiar both in Egypt on the one hand and in the Homeric poems on the other makes it highly probable that they were in use among the upper classes in Crete. A low plaster platform in the corner of a small room of the Residential Quarter at H. Triadha, measuring 6 ft. 8 in. by 3 ft. 2 in. (203 by 97 cm.), it has been suggested, was used as a bed by piling blankets upon it (Fig. 11); but it would have served equally well as a platform for a wooden bed, as in contemporary Egyptian houses at Amarna. Though smaller, 5 ft. by 2 ft. 8 in. (150 by 80 cm.), the platform in the room of the toilet in the Residential Quarter at Knossos may also have been so used (Fig. 12). Evans originally called this the "Room of the Plaster Couch." In general, however, bedrooms were probably on the upper floors.

Chests of many forms, and often finely decorated, were used in Egypt from early times. We may be sure that they were common also in Crete, and used for many purposes. In the

---

[6] *DMG*, pp. 342-343, nos. 241-242.
[7] *DMG*, p. 346, fig. 23.
[8] *DMG*, p. 349, Vn851 (under no. 251).

Odyssey "Helen went to the chests which contained her embroidered dresses, the work of her own hands, and from them, she lifted out the longest and most richly decorated robe, which had lain underneath all the rest, and now glittered like a star."[9]

Remains of wooden chests together with bronze hinges and loop handles have been found at Knossos, but never well enough preserved to give any accurate impression of their size or form. Inscribed tablets were kept in several wooden boxes in a deposit found in the Palace of Minos, and two chests containing arrows, discovered in the "Armory" northwest of the palace, had clearly been tied and sealed.[10] The Town Mosaic, Evans suggested, may have formed part of the inlay decoration of a wooden chest, and classical scholars will be reminded of the elaborate scene depicted on the Corinthian "Chest of Cypselus." The appearance of one common form of Cretan chest is almost certainly represented, translated with obvious literalness from a wooden prototype, in clay coffins of a type much used in the Late Minoan period; a handsome example is illustrated in Fig. 140, D.

Bathrooms were, as we have seen (Ch. v, 3), fairly abundant, but strangely few bathtubs have been found in the houses or palaces. The reason, perhaps, is that they were valuable, readily portable, and could be used in the next world as well as in this —the dead were often buried in them.[11] One tub found in the Palace of Minos (Fig. 140, C) was almost five feet (145 cm.) long; it compares favorably in size with our modern tubs, and is certainly more handsome. Most tubs were however considerably shorter.

A number of candlesticks of various shapes have been found in Crete, but artificial light was ordinarily supplied by lamps burning olive oil.[12] Lamps of many sizes and forms, made of clay, stone, or bronze, were in use. Shallow, open bowls of clay with a projecting nozzle for the wick, and loop or shaft handles,

---

[9] *Odyssey*, 15, 104-108 (Rieu translation).
[10] *Knossos*, IV, pp. 617, 836; cf. III, p. 409, and I, p. 452.
[11] Cf. *DMG*, pp. 338-339; Platon, *Guide*², p. 121.
[12] *Knossos*, II, p. 127 and note 2.

were common (Fig. 140, B). A bronze lamp of this type with a simple incised pattern on the rim has a very long thin handle which could be thrust into a wall to support it (Fig. 140, A); wall niches were perhaps commonly used as a place to put lamps, as in the bathroom of House E at Mallia (Ch. v, 3). Stone lamps were often handsomely decorated (Fig. 140, G), and sometimes were made in one piece with a tall stand (Fig. 94, right foreground). This latter form includes the aristocrats of Minoan lamps. The stone, often of a fine purple variety, is sometimes carved in the form of a column with spreading foot, decorated shaft, and distinct capital (Fig. 140, J), clearly influenced by Egyptian column forms.

The finest known pedestaled lamp has a shaft adorned with ivy leaves and a hollow spiral groove, and was found in the Pillar Crypt of the Southeast House at Knossos.[13] Lamps have frequently been found in these dark, ground floor cult rooms, also in bathrooms (Fig. 81), and in association with stairways. A fine pedestaled lamp was found in position on a step leading to the dais in the Hall of the Royal Villa.[14]

Heat was supplied by portable clay hearths on three legs, or by small clay braziers with a handle for easy carrying (Fig. 140, E).[15] One "tripod hearth" from Knossos had a diameter of three feet (90 cm.), but this is small in comparison with the great fixed hearths in the megarons of the colder Mycenaean mainland (Fig. 150); one at Pylos measures thirteen feet across (4.02 m.). A specimen in the "Tomb of the Tripod Hearth" at Knossos still contained some of the charcoal fuel (Fig. 140, F). Fire rakes and tongs are mentioned in the Linear B tablets.[16]

No built fireplaces for cooking have been found in the service quarters of the palaces or houses (Ch. vii, 1). A common type of cooking pot, evidently to be placed directly over the fire, is

[13] *Knossos*, II, p. 481, fig. 288a; Platon, *Guide*², pl. 6, 2.
[14] *Knossos*, II, p. 404.
[15] Fixed hearths are rare; one was reported at Mallia, House Zb, *Mallia, Maisons*, II, p. 12.
[16] *DMG*, p. 337, no. 237.

a bronze cauldron mounted on three legs. Two types are illustrated in Fig. 140, H and K. The later form, H, is the prototype of the Classical Greek tripod, often used as a prize from Homeric times on, and already known under that name by the Mycenaean Greeks, for a tablet found recently at Pylos mentions tripods several times and accompanies the text with perfectly recognizable little pictures (ideograms) of Bronze Age types of tripods (Fig. 140, I); they are further described as "of Cretan workmanship."[17] As a matter of fact the correspondence of the reading "t(i)-ri-po-de" and the ideogram on this tablet (Fig. 147), found after the decipherment had been announced, helped to prove that the language of the tablets had been correctly identified as an early form of Greek.

Clay pots in a wide assortment of shapes and sizes were provided for the cook, and many strange objects whose use is difficult to determine. Some have been ingeniously identified by excavators who have carefully noted any traces of the original contents of a vessel, or have observed similar objects still in use among modern peoples.[18] Various types of pots are shown in Fig. 141, also a funnel, an egg stand (?), a grill, and a spit support (M) for roasting those succulent morsels of lamb the Greeks today call "souflahkia." Bronze Age heroes enjoyed them too, and Homer describes the process with evident appreciation: Achilles "sliced well the meat and pierced it through with spits, and (his squire) made the fire burn high. Then when the fire was burned down and the flame waned, he scattered the embers and laid the spits thereover, resting them on the spit-racks, when he had sprinkled them with holy salt" (*Iliad*, 9, 210-214).[19]

The circular object about a foot and a half (44 cm.) high and a little less in diameter, illustrated in two views in Fig. 141, A, was obviously designed for some specific purpose. The

[17] *DMG*, p. 336, no. 236.
[18] Chapouthier, *REA*, 43 (1941), pp. 5-15.
[19] The identification and the references to modern and Homeric practice are due to Chapouthier, *idem*, pp. 12-14. A grill similar to Fig. 141, D, has recently been found in Attica, *Praktika*, 1955, p. 114, pl. 36d; it is dated E.H. III.

shallow bottom compartment was intended for the fire, no doubt of charcoal; the deep upper compartment, readily accessible through a large slot in the side, was perhaps designed for long slow cooking, somewhat like a modern "deep-well cooker."[20] The object from Palaikastro (Fig. 141, B) must have served a similar purpose.

Storage jars and vessels were abundant and varied. Characteristic examples are the two-handled "amphoras" no doubt often used for wine (Fig. 141, F); and the huge yet often handsomely decorated "pithoi" already discussed in connection with storerooms (Ch. VII, 1, and Fig. 92).

Metal vessels are rarely preserved. Typical forms of pans, bowls, pitchers, ewers, etc. are illustrated in Fig. 142. Four huge bronze cauldrons made out of large sheets of metal riveted together, and in places repaired with bronze patches, were found in one of the rooms of House A at Tylissos. Three of these were round and had diameters ranging from 2½ to 3½ ft. (72 to 105 cm.); the fourth was hemispherical (Fig. 142, G) with a diameter of 4½ ft. (ca. 140 cm.) and a weight of 115 lbs. (52 kg.).[21]

Pitchers, bowls, cups, and goblets in a wide range of shapes and sizes were available for eating purposes (Figs. 141, 143). The forms even in plain ware are often very pleasing; the finer ware was decorated with that Minoan eye for beauty which made it by far the handsomest pottery of its day. The earlier "Kamares" style pottery (M.M. II) was painted with a fine feeling for color, movement, and the relation of the design to the shape of the vase (Fig. 153, A). In the later Palace Period (L.M. I-II) equally attractive effects result from informally arranged motives derived from natural forms: octopus, nautilus, starfish, molluscs, and plant life from both sea and land (Fig. 153, B). To find the Cretans using graceful vases with small holes in the bottom, surely flowerpots, is therefore no great surprise (Fig. 141, J).

[20] *Mallia, Maisons*, I, pp. 91-92, pls. 39, 1 and 2; 58, 4.
[21] *Knossos*, II, pp. 569-570, fig. 355: *Ephemeris*, 1912, p. 221, fig. 29.

The looting of the palaces and the failure to locate any intact royal burials has left us with no fine examples of vessels of gold or silver found in Crete. A small silver pitcher and three bowls, one decorated with a simple spiral pattern, were excavated in the South House at Knossos;[22] and recently a gold bowl with similar design has been found in a grave.[23] A few shallow loop-handled bowls in bronze give us an idea of the perfection of design and craftsmanship to be expected, although these exhibit only simple patterns (Fig. 142, I).

The dearth of fine quality metalwork from Crete is in strange contrast to the wealth of material from the late Middle Bronze and Late Bronze Age mainland: the gold and silver vessels (we are not concerned here with the magnificent metal daggers, decorative pieces, masks, etc.) from the two Shaft Grave Circles at Mycenae (ca. 1600 B.C.),[24] the Octopus Cup from Dendra,[25] and the superb pair of Vaphio Cups from a tomb near Sparta (Fig. 143, F), to mention only a few of the finest. The Minoan style and subject matter of much of this metalwork can only mean that it was the product "of Cretan workmanship," as the Pylos Linear B tablets put it. Possibly such precious objects were acquired by the Mycenaean Greeks through legitimate trade or during the period of their occupation of Crete, but, remembering that the Homeric heroes were numbered among their descendants, it is likely that often they were the rewards of piracy or war.

No attempt has been made in our account to speak of cult objects used in the ubiquitous small shrines: altars, small idols, cult symbols, incense burners, libation vessels, and so on (Figs. 100, 101). Nor have we included small objects of personal use such as mirrors, caskets for jewelry or beauty lotions, toilet articles, razors, etc., nor the tools of craftsmen or agriculturists, found in the palaces or houses. If the reader has obtained some

[22] *Knossos*, II, p. 387, fig. 221.
[23] *BSA*, 51 (1956), pp. 87-92, fig. 5 and pl. 13.
[24] Mylonas, *Anc. Myc.*, chapters v and vi.
[25] Persson, *Royal Tombs at Dendra near Midea*, pp. 43-46, pls. 9-11.

idea of the kind of furnishings characteristically found in the living quarters, public halls, kitchens, and service rooms of upper-class dwellings, that is as much as can be hoped for even after sixty years of excavation and discovery.

2. WATER SUPPLY AND DRAINAGE

Our knowledge of how the Minoan palaces were supplied with water for drinking and other purposes is almost entirely confined to Knossos. A few cisterns have been discovered at Phaistos,[26] but no wells or springs, owing to the nature of the ground. The only drainage system of any complexity is also a feature of the Palace of Minos.

Even at Knossos the sources and methods of supplying water are only partially understood. Several wells have been discovered in the palace area, and one a little to the northwest of the Little Palace. The last, cleaned out to its original three-foot (1 m.) diameter and forty-two foot (ca. 12½ m.) depth, continues to furnish an excellent supply of drinking water.[27]

That the inhabitants at Knossos did not rely on wells alone but were supplied with running water is indicated by the discovery, beneath the palace floors, of lengths of terracotta piping. The clay pipes, made in sections about 2 to 2½ ft. long (60 to 75 cm.), were carefully flanged to fit into one another, and the joints were tightly cemented (Fig. 139, A). This would make a pressure system feasible. That the Minoans did understand and utilize the principle that water seeks its own level is further shown "by the discovery of the Minoan conduit heading towards the Palace from the pure limestone spring of Mavrokolybo and implying a descending and subsequently ascending channel."[28]

[26] The "cisterns" at the southwestern corner of the Palace of Mallia are surely granaries (in any case this is not the corner to pick for keeping water cool, though excellent for keeping grain dry)—see Ch. VII, 1, note 11. Lawrence believes that the very deep stone-lined pits ("keeps" Evans called them) at Knossos were really cisterns, *Gk. Arch.* p. 298, note 2; *JHS,* 62 (1942), pp. 84-85.

[27] *Knossos,* III, p. 254.

[28] *Knossos,* III, p. 252. R. W. Hutchinson thinks that the Knossos water-supply came from the "excellent and perennial spring on Gypsádhes," which served the Caravanserai; "an extension of this conduit could well have been carried along

The sections of clay pipe resemble those in use in Classical Greek times, though Evans claims they were more efficiently designed; each section was rather strongly tapered toward one end, with the purpose of increasing the speed of flow of the water and thus helping to flush any sediment through the pipe.[29]

The clay tubs in the Minoan bathrooms must have been filled and emptied by hand (Fig. 140, C). However, in the "Caravan-serai," a rest house on the cross-island route just south of the palace, a footbath for the weary traveler was supplied by a direct pipe, and the overflow was taken care of by another conduit; a branch of the water channel also served a drinking trough (Fig. 3). Nearby Evans excavated a Spring House consisting of a well-built stone chamber. Within this was a stone-lined basin, a foot and a half deep (45 cm.), through whose pebble bottom a spring welled up, and indeed still does to some degree; the stones of the basin were deeply worn by those who came there to fill their jars in the days of Minos.[30]

Rainwater from the flat roofs of the palace at Knossos was carried off by vertical pipes, one of which in the eastern wing emptied on to a stone drainhead from which a stone channel carried the flow of water.[31]

Surface water from part of the Central Court of the Palace of Minos was taken care of by a very capacious underground channel built of stone and lined with cement, which ran beneath the passage leading from the North Entrance and received several affluents from various quarters. The most fully explored portion of the palace drainage system is that which ran beneath the floors of the Residential Quarter (Fig. 12).[32] This formed a great loop with its high point under the light-well beside the Grand Staircase, and emptied via a combined channel down the slope to the east of the palace. In the area of the Hall of the Double-Axes and the Queen's Hall with its associated chambers

the viaduct across the bridge and so to the southern limits of the palace," *Town Planning Review*, 21 (1950), p. 212.

[29] *Knossos*, III, pp. 252-253.   [30] *Knossos*, II, pp. 123-128.

[31] *Knossos*, I, pp. 378-379.   [32] *Knossos*, I, pp. 226-230.

it received the drainage water from no less than five light-wells; it served a toilet on the lowest floor, and was connected with three vertical shafts which evidently received rainwater from the roof and were also probably connected with toilets on the upper floors. The drain was built of stone blocks, lined with cement, and measured about 31 by 15 in. (79 by 38 cm.) in section, quite large enough to permit men to enter it, for cleaning purposes, through manholes provided for the purpose. Airshafts at intervals also helped to ventilate the drains.

CHAPTER XIII

PROCEDURES AND PRINCIPLES

1. MEASURING AND PLANNING THE PALACES

ONE OF THE MOST intriguing yet most dangerous intellectual pastimes the archaeologist can indulge in is the attempt to determine what unit of measurement was employed in the planning and construction of the architectural remains he is studying. With a little luck and a considerable amount of ingenuity (with which he is often overly supplied) the well-meaning but incautious investigator can evoke the most astonishing results from the most unpromising set of data.

On the other hand if he is too cautious he may over hastily conclude that no unit of measurement was used at all, or one so imprecise or so laxly applied that it cannot be detected by an examination of the architectural remains. In general, the more regular and uniform the workmanship—accurate right angles and close coincidence of dimensions between similar elements in the plan, well dressed masonry laid in regular coursing, and so on—the more reasonable it will be to assume that some definite unit was actually employed in the construction, and the greater the chance of being able to detect it.

The solution may come much more quickly if a known unit with a known value or range of values is likely to have been in use in the area under investigation, for then one can test these values of the unit directly on the data being studied. This was the situation when, some years ago, I was studying for publication a series of houses of the fifth and fourth centuries B.C., excavated at the site of Olynthos in northern Greece.[1]

---

[1] *Olynthus*, VIII, pp. 45-51.

It was the practice of the house builders in this city to paint the upper part of the plastered wall, in the better rooms of the better houses, in a single color, usually red; and the lower part of the wall in a contrasting color, commonly white. This white dado was evidently an imitation of a course of masonry blocks supporting a wall of some other material, and it was therefore often marked off with accurately ruled horizontal and vertical lines, incised in the surface of the plaster before it had set. It was obvious that the intervals between the vertical incised lines, suggesting the individual blocks, had in some cases been carefully measured, for the same length often occurred repeatedly on the walls of the same room and, even more significantly, on the walls of rooms in different houses. Surprisingly, however, not one but two sets of measurements, each apparently incommensurate with the other, were found: one approximating 2 ft. 10¾ in. (88 cm.), the other 3 ft. 2½ in. (98 cm.). But the answer was not far to seek. Two foot-standards were in common use in Greece at this period, and both must have been current contemporaneously at Olynthos: a shorter "Ionic" foot of 11⅝ in. (29.5 cm.), and a longer "Doric" foot of 12⅞ in. (32.7 cm.). Both sets of wall blocks were therefore measured in three-foot intervals ($3 \times 29.5 = 88.5$ cm.; $3 \times 32.7 = 98.1$ cm.).

This then is one type of measurement which the investigator may hope will yield a determination of the linear unit, namely comparatively short and closely measurable distances set out in *whole* numbers of that unit, and repeating frequently enough to avoid any danger of mere coincidence.

At the same site many complete blocks of identical dimensions were discovered, and such blocks, as we know from other regularly planned Greek cities, were usually laid out in round numbers of feet, such as 200 by 120. The Olynthian blocks were evidently designed to measure 300 by 120 "Ionic" feet; the width of a block, ca. 35½ m., divided by 120, yields a foot of between 29.5 and 29.6 cm. (11⅝ in.).

Here then is a second type of measurement that may be expected to assist in determining the standard of length, namely a comparatively long interval laid out in *round* numbers of the unit, recurring with sufficient frequency to rule out the possibility of coincidence.

But to return to our Bronze Age palaces—here we are forced to work almost entirely in the dark even as to the general unit likely to have been employed. The cubit is known to have been in use at this period in Egypt and the Near East with values in the neighborhood of 20 in. (ca. 50 cm.). Of the foot used as a linear standard before the Iron Age no reliable evidence has so far been presented; on the other hand, there is no good reason for believing that it may *not* have been in use in the Bronze Age.

The solution I propose was not reached as a result of a deliberate search for a linear unit, but was the by-product of a series of precise measurements made in studying the recesses of the west façades of the palaces and the related problem of windows (Ch. ix, 1). The west front of the Magazine Block at Phaistos (Fig. 48), with its symmetrical recesses, was found to repeat the same measurement very accurately four times: 3.34 m., or, on the English foot-standard, 10 ft. 11¼ in. After trying vainly to fit this to a system of cubit measures the next step was clearly to test the possibility that the Minoan builder had measured this interval as eleven feet on his scale. This would mean a foot actually much closer to the value of the modern English foot than were the Classical Greek feet mentioned above, in fact only about ¹⁄₁₆ in. (a little over 1 mm.) short. The near coincidence is of course of no significance, except to show that the proposed Minoan foot-length is a perfectly reasonable one.

Proof or disproof of the use by the Minoan Cretans of a foot of approximately 11¹⁵⁄₁₆ in., or 30.36 cm., can only be obtained by a systematic and intensive testing of all the available data. Here there is space to give but a few examples.[2]

On the south side of the same projecting block at Phaistos another recess measures 3.02 m. = 9 ft. 11½ in. = almost exactly 10 Minoan feet, or "10 M. ft." as we will abbreviate it. To the north of the Grand Propylon another recess and the two adjacent wall faces repeat the measurement 2.74 m. three times; 2.74 m. = 9 M. ft. (In this and in what follows we omit giving the measurement also in English feet, in order to avoid confusion.)

Further support comes from the palace at Mallia where the spacing, 3.31 m., nearly identical with the 11 M. ft. interval with which we started at Phaistos, occurs twice on the west front (Fig. 58). Just south of this the main projecting element of the façade has a broad central recess balanced by two plain units of wall on either side; the recess measures 6.06 m., the wall units, 6.03 and 6.09 m., each approximately 20 M. ft. (6.072 m.). The width of the entire element is 18.19 m. or 60 M. ft.; 60 × 30.36 cm. = 18.216 m.

As the reader will have observed, the evidence provided by the length of the recesses and the adjacent wall faces is strictly analogous to the even three-foot intervals marked on the wall plaster, which were found to be a useful guide to the foot-standard in use at Olynthos. (Actually some of the intervals between incised lines on Minoan stuccoed walls are measurable in even numbers of Minoan feet, but they are too few to avoid the possibility of coincidence.) It will be equally clear that the sixty-foot width of the projecting façade element at Mallia finds its analogy in the long intervals, expressible in round numbers of feet, found in the dimensions of the Olynthian blocks.

Nor is this likely to be mere coincidence. For the 18.19 m. = 60 M. ft. long façade element at Mallia reappears on the west

[2] For a more detailed discussion see *AJA*, 64 (1960), pp. 335-341.

façade at Gournia—18.13 m., and in the earlier palace at Phaistos—18.24 m., while at Knossos the two main projections of the façade amount to 36.23 m. = 120 M. ft., and four projecting elements amount to 60.54 m. = 200 M. ft. (Fig. 83).[2a]

If the elements of the palace west façades were laid off in round numbers of Minoan feet, the possibility suggests itself that other of the more regular parts of the palaces were similarly designed, and if so perhaps we can get some idea of the Minoan architect's procedure in planning a palace.

Of the three major palaces the most promising one with which to begin the experiment is the last palace at Phaistos, since it gives the impression of having been designed as a unified whole, or nearly so.[3] An extensive series of measurements made on the site in 1959 is the basis of the results shown in Fig. 144, and these do in fact appear to indicate that the areas of the palace to the west and immediately to the north of the Central Court, that is the most regularly planned parts of the palace, fall into a system of round numbers of Minoan feet.

It looks as if the unknown architect of the Phaistos palace had proceeded more methodically than his celebrated colleague, Daedalus, who built the Labyrinth at Knossos. Hypothetically we can trace his procedure somewhat as follows. First he laid out two base lines or axes, one running north to south, the other, exactly at right angles to this, east to west; the point of intersection, the focus or "origin" of the system of coordinates, may be termed "X." He then measured off a distance of 170 M. ft. on the north-south line south of X to mark the west edge of the west stylobate of the Central Court,[4] while on the east-west line he measured off 80 M. ft. east of X to determine the line

[2a] The frequency of the occurrence of 60, and once of 120, is noteworthy, and finds a parallel in numerals on Linear A tablets: "Minoan numbers follow a decimal system, and there is no doubt that the Minoans counted in hundreds. . . . That the Minoans also counted sexagesimally for some purposes is not only likely in itself, but also witnessed by a tablet from Phaistos (Ph. 2) where the account is composed of three items of sixty each," *BSA*, 55 (1960), p. 204. Cf. Palmer, *Mycenaeans and Minoans*, pp. 118-119.

[3] Cf. *Festòs*, II, pp. 13-14.

[4] *Festòs*, II, p. 8.

of façade at the north end of the Central Court, and 100 M.ft. west of X to define the south face of the north wall of the Magazine Block (Fig. 144). The east and south boundaries of the Central Court could then be determined by projecting them from the points already established.

Next the north-south width of the Magazine Block was established at 50 M.ft., and this block constructed with very thick walls because of the importance and height of the three storeys they were designed to carry (Ch. vi, 1). North of this block 45 M.ft. were assigned to the monumental stairway of approach. Parallel to and 60 M.ft. west of the north-south axis through X a line was drawn to mark 1) the west face of the great columned opening at the head of the stairway 66-67; 2) the west face of the heavy transverse wall running between 30-36 and 31-37 in the Magazine Block (probably intended to support a pier-and-door partition in the hall above); and 3) the west façade of a block of rooms to be built to the south of the Magazine Block. South of this last block another block was constructed with its west façade laid out 70 M.ft. west of the north-south axis; the combined length of the two blocks south of the Magazine Block from north to south was set at 120 M.ft.

Finally the wall lines forming the north side of the Propylon were projected eastward and returned southward to form the north and east walls of the important block of rooms north of the Central Court, in the upper storeys of which, we have suggested, the Banquet Hall or Halls were located (Ch. vi, 2).

The rest of the palace is less regularly laid out, and it would be useless to attempt to follow our architect further, except to note once again that the elements of the elaborate façade at the north end of the Central Court were carefully worked out in a symmetrical scheme in even numbers of Minoan feet (Figs. 50, 145, and Ch. ii, 2, p. 37).

The lines and measurements established by the architect were not always precisely adhered to by the builders, sometimes for good practical reasons, sometimes probably through sheer care-lessness. Thus the actual position of some of the details of the symmetrical façade just mentioned vary somewhat from their "predicted values," partly perhaps to improve the position of the south window of the Banquet Hall; the west line of the west stylobate of the Central Court veers off about one foot too far to the east at X, possibly to allow Stairway 39 a little extra width; and the south face of the north wall of the Magazine Blocks works somewhat south of its true position. But the original design is still discernible in the completed work to a remarkable degree.

The more complicated history of partial rebuilding and re-peated repair, plus modern restorations, would be sufficient to obscure the planning of the Palace of Minos, with the exception of the dimensioning of the west façade already spoken of. But Mallia, as our Fig. 146 shows, seems to illustrate a process of planning parallel to that more fully visible at Phaistos.

In closing it may be pointed out that the designing of build-ings in round numbers is not only a procedure which appeals to the reason, but for which there is good precedent. The builder of the Great Pyramid, a millennium earlier, laid out each side of the base to be 440 cubits, its height to be 280 cubits, and the dimensions of the king's chamber to be 10 by 20 cubits.[5] And about 1400 B.C. Amenhotpe III determined the dimensions of the lake to be built for his wife as 3700 by 700 cubits.[6]

Whether the Mycenaeans used a foot with the Minoan value is not yet clear, though the uncertainly translated description of tables in the Linear B tablets as "six-*footers*" and "nine-*footers*" may indicate that at least they did use a foot as a linear measure.[7] It certainly would be natural to suppose that

[5] Badawy, *A History of Egyptian Architecture*, I (1954), p. 135. The maximum error in the length of the four sides of the base amounts to about two-fifths of a cubit (7.9 in.).

[6] Baldwin Smith, *Eg. Arch.*, p. 219.

[7] *DMG*, pp. 339-341, nos. 239-240. However, Emmett Bennett, a leading authority on Linear B, has recently pointed out to me that the "feet" always occur in multiples of three, and he therefore suspects that each leg of a three-legged

the use of the foot as a standard of measurement was inherited by the Classical Greeks from their Bronze Age predecessors, and therefore it may not be merely a coincidence that, according to Oscar Broneer (*AJA*, 72 [1968], p. 159), the stadia at Epidauros and the Isthmia and probably the Temple at Nemea—all three sites in an area of strong Mycenaean traditions—were laid out on a foot of 30.2 cm., i.e. only about one and a half millimeters short of the Minoan foot. See further **Addendum 5**.

2. THE ORIGINS OF MINOAN ARCHITECTURE

Before going on to consider the principles of Minoan architecture it may be wise to see whether some light can be shed on this difficult subject by a discussion of the origins of the Cretan palaces, for it is a reasonable supposition that an examination of their prototypes, if they can be found, should reveal something of the essential character of Cretan palace planning.

It has often been remarked that the Minoan palaces seem to appear with something of the sudden maturity of an Athena born full-armed from the head of Zeus. This suddenness can be explained on various hypotheses: that we have simply failed to find the earlier stages belonging to the Early Minoan period —and it must be admitted that we know little enough[7a] of Cretan architecture in the third millennium B.C.; that the palace type was evolved somewhere outside Crete and was imported as an almost ready-made foreign product; or that in response to certain needs the palace plan was suddenly created at, say, Knossos,[8] emerging fully formed (or nearly so) from the brain of some Cretan Daedalus, in much the same fashion as the first

---

table may have been decoratively equipped with more than one "foot"; such a table could therefore have been described as "six-foot" or "nine-foot."

[7a] Add now P. Warren, *Myrtos: An Early Bronze Age Settlement in Crete* (London, 1972), and A. Zois' recent work at Vasiliki.

[8] So Rodenwaldt suggested in a review of *Mallia*, I, published in *Gnomon*, 5 (1929), pp. 177-184 (especially p. 183), with much of which I find myself in agreement in the present section.

great complex of stone buildings was created for King Zoser by the genius of Imhotep a century earlier than the building of the Pyramids of Giza.

Against the first possibility is the fact that no considerable buildings earlier than the beginning of the Middle Minoan period have been uncovered on the sites of the three major palaces. However the recent discovery of two palaces earlier than the one known for half a century as the "First Palace" at Phaistos, in the course of exploring deeper levels at that site, warns us that more surprises of this sort are not impossible. Indeed the unsatisfactory state of our knowledge of the chronology of the palaces and of their form even in the Middle Minoan period, plus the recent doubts cast on the dating of the final stages of the Palace of Minos, has discouraged any effort to trace the evolution of palace architecture in the present study. It is essential, we believe, first to understand as completely as possible the palaces in the final forms that the excavators' spades have revealed.

The second possibility mentioned above is that the palace type originated elsewhere and was simply imported into Crete; and this indeed is what Sir Arthur Evans supposed: "We see, in fact, the more or less simultaneous introduction into the Island at various points of an already stereotyped model. That this model was derived from an Eastern source is a reasonable conclusion."[9] Sir Arthur believed that the earliest form of the Palace of Minos was a series of blocks or *insulae* built around a large court; only gradually did this coalesce into a single coherent structure which, however, continued to betray its earlier condition by a pattern of vestigial corridors. The plans of the palaces at Mallia and Phaistos fail to support the *insula* hypothesis, and few if any students of Minoan architecture still adhere to this view.

The theory that the Cretan type of palace was imported ready-made has not disappeared, however. Sir Leonard Woolley, on the basis of his recent excavations at Alalakh (Tel Atchana)

[9] *Knossos*, II, p. 269.

in Syria, has restated this view in a particularly violent form: "We are bound to believe," he tells us, "that trained experts, members of the Architects' and Painters' Guilds, were invited to travel overseas from Asia (possibly from Alalakh itself, seeing that it had its Mediterranean harbour) to build and decorate the palaces of the Cretan rulers."[10] Other British excavators, Seton Lloyd and James Mellaart, who are excavating a Bronze Age palace at Beycesultan in western Turkey (Fig. 1, inset), have been almost equally positive about the close resemblance of their palace to the Cretan.[11] Nevertheless the Alalakh and the Beycesultan palaces bear no resemblance to one another. The excavator at Mari on the Euphrates, M. Parrot, has compared his palace (Fig. 148) with the Minoan, though he gives no details. Others have followed suit. Thus Hood of the British School, in a review of *Festòs* II, remarks that "the similarities in methods of construction, and even in details of design and decoration, between the Palace architecture of Crete and that of the contemporary Near East (e.g. the Palaces at Mari and Atchana) are in fact very striking, and might have been worth elaborating in so full a study as this" (of the last palace at Phaistos).[12] L. R. Palmer likewise uses the similarity between the Beycesultan and the Cretan palaces, claimed by the British archaeologists, as further evidence for the Luvian character of the Minoans.[12a]

That resemblances do exist between the Cretan and the Near Eastern palaces in some respects can scarcely be denied, and likewise, as Lawrence declares in his recent book on *Greek Architecture*, between Cretan and Egyptian architecture.[13]

There are resemblances of a general nature, especially be-

[10] Woolley, *A Forgotten Kingdom*, London, 1953, p. 77. The definitive publication, *Alalakh* (1955) fails to provide specific proof of the connection between the palaces of Alalakh and Crete (cf. pp. 116, 228).

[11] *Anatolian Studies*, 5 (1955), pp. 39-92; 6 (1956), pp. 101-135; 7 (1957), pp. 27-36; 10 (1960), pp. 31-41; *London Times*, Sept. 24, 1954, pp. 9-10; Aug. 1, 1955, pp. 7, 9.

[12] *Gnomon*, 26 (1954), p. 375.

[12a] *Mycenaeans and Minoans*, pp. 239-240.

[13] pp. 22, 23, 28, 34, 39, etc.; cf. *BSA*, 46 (1951), p. 83.

tween the Mari palace and the Minoan (Fig. 148): rooms are arranged around courts; different quarters of the palaces are used for specific purposes—storage, work, worship, residence, etc.; there are bathrooms with clay bathtubs, audience halls; and so on. But within the limits of this broad likeness the differences are so profound and so deep-rooted that who can positively say whether one type of palace architecture is really influencing the other to any significant degree? Certain general methods of construction are also widely spread, such as "half-timbering" and the use of orthostates; but where these arose and when and how they spread, again who can definitely say?

There are also some resemblances in detail, between, for example, the clay pipe sections at Mari and Knossos (Fig. 139, A), or between Cretan fluted column shafts and possibly some capitals (if the capitals on some Cretan stone lamps were also employed in architecture) and Egyptian columns; mural painting is also an area of contact to a limited extent.

But all this is very far from substantiating the extreme claims of the Alalakh and Beycesultan excavators. The comparisons they themselves have drawn between their palaces and the Cretan are often very forced, and even taken cumulatively are, in my opinion, practically valueless. To discuss the matter in detail would be impossible in the space available here, and, since the results would be almost entirely negative, would achieve no useful purpose.[14]

The available evidence suggests, to my mind, that when the palaces first came into being around 2000 B.C. the Cretan architects, though aware in a general way of palace architecture elsewhere, created forms suited to, and determined by, Cretan needs and the Cretan environment, and employed constructional techniques traditional to the eastern Mediterranean and with which they were already in general familiar. In the course of construc-

[14] For a detailed discussion, see my paper "The Relations of the Minoan Palaces to the Near Eastern Palaces of the Second Millennium," published in E. L. Bennett (ed.), *Mycenaean Studies* (Madison, Wisconsin, 1964), pp. 195-215.

tion and reconstruction in the centuries that followed, the architects, reacting to changing needs and to the experience gained from long habitation of the palaces, developed more efficient and more peculiarly local forms, forms which were in some measure affected by the architecture of their overseas neighbors, as increasing wealth and culture in Crete fostered a desire to make the structures more comfortable and more pleasing to the eye. For new decorative forms they turned especially to Egypt, as Mycenae would later draw upon Crete, and Rome in turn on Greece. The possible adoption of the Egyptian type of banquet hall when Minoan kings wished, in imitation of the pharaohs, to add this luxury feature, would fall in the same category (Ch. VI, 2).

We have thus moved to the third possibility mentioned at the beginning of this section as to the most probable explanation for the sudden appearance of the Cretan palace type in an already well developed form, namely that in its main outlines it was created by some Cretan Imhotep for his Cretan Zoser. The outside influences mentioned above do not alter the essentially native character of Cretan architecture, which seems to have arisen and developed as independently of "foreign aid" as the Cretan system of writing. The truly distinctive features of the Cretan palaces are not derived from other architectures, for example the "Cretan Hall," the pier-and-door partition, the light-well, the use of alabaster veneering, the sunken bathroom or lustral chamber, the downward tapering column, the column oval in cross-section, the porticoed central courts, the alternating pier-and-column scheme, the columned propylon, the terraced and porticoed gardens of the residential quarters, the use of monumental stairways, and the system of putting the main public rooms on the upper floors.

If our conclusions regarding the native character of Cretan palace architecture are correct we must abandon any hope of assistance from foreign archetypes in the study of the principles of Minoan architecture, the topic of our final section.

3. PRINCIPLES OF MINOAN
ARCHITECTURE

To some students of Minoan architecture the title of our final section may appear highly misleading. How can Minoan architecture, they will ask, lay claim to being founded on any "principles"—an architecture which has been termed "incomprehensible, confusing, illogical, irrational, primitive"?[15] There are those who regard the development of the Minoan palaces as little more than the casual growth of groups of rooms about an open space; Zervos pictures the palace as enlarging spasmodically in much the way a city enlarges in response to increases in population, wealth, and material importance.[16] Lawrence in his recent handbook on *Greek Architecture* refers to the palaces as "confusedly planned," as an "apparently insane jigsaw," as a "senseless agglomeration," and as an "illogical disorderly growth."[17] One might infer that the tale of Daedalus building the Labyrinth to confuse the Minotaur is to be understood as a symbolic statement of the normal procedure of the Minoan architect.

That critics familiar with Classical Greek architecture should be shocked and baffled by the Minoan palaces is not surprising. The principles of design embodied in a building like the Parthenon are immediately apparent: bilateral symmetry, like a living organism; a single chamber for its divine occupant, balanced by a porch at either end; outside, from whatever point of view, a continuous circuit of columns closed above by the horizontal lines of the roof—simplicity, clarity, unity.

---

[15] *Festòs*, II, p. 475, quoting Rodenwaldt and Snijder.

[16] *L'art de la Crète*, p. 497.

[17] Lawrence, *Gk. Arch.*, pp. 34, 41, 291, and *BSA*, 46 (1951), pp. 81, 83. Yet Hugh Plommer in his recent book *Anc. and Class. Arch.*, p. 75, remarks that "Cnossus was admirably planned." Seton Lloyd has also recently written, "Cretan planning has been described by the adjective 'agglutinative,' and the familiar association of the Palace of Minos with the legend of the Labyrinth has perhaps tended to over-emphasize the complexity of its arrangement and come to suggest a haphazard and unconsidered agglomeration of miscellaneous units. That this impression is a false one has in the past frequently been shown by intelligent analyses and comparisons of the buildings concerned," *Anatolian Studies*, 6 (1956), p. 119.

It is only natural that such critics should seek for some simple unifying principle of logic and order in the architecture of the Cretan palace and, failing to find it readily, declare that the corresponding Minoan trinity must be complexity, obscurity, multiplicity.

As a preliminary move to a fresh consideration of the problem let us clear the ground by making a few general observations. In the first place we must bear in mind that the "horrifying complexity of what remains," as Lawrence puts it, is made up of little but the "basement."[18] For, though not really an excavated "cellar" in the modern sense, most of the ground floor was used for service purposes: storerooms, workrooms, small shrines, and the like. Almost the only important rooms in this storey were those composing the principal floor of the residential quarter. Secondly, it should be noted that most discussions of palace aesthetics have been based largely or entirely on the Palace of Minos, and a glance at the plans (Fig. 7) is sufficient to show how much more labyrinthine was its ground floor than that of its sister palaces. This was at least in part due to the frequent partial rebuildings to which Knossos was subjected as the result of repeated damage from earthquake or hostile attack.

Again we must remember that these palaces served a multiplicity of purposes. They were not merely the residence of the sovereign, they were storehouses for the king's wealth; factories for the production of quality goods for royal use; sanctuaries where the cult of the gods, whose chief concern was the king, was centered; administrative offices where the records of the state were kept and the daily routine of government was conducted; possibly courts where the monarch dispensed justice to his subjects;—in addition they must express the power and dignity of the king, and contain facilities for worthily receiving and entertaining important visitors from home and abroad. It is a simple matter for a one-purpose building, such as a temple or a pleasure palace like that of Akhenaton at Amarna, to be

[18] *Gk. Arch.*, p. 34.

simple, unified, and symmetrically planned (Fig. 149); sweeping generalizations on the basis of the plan of the Palace of Minos, such as the one "that the Cretan genius is asymmetric," should not be too hastily adopted.[19]

The complexity of the present remains, then, should not cause us to leap to the conclusion that the palaces were virtually unplanned. Indeed the remarkable similarity in the general design of the three major palaces as well as in detailed parts such as the residential quarter, the orientation and size of the central court, the arrangement of magazines, etc., would be difficult to explain except as the result of deliberate planning.

To attempt to discover the nature of that planning it will be best to turn first to Mallia and Phaistos, where the last state of the palaces appears to represent, by and large, a single stage of planning and construction, comparatively free from the complications met with in the Palace of Minos. They may be taken as illustrating an approximation of the "ideal" Minoan palace plan.

Let us begin with the palace at Phaistos (Fig. 4). Unfortunately its ground plan is not quite complete, for whatever rooms may have existed along the south end and the southern part of the east side of the Central Court have been lost to erosion. The remainder falls quite easily into fairly clearly marked areas or quarters: 1) guest rooms and cult rooms, west of the Central Court and south of Corridor 7; 2) magazines and entranceway, north of the same corridor; 3) service rooms, the area north and northeast of the Central Court except north of Court 48; 4) main residential quarter, north of Court 48; 5) secondary residential quarter, east of the Central Court; 6) the Central Court, 40. Above 2), part of 3), and possibly above 1), were the main public rooms.

[19] An instructive example is provided by the "Palace of the Rulers" at Eshnunna in Mesopotamia, built about 2000 B.C., which exhibits no symmetry of design, yet the two contiguous and contemporaneous temples on either side present almost perfect illustrations of bilateral symmetry about a medial axis, Frankfort, op.cit., fig. 19.

The Mallia palace also exhibits clearly marked quarters (Fig. 162): 1) cult rooms, vi and vii, west of the Central Court; 2) storerooms, i, viii, xx, along the west façade; 3) cult rooms (?), xviii, at the southwest corner of the palace; 4) storerooms, x-xii, east of the Central Court; 5) residential quarter, iii, at the northwest corner of the palace; 6) storerooms and workrooms, xxi, xxii, xxiv-xxviii, at the north end of the palace; 7) the Central Court. Above i, viii, and ix, were the main public rooms, i.e. to the north and west of the Central Court.

Even at Knossos a similar arrangement in quarters can be discerned (Fig. 2): storerooms along the west side; cult rooms west of the Central Court; the northeast quarter given over to workrooms and storerooms; and the southeast to the Residential Quarter. The public rooms were mostly above the rooms west and north of the Central Court.

It therefore seems evident that considerable deliberate planning must have preceded the actual construction of these buildings. It also seems evident that the focal point of the plan was the central court, and around this and facing on it most of the quarters were built. Further groups of rooms built beyond these were served by corridors or by smaller courts.

Support for the view that the palace was planned in units radiating from the central court has been presented in the first section of this chapter. It was suggested there that in the palace at Phaistos a pair of straight lines crossing one another at right angles was first laid out to mark the west and north boundaries of the Central Court, and that from these as base lines the most important quarters were planned in round numbers of Minoan feet (Fig. 144). The available evidence at Mallia indicates a comparable procedure of planning (Fig. 146), and something of the same sort at least can be made out for Knossos on the basis of the scantier data. Deliberate planning in detail, accompanied by definite dimensioning, can also be followed, and has already been described (Ch. ii, 2), in the laying out of the symmetrical façade of the north end of the Central Court at Phaistos (Figs. 50, 145).

However, the guiding principle in this planning of the quarters about the central court was not aesthetic—there is no attempt to arrange them symmetrically, for example—but practical. The efficient arrangement of these quarters in a well coordinated whole evidently took precedence over any theoretically conceived architectural scheme; and whether the modern eye censures the results as untidy and illogical, or praises them for their variety and interest, is strictly irrelevant.

Another conspicuous feature of the palace plans which seems to violate normal principles of design, and which has therefore frequently provoked the surprised comments of critics is the bizarre irregularity of the "trace" or outline of the exterior walls, particularly along the west façade; the clearest illustration of this is the palace at Mallia (Fig. 6). In lack of symmetry Near Eastern palaces resemble the Minoan, but in this respect they differ, for they are normally firmly bounded by a more or less regular, often rectangular, enclosing outline (Fig. 148). Lawrence's explanation of the indentations along the west façade as either aesthetic, showing "an architectural sense," or structural—"long stretches of wall were avoided, probably because the builders distrusted their stability"—are not satisfying.[20] The explanation given by Evans and others, that the projections were a vestigial architectural legacy from times when the walls were fronted by defensive towers, is no longer in favor; indeed it was due to the very fact that the Minoan palaces were not fortified, that they were under no compulsion to assume the compact form and tight-drawn outline seen in Near Eastern palaces like that at Mari.

The correct explanation of the "indented trace" is surely the one already clearly enunciated by the French excavators at Mallia: "The indented line of the outer wall is easily explained if it was desired to place around the central court quarters of different importance; it is not, in fact, toward the exterior that the apartments face; the true façade gives on an interior court, on the large or the small court (that is, the Central and North

[20] *BSA*, 46 (1951), p. 81.

Service Courts at Mallia). The exterior wall marks only the rear of the building; each quarter—often conceived, if isolated, as a complete rectangle—projects to a greater or less degree in accordance with its own depth."[21]

This indented outline or uneven projection into horizontal space, so characteristic of the Cretan palaces, was repeated in a vertical sense; in other words the roof levels were far from uniform over the whole building. For it is quite clear that the number of storeys (and the height of the individual storeys) varied considerably, for purely practical reasons, in the different quarters, from one storey (probably) along the whole south end of the palace at Mallia (Fig. 58), for example, and perhaps east of the Central Courts at Phaistos and Mallia; two storeys were common but three were rare even at Knossos and Phaistos (Fig. 58). Exaggerating this differential in elevation, the palaces were built on a succession of terraces, partly from necessity, partly it would seem from deliberate choice. The excavators reckon the number of terraces at Phaistos and H. Triadha at seven and eight respectively.[22]

The irregularity of outline in plan and the disparity in the roof levels in Minoan architecture was encouraged by the apparently universal Cretan practice of flat roofs. In these features, as in others, Cretan palaces and houses bear a strong resemblance to the type of houses still common in many of the Greek islands, including Crete,[23] though in a more regularized and sophisticated form, and, in the case of the palaces, with the addition of inner courts. Such houses, or agglomerations of houses, are often veritable labyrinths of small rooms, the flat roofs of the inner rooms being built higher in order to be lighted, clerestory

[21] *Mallia*, III, pp. 71-72. This is not quite exact for the indented line of the west façade at Mallia and Knossos. There the irregularity is caused by the difference in size among the great halls of the Piano Nobile (Ch. VI, 1), and these front not on the central court but on the long north-south corridor of the magazines. Nor can the west façade be described as the "rear" of the building.

[22] *Festòs*, II, p. 478.

[23] E. Heinrich has recently studied this "Inselarchitektur" and has noted examples extending from the 4th millennium B.C. in the Near East to modern towns in Greece and Italy; it is not clear that all these are actually related, *AA*, 73 (1958), cols. 89-133.

fashion (Fig. 152); indeed this clerestory principle may have been used as a supplementary device for lighting the great halls of the Piano Nobile, as represented in our restoration of the Palace of Mallia (Fig. 58).

A few examples of clusters of rooms similar, at least in plan, to the modern "Island-architecture," and dated to the pre-palatial period (third millennium B.C.), have been found in Crete (Fig. 33); Lawrence refers to the "interminable chaotic rambling" plan of one of these and suggests them as prototypes of the palaces.[24] A kind of embryonic survival of this primitive "agglutinative" principle might help to explain the existence of such a maze of small rooms as that at the south end of the palace at Mallia, or to the west of the Central Court at Knossos. But the planning of the last Palace of Phaistos, for example, had surely reached a far more advanced level of architectural design.

So far in our search for principles determining the form of the Cretan palaces in their final stages we seem to have found them to be mainly functional rather than aesthetic in character; but, although practical considerations may have dominated the Minoan architect, aesthetic considerations were also bound to claim his attention. For one thing, the living quarters of the royal family must be commodious and, in a civilization as advanced as the Minoan, pleasing to the eye. As a matter of fact there was not a little "keeping up with the Joneses" even in those days; kings kept their eye on the palaces built by their brother monarchs and strove to rival or surpass them in magnificence. For example we read in an ancient text that the king of Ugarit in Syria sent his son, about 1700 B.C., to see the palace of Zimrilim, king of Mari, and bring back some ideas which he could apply for the improvement of his own residence.[25]

So successful was the Cretan architect in beautifying the residential quarter that some have seen in the main room of these apartments—the "Minoan Hall," as we have called it (at

[24] *Gk. Arch.*, p. 22.
[25] *Syria*, 18 (1937), pp. 74-75.

Knossos it was the Hall of the Double-Axes)—or in this Hall together with the associated sequence of rooms, the dominant aesthetic principle of Minoan palatial architecture. However exaggerated we may consider a view which suggests that so small a tail should wag so large a dog, we must grant that the aesthetic effect of these apartments must have been very striking, and not only for the rich decoration in gleaming alabaster and the painted stucco surfaces of floor, walls, and ceiling. A far more original feature is the ability to open at will entire walls, composed of rows of double doors, in order to reveal views of terraced gardens and distant landscapes. Complex patterns of light and shade were created by series of such pier-and-door partitions, by light-wells, windows, corridors, porticoes, etc. (Fig. 151). Schweitzer suggests that "these spatial shadings developed into a very finely felt instrument on which, as on a light-organ, the architect could compose fugues as he liked."[26] Whether the Minoan was in fact consciously sensitive to "photo-fugues" we have no way of knowing, but it would be dangerous to elevate this to the level of a determining principle guiding the Cretan designer in his architectural compositions.

The desire to impress the king's power and magnificence upon visitors, native or foreign, introduced another stimulus to aesthetic treatment in palace design.

The principal exterior façade of the three major palaces was the west. Along this side, in the Piano Nobile, were the state reception halls, and here was located the main entrance to the palace, except in the less pretentious palace at Mallia. The comparatively lofty walls rising above the heavy orthostate course must have been impressive, and their massiveness would have been increased by the strong contrasts of light and shadow created by boldly projecting room forms and by the shallower recess in the face of each façade element (Figs. 55, 58).

The west entrance at Knossos was further dignified by a broad porch with a single central column, at the rear of which

[26] *Die Antike*, 2 (1926), p. 305.

opened the Corridor of the Procession (Fig. 128). After two right-angle turns this corridor reached a formal Propylon (Fig. 42); at the rear of this a broad stairway led to the Piano Nobile, which was approached by still another fine stairway opening directly from the west side of the Central Court (Fig. 44).

Far more monumental is the approach to the state apartments at Phaistos. At the northeast corner of the West Court a great forty-five foot broad stairway of a dozen steps leads up to a grandiosely proportioned portal, and all this is balanced by the adjacent massive three-storeyed block to the south (Fig. 48).

Impressive and effective as these stairways and others, such as the Grand Staircase to the Residential Quarter at Knossos, must have been, it is unrealistic to elevate them, as Rodenwaldt suggested doing, into a dominant principle of palace composition.[27] They do constitute an important element, but the palaces were certainly not planned around a series of grand stairways.

Nor must we neglect, in estimating the aesthetic effect of the Cretan palaces, to take account of the central courts, which were certainly designed with appearance as well as usefulness in mind. Long porticoes with columned galleries above not only conveniently accommodated the spectators of the various sports and ceremonies which took place there (Ch. IV), but relieved the otherwise long monotonous walls with a variegated pattern of light and shade. On the west side the columned and pillared façades of the Tripartite Shrine at Knossos (Fig. 44), of Room 25 at Phaistos, and of Room vi 1 at Mallia, plus the broad stairways to the Piano Nobile at Knossos and Mallia, further enhanced the central courts; the handsome symmetrical north façade of the court at Phaistos, with its axial doorway flanked by half-columns, also added a decorative element (Figs. 50, 51).

It is clear that many features contribute elements of beauty to the Cretan palaces: the Halls of the residential quarters, the alabaster-lined bathrooms, the long porticoes of the central courts, the monumental stairways, the columned entranceways.

[27] *Gnomon*, 11 (1935), p. 331.

In fact it is commonly recognized that much of the aesthetic appeal of these buildings lies in details such as these. It is in general organization that their architectural design appears weak to us: in a well balanced relationship between the parts, in a proper subordination of lesser features to more important ones. The richly detailed diminutive shrine on the west side of the Central Court at Knossos, set in a framework of comparatively massive porticoes and a monumental stairway to the Piano Nobile, is a good illustration of architectural inappropriateness, at least to modern feeling (Fig. 44).[28] The narrow, winding Corridor of the Procession, forming, in spite of its richly decorated walls, an inadequate approach to the South Propylon at Knossos, and the reverse situation at Phaistos of a grandiose Propylon leading up to an area whose only exit consisted of three moderate-sized doorways, are further examples of architectural inexperience and naïveté.

We are reminded of the analytic approach of all early drawing and low relief, including the Minoan. Each detail may be done correctly enough, but the synthesis, the combination of the parts to form the whole, is awkwardly managed: full-front eyes in profile heads (Figs. 131, A, B), full-front bodies on side-view legs; even, in Egypt, left hands on right arms or right feet on left legs.

Yet it may be that this loose, uncoordinated architectural syntax, this imbalance of the component parts, was in part, at least, deliberate, "wilful irregularity." "Surely," says Snijder in his penetrating study of Cretan art, "*if he* (the Minoan designer) *had wanted to*, if the disciplined, centralizing architectural-style of the Orient had impressed him as something essential, important, unqualifiedly necessary, he would have succeeded. He had evidently not so wished, and therefore we must probably conclude from this fact that 'the power to create plastically unified compositions out of which all later European architecture grew' was foreign to him and remained so."[29]

[28] Karo, *Greifen am Thron*, p. 26.
[29] *Kretische Kunst*, p. 81.

Although this fact is rarely noticed, the Cretan architect certainly did understand the principles of formal balance and symmetry, and occasionally used them in details of his composition, yet he never thought of forcing his whole plan into such a rigid system. Instances readily come to mind, such as the recesses in the west façades at Mallia, and the double recessed Magazine Block at Phaistos (Fig. 48); even, to a degree, the recesses at Knossos. The symmetrical arrangement of important entrances, particularly the one at Phaistos with its single central column, its two portals, and the three columns of the light-well behind, is another example; symmetrical also is the front of Room 25 in the same palace, with its central column and pairs of pillars on either side (Fig. 50). But the most conspicuous instance is the nearby north façade of the Central Court; the formal balance here has been carefully thought out: axial door, half-columns, niches, and recesses. If the execution was not precise in its measurements this was not the fault of the designer, and the discrepancies would not have been readily apparent to the observer.

Symmetrical designs appear in other Cretan arts, such as the pottery both of the Middle and the Late Minoan periods. But the informality and asymmetry which were, it seems, particularly congenial to the Minoan temperament, may be best brought out by comparing the Minoan with the Mycenaean Greek treatment of the same theme. On a Cretan vase of the L.M. II period the octopus swims slantwise with writhing tentacles amid a litter of marine vegetation (Fig. 153, B); the contemporary mainland version sets the octopus firmly upon the axis of the vessel, combs out the tentacles into an ordered symmetry, and arranges the seaweed particles in forms carefully calculated to fill the vacant spaces (Fig. 153, C).[30] The Cretan genius delights in life and movement, in a baroque feeling for variety and unexpected effects; the Greek, whether Mycenaean or Hellenic, prefers balance and order, symmetry and formal pattern.

[30] Cf. Furumark, *Op. Arch.*, 6 (1950), pp. 157-159, fig. 3.

In Minoan architecture too the unexpected prevails. Doors tend to be placed near corners, not on the axis; columns alternate with piers in long porticoes; corridors bend in "dog's-leg" forms (Evans); the straightness of column shafts may be denied by spiral fluting; stairways wind and twist from storey to storey; rooflines rise and fall in constant oscillation; façades sway in and out in a shimmering mass of lights and shadows; and even more kaleidoscopic patterns are set adancing through the labyrinths of door openings, windows, pillared porticoes, and light-wells reflecting on the polished alabaster surfaces of floors and walls—all creating an atmosphere of restless movement, or in the architectural philosopher's language, "a motoroptical experience of spatiality."[31] Masses are broken up by the interplay of light and color. The very outlines of the buildings are loosely drawn; flickering forms advance and retreat both outwards into the surroundings and upwards into the sky. The general effect is pictorial rather than plastic (Figs. 55, 58).

Miss Banti sees this pictorial tendency particularly strong in the Phaistos palace, and finds in it a unifying principle which raises it from a merely clever work of construction to the level of a work of art. "The architect has made clear in his work and infused into it his essentially pictorial spirit, which is revealed in this center of southern Crete better and more clearly than elsewhere, and gives artistic unity to the vast complex." The construction of the palace in a series of terraces contributes to the effect, "the lines, surfaces, volumes join together to lend variety, movement—to take away from the mass all excessive heaviness. It is the modern architectonic conception in opposition to the classic. . . . The Minoan architects reveal here (at Phaistos) a technical ability and resource that is truly remarkable. It is wrong in reference to them to speak of empiricism, of primitiveness: they exhibit remarkable experience which, though it does not coincide with classical experience, is not inferior to that of any other people of antiquity."[32]

[31] Snijder, *Kretische Kunst*, p. 87, "ein motorisch-optisches Erleben der Räumlichkeit."

[32] *Festòs*, II, pp. 480, 478, 479.

Snijder concludes his analysis of Minoan architecture some-what as follows: "Such an art of building makes sport of all our architectural conceptions, and defeats all attempts to force it into a logical, rational system. Yet it captivates even modern man and delights him with its charm. The Palace of Knossos is to the adult an adventure in the grand style, while it reminds him of his youth when as a child he reconnoitered the old-fashioned house of a friend and kept discovering it full of charms, new rooms, secret nooks, unexpected cupboards and passages, without his coming to understand the arrangement as a whole. So the modern investigator is charmed and delighted —until he remembers that it must yield some design; that he must discover the logical thread of Ariadne. Then he begins his researches and forgets that it is the irrational in these dwellings that constitutes their excellence and charm. Inevitably these logical attempts come to nought, and the investigator takes refuge in a world of dreams and fairytales, a gay world of change and movement far from restrictions of logic and reality."[33]

It is easy to romanticize the impressions that Cretan art makes on us, and in the absence of any written record of their own thought and feelings we shall never know how sensitive the Minoans actually were to such effects and to what extent they intentionally expressed them in their art. We must not forget that the voices that speak to us are but those of the stones themselves, not those of the people who built with them.

We have confined our discussion of Minoan architectural principles to the palaces, but much would apply likewise to house architecture: the division into "quarters," the irregularity of outline (with occasional exceptions such as Mallia Za, Fig. 25), the variations in the height of the flat roofs, and the lighting effects in the "Cretan Hall." In many ways the house is the palace on a small scale—the resemblance of the living quarters to those of the palaces is a striking illustration of this (Ch.

---

[33] *op.cit.*, pp. 89-90.

v, 1)—though the absence of a court in all but a few of the largest houses is a significant point of distinction. The Cretan house was of course far less complex than the palace. Its unpretentious, unsymmetrical design is to be expected; so even in Classical Greece, where monumental architecture represents the epitome of formalism, houses preserve a non-axial plan.[34]

The sensitive, volatile Gallic temperament has, we may fancy, not a little in common with the ancient Minoan. It is fitting then to close our account of the palaces of Crete by quoting the discriminating sentiments of M. Gustav Glotz in his account of *The Aegean Civilization* (p. 119).

"To estimate the level reached by Cretan architecture and to enjoy its charm one must first forget those intellectual qualities of order, symmetry, and balance which give Greek buildings their incomparable beauty. The Cretan architect made no effort to offer to the gods temples worthy of them. He wanted to build comfortable houses and mansions and magnificent palaces, in which the master could conveniently accommodate his whole family, an army of servants, and the offices of a complicated administrative system, and display his wealth by brilliant entertainments. The great artistic skill with which all crafts combined their resources at the call of the Cretan architect is clearly shown not so much in the majesty of the general effect or even in the splendour of the external decoration as in the perfect adaptation to climatic conditions, happy distribution of light and shade, and intelligent ventilation and drainage, in the ease of communication between the countless rooms, the arrangements made to satisfy quite modern notions of comfort, and the harmonious opulence of detail, and finally in a sure sense of the spectacular and picturesque which indulges in monumental entrances, the elegant ordering of terrace upon terrace and vistas of noble landscapes on every side."

[34] *Olynthus*, VIII, p. 147.

ADDENDUM 1.

THE NORTHWEST ENTRANCE, KNOSSOS

(See pp. 30, 118f.)

THE THIRTEEN southernmost magazines that could be reached from the Corridor of the Magazines at Knossos (Fig. 157) contained for the most part (both magazines and corridor) large pithoi and cists beneath the floor. One point that is not immediately clear is how goods stored here were brought in or out of the palace. An examination of the plan will show that only by a very circuitous route could porters have made their way to either the north or south end of the building, and then only via the Central Court.

In a recent paper—to which I refer the reader for details—I propose a route that is more direct and provides, I believe, a better solution for certain architectural features than those proposed many years ago by Evans and his colleagues.[1] Briefly, I suggest that the principal entrance to the magazines was at the northwest corner of the palace by way of a ramp—possibly a stepped ramp—now disappeared but originally sloping up southward between the exterior palace wall opposite Magazines 17-18 and the massive stone buttress projecting northward some nine meters from the northwest corner of Magazine Block 11-16 (Figs. 157, 158). Immediately at the head of this conjectural ramp a doorway would have opened on a rectangular area about 7 by 4 m. (created by shortening Magazine 15), which would have provided a convenient place for receiving and checking goods, in conjunction with Magazine 15 where, significantly, a deposit of Linear A tablets (relating to textiles) was found. Once through the check-points porters would have carried the goods through the corridor numbered "Magazine 16" (which, appropriately, seems to have been found empty), and thence, via the east end of Magazine 17, into the north end of the Corridor of the Magazines.

Instead of the ramp I suggest, following the general north-to-south upward slope of the ground, Evans proposed a stairway leading up to a hypothetical doorway at the level of the great halls of the Piano Nobile (Fig.

---

[1] *AJA*, 83 (1979), pp. 49-63.

85). Such a stairway would have been impossibly steep and, in any case, would not have opened into any such system of corridors and stairways as Evans imaginatively created over the area occupied by Magazines 11 to 16, but rather into a single vast room, the Northwest Hall (Fig. 86).

ADDENDUM 2.

PALACE AT KATO ZAKRO

(See p. 46)

THE DISCOVERY in a farmer's field of several gold objects of great beauty and skillful technique induced the then ephor of Crete, Nikolaos Platon, to commence excavations there that resulted, in 1962, in the identification of another Minoan palace on a deserted site at the east end of the island known as Kato Zakro. Since there is little or no arable land in the area, Platon supposes that the basis of the palace's economy was trade by sea, both local and overseas, especially with Syria, and objects found in the ruins bear out his thesis.[1]

Since the palace was discovered just after the publication of *Palaces of Crete* (1962) it provided an unexpected but welcome opportunity to test some of the conclusions arrived at on the basis of other, longer-known palaces. Zakro was evidently abandoned in haste about 1450 B.C. due to some catastrophe, and although the inhabitants managed to save themselves and to carry off most of their belongings in the form of precious metals, they seem to have made little or no attempt afterwards to search among the ruins for other valuable objects of clay, stone, or bronze. Though such valuables are not the prime interest of this study, they often provide useful clues as to the function of particular rooms.

Since the palace has not yet been thoroughly investigated, let alone published, we must depend on Platon's preliminary but excellent accounts, combined with visits to the site, and discussions with Platon himself and with his principal architect, J. W. Shaw; many of the objects, too, are now well displayed in the Herakleion Museum. As at Mallia and at Phaistos, no wall paintings with figuré scenes have been found.

Though considerably smaller than the other three palaces, Zakro offers many points of similarity in general plan (Fig. 166). Dominating, as usual, is the Central Court, though less than one-third the area of the court at Mallia; north to south it runs quite precisely 100 M.ft., and east to west an even 40 M.ft.—providing further confirmation for the value of the Minoan unit of length (30.36 cm.) as determined at Phaistos and Mallia.

---

[1] N. Platon, *Zakros* (New York, 1971), pp. 240-246.

The principal entrance to the palace was at the northeast corner of the court, where a ramp is connected with the Zakro harborage.

Immediately west of the Central Court is a suite of large rooms (XXVIII, XXIX) with attractively designed floors and a painted spiral cornice around the inner walls of XXIX, possibly used, to judge from objects found in it, for some kind of ceremonial libations, though Platon calls it a Banquet Hall. At the northwest corner of the suite is a columned light-well, and at the northeast a stairway leading up to an upper suite of rooms or, as I think more likely, to a flat roof. The position of the Reception Halls at the level of the court rather than in the Piano Nobile constitutes a departure from the usual planning practice at the other sites, but it is a welcome change since it provides us with more preserved evidence to help us visualize the appearance of the *salles d'apparat* of a Minoan palace.

West of the great halls is a number of smaller rooms devoted to religious practices: a central shrine (XXIII), a lustration chamber with a descending flight of steps (XXIV), an archives room with many tablets—only 13 still legible—and a storage room (XXV) with several bins containing stone, rock crystal, and clay vessels of sacral types of great interest and beauty. Other rooms to the west and north were work and storage rooms; finds included three elephant tusks and six bronze ingots each weighing about 30 kg. (65 lbs.). More workshops occurred to the south of the Central Court, and to the southeast are a well and spring chamber.

The north half of the east side of the Central Court contained the Residential Quarter. According to Platon, XXXVIII is the King's Hall and XXXVI the Queen's; both contain pier-and-door partitions, and both face on a narrow portico that opens on the court. At the south end of XXXVIII, Platon identifies a light-well, and another at the east end of XXXVI; but in the latter, which has no drain and is reached by two steps down, Shaw would, with greater likelihood, see a bathroom. The King's Hall faces east by a narrow portico on a large walled area in whose center is a stone-built basin, 5 m. in diameter, with steps descending to a flagged floor. The resemblance of the basin to a circular basin of similar dimensions in an unexcavated palace (?) at Arkhanes near Knossos,[2] is remarkable; both were perhaps used for bathing in the hot Cretan summers—perhaps particularly by the children of the royal family.

Near the palace entrance at the northeast corner of the Central Court and some eight meters north of the Residential Quarters is a small suite of rooms, LVIII, LIX, and LX, the first reached by a flight of a half-dozen steps down, and decorated with columns on two sides and with painted sacral horns. The position and character of the suite suggests identifying it rather as a "lustral chamber," with primarily ceremonial functions than as

[2] *Knossos*, II, pp. 64f., figs. 29f.

a bathroom forming part of the Residential Quarters—as Platon would see it.

At the north end of the Central Court, a large room, XXXII, ca. 30 by 40 M.ft., with six rough sub-bases, two in each row, was immediately identified by Platon as a kitchen because of the remains of a hearth, meatbones, culinary equipment, and masses of pottery for eating, drinking, and cooking found in the small rooms to the east. Also adjacent to XXXII on the east is a short portico from which a stairway runs up no doubt to an upper gallery, providing access to a large room, the "Banquet Hall" above XXXII; a service stairway is probably to be recognized in a room to the north of XXXII. The arrangement of rooms north of the Central Court at Zakro and at Mallia is so similar that both sets of rooms must have been used for the same purpose. Our guess as to what that purpose was, we set out in an article in 1961,[3] namely a dining or banqueting area; surely Platon's new palace has presented us with a more than adequate confirmation of this hypothesis.

[3] *AJA*, 65 (1961), pp. 165-172.

ADDENDUM 3.

THE WEST ANNEX OF THE LITTLE PALACE

(See pp. 51f, 128)

EVANS' EXCAVATIONS to the west of the Little Palace revealed the east outside wall, constructed of excellent limestone masonry (comparable to that of the Little Palace itself), of an adjacent building he refers to as the "Unexplored Mansion."[1] Since its recent thorough excavation by Popham and Sackett of the British School, a more appropriate name might be the West Annex (of the Little Palace).[2] The Annex seems to have been built a little later than the main building. It was laid out at a somewhat different orientation, and was separated from the original construction by an irregular space several meters wide. In spite of this separation, the two buildings were actually connected near their south end by a kind of bridge whose function was suspected by Evans and proved by Popham and Sackett. Indeed the doorway at the west end of this bridge forms the only entrance yet found to the West Annex.

The ground floor of the Annex consisted of a large central room, 7, with four square pillars, flanked on both north and south by a row of small

[1] See pp. 51f, *supra*, and *Knossos*, II, pp. 513-546.
[2] *JHS, Archaeological Reports for 1972-73*, pp. 50-61; see my comments on the report, *AJA*, 79 (1975), pp. 141-144.

storage and work rooms, 1-4 and 11-14. Large amounts of pottery, both coarse and fine, were found in 7 as well as elsewhere on the ground floor. Two service stairways, 5 and 12, led to the upper floor; a third is much better built and led, we feel sure, to a large four-columned hall, 7 ft., above 7. The essential resemblance of this whole complex of rooms and stairways to the complex of rooms north of the Central Court at Mallia strongly suggests that we have here a further example of a dining hall on the second storey, combined with the appropriate storage and service rooms.

Such a complex would form a suitable complement to the handsome suite of reception halls uncovered by Evans along the east front of the Little Palace. Though we may doubt that the structure as a whole represents merely a particularly lavish example of a Minoan urban mansion, there seems to be no clue in the remains just what its function may have been; Evans' term for it, "Little Palace," is perhaps a suitably noncommital designation suggestive of a certain splendor.

ADDENDUM 4.

THE ARKHANES MODEL

(See p. 72)

EXCAVATIONS conducted in 1970 in the village of Arkhanes, about ten km. south of Knossos, by the at that time local epimelete, Miss Aggeliki Lembesi, brought to light a well-preserved house model of great interest dated, by the context in which it was discovered, to the late M.M. IIIA period, a little before 1600 B.C. The model received a publication worthy of its importance by the discoverer in the 1976 number of the *Archailogike Ephemeris* (pp. 12-43), with numerous drawings and photos in both black and white and color.

The model measures 31.3 by 28.7 by 23.5 cm., and the ground floor contains three rooms and a but-and-ben entranceway. The largest room has a central column and one window; the second, also with one window, has a ramp leading up to the roof; the third, with two windows, is divided near one end by a row of three pillars, like a pier-and-door partition, and beyond this is a light-well walled to about half the height of the room.

The ramp from the second room emerged onto the flat roof sheltered by a protective hood or stairhead. The edges of the roof were guarded by a parapet on which rested a series of piers and columns, the purpose of which, according to Miss Lembesi, was to support a light canopy of reeds to provide shelter from the hot Cretan sun—a common practice at the present day. A particularly interesting feature is a small balcony, reached from the roof by three steps, on which stands a fragment of a small clay figure probably not so much looking out as being looked at from below. In other words we may have here a minuscule version of what we have suggested was represented on a grand scale at the Grand Propylon at Phaistos, namely the "Window of Appearances." If this is correct then the Arkhanes Model is not literally a "model" or design of a structure to be built but a representation of an existent type of building having a specific purpose, religious or regal or both.

ADDENDUM 5.

MINOAN LINEAR MEASUREMENT

(See pp. 222-229)

THE HYPOTHESIS that, during at least part of the second millennium B.C., the foot was used extensively, if not ubiquitously, on the island of Crete as a unit of linear measurement was first advanced in an article published in 1960[1] and, in less detail, in the *Palaces of Crete* two years later. It was also proposed that the value of the Minoan foot (M.ft.) was approximately 30.36 cm. A good many scholars accepted this hypothesis as more or less probable, and recognized its important bearing on our understanding of how the palaces were planned.

By a stroke of good fortune a means of testing the validity of the hypothesis was shortly afterwards offered by the discovery of a fourth major palace excavated in the 1960s by Nikolaos Platon at Kato Zakro (**Addendum 2**). The Central Court of this new palace proved to measure, within a matter of centimeters, on the basis of the proposed 30.36 cm. foot, 100 by 40 M.ft. (Fig. 166). In view of such obviously intentional round numbers it would be difficult for even the most skeptical to deny the existence and approximate value of the Minoan foot.

At the Second Cretological Conference in 1967 I presented a paper based on a study of the very regularly laid out porticoes along the east sides of the Central Courts at Phaistos and Mallia and along the front of the L.M. III portico near the Villa of Hagia Triadha (Fig. 163). All three porticoes consist of alternating piers and columns. The length, north to south, of the rectangular bases on which the wooden piers were supported quite consistently measures 1.00 m. at Phaistos, 0.77 m. at Mallia, and 0.86 at Hagia Triadha, or, expressed in Minoan feet, 3⅓, 2½, and 2⅚, respectively. But we can be quite certain that the Minoans, instead of using such fractions as ½, ⅓, and ⅚—which the Ancients always found difficult to deal with—would have subdivided the unit into six, or some multiple of

[1] *AJA*, 64 (1960), pp. 335-341.

six, parts; and since like ourselves the Romans possessed a foot (*pes*) composed of twelve *unciae*, inches, we might reasonably assume that this was, like the foot itself, an inheritance from the Minoan system of mensuration. The matter is, however, not quite so simple, for Herodotos tells us that the Greek foot of his day was divided into four "palms," and each palm contained four "fingers," *daktyloi*; thus there were sixteen, not twelve, parts in a Πούς *foot*. To add to the uncertainty we have no proof that the Mycenaean Greeks adopted the Minoan foot, though this would be a reasonable assumption, somewhat strengthened by the fact that the height of the great doorway of the Treasury of Atreus at Mycenae is about 5.40 m., i.e. nearly eighteen M.ft., while its width at the bottom of the opening is 2.70 m. or nearly nine M.ft.; it may also be significant that the outside diameter of the enclosure walls of Shaft Grave Circles A and B at Mycenae may have been intended to measure 100 M.ft.—the matter is very uncertain, however, since A is only very roughly circular, and B is, in addition, very badly preserved.

ADDENDUM 6.

BATHROOMS AND LUSTRAL CHAMBERS*

(See pp. 99-108)

"THE QUESTION should not (be) whether these rooms were 'bathrooms *or* lustral chambers,' for they were both at once, though the relative emphasis doubtless varied in the individual instances."[1] This was the general conclusion I put forward in 1962 with respect to the small rooms frequently found in Minoan palaces and houses, usually some two to three meters square, and characterized by sunken floors to which several steps descended from an adjacent larger room. In order to have a brief and neutral term by which to refer to the score or more of these low-level chambers or basins,

---

* This article, which first appeared in *Greece and the Eastern Mediterranean in Ancient History and Prehistory*, ed. by K. M. Kinzl, © Walter de Gruyter, Berlin, 1977, is here reprinted by kind permission of the publishers, to supplement the discussion in the text, pp. 99-108. N.B. that Figs. 1, 2, and 3, referred to on the second and third pages of the article, correspond to Figs. 12, 10, and 11, respectively, in the text.

[1] Abbreviations: *Europa* = N. Platon, "Bathrooms and Lustral Basins in Minoan Dwellings," in: *Europa; Festschrift E. Grumach. Studien zur Geschichte und Epigraphik der frühen Ägäis*, ed. W. C. Brice, 1967, 236-245. –*KHC* = S. Alexiou, "About the Minoan 'Lustral Chambers,' " Κρητικά Χρονικά 24,1972, 414-434. – *PoC* = J. W. Graham, *The Palaces of Crete*, 1962 (repr. with *Addenda* 1969). – *PoM* = A. J. Evans, *The Palace of Minos at Knossos*, 1929-1936 (repr. 1964).

The quote is from *PoC* 108.

occurring usually in the residential quarters, I shall speak of them in this paper as the BR/LBs, i.e. the bath-rooms and/or lustral basins.

Let me say at the outset that it is still my opinion that most of the BR/LBs formed part of what are usually referred to as the women's apartments, and that most of them were used for ordinary washing or bathing, though this might often, if not always, be accompanied to a greater or less degree by an awareness that it was at the same time a religious act involving a purification of the soul as well as of the body. On the other hand, in perhaps as many as five instances, where the room was larger, deeper, more elaborate architecturally, and sometimes included the display of religious symbols such as the double-axe, the BR/LB may appear to have functioned primarily, or even exclusively, as a place for the ritual performance of an act of lustration or of some related form of religious ritual involving the use of a liquid cleansing agent.[2] Between these two extremes of usage the relative degree of emphasis—practical or religious—might vary widely in the specific case. A wide variation may also have occurred in the amount and nature of the purifying agent employed. Near Eastern analogies would suggest water, whether sanctified or not, as the most likely or most common liquid to be so employed, though in the Aegean area a perfumed unguent is another distinct possibility. In view of our profound ignorance of the details of Minoan religious ceremonial it would be unwise to attempt to be more specific on these points.[3]

Although my conclusions, as expressed in the *Palaces of Crete* (99-108), have received considerable approval as a reasonable interpretation of the available evidence, nevertheless, partly as a result of new facts brought to light in the excavation of the recently discovered palace at Kato Zakro, two eminent specialists in Minoan archaeology have raised a number of questions regarding certain details of my interpretations, namely Prof. Nikolaos Platon, former Ephor of Cretan Antiquities, and Dr. Stylianos Alexiou, the present ephor.[4] Some of their contentions have been anticipated in my study mentioned above, and to it the reader is referred for further details.

I shall discuss first the points raised by Platon since we are, I am happy to say, in essential agreement on most matters, such as the identification and function of most of the BR/LBs, the possible use in them of clay bathtubs (but on this see below), and the raising of the floor-level in several of these rooms to the level of the adjacent room without change of their function—an alteration datable to the late Middle Minoan or early Late Minoan period.

[2] The two most outstanding examples, architecturally, are the North Lustral Chamber and the Lustral Chamber off the Room of the Throne, both at Knossos (*PoM* 1, 405ff. and 4,907f.).

[3] *KCh* 425f.

[4] See both *Europa and KCh*.

Our agreement is complete, I believe, on the interpretation of a crucial example of the BR/LB in the Residential Quarter east of the Central court at Knossos (Fig. 1). A broad stairway (the "Grand Staircase") descends from the Central Court to the main (i.e. lowest) floor of the Residential Quarter (Evans' "Domestic Quarter"), and from a long East-West Corridor one turns south at right angles into ABC, the Men's or King's Hall (Evans' "Hall of the Double Axes"), which is provided with a typical Cretan light-well (or ventilation-shaft), C, and with several "pier-and-door partitions" leading out to an exterior portico, H, with a fine view of the valley below. Near the south-west corner of B a door opens at right angles into a corridor, D, at whose end another door opens, again at right angles, into a smaller room, E, which has generally been referred to as the Women's or Queen's Hall (Evans' "Queen's Megaron"). Off this room, to the west, opens a small room, F, with a parapet supporting a small column,[5] which is commonly identified as a bathroom, following Evans, who himself did so chiefly because of the size and shape of the room and because a decorated clay bathtub was found in fragments not far away in Ea.[6] Finally, from E another long corridor leads westward to a room containing a toilet, G.

Turning next to the palace at Phaistos we proceed to the peristyle (74) in the northern part of the building. From this we descend a flight of stairs (Fig. 2) to an East-West Corridor (76) and turn north at right angles into the King's Hall, ABC (79, 77, 78), equipped with a light-well, C, pier-and-door partitions, and an exterior portico, H (85). Near the south-west corner of the King's Hall, A, a door opens at right angles into a corridor, D (80), at whose north end another door opens at right angles into a smaller room, E (81), which has generally been called the Women's or Queen's Hall. Off this, to the south, steps lead down past a parapet with column-

[5] As the room now appears there is no low-level floor and no stairway down (but see below with n. 42).

[6] For general account see *PoM* 1,325-359; 3,282-390; and *PoC* 84-88. There seems a slight discrepancy as to where the tub fragments were found. Unfortunately Mackenzie does not mention them in his daybooks. The earliest mention seems to be *BSA* 8,1901/02,54, "considerable remains of a large painted terracotta bath were found in the portico of the neighboring hall, having doubtless been turned out when the bath-chamber was used as a lime-store"; from the context this clearly means the "portico," Ea,—better, the "corridor"—between the Queen's Hall (Queen's "Megaron"), E, and the eastern lightwell, Eb. However, in the final publication (*PoM* 3, 385) the tub fragments are said to have been found "by its entrance and in the adjoining section of the 'Megaron,'" by which is meant the entrance to the bathroom, F, and the Queen's Hall, E. Considering Evans' tendency in his later writings, particularly in the *Palace of Minos*, to improve on the evidence of excavation I think we must choose the earlier provenience, i.e. the one given in *BSA* 8,1901/02,54, even though it is slightly less favorable to our argument; in any case there is no other suitable room anywhere nearby for the tub to have been used in.

base to F (83), a BR/LB; beyond E to the west are two small rooms (82) in the northern one of which are the remains of what appears to be a latrine, G.[7]

At Mallia a similar arrangement of similar rooms is to be seen in the north-western area of the palace (Fig. 3). Unessential points of difference are that there is no terracing and no stairway descending to the Residential Quarters since the palace is built on level ground; likewise the rooms are less well decorated, in line with the generally greater simplicity of the palace. Readily identifiable components of the Residential Quarter are the King's Hall, AB (III 7), with light-well, C; pier-and-door partitions; an exterior portico, H; a corridor, D, connecting the King's Hall with the Queen's Hall, E (III 1); a BR/LB, F (III 9) with sunken floor entered by steps down from E; and probably a toilet in G (III 2).[8]

The similarities in general plan and even in detail among the rooms of the Residential Quarter, ABCDEFGH, in all three palaces, Knossos, Phaistos, and Mallia, are, as we have seen, so consistent and so nearly identical that one would think it could be taken to be virtually axiomatic that however the function of each of the principal elements were to be identified their function individually would have to be regarded as the same in all three palaces,[9] that is, if E is the "Women's Hall" in any one of the three then it is the "Women's Hall" in all three. In spite of this Platon calls E at Knossos the Queen's Hall, while at Phaistos and Mallia he describes E as the "Anteroom to the Bath."[10] The Queen's Hall at the latter two sites he locates elsewhere, as we shall see.

Although Platon concedes, in his article on "Bathrooms and Lustral Basins in Minoan Dwellings," that my "opinions are basically right," he attributes our remaining points of difference to my "bias to one side."[11] But I would suggest the possibility that they may rather be the result of his own arbitrary definition of what constitutes the indispensable characteristics of the Minoan "main living-rooms," i.e. a definition intended to cover both Men's and Women's Halls, ABC and E. They are, he asserts, "recognizable by their tiers of doors (his term for pier-and-door partitions), light-wells, and sometimes by their external colonnades" together with "a characteristic room provided with a descending staircase separated by a

---

[7] L. Pernier and L. Banti, *Il palazzo minoico di Festòs*, 2, 1951, 254-304; *PoC* 89f.

[8] F. Chapouthier and P. Demargne, *Fouilles exécutées à Mallia*, 4, 1962, 32-36; *PoC* 91.

[9] In general see J. W. Graham, *AJA* 63, 1959, 47-52.

[10] *Europa* 238. The application of the term "antechamber" to room E seems to stem from the first French preliminary report by Chapouthier and J. Charbonneaux, *Fouilles exécutées à Mallia*, 1, 1928, 13, where it is described as a "sorte d'antichambre . . . au petit sanctuaire III₄," i.e. F. Similarly, in early accounts, the Room of the Throne at Knossos was referred to as the anetchamber to the bath.

[11] *Europa* 238.

parapet ending in a pillar carrying a column" (i.e. a BR/LB).[12] Platon further declares that I "misjudge the character of the chambers outside the bathrooms," and that I am wrong in locating "in two main cases (he means Mallia and Phaistos) the women's royal apartment there."[13] This might be granted *if* all the features which he attributes to both Men's and Women's Halls were really to be considered essential to their identification; personally I do not find them essential, and Platon gives no reasons why they must be so accepted. I would, on the contrary, see the decisive evidence for determining the function of E in the extraordinary similarity of this room in all three palaces. The essentially identical features are the following: 1) each is reached from the Men's Hall (A or B) by a narrow corridor, D, with a door at each end (the presence of an actual door is certain at Knossos and Phaistos); 2) the dimensions of E (excluding the light-wells at Knossos) are similar, absolutely, to each other, and relatively to the dimensions of AB in each case; 3) the character and quality of E, as indicated by the surviving remains, especially in regard to the flooring and the wall-facing, were similar to those of ABC, and quite superior to those of other nearby rooms; 4) in each case a BR/LB opens off one side of E,[14] and its decorative quality and character is also in harmony with that of E and AB in the same suite.

This remarkable coincidence of characteristics indicates to me that E performed the same function in the three palaces. Yet Platon identifies E at Knossos as the Women's or Queen's Hall while disqualifying E at Phaistos and Mallia on the grounds that they contain no light-wells or pier-and-door partitions,[15] and demoting them to the position of "Anterooms of the Bath." Moreover he clearly regards this as signifying not a mere difference of name but denoting a real difference in function for he proceeds to identify the rooms which properly (in his opinion) constitute, at Phaistos and Mallia, the Queen's Halls.

Let us examine Platon's candidates to see how well they meet his own specifications.

At Mallia, as we have seen, I would consider E as the Queen's Hall, with F as the bathroom. Rejecting this, Platon sees as the Queen's Hall GJK, a series of rooms or spaces immediately to the west of EF, and within the bounds of GJ he claims to be able to recognize a light-well and an external portico, which form part of what "evidently was the Queen's apartment, communicating immediately with that of the king."[16] It is unfortunate that

---

[12] *Europa* 238.   [13] *Europa* 238 n. 9.

[14] The BR/LB in the Residential Quarter at Knossos is an apparent exception since it has no steps down and no lower floor (but see below).

[15] Note that the rooms at Mallia and Phaistos opened directly on the north portico and so did not have the same need for extra lighting as E at Knossos did.

[16] *Europa* 238 n. 9. Platon has been misled, it seems, by a remark in the French publication, "la liaison étroite du 'mégaron' et du 'bain' n'est connue qu'ici dans le palais de

Platon has not been a little more specific for as it stands this identification is very puzzling in a number of ways: 1) I find it impossible to recognize any sign of a typical Cretan light-well in the area GJK; 2) there seems to be no suitable space for the Queen's Hall itself; 3) there is certainly no direct connection (*pace* Platon) between GJK and the King's Hall, ABC, for rooms EFD lie directly between; 4) there are no pier-and-door partitions; 5) the bathroom, F, opens off E, not off any part of GJK; 6) the "external portico" presumably would be the space west of G, i.e. K, bounded on the west by two column bases—but the Mallia publication seems correct in reporting of area K that it was "en dehors des limites du palais"; that it was "à un niveau inférieur (0 m. 90 envir.)," i.e. below the level of G; and that it was "antérieur au dernier état du palais."[17] Aside from these objections in detail to Platon's identifications there is no resemblance whatever in general plan between the confused and poorly preserved area GJK and the area of the Queen's Hall at Knossos, E, Ea, Eb, Ec, which must be his touchstone of comparison.

Clearly Platon's recognition of the Women's Quarters at Mallia is far from self-evident, and it is clear too that he must have been induced to propose such an identification in order that he might find at Mallia a pattern conforming to what at Phaistos he believed he could recognize as the Women's Quarters. And, to be sure, he can present a more reasonable case at Phaistos than at Mallia, for at Phaistos he locates the Women's Quarters in LMN (50) which, he says, "is paralleled in the Queen's Hall of the Palace of Knossos."[18] For all that, I believe that the resemblance in plan he postulates is more apparent than real, for the following reasons: 1) there are no "tiers of doors" at Phaistos but rather four columns flanking M; 2) the light-well at Phaistos, M, is in the center of the suite of rooms and between the two pairs of columns,[19] whereas at Knossos there was a light-well along

---

Mallia" (*op.cit.* [n. 8], 35 n. 1). EF are not really nearer ABC at Mallia than at either Phaistos or at Knossos itself; in each case there is the separating corridor, D. This error seems to have been encouraged by a misplacement of the door from B at Mallia into D; the position of this doorway should be about a meter and a half farther south than it is placed on the French plans, e.g. on Plan II of *op.cit.* (n. 8), where it is put at a gap in the wall instead of where there is a single block, surely a threshold, still in situ. See also the new plan (VII) published in *Etudes crétoises*, 19 (Plan du site, plans du palais, indices), 1974.

[17] *Op.cit.* (n. 10), 13. This is in approximate agreement with the new plan referred to above n. 16; on this plan the top surface of one of the two bases is 1.05 m. lower than the floor of E.

[18] *Europa* 238 n. 9. On LMN (50) see *PoC* 90 and *op.cit.* (n. 7), 258-268.

[19] From the plan of the palace one might suppose that N, not M, was the light-well, but the evidence of a drain and of the wall construction indicates that the Italians are right in taking M to be the light-well (a similar arrangement occurs at Hagia Triada, *PoC* 98).

the side and another at the far east end; 3) Ea at Knossos is a corridor leading to H, not a part of the living-space of the Queen's Hall, and the light-well, Eb, was evidently intended principally to light the corridor Ea and the stairway to the upper storey; 4) the stone bench around the two walls of L at Phaistos finds its parallel not with the Residential Quarters at Knossos but with the room at the east end of the Men's Hall at Hagia Triada; 5) there is no BR/LB off LMN, and, although Platon explains this by means of his postulate that a BR/LB can occur either off the Queen's Hall or off the King's Hall, yet the BR/LB, F, is no more closely associated with the Men's Hall, ABC, at Phaistos, than it is at Knossos or at Mallia, for there is the same intervening corridor, D, in all three cases;[20] 6) LMN does not have the privacy that characterizes E at Knossos or Mallia, or E at Phaistos itself, for it is entered through a wide doorless opening, flanked by a column and a window-like space, directly from the stairway (76) descending to the Men's Hall, ABC. Thus, although its position suggests that LMN *may* have formed some part of the Residential Quarters, to attempt to explain it more specifically as constituting the Women's Quarters raises more objections that it settles. I am therefore content to leave its true function unsolved, at least for the time being, for I can see no helpful parallel to it in the other palaces. On the other hand I can see no objection whatever to recognizing in EF at Phaistos, as at Knossos, a suite forming part of the Women's Quarters.

In summary, then, I am firmly convinced that the Residential Quarters of the three major palaces are so similar that Platon's suggestions represent a step backward rather than forward in the interpretation of the function of the rooms of which they are composed. The rooms I have designated as E on the plans will, I repeat, surely have had the same purpose in all three cases. Whether that purpose is best described by the terms Queen's Hall, Women's Hall, Ladies' Dressing Room, Private Sitting-room of the Royal Family, or even Anteroom to the Bath, is a matter on which there is plenty of room for a difference of opinion, though personally I think the term Anteroom to the Bath does less than justice to the importance of the room.[21]

It may be added with regard to the newly found palace at Kato Zakro that its excavator, Platon, is probably right in recognizing the Men's and Women's Halls in rooms 37 and 36, respectively, which form part of a badly preserved area east of the Central Court.[22] But it is not clear whether

---

[20] See above n. 16. The BR/LB is off the King's Hall only when there is no Queen's Hall, as in Tylissos A.

[21] In their study of the houses at Amarna (first half of the fourteenth century B.C.) Peet and Woolley (*The City of Akhenaten*, 1, 37) conclude that a room, smaller than the main Living Room but similarly furnished was "clearly an inner and more private Living Room"; the analogy between these two halls and the primary and secondary halls (men's and women's halls) in the Minoan palaces and houses is extraordinarily close.

[22] N. Platon, *Zakros: The Discovery of a Lost Palace of Ancient Crete*, 1971, 174-184.

the BR/LB (58), some distance to the north of these rooms, together with its anteroom (59)—certainly as "anteroom" in this case—is to be considered as a bathroom belonging to the Residential Quarters or as a lustral chamber to be associated with the main entrance of the palace. Its form, decoration, and finds, as well as its isolation from 37 and 36 would suggest that the latter alternative is a distinct possibility.[23] But, as Platon himself says, "the distinction between bathroom and lustral chamber is not always easy."[24]

Another instance of this difficulty is to be found in the pair of BR/LBs in the south-western quarter of the palace at Phaistos, 19 and 21. These have been interpreted by their Italian excavators as bathrooms for the palace staff,[25] but as Platon remarks, "there are no living quarters nearby."[26] Instead, as he further notes, the nearby rooms along the Central Court, 22-24, and the block of four rooms facing on the West Court, 8-11, appear to have had religious functions. Nevertheless, although I would agree that these two BR/LBs, like perhaps all "bathrooms," may have possessed religious associations to a certain degree, I see no strong reasons either in the form of the rooms or in the finds made in them to view 19 and 21 as *primarily* ritual rooms, as Platon does—in this instance approaching the views of Alexiou (see below). For the two suites of rooms of which the BR/LBs form a part, i.e. rooms 17, 18, 19, and 16, 20, 21, appear to have no physical connection with rooms 8-11 or 22-24; their exit and entrance, in fact, is by way of 12-15, a series of corridors which connect with the main entrance, 7, from the West Court into the Central Court.[27] Platon seems not to have noticed my suggestion that the complex of rooms 16-21 constituted two guest-suites, consisting, we might say, of sitting-room, bedroom, and bath, entered from a common anteroom, 15. I still see this as the solution that best fits the known facts, hypothetical though it must remain unless some further evidence turns up.[28]

The views of Alexiou take quite a different turn from those of Platon. Alexiou's principal thesis is that none of the BR/LBs was used for ordinary bathing, but solely for some ritual purpose or purposes. He thus reverts essentially to the position of Evans and his followers who regarded these rooms as lustral basins or chambers rather than as bathrooms. The bathing of the body for the ordinary purposes of cleansing would have taken place,

[23] Platon sees it as "serving both as an ordinary bathroom for the royal family and occasionally for ritual purification," *op.cit.*, 183.

[24] *Europa* 239.

[25] *Op.cit.* (n. 7), 122-130.

[26] *Europa* 243.

[27] *PoC* 112.

[28] My suggestion was made quite independently of a similar identification by Mr. and Mrs. Hawes, *Crete the Forerunner of Greece*, 1911, 81.

according to Alexiou, in clay tubs which could be placed almost anywhere in the palace or house, although rarely, it would appear, in the Residential Quarters.[29]

One of Alexiou's principal reasons for adopting this view is that the BR/LBs had no drain and therefore could not have been used, he says, for any such practical purpose as bathing.[30] This is not a new argument, and Platon and I have alrealy pointed out that it would have been very difficult and expensive to build and to maintain in operation a drain at such a depth below the general surface.[31] However that may be, we do not subscribe to Alexiou's view that the lack of a drain would have ruled out the possible use of the BR/LBs as actual bathrooms. Drains would have been a convenience (until they became blocked), but were not a necessity. For example, in the classical Greek houses of Olynthos, where *built-in* tubs were used, less than half of the two dozen bathrooms excavated at that site were provided with drains, and these would have done no more than help to keep the *floors* dry—it would still have been necessary to bail and sponge out the *tubs*.[32] The same is true for the bathroom in the Palace of Nestor at Pylos, which had a built-in tub and a drain for the floor.[33] Egyptian practice varied: sometimes there was a drain, sometimes a jar cemented into the floor—which would have had to be bailed out in order to be emptied.[34]

The need for some method of drainage would have been much reduced if, as I have previously suggested, clay bathtubs were used in conjunction with these BR/LBs, for the tubs could have been carried out by their handles or their projecting rims and emptied[35]—indeed the provision of handles might be taken to indicate that some such practice was followed. And, although Alexiou may be right in objecting that the tubs of water would have been excessively heavy and awkward even for four men to carry up the narrow stairways (usually involving a right-angled turn),[36] this objection is not really serious inasmuch as only a relatively small amount of water would have been used since a "Sitzbad" was not intended for

[29] *KCh* 420.

[30] Cf. Platon's comment (*Europa* 237): "Graham rightly noticed that neither the lack of drainage nor the covering of the walls and floors with gypsum constitutes an argument supporting the theory of lustral places . . ." Platon says that the BR/LB in Tylissos C does have a drain.

[31] *Europa* 245; *PoC* 103. Not that it would have been at all impossible for a people who built the drainage system in the Residential Quarter at Knossos; yet even there it had not been felt desirable to connect the bathroom with this system.

[32] D. M. Robinson and J. W. Graham, *Excavations at Olynthus*, 8, 1938, 202.

[33] C. W. Blegen and M. Rawson, *The Palace of Nestor at Pylos in Western Messenia*, 1, 1966, 185-189.

[34] J. D. S. Pendlebury, *Tell el-Amarna*, 1935, 106f.

[35] Platon notes that "the use of bath-tubs reduced the need for drainage," *Europa* 237.

[36] *KCh* 421.

immersion, modern style. In any event they could have been lightened, or even have been completely evacuated, by bailing—just as built-in tubs necessarily were—thus making it unnecessary to carry out the tubs at all.

More serious is Alexiou's further argument against the use of tubs that no tubs, and more significantly (since complete specimens would have been retrieved from the ruins), no fragments of tubs have ever been found, or at any rate seem to have been reported as found, in the BR/LBs.[37] He suggests, therefore, that the BR/LBs were not designed for the use of clay bathtubs, or indeed for bathing at all, but rather for ceremonial purifications or perhaps for rain-magic rituals (in conjunction with the rhyta so often found in or near these rooms), the performance of which need have involved only symbolic amounts of liquids.[38]

The comparatively few and very fragmentary bathtubs, mostly in LM I-II contexts,, that have been mentioned in publications, Alexiou concludes from their place of finding, were used almost indiscriminately in one or another of the rooms of the Minoan palaces or houses.[39] At any rate there fewness contrasts strongly with the mass of tubs of LM III date found for the most part in burials of that period, where they were used, or reused, as coffins.[40]

As relevant to the discussion we should at this point consider the significance of a peculiar phenomenon that has been observed in Houses A and C at Tylissos, in the Villa of the Lilies at Amnisos, and in the South House at Knossos.[41] In each of these four houses the deep basin, F, of their BR/LBs was eliminated by backfilling with earth, thus elevating their floor-level to match that of the adjoining room, E, from which they were entered, and completely concealing the stairway except for the top of the parapet at the edge of the stairway and the column, or the base on which the column had rested. The existence of such a parapet and column-base in F in the Residential Quarter of the Palace of Minos renders it highly probable that, although the present floors of E and F are at the same level, a trial excavation below the floor of F would reveal that here too a similar change had occurred.[42]

In the four certain instances, just mentioned, in which the low-level floor of the BR/LB was eliminated we still have no decisive evidence to indicate what purpose the room served even in its later form. In the fifth and still uncertain instance, however, i.e. the one in the Residential Quarter at Knossos, a fragmentary clay bathtub in LM IIIA style was found nearby,

[37] *KCh* 419f. [38] *KCh* 428.
[39] The significance of such scattered finds of tub fragments is debatable.
[40] *KCh* 419f.
[41] *Europa* 237-239; *PoC* 102f. The two at Tylissos and the one at Amnisos were first recognized by Platon.
[42] *Europa* 239 with n. 12; *PoC* 103.

in Ea,[43] and it was this fact, coupled with the dimensions, location, and form of the room, that induced Evans to identify F here as a bathroom, an identification that he maintained from first to last.[44] If, then, Alexiou excavates here (as he plans to do) and finds traces of stairs and/or a low level floor it would be natural to infer that the room in its earlier form (i.e. with sunken floor) was also used as a bathroom, and natural too to infer that at least all the BR/LRs in the Residential Quarters were likewise so used.[45]

This change in the form of the bathroom—if bathroom it was in both stages—could be understood as reflecting a change in the style of bathing.[46] The fact that, as Alexiou has pointed out, clay tubs seem to have been rare before the LM period might suggest that their appearance was also connected with this change in the physical form of the room. In that event it may be conjectured that in the earlier stage, and possibly under the influence of the Egyptian practice, water was poured over the bather, while in a standing or crouching position, by an attendant.[47] With an eye to increased physical comfort the Cretans will have improved upon this method by sinking the floor of F, where the bather stood, below the level of the room, E, from which it was entered. Thus the attendant would have been able to stand at a higher level and so more conveniently and more effectively pour the water—or even sprinkle it from a perforated container—over the head and shoulders of the bather.

This would also provide a more adequate explanation for the Cretan's going to so much trouble to sink their BR/LBs several feet beneath the general level than any of the explanations offered previously, such as to avoid draughts, to prevent splashing the surroundings, or to ensure privacy—though one or more of these may have been a consideration.[48] This will also provide a reasonable explanation for an otherwise puzzling feature of the carefully designed and finished BR/LB in the North Residential Quarter at Phaistos.[49] The entrance to the basin in F is, in quite

[43] See above (n. 6).   [44] *PoM* 3, 385.

[45] Cf. *Europa* 237: "as we know that many rooms with a staircase have been altered by being filled up with earth and thus making a new floor, such an interpretation would lead us to admit the transformation of the lustral places into bathrooms, which seems very unlikely"; the interpretation he here refers to is that "all the rooms provided with a staircase leading down into them should be lustral places."

[46] Platon, *Europa* 245, seems to suggest a change in bathing habits: "it is possible that in earlier times the basin was filled with water" (on this see below, n. 51), while "the use of bath-tubs is very likely during the last period."

[47] Pendlebury, *op.cit.* (n. 34), 106f.: "the bath itself is a stone slab in one corner surrounded by a screen wall over which a slave would pour the water on his master."

[48] *PoC* 105f.; *Europa* 237. In a short discussion of the problem of the BR/LBs Bogdan Rutkowski explains the sunken basins as a means "to prevent the water from escaping" (*Cult Places in the Aegean World*, Warsaw 1972, 231).

[49] Pernier and Banti (*op.cit.* [n. 7], 303) also admit being puzzled and make a very unlikely suggestion.

normal fashion, via a stairway along its west side, at the head of which is a doorway entered from E; but, in addition, on the opposite (east) side, there is a broad ledge at the same level as the floor in E entered, like the stairs, by a doorway from E. Surely this ledge, whose level is about a meter above the floor of the basin, F, would have provided an excellent location for the attendant to stand when administering the douche.

It should also be observed that the suggestions just made to explain the function of these low-level basins would apply well for a ceremonial as for a practical usage.

Some, however, will perhaps be inclined to object to this proposed method of bathing on the ground that, as has often been asserted, gypsum is so soluble to water that the thin alabaster lining of the Minoan BR/LBs would soon be eroded away.[50] But this danger has been greatly exaggerated: a finegrained, smooth-finished gypsum slab would resist the dissolving power of water almost indefinitely. Moreover, such a "shower" bath—which would be quite a different thing from an "immersion" bath—would not have meant filling or even partly filling the basin, nor allowing water to stand to some depth in it for some length of time before it was emptied. Probably not more than a couple of gallons of water would have been used for a single douche, and even five gallons (20 to 25 liters) would not have covered the floor of the basin in such a BR/LB as that in the North Residential Quarter in Phaistos to a depth greater than half a centimeter (one fifth of an inch).[51] To sponge up this amount promptly after the bath would surely not have unduly taxed the attendants of the royal bath. They may even have, on occasion, allowed the water to disappear through evaporation or by seepage between the slabs of the floor.

When, at a later date, possibly under Near Eastern influence, the convenience of bathing in a tub came to be appreciated, it must also soon have been realized that, as Alexiou has pointed out, to carry the tub up the

[50] On the use of gypsum see *PoC* 104; *KCh* 415; and *Europa* 237 ("gypsum slabs . . . had the practical advantages of being durable and easily renewed.") J. W. Shaw, "Minoan Architecture: Materials and Techniques," *ASAtene* 33, 1971, 21-33 takes a more cautious approach.

[51] Even a royal Minoan bather would be unlikely to use nearly as much water as the modern bather who is accustomed to unlimited amounts of water, hot or cold, at the turn of a tap. Platon's suggestion that "it is possible that in earlier times the basin was *filled* [my italics] with water" should surely be rejected because of the amount of water involved (cf. above, n. 46): the BR/LB in the North Residential Quarter at Phaistos, for example, would contain when full some 1200 imperial gallons or about 5500 liters! If the basin were not emptied after each such use (at what labor!) one can readily imagine the condition of the water after a week or two in the heat of summer. Pendlebury also remarks of the north "lustral area" at Knossos that "it can never have been filled with water—the gypsum paving and wall-slabs would not have stood it" (*Handbook to the Palace of Minos*, ²1954, 44).

stairs to be emptied, or even to bail the water into buckets to be carried out, was a needlessly laborious task. The obvious remedy was to bring the floor-level of the BR/LB up to the level of the adjoining room, E, the Women's Hall. As we have already seen, this change in level seems to have been carried out in LM times in five out of the score or more BR/LBs so far excavated.

A solution along these lines, it seems to me, is more in keeping with the realities of the situation than to accept Alexiou's explanation that the palaces and mansions of Minoan Crete had no special bathrooms—palaces which, as the late Friedrich Matz wrote (perhaps with some exaggeration) in the *Cambridge Ancient History*, display a "domestic luxury with which the palaces of Egypt and the Near East have nothing comparable."[52] Alexiou's view, if correct, would suggest instead that in this aspect of private life Crete was extraordinarily backward in the physical amenities, in consideration of the fact that specially constructed bathrooms were provided in mid-fourteenth century Egyptian houses at Amarna, in the palace in Mari on the Euphrates in the time of Hammurabi (18th century B.C.), in a LM III private house excavated by Alexiou himself at Katsamba, a seaport of Knossos,[53] and in the Mycenaean palaces at Pylos, Tiryns, and (perhaps) Mycenae, even if one leaves out of account their frequency in quite modest private houses of the Hellenic and Hellenistic period at Olynthos and Delos.

It is also very difficult to accept Alexiou's point of view that even the BR/LBs in the very heart of the Residential Quarters, both in the palaces and in many of the private houses, should have been used *exclusively* for religious or ceremonial purposes.[54] Nor does this view seem consistent with his remark that "the position of the 'basins' (i.e. the BR/LBs) is not always so near the residential apartments that the conclusion may be drawn with certainty about their domestic usage,"[55] for this would seem to imply that the BR/LBs did often occur within the Residential Quarters and that in such instances they were in fact used for domestic, i.e. bathing, purposes.

As for the alteration in the floor-level of several of the BR/LBs it seems easier to suggest a reason for this change in terms of a change in bathing habits than to attempt to explain it as due to some hypothetical alteration in religious fashions.[56] Indeed the naturally conservative character of religious practice would favor the retention of the system of purification by

[52] *CAH* 2³, 1, 1973, 559.

[53] *Praktika* 1955, 312f. For Mari see A. Parrot, *Mission archéologique de Mari*, 2, 1958, 202-205, and note that the Homeric word *asaminthos* (now attested in Linear B) with its 'Minoan' ending has recently been referred to Akkadian namasittu, 'wash-basin, tub,' by O. Szemerényi, *JHS* 94, 1974, 149.

[54] *KCh* 425; 433.   [55] *KCh* 422.

[56] As Alexiou would do, *KCh* 434.

sprinkling rather than encourage a change to tub bathing, thus explaining why rooms which were used primarily or exclusively for ritual ceremonies, such as the Lustral Basin off the Throne Room at Knossos, would have kept their sunken floors.

In this connection I should admit that it was probably my attempt to sum up my position too briefly in the sentence quoted at the beginning of this paper that caused Dr. Alexiou to misunderstand me. Taking me too literally as meaning that *every* BR/LB must have served both religious and domestic purposes he pointed to the in that case anomalous position of the BR/LB off the Room of the Throne at Knossos when so much space was available elsewhere in the palace for a bathroom, and when the Residential Quarters were so remote.[57] What I meant to suggest was that bathing in even the simplest and most domestic surroundings might involve some degree of religious experience; on the other hand I did not mean to be understood as declaring that even the most elaborate BR/LB must have been available on occasion for the purpose of ordinary bodily cleansing.

One other rather captious objection that Alexiou finds is that if EF had a ceremonial use then E would have functioned as a waiting-room for worshippers waiting to undergo the ritual bath or anointment in F; whereas if F were merely used for ordinary purpose of bathing then he can see no useful function for E to play.[58] Is it not reasonable, however, to suppose that in the numerous cases where the BR/LB was located within the Residential Quarters the women of the house or palace would have used E as a kind of private sitting-room or dressing-room? Evans evidently thought so, to judge from the restoration of this room which he published,[59] and so surely have most writers on Minoan domestic architecture.

In conclusion I would suggest that the history of the usage of the BR/LBs ran somewhat as follows:

Sometime probably early in the period of the "new palaces" (MM IIIA)—if not earlier—and possibly under Egyptian influence, the practice was adopted of constructing a room specifically for bathing and located off the secondary ("women's") hall, or, if that were missing, e.g. in Tylissos A, off the primary ("men's") hall. Water was poured over the bather by an attendant, as was done in Egypt, but this procedure was improved upon by sinking the floor of the bathroom, F, several feet below that of the main hall, E, and connecting the two rooms by a short flight of steps; thus the attendant, standing on the higher level in E, could pour the water over the bather in F more effectively, providing a kind of overhead douche or shower-bath.

[57] *KCh* 417; 422.
[58] *KCh* 433.
[59] *PoM* 3, frontispiece. Cf. the arrangement of the Amarna houses (see above, n. 21).

Due to the widely-held belief that the soul as well as the body could be cleansed by washing it is not surprising that rooms similar to the bathrooms with sunken floors should also have been developed for ceremonial or ritual cleansing in connection with state or official functions. Naturally, too, such rooms tended to be built larger, deeper, and in a more pretentious architectural style than those built for private or domestic use only.

Apparently in MM III B times the introduction of bathing in clay tubs began, perhaps due to Near Eastern influence, and this in turn led to giving up the use of the sunken basins. For ritual purposes, however, religious conservatism would have tended to perpetuate the older procedure of pouring water over the worshipper, and so we may assume that there would have been no compelling reason to alter the physical form of the ceremonial type of room, that is of the "Lustral Basin." And it is true that the four or five instances so far recognized where the floor of the basin, F, has been adjusted upward have all been clearly of the domestic rather than of the ceremonial character, while there seems no clear evidence that the floor-level of any of the purely or primarily ritual BR/LBs was ever so elevated.[60]

[60] Platon, to be sure, does claim that the BR/LB in the Little Palace at Knossos (which should probably be reckoned as a lustral basin rather than as a domestic bathroom) "during the Post-palatial period was changed into a shrine by filling in the inner space and thus covering up its staircase . . ." (*op.cit.* [n. 22], 181; and similarly *Europa* 241). But this view is based on a somewhat obscurely worded passage in the *PoM* (2,522f.) where Evans is really referring to the floor-level of the bottom of the basin, not, as Platon understands him, to a hypothetical later floor built at a higher level in the "Reoccupation" period. It is true that in this late period certain alterations in the room were made, such as walling up some doorways and closing the intervals between the row of fluted wooden columns standing on the east parapet of the basin, but that no raising of the floor-level occurred is made clear by Evans' comparison to the BR/LBs of the Room of the Throne and of the North Lustral Area (no one, I think, has ever claimed that either of these was at any time rebuilt with a high-level floor), as well as by a careful reading of Mackenzie's eye-witness account of the excavation of the BR/LB of the Little Palace (daybook 1905, May 3-5) where he describes its clearing in explicit detail.

BIBLIOGRAPHY

BRIEF LIST OF RECENT BOOKS AND ARTICLES

Cottrell, Leonard, *The Bull of Minos*, London, 1953.

Dinsmoor, *Architecture of Ancient Greece*, 3rd ed., London, 1950.

Graham, J. W., "The Phaistos 'Piano Nobile,'" *AJA*, 60 (1956), pp. 151-157.

———, "The Central Court as the Minoan Bull-Ring," *AJA*, 61 (1957), pp. 255-262.

———, "The Residential Quarter of the Minoan Palace," *AJA*, 63 (1959), pp. 47-52.

———, "Windows, Recesses, and the Piano Nobile in the Minoan Palaces," *AJA*, 64 (1960), pp. 329-333.

———, "The Minoan Unit of Length and Minoan Palace Planning," *AJA*, 64 (1960), pp. 335-341.

———, "The Minoan Banquet Hall," *AJA*, 65 (1961), pp. 165-172.

———, "Mycenaean Architecture," *Archaeology*, 13 (1960), pp. 46-54.

Hutchinson, R. W., "Prehistoric Town Planning in Crete," *Town Planning Review*, 21 (1950), pp. 199-220.

*Karo, Georg, *Greifen am Thron, Erinnerungen an Knossos*, Baden-Baden, 1959.

Lawrence, A. W., *Greek Architecture*, Penguin Books, 1957.

———, "Alleged Minoan Fortifications," *JHS*, 80 (1942), pp. 84-85.

———, "The Ancestry of the Minoan Palace," *BSA*, 46 (1951), pp. 81-85.

**Marinatos, Spyridon, and Hirmer, Max, *Crete and Mycenae*, New York, 1960.

Matton, Raymond, *La Crète au cours des siècles*, Athens, 1957.

*Matz, Friedrich, *Kreta, Mykene, Troja*, Stuttgart, 1957.

Palmer, L. R., *Mycenaeans and Minoans, Aegean Prehistory in the Light of the Linear B Tablets* (London, 1961).

Pendlebury, J. D. S., *Archaeology of Crete*, London, 1939.

———, *A Handbook to the Palace of Minos*, 2nd ed., 1954.

Pernier, Luigi, and Luisa Banti, *Guida degli scavi italiani in Creta,* Rome, 1947.

**Piggott, Stuart (ed.), *The Dawn of Civilization* (ch. VII, M. S. F. Hood, "The Home of the Heroes, the Aegean before the Greeks"), London, 1961.

Plommer, Hugh, *Ancient and Classical Architecture,* London, 1956.

Press, Ludwika, "Les maisons et les palais de Crète à l'époque du néolithe et du bronze," *Archeologia,* 9 (1957), pp. 1-31 (in Polish, with French summary, pp. 33-34).

————, "Les sites et les villes de la Crète aux IIIe et IIe millénaires avant notre ère," *Archeologia,* 10 (1958), pp. 28-58 (in Polish, with French summary, pp. 60-61).

*Rau, Heimo, *Kretische Paläste, Mykenische Burgen,* Stuttgart, 1957.

Renault, Mary, *The King Must Die,* New York, 1958.

Snijder, G. A. S., *Kretische Kunst,* Berlin, 1936.

*Zervos, C., *L'Art de la Crète,* Paris, 1956.

* The items marked with an asterisk are particularly valuable for their illustrations; a double asterisk indicates color as well as black and white illustrations.

SELECT ADDENDA, 1968

Alexiou, S., "Minoan Flagstaffs," *Kret. Chron.* 17, 1963, pp. 339-351.

————, *Minoan Civilization with a Guide to the Palaces of Knossos, Phaistos, and Mallia* (in Greek), Herakleion, 1964.

————, Platon, Guanella, von Matt, *Ancient Crete,* New York, 1968.

Alsop, J., "A Reporter at Large, Kato Zakro," *New Yorker,* Aug. 13, 1966, pp. 32-95.

Baumann, H., *Lion Gate and Labyrinth,* London, 1967.

Bowman, John, *Crete,* London, 1962.

Graham, J. W., "The Relation of the Minoan Palaces to the Near Eastern palaces of the Second Millennium," *Mycenaean Studies,* ed. E. L. Bennett Jr., Madison, 1964, pp. 195-215.

————, "A Banquet Hall at Mycenaean Pylos," *AJA* 71 (1967), pp. 353-360.

————, "Further Notes on the Minoan Foot," *Second International Cretological Conference,* Athens, 1967, pp. 157-165.

————, "The Cretan Palace: sixty-seven years of Exploration," *A Land called Crete* (Smith College Studies in History, XLV), Northampton, Massachusetts, 1968, pp. 17-34.

**Hawkes, J., *Dawn of the Gods*, Toronto, 1968.

**Higgins, R., Minoan and Mycenaean Art, New York, 1967.

**Hood, S., *Home of the Heroes, the Aegean before the Greeks*, New York, 1967.

Hutchinson, R. W., *Prehistoric Crete*, Harmondsworth, 1962.

Matz, F., "Minoan Civilization: Maturity and Zenith," *Cambridge Ancient History*², Cambridge, 1962, pp. 3-48.

**————, *Crete and Early Greece*, London, 1962.

Press, L., "Architecture of Minoan Crete, State of Research," *Archaeologia* 11 (1959-60), pp. 222-233 (in Polish).

————, *Aegean Architecture*, Warsaw, 1964 (in Polish).

————, *Architecture in Prehellenic Iconography*, Warsaw, 1967 (in Polish).

**Platon, N., *Crete*, Cleveland and New York, 1966.

————, *Encyclopedia of World Art* IV, New York, 1961, pp. 75-114.

————, "Comparative Chronology of the Three Minoan Palaces," *Kret. Chron.* 15, 1961-62, pp. 127-136.

————, "Bathrooms and Lustral Basins in Minoan Dwellings," *Europa*, ed. W. C. Brice, Berlin, 1967, pp. 236-245.

Schachermeyr, F., *Die minoische Kultur des alten Kreta*, Stuttgart, 1964.

Schott, A., "Minoische und mykenische Palasthöfe," *Jb. Oest. Arch. Inst.* 45 (1960), pp. 68-80.

Tiré, C. and Van Effenterre, H., *Guide des fouilles françaises en Crète*, Paris, 1966.

Ward, A., "The Cretan Bull Sports," *Antiquity* 42 (1968), pp. 117-122.

SELECT ADDENDA, 1971

Branigan, K., *The Foundations of Palatial Crete*, New York, 1970.

Graham, J. W., "Egyptian Features at Phaistos," *AJA* 74 (1970), pp. 231-239.

BIBLIOGRAPHY

Hood, S., *The Minoans, Crete in the Bronze Age*, London, New York, 1971.

Palmer, L. R., *A New Guide to the Palace of Knossos*, London, New York, 1969.

————, *The Penultimate Palace of Knossos*, Rome, 1969.

Sinos, S., *Die vorklassischen Hausformen in der Ägäis*, Mainz am Rhein, 1971.

SELECT ADDENDA, 1986

Alexiou, S., *A Guide to the Minoan Palaces*, Herakleion, n.d.

————, *Minoan Civilization*, Herakleion, 1969.

————, "Masts of Minoan Shrines and Egyptian Pylons," *Athens Annals of Archaeology*, 2 (1969), pp. 84-88 (in Greek with French summary).

————, "Sulla funzione di alcuni ambienti nei palazzi minoici," *Antichità Cretesi*, I, Università di Catania, Istituto di Archaeologia, 1973, pp. 60-64.

Amouretti, M.Cl. *Fouilles exécutées à Mallia, le centre politique, II, la crypte hypostyle*, Paris, 1970.

Cadogan, G., *Palaces of Minoan Crete*, London, 1976.

————, "Pyrgos, Crete, 1970-77," *JHS Archaeological Reports*, 1977-78, pp. 70-84.

Chapouthier, F., et al., *Fouilles exécutées à Mallia, quatrième rapport, exploration du palais (1929-1935 et 1946-1960)*, Paris, 1962.

Davaras, C., *Guide to Cretan Antiquities*, Park Ridge, New Jersey, 1976.

Dow, S., Graham, W., Shear, L., Vermeule, E., *A Land Called Crete, A Symposium in Memory of Harriet Boyd Hawes, 1871-1945*, Northampton, Smith College, 1968.

Ecole française d'Athènes, *Études crétoises, XIX, 1974, Mallia, Plan du site, Plans du palais, indices*.

Graham, J. W., "A New Arena at Mallia," *Antichità Cretesi*, I, Università di Catania, Istituto di Archeologia, 1973, pp. 65-73.

————, *Minoan Crete*, Keramos Guides, Athens, 1974.

————, "The Banquet Hall of the Little Palace," *AJA*, 79 (1975), pp. 141-144.

————, "Bathrooms and Lustral Chambers," *Greece and the Eastern Mediterranean in Ancient History and Prehistory*," ed. K. H. Kinzl, Berlin, 1977, pp. 110-125.

————, "Further Notes on Minoan Palace Architecture: 1. West Magazines and Upper Halls at Knossos and Mallia; 2. Access to, and Use of, Minoan Palace Roofs," *AJA* 83 (1979), pp. 49-69.

273

Hallager, E., *The Mycenaean Palace at Knossos*, Stockholm, 1977.

Laviosa, C., "La casa TM III a Festòs: osservazioni sull'architettura cretesi in età micénea," *Antichità Cretesi*, I, Università di Catania, Istituto di Archeologia, pp. 79-88.

Lawrence, A. W., *Greek Architecture³*, Penguin Books, 1973.

Lembesi, A., "The Archanes House-model" (in Greek), *Ephemeris*, 1976, pp. 12-43.

Levi, D., *Festòs e la civiltà minoica*, Rome, 1976.

Pelon, O., *Mallia, Exploration des maisons et quartiers d'habitation (1963-1966), troisième fascicule*, Paris, 1970.

————, *Le Palais de Malia*, Ecole française d'Athènes, Etudes crétoises, XXV, 1980, Paris.

Platon, N., "Chronological Problems of Minoan Palaces" (in Greek) *Ephemeris* 1968, pp. 1-58.

————, "About the Problem of the Site of the Minoan Bullgames" (in Greek), KERNOS, presented to Prof. George Bakalakis, Thessalonike, 1972, pp. 134-148.

————, *Zakros, The Discovery of a Lost Palace of Ancient Crete*, New York, 1971.

Popham, M. R. et al. *Minoan Unexplored Mansion at Knossos, Supp. vol. 17*, British School of Archaeology at Athens, Thames and Hudson, 1984.

Press, L., *Material Culture of Ancient Greece, I, The Aegean Settlements*, Warsaw, 1977 (in Polish).

Shaw, J. W., *Minoan Architecture: Materials and Techniques (Annuario della Scuola Archeologica di Atene, 33, 1971)*.

————, "The Orientation of the Minoan Palaces," *Antichità Cretesi*, I, Università di Catania, Istituto di Archeologia, 1973, pp. 47-59.

————, "Sliding Panels at Knossos," *BSA*, 73, (1978), pp. 234-248.

————, "Evidence for the Minoan Tripartite Shrine," *AJA*, 82, 1978, pp. 429-448.

van Effenterre, H. and M., *Fouilles exécutées à Mallia, le centre politique I, l'Agora*, Paris, 1969.

————, "Arène ou Agora?" *Antichità Cretesi*, I, Università di Catania, Istituto di Archeologia, pp. 74-78.

————, *Le Palais de Mallia et la cité minoenne*, Rome, 1980.

Warren, P., *Myrtos: An Early Bronze Age Settlement in Crete*, London, 1972.

————, *The Aegean Civilizations*, Oxford: Elsevier-Phaidon, 1975.

For a comprehensive bibliography with summaries of sites and architecture in the decade 1965-1977 see Stefan Hiller, *Das minoische Kreta nach den Ausgrabungen des letzten Jahrzehnts*, Vienna, 1977, especially pp. 27f., and chap. IV.

ABBREVIATIONS

PERIODICALS

AA	*Archäologischer Anzeiger*
AJA	*American Journal of Archaeology*
Annuario	*Annuario della R. Scuola Archeologica di Atene*
Ath. Mitt.	*Athenische Mitteilungen*
BCH	*Bulletin de correspondence hellénique*
BSA	*Annual of the British School of Archaeology at Athens*
Ephemeris	Ἀρχαιολογικὴ Ἐφημερίς
JHS	*Journal of Hellenic Studies*
Kret. Chron.	Κρητικὰ Χρονικά
Mon. Piot	*Monuments et Mémoires Piot*
Op. Arch.	*Opuscula Archaeologica*
PdP	*Parola del Passato*
Praktika	Πρακτικὰ τῆς Ἀρχαιολογικῆς Ἑταιρείας
RA	*Revue archéologique*
REA	*Revue des études anciennes*
To Ergon	Τὸ Ἔργον τῆς Ἀρχαιολογικῆς Ἑταιρείας

MISCELLANEOUS

A. of C.	Pendlebury, J. D. S., *Archaeology of Crete*, London, 1939.
C. and M.	Marinatos and Hirmer, *Crete and Mycenae*, New York, 1960.
DMG	Ventris and Chadwick, *Documents in Mycenaean Greek*, Cambridge, 1956.
Guida	Pernier and Banti, *Guida degli scavi italiani in Creta*, Rome, 1947.
Guide²	Platon, *A Guide to the Archaeological Museum of Heraclion*, 2nd ed., Heraclion, 1957.
KMT	Matz, *Kreta, Mykene, Troja*, Stuttgart, 1957.
Minoica	Grumach, editor, *Minoica, Festschrift zum 80. Geburtstag von Johannes Sundwall*, Berlin, 1958.
MMR²	Nilsson, *Minoan-Mycenaean Religion*, 2nd ed., Lund, 1950.

PRINCIPAL SITES

Alalakh	Woolley, *Alalakh*, Oxford, 1955.
Festòs, I	Pernier, *Il Palazzo Minoico di Festòs*, I, Roma, 1935.
Festòs, II	Pernier and Banti, *Il Palazzo Minoico di Festòs*, II, Roma, 1951.
Gournia	Hawes, and others, *Gournia*, Philadelphia, 1908.
Knossos, I-IV	Evans, *The Palace of Minos at Knossos*, vols. I-IV (in six) and Index volume, London, 1921-1936.
Mallia, I	Chapouthier and Charbonneaux, *Fouilles exécutées à Mallia, premier rapport (1922-1924)*, Paris, 1928.
Mallia, II	Chapouthier and Joly, *Fouilles*, etc., *deuxième rapport, exploration du palais (1925-1926)*, Paris, 1936.
Mallia, III	Chapouthier and Demargne, *Fouilles*, etc., *troisième rapport, exploration du palais bordures orientale et septentrionale (1927, 1928, 1931, 1932)*, Paris, 1942.
Mallia, Maisons, I	Demargne and Santerre, *Fouilles*, etc., *exploration des maisons et quartiers d'habitation (1921-1948), premier fascicule*, Paris, 1953.
Mallia, Maisons, II	Deshayes and Dessenne, *Fouilles*, etc., *Exploration des maisons et quartiers d'habitation (1948-1954), deuxième fascicule*, Paris, 1960.
Mari, II	Parrot, *Mission archéologique de Mari*, II, *Le Palais*, Paris, 1958.
Mochlos	Seager, *Explorations in the Island of Mochlos*, Boston and New York, 1912.
Olynthus, VIII	Robinson and Graham, *Excavations at Olynthus*, VIII, *The Hellenic House*, Baltimore, 1938.
Palaikastro	British School at Athens, Supplementary Paper No. 1, *The Unpublished Objects from the Palaikastro Excavations 1902-1906*, Part I, London, 1923.
Phylakopi	Society for the Promotion of Hellenic Studies, Supplementary Paper No. 4, *Excavations at Phylakopi in Melos*, London, 1904.
Tylissos	Hazzidakis, *Les Villas minoennes de Tylissos*, Paris, 1934.

ILLUSTRATIONS:

SOURCES, CREDITS, DIMENSIONS

1. Drawn for Palaces of Crete by W. S. Schoonhoven
2. Knossos, IV, p. xxvi; by permission Macmillan & Co.
3. Redrawn by Juliana Bianco.
4. Drawn by JWG, after *Festòs, Tavole*, pl. 2.
5. Drawn by JWG.
6. Redrawn by Juliana Bianco.
7. Combination of Figs. 2, 4, 6.
8, 9. *Gournia*, plan and fig. 10.
10–12. Drawn by JWG.
13. From *JHS, AR 1972-73*, p. 51, fig. 3, by permission.
14. *Knossos*, II, fig. 227; by permission.
15. *Knossos*, II, fig. 208; by permission.
16. *Knossos*, II, fig. 224; by permission.
17. *Knossos*, I, fig. 306; by permission.
18. *Knossos*, II, fig. 251; by permission.
19, 20. *Tylissos*, pls. 6, 11.
21. Drawn for *Palaces of Crete* by Frances Brittain.
22. *Mallia, Maisons*, I, pl. 63; by permission.
23. Drawn by JWG, after *Mallia, Maisons*, II, plan 7.
24. *Mallia, Maisons*, II, plan I; by permission.
25. *Mallia, Maisons*, I, pl. 66; by permission.
26. Drawn by JWG, detail of preceding.
27. *Mallia, Maisons*, II, plan 3; by permission.
28. *BSA, Supplement* I, pl. I.
29. *BSA*, 8 (1901-1902), pl. 20.
30. Drawn by JWG, after *BSA*, 20 (1913-1914), pl. I.
31. *Knossos*, II, fig. 167; by permission.
32. Drawn by JWG, after *Ephemeris*, 1939-1941, p. 71, fig. 4.
33. Drawn by JWG, after Pendlebury, *A. of C.*, fig. 5.
34–42. Photos by JWG.
43. Mural in Royal Ontario Museum, by Sylvia Hahn, after *Knossos*, III, frontispiece; by permission R.O.M.
44, 45. Water-colors in Herakleion Museum; by permission of Piet de Jong and Nikolaos Platon.

46, 47. Photos by JWG.

48. Redrawn by Sylvia Hahn after perspective by JWG.

49. Photo by JWG.

50. Redrawn by Juliana Bianco after perspective by JWG.

51–53. Photos by JWG.

54. *Knossos*, III, fig. 129; by permission.

55. Drawn by Prof. Hugo-Brunt for *Palaces of Crete*.

56, 57. Photos by JWG.

58. Redrawn by Juliana Bianco after perspective by JWG.

59–80. Photos by JWG.

81. *Knossos*, III, fig. 255; by permission.

82. Photo by JWG.

83–84. Drawn by JWG.

85. From J.D.S. Pendlebury, *Handbook to the Palace of Minos*, plan 3.

86. Drawn by JWG.

87–88. Drawn by Juliana Bianco.

89–90. Drawn by JWG.

91. *Mallia*, III, pl. 1; by permission.

92. *Mallia*, III, pl. 14; by permission.

93. Photo by JWG.

94. Marinatos and Hirmer, *C. and M.*, fig. 62; by permission.

95, 96. Photos by JWG.

97. *Knossos*, II, fig. 235; by permission.

98, 99. Photos by JWG.

100, 101. *DMG*, fig. 15.

102. Photo by JWG.

103. Drawn by JWG, after *Knossos*, I, fig. 226, A, B.

104. Drawn by JWG, after: A) *Mallia*, II, fig. 12 B) *Festòs*, II, fig. 32 C) *Alalakh*, p. 118, fig. 48. Dimensions: A) 16 cm. diam. B) 11 cm. diam. C) not given.

105–107. Drawn by JWG.

108–111. Drawn by M. Hugo-Brunt.

112. Photos and model by JWG.

113A. Drawn by JWG, after *Knossos*, II, fig. 214.

B. Drawn by JWG.

C. Drawn by JWG, after Pendlebury, *Handbook*, plan 8.

114. Drawn by JWG.

115–128. Photos by JWG.

129. Drawn by JWG.

130. *Knossos*, IV, Part II, frontispiece; by permission.

131A. *Knossos*, I, fig. 311; by permission.

B. *Knossos*, II, pl. 12; by permission.

132. *Knossos*, I, fig. 393; by permission.

133. *Knossos*, III, pl. 16; by permission.
134. *Knossos*, I, fig. 391; by permission.
135. Photo by JWG.
136. Drawn by JWG. A) Tomb of Clytemnestra, Bossert, *The Art of Ancient Crete*, fig. 24. B) From *Knossos*, II, fig. 368. C) From *Knossos*, III, fig. 35. D) From *Knossos*, I, fig. 226, I. EFK) From Grandstand Fresco, see Fig. 133. GH) *Archaeology*, 7 (1954), p. 152. I) Wace, *Mycenae*, figs. 49-51. J) *Knossos*, III, fig. 209. L) H. Triadha Boxer Vase, *Knossos*, I, fig. 508.
137, 138. Photos by JWG.
139. Drawn by JWG. A) From *Knossos*, III, fig. 173. BC) From *DMG*, fig. 23. D) *Knossos*, IV, fig. 890. E) See Fig. 101. F) *Knossos*, IV, fig. 899. G) *Knossos*, IV, pl. 31. H) *C. and M.*, fig. 207; *Knossos*, IV, fig. 329. I) *DMG*, p. 234. Dimensions: A) Length of each section, 70 cm. BC) Each 36 cm. long. D) Total ht. 1.38 m. F) Length 55 cm., ht. 13 cm.
140. Drawn by JWG. A) *Knossos*, II, fig. 401. B) *BSA, Suppl.* I, pl. 28F, fig. 112, I. C) *Knossos*, I, fig. 424. D) *Archaeologia*, 9 (1905), p. 398, fig. 3b. E) *ibid.*, p. 439, fig. 46. F) *Knossos*, II, fig. 398, a. G) *Mallia, Maisons*, II, pl. 17, 2. H) *Knossos*, II, fig. 398. I) *DMG*, fig. 16. J) *Knossos*, III, fig. 14. K) *Knossos*, II, fig. 392. Dimensions (where available): B) Length ca 13 cm. C) Length 1.45 m. D) Similar one 95 cm. long. E) Ht. 15 cm. G) Diam. 19.3 cm. K) Ht. 19.3 cm.
141. Drawn by JWG. A) *Mallia, Maisons*, I, pl. 39, 1, 2. B) *BSA*, 9 (1902-1903), p. 325, fig. 25. C) *Knossos*, II, fig. 178. D) *BSA, Suppl.* I, p. 73, fig. 58c. E) *Festòs*, II, fig. 232. F) *Knossos*, II, fig. 176, A. G) *Gournia*, pl. 2, no. 70. H) *Mallia, Maisons*, I, pl. 30, fig. 5. I) *ibid.*, pl. 30, fig. 2. J) *Knossos*, III, fig. 186. K) *BSA, Suppl.* I, p. 73, fig. 58. L) *Mallia, Maisons*, I, pl. 30, fig. 2. M) *Mallia*, III, fig. 28. Dimensions (where available): A) Ht. 44 cm., top diam. 40 cm. B) Ht. ca. 24 cm. C) Diam. 25 cm. D) Length 37.5 cm. G) Diam. ca. 24 cm. H) Ht. ca. 16 cm. I) Ht. ca. 13 cm. J) Ht. ca. 18 cm. K) Ht. 12.5 cm. L) Ht. ca. 18 cm. M) Ht. 15 cm.
142. A–H drawn by JWG; I) from *Knossos*, II, fig. 403, by permission. A) *AJA*, 13 (1909), p. 287, fig. 10. B) *Knossos*, II, fig. 394. C) *Knossos*, II, fig. 396. DE) *Knossos*, II, fig. 398. F) *Knossos*, II, fig. 400. G) *Knossos*, II, fig. 355. H) *Knossos*, II, fig. 398. Dimensions (where available): A) Diam. 31 cm. B) Diam. ca. 45 cm. C) Diam. ca. 18 cm. G) Diam. 1.40 m.; wt. 52.564 kg. I) Diam. ca. 39 cm.
143. Drawn by JWG. A) *Festòs*, II, fig. 171. B) *Knossos*, II, fig. 398, n. C) *Knossos*, IV, pl. 31. D) *Mochlos*, fig. 31. E) *Knossos*, I, fig. 435.

F) *C. and M.*, fig. 178-185. G) *Festòs*, II, fig. 46. H) *Mallia*, III, fig. 24. Dimensions (where available): D) Diam. 11.5 cm. F) Ht. ca. 8 cm. G) Ht. 43 cm. H) Diam. ca. 55 cm.

144–146. Drawn by JWG.

147. *Archaeology*, 7 (1954), p. 18 fig. 3; by permission.

148. Parrot, *Mari* (Paris, 1953), plan 3; by permission.

149. Smith, E. B., *Eg. Arch.*, pl. 71; by permission.

150. Drawn by JWG.

151. Photos and model by JWG, scale of model 1: 40; figure by Sylvia Hahn.

152. Photo by JWG.

153ABC. Drawn by JWG.

154. Photo by JWG.

155–156. Drawn by JWG.

157. From *BSA*, 10 (1903-1904), fig. 13.

158. Plan by J. W. Shaw, by permission British School of Archaeology.

159. Drawn by Juliana Bianco.

160. From H. and M. van Effenterre, *Fouilles exécutées a Mallia. Le centre politique*, I, *L'Agora* (Paris, 1969), fig. 160 by permission.

161. From École française d'Athènes, *Mallia, Plan du site, Plan du palais, Indices* (Paris, 1974), plans VII, VIII (dimensions and dashed lines added).

162–163. Drawn by JWG.

164. From *Festòs*, I, fig. 8, by permission.

165. Detail from fig. 164, drawn by JWG.

166. From plan by J. W. Shaw, by permission of N. Platon.

Special acknowledgements should be made to the following: to M. Georges Daux, Director of the French School of Archaeology at Athens for kind permission to reproduce Figs. 22, 24, 25, 27, 91, and 92 from the *Mallia* publications; to Nikolaos Platon and Piet de Jong for Figs. 44 and 45 (drawn by the latter under the supervision of the former); to M. André Parrot and the Librairie Orientaliste Paul Geuthner, Paris, for permission to reproduce Fig. 148; and to the Istituto Poligrafico dello Stato, Libreria dello Stato, Roma, for permission to reproduce Fig. 8 from *Palazzo Minoico di Festòs*, vol. 1 (riproduzione autorizzata dall'Istituto Nazionale di Archeologia e Storia dell'Arte, Roma); to Hirmer Verlag, Munich, for permission to reproduce Fig. 94; to the Cambridge University Press for permission to reproduce Figs. 100, 101; and to Macmillan & Co. Ltd. for permission to reproduce Figs. 2, 13-18, 31, 54, 81, 97, 130, 131A, 131B, and 132-134. The following figures have appeared in my articles in the *AJA* and by kind permission are here reproduced, some in somewhat altered form, and two redrawn (Figs. 48,

50): Fig. 4, *AJA* 64 (1960), pl. 96, fig. 10; Fig. 11, *AJA* 63 (1959), pl. 16, fig. 3; Fig. 12, *AJA* 63 (1959), pl. 16, fig. 2; Fig. 48, *AJA* 60 (1956), pl. 59, fig. 4; Fig. 50, *AJA* 61 (1957), pl. 79, fig. 14; Fig. 52, *AJA* 61 (1957), pl. 79, fig. 10; Fig. 83, *AJA* 64 (1960), pl. 93, fig. 3; Fig. 84, *AJA* 64 (1960), pl. 94, fig. 5; Fig. 85, *AJA* 64 (1960), pl. 97, fig. 12; Fig. 86, *AJA* 64 (1960), pl. 97, fig. 13; Fig. 87, *AJA* 65 (1961), pl. 62, fig. 4; Fig. 88, *AJA* 65 (1961), pls. 62, 63, figs. 6, 8; Fig. 89, *AJA* 65 (1961), pl. 63, fig. 7; Fig. 90, *AJA* 65 (1961), pl. 61, fig. 3; Fig. 99, *AJA* 65 (1961), pl. 64, fig. 11; Fig. 144, *AJA* 64 (1960), pl. 95, fig. 7; Fig. 145, *AJA* 64 (1960), pl. 95, fig. 8; Fig. 146, *AJA* 64 (1960), pl. 96, fig. 9.

INDEX

Bold-faced type is used for principal discussions where the references are numerous, and to refer to the **Addenda** (**Add.**).

workrooms, 32, 38, 44f, 127f, **129-137**;
  see also service areas
writing, 7, 12, 16f, 233; Linear A, 7,
  226; Linear B, 14, 68f, 136, 211-213,
  215f, 218, 228; *see also* tablets
Wroncka, Teresa, 4

Xanthoudides, S. A., 58, 161

yew, 213

Zakros, 4, 19, 72, 169, 191, **Add. 2**
Zervos, C., 234
Zeus, 5, 17f, 23, 25
Zimrilim, 240
Zoser, 230
Zou, 72

PLATES

LIST OF SITES

1. APODHOULOU
2. H. TRIADHA
3. PHAISTOS
4. GORTYN
5. KAMARES CAVE
6. SKLAVOKAMBOS

7. TYLISSOS
8. PRASA, KATSAMBA
9. KNOSSOS
10. ARKHANES
11. VATHYPETRO
12. KANLI KASTELLI
13. AMNISOS

14. NIROU KHANI
15. MALLIA
16. PLATI
17. KEPHALA
18. GOURNIA
19. VASILIKI
20. PSEIRA

21. MOCHLOS
22. SITEIA
23. ZOU
24. PALAIKASTRO
25. ZAKROS
26. MONASTIRAKI

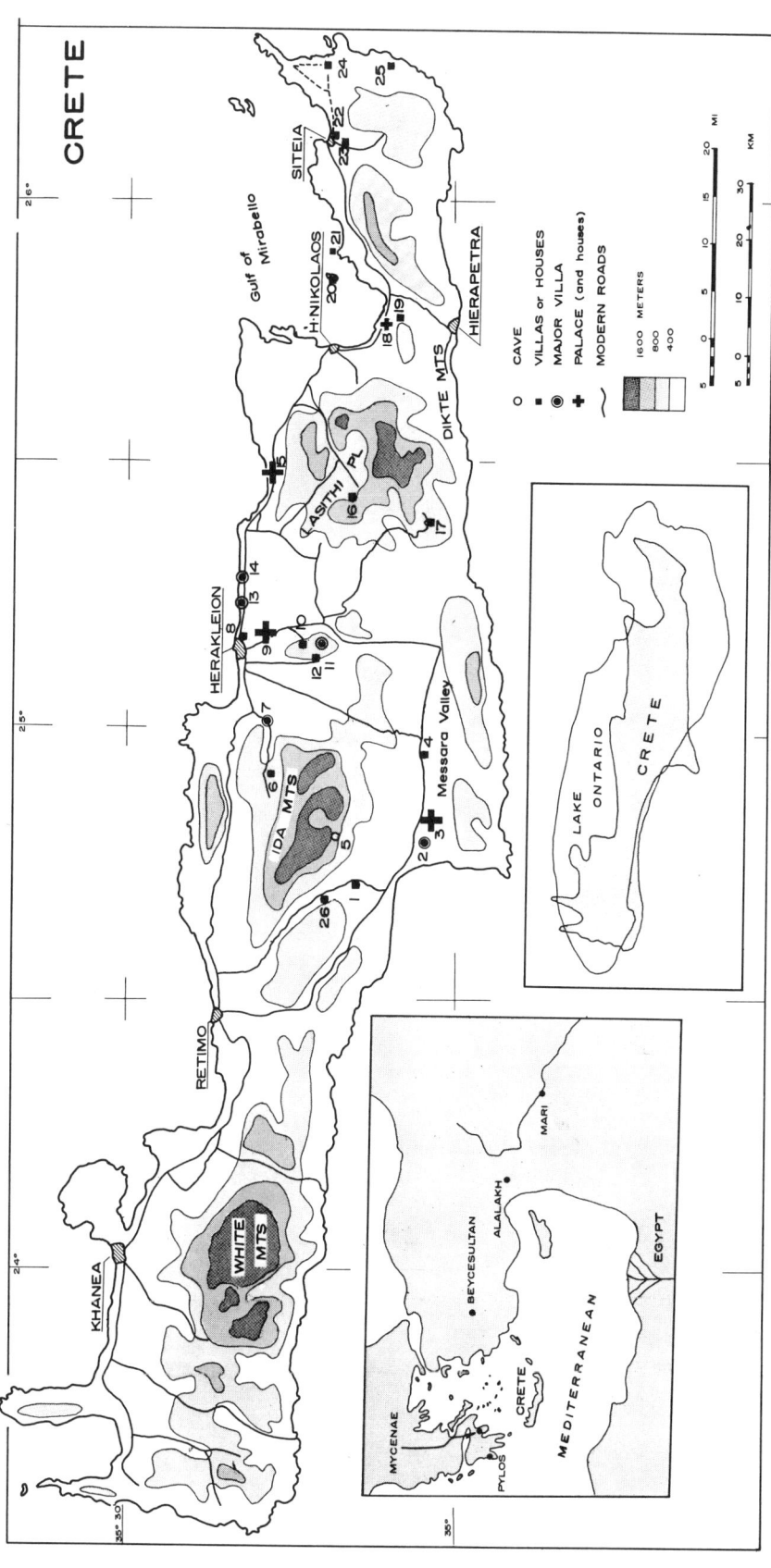

1. Relief map of Crete showing principal modern roads and Minoan sites. The newly found palace of Kato Zakro lies at the extreme eastern end of the island (25)

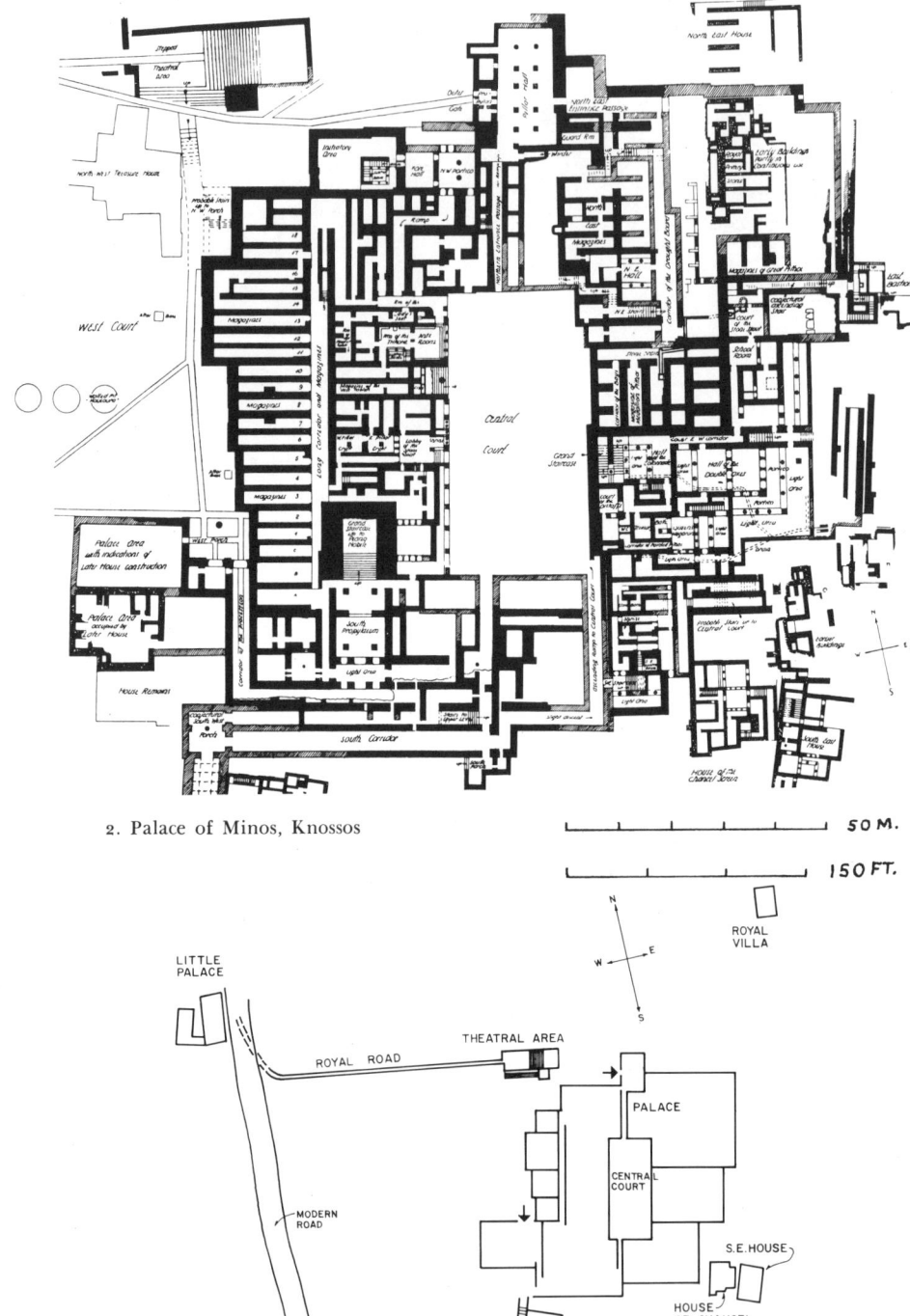

2. Palace of Minos, Knossos

50 M.

150 FT.

3. Environs of Palace of Minos

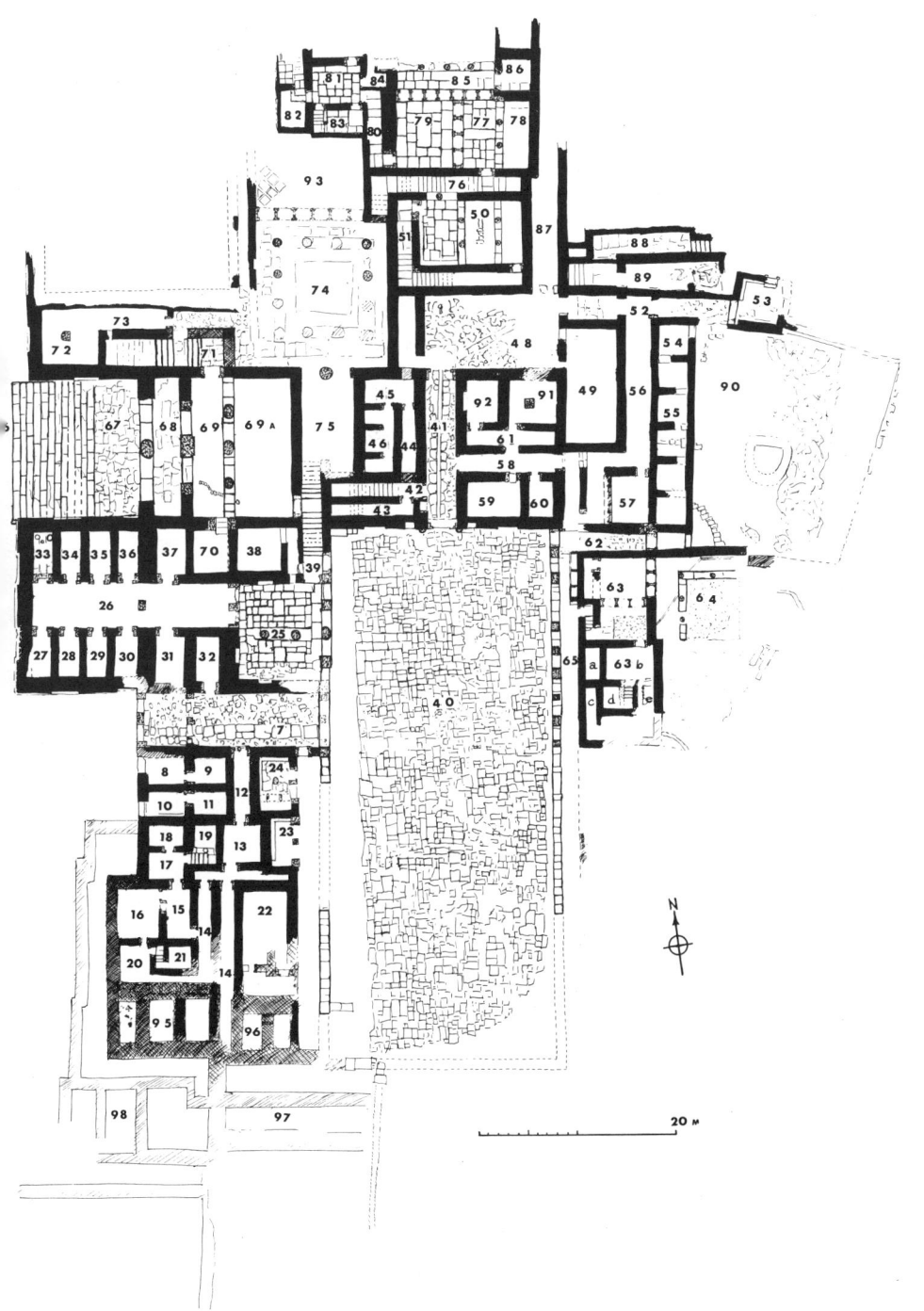

4. Last Palace of Phaistos

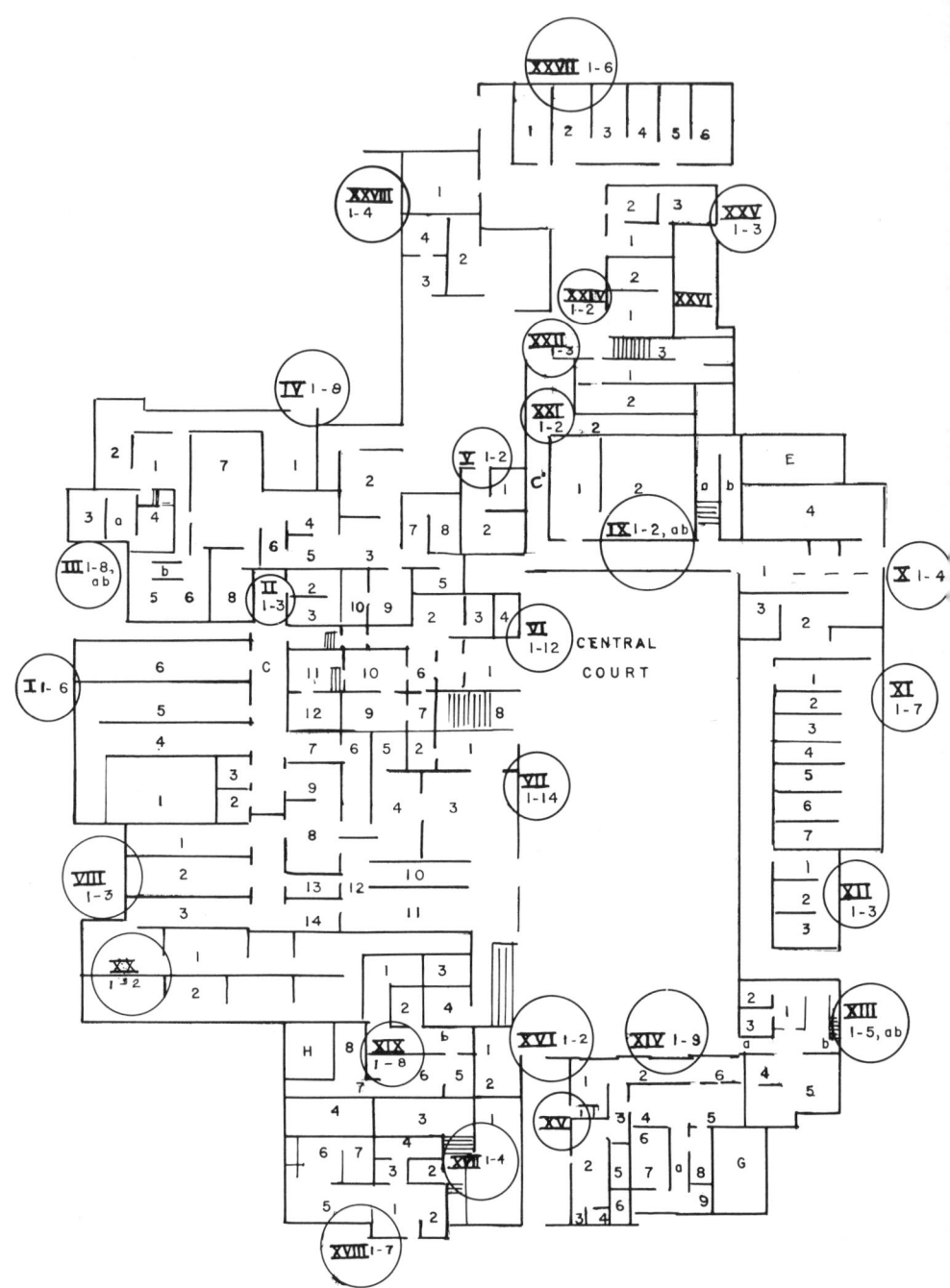

5. Key to plan of Palace of Mallia

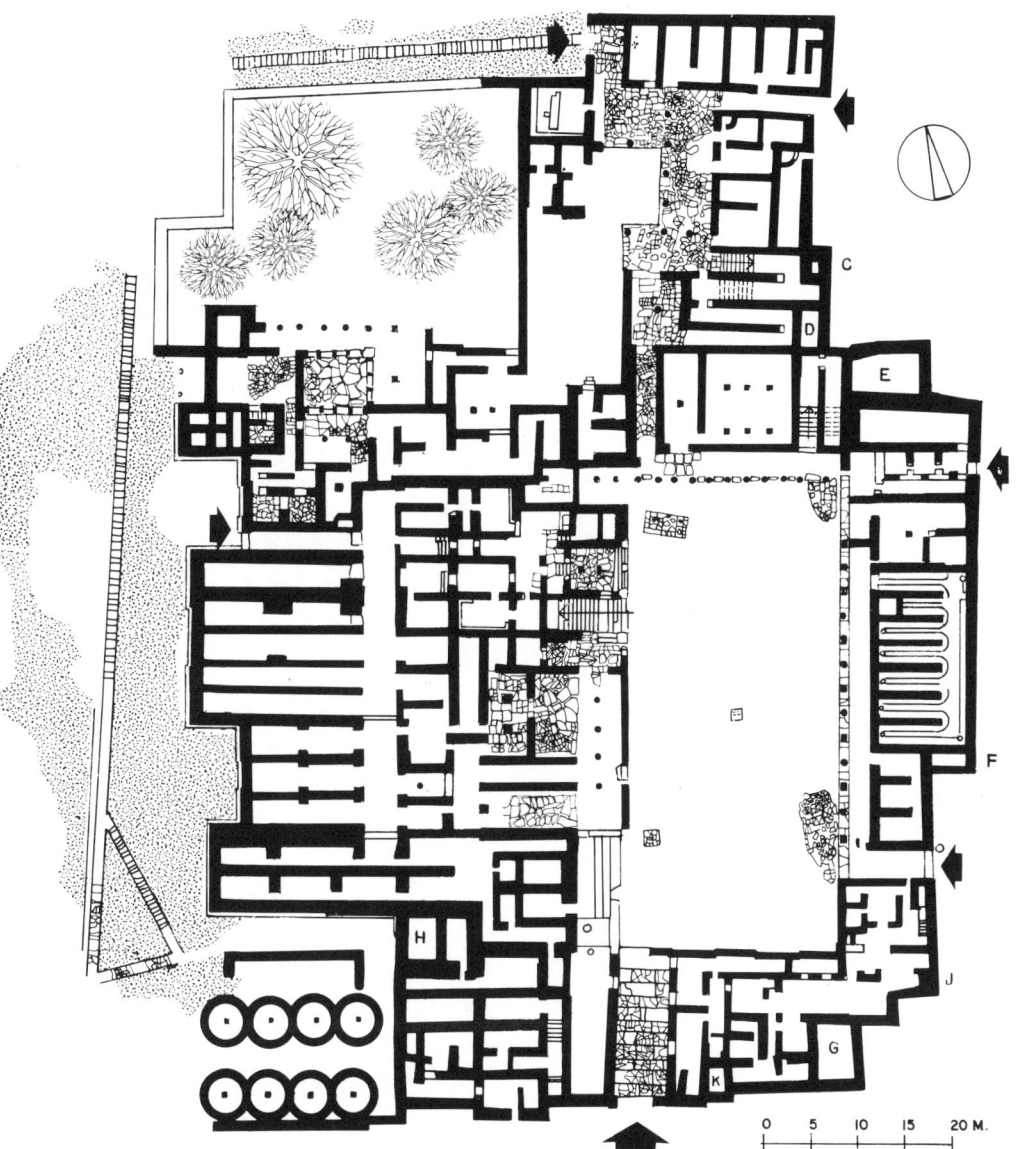

6. Palace of Mallia

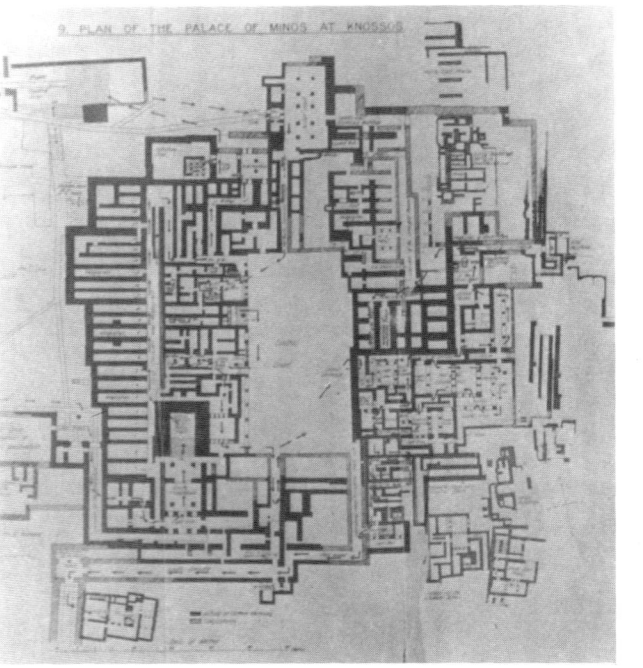

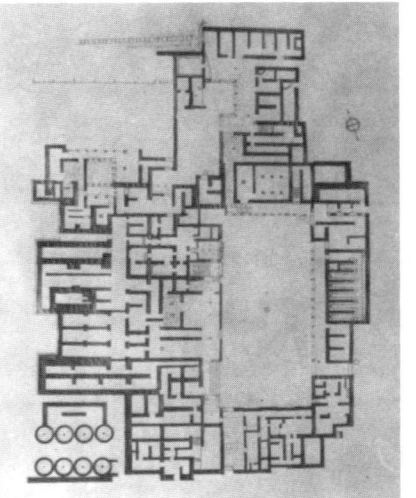

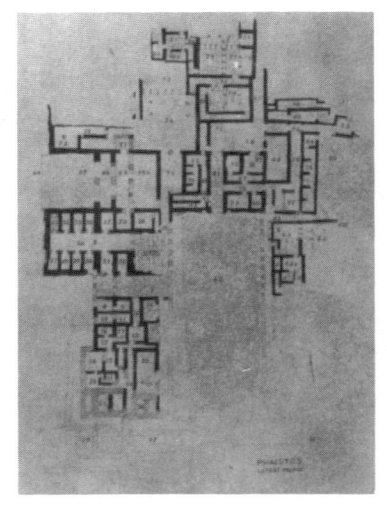

7. Plans of the three major palaces, Knossos, Mallia, and Phaistos, at the same scale
(See Figs. 2, 6, 4, for enlargements)

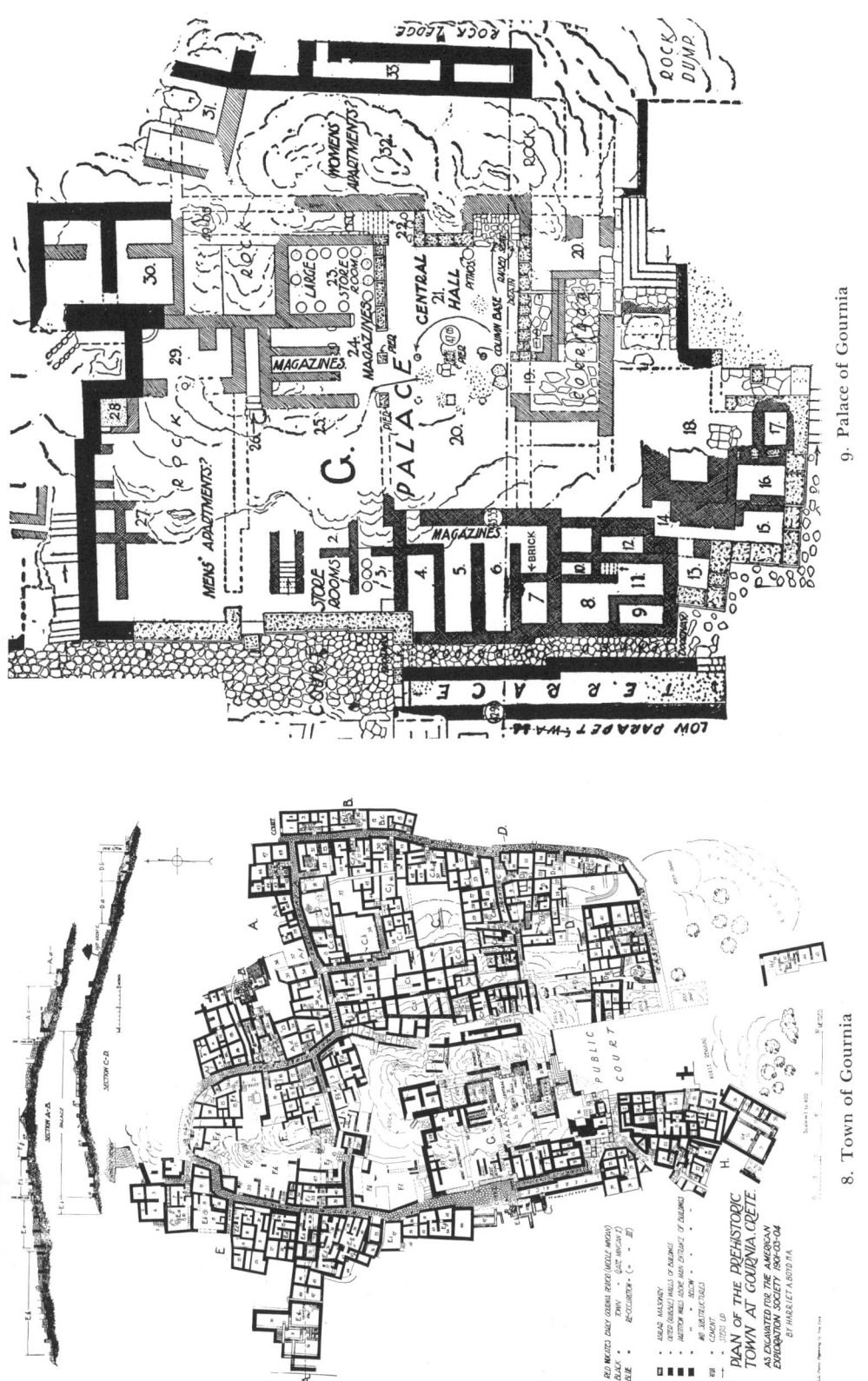

9. Palace of Gournia

8. Town of Gournia

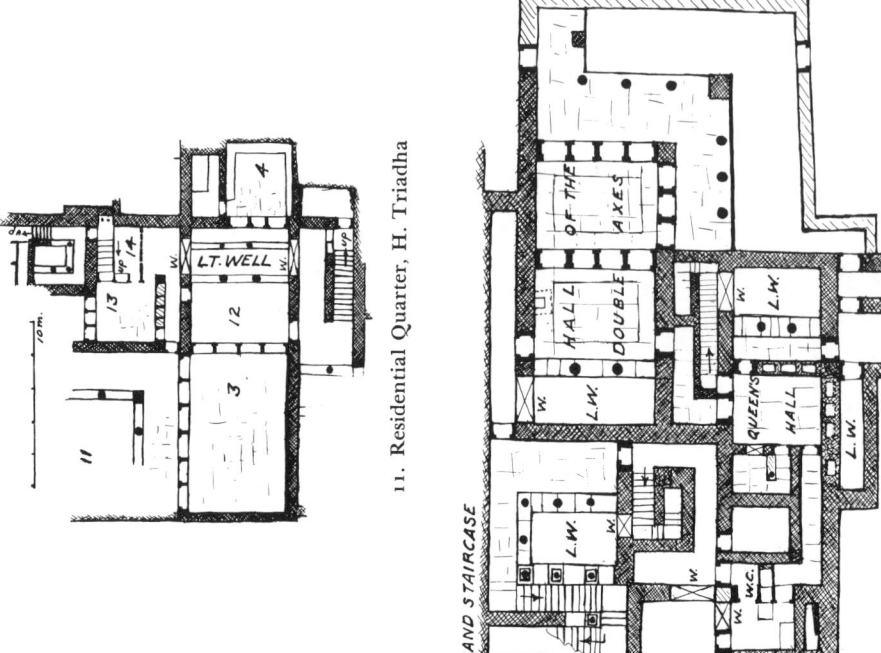

11. Residential Quarter, H. Triadha

GRAND STAIRCASE

12. Residential Quarter, Palace of Minos. North at top

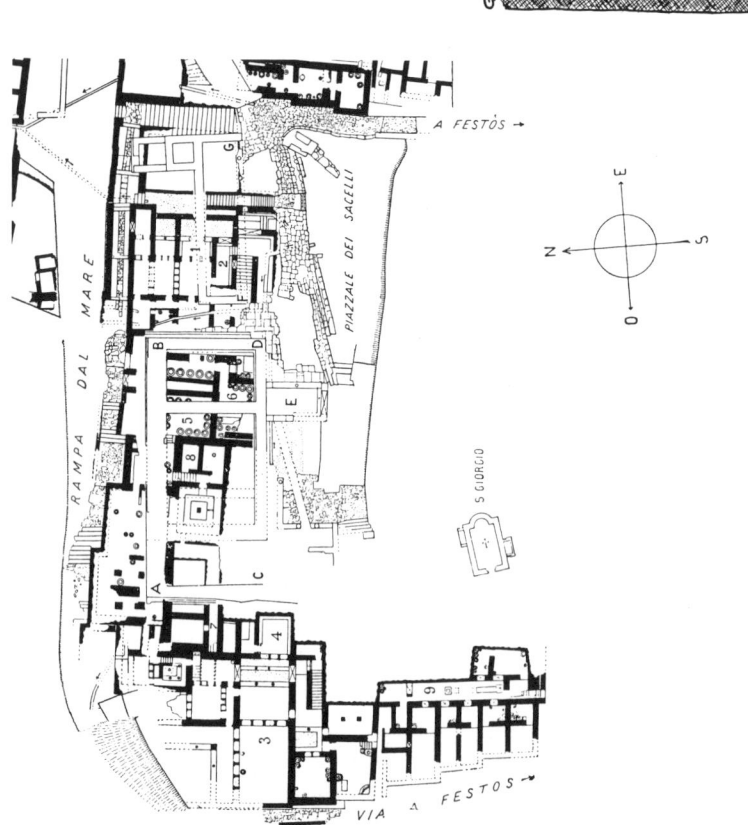

10. Villa of Hagia Triadha

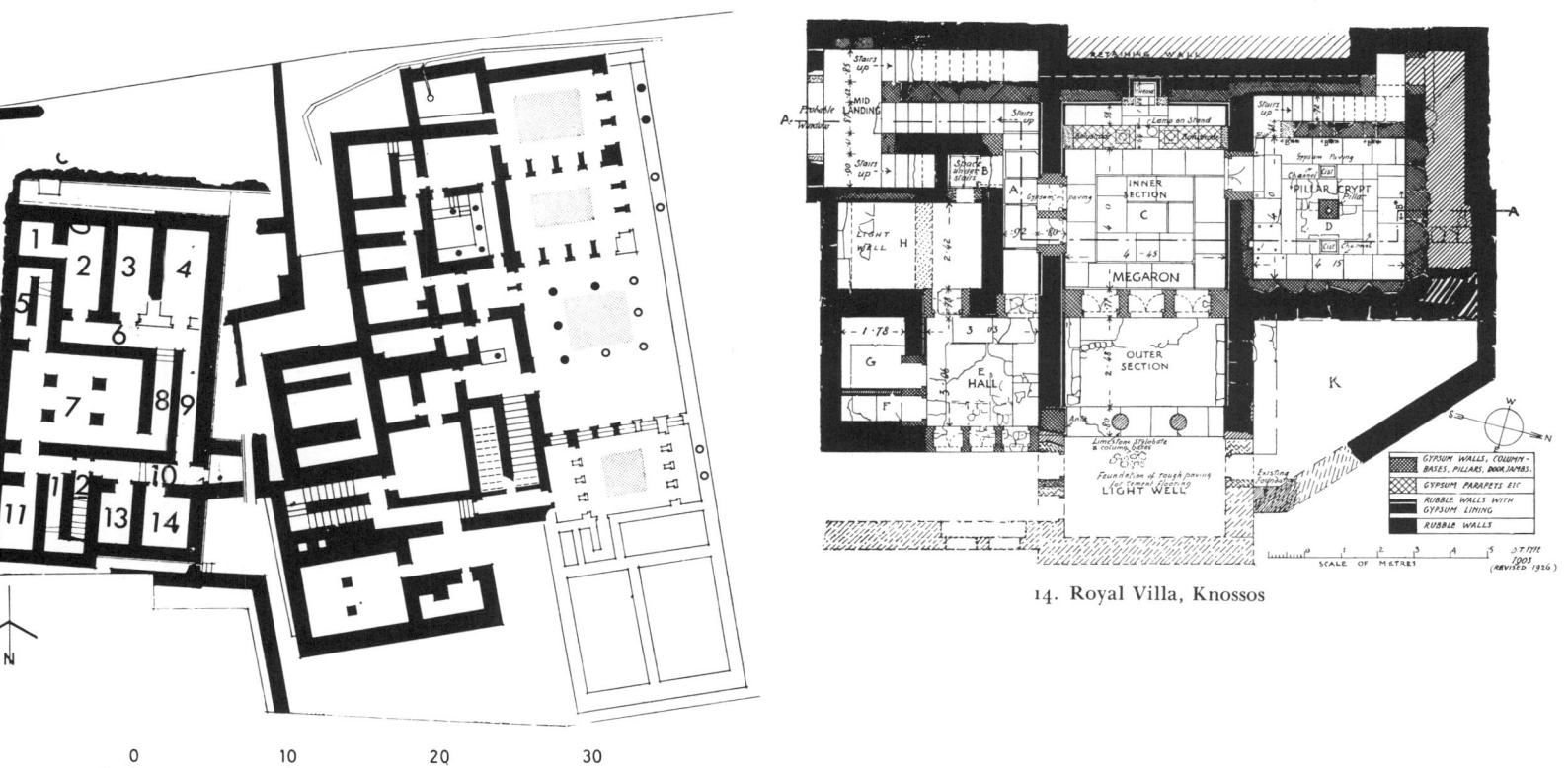

14. Royal Villa, Knossos

13. Plan of Little Palace, Knossos, together with "Unexplored Mansion" or "West Annex." From *AR 1972-73*, 51, fig. 3, by permission

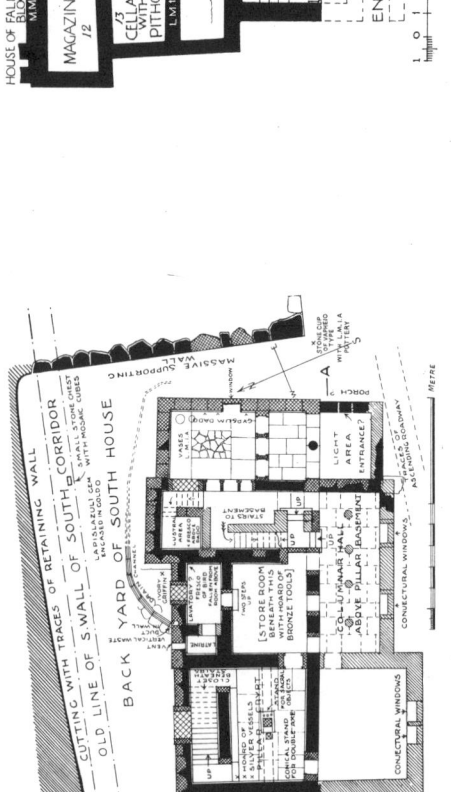

15. South House, Knossos

16. House of the Chancel Screen, Knossos
North at right

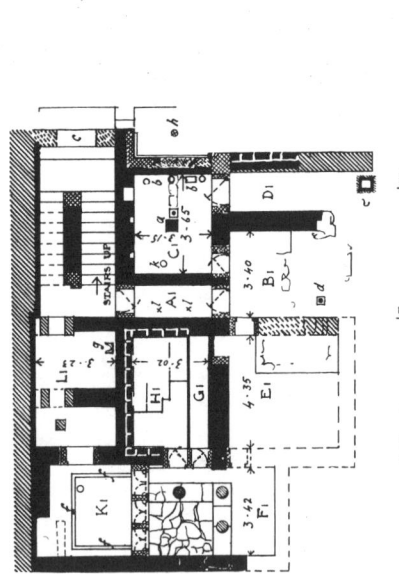

17. Southeast House, Knossos
North at right

18. House of the Frescoes, Knossos
North at left

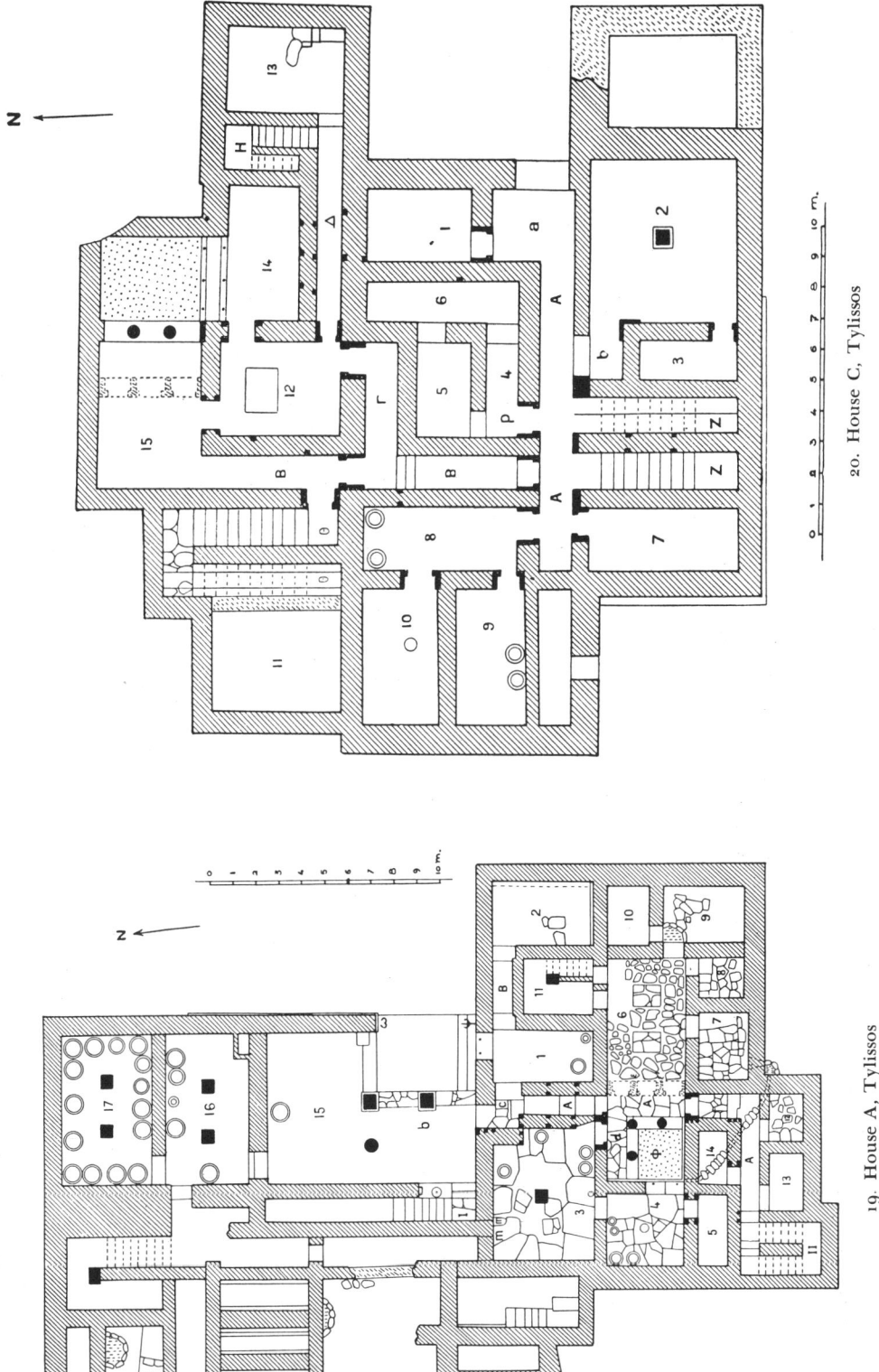

20. House C, Tylissos

19. House A, Tylissos

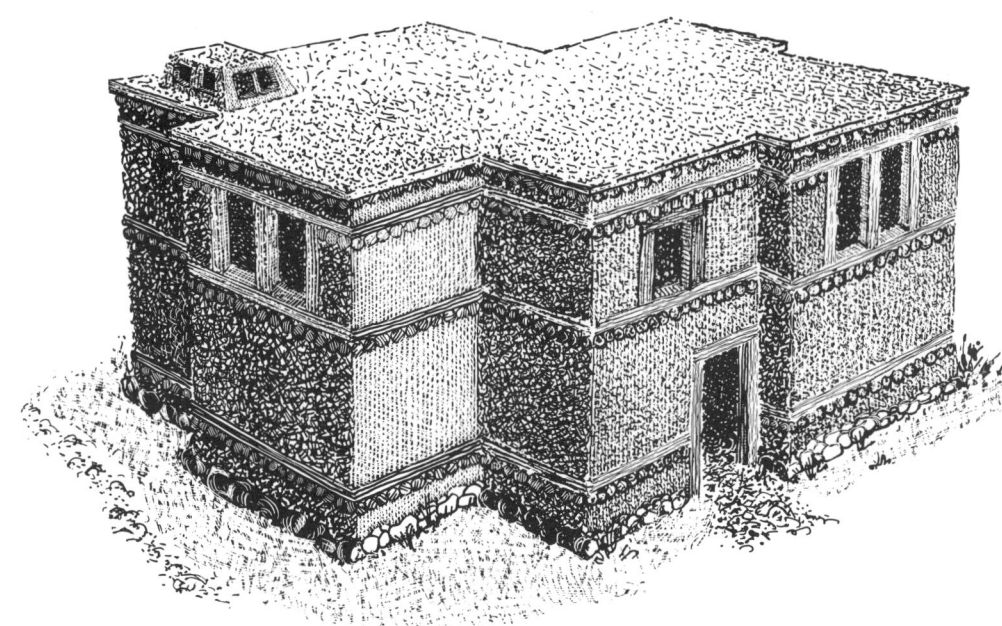

21. Restoration of House Da, Mallia, from northwest

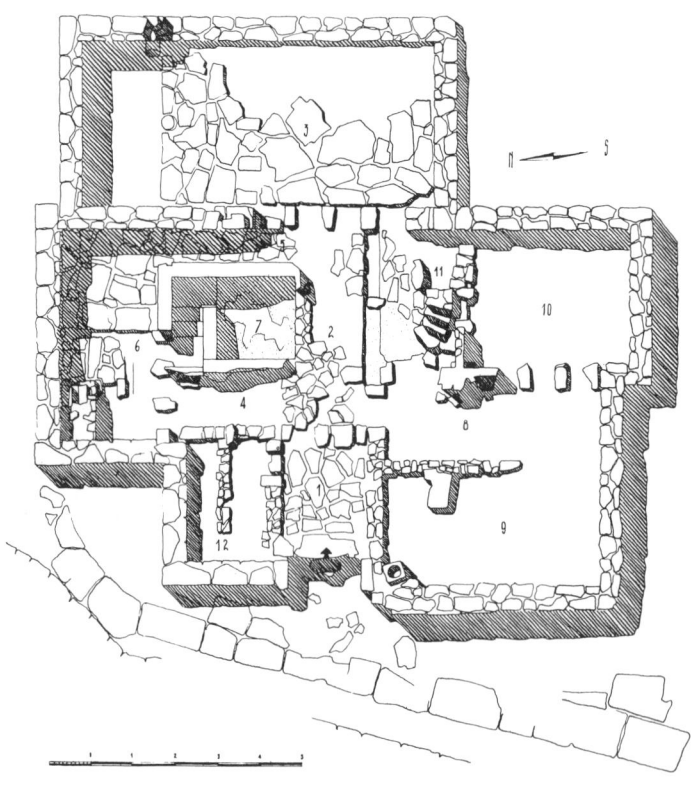

22. House Da, Mallia

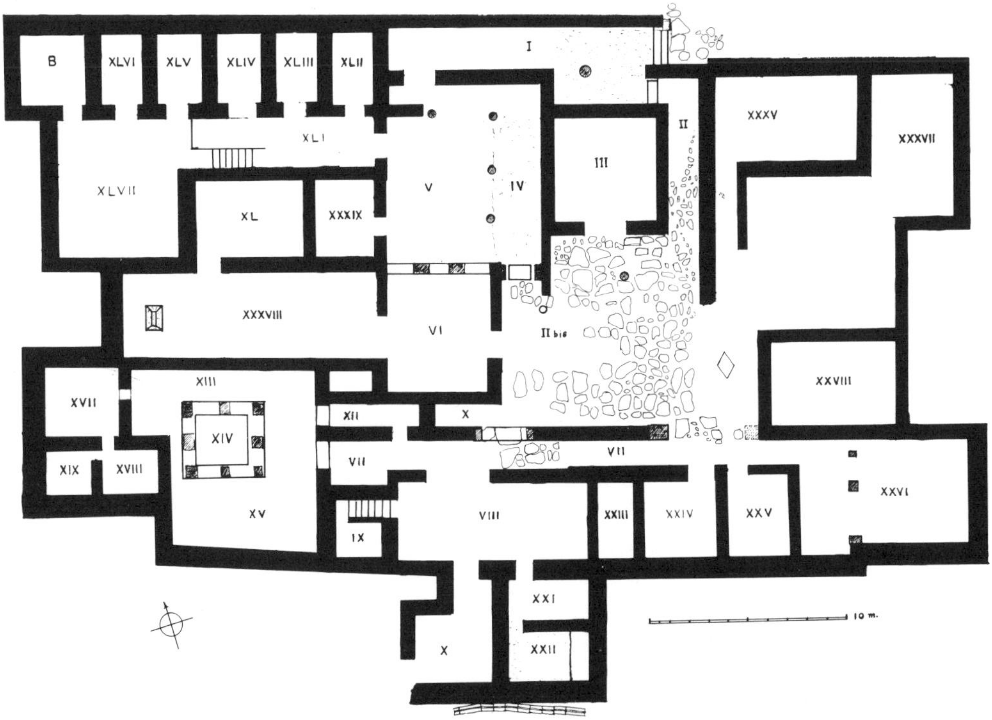

23. House E, Mallia (simplified plan)

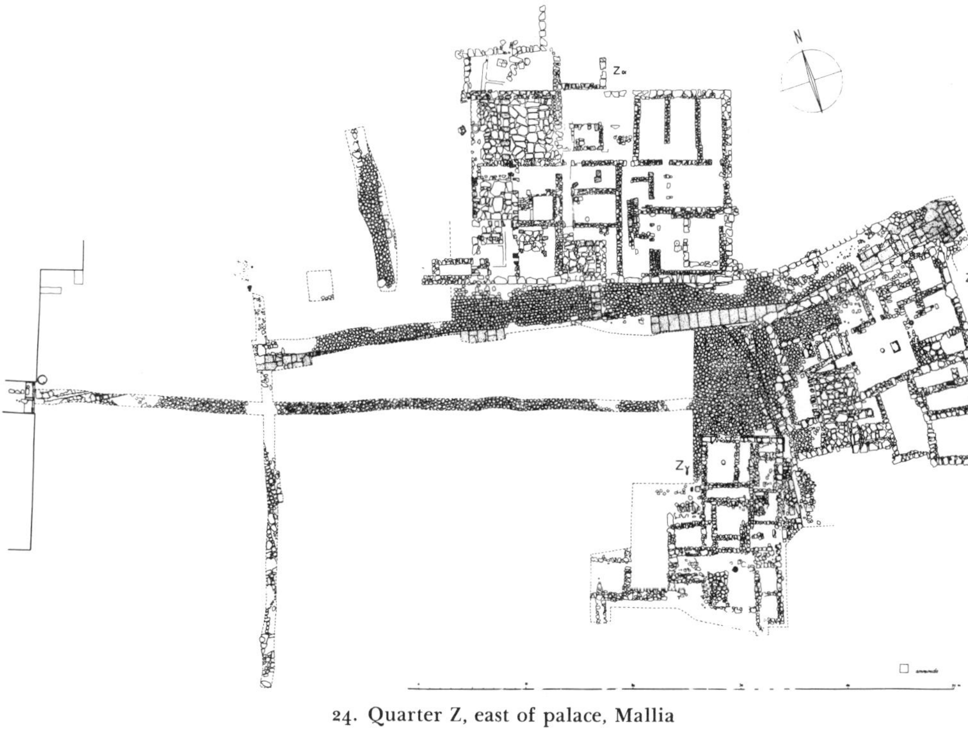

24. Quarter Z, east of palace, Mallia

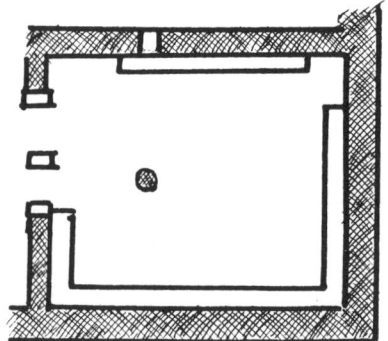

25. House Za, Mallia

m 0 1 2 3 4 5 6 7 8 9 10 11 12 13 14 15 m

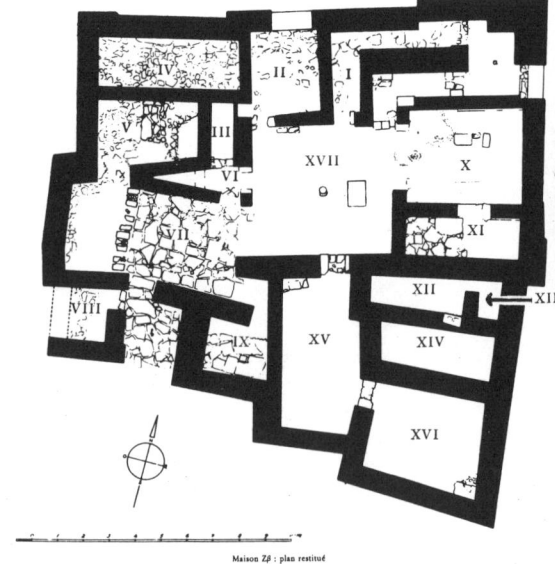

26. Room 24, House Za, Mallia

Maison Zβ : plan restitué

27. House Zb, Mallia

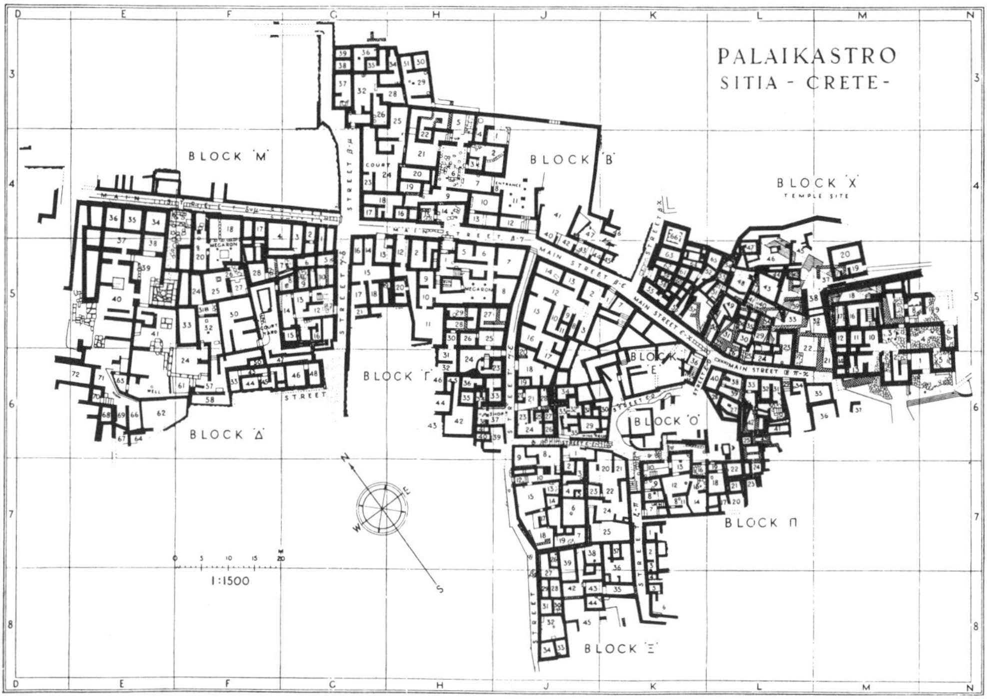

28. Town of Palaikastro; squares 20 m. (ca. 65 ft.) to a side

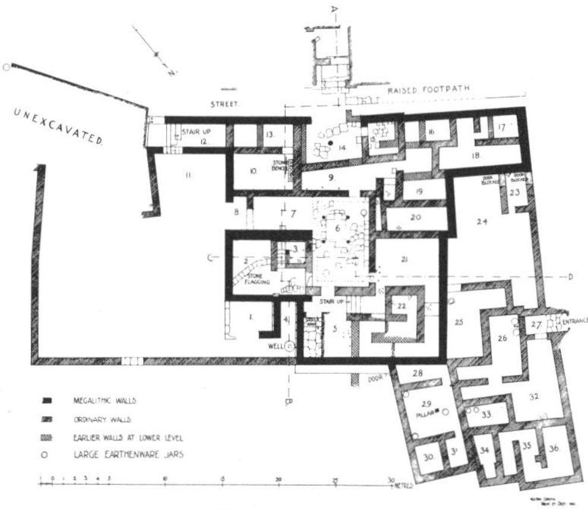

29. House B, Palaikastro

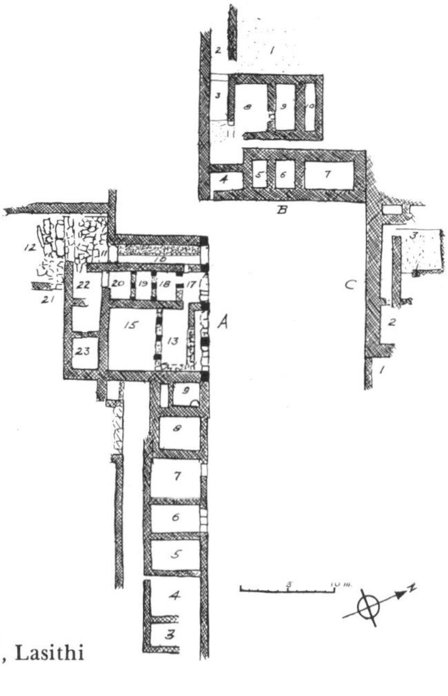

30. Building at Plati, Lasithi

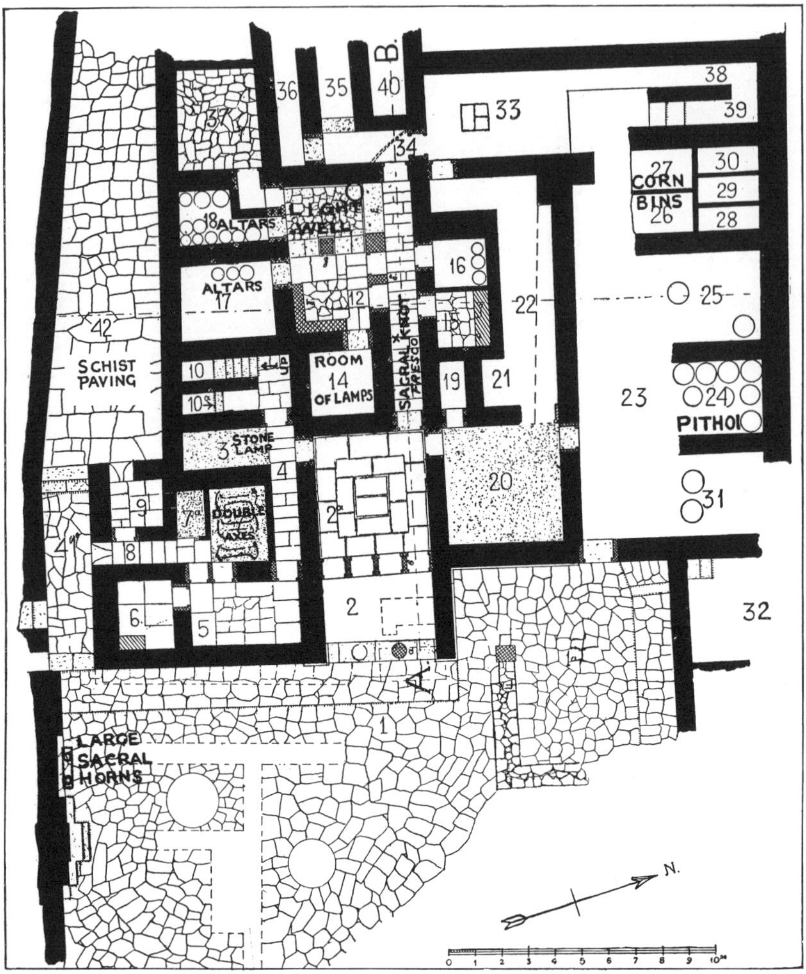

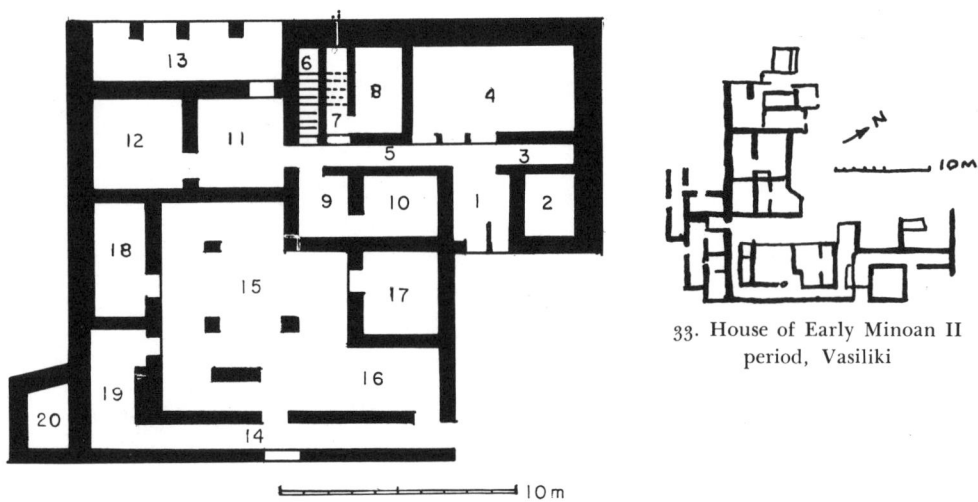

31. House at Nirou Khani

32. House at Sklavokambos. North at top

33. House of Early Minoan II period, Vasiliki

34. White Mountains and river in west Crete

35. Mountains and Gulf of Mirabello west of Gournia

36. View from hill east of Knossos: a) Palace of Minos b) Royal Villa
c) Little Palace d) New Hospital e) Herakleion

37. Palace of Minos from hill to east (telephoto)

38. Grand Staircase of Residential Quarter, Knossos

39. Hall of Double-axes from light-well, Knossos

40. North Pillar Hall, Knossos, from southwest

41. Theatral Area, Knossos, from northwest

42. Restored South Propylon, Knossos, from southeast

43. Queen's Hall in Palace of Minos, painting in Royal Ontario Museum

44. Restoration of west side of Central Court, Knossos, by Piet de Jong under supervision of Nikolaos Platon. The third storey should be eliminated

45. Restoration of east end of Hall of the Double-axes, by Piet de Jong under supervision of Nikolaos Platon

46. Palace of Phaistos and Messara Valley from northwest

47. North Residential Quarter, Phaistos, from southeast

48. Restoration of Grand Propylon, Phaistos, from northwest

49. West Court and main entrance of Palace of Phaistos, from the west

50. Restoration of north end of Central Court, Phaistos, from southeast

51. Central Court and range of Ida from south, Phaistos

52. Northwest corner of Central Court, Phaistos

54. Minoan gem with scene from bull games

53. Niche and half-column west of Corridor 41, Phaistos

55. Palace of Phaistos from southwest, axonometric restoration

56. Site of Mallia from south (telephoto): palace in middle ground, Chrysolakkos necropolis near sea

57. Central Court of Palace of Mallia from northwest; modern shed over East Magazines at left

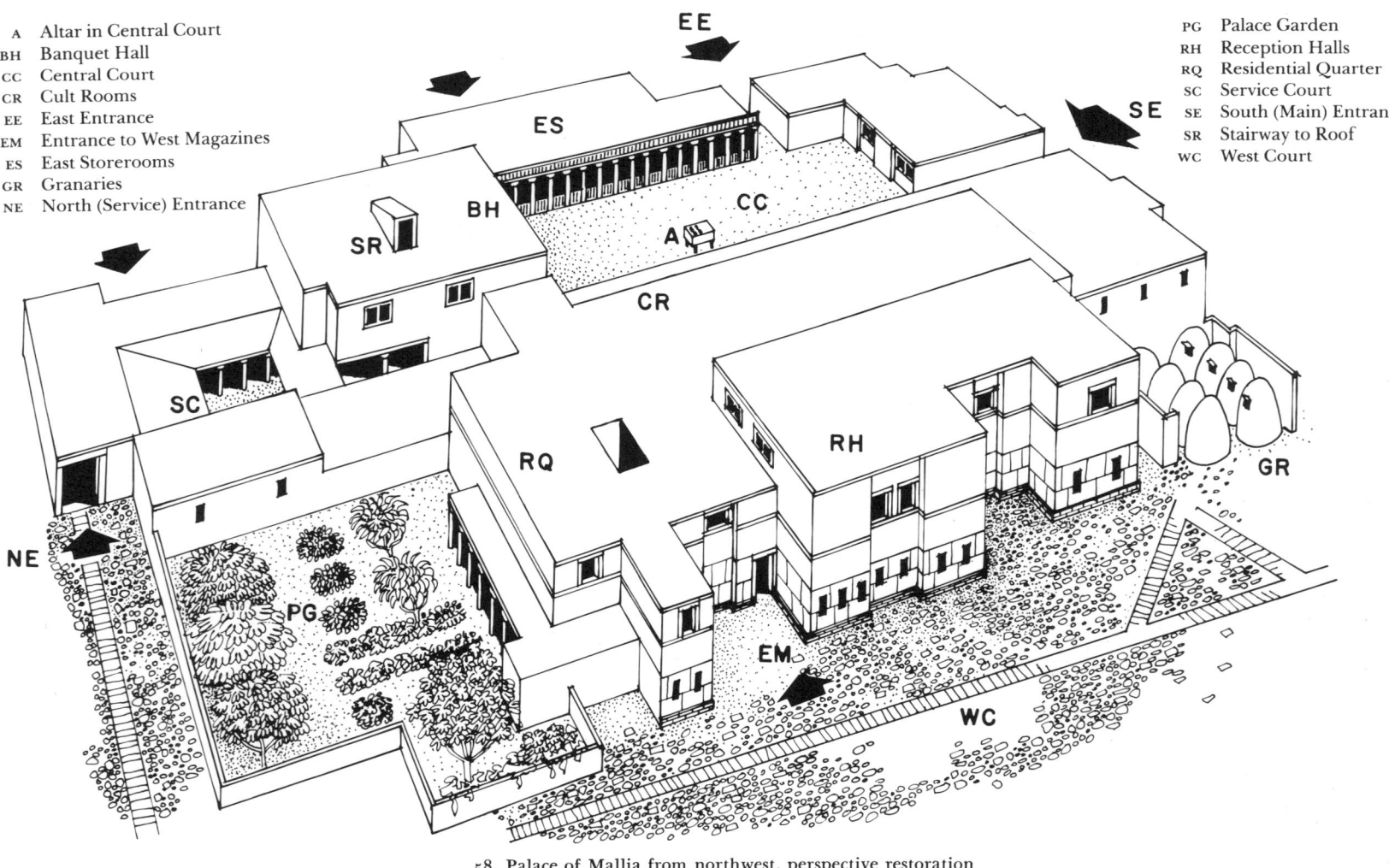

A	Altar in Central Court	PG	Palace Garden
BH	Banquet Hall	RH	Reception Halls
CC	Central Court	RQ	Residential Quarter
CR	Cult Rooms	SC	Service Court
EE	East Entrance	SE	South (Main) Entrance
EM	Entrance to West Magazines	SR	Stairway to Roof
ES	East Storerooms	WC	West Court
GR	Granaries		
NE	North (Service) Entrance		

58. Palace of Mallia from northwest, perspective restoration

59. Rooms ix 1 and 2 from northwest, Palace of Mallia

60. Stairs xxii 3 from west, Palace of Mallia

61. Circular stone with cups at southwest corner of
Central Court, Palace of Mallia

62. Granary at southwest corner of Palace of Mallia

63. Site of Gournia and Mirabello Bay from southeast

64. Little Palace, Knossos, from southwest

65. H. Triadha and view toward Ida, from south

66. Villa of H. Triadha from northeast

67. South wall of Room 3, H. Triadha

68. Queen's Hall from southeast, H. Triadha

69. Room 4 from west, H. Triadha

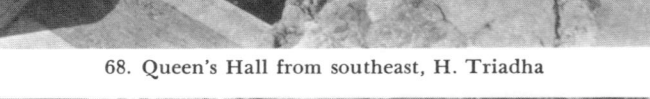

70. Light-well and window, Room 12, from northwest, H. Triadha

71. South House from southwest, Knossos

72. East half of South House from north, Knossos

73. Staircase of Royal Villa from south, Knossos

74. Balustrade in Hall (C) of Royal Villa, Knossos

75. Main Hall (2) from east, Nirou Khani

76. Villa of the Lilies from west, Amnisos

77. Hall with light-well and window from northwest,
House C, Tylissos

78. Exterior wall west of Hall, House C, Tylissos

79. Drain from toilet, House C, Tylissos

80. Southeast House from southeast, Knossos

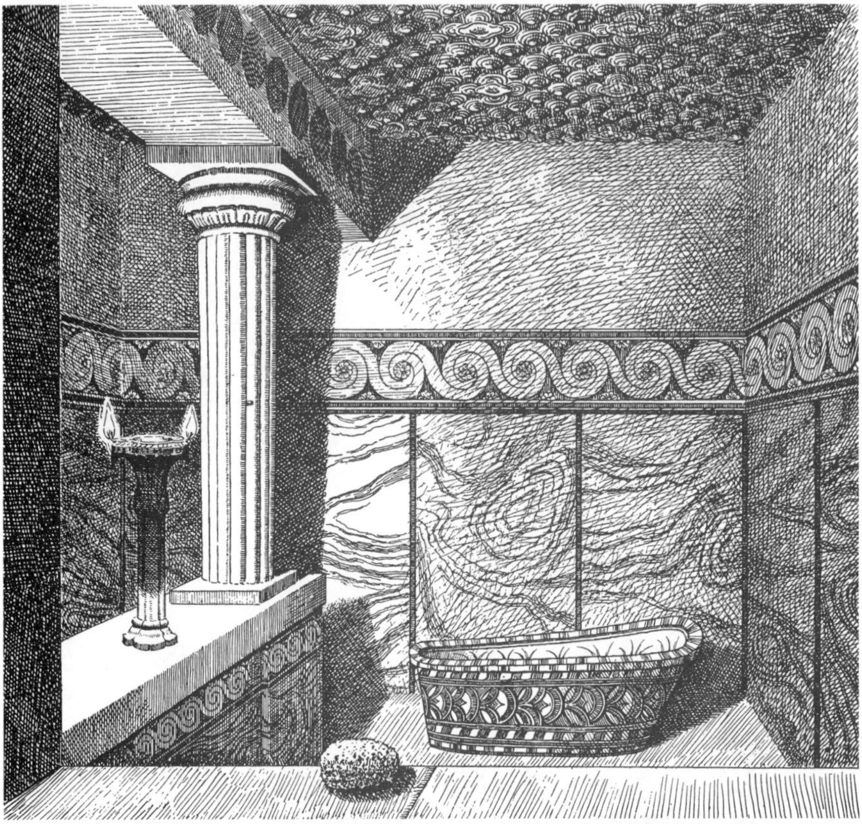

81. Restoration of bathroom in Residential Quarter, Knossos

82. Bathroom and Queen's Hall in North Residential Quarter from south, Phaistos

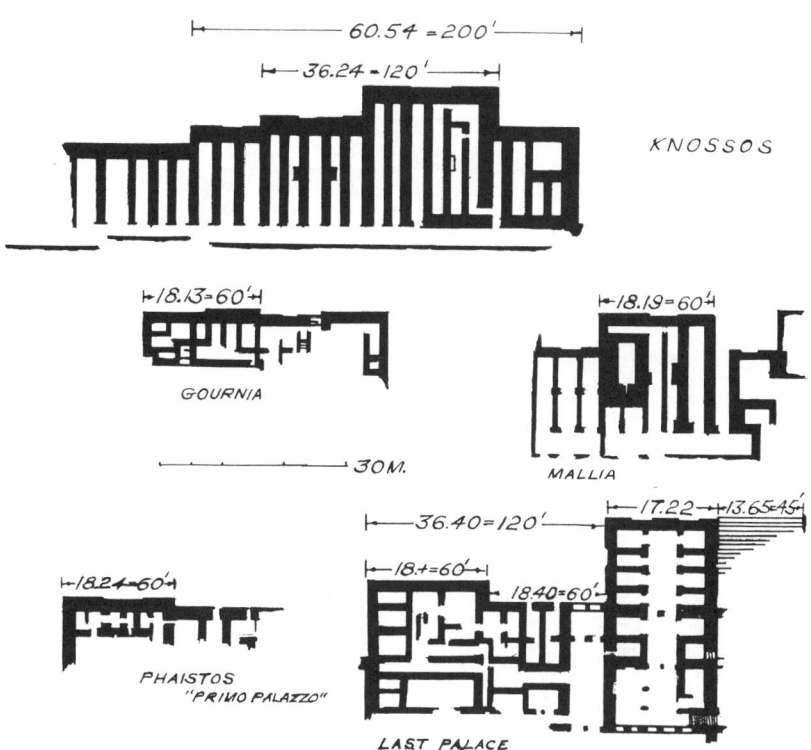

KNOSSOS

GOURNIA

18.13=60'

30M.

MALLIA

18.19=60'

PHAISTOS
"PRIMO PALAZZO"

1824=60'

36.40=120'

18.4=60'

1840=60'

17.22   13.65=45'

LAST PALACE

83. Plans of rooms along west façades of five palaces

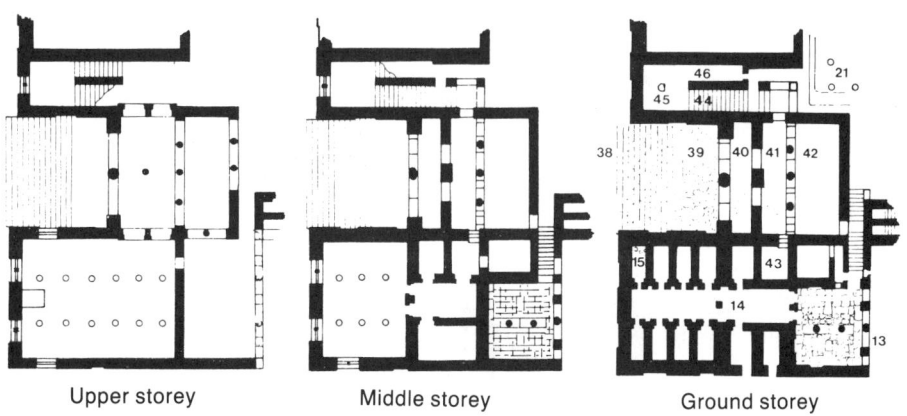

Upper storey   Middle storey   Ground storey

METERS
0   5   10   15   20

0   50   100
FEET

84. Plans of Propylon-Magazine Block, Phaistos, at three levels

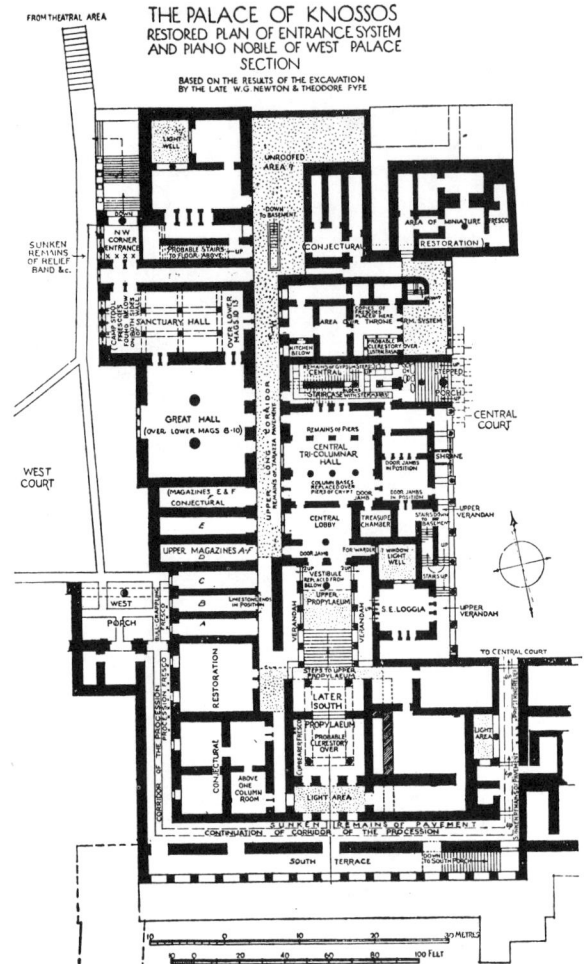

85. Restored plan of Piano Nobile west of Central Court. By Newton and Fyfe, from J.D.S. Pendlebury, *Handbook to the Palace of Minos*, plan 3

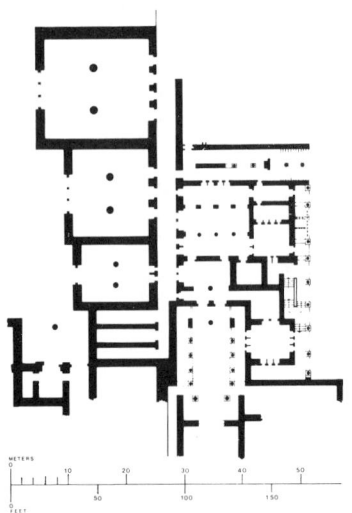

86. Restored plan of West Halls of Piano Nobile at Knossos. From J. W. Graham, *Minoan Crete* (1974), p. 36; north at top

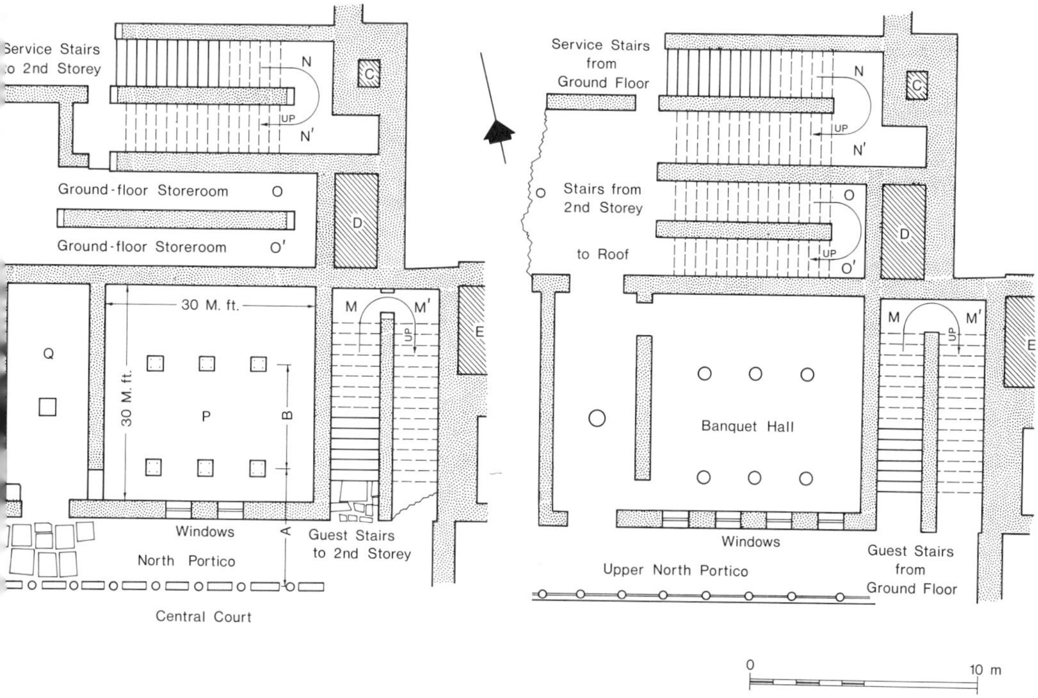

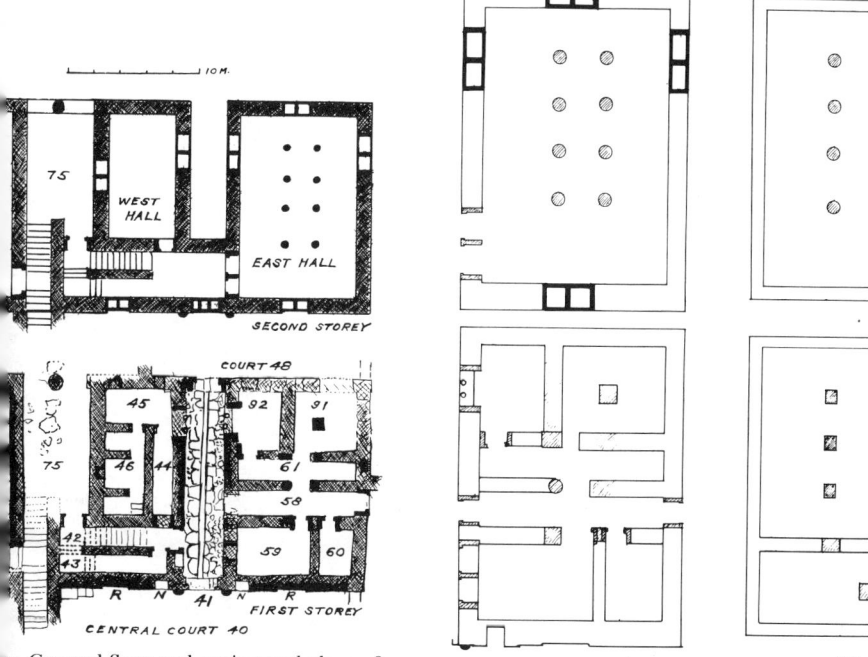

87 and 88. Plan of area north of Central Court at Mallia, and proposed restoration of Upper Storey

89. Ground floor and conjectural plans of upper floor north of Central Court, Phaistos

90. Conjectural plans of Banquet Halls at Phaistos (left) and Mallia (right) at same scale

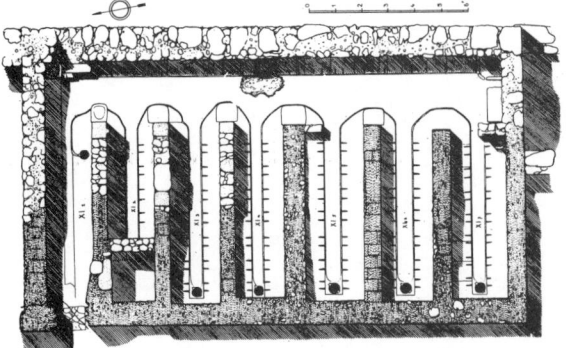

91. East Magazines, Palace of Mallia

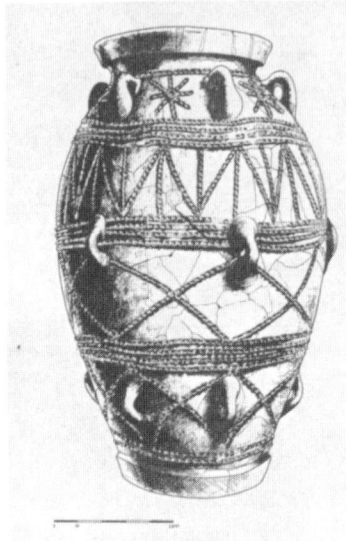

92. Pithos from Mallia

93. West Magazines, Palace of Minos

94. Wine press, Vathypetro

95. Pillar Crypt (vii 4) from southeast, Mallia

96. Room 23 from southeast, Phaistos

97. Pillar Crypt of Royal Villa, Knossos, restored
view from northeast

98. South pillar in vii 4 from
northeast, Mallia

100. Scene from H. Triadha Sarcophagus: offerings

102. Figurine of bull in terracotta from Pseira

99. Niche in wall of Room 46, Phaistos

101. Scene from H. Triadha Sarcophagus: bull sacrifice

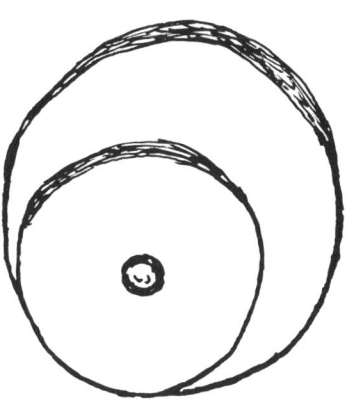

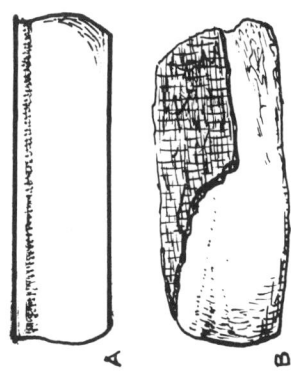

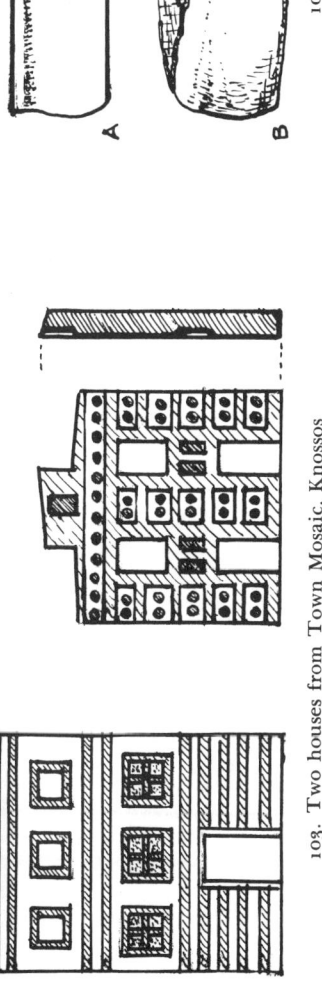

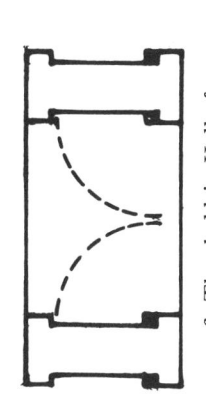

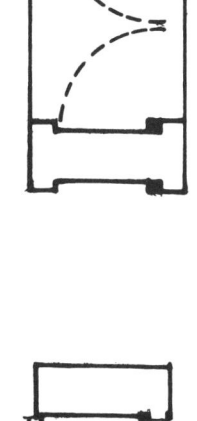

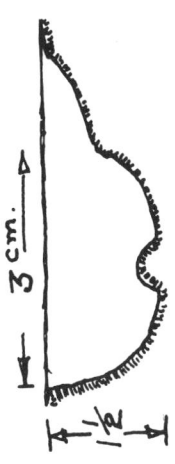

104. Three door-pivot caps: A. from Mallia
B. from Phaistos C. from Alalakh, Syria

106. Threshold in Hall of
Double-axes, Knossos

107. Pivot-hole in threshold of
Room iv 3, Palace of Mallia

103. Two houses from Town Mosaic, Knossos

105. Threshold of Room 22,
Phaistos

PLAN

ELEVATION

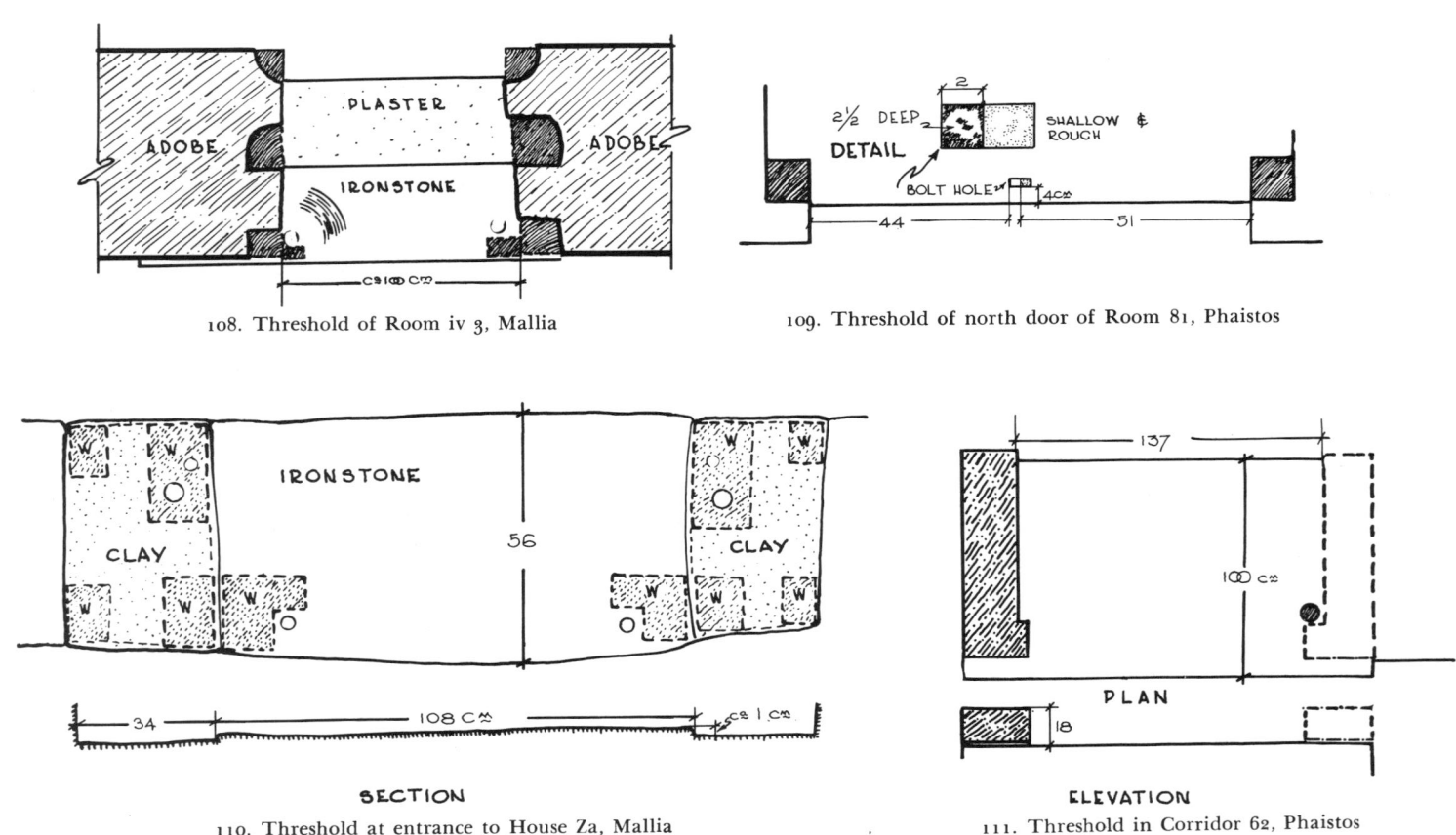

108. Threshold of Room iv 3, Mallia

109. Threshold of north door of Room 81, Phaistos

SECTION

110. Threshold at entrance to House Za, Mallia

ELEVATION

111. Threshold in Corridor 62, Phaistos

A

B

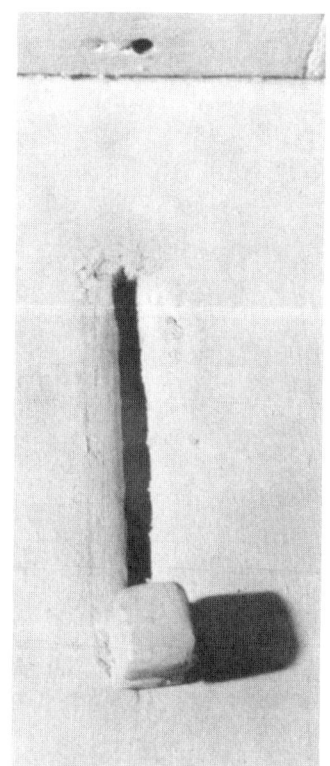

C

D

112. Four views of model of lock to basement room, South
House, Knossos

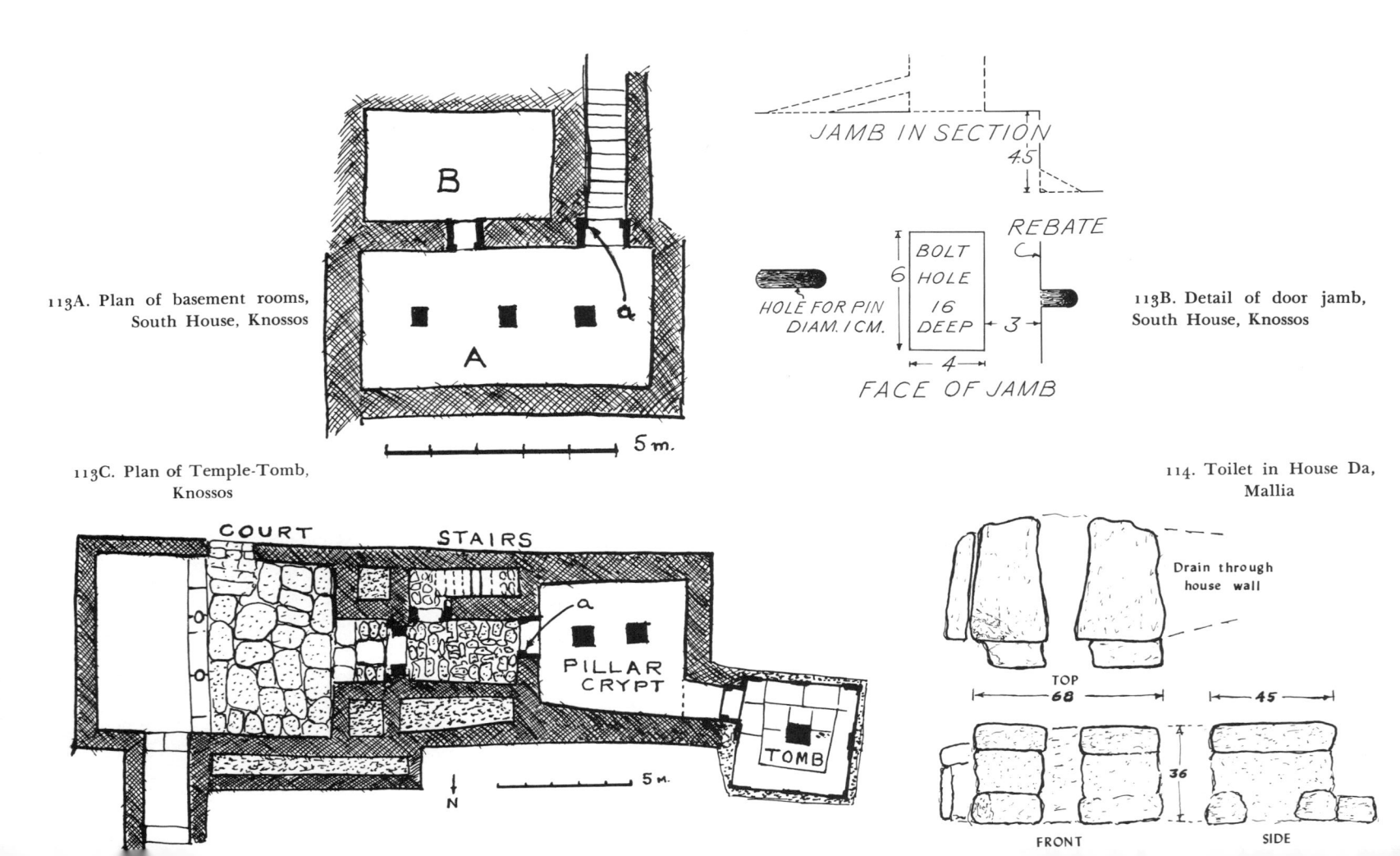

113A. Plan of basement rooms, South House, Knossos

B

A

5 m.

JAMB IN SECTION

4.5

REBATE

HOLE FOR PIN DIAM. 1 CM.

BOLT HOLE 16 DEEP

6

3

4

FACE OF JAMB

113B. Detail of door jamb, South House, Knossos

113C. Plan of Temple-Tomb, Knossos

COURT

STAIRS

PILLAR CRYPT

TOMB

N

5 m.

114. Toilet in House Da, Mallia

Drain through house wall

TOP

68

45

FRONT

36

SIDE

115. Base in Magazine 15 from west, Palace of Minos

116. Restored Central Hall from southeast, Palace of Minos

117. Eroded gypsum base, Southeast House, Knossos

118. Construction of west orthostate wall, Palace of Minos

119. Tiny mason's mark, Phaistos

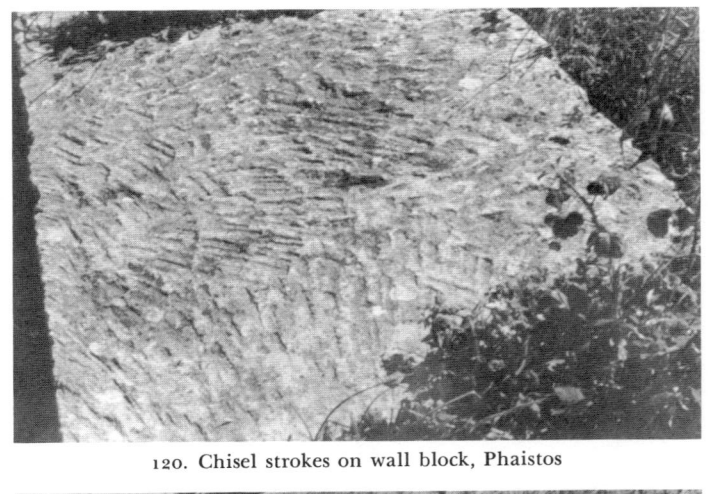

120. Chisel strokes on wall block, Phaistos

121. Stuccoing of wall blocks, Phaistos

122. Recess in north façade of Central Court, Phaistos

123. Bases with mortises, H. Triadha

124. Present day house in Delphi, Greece

125. Gypsum quarry near H. Triadha

126. Room 93 and Peristyle 74 from northwest, Phaistos

127. Alabaster floor of Room 79, Phaistos

128. Flagged West Court from north, Knossos

129. Diagrams of wall decoration:
A. House of Frescoes, Knossos
B. Room 71, Phaistos
C. Magazine 12, Knossos

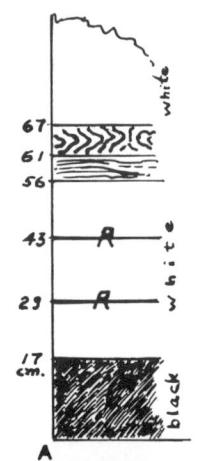

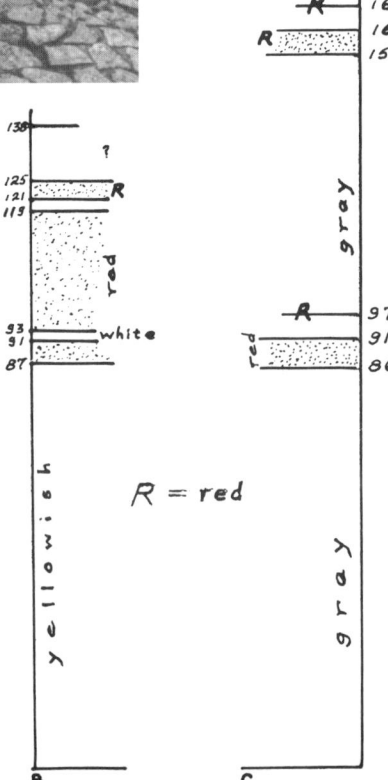

$R = red$

130. Restored Throne Room, Knossos

131A. "La petite Parisienne," Palace of Minos

131B. The Cupbearer, Palace of Minos

132. Flying Fish Fresco, Melos

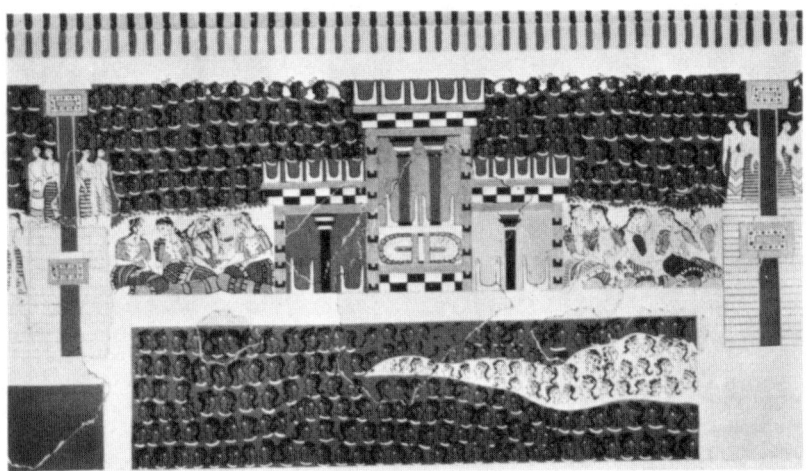

133. Grandstand Fresco, Knossos

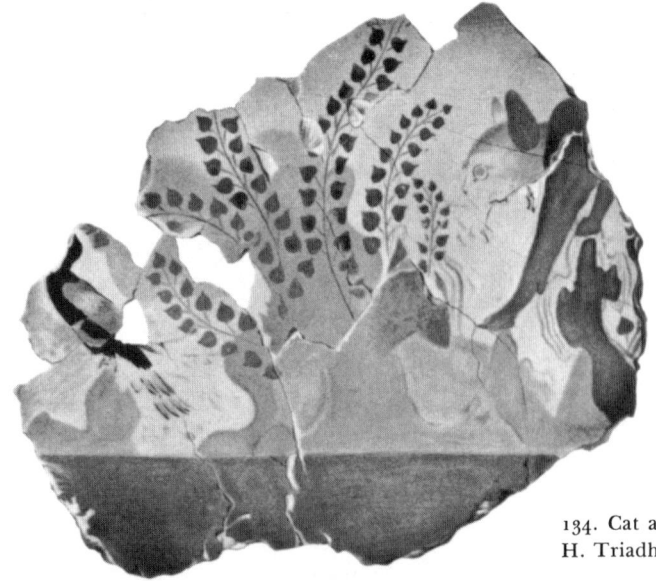

134. Cat and Bird Fresco, H. Triadha

135. Detail of Lion Gate, Mycenae

136. VARIOUS ARCHITECTURAL DETAILS: A. Half-rosette frieze, Mycenae B. Half-rosette frieze, Knossos C. Fresco fragment, Knossos D. Door, Town Mosaic detail E. Detail of Tripartite Shrine, Grandstand Fresco F. Column from same GH. Ivory column fragments, Mycenae I. Treasury of Atreus half-column, detail J. Spiral column, gem KL. Rectangular capitals from Grandstand Fresco and Boxer Cup M. Tomb doorway, Knossos N. Floor pattern, Room 79, Phaistos

137. Horizontal curvature in Stairway 66, Phaistos, from west

138. Stairways 66 and 6 from south, Phaistos

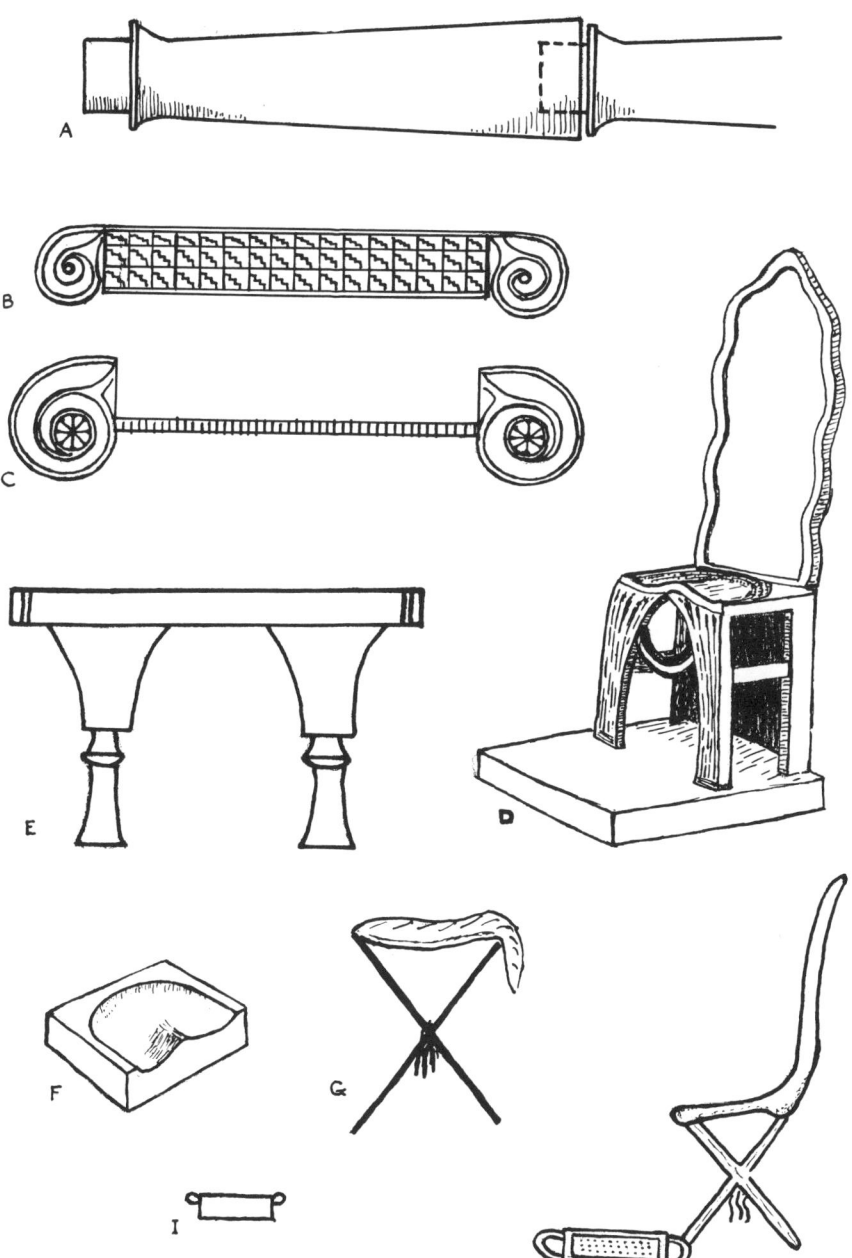

139. MINOAN PIPE AND FURNITURE: A. Terracotta pipe sections BC. Ivory appliqué for foot-stools (?) D. Wooden throne, based on Knossos stone throne E. Table from H. Triadha Sarcophagus F. Stone seat, Knossos G. Folding stool, fresco detail, Knossos H. Chair and footstool, gem I. Footstool, Linear B ideogram

140. VARIOUS FURNISHINGS: A. Bronze lamp B. Clay lamp C. Clay bathtub D. Clay sarcophagus in form of wooden chest E. Portable clay charcoal burner F. Clay tripod hearth GJ. Stone lamps HK. Bronze tripods I. Linear B tripod ideograms

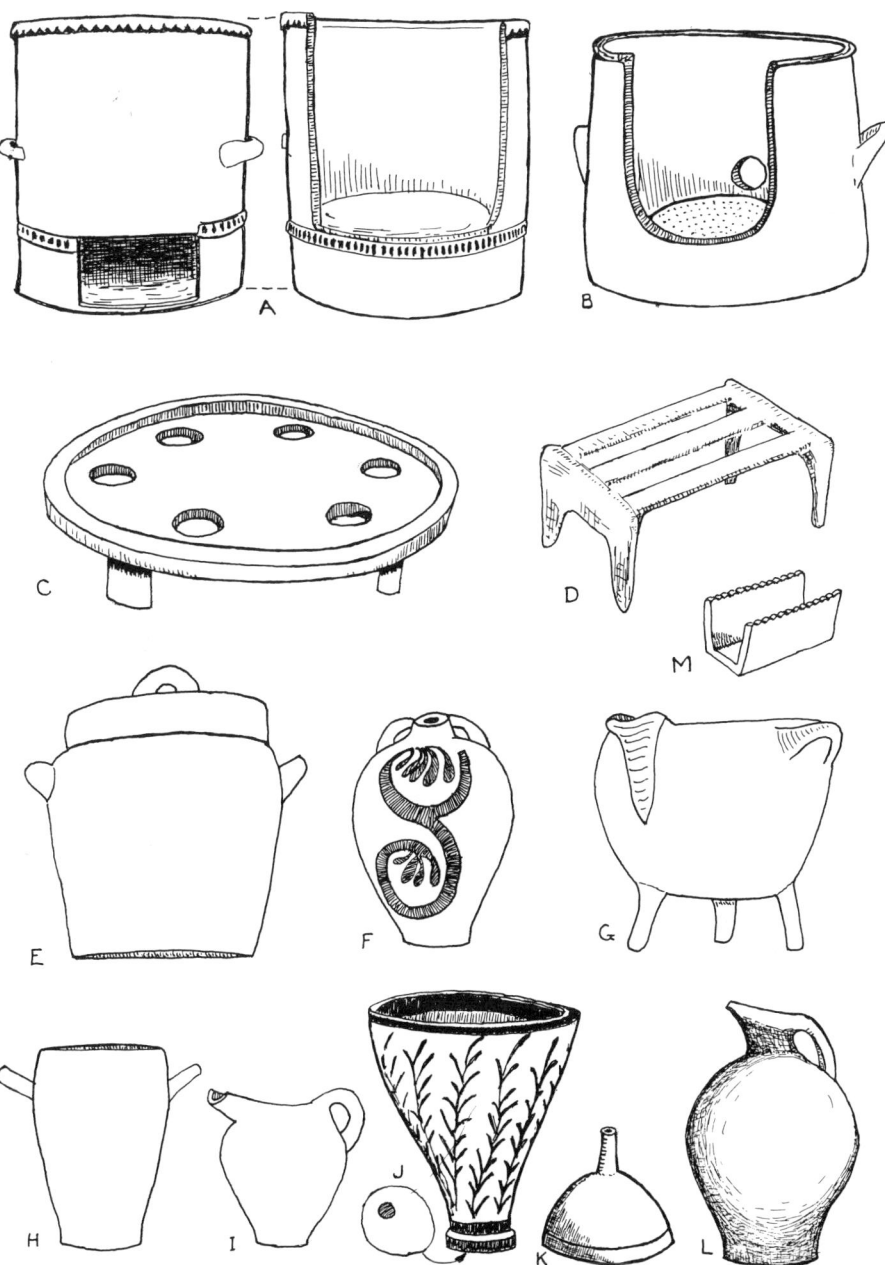

141. CLAY OBJECTS FOR COOKING, ETC.: AB. Ovens C. Egg tray (?) D. Grill E. Stewpot
F. Amphora G. Spouted tripod pot H. Two-handled jar IL. Pitchers J. Flower-pot
K. Funnel M. Spit support

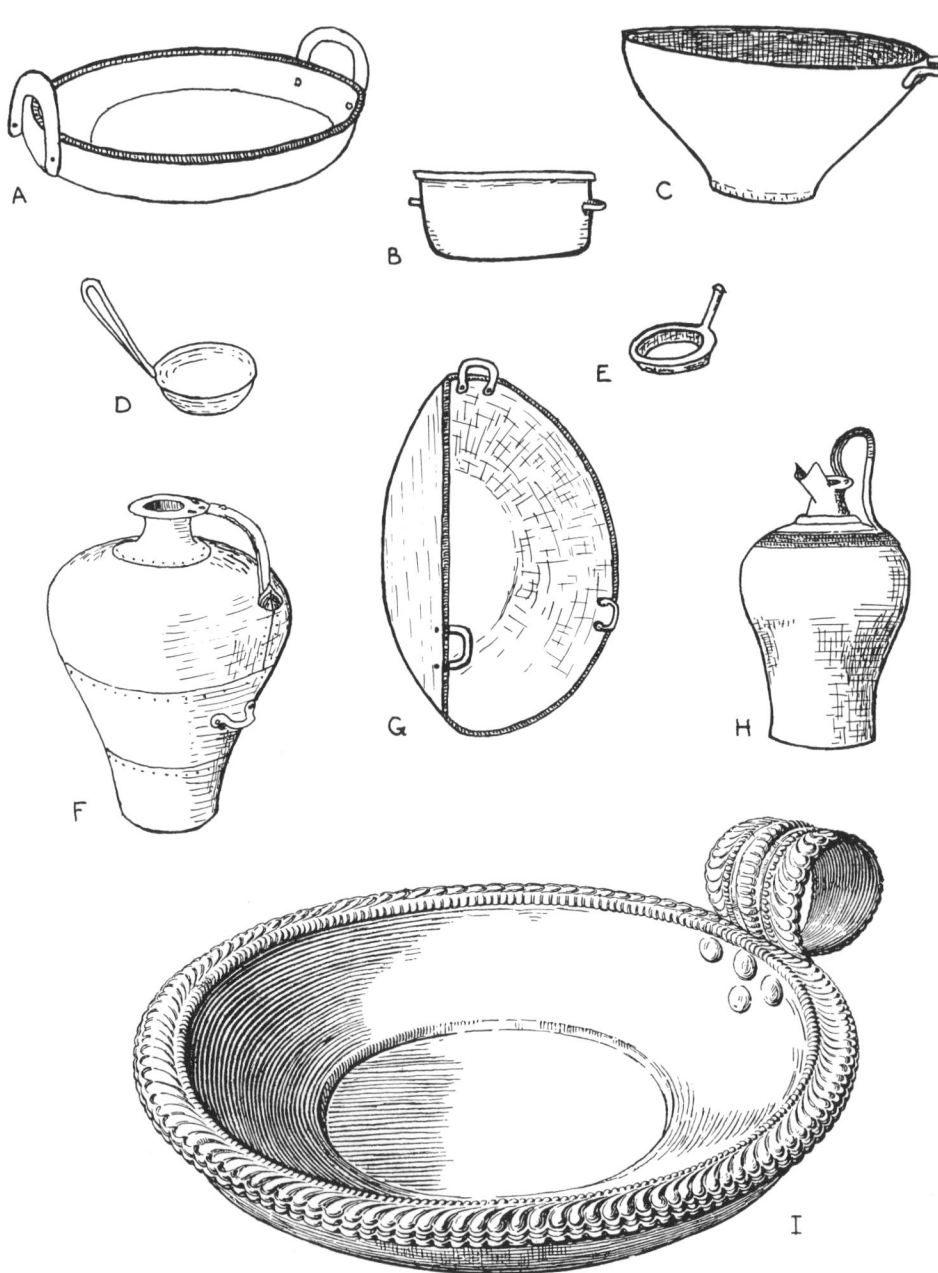

142. Minoan bronze vessels: D. Ladle   FH. Pitchers   G. Large cauldron
I. Cup with fine cast detail

143. CLAY AND METAL OBJECTS: AE. Clay cups   BD. Bronze cups   C. Cup from Campstool
Fresco   F. Gold cup from Vaphio, near Sparta   G. Clay stool   H. Oil separator   (clay)

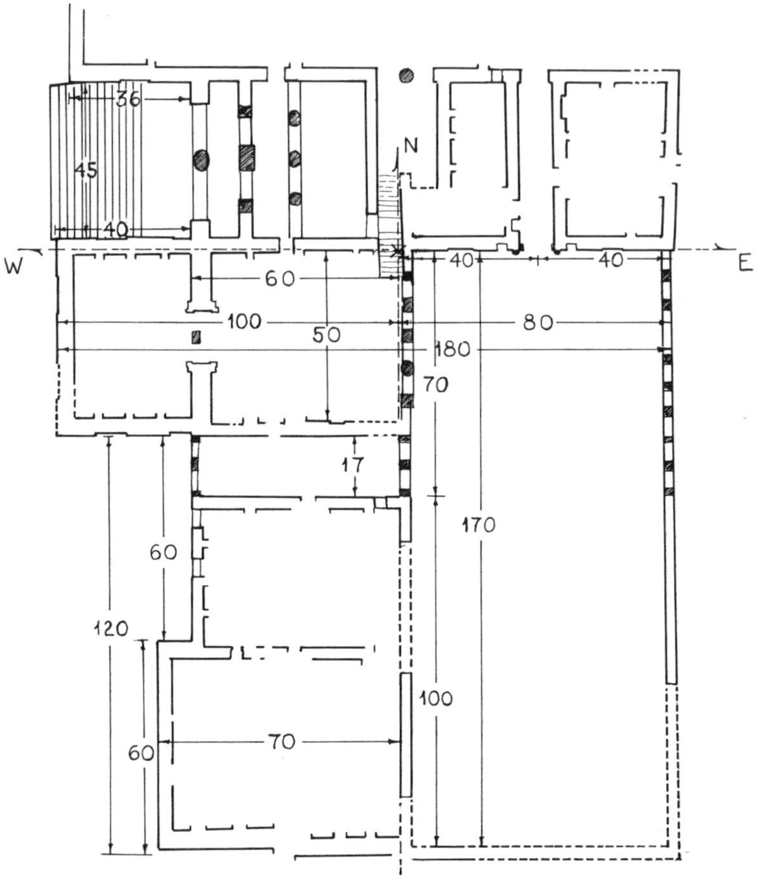

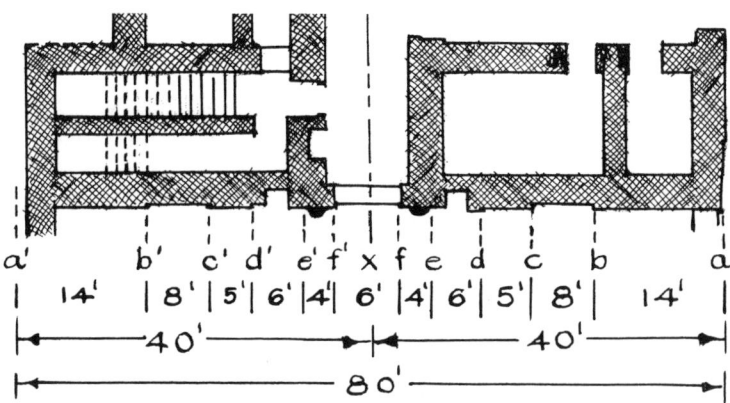

144. Diagram of part of Palace of Phaistos with dimensions
in round numbers of Minoan feet

145. Diagram of north façade of Central Court, Phaistos,
with dimensions in Minoan feet

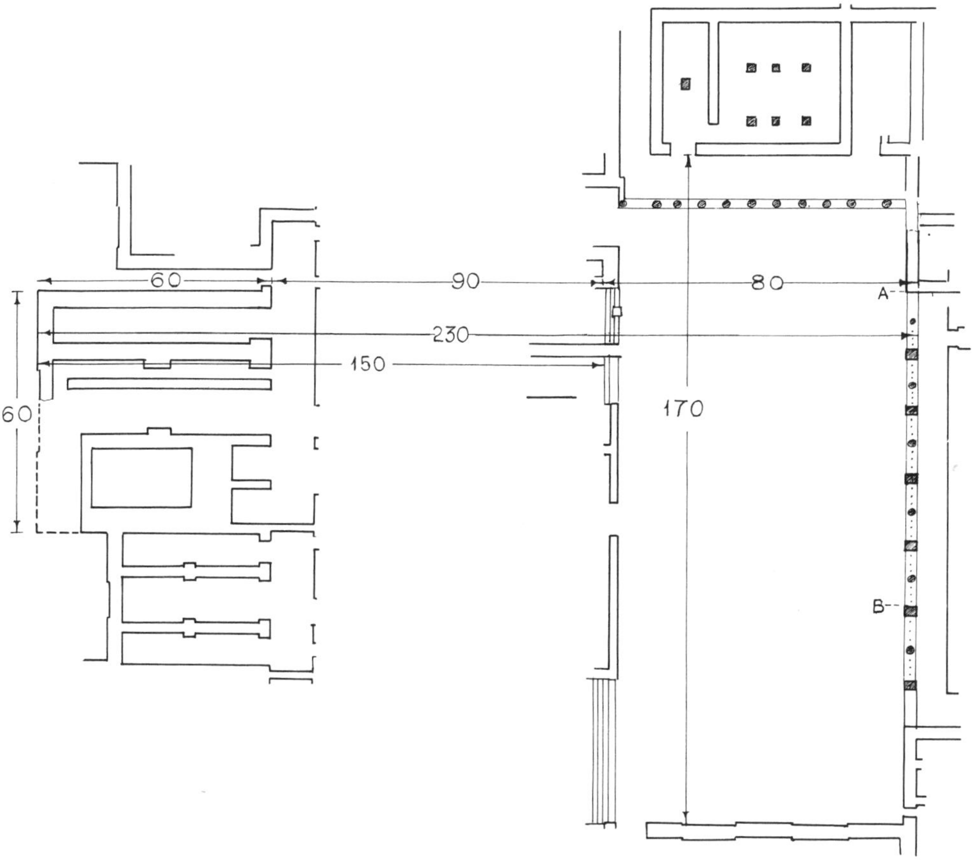

146. Diagram of part of Palace of Mallia with dimensions
in round numbers of Minoan feet

147. Linear B "Tripod Tablet" from Pylos

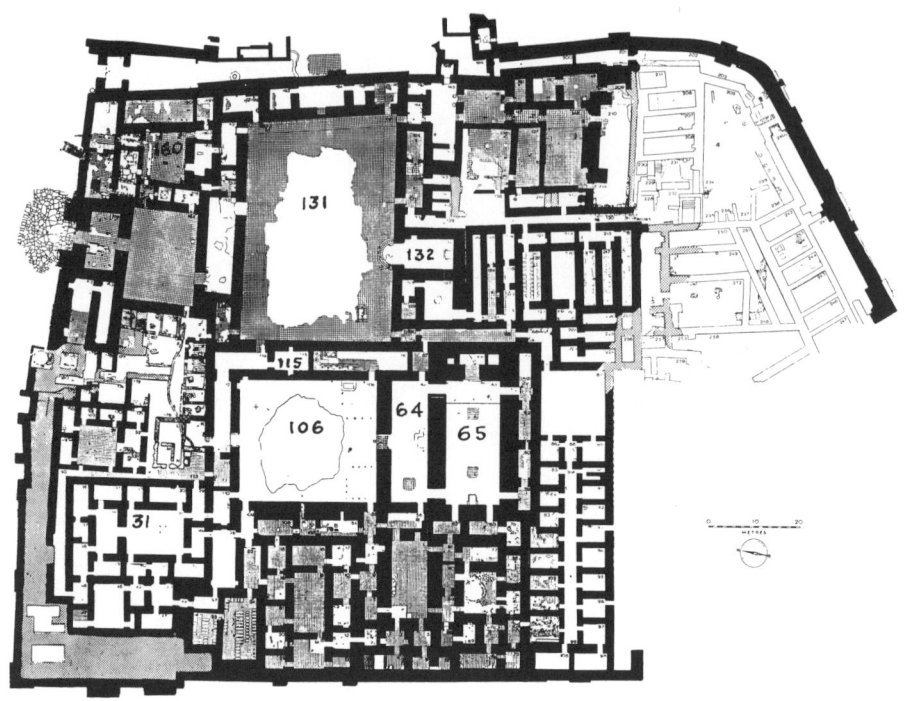

148. Palace of Mari on the Euphrates

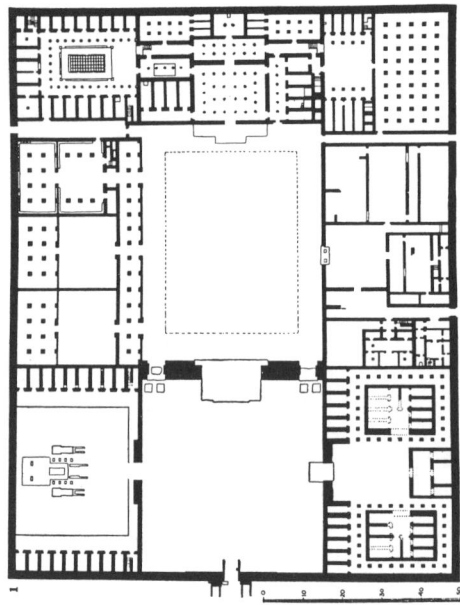

149. North Palace at Amarna, Egypt

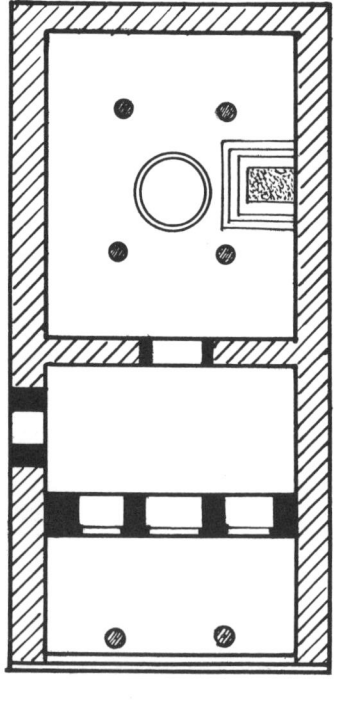

150. Megaron of Palace of Tiryns, Greece

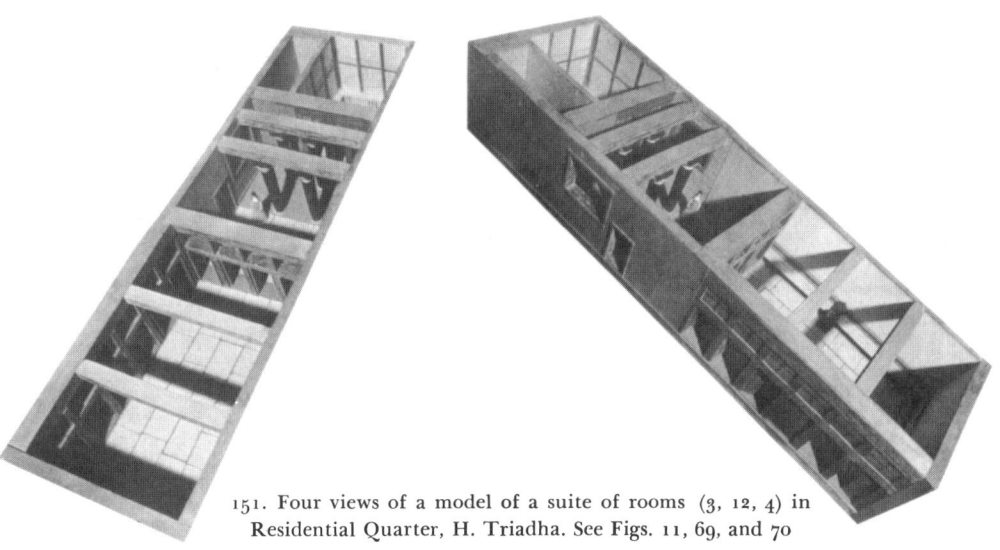

151. Four views of a model of a suite of rooms (3, 12, 4) in
Residential Quarter, H. Triadha. See Figs. 11, 69, and 70

152. Present day town in the Greek islands

154. Doorway in Residential Quarter, H. Triadha

A

B

C

153. DECORATED POTTERY: A. Kamares vase, Middle Minoan II B. Stirrup jar from Gournia, Late Minoan Ib C. Amphora from Greek mainland, Late Helladic II

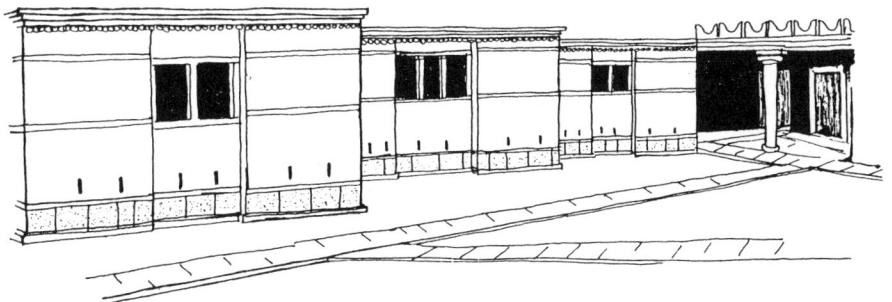

155. West façade and west entrance to Palace of Minos, from west court

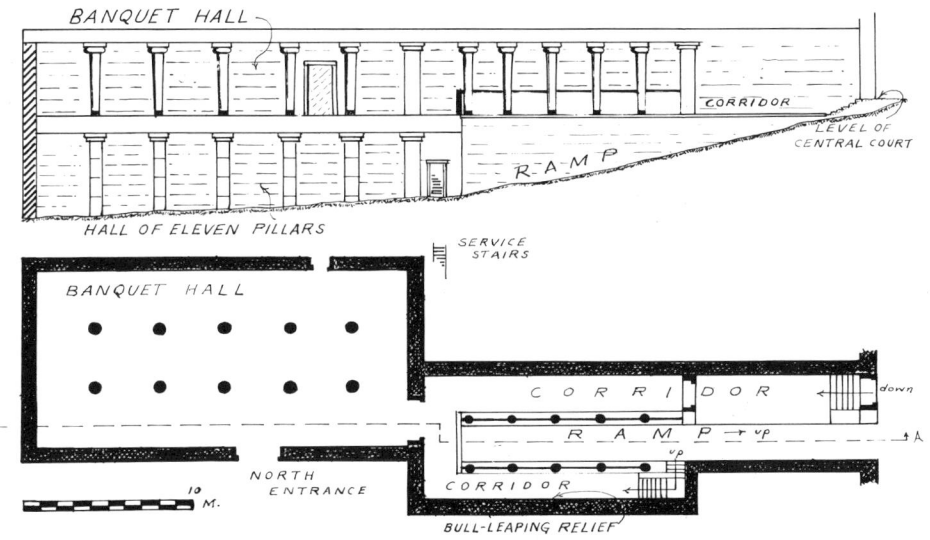

156. Conjectural Banquet Hall at Knossos, with access from Central Court

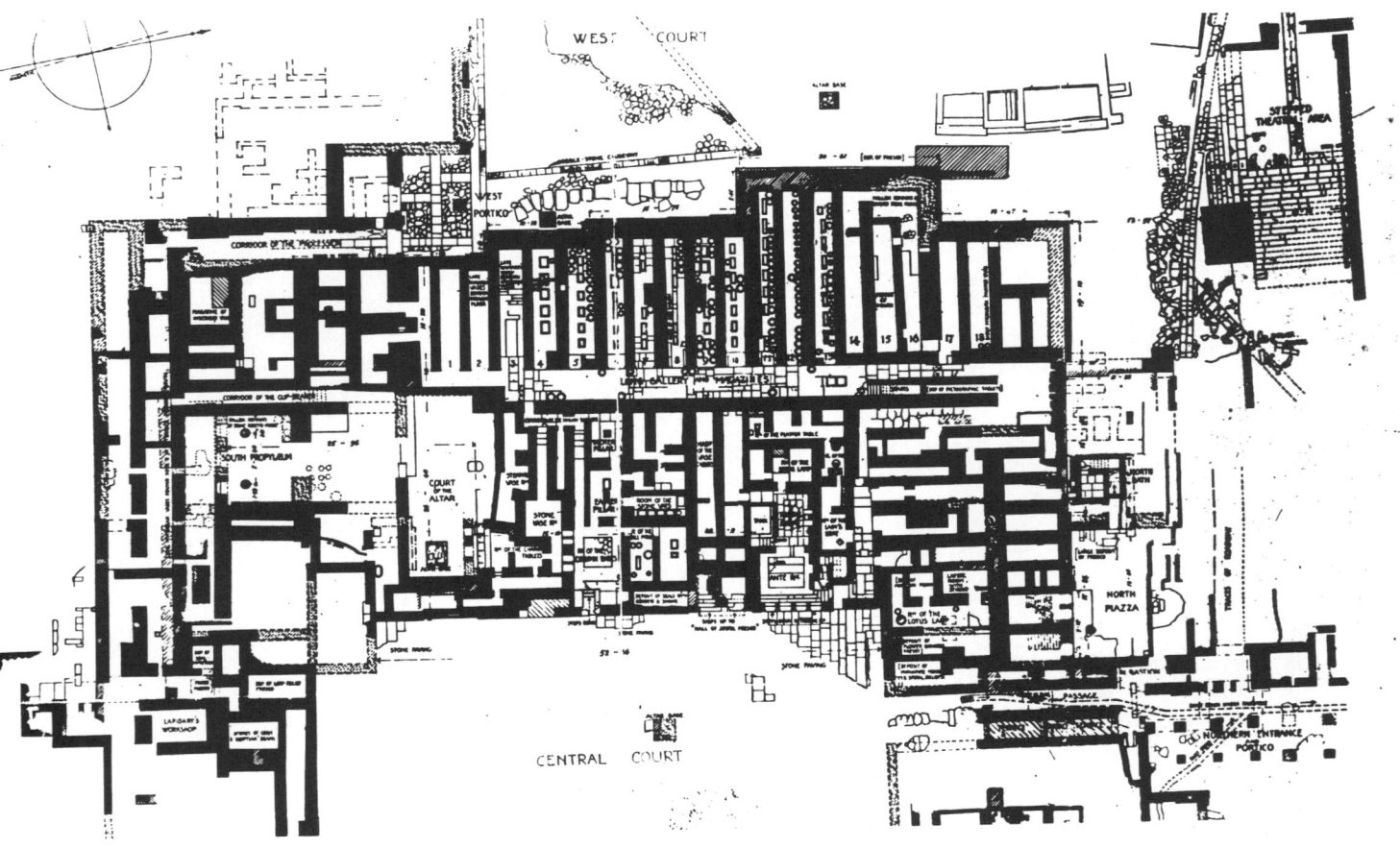

157. Plan of Palace of Minos west of Central Court. From Th. Fyfe, *BSA* 10 (1903-1904), fig. 13; north at top

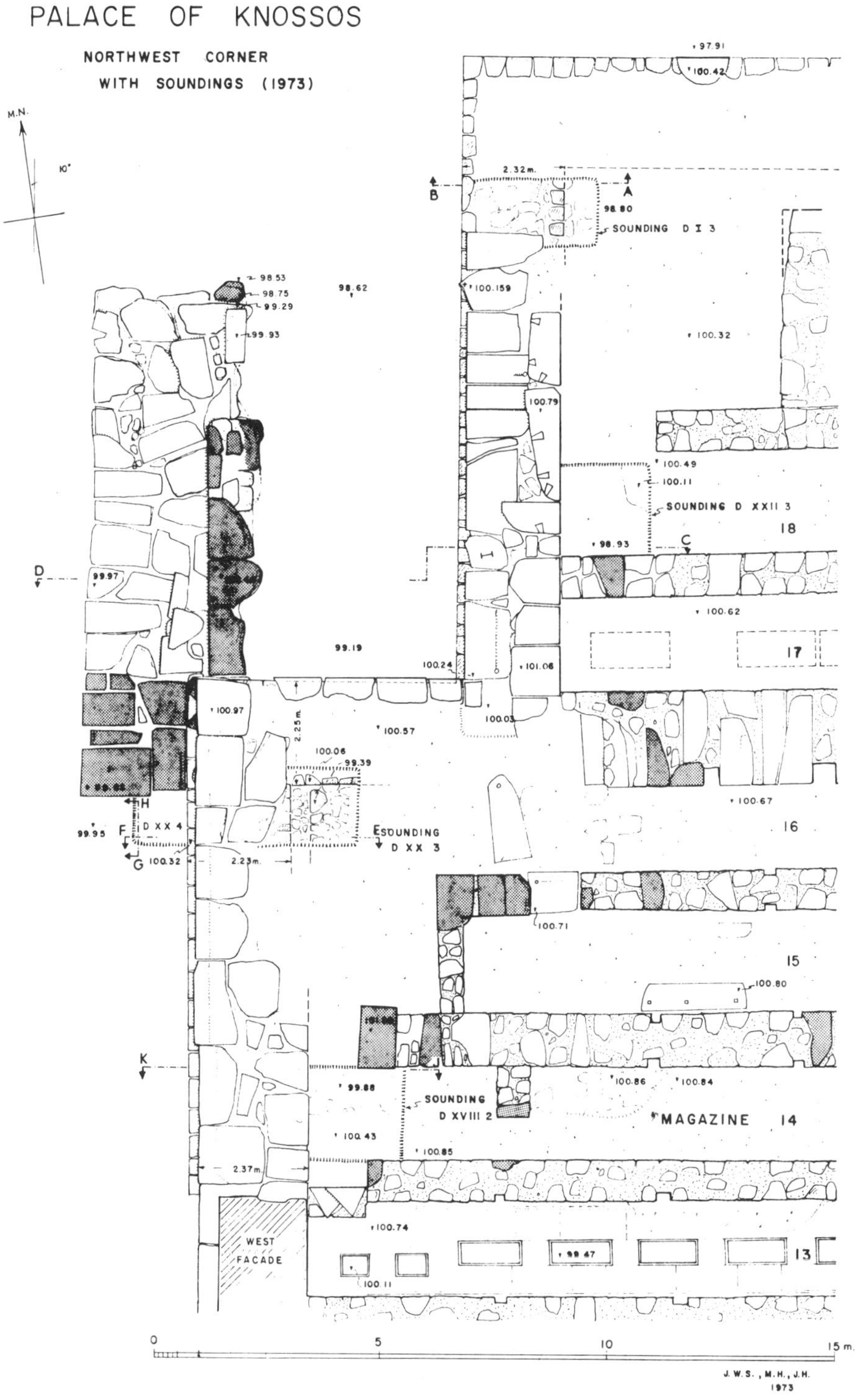

PALACE OF KNOSSOS

NORTHWEST CORNER

WITH SOUNDINGS (1973)

158. Unpublished present-state plan of NW corner of Palace of Minos.
By permission of British School of Archaeology at Athens.

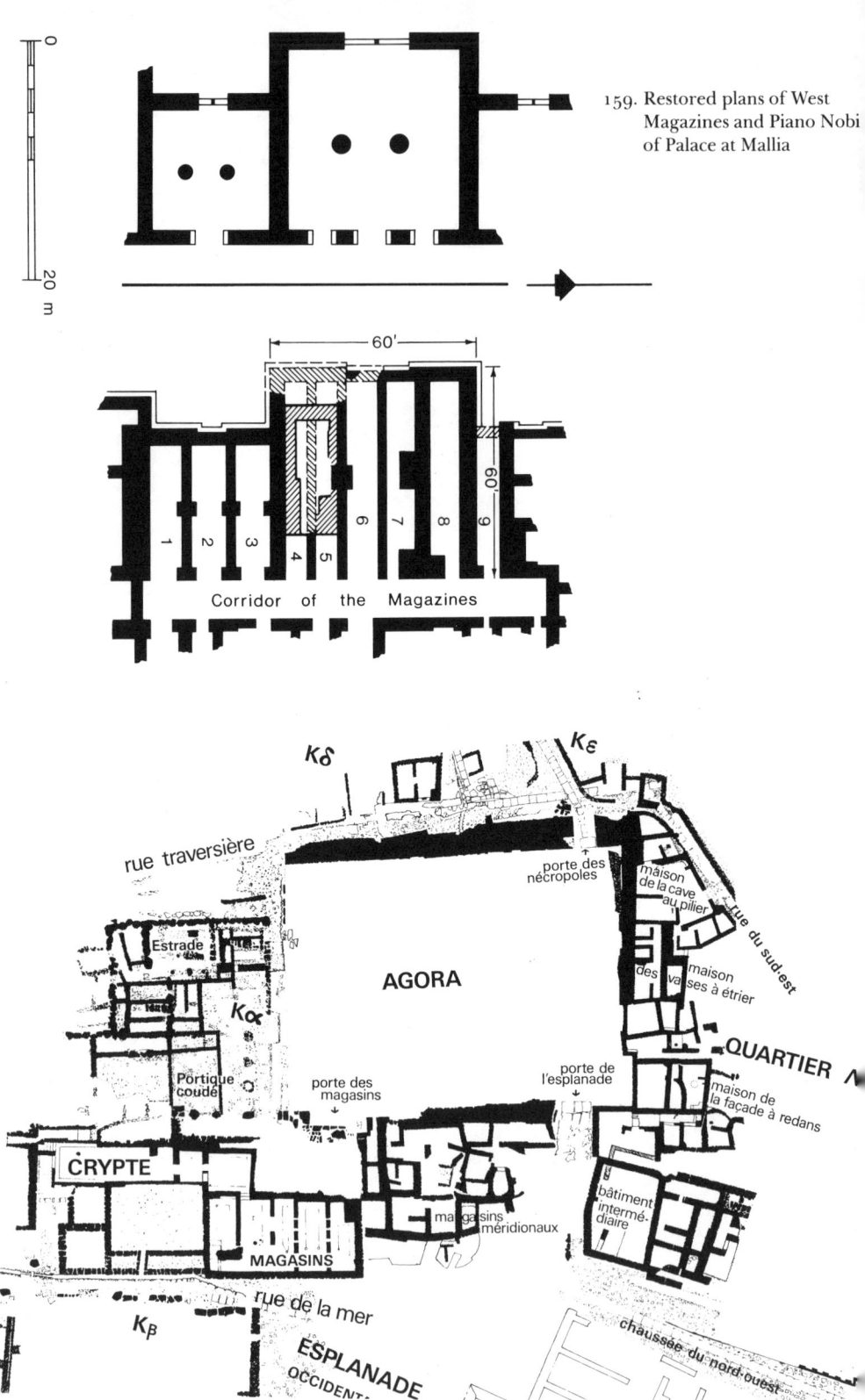

159. Restored plans of West Magazines and Piano Nobi of Palace at Mallia

60′

60′

1 2 3 4 5 6 7 8 9

Corridor of the Magazines

Kδ Kε

rue traversière

porte des nécropoles

maison de la cave au pilier

rue du sud-est

Estrade

AGORA

des vases à étrier

maison

Kα

QUARTIER Λ

Portique coudé

porte des magasins

porte de l'esplanade

maison de la façade à redans

CRYPTE

magasins méridionaux

bâtiment intermédiaire

MAGASINS

rue de la mer

Kβ

ESPLANADE OCCIDENTALE

chaussée du nord-ouest

160. "Agora" area northwest of Palace at Mallia

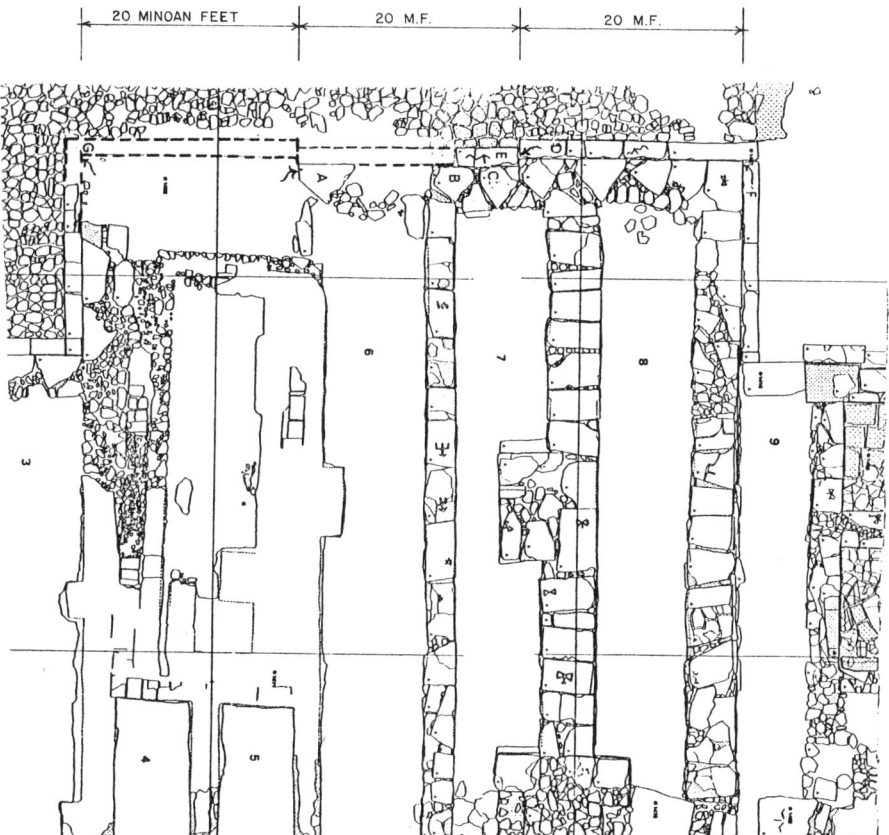

161. Present-state plan of West Magazines beneath Central Hall of Piano Nobile at Mallia (slightly modified and restored). By permission of French School of Archaeology; north at top

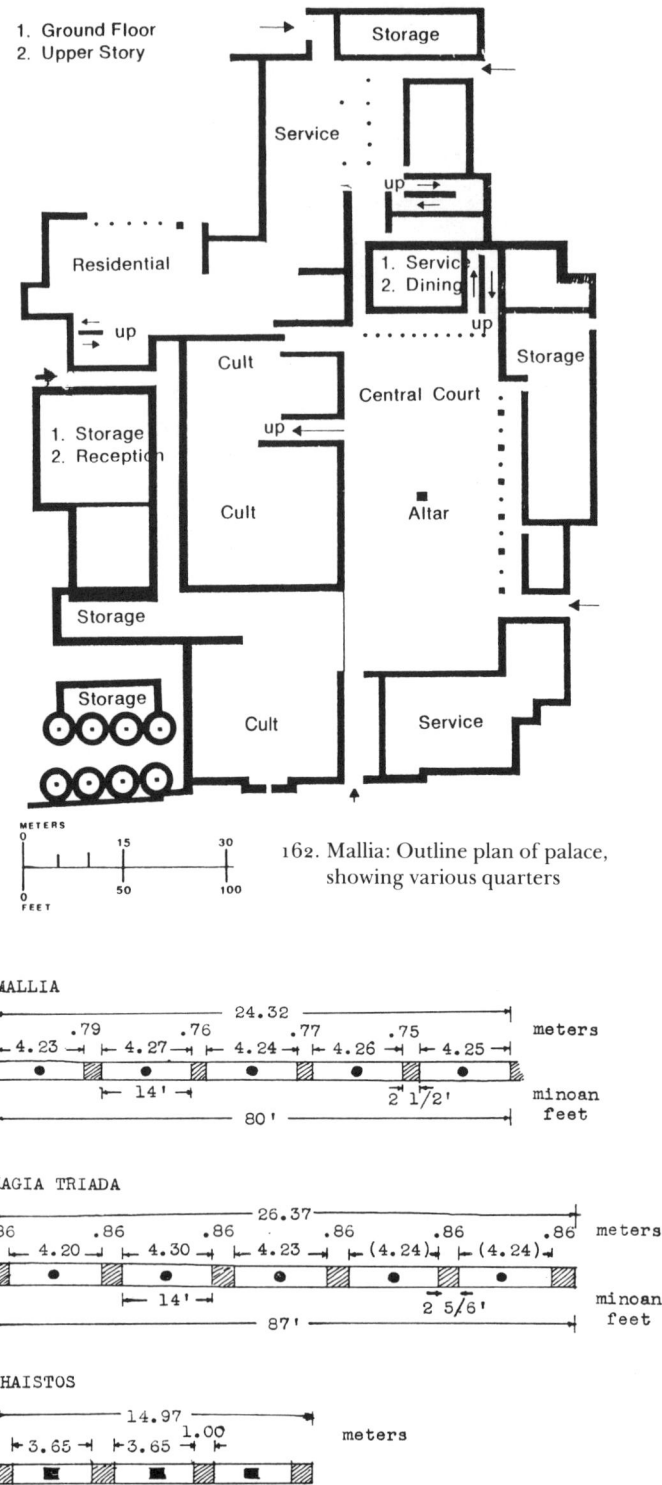

1. Ground Floor
2. Upper Story

Storage

Service

up

1. Service
2. Dining

up

Residential

up

Storage

Cult

Central Court

1. Storage
2. Reception

Cult

Altar

Storage

Storage

Cult

Service

METERS
0   15   30
0   50   100
FEET

162. Mallia: Outline plan of palace, showing various quarters

MALLIA

|————— 24.32 —————|
.79   .76   .77   .75
|—4.23—| |—4.27—| |—4.24—| |—4.26—| |—4.25—|

meters

|— 14' —| 2 1/2'

minoan feet

|————————— 80' —————————|

HAGIA TRIADA

|——————— 26.37 ———————|
.86   .86   .86   .86   .86   .86
|— 4.20 —| |— 4.30 —| |— 4.23 —| |—(4.24)—| |—(4.24)—|

meters

|— 14' —| 2 5/6'

minoan feet

|————————— 87' —————————|

PHAISTOS

|——————— 14.97 ———————|
                     1.00
|—3.65—| |—3.65—| |—|

meters

|—12'—| 3 1/3'

minoan feet

|————— 49 1/3' —————|

163. Details of three Minoan porticoes

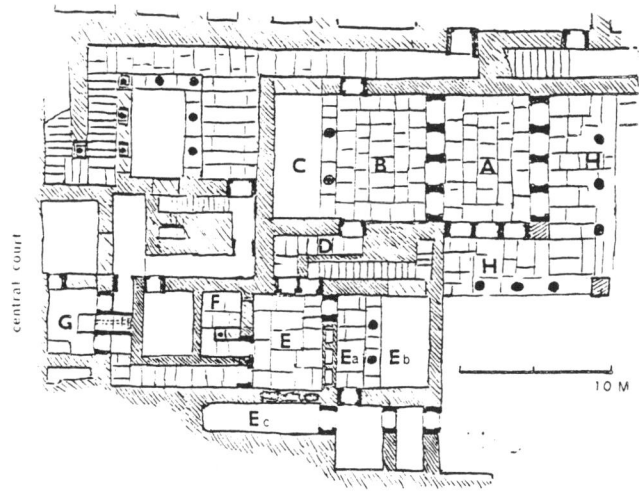

KNOSSOS

164-166. Residential quarters of three palaces

AB	King's Hall
C	Light-well
D	Corridor to
E	Queen's Hall
F	Bathroom
G	Toilet
H	Porticoes
LMN	Secondary Suite

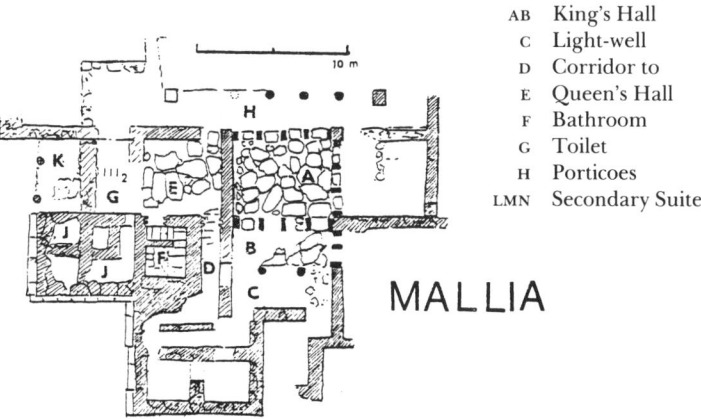

MALLIA

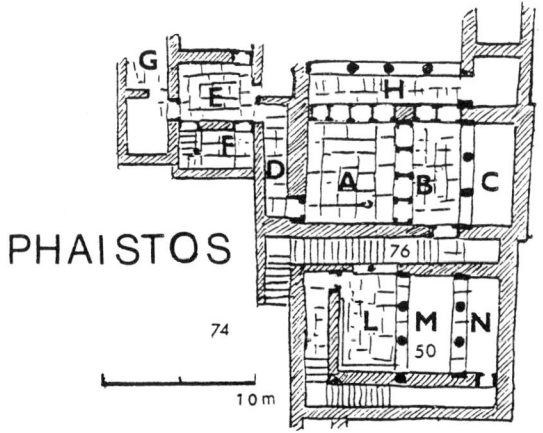

PHAISTOS

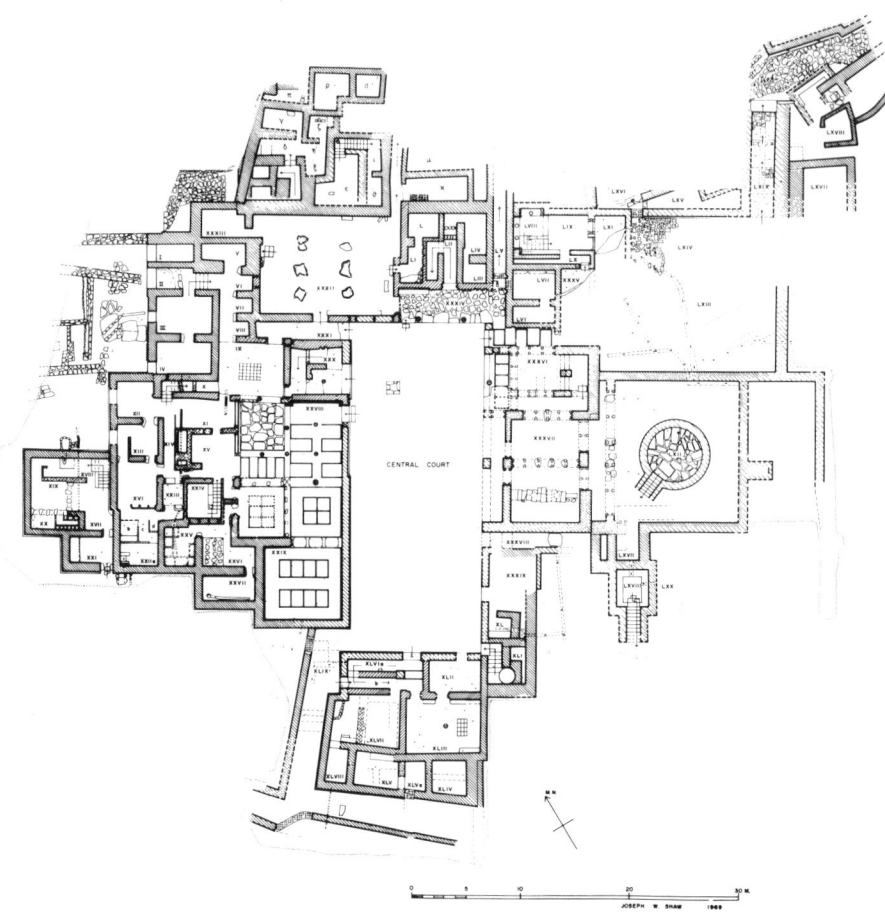

167. Palace at Kato Zakro. By permission of Nikolaos Platon

WORKING IN INDIAN COUNTRY

Building Successful Business Relationships With American Indian Tribes

LARRY D. KEOWN

HUGO HOUSE PUBLISHERS, LTD.

DISCLAIMER

The purpose of this book is to educate. The author and/or publisher do not guarantee that anyone following these techniques, suggestions, tips, ideas, or strategies will engender success. The author and/or publisher shall have neither liability nor responsibility to anyone with respect to any loss or damage caused, or alleged to be caused, directly or indirectly by the information contained in this book.

Library of Congress Control Number: 2010939018

ISBN: 978-1-936449-00-2

Cover Design and Interior Layout: www.taylorbydesign.com

Hugo House Publishers, Ltd.
Englewood, Colorado
Austin, Texas
(877) 700-0616
www.HugoHousePublishers.com

What Readers Are Saying about *Working in Indian Country*

I think that you make many interesting and perceptive observations, which will be valuable to non-Indians who do not have much experience working with tribes. You have put an impressive amount of time and effort into thinking about this topic based upon your experiences and listened carefully to what Indian people have had to say. All of this is reflected in your book and you provide a unique perspective on the challenges and rewards of meaningful consultation with Indian tribal nations.

Jack Trope
Executive Director
Association on American Indian Affairs

Practical, informative, highly readable road map to achieve success in Indian country. Every organization dealing with American Indian tribes should have a line of top management people who are familiar with the contents of this book.

Jeff Sanders
Chair Department of Sociology, Political Science, Native American Studies, and Environmental Studies
Montana State University–Billings

[This book] should be required reading for all non-Indian government people before they're allowed to work with tribes.

Jim St. Arnold
Past Tribal Chairman and Council Member
Keweenaw Indian Community, Ojibwa, Michigan

It's great, easy reading, very colloquial, and has both common sense and expert sense. It belongs on every line officer's library shelf in every agency.

Alan Dorian

About the Cover

The cover art for *Working in Indian Country* was created by Eugene J. Ridgely (Ridge Bear) specifically for this book. Each symbol has a specific meaning but when combined they represent the bonding and trust between two parties. The buffalo hide and tail are used by many Plains Tribes in spiritual ceremonies. The hide is often used as an altar where spiritual ceremonies take place. The pipe has historical significance and, when smoked by all parties, was used to validate treaties. It illustrates trust, respect, honor, and friendship. The four feathers hanging from the pipe represent the four races–red (indigenous), white (Caucasian), black (African), and yellow (Asian) people. Finally, the two feathers in each corner symbolize friendship between two people.

About the Artist

Eugene J. Ridgely Jr. (Ridge Bear) is a member of the Northern Arapaho Tribe. He has resided all his life on the Wind River Indian Reservation in Wyoming and continues to live there with his wife Rowena and four grown sons, one daughter, and fourteen grandchildren. Eugene is a past educator in the private and public school systems on the reservation. He received a BA in Education from the University of Wyoming in 1975. Eugene is a noted artist and musician and has promoted both of his artistic passions for the past thirty-three years in local, regional, and national art shows, galleries, and markets. He is proud to have been selected by the Northern Arapaho Tribe to have designed the Tribal Logo that now appears on tribal letterheads and stationary, signage, clothing, apparel, and gift souvenirs.

Eugene is a descendent of "Lame Man" from the "Sand Creek Massacre" that tragically happened in Colorado on November 29th, 1864.

Mr. Ridgely can be contacted at ridgebear@ymail.com.

Dedication

To all in the American Indian community who led me on this journey—those who taught, those who exhibited untiring patience, and those who trusted.

You became my teachers, my mentors, and most importantly, my friends.

Contents

PART ONE—A NEW PARADIGM

PART TWO—TRUST: THE FOUNDATION OF A GOOD RELATIONSHIP

Chapter 4

Chapter 5

PART THREE—THE BUSINESS ENVIRONMENT

Acknowledgments

This book, *Working in Indian Country*, could not have been written without the support, teaching, counsel, and advice of many in both the American Indian and non-Indian community. There are literally twenty years of information accumulated from personal accounts, experiences, interviews, presentations, personal conversations, stories, and books that make up this work. Were it not for the generosity of many individuals this effort would have never come to fruition. So, I begin by acknowledging those who have guided and assisted me on this long journey.

First, to the many technical advisors over the years, to whom I refer as my teachers in or associated with the American Indian community and who shared with me the lessons in this book. Not only did they teach me the proper protocol but accepted my efforts to put them into practice. My deepest gratitude goes out to these people whose teachings are the foundation of this work:

Steve Brady, Otto Braided Hair, the late Luke Brady, and the late Dr. Bill Tall Bull, Northern Cheyenne Tribe, Montana; Gerard Baker, Mandan Hidatsa, North Dakota; Jim St. Arnold, Keweenaw Indian Community, Ojibwa, Michigan; Ivan Posey, Tribal Chairman, Eastern Shoshone Business Council, Wyoming; the late John Tarnese and Hamen Wise, Eastern Shoshone Tribe, Wyoming; Eugene Ridgely and the late Francis Brown, Northern Arapaho Tribe, Wyoming; Jerry Flute, Sisseton/Wahpeton Sioux Nation, South Dakota; the late George Sutton, Southern Arapaho, Oklahoma; John Pretty On Top, Shawn Real Bird and the late John Hill and Arthur Big Man, Crow Tribe, Montana; Robert Thrower, Poarch Band of Creek Indians, Alabama; Perry Mathews, Quapaw and Seneca-Cayuga Tribes, Oklahoma; Barbara Sutteer, Northern Ute/Cherokee Tribes; Susan Johnson, Three Affiliated Tribes of the Fort Berthold Reservation, North Dakota; Antone Minthorn, past chair, Confederated Tribes of the Umatilla Indian Reservation,

Oregon; and Jack Trope, Executive Director of the Association on American Indian Affairs.

A special admiration goes out to my past associate Velma Real Bird, Crow Tribal member in Montana, who graciously proffered endless time and patience to me during our planning efforts and travels, adding content, depth, and value to American Indian history and the cultural protocols presented in this book.

I have been honored to interview numerous tribal leaders and have used their quotations or the information they provided to me in this book. They provided many insights on how to work successfully with tribes, build trust, and develop those critical relationships. I am grateful for both their time and the permission to use their words of wisdom. Thank you to:

- Aaron Miles, Director of Natural Resources, Nez Perce Tribe, Idaho
- Albert White Hat, Sante Gleska University, Rosebud, South Dakota
- Ben Speak Thunder, Past Tribal Chairman, Assiniboine-Gros Ventre Tribes, Fort Belknap Indian Reservation, Montana
- Bobby Gonzalez, Native American Graves Protection and Repatriation Act Coordinator, Caddo Nation, Oklahoma
- Bruce Sun Child, Tribal Councilman, Chippewa-Cree Tribe, Rocky Boys Indian Reservation, Montana
- Arthur "Butch" Blazer, New Mexico State Forester, Mescalero-Apache Tribe, New Mexico
- Curley Youpee, Director Cultural Resources, Assiniboine and Sioux Tribes, Fort Peck Indian Reservation
- Eddie Tullis, Past Chairman, Poarch Band of Creek Indians, Atmore, Alabama
- Eugene J. Ridgely, Jr., Northern Arapaho Tribe, Wyoming
- George Sutton (deceased), Southern Arapaho Tribe, Oklahoma
- Gerri Grady, Accounting Coordinator, Eastern Band of Cherokee Indians, North Carolina

- Ivan Posey, Chairman, Eastern Shoshone Tribe, Wyoming
- James Bird, National Park Service, Eastern Band of Cherokee Indians, North Carolina
- Jim St. Arnold, Keweenaw Indian Community, Ojibwa, Michigan
- John Pretty On Top, County Commissioner, Crow Nation, Montana
- Marguerite Teller, Kanosh Band, Paiute Tribe of Utah
- Matthew Gachupin, Pueblo of Jemez, New Mexico
- Mic Isham, Councilman, Lac Courte Oreilles Band of Ojibwe, Wisconsin
- Poncho Bigby (deceased), Assiniboine-Gros Ventre Tribes, Fort Belknap Indian Community, Montana
- Ray Gachupin, Pueblo of Jemez, New Mexico
- Robert Thrower, Tribal Historic Preservation Officer, Poarch Band of Creek Indians, Atmore, Alabama
- Russ Townsend, Tribal Historic Preservation Officer, Eastern Band of Cherokee Indians, North Carolina
- Solo Greene, Education Specialist, Environmental Restoration and Waste Management, Nez Perce Tribe, Idaho
- Terry Cole, Tribal Historic Preservation Officer, Choctaw Nation, Oklahoma
- Travis Parashonts, Paiute Tribe of Utah
- Victor Douville, Sante Gleska University, Rosebud, South Dakota

There are dozens of other tribal leaders I have had the honor of interviewing whose quotations are not included in this work due to space or suitability of topic. However your contributions, although invisible, are included in the discussions through what you have taught me. I hope I have honored your teaching in this work.

I would like to give a special thank you to Debra Croswell of the Confederated Tribes of the Umatilla Indian Reservation for permission to use their Points of Protocol for Working with Tribes, and LaDonna Brave Bull Allard of the Standing Rock Tourism Office for permission to use their Cante Etanhan Owaglake, Speaking for the Heart, Customs and Norms for the Standing Rock Sioux Tribe. Selected excerpts allowed me to introduce the protocols in chapters 6 and 7 with the traditional protocols of these tribes. Also, appreciation goes to Dr. Ted Vlahos for his permission to use his Guest Opinion—Raymond's Story. This story has had a significant impact on many people by creating a real paradigm shift in their thinking about other cultures.

There are those in the non-Indian community that have been very supportive of the work on the Sacred Circle, sponsoring and offering workshops, reviewing the manuscript as an end user, or just getting the word out about the importance of tribal relations. This list goes back almost twenty years and includes hundreds of individuals. At the risk of inadvertently omitting just one individual I offer to those who have been a part of this effort a fond thank you for your support and contributions.

I am very indebted to Dr. Patricia Ross, my editor (and professor), the one who taught me that anyone can be an author but not necessarily a good writer. She took the hundreds of paragraphs and thousands of words and magically gave them meaningful organization and context to make the book fluent and motivating.

Patience, understanding, and support are a few of many family virtues. My wife and children exhibited all these over the past twenty years of me being away from our family to attend tribal meetings, interview tribal leaders, or offer workshops across the country. However, their encouragement for this work never waivered, and I extend my deepest appreciation to my wife Carol and children Kim, Kelly, and Josh. I am always honored when they never fail to ask me, "How's the book going?" Now I can say, thanks to them, "It's finished!"

Foreword

Doe-shaa (Greetings),

When I started working with the government over thirty-four years ago, being a new college graduate and a member of the Three Affiliated tribes of North Dakota on the Fort Berthold Indian Reservation, I never thought too much about the relationship between tribes and federal agencies and if they knew how to "talk" to one another. I soon discovered that most Government leaders had no idea of how to establish Government-to-Government relations with tribes.

I can still remember sitting in some meetings regarding tribes, where the tribes were not even present, and my thought was, as usual, "We Indians are not even invited to the table, but they are making decisions for us!" I was not paid too much attention to in those meetings as a young seasonal with no experience, but the government officials thought it was great, as I was an Indian—as if my presence alone was all that was needed. It was evident at that time that the U. S. Government leaders had no idea, nor was there too much concern about, "getting it right."

Over the years there have been some attempts at "getting it right," and while there are some fairly good books out there, nothing has the depth of *Working in Indian Country*.

I am a member of a generation that still had the opportunity to grow up in a log house. In my very early years, we had no electricity or running water, and I have always thought this was some evidence of the leftover village days at Knife River, when our people lived together as a group. Back then, of course, we all knew the proper etiquette of communication and making decisions. I say this because we always had visitors, mostly relatives from all of the reservation, but also other members of our tribe, many being elders.

My father was from the Flint Knife Clan of the Mandan and my mother from the Low Cap clan of the Hidatsa. I can remember my father being the translator for the elders when our community had public meetings with the Government folks. It was always fun to watch the government folks before the meetings looking scared and, for some reason, mad. As the meetings progressed they looked very uncomfortable. Later, I recognized that they were just unprepared and out of their element.

As I look back on it now, it was the best of times and I do believe that I truly heard and learned from my elders many things including how to communicate with these elders. I would use these lessons later in my government career when I, too, would have to work with tribes. I later realized that these elders, the elders who would sit and visit with my father and mother, were the same Indian leaders that had to communicate with the government and deal with their procedures. These elders were the leaders in the 1930's, 40's and 50's, and I also realized their lessons were not available to most of those government workers at that time. Now, Larry Keown's *Working in Indian Country* brings out those much needed lessons in a straight-forward discussion using his experiences, his mistakes, and his successes.

I remember when my folks had to work and talk with the "government man" as the folks would call him. He would always show up in a very black car, kicking up dust as he drove down our dirt two-track (later gravel) road, and the guy always had on a black suit with a very white shirt and of course a black tie. I never knew how they approached my father, as he was the head of the house, because my mother always told my sister and me to go hide. But I am pretty sure the communications and actions of the "government man" were not up to par! As I got older and paid a little more attention, I did take notice of these men. They were usually people who knew nothing about us, and many times it appeared to my young mind a bit insulting as they tried to communicate with my dad and the other men that sat in our old log home. They definitely were not like the elders who would come and sit at the table. I remember one time that it got so bad with this "government communication," or lack thereof, that my father and the rest of the Indian men started to talk nothing but the Hidatsa language and the government man finally got mad and left. We have improved since that time, and now with the true understanding and honest teaching in this book, the reader should be able to have very successful relationships with tribes and tribal people.

Larry has learned the hard way, which in this case, is the best way to learn. He is a non-Indian (a white guy), but in all of my years of teaching these very subjects, from an Indian side I may add, I have never run across a person who has captured these abilities and knows how to present it so we can all continue to learn from it.

I have realized that over the years it takes someone like Larry and his experiences in working with tribal leaders in Indian country to bring that across to others. Through Larry I have learned that we all need to take a different approach and maybe listen in a different way. He talks about his mistakes and what he learned from them, and how he used his lessons to work with Indian leaders. Now he is passing it on in a very educational and practical and positive manner. He accomplishes this the way most American Indian leaders do, to the point and with explanation.

There is a danger, it seems, in this day and age of wanting to follow the right protocol, but most are not really sure how to go about it especially with all the political correctness in the air. All these years, government leaders have tried, mostly unsuccessfully, to communicate with American Indian leaders, elders, the youth, and Tribal Governments. Even in my fifteen years as superintendent in a government agency and as an American Indian superintendent and hopefully a teacher of the same subject matter, I have not learned how to be as effective as Larry. I have found that is just the way it is. I appreciate the way that Larry takes the approach of really using what he learned from the best teachers in the universe—the traditional elders, the tribal council members, and Indian people in general, covering the most complicated issues. He asks the simple question that makes all the difference in the world—how do we get along and how do we talk to make this a better world for the next generation of government leaders who have the responsibility to work with Tribal folks as well as the citizens in Indian country?

Foreword

As I read and re-read this book, each time it was more and more like sitting in our old log house and watching and listening to the elders, learning from them how I was to approach and visit with them with all the respect and honesty they deserve. It is not easy when you first work with tribes. You are coming into a very different world, especially if you did not grow up that way. Larry gives rock-solid advice—this is a guide and a message—that now is the time to understand and acknowledge the necessity of working with tribal people on their terms. If you really do want to create a working relationship that is honest and productive, it is time to understand the American Indian people, to not only be able to work with them, but to work with them on their terms.

Gerard A. Baker—Mandan-Hidatsa
Retired, National Park Service Assistant Director of American Indian Relations
and Superintendent, Mount Rushmore National Memorial

Introduction

The Journey Begins

Nineteen ninety-one was a signature year for me. As a federal employee, I arrived at my new position in the U.S. Forest Service in March and was immediately assigned to develop a long-term management plan for an American Indian sacred site called the Sacred Circle.[1] The plan was supposed to be developed with the local American Indian tribes, and I couldn't wait to roll up my sleeves and get to work. I spent hours trying to figure out the best way to work with the tribes. I didn't consult them on the process because I didn't think I needed to. I knew I was going to lead it through to the best conclusion possible.

I couldn't have been more wrong.

I was extremely curious about the site. A powerful place revered by American Indians for centuries, I was told that the Sacred Circle was considered by many to be a place where one lays down his weapons and comes in peace, a place where one communicates with the Great Spirit, a place to pray. At 10,000 feet atop a long ridge the elements of nature test one's physical and spiritual strength. Many times American Indians

---

[1] I have taken the liberty to use this anonymous name, Sacred Circle, in deference to the wishes of the American Indian community. In our collaborative effort to develop a long-term management plan we agreed that one of the best ways to protect this sacred site was to avoid calling attention to it and attracting more visitors. Increased visitation, the potential for vandalism, and illegitimate use detracts from and threatens the fragile environment, structure, and integrity of this sacred site.

would literally spend days challenging nature's best—wind, rain, snow, sleet, hail or fog to reach out and communicate with the Great Spirit. I remember the first time I made the trek. I was actually surprised. At first glance, I didn't recognize the meaning of how the Sacred Circle is laid out—a circle of stones about eighty feet in diameter with twenty-eight spokes radiating from a central cairn. The central cairn has been dated at about 7,500 years old with the peripheral structure dating in the hundreds of years. There are four cairns on the outside ring of stones oriented in the four cardinal directions—north, south, east, and west. When standing in or near the Sacred Circle, one can view the landscape for a hundred miles in three directions. It is awe inspiring.

Prior to my arrival in 1991, the agency had prepared a Draft Environmental Impact Statement (commonly known as a DEIS) outlining management options for this sacred place. Little did I realize until meeting with tribal representatives how volatile the situation was. My first encounter was at a meeting in Billings, Montana where we were holding an open house for tribes to visit with us about the DEIS. The first person I had an encounter with was a tribal representative connected to the site named Dr. Bill Tall Bull, an elder with the Northern Cheyenne tribe in Montana. My colleagues pointed him out at a table and suggested I introduce myself. Made sense. He was a representative of one of the tribal organizations we were working with on the project. I walked up to Bill, extended my hand and said, "Bill, I'm Larry Keown, the new kid on the block and will be working with you on the Sacred Circle."

His response was abrupt and to the point, "You're just another white man who breaks treaties and I don't want anything to do with you!" I was totally taken aback. I felt rejected but I was determined to move forward. I had a job to do.

Our next open house was in Riverton, Wyoming, with the same objective as the Billings' open house. Unfortunately, very few tribal members showed up. I was disappointed. We had put a ton of work into planning the event. A young Eastern Shoshone woman who was there took it upon herself to approach me. She gave me the same tongue lashing I had received from Dr. Tall Bull. She lectured me on the atrocities of what the government had done to American Indians and about us not listening to their real concerns.

This time I thought I was prepared for such a response. I told her we were there to listen but no one showed up. She replied, "Well, it's Sundance and Powwow season and everyone is gone until it ends around the autumnal equinox in September!"

"Uh oh," I thought, "why didn't we know that?" I vowed to do better.

Later that fall, I thought it might be beneficial if I visited with each tribal leader individually. So, I hit the road and my first appointment was with the late Francis Brown, a Northern Arapaho elder and president of the coalition representing numerous tribes on the Sacred Circle project. I had never met Francis and wanted to visit with him about what we could do to move the planning process forward with the tribes. Everyone told me I would know Francis when I walked in the door—"He'll be the big guy wearing a cowboy hat, smoking a cigarette and drinking coffee." Sure enough, as soon as I walked into JB's Big Boy in Riverton, Wyoming, there he was. We chatted cordially about "stuff," and then I asked the inevitable question: "Why is the Sacred Circle so important to American Indians?"

His response was curt: "You'll learn in court!"

I was again taken aback, but I had another question prepared and I was determined to ask it: "What would proper management of the site look like? I mean how should it be managed?"

His response, "You'll learn in court!"

Now I was at a loss, so I went for broke: "What can we do to work together?"

You guessed it. His reply: "You'll learn in court!"

Every question I asked that day was answered the same way: "You'll learn in court!"

I learned later, and very much the hard way, that Francis was sending me a message that tribes were fed up with the way they had been treated in the planning process. They were tired of feeling that they were ignored, tired of answering questions that they felt the government was asking only because it was required to. Above all, they were totally fed up with all the failed commitments on this project. In the end, Francis' message was that he was fed up and ready to settle the issue in court. I was going nowhere fast.

But I still had a job to do. Soon after, I called a team meeting. We candidly discussed what we could do to get this project off dead center and moving forward. We decided we should have a big meeting in Billings and invite all the interested tribal representatives and non-Indians from the local communities. We decided the best format would be a traditional workshop format where we would group people together and have them provide ideas and proposals. We also decided that we would hold it over a weekend so people could attend without interrupting their work schedules. It was perfect—a big, two-day brainstorming session! So, we made the contacts, developed an agenda, prepared flip charts with questions, arranged for a facilitator, and awaited the big day. We were excited that a captive audience for two days would give us both the information needed and get people working together. Boy, were we wrong!

As people began registering for the workshop we noted that there were American Indian lawyers, professors, chairmen, elders, and interested individuals from across the country. How had these people found out about our little workshop? We only invited the local tribal representatives to attend.

We also started late, a sure sign, I thought, that things would not go well. We were supposed to start at 9:00 a.m., but at 10:00, people were still drifting in, drinking coffee, socializing, and wandering around greeting old friends. I was getting impatient knowing we had a lot of work to do in the next couple of days. I finally had enough. I had the facilitator call everyone together to be seated and began with *our* opening comments so we could move to the next step—break out into small groups, roll up our sleeves, and get to work.

We never got there.

For the next two days it was speech after speech with me being the primary target. I was called the "Custer of the World," accused of genocide, and breaking treaties. As I stood in front of the group I said to myself, "How can these people say these things about me? They don't even know me." Finally, into the second day an elder got up and started making a statement about our lack of respect and appreciation towards the Sacred Circle. I interrupted and told him that was not true. It took only a second for me to realize that I had just poured gas on an already inflamed Indian community.

Finally, the meeting ended. I was feeling pretty lousy. Actually, to this day, I rate that meeting up there as one of the most emotional experiences of my life, ranking next to getting married and having my kids. The latter two were happy experiences. This time, I was completely dejected. I thought I had accomplished nothing. All that happened was a lot of venting about what a terrible job we were doing and how the government had screwed these people. Fortunately, there were a few tribal representatives who decided to help me out. Francis Brown, the Northern Arapaho elder who had kept threatening me that he would "see me in court," came up to me and placed his hand on my shoulder and said, "Larry, this had to happen. Now we can get to work on the Sacred Circle." He told me the attacks weren't against me personally but who I represented—the government. "And," he said, "people have so much pent-up emotion about what has happened in the past that they had to let it out." He paused, then said something that really made me stop and think: "So don't take it personally."

It was my first lesson on how to really work in Indian country.

The next morning I received a call from John Hill, a Crow elder, asking me if he and Arthur Big Man could drive down and hold a prayer ceremony for me. They had attended the meeting in Billings and were obviously concerned about what I had gone through. I eagerly accepted, and they arrived a couple of hours later. John loaded and lit a sacred pipe with native tobacco and began praying for the Great Spirit to give me the strength on the long road to working with tribes on the Sacred

Circle. To this day, I feel much honored that John and Art would take the time to perform such a wonderful act of kindness.

But things still weren't moving quickly. By summer I was completely exasperated since very little progress was being made, at least in my "business as usual" way of thinking. In fact, to us progress was nonexistent because, to our way of thinking, we had very few successes. Little did we realize that a very important process was going on in the American Indian community. As the "new guy on the block," I was being tested. The Indian community was going through their process of building trust with me and my team. They were working on developing personal relationships with all of us to determine if we were sincere and worthy of the task at hand.

Then something happened. I didn't realize it at the time, but it was pretty important. Perry Mathews, an American Indian from Oklahoma and the governor's liaison for the Wind River Reservation tribes in Wyoming, called that same summer and asked me if I would take him to the Sacred Circle. He told me he'd never had the opportunity to visit the site. I readily agreed and vividly remember the day we met. As soon as we got there, Perry told me he wanted to walk over to the cliffs to offer a prayer. He left the truck and walked into the thick fog enveloping the mountain where the Sacred Circle rests. I soon lost him in the thick fog toward the cliffs to the west.

As I sat waiting for Perry, I contemplated my recent experiences. As a federal official, I was charged with the task of facilitating a long-term management plan for the Sacred Circle with numerous Indian tribes and federal, state, and local government agencies. Here a sacred place sits on federal lands. It was supposed to bring peace to all those who gathered there, but I couldn't help but think of the irony. Peace was the last thing that was happening between our "tribe"—the U.S. government—and theirs. In fact, it was quite the opposite. The tribes, government agencies, and local communities all disagreed on how to manage this sacred site. There were so many issues to resolve: misperceptions of one another's true feelings, differing philosophies about grazing, economic development, recreation, race, and history. How could one facilitate such a task when the desired outcomes by all the parities involved were so vastly different?

I knew by this point I was facing a daunting task because it was all compounded by centuries of broken promises, conflict, anger, hatred, and mistrust between tribes and governments. I had already been the target of these emotions felt by the American Indian community for the previous year. Others before me had tried and failed, and the volatility of the issues were, time and again, articulated by tribal representatives with the phrase "We'll see you in court!"

Then there were the personal issues I had to deal with. Billings was not the last time that I was called the "Custer of the World" or "Treaty Breaker." The one that hurt most was, "You're just another white man who breaks treaties," even though Francis told me not to take it personally.

Again I thought, "How could people in the Indian community make such statements (which I considered shocking) when they didn't even know me?" It hit me hard—both heart and soul—and many before me had failed to endure the heart wrenching process of working in Indian country. Would I just become another casualty of the process?

Suddenly, Perry's shadow appeared through the fog. As he drew nearer, the fog split, much like Moses' parting of the Red Sea, and I could see the mountain ranges a hundred miles to the west through the narrow band of bright sky. As Perry came nearer, the fog closed again and enveloped the mountain and Sacred Circle.

As Perry arrived at the truck I was confused by what I had just seen. I was not able to even begin to rationalize what happened let alone fully grasp the meaning of it all. So I asked Perry, "What just happened here?"

In a calm, nonchalant voice he replied, "I just finished my prayer, that's all."

There was something ineffable and mysterious about that moment. I had been in these mountains long enough to know that fog doesn't part like that, normally. There was a power in that place that was breathtaking. After that, I asked others if they had experienced anything at the site. They confided to me their unexplained experiences. In most cases, there were no rational explanations. It helped me understand why the American Indian tribes were so protective of this site, and it also prompted me to start asking the real questions, the ones I should have asked at the very beginning: How does one take an analytical and collaborative planning approach to a place that refuses to give rational explanations to its secrets? How does one address sacred secrets deeply rooted in American Indian spiritual values, spiritual secrets that have no physical tangible substance that one can readily see and touch, spiritual secrets they don't teach you how to balance with other natural resources in college?

As I pondered these questions, it became clear the future would be difficult and uncertain. Then it hit me. Suspicion and mistrust! Two words that nagged at me most. The answer had to be hidden somewhere in those words. This notion deserved to be explored further. How do you obliterate centuries of suspicion and mistrust? How do you build an effective working relationship with American Indian tribes? The answers are simple enough, and I would soon learn them the hard way.

The next six years taught me many of those lessons. Fortunately, there were many tribal individuals who were willing to open the door, however small the opening, and give me that chance. It was my choice to walk through that opening and receive the teaching, wisdom and mentoring that would forever change my thinking and feelings about working in Indian country.

And eventually, Francis Brown was correct. We were able to roll up our sleeves and get to work with a smaller group of tribal representatives. The road was long and rocky in many places, but also a journey that I now look back upon and greatly value.

What is the biggest lesson I learned in that first year? That our "business as usual" approach does not work in Indian country. Issues of cultural protocol, history, past actions of others, communication, and the lack of trust coupled with a non-existent working relationship clouded our efforts to work effectively with the tribes. We finally did come to an agreement on how to best manage the Sacred Circle, one that all parties were happy with, and there were no court cases involved.

But it wasn't the success of the project that was most important to me. Rather, it was the journey—the teaching and wisdom imparted to me by elders, the lessons on trust and relationships taught by tribal leaders, and most importantly the friendships of those in the American Indian community that will live with me forever.

Since that time I also have had the honor to meet, interview, and collaborate with many American Indian tribal representatives across the country. I've interviewed dozens of tribal leaders asking, "How do you work effectively in Indian country?" What I have learned is priceless, and it's those lessons that I want to pass on to you because, if you are reading this, you are either already involved in a project or are starting on your journey of working with an American Indian tribe. And I can save you much of the trouble I first encountered.

Working in Indian country can be immensely rewarding. You learn about other cultures and traditions; it makes you step outside of your comfort zone, and that can help you see your own culture and traditions in a new light. I have broken this book into three parts—why, how, and what to do. The "why" is helping you change your thinking, a new paradigm if you will, of how to do business. The "how" is the nuts and bolts. This section comprises the longest part of the book because it gets into the core of how to build a trusting relationship between yourself and the tribe you've elected to work with. The last section takes all that you've learned in the "why" and "how" and applies it to situations that I have over the years come to see as typical. I hope you find it as helpful as the many participants in my workshops have over the years.

For I want you to be successful in your venture. Some of the most memorable moments of my life have come from my work with various American Indian tribes across the United States. But right now, you have a choice. You can continue to take the "business as usual" approach, or you can learn from what I did, and save yourself and your project a lot of grief and time. I hope you choose the latter.

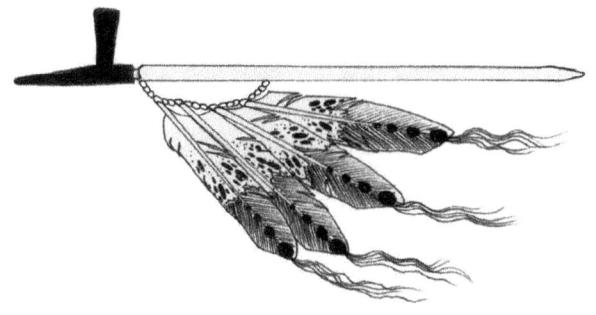

— PART ONE —

A NEW PARADIGM

Successfully working in Indian country requires that you re-examine the way you do business as well as the way you think about Native Americans. The purpose of part one is to help you shift your thinking in both those areas. In other words, I'm asking you to experience a paradigm shift.

A paradigm is simply a way of thinking. For example, the paradigm of the European Middle Ages was that the earth was flat. Explorers of the time helped change that paradigm when they began to use their crude instruments and observation skills and figured out the earth was curved. In the process of proving they could sail from Spain or Portugal to India without falling off the edge, they bumped into a whole new land mass. The people they found on that continent experienced, for good or for ill, a paradigm shift as well. Thus a paradigm shift is simply changing your thinking from one way to another.

The paradigm shift I present in part one is about developing connection and trust in your business relations with American Indian tribes.

1

Beyond Business as Usual: Redefining Leadership

You ultimately chose this book on working in Indian country because you have a desire, wish or even a government or corporate mandate to work with American Indian tribes. Or you may have a simple curiosity about tribal relations in general. Regardless of your motivation you are about to realize the often stark differences between what I have been calling the "business as usual" approach versus a successful "working in Indian country" approach.

Many, if not most, of us work and operate in a traditional business environment defined by social and business norms. Those who travel abroad realize that the business environment in other countries often contrasts with that of ours. However, what few realize is that in our own country there are cultural microcosms—American Indian tribal governments, for one, where the business environment may differ significantly from what we practice on a broader scale. Applying our "business as usual" approach when working with and within another cultural microcosm is not always effective and can lead to disappointing results. But because it is so prevalent in our contemporary style of doing business, I want to spend some time pointing out what "business as usual" is.

In our "business as usual" model we define a leader as one who is visionary, a motivator, a change agent, one who influences others, has power over others, is prominent, or holds a position of status. We look at a leader to inspire others and chart a path into the future. And we use a particular style of communication. However, this traditional model of you setting yourself up as the authority figure does not work well in Indian country for this reason—you are working with a sovereign entity! Tribal sovereignty is inherent and has been affirmed and validated by the Supreme Court of the United States. This means you are dealing with an independent organization, one that is self-governing and not ruled by any other state, much less you or your organization. Because this key concept is overlooked, we fail to redefine leadership to accommodate tribal sovereign rights. You cannot impose a vision on a tribe, exercise power and authority over a tribe, or even change a tribe without their participation and willingness. But because this so often occurs, let me paint you a portrait of what typically happens when our "business as usual" tradition of leadership collides with cultural differences and tribal sovereignty.

You might be a federal or state official wanting to offer a program or project to a tribe; a county official wanting to partner on a grant with a tribe; a banker seeking to expand business to a reservation; an energy official desiring to develop mineral resources on a reservation; a telecommunications company employee wanting to expand services to a tribe; a power company executive needing an easement or right-of-way across a reservation; or, an employee of a non-governmental organization wishing to partner with a tribe on social, health, or environmental issues. Regardless of your motivation, you will soon realize the ineffectiveness of a "business as usual" approach.

So, at the inception of an idea to work with a tribe we begin the typical steps of our "business as usual" approach. We've been taught that we must demonstrate leadership in our programs. And what is one of the greatest attributes of leadership? We're taught that great leaders are visionary—after all Bill Gates had a vision that everyone would have a computer in their house; President Kennedy had a vision to put a man on the moon within ten years, and government officials have a vision for their agency. A "great leader" always articulates that vision, bringing it to life. So, individually or as a group, we sit down and outline our presentation for the tribe with a visionary approach of what we can do for the tribe, what is best for them, and all the great places it will take them in the future. This becomes the foundation of our approach. After all, we are the experts and know what's best for the tribe and their people—right?

We continue our approach with goals, objectives, options, benefits, budgets and more; after all, to us leadership means being able to articulate our vision through sound goals and objectives. Our goals and objectives are mostly self-centered in how they will benefit our organization but often outline how they will benefit the tribe as well. In other words we decide what we think is best for the tribe. This is often accomplished in a vacuum without a thorough understanding of the potential cultural implications, and since we're either unaware of those implications or choose to ignore them, "business as usual" keeps happening.

We then prepare our presentation to the tribe. It may be to a full tribal council, a committee, or group of individuals we feel might be interested. We have handouts of graphs, tables and charts, and an accompanying slideshow presentation to sell our product. It's the perfect presentation, we think. It demonstrates we are truly the experts and know what's best for the tribe.

The big day arrives. We show up early for our appointment and wait, and wait ... and wait. Finally we go before the tribal group and begin the presentation. All goes well but some important cues begin to make us wonder what is going on. First, there is no physical acknowledgement of our important points. Sometimes there are just stares or even no eye contact. No nodding of the heads to signify to us that they are even remotely interested. We become condescending, thinking that they just don't get what we have to offer. After all, this is a great program! So we keep talking and explaining things in simpler terms. Unknowingly, we become patronizing, talking down to the tribal officials as if they just don't comprehend what we are offering. Finally, a tribal leader stands and begins to lecture us on all the atrocities American Indians have been through the past two hundred years and how we could never begin to relate to their problems and issues. "What makes you any different than any other government or corporate official in the past that has broken promises or exploited the tribe for monetary gain?" the tribal leader asks. In the "business as usual" model, we're unprepared to answer that.

Our presentation ends and we are dismissed with a simple "thank you." No further discussion, no questions, no comments. Just a "thank you" and "we'll get back to you." We walk away feeling exasperated, disappointed, and rejected. We thought this was going to be easy! We think it's obvious from the cues that the tribe is not interested in what we have to offer. Or we might start thinking in stereotypes—that American Indians just don't understand and appreciate what we can do for them, that they just cannot get over the past, or that they want to continue to live in the Dark Ages and not capitalize on what we have to offer.

What we don't stop to look at is our attitudes about the tribe in question. You might have come in and by overtly presenting your program as an ultimatum, "Here's what you have to do," you came across as being pushy and not recognizing the tribe's sovereignty. Or, you might have benignly offered a suggestion that violates the cultural standards for that tribe. In either case, the end result might be the same, the tribe's enthusiasm is less than you had anticipated and you come away thinking, "We were warned by others in our organization that this tribe just doesn't get it." "Well," we say to ourselves because we don't know how to think any differently, "it's their loss!"

Changing Our Thinking

For you to get the participation and willingness that you want, you need to build a respectful, culturally-based relationship and earn the trust of individual tribal leaders. If we analyze what happened in this example, it becomes obvious why things turned out the way they did. The response from the tribe—lack of physical and verbal cues, no questions, discussion or comments, and being dismissed with a simple "thank you"—is a strong indicator of our "business as usual" approach clashing head-on with a successful, culturally-based, "working in Indian country" approach. What you might have missed in your typical "business as usual" approach and classic leadership role is the stark cultural and historical differences that have an effect on how we are received and eventually accepted.

So how do we get past this? To begin with, we must change our thinking about how we do business in Indian country and our concepts of leadership. We have to pay attention to their history and to their communication protocols and rituals. For example, to a tribal leader, "listening" means never interrupting, which can leave you with a feeling that a passive response to your proposal means rejection. I'm not going to elaborate on these protocols and rituals here because that will be handled in subsequent chapters.

But the beauty of what I am about to share with you is that anyone can be successful—despite your role or status in your organization, your current mindset about leadership, or how you conduct business. It's about you and your willingness to change your thinking about the American Indians and their experiences. It is up to you to experience a paradigm shift in the way you carry out business in Indian country.

Let me give you another example of what I'm talking about. Many of the tribal governments are culturally-based and stand on a foundation that may be centuries old, older than the Constitution of the United States itself. A few years back I was leading a community assessment for a tribe in Wyoming. A tribal official described how their "resolution" form of government operated: the tribal council made decisions for the people but these decisions could be overturned with a vote of the people. The tribal council is an elected body but the general council included all enrolled members of the tribe.

I asked the tribal leader why the tribe did not choose to form a constitutional form of government, one that mimics our United States model, as many tribes have under the Wheeler-Howard Act (Indian Reorganization Act) of 1934. I was told, sternly but politely, that the tribe's great-grandfathers had created this resolution form of government. They had operated this way effectively for centuries; they were not about to change.

I had to change my thinking about how tribes "should" operate. Many American Indian tribes in the United States choose to operate under their traditional forms of government that are historically and culturally based. And they have the right to do so based upon treaties and the principles of sovereignty. This tribe represents a cultural and governmental microcosm that operates differently from the business environment we are most familiar with. Therefore, it becomes imperative that we, in the non-Indian community, learn and understand how to conduct business in these different environments in order to be successful.

Above all, we must keep in mind that the Indian community is often skeptical about the intentions of government officials and business leaders. This has evolved from a long history of governments trying to mold tribes into a contemporary society, as it existed at that point in time. I say "that point in time" because this problem has persisted for centuries (again, more about this in the next chapter). Ben Speak Thunder, past tribal chairman of the Fort Belknap Indian Community, illustrated this point when he once told me:

> *The non-Indian, the Anglo civilization, has always wanted to help the Native Americans. They helped us so much they just about helped us out of existence. And, I think their way of assistance in helping is premeditated, especially in the early years ... .*[2]

From a business standpoint, there is a sad history of governments and businesses exploiting tribes for profit. It still happens today in many areas of business:

- In energy, by not paying fair royalties for oil, gas, or coal
- In telecommunications by acquiring rights-of-way at less than fair market values
- In gaming by initially reaping profits and then leaving the tribe high and dry
- In construction projects by agreeing to hiring practices and not honoring those practices, and more.

---

[2] Speak Thunder, Ben. 2002. Interview by author. Video recording. April 11. Fort Belknap Indian Community Tribal Office, Harlem, Montana

It is no wonder many tribes are developing their own business infrastructure and not relying on outside business services or opportunities. Tribes have become very savvy and may require protective stipulations when conducting business with government and corporate entities.

As. we have seen, too many government and business leaders approach tribes with a "business as usual" attitude of "We know what's best for you" or "We're here to help." In our new role as collaborative leaders, we must resist these temptations to tell a tribe what's best for them. Would you like someone who doesn't know you to tell you what's best for you? Instead, we need to exhibit patience and a willingness to listen and understand.

What I am about to teach you throughout this book departs significantly from our typical "business as usual" approach to working with organizations. The foundation is simple—build relationships and never say, "Here is what I am going to do for you." Instead, focus on "Here is who we are and what we do, and does it fit with your needs, goals, and culture?" Be aware of the history, the abuses Indian people experienced, the broken treaties and promises, and the culture. More on all this in detail later, but, regardless of whether you simply want to partner with a tribe on a grant or open a branch bank on a reservation, the principles are the same. It's the way I was taught by tribal elders and leaders to build and conduct a successful business venture with a tribe. It's about redefining leadership that might be in contrast to our traditional way of thinking and operating in the American Indian business environment. They may be tough lessons to learn—mine were—but in the end they will help engender success for your project.

Redefining Leadership

As I mentioned earlier, we often equate the term leadership in our own organization or business as a position of authority with the ability to lead and motivate people, resolve conflicts, and provide vision and direction. Working in Indian country requires a leadership approach similar to, yet different from, what we read or learn in a classroom setting. Butch Blazer, State Forester in New Mexico and a member of the Mescalero-Apache Tribe, defines leadership when working with tribes:

> *When I say leadership I'm referring more to that cultural understanding of how to effectively interact with tribal leadership. It's not something that's that easy to do.*[3]

The cultural understanding Mr. Blazer refers to is so critical. It's because culture often defines how tribal governments operate, which in turn defines our business and leadership approach. Only through understanding the culture, and in turn the tribal protocol, can we adjust our approach to *effectively interact* with American Indian tribes.

In his book, *Leadership Without Easy Answers,* Ronald A. Heifetz, helps us understand how we can redefine leadership. Heifetz states,

> *Rather than define leadership either as a position of authority in a social structure or as a personal set of characteristics, we may find it a great deal more useful to define leadership as an activity. This allows for leadership from multiple positions in a social structure. A President and a clerk can both lead. It also allows for the use of a variety of abilities depending on the demands of the culture and situation.*[4]

In his definition, Heifetz makes two vital points that are applicable to working in Indian country. First, leadership is a set of activities or skills that are adjusted to meet cultural situations. Second, anyone can provide leadership despite his or her standing in an organization. In other words, Heifetz's idea of leadership is that it can be done by anyone in an organization and can be adjusted to fit any culture—internally to an organization or externally when dealing with different social cultures such as the American Indian community.

Let's first explore what these leadership activities or skills are and how we can redefine our leadership approach in Indian country. In a traditional sense, leadership might include the way we engage in dialogue, negotiate, make decisions, exercise authority, conduct meetings, articulate

---

[3] Blazer, Arthur "Butch." 2004. Interview by author. Video recording. July 14. New Mexico State Foresters Office, Santa Fe.

[4] Ronald A. Heifetz. 1994. *Leadership Without Easy Answers.* The Belknap Press of Harvard University Press.

visions, and more. The means by which we conduct these activities or skills does not always fit culturally with tribes. This is because, as I mentioned earlier, you cannot impose a vision, make decisions for, or expect to conduct business directly with a tribe. What you will accomplish by merging these redefined leadership activities and skills with American Indian cultural elements is earned respect from tribal leaders—the key to success when working in Indian country. The bottom line is that you will be entering the world of a culturally based "collaborative leadership" style.

As I look at how to usefully redefine these activities or skills for application in Indian country, I am reminded of the various Native American cultures we need to honor and respect. First and foremost is the need to respect the inherent sovereignty of tribes and remind ourselves that we have no formal authority over tribal programs and operations. With that said, our focus needs to be on how we communicate, honor cultural protocols, and ultimately build trust and strong social and business relationships. Specifically, this means how we listen, ask questions, make statements, make decisions, collaborate, present programs or projects, begin, conduct and end meetings, cope with time issues, manage conflict, appreciate social encounters, respect spiritual etiquette, and so much more. In summary, the redefined collaborative leadership activities and skills in this book lead us to that end—learning how to effectively communicate, build trust and relationships, and operate in a business environment that may be significantly different from what we are used to.

Finally, Heifetz's concept that anyone can be a leader also applies well to working in Indian country. If you are the authority figure in your organization, these principles apply. If you are a staff person or executive assistant without any authority or power, the good news is the same principles apply. I have seen many people in organizations at various levels function very effectively with American Indian tribes because they implement many of the collaborative leadership activities and skills I address in detail throughout this book. They have a sound relationship with the tribe in a social and business context and are trusted. They become a conduit of information, relationships, trust, and communication for their organization. They are the linkage to higher levels of the organization and prepare their organization's authority figure with the new protocols for meeting with the tribe's authority figures.

The key to success, however, lies in your ability to bridge your own organization. The knowledge of these new protocols must flow through your organization so they are applied uniformly amongst you and everyone else interacting with the tribe. An often fatal mistake is made when someone in an organization earns the respect and trust of a tribe by applying these redefined collaborative leadership activities and skills and then the authority figure arrives and defaults to a traditional leadership role, telling the tribe what's good for them, making decisions for them or being arrogant. This undermines all the trust and relationship building you have accomplished probably over many years. That is exactly what I don't want to have happen. Anyone exercising these new skills can work successfully with American Indian tribes if they follow the principles outlined in this book.

The following chapters contain the lessons and teachings I have learned from a cautious but patient Indian community and from tribal members who have become friends, teachers, and mentors to me. I cannot over-emphasize that I am not an expert in American Indian culture. However, at least a superficial awareness is essential to effectively apply the concepts I will be presenting. Keep in mind that this writing is from a non-Indian perspective; someone who has been in your shoes working in both the government and corporate environments.

As we begin pondering our new business paradigm, we need to keep in mind some caveats, some firm rules, which are necessary for you to understand when you begin your journey into Indian country and which will become the foundation of working successfully with American Indian tribes.

First, tribes are unique and each has its own history, culture, government, protocol, and structure. Protocols that work with one tribe may not work with another because of these differences. Although American Indian tribes may have experienced a similar history in this country we must recognize the cultural and traditional uniqueness of each. Butch Blazer describes the differences in tribes:

> *One should understand that every tribal entity is very unique. They have their own priorities, they have their own culture, they have their own traditions, and all those things are going to impact the way they interact with non-tribal entities, whether they be federal, state or private. Again, that understanding and respect that has to be given to tribes in allowing them to explain what their particular positions are in regards to a certain issue are important. Whether or not people become frustrated or not, [they are] still a sovereign nation and they have to be given that respect.[5]*

Therefore, our leadership approach must respect and honor these differences and avoid the temptation to lump tribes into a single category of "American Indians." Never think, "I've learned to work with the Caddo Nation in Oklahoma so now I can use the same principles to work with the Ojibwa in Wisconsin."

Second, the opinions, practices, and recommendations presented in this book by individual tribal members, and myself, represent those individuals only and not necessarily those of any tribe, tribal government, or Indian community as a whole. Throughout this book you will read a number of tribal perspectives about various topics relating to culture, communication, trust and relationships, as well as their individual protocols. Most of the individuals interviewed are tribal leaders or past leaders and served as tribal chairs, councilmen, or staff. As I interviewed these individuals I would explain my intent and always offer this question; "As a government official or business leader, what must I do to build trust and work effectively with your tribe?" In virtually every case, these individuals were excited that someone asked them the question, rather than telling them what *they* need to do.

However, we need to keep in mind that, individually, we all have different perspectives of history, culture, values, and other factors that come into play when we offer our opinions about a subject. It might

---

[5] Blazer, Arthur "Butch." 2004. Interview by author. Video recording. July 14. New Mexico State Foresters Office, Santa Fe.

be useful to describe this concept as it is found in nature. A stand of aspen grows in a clone—a group of trees joined by a common root system. But, each tree is an individual growing by itself subject to environmental factors such as sunlight, exposure to disease or insects, fire, and browsing of its leaves by deer or elk. Each tree is an individual growing differently than others, but joined and dependent on their common root system. A community of people can be like an aspen grove—a group of individuals rooted together by a common value or cultural system. But, each person as an individual is influenced by family values, history, traditions, cultures, and personal experiences that shape their way of thinking. Often times these perspectives become skewed due to their biases, lack of objectivity, or even level of knowledge. This is exactly the reason I use the words "many," "often," or "some" to avoid the conclusion that all individuals or tribes are exact duplicates of one another. The perspective a tribal representative offers, however, lends us a culturally diverse viewpoint of the American Indian community that we should value and take to heart. Therefore, I cannot over-emphasize the importance of consulting with local tribal representatives for customary practices and protocol. John Pretty On Top, a former cultural director of the Crow Tribe in Montana and currently County Commissioner, makes the point clearly:

> *What I'm saying is what I know of my people and some small experiences with other people and other tribes. Everywhere I go I start with "I'm a Crow Indian and I'm here to speak about the Crows." Especially in Europe, when I go over there they ask me so many things about other tribes and I say "I don't know, I don't know them, I cannot speak for them [because] I might say something against their way."*[6]

Third, the complexity or simplicity of an issue will determine the extent of effort that is necessary to develop an effective working relationship with an Indian tribe or organization. For example, developing a long-term management plan will probably require application of many more leadership skills than merely requesting a tribal representative to

---

[6] Pretty On Top, John. 2001. Interview by author. Video recording. April 4. Crow Tribe Senior Center, Lodgegrass, Montana.

serve on a discussion panel. Your approach must identify the situation and employ the appropriate activities necessary to meet your objective.

And fourth, a definition of Indian country is in order because there are so many definitions, and it is important to understand the grand scale of what I am talking about. In its narrowest sense Indian country can be defined within the bounds of an Indian Reservation. There are literally hundreds across the country. In the broadest sense, Indian country covers a vast area that includes reservations, ceded lands, and traditional areas that tribes have historically occupied. The phrase "working in Indian country" can have many connotations other than geographic, such as a particular Indian community or even an Indian organization. So look at Indian country not as a place, but as a concept that incorporates place, culture, history, sovereignty, and most importantly, its people.

You will find in this book that many of the lessons I present are repeated because of their importance in many different areas. For instance, you will find the topic of communication discussed in "Communication," "Trust and Relationships" and "The Business Environment." Since many lessons overlap it is important that they be repeated, rather than addressed only once in any given chapter.

Finally, I would be remiss not to share the greatest leadership lesson I have learned, as this is the foundation for all the others that follow. Before I offer this lesson, I must explain the importance of what I am about to share. In our government and corporate "business as usual" approach, we often feel we need to be analytical and detached in our thinking and approach to issues. We dissect issues to ensure an "objective," "non-biased" view. When someone mentions any descriptor about heart, relationship, spirit, or wisdom we tend to close our minds and, most importantly, the door to receiving the lessons imparted by tribal leaders. There is an old management adage that says "think with your head, not your heart." I tend to think of it as "think with your mind, not with your heart," but no matter if you use "head" or "mind," I want to analyze this and show how thinking with your mind versus thinking with your heart applies to working in Indian country. Those who think with their minds focus on facts, figures, numbers, bottom lines, and do not always end up doing what is right, but only what the rational approach leads them to do. Those who think with their hearts focus on emotions, feelings, social relationships, and trust. Working in Indian country requires a sensible dose of both, but leaning heavily towards heart. I can emphatically say that if you are a "mind" oriented person, your success in Indian country will most likely be limited. I have seen many government and business leaders approach tribes on the basis of numbers, facts, regulations, and bottom lines, only to be disappointed that the approach was not well-received. Travis Parashonts, a past tribal leader from the Paiute Tribe in Utah, once related to me the following:

> *Indian people are ... closer to Mother Earth and are more sensitive to the spirit, the creator ... and spiritual things. They're more in tune with that than they are with black and white paper stuff. And so, a lot of times when politicians come to a meeting they want to get right to the business and certain issues. But, a lot of times when you come to tribes that doesn't really happen because [of] the way we are, and the way we are is that a lot of time we see things more spiritually than tangible, I guess, which issues can be. So, Indian people are going to come and voice more about their emotions, passions, and spiritual things on issues. But I think politicians have to listen closely because what's in that passion is some of the things they need to hear in order to make a decision on an issue.*[7]

In short, Indian people tend to be more "heart" oriented than "mind" oriented, and this takes some getting used to especially because we're so used to working from the "mind" first. But what makes this a particularly tough issue is that when working in Indian country, we want to, above all, avoid putting Native American people automatically in either category. While the distinction between has always been helpful to me, I also recognize that there are many in the American Indian community who are more mind-oriented because of many different factors—age and place of education amongst them—and as such will

---

[7] Parashonts, Travis. 2001. Interview by author. Video recording. August 27. Paiute Tribe of Utah Tribal Office, Cedar City.

respond well to fact-based or "mind" oriented presentations. It becomes incumbent upon you to know something about the tribal leaders and the tribe. However, you can never go wrong by showing respect, being honest, and never being patronizing.

Eugene Ridgely, a friend of mine and member of the Northern Arapaho Tribe in Wyoming, shared with me a proper approach when initiating a working relationship with tribes:

> First of all I would tell you, take it slowly. Slowly introduce yourself. Don't be too pushy. If you are going to be pushy they are going to have second thoughts about you, they might not trust you.... You have got to be sincere, slowly work yourself into that relationship and that trust with that tribe or those individuals. Then, that is when you can start asking your questions.[8]

You'll learn more about how to do that in a bit, but what Eugene was saying is that, in the beginning, trust and relationship building—what I call the heart side—are more important than the facts, figures and bottom lines—what I call the mind side. This is due to the suspicion and mistrust that has evolved in the Indian community towards government and business leaders over centuries. Bruce Sun Child, a Chippewa-Cree tribal Councilman for the Rocky Boy's Indian Reservation in Montana, once told me,

> I guess that comes from many years of mistrust...and we're always apprehensive when there's something going on.[9]

So, through the following words, I hope to teach you the lessons of leadership based upon a balanced "mind and heart" approach. I humbly ask that you respectfully listen with your heart, be patient, and receive the wisdom that follows.

---

[8] Ridgely, Eugene. 2002. Interview by author. Video recording. September 4. Wind River Tribal College, Ethete, Wyoming.

[9] Sun Child, Bruce. 2002. Interview by author. Video recording. May 6. Chippewa-Cree Rocky Boys Indian Reservation Tribal Council Office, Box Elder, Montana.

2

History from a Different Perspective: The Importance of American Indian History

Many of us hated history in school because we thought it was boring. Who cared who won what battle in whatever war? We in the non-Indian community were taught that history was something that happened in the past. It's definitely more interesting when the History Channel makes it all come alive on the small screen, but for the most part we tend to view history as something separate from ourselves. Now whether this is true philosophically is not the issue here. What is true is the fact that history is a living breathing entity to many American Indian tribes. What happened in the past bears directly on how they handle the present. That makes it something vital to pay attention to for anyone wanting to work successfully in Indian country.

When it comes to American Indian history, there are also some stark differences in how we remember that history. We, in the non-Indian world, look at the history of American Indian relations on the basis of past Indian wars, how American Indians were placed on reservations, or the era of the settling of this country. Tribes on the other hand might view this history totally differently—a time of broken treaties and promises, land taken away, and the government treating them as non-citizens in a country they had lived in for thousands of years. As I did, you will come smack up against that history, and until you accept it, you will be faced with skepticism and lack of trust of you as a government or corporate representative.

In the last chapter, I talked about the necessity of a paradigm shift in your thinking. The first element of that shift is toward leadership; the second is regarding how history is perceived. For in order to have an effective collaborative leadership approach with tribes, it is essential to have an accurate and truthful perspective of history as it is viewed through the eyes of American Indians. The truth is, whether we like to admit it or not, there are some painful and appalling events that were perpetrated over the past two hundred years upon the American Indian community. They include broken treaties, removal, and attempts at forced assimilation, all of which led to not only loss of traditional lands and homelands but also rights and culture.

Any or all of these factors may have an affect on your ability to successfully work in Indian country. And it gets more complicated. Each tribe not only has its own history—just as sovereign nations throughout the world have theirs—but the magnitude of the historical events on each tribe is different, and tribes view history and its significance differently as well. That is why it is so important to become familiar with the specific history of individual tribes to understand the attitudes you might encounter.

Now, having said all that, I realize that what I'm about to tell you is a contradiction, but please bear with me. This chapter is merely an overview, a historical sketch if you will, that encompasses all tribes. It is not intended to be exhaustive. It includes the salient points of history that may reflect tribal attitudes that result in suspicion and mistrust today. If you have an interest in the finer points of American Indian history, I encourage you to pursue the many resources available, such as books, videos, college courses, and cultural events as well as the information available through individual tribes. But I do know from individuals who have attended my tribal relations seminars that what you are about to learn can help you. I've had many of my participants, people in government and the private sector, comment that they wish they had known this historical information, as it would have helped them understand what was going on when meeting with tribes or tribal representatives.

The Different Perspectives

We tend to think of history as a chronological record. But the first major point I want to impress upon you is that it is not the chronological records that are necessarily important, but the differences in how American Indians and non-Indians view history. In its simplicity, our historical memory is based upon what we learned in school, books we have read, or even movies or TV shows that we have watched. The historical memories of American Indians, on the other hand, are based upon oral histories passed down to many generations, of how their ancestors were treated or mistreated by government and corporate entities as well as individual settlers. This difference in perspective is further compounded by the sad fact that many of us in today's generation were raised with a very slanted perspective of the American Indian community because it was shaped by old Western television shows and Hollywood stereotypes. In addition, what we learned in school about American Indians focused on Columbus discovering America, the first Thanksgiving with the Pilgrims, Sacajawea accompanying Lewis and Clark, famous warriors and chiefs, and massacres of non-Indian people. Basically, our non-Indian perspective of American Indian history is framed within what we have been taught and what we have experienced in our short lifetimes.

On the other hand, the American Indian perspective of history is different. Today, an American Indian's memory might be fraught with broken treaties, massacres of American Indian women and children, traditional land being taken for non-Indian settlement, removal of tribes hundreds and thousands of miles from their homelands, placement on reservations in inhumane conditions, diet changes resulting in long-term health issues, surrendering rights and freedoms, and so much more. More importantly, they learned of these events through oral histories passed from generation to generation, not in the public school classroom or from a textbook. Their ancestors, their great grandparents, most likely lived through these events directly. Consequently, their memories are long and accurate, often going back centuries.

Second, tribal leaders have provided me a diversity of opinions about American Indian history. Some have told me that history is important and needs to be retold to remind government and business officials what the American Indian community has suffered through in order to avoid reoccurrence of the past. In your dealings with tribes, you may be required to listen to tribal leaders articulate the linkages of past government and business actions, policies, and events toward American Indians which have led to the suspicious Indian community today. Other tribal leaders will say history is in the past and we just need to move forward and focus on the future. In either case, you need to understand how certain historical events have shaped these current attitudes.

Finally, one element of history that everyone needs to keep in mind is that of intentions. In the past, there were many in the United States government who, unfortunately, had bad intentions towards the American Indian community. Many in government had overt intentions to simply eradicate the American Indian community and culture in favor of westward expansion. Their viewpoint was American Indians were merely a problem that had to be overcome at any expense to accomplish this goal. They looked upon the American Indian culture as barbarous, uncivilized, weak, and a problem to the newly formed United States government seeking to expand its borders west. There were other government officials who had arguably good intentions but looked at the Native community through decidedly Western eyes. These men and women felt they were doing what was best for the Indian community by "civilizing" them to the social norm at the time. And their proposals and actions in the end, although in their minds were for the good of the American Indian people, were destructive to the culture, traditions, beliefs and people as a whole. This was especially evident when these proposals and actions were converted to policy and legislation, such as removal, assimilation, the Dawes Act (which I will discuss in more detail in a bit), and rules of behavior specified by Indian courts. The point is that many of the government officials' intentions, good or bad, resulted in the same or similar destructive consequences—and that mistrust continues to this day.

I cannot put too fine a point on this. The contrast in these viewpoints of history creates challenges for all of us who have a desire to work effectively in Indian country. As you read this chapter, I hope you understand that our perspective of history and an American Indian's perspective of history may be totally contrary to each other. For example, you may look at the first contact between Natives and Europeans as an idealistic time of the first Thanksgiving or settlement of the West. An American Indian may look at it as a time of tragedy and suppression. The whole point of this book is to help you develop trust with the specific tribe you're working with. As you understand history from the American Indian perspective, you are better prepared to avoid repeating those historical events, actions, and behaviors that can get in the way of building the desired working relationship.

There are three major historical areas that affect trust and relationship building. They are Geographic History and Displacement of Tribes, the Loss of Rights and Related Government Polices, both of which I will address in this chapter, and the historic consequences of working with tribes today which I will cover in the next chapter.

Geographic History and Displacement of Tribes

For thousands of years Indian people lived in organized societies, each with their own form of government. Tribes were often subdivided into bands or clans that lived within geographic vicinities often referred to as traditional territories. Many of these subdivisions exist today within Indian reservations. We often recognize these governments as "tribal councils" with a chief or chiefs, governor, president, chairman or chairwoman.

American Indian tribal lands, however, are not so easy to discern, but they are an integral part of their culture, their history, even their spiritual values. Because of that, tribal geographic history, while difficult to understand, is the backbone of any historical knowledge you gather about the tribe you're dealing with.

Before the Europeans came to take control of North America for their respective monarchies, the hundreds of American Indian tribes were a mosaic of communities of indigenous people living off the land within certain geographic areas that many times overlapped with other tribes. From a general standpoint, travel was often extensive, even for those tribes who were not considered nomadic. Granted, many tribes were migrant, especially those that depended on migrating species of wildlife, such as the buffalo. For example the northern plains tribes could be considered migrant while following herds of buffalo. These tribes depended heavily on the buffalo for their survival as well as their economy. However, other tribes across the country were relatively stationary, particularly where agriculture was the primary focus. Extensive travel occurred for purposes of trade with other tribes, seasonal gathering, hunting or sometimes exploration.

It was not uncommon for tribes to travel long distances to acquire important resources. For example, an Eastern Shoshone elder in Wyoming told me her grandparents would tell stories about traveling to the Great Salt Lake in Utah to gather salt. Another example is the Nez Perce tribe in Idaho whose economic mainstay was the salmon and steelhead fishery of the Columbia, Snake and Salmon River systems. However, Nez Perce hunters would traverse the Bitterroot Mountains into Montana to harvest buffalo. On the other hand, Salish-Kootenai tribal members in Montana, whose economy depended on the buffalo, would traverse the same trail into Idaho for salmon.

One of the important common denominators concerning geographic history is that each tribe depended upon the natural resources of a particular geographic area for their survival and economy. For example, and as mentioned earlier, the northern plains tribes depended extensively on the numerous buffalo; north central tribes in Wisconsin and Minnesota on fish and wild rice; southern tribes on white-tailed deer; northwestern tribes on salmon and steelhead; and southwestern tribes on corn and smaller game. Other than meat, many parts of the animals harvested were made into useable materials such as hides for clothing and shelter, bones for utensils, body organs for containers, and sinew for ropes and bow strings. All tribes were familiar with a variety of plant species that supplemented their diets and were used for medicinal purposes, as well as in the manufacturing of tools and weapons.

That mosaic of communities changed, and drastically, with the advent of non-Indian settlement and expansion into this country. With more and more settlers from the East demanding the same land and natural resources American Indians had depended upon for centuries, tension was bound to erupt.

In its infancy, the United States government delegated the responsibility of addressing American Indian issues to the jurisdiction of the War Department (Establishment of the War Department, August 7, 1789) in a generic sense stating " … as the President of the United States shall assign to the said department [War Department] … relative to Indian affairs … "[10] The War Department, therefore, had the jurisdiction to enforce rules established by law and policy. It wasn't until 1824 that Secretary of War John C. Calhoun created a Bureau of Indian Affairs within the War Department with duties to oversee appropriations for annuities, expenses, and warrants having to do with American Indian tribes.

Those formative years witnessed the United States initiating and expanding policies and legislation that focused on segregation—separating the American Indian community from settlers moving westward from the east coast. This was accomplished by treaties that allotted land for American Indians and settlers in separate areas intended to minimize interaction between the two. The Trade and Intercourse Act of March 30, 1802 clearly articulated this policy:

> *Sec. 2. And be it further enacted, That if any citizen of, or other person resident in, the United States, or either of the territorial districts of the United States, shall cross over, or go within the said boundary line, to hunt, or in any way destroy the game; or shall drive, or otherwise convey any stock of horses or cattle to range on any lands allotted or secured by treaty with the United States, to any Indian tribes, he shall*

---

[10] *An Act to establish an Executive Department, to be denominated the Department of War, U.S. Statutes at Large 1 (1789).*

forfeit a sum not exceeding one hundred dollars, or be imprisoned not exceeding six months.[11]

The government was instituting a sort of "separate but equal" clause in terms of tribal lands, and it is clear that in 1802, at least, the government still held that the American Indians had some claim to their lands.

That didn't last for long. In the 1820's, subsequent to the purchase of the Louisiana Territory and the Lewis and Clark expedition, pressure continued to mount for a removal policy of eastern tribes to lands west of the Mississippi River. Although the argument was framed for the "benefit of the American Indians," the underlying desire was to acquire land for expansion, settlement, and farming and to penalize certain tribes for aligning with Great Britain during the Revolutionary War. The removal policy resulted in the many "Trail of Tears" accounts made most legendary by the removal of the Cherokee Nation from Georgia, North Carolina, and Tennessee to Oklahoma. In all, fifteen thousand Cherokee began the march to Oklahoma with over four thousand casualties attributed to starvation, exposure, and disease—much of it due to the failure of supplies being sent by the government to various resupply points along the trail. The Cherokee refer to it as Nunna daul Isunyi—"The Trail Where They Cried." Many other tribes suffered the same fate and can recount their own Trail of Tears, such as the Delaware, Choctaw, Seminole, and Creeks. In all, over forty tribes were removed from their homelands from across the country to what is now the state of Oklahoma.

But there was a huge problem. The government and the settlers wanted the American Indians moved west of the Mississippi, but what do you do with the tribes that are already occupying those lands? You move them too—creating all sorts of havoc. For example, the Caddo Nation historically occupied a geographical area along the Red River in southeastern Oklahoma and northeastern Texas. The Choctaw people, on the other hand, historically resided in Mississippi and Louisiana. The government's first step was to relocate the Caddo people to western

---

[11] *An Act to regulate trade and intercourse with Indian tribes, and to preserve peace on the frontiers, U.S. Statutes at Large* 1 (1802).

Oklahoma around the current town of Binger. Then, they relocated the Choctaw people from Mississippi and Louisiana to the Caddo's traditional homeland in southeastern Oklahoma near the Red River. If your head is spinning, good. You get the idea of how complicated this all is.

And it gets worse. The persistent westward expansion of the United States beyond the Mississippi River was led by the settlers' demand for land, furs, gold and other assets. Non-Indian settlement continued regardless of the treaties banning non-Indians from trespass or occupation on Indian lands. At this point, many tribes felt backed into a corner and fought back when the fear of the unknown became amplified. Albert White Hat, a professor at Sinte Gleska University in South Dakota, shared with me,

> I don't think people knew what kind of influences were coming with the outside in the beginning. They had some hints of it with the trappers, the early missionaries. And when these trails were established, I think probably the biggest fear was the disease, the sickness that came with it.[12]

It is interesting to note that early in the era of wagon trains many tribes ensured settlers safe passage as long as they stayed on established trails, did not hunt or graze their cattle, horses and oxen, or settle on adjacent lands. The history books don't tell you that, but what you do know is what happened later. Abuses by the settlers inevitably occurred, and friction between settlers and tribes escalated. One of the first recorded conflicts between settlers and Indian tribes occurred in Wyoming over a cow and is referred to as the Grattan Fight. The story goes like this,

> The fight broke out when Brevet 2nd Lt. John L. Grattan and 28 soldiers attempted to arrest a Sioux Indian for killing a crippled cow belonging to a wagon train. An allegedly drunken interpreter, who had grievances against the Indians, apparently mistranslated an offer by Chief Conquering Bear to replace the cow with a sound pony of his own. Grattan ordered his men to fire and when the gun smoke

---

[12] White Hat, Albert. 1998. Interview by author. Video recording. February 12. Sante Gleska University, Rosebud, South Dakota. © National Historic Trails Center, Casper, Wyoming. Used with permission.

cleared, Grattan, almost his entire command, and the chief lay dead. This August, 1854 incident led to years of intermittent hostility along the trail.[13]

Furthermore, the trails used by settlers began fragmenting the vast herds of buffalo and causing ever more stress between tribes in the Upper Great Plains. Victor Douville, a professor at Sinte Gleska University in South Dakota states,

> *... always our focal point was the buffalo ... wherever it went to, wherever it wound up, that is where our people went ... With the coming of the trail[s] [Oregon, Mormon, Immigrant, Bozeman, and other trails], it really diminished that and it forced our people to scramble, to look elsewhere and expand beyond our tribal limitations, going all the way up to Yellowstone and beyond ... And, they'll intrude on other tribes' area[s], but they really, really hard pressed us. So, in that way we were able to intrude on other areas and cause a lot of ill feelings ... Our only hope and desire was to be able to survive ...* [14]

Stress between tribes and settlers continued to increase and the military was again engaged to help settle the "Indian problem." Tensions continued throughout the next fifty years with numerous conflicts, battles, and raids ensuing.

In the meantime, many treaties were being negotiated but not necessarily in good faith from an American Indian perspective. In a North American Review article published in 1879 Chief Joseph of the Nez Perce Tribe was quoted describing the results of the negotiations this way.

> *If we ever owned the land we own it still, for we never sold it. In the treaty councils the commissioners have claimed that our county had been sold to the Government. Suppose a white man should come to me and say, "Joseph, I like your horses, and I want to buy them."*

---

[13] U.S. Department of Interior, Bureau of Land Management, *Tour the Trails in Wyoming.* http://www.blm.gov/wy/st/en/programs/nlcs/Historic_Trails/trails_tour.html

[14] Douville, Victor. 1998. Interview by author. Video recording. February 12. Sante Gleska University, Rosebud, South Dakota. © National Historic Trails Center, Casper, Wyoming. Used with permission.

I say to him, "No, my horses suit me, I will not sell them."

Then he goes to my neighbor, and says to him: "Joseph has some good horses. I want to buy them, but he refuses to sell."

My neighbor answers, "Pay me the money and I will sell you Joseph's horses."

The white man returns to me, and says, "Joseph, I have bought your horses, and you must let me have them." If we sold our lands to the Government this is the way they were bought.[15]

The end result was that Chief Joseph was instructed to give up his coveted homeland in the Wallowa Valley in Washington to live on another band's homeland near Lapwai, Idaho. He refused, and he and his band were considered non-treaty Indians and subject to forced measures. This "divide and conquer" strategy was used all too often across the West affecting many tribes. Friction was further compounded by the fact that the United States Senate did not ratify treaties negotiated in the West in a timely manner and goods, services, and monetary compensation for ceded land promised in the treaties were often delayed by literally years or even never delivered. Promises made in the treaties were often not kept by the government. Chief Joseph's feelings, I'm sure, were echoed by many tribes across the country.

The white people have too many chiefs. They do not understand each other. They do not all talk alike ... I cannot understand why so many chiefs are allowed to talk so many different ways, and promise so many different things.[16]

One of the many instances of treaties being compromised is the Fort Laramie Treaty of 1851. Consummated between the numerous Sioux or Dahcotahs, Cheyennes, Arrapahoes, Crows, Assinaboines, Gros-Ventres, Mandans, and Arrickaras, this treaty defined western North and South Dakota, western Nebraska and northeast Wyoming

---

[15] The North American Review, Volume 0128, Issue 269, April 1879, *An Indians View of Indian Affairs*, Courtesy of Cornell University Library, *Making of America Digital Collection*, http://digital.library.cornell.edu/cgi/t/text/text-idx?c=nora;idno=nora0128-4

[16] Ibid

as lands the Sioux or Dahcotahs would own (sic). It was aptly called the "Great Sioux Nation," but a later treaty at Fort Laramie in 1868 redefined the "Great Sioux Nation" as something not so grand. The Sioux were now relegated to basically western South Dakota (a line from the North Dakota–South Dakota border along the Missouri River to the South Dakota–Nebraska border west to the Wyoming–Montana border and back to the Missouri River). This treaty expressly states in Article 2,

> ... Shall be ... set apart for the absolute and undisturbed use and occupation of the Indians herein named. The U.S. now solemnly agrees that no persons except those herein designated and authorized to do so ... shall be permitted to pass over, settle upon, or reside in the territory ... [17]

Article 16 continues,

> The U.S. hereby agrees and stipulates that the country north of the North Platte River and east of the summits of the Big Horn Mountains shall be held and considered to be unceded Indian territory, and also stipulates and agrees that no white person or persons shall be permitted to settle upon or occupy any portion of the same ... And it is further agreed by the U.S. that within ninety days after the conclusion of peace with all the bands of the Sioux Nation, the military posts now established in the territory in the article named shall be abandoned, and that the road leading to them and by them to settlements in the territory of Montana shall be closed. [18]

All seemed to be well until 1874 when gold was discovered in the Black Hills of South Dakota. The area, sacred to the Sioux and closed to non-Indian entry or settlement by treaty, was worth the risk by many gold prospectors desiring to "strike it rich." Despite efforts of the military they were unable to contain this desire for gold. Finally, the Sioux were forced to negotiate a successive agreement in 1882 that stated, "The said Indians do hereby relinquish and cede to the U.S. all of the Great

---

[17] Kappler, C. J. 1904. *Indian Affairs: Laws and Treaties, vol. 2: Treaties. Treaty With The Sioux [etc.] 1868.* Washington, DC: Government Printing Office.
[18] Ibid.

Sioux Reservation—as reserved to them in the Treaty of 1868 ... "[19] In all, the Sioux people negotiated and re-negotiated four treaties and/ or agreements. Each significantly reduced the size and scope of their original homeland in Wyoming, Montana, South Dakota, North Dakota and Nebraska to what remains today primarily in South Dakota.

Finally, treaty-making between American Indian tribes and the United States was extinguished in 1871 by Congress (The Treaties Statute of 1871). A sample paragraph states,

> *Future treaties with Indian tribes—No Indian nation or tribe within the territory of the United States shall be acknowledged or recognized as an independent nation, tribe, or power with whom the United States may contract by treaty ...* [20]

This statute did let stand and honor treaties negotiated prior to March 3, 1871, but this one clause effectively shut down any ability for the tribes to renegotiate lands with the U.S. Government.

It gets worse again. Shortly after treaty-making was extinguished, Congress began to pass laws in an attempt to assimilate American Indian people into the mainstream culture by eliminating the communal custody of land. Numerous American Indian tribal cultures historically did not recognize the European concept of land ownership. Owning a parcel of land was equated to owning the sky. How could one own a piece of "Mother Earth" anymore than you could own a piece of "Father Sky?" Land was sacred, not something you bartered, sold or owned. Then in 1887, one of the most significant federal laws, referred to as the General Allotment Act, or Dawes Act, attempted to break up communal ownership of reservations by deeding parcels of land to individual ownership. The intent was to pressure American Indians to abandon their nomadic lifestyle and convert them to an agricultural lifestyle, as well as to open newly-created "surplus" land to non-Indian settlement. It is a prime example of the patronizing attitude many in

---

[19] Ibid. *Agreement With The Sioux Of Various Tribes*, 1882-1883.
[20] *An Act Making Appropriations for the current and contingent Expenses of the Indian Department, and for fulfilling Treaty Stipulations with various Indian Tribes*, U. S. *Statutes at Large 16* (1871).

power held about American Indians. Many in government felt that this was the best way to "civilize and teach" American Indians about farming and ranching—by breaking up the land, locating settlers on adjacent lands, and teaching by example. Those tribal members that yielded to this policy were given farm implements and cows, what they called the "white man's poor buffalo."

The Dawes act began not only a geographic but a significant cultural shift in most American Indian tribes. Many tribal members did not exercise the option to own land and so forfeited their rights as specified in the General Allotment Act. Or, if they did stay on the land, they either did not understand the idea of property taxes or did not have the means to pay them. Whatever the reason, land on many reservations was either not claimed by resident Indian people or reverted to the U.S. government who then opened it up to settlement and homesteading by non-Indians. The loss of land was catastrophic. Tribes lost ninety million acres of reservation land, previously negotiated in treaties, to homesteaders between the late 1800's and early 1900's.

I often ask my workshop participants—how would you like it if you owned land, considered it yours because your family had homesteaded it for hundreds of years, but then the government came and told you that you no longer owned the land because someone else "better" than you wanted it?

American Indian history is filled with many accounts and events of a shrinking land base and the displacement of tribes. It is etched in the memories of many American Indian people. And this is the salient point to remember: Just because it happened to their great, great, great-grandfathers doesn't dilute the fact that it is still important today, nor does it mean that you can brush it off as simply unfortunate. Stories, teachings, speeches, discussions, arguments, and even litigation, remind us relentlessly, and rightly so, that the American Indian community will never forget these unjust historical takings of land. They will affect your ability to successfully work in Indian country today so it is imperative that you work to understand them, both from a "history book" perspective and from the oral histories that are still passed on today.

Loss of Rights and Other Related Government Policies

While the loss of land and the displacement of American Indians in the United States remains fresh in an Indian's memory, there were other, arguably more egregious, historical injustices perpetrated on the American Indian populations. It is another chapter of history that has an equal bearing on your ability to work successfully in Indian country, and it started with the Dawes act mentioned earlier. These injustices involved the loss of human rights and the policies implemented by the United States to "civilize" the American Indian community.

It was practically inevitable. When one culture, in this case the European culture, meets head-on with a completely foreign culture, such as the American Indian culture, an assortment of misunderstandings and intolerances ensues. Words used to describe this newly contacted foreign culture that did not meet the European cultural norms or standards of behavior, were telling. Government document after government document uses words such as "uncivilized," "savage," "barbarous," "fierce," "uneducated," "wandering," and "heathen," to describe the American Indian. As the land mass of the United States was being settled, many in government felt that tribes needed to be conquered and brought into the fold of the U.S. government. Even the Supreme Court in 1823 (Johnson and Graham's Lessee v. William McIntosh) described in detail the typical outcome between two opposing parties and how this model did not fit the American Indian community.

> *The title of conquest is acquired and maintained by force. The conqueror prescribes its limits ... Most usually, they [the conquered] are incorporated with the victorious nation, and becoming subjects or citizens of the government with which they are connected. The new and old members of the society mingle with each other; the distinction between them is gradually lost, and they make one people ... But the tribes of Indians inhabiting this country were fierce savages, whose occupation was war, and whose subsistence was drawn chiefly from the forest. To leave them in possession of their country, was to leave the country a wilderness; to govern them as a distinct people, was impossible, because they were as brave and as high spirited as they*

were fierce, and were ready to repel by arms every attempt on their independence.[21]

In other words, the court realized that to govern the American Indian community as a "distinct people," by removal or segregation, would not work. So the United States government initiated many efforts to "civilize" the American Indian community through a policy of assimilation. The government became the arbiter of culture, in other words, by using education, religious conversion, lifestyle changes, and governance, they worked to change American Indian habits and customs to European-American conventions. The consequence of these actions, however, resulted in a culture shift that compromised the rights of the American Indian people as a whole.

The enormity of this cannot be overstated. For example, American Indians during and after treaty-making, were not considered citizens of the United States, but rather wards of the government. They did not enjoy the protections of the United States Constitution and law. American Indians were not considered citizens, they could not vote, they could be detained by government officials without cause (habeas corpus), they were prohibited from practicing spiritual (religious) ceremonies, prohibited the right of assembly, and more. An illustration of the government's policy toward spiritual values or religion is contained within Secretary of Interior Henry M. Teller's (1883) imposition of the following rules that were subject to severe punishment:

Any Indian who shall engage in the sun dance, scalp dance, or war dance, or any other similar feast, so called, shall be deemed guilty of an offense and upon conviction thereof shall be punished ... [22]

And,

Any Indian who shall engage in the practices of so-called medicine men, or who shall resort to any artifice or device to keep the Indians of the reservation from adopting and following civilized habits and pursuits, ... or shall use any arts of a conjurer to prevent Indians from

---

[21] Johnson v. M'Intosh, 21 U.S. 543, 5 L. Ed. 681, 8 Wheat. 543 (1823)

[22] Prucha, Francis Paul, 2000, *Documents of United States Indian Policy*, 3rd Edition, University of Nebraska Press

abandoning their barbarous rites and customs, shall be deemed to be guilty of an offense ... [23]

This policy is akin to another country taking over the United States and prohibiting religious ceremonies, such as Holy Communion in the Christian Church or even celebrating Christmas or Easter. Such a policy clearly violated the First Amendment of the United States Constitution that states, "Congress shall make no law respecting an establishment of religion, or prohibiting the free exercise thereof; ... " But this is what the American Indian community was up against.

Assimilation also continued in a social context. Churches and boarding schools sprang up on reservations. This was a result of an 1872 "Annual Report of the Commissioner of Indian Affairs" that apportioned Indian agencies among missionary societies and religious denominations. The purpose was to " ... assume charge of the intellectual and moral education of the Indians ... "[24] Children were taken from parents and placed in boarding schools to learn the "new way." They were prohibited from speaking their native language and their hair was cut. This might not seem so bad until you realize that long hair is an honor to many Indian youth, especially males.

The fallout from this kind of cultural repression is truly sad. I interviewed a Northern Arapaho elder of eighty-plus years. I asked Joe, "Can you tell me about Indian life before explorers, trappers, missionaries, and settlers moved west?"

He replied, "I don't know."

I reframed the question, "Well, what are some of the stories your great, great, great, great-grandparents told you about life before explorers, trappers, missionaries and settlers moved west?"

Again, he responded, "I don't know."

I tried a different approach, "Didn't you hear stories from your grandparents about Indian life say two-hundred years ago?"

---

[23] Ibid

[24] Ibid

Joe said, "We didn't know because teachers told us to forget the past. Let it go, we teach you a new way, white man way ... And that's why I forget a lot of that, Indian stories."

I learned Joe was placed in a boarding school at six years of age. In Indian schools, American Indian children were prohibited from speaking their native language. That led to many American Indian parents not teaching their children the native language for fear of their children being punished. The ramifications of this are far-reaching and it was done with malicious purpose. If your culture is passed on orally through stories, and you take away the vehicle through which those stories can be told, you have, in essence, annihilated that culture. It has no way to carry forth its customs.

Finally, in 1924 through the Indian Citizenship Act, American Indian people were given full citizenship status in the United States. The irony of this political act is that innumerable American Indian people were at that time very patriotic to the United States. World War I saw many American Indian people (who did not yet enjoy American citizenship status) enlisting in the armed forces to fight alongside non-Indian United States soldiers. Their reward? If they survived, they were given the option of citizenship for their service to the United States. The most memorable example of American Indian patriotism was the Code Talkers of World War II. The previously forbidden Navajo, Cherokee, Choctaw, and Comanche languages were used to communicate sensitive messages about troop movements, tactics, and strategies and could not be understood or broken by the enemy forces.

An important point to keep in mind is that today American Indians enjoy multiple levels of citizenship. They are citizens of their tribe, of the United States, and of the state in which they reside. As an example, an enrolled tribal member can vote for the chairman, chief, or governor of their tribe, the President of the United States, and Governor of their state.

1934 saw the passage of the Wheeler-Howard Act, commonly known as the Indian Reorganization Act (IRA). The preamble of the Act states:

An Act to conserve and develop Indian lands and resources; to extend to Indians the right to form businesses and other organizations; to establish a credit system for Indians; to grant certain rights of home rule to Indians; to provide for vocational education for Indians; and for other purposes.[25]

Although a major purpose of the act was to invalidate the General Allotment Act (or Dawes Act) of 1887, the Indian Reorganization Act granted tribes the rights of home rule. Specifically the Act states:

Any Indian tribe, or tribes, residing on the same reservation, shall have the right to organize for its common welfare, and may adopt an appropriate constitution and bylaws ... [26]

Tribes were given the option to adopt constitutional forms of government. Many tribes adopted this new form of government, however many chose not to. These new government structures sometime fit uneasily with tribal traditions and created conflict that often played itself out within tribal communities, and which can also impact how they currently interact with outsiders.

While the Indian Citizenship Act of 1924 and Indian Reorganization Act of 1934 seemed to make great strides in giving the American Indian community some of their rights back, it was all destroyed in the 1950's. We think that most American Indian atrocities happened back in the Wild West, in the 1700's and 1800's. But a mere sixty years ago witnessed an even more aggressive assimilation policy. It came in the form of a declaration of Congress that is commonly referred to as "termination." House Concurrent Resolution 108 declared in 1953,

That it is declared to be the sense of Congress that, at the earliest possible time, all of the Indian tribes and the individual members thereof ... should be freed from Federal supervision and control and from all disabilities and limitations specially applicable to Indians ... [27]

This was simply a politically correct way of stating that all treaties mentioned in Resolution 108 are null and void and that all provisions of the treaties relating to trust lands, education, health, hunting and

---

[25] , *Wheeler-Howard Act (Indian Reorganization Act), U.S. Statutes at Large* 48 (1934).
[26] Ibid
[27] *H. Con. Res 108, U.S. Statutes at Large* 67 (1953).

gathering rights, and other trust and fiduciary matters were now being transferred to the individual American Indian. While this sounds like a good thing—the federal government was washing its hands of being a caretaker of the Indian Community—devastation happened in the name of termination. Basically, it was a means of de-tribalizing American Indians and carving away at tribal sovereignty.

The Paiute Tribe of Utah was one of approximately one hundred tribes that experienced the destruction this policy wrought. Marguerite Teller from the Paiute Tribe of Utah shared with me her perspective of how termination came about with the Paiute people:

> *Termination happened in 1954 and the Senator that was introducing legislation came from Utah. So the people in Washington, D.C. said, "Well if it's so great let's see you terminate your tribes in Utah." And that's exactly what he did. They came around to the Paiute people and the Ute Tribes and the Goshutes … And that was the problem with the Paiute people … that then in 1954, '53 … I'd say probably eighty percent of the Paiute people spoke Paiute and didn't understand English. So, when those people came down from the Senator's office they would talk to the Indians and they really didn't know … they didn't really have the full comprehension or understanding of what would really happen. And of course there were some things said that, … like there would be no taxes on band lands … which was not true.[28]*

Travis Parashonts, also from the Paiute Tribe of Utah, continued regarding the consequences of termination. "We lost some rights … because we lost our treaties, we lost our land, we lost our water, our hunting and fishing."[29]

The Paiute Tribe of Utah was finally reestablished by the Paiute Indian Tribe of Utah Restoration Act (1980) by stating, "To restore to the Shivwits, Kanosh, Koosharem, and Indian Peaks Bands of Paiute

---

[28] Teller, Marguerite. 2001. Interview by author. Video recording. August 27. Paiute Tribe of Utah Tribal Office, Cedar City.

[29] Parashonts, Travis. 2001. Interview by author. Video recording. August 27. Paiute Tribe of Utah Tribal Office, Cedar City.

Indians of Utah, and with respect to the Cedar City Band of Paiute Indians of Utah,

> *to restore or confirm, the Federal trust relationship, to restore to members of such Bands those Federal services and benefits furnished to American Indian Tribes by reason of such trust relationship, and for other purposes.*[30]

The Act merely recognized the tribes as federally recognized and bestowed eligibility for the same government services provided to other sovereign American Indian nations. The Act did not restore hunting, fishing, gathering, or land rights lost during termination.

Parallel with termination was the Indian Adoption Project of the 1950's and 1960's. The project was an agreement between the Bureau of Indian Affairs and the Child Welfare League that allowed placement of American Indian children into non-Indian foster homes. In a Denver Post (November 29, 2009) article, this program was described by numerous American Indians who experienced the policy.

> *The idea ... to rescue American Indian children from poverty and challenging social conditions and give them access to the resources of the white middle class ... the Indian Adoption Project may have been well-intentioned. But mostly it allowed non-Indians to pass judgment on reservation families and break them up as they saw fit ...* [31]

The result of this experiment was that hundreds of American Indian children were taken from their biological parents and adopted by non-Indian families. Finally, in 1978, the Indian Child Welfare Act corrected the misdeeds of the program, established standards for the placement of Indian children in foster or adoptive homes, prevented the breakup of American Indian families, and addressed the widespread abuses by state child welfare agencies and courts. In all fairness I need to acknowledge a 2001 speech when the Child Welfare League described

---

[30] *Paiute Indian Tribe of Utah Restoration Act.* Public Law 96-227. *U.S. Statutes at Large* 94 (1980).

[31] Whaley, Monte. 2009. *Forcibly adopted American Indians torn between cultures,* The Denver Post, November 29..

the experiment as "catastrophic and unforgiveable" and expressed their deep and sincere regret.[32]

By the 1970's and '80s, many legislative efforts, executive orders, and regulatory rules of the United States government made efforts to right the wrongs of the past two centuries. Legislation was passed, such as the Indian Self-Determination Act, the American Indian Religious Freedom Act, the Archeological Resources Protection Act, the Indian Land Consolidation Act, the Native American Graves Protection and Repatriation Act, as well as many claims settlement acts and others. There were also Executive Orders, one of which was Consultation and Coordination with Indian Tribal Governments. Regulatory rules on Indian policy, consultation, federal acknowledgement, and recognition have all paved the way for tribes to achieve the ultimate goal today of self-determination. For example, the preamble to the 1975 Indian Self-Determination and Education Assistance Act is most important and states:

An Act to provide maximum Indian participation in the Government and education of Indian people; to provide for the full participation of Indian tribes in programs and services provided by the Federal Government for Indians and to encourage the development of human resources of the Indian people; to establish a program of assistance to upgrade Indian education; to support the right of Indian citizens to control their own educational activities and for other purposes.[33]

This act, Public Law 93–638, led to what is often referred to as "638 Contracting." Today, tribes have the option to contract with the federal government to offer services directly to tribal members rather than through the Bureau of Indian Affairs or Indian Health Service. For example, the Indian Health Service, a federal agency, states that:

Indian Tribes obtain health care for their members from the federal government through direct services, contracts, or compacts. Specifically,

---

[32] Bilchik, Shay. 2001. *Coming Together in Humility: Steps towards Healing.* Child Welfare League of America, NICWA Conference, Anchorage, Alaska. April 24.

[33] *Indian Self-Determination and Education Assistance Act,* Public Law 93-638, *U.S. Statutes at Large* 88 (1975).

Tribes can choose to: (1) receive health care services directly from the Indian Health Service (IHS), (2) contract with the IHS to assume control over administration and funding for individual programs and services the IHS would otherwise provide (referred to as "Self-Determination Contracts"), or (3) compact with the IHS to assume control over health care programs the IHS would otherwise provide (referred to as "Self-Governance Compacts"). Self-Governance affords Tribes the most flexibility to tailor health care services to the needs of their communities. [34]

Many other government agencies have similar policies. Programs that can fall under "638 Contracting" may include housing, health, social, natural resources, law enforcement, education, transportation, economic development, culture, and many others.

Despite what many American Indians and tribes refer to as atrocities and misdeeds of the past, many are exercising their legal rights which were previously denied. Tribes are becoming competitive in the market place, buying back historical land holdings at their own expense, challenging policies and legislation which infringe on treaties, implementing social programs for elders and children, reviving native languages and traditions, effectively governing, and more.

If your head is really spinning at this point, I understand. This is a mountain of information that you must wade through. Additionally, it is up to you to learn all the facts—the tribe you work with won't automatically teach them to you. But when you have taken the responsibility to learn the history of the tribe you're destined to work with, then you will be successful when working in Indian country.

---

[34] Indian Health Service, *IHS Fact Sheets*, http://info.ihs.gov/TrblSlfGov.asp

3

Bringing History
Into the Present

In our Euro-centric view of the world, we tend to ignore history. It is why the adage, "those who fail to learn from history are doomed to repeat it," holds more true than most are comfortable with. However the Native American view of history is, as I have said, very different. They don't ignore their history. History is a living entity to the American Indian; historical memory is long precisely so that history won't repeat itself. They don't want to suffer cultural devastation and personal degradation again. And I don't blame them—I wouldn't either. And that is the purpose of this chapter, to share with you the current implications of Native American history—in other words to make the history I gave you in the previous chapter relevant to our present moment. It has affected my ability to work successfully in Indian country and it will yours, too.

For the first couple of years while working on the Sacred Circle, I was lectured repeatedly about the loss of traditional Indian land, the compromising of rights to fish, hunt, gather, and practice spiritual rites, the degradation of sacred sites, the demise of language and culture, the breaking of treaties and commitments and much more. All of these have a foundation in history and in the eyes of many American Indians it happened yesterday—not long ago, but yesterday! These events happened to most of their grandparents, many of their parents, and to the few elders remaining today. I learned about many of these historical events by listening to countless speeches. Many of these speeches were directed pointedly at me as if I had committed those offenses myself. But I quickly learned that the finger was not pointed just at me, but at everyone in government and business that symbolized those past linkages. Our first reaction was typical, "Why are we the target for things that happened in the past that we had nothing to do with?" And, "What do these historical events have to do with us and our work on the Sacred Circle?"

If you think you are immune to these history lessons, you might want to listen carefully. All of this recounting of history is really a symptom of a deeper-rooted paradigm—that of mistrust—that can affect all of us in government and in business. This paradigm manifests itself in phrases and statements to government and business officials, such as: "You took advantage of us and stole our land and homeland … you lied to us … you broke commitments and treaties to us … you think you know what's best for us," or "your arrogant attitude is patronizing."

What are the messages here? John Pretty on Top, a friend of mine from the Crow Nation, explained to me the reasons for these history lessons and how they result in very pointed statements.

> *It starts right off with a debate … because they're not there with trust, they're thinking they're going to get stabbed in the back again. And, they have been through that so many times [historically]. Some of the younger ones are just bitter over it, they've seen so much of it, they've seen their elders abused, they've seen their tribe abused, [and] they [grew] up watching it. And when it comes to their time, their turn to talk, they're bitter.[35]*

So, I had to keep asking myself, "How do we get beyond these hard feelings about history and beyond the mistrust in order to begin working together?" The answer was revealed to me when the late George Sutton, a Southern Arapaho friend and mentor from the Cheyenne and Arapaho

---

[35] Pretty On Top, John. 2001. Interview by author. Video recording. April 4. Crow Tribe Senior Center, Lodgegrass, Montana.

Tribes of Oklahoma, shared with me how to take these history lessons from tribal leaders.

Take it as a tool or something to use for learning. And, most of the time they are blunt and to the point. But, they have a reason for saying that because [of] some things that happened before and that sticks in their mind.[36]

Both John and George share a couple of very important points to help us understand the relevance of history. First, when trust is lacking the bitterness of history comes out—that relentless recounting of abuses and injustices. It becomes an obvious conclusion that mistrust is ingrained in history. Second, you should take it as an opportunity to learn. Therefore, by accepting these premises you demonstrate a willingness to listen, learn, and understand.

So what are the implications of these historical accounts today? And, how might they relate to your ability to build trust and strong working relationships with American Indian tribes? As I have said repeatedly, I believe the first and most obvious aspect is the lack of, or hesitancy to, trust government officials and business leaders. American Indian people have told me often that, "I can't work with you if I don't know you." At the heart of knowing someone is to trust him. Recognizing, understanding, and acknowledging these historical accounts become the foundation of building trust. Simply put, by understanding a tribe's specific history you will avoid repeating the behaviors, actions, and arrogance (the stance that many take that they know what is best for that tribe—something you should never do) that have eroded trust in the past.

The present moment is what is important, thus this chapter gets specific on how these historical implications affect your ability to build trust and develop relationships today. As I said, this history is deeply rooted and includes many more historical events than just those listed. All are too important to be ignored.

---

[36] Sutton, George. 2006. Interview by author. Video recording. January 11. Watonga, Oklahoma.

The Settlement of the West

What we learned from the settlement of the West is that tribes may still harbor ill feelings about being taken advantage of. What started off as friendly overtures to the Lewis and Clark party led to a mass western movement of settlers claiming, settling, and occupying traditional homelands held dear by generations of tribes. Even today, we will be reminded by tribal leaders of what was taken away from their ancestors and that what remains is a mere fraction of historical holdings. So, the fallout is that when a government or business leader asks something from a tribal leader, the immediate reaction might be a recounting of what was taken from their ancestors historically.

Loss of Land

The difficulties today in building trust and relationships tie directly, in many cases, back to the historical treaty-making events that significantly reduced the traditional land holdings of tribes. Many tribes, such as the Crow, Ojibwa, Blackfeet, Shoshone, and many others, will articulate the loss of their ancestral homelands. Dialogue will often be framed in terms of, "We have lost so much land, our homelands were taken, and we will do whatever to protect what's left." You, as a government or business leader may have to face and address these issues, particularly where land use issues are involved.

You might ask yourself: Why is land so important to American Indians? Why is it considered so sacred? John Pretty On Top, Crow Tribe in Montana, explains it this way:

I can remember the stories I've been told by the elders of the tribe. We were instructed to sit with the chosen elder to listen and learn the importance of life. The most important was our mothers, I say mothers because although we were born from our mother, we have three mothers and we were taught to respect those three mothers and hold them sacred as they are the providers of life.

Our First Mother is the woman from whom we are born, from whom we come into this world. This woman is our first mother [who] cares

56

for us, nourishes us, cuddles us, keeps us clean, and gives us all necessary ways of life.

After we grow up and mature and leave the mother and start our own life, we are provided with a lodge or a teepee. Then this lodge becomes our Second Mother, as in this lodge we are provided with all things our first mother provided for us—shelter, comfort, warmth, and love.

And the third and most sacred is Mother Earth. Mother Earth, who gives and provides everything our first two mothers [gave us]—everything needed to bring us life. We are taught to walk gently on earth and to respect everything that comes from earth as a way of life, a giver of life, and in the end we return to its womb where we first came from.[37]

The sacredness of land cuts two ways, culturally. On one extreme you have the Judeo-Christian philosophy based on man owning and having dominion over the land and all creatures. On the other hand, the American Indian philosophy focuses on harmony between man and the land where one receives sustenance, shelter, and clothing. These two philosophies collide when you begin imposing one over the other—in this case the Judeo-Christian philosophy over the American Indian philosophy. The former considers it simply land, a possession to manage and control, while the latter considers it Mother Earth, sacred, and a means of sustaining life. The hard truth is the philosophy of considering land as a possession to be owned resulted in the loss of millions of acres of sacred tribal lands and was culturally devastating to many tribes. With the loss of their tribal land, the American Indian traditional way of life was basically in ruin.

Today, the anger and frustration expressed by tribes about losing their sacred land is typically in proportion to the amount of those historical takings. The loss of land transcends present-day issues relating to sacred sites, land development, or land-management decisions. For instance, when working with tribes on the Sacred Circle, we were

---

[37] Pretty On Top, John. 2010. Personal communication. May 11.

reminded many times, and rightfully so, that tribes lost millions of acres through the treaty-making process. We were also asked repeatedly, "Why is the government so reluctant to set aside a few hundred or a thousand acres to protect this sacred site?" It's a good question and the reluctance lies, I believe, in the difference between the two different philosophies of how we perceive the importance of land. When you work to understand and allow for these differences in philosophy, you are better able to understand and value the American Indian viewpoint relating to the sacredness of land and work more effectively within those parameters.

Removal and Assimilation

Removal and assimilation created yet another conundrum that continues today. As tribes such as the Cherokee, Delaware, Choctaw, Creeks, and others were relocated to different areas around the country, they continued to retain an interest in, and paid attention to, their traditional homelands. For example, the Cherokee Nation and United Keetoowah Band of Cherokee in Oklahoma have a vested interest in what is happening to their homelands in North Carolina, Georgia, Tennessee, and Alabama. The lesson we learn from removal is that just because a tribe resides in a location today does not mean they are historically limited to that geographic area. Therefore, contemporary issues important to a particular tribe may be evident hundreds or thousands of miles away.

As we have learned, assimilation was a means to break up communal ownership of lands held by American Indians and transfer these lands to individual ownership—a principle that was not well-understood or embraced by the Indian community. Land on reservations deeded to non-Indian settlers under the Dawes Act has created a maze of ownership within reservations today. Within a reservation's boundary, you can find a non-Indian rancher next door to an American Indian rancher. The hard feelings that ensue are the result of the non-Indian rancher working land that was historically Indian land. The implication is that many tribes want their land back, especially those lands within reservation boundaries. And today, many tribes are acquiring these non-Indian-owned parcels and placing them in trust for use by the tribe and tribal members.

Broken Treaties and Promises

The long history of broken treaties and promises is the reason for much of the mistrust and suspicion today towards government officials and business leaders. Many times I have experienced Indian people comparing historical accounts of broken promises and treaties to examples of broken commitments that take place today. Therefore, it is sometimes difficult for government and business leaders to approach tribes, even with good intentions, and not have their motives closely scrutinized.

The animosity felt by American Indians today is understandable when looking at treaties in an international context. Treaties ratified by the United States Senate are considered extremely important and strictly adhered to. Very rarely are treaties broken or compromised with other countries. The benefits of treaties with the United States and other countries that were initiated at the end of World Wars I and II have been financially and socially beneficial to those countries. They have flourished economically by our investments of billions of dollars in aid and support. Just the opposite has happened in the United States with our American Indian neighbors. Many of the commitments made in treaties were never fulfilled or were changed to benefit the influx of settlers moving west. And even today litigation continues in many areas, challenging the government to fulfill the obligations spelled out in these past treaties to American Indians. It is, therefore, important to understand the reluctance of American Indian tribes to put much trust and faith in American government politics.

Reserved Rights

On another note relating to treaties is the matter of reserved rights. Reserved rights have a strong historical foundation and are an issue that we need to be sensitive to today. As mentioned earlier, tribes often negotiated to reserve or retain these rights to continue their traditional practices, such as hunting, fishing, gathering, and spiritual ceremonies.

The exercise of these rights, documented in the treaties, often included traditional areas that went beyond the reservation boundaries. Today these rights may be exercised on what are referred to as unclaimed lands, in other words, lands that are not held in private ownership but owned and managed by the federal government. They may include national forests, public lands, wildlife refuges, and national parks. A grave error often made today by government officials and business leaders is to refer to these rights as "given rights" in the treaty-making process. These rights were not given but retained by tribal leaders through a tough negotiating process. Mic Isham, a tribal councilman from the Lac Courte Oreilles Band of Ojibwe in Wisconsin, explains it very well:

A lot of people when they come into the job ... they think treaty rights are these special rights given to the tribes ... well, these are rights that we retained, we've always had them, they are not special rights given to us, we've always had them ... These are rights our chiefs negotiated long and hard for and knew that our culture and our way of life depended on it.[38]

So, a wise person is sensitive to his or her choice of words. Choosing your words with a good understanding of the historical linkages of the past will prevent you from being perceived as indifferent, apathetic, or insensitive in today's environment.

Historical Distortions

There are many realities that have become distorted as a result of historical incidents. As an example, I have heard non-Indian people say about the Sacred Circle, "I've never seen an Indian up there so how can they claim it as theirs? Not only that, but my great-grandparents never saw an Indian up there." Putting two and two together becomes rather simple if we understand the history. Most of these people's great-grandparents were born in the late 1800's or early 1900's, during the time when Indian people were prohibited from practicing traditional and spiritual ceremonies. At that time, American Indians avoided, or secretly visited, well-known sacred places such as the Sacred Circle. Also, ceremonies

---

[38] Isham, Mic. 2003. Interview by author. January 17. Lac Courte Oreilles Casino, Lodge, and Convention Center, Hayward, Wisconsin.

were often held in secret locations where the fear of being caught and punished was minimized. That's why your great-grandparents never saw an Indian at the Sacred Circle, and most importantly, why we should not draw conclusions without knowing the whole history.

If we let our beliefs become clouded by one side of the story, we can overlook the true underlying principle of why things happened the way they did. Accurately understanding what American Indian people endured during the era of military control and occupation provides us insights to the attitudes of today.

Government Controls Over American Indians

Historically, strong governmental controls still leave many Indian people with a perception that they are being treated differently and are subject to special rules. A Northern Cheyenne friend one time told me that tribes often feel they are treated as "secondary citizens." I think this goes back, again, to the issue of government and business leaders judging what they believe progress in Indian country should look like. If tribes do not meet our expectations or rules in the business environment, such as structure, time, protocol, or procedure, we might make subtle judgments and exhibit behaviors that reinforce the "secondary citizen" syndrome. This might be particularly true for elders and older people who have experienced some of the more recent suppression.

For example, during a meeting with tribes on the Sacred Circle a group of traditional elders approached me and asked for a camping permit. I asked why they wanted a permit to camp. Their response was "We have always been required to have a permit to camp in the area and practice our ceremonies." Other questions raced through my mind as to why someone today would ask such a question. To us non-Indians, we simply look at something like that as a question of unnecessary regulation on public land. We're very quick to ask questions like, "Why can't we camp here?"

But I didn't want to make any assumptions at that point, so I asked the elders, "Why do you need a permit to camp when no one else does?"

Their response was, "Because we've always had to."

After some introspection, it dawned on me that the historical controls placed on Indian people leave perceptions by many Indian people (particularly elders who were born in that era) that these controls still exist today. My response to them was, "No one is required to have a permit to camp as long as they follow the regulations applicable to every individual utilizing *your* public lands."

The Era of Termination

Another historical event that continues to create anxiety with tribes today is termination. It happened once and many believe that it could happen again. All it would take is an Act of Congress to invalidate the existing treaties signed in the 1800's. So, many tribes feel, not unrealistically, that the fight to protect sovereignty must be waged on a daily basis. Therefore, any program proposed by government officials or business leaders that threatens existing treaties, retained rights, tribal sovereignty, land, or culture will be looked at with a jaundiced eye. Tribes must be respected as a full partner with all the powers of an independent government in any collaborative environment.

Tribal Governance

History also plays a significant role in how tribes govern today. The passage of the Indian Reorganization Act of 1934 sought to promote tribal self-governance and encourage tribes to adopt constitutions. Many tribes accepted and many rejected the opportunities provided in the Act. As a result, today one observes a diversity of tribal government structures and levels of self-determination. Tribes are structured and operate in many different ways. Some have retained their traditional form of government aligned with traditional values while others have adopted more contemporary practices of governing. This is neither right nor wrong; it's just the way individual tribes choose to exercise their sovereignty and freedom in how they govern. Each tribe is in the process of trying to develop an effective form of government that works for its community. What is important is that you recognize the differences in the way tribes choose to govern and work within their specific framework.

Another element of tribal governance is how much responsibility tribes are willing to accept through the Bureau of Indian Affairs (BIA), Department of Housing and Urban Development (HUD) and Indian Health Service (IHS) in the management of a multiplicity of programs, such as transportation, education, natural resources, lands, housing, and more. Many tribes have taken advantage of and operate under the "638 Contracts" law (after Public Law 638) that delegates the administration and management of many programs directly to the tribe. As a result, these tribes sometimes have extensive staff to administer and manage these programs much like their federal government counterparts. One will find many combinations in between, where the BIA, HUD and IHS continue to have an active role in some programs and are limited or non-existent in others. The significance of this is that tribes are better able than federal entities to link the services provided to matching cultural matters. In other words, tribes are better able to complement traditions and culture when pursuing their own future in managing programs.

As an illustration, I once was part of a Community Assessment team for a tribe to assist them in defining their future direction. The tribe requested this assessment to assist them in defining a future direction for many tribally-run programs. We were told that the tribe historically lived in family units in different geographic locations. One family might live on Elk Creek and another on Lodgepole Creek. Each unit was defined by the extended family that could include grandparents, parents and children, aunts and uncles, and cousins. This allowed grandparents to care for children while parents were working and sustaining the family unit; for parents to care for elders; for aunts and uncles to care for displaced children; and cousins to become as close as brothers and sisters. When HUD came in to construct a housing development for the tribe, the decision about who would get the new houses was based on regulatory factors, financial need, first-come first-served, or other social criteria. As a result of this policy the family units became fragmented. Grandparents ended up living in the new development while parents lived miles away, making the traditional elder/child care system difficult to impossible—a care system that had evolved over centuries. A tribe administering their own housing authority has the ability to consider and account for these important historical, cultural, and social needs.

Housing can be prioritized on the basis of family unity to retain important cultural norms, rather than a federal agency's rules.

Today, many tribes are making efforts to mesh traditional and cultural models of governing with more contemporary forms of governing. A tribal chairman some time ago related to me that many tribal governments have progressed rapidly in an attempt to align their governing structures with federal, state and local governments. He said that the United States government has had over two hundred years of practice to perfect operating within a constitutional form of government while tribes have been practicing for only forty to fifty years—a good lesson to keep in perspective when we become perplexed at how different tribes choose to operate.

Historical Trauma

We often read or hear in the media about the shock and distress suffered by Holocaust survivors, Japanese internment camp residents, even those who have experienced combat. They all are experiencing what is often referred to as *trauma*. Trauma is "an emotional shock causing lasting and substantial damage to a person's psychological development."[39] *Historical* trauma is when this damage is done to an ethnic or religious group, and the damage in the past is still relevant and applicable to the group's descendants today. The Holocaust and its effect on the Jewish community today is a stark example of historical trauma. While it is not my intent to diminish anyone's traumatic experiences, I must acknowledge that seldom or never do we hear about the historical trauma experienced by American Indians today as a result of the historical events described earlier. Consequently, it is important for you to understand how historical trauma has affected Indian people today, and the effects it might have on relationship building.

Dr. Maria Yellow Horse Brave Heart at Columbia University is recognized as one of the foremost authorities on the subject of American Indian historical trauma. According to her, historical trauma is:

---

[39] Webster's Dictionary and Thesaurus, Copyright © 1997 V. Nichols.

... [the] cumulative emotional and psychological wounding over the lifespan and across generations, emanating from massive group trauma. Native Americans have, for over 500 years, endured physical, emotional, social, and spiritual genocide from European and American colonialist policy.[40]

The specific events that led to historical trauma for American Indians may include, but are not limited to, forced boarding school attendance, outlawed spiritual practices, introduction of diseases, flooding of homelands (when dams were built on ancestral lands), and of course the attacks and killings in tribal communities.[41] You should be aware of many of these events from what I have presented previously. However, the impact of historical trauma can occur at the individual, family, and community levels depending on the scope of the traumatic event.[42] Even events today (broken promises, taking advantage of tribes, unfair practices, law enforcement actions, discrimination, and others) tend to remind and reinforce this concept for some current tribal leaders.

Coupled with the issues inherent in historical trauma, there is also the aftermath of something that is commonly referred to as the *"white man's burden."* Here's a definition:

n. The supposed or presumed responsibility of white people to govern and impart their culture to nonwhite people, often advanced as a justification for European colonialism.[43]

Many of our historic and contemporary leaders believed and advanced this incredibly patronizing concept through policies, legislation, and even self-imposed actions. The linkage between historical trauma and the white man's burden is important to understand. First the trauma: non-Indian settlers took tribal land. This led to the removal

---

[40] Yellow Horse Brave Heart, Dr. Maria. *Welcome to Takini's Historical Trauma*, http://www.historicaltrauma.com/ (accessed May 3, 2010).

[41] Evans-Campbell, Teresa, *Historical Trauma in American Indian/Native Alaska Communities: A Multilevel Framework for Exploring Impacts on Individuals, Families, and Communities.* J Interpers Violence 2008: 23; 316.

[42] Ibid

[43] White man's burden. Answers.com. The American Heritage® Dictionary of the English Language, Fourth Edition, Houghton Mifflin Company, 2004. http://www.answers.com/topic/the-white-man-s-burden, accessed May 03, 2010.

of entire tribal communities to reservations. The non-Indian "powers that be" also decided that Indian children needed to be separated from their families and placed in boarding schools. These same powers prohibited the practice of spiritual beliefs and so on. This all led to the annihilation of the Native American culture in question. Then you have the white man's burden that prescribed the compulsory actions of European culture to impose what they believed was best for non-whites and make them dependent on the Europeans regardless of their wishes. The compulsory aspect of the white man's burden compounded the historical trauma. But it gets worse because both together fly directly in the face of inherent tribal sovereignty. Sovereignty means "to be independent, autonomous, and self-governing." But when you impose behavior, culture, rules, and other actions onto a culture that is not yours, you are not acknowledging that sovereign right—in fact you are taking it away, and that worsens the effects of historical trauma. It's no wonder trust has eroded so much over the past one hundred years, and it directly affects your ability to work easily in Indian country.

Given that fact, let's focus on how historical trauma affects your ability to build respectful working relationships today with American Indians. The typical reaction we can expect from those experiencing historical trauma will be anger—anger towards those responsible for, or linked to, the traumatic events that took place. That means you in government and/or you in the corporate world. I believe this anger is the basis for many of the blunt statements that we in the non-Indian culture may receive. However, there are other responses we need to be aware of. They might include discomfort around non-Indians manifested as silence, fear, or even avoiding those outside the American-Indian community.

Historical trauma is not something that is easily handled. But neither is it insurmountable. For those of us trying to build a relationship with an individual or a tribe that is experiencing historical trauma, we must be patient, show respect, and be resilient—in other words, work diligently and hard toward building trust. Without that trust, no business, nothing, is going to take place.

Some Final Thoughts

As you can see, American Indian history over the past two hundred years has not been a pretty picture. It is what I call bittersweet—a picture that has been glamorized by Hollywood and yet minimizes the human injustices and prejudices of the past. But on the sweet side, the future is promising as tribes become savvy in governing, exercising their sovereign rights, economic development, caring for the people, and protecting the traditional cultures and practices that make them what they are today—a proud people.

I cannot put too fine a point on this. You must appreciate and understand that these historical accounts have a bearing and impact on the collaborative environment today, and as I said in the previous chapter, it becomes incumbent upon you to research and learn specific tribal histories—each tribe having its own historical record. Recall that the Cherokee suffered the "Trail of Tears" tragedy in contrast to the Paiute Tribe of Utah whose treaty was terminated, which was how their land and rights were taken away. Both are horrendous; both are unique. Each tribe is as unique in its history as in its culture.

So you might ask, "What do these historical events have to do with my program to acquire a right-of-way, open a branch bank, or manage a sacred site on or off a reservation?" The answer is "Plenty!" Our first thoughts are usually along the line of, "Why am I the target for things that happened in the past and that I had nothing to do with?" Or, "What do these historical events have to do with me and the program I'm presenting?"

Never forget, unless you have directly or intentionally done something to offend a tribe or individual, you are a target because of whom you represent—not who you are. So put these questions aside and take the advice of the late George Sutton, "Take it as a tool or something to use for learning."[44] By understanding and appreciating the past you will

---

[44] Sutton, George. 2006. Interview by author. Video recording. January 11. Watonga, Oklahoma.

be in a better position to exercise patience and tolerance in the face of harsh criticism or condemnation over historical events.

Moving Forward

I have been asked many times after presenting my brief treatise on American Indian history in my workshops if I, as a non-Indian, should personally feel guilty or responsible for the many historical abuses that took place. My answer is no. I always tell participants, "American Indian history contains many dreadful lessons we do not want to repeat." But I make sure that they understand, as I have helped tribal representatives understand, that I personally did not partake in those historical actions and can not be held accountable for them. However, I do acknowledge that it did happen. I am sorry it happened, and I feel bad it happened. Above all, my responsibility is to the future, to help ensure American Indian people and their governments are treated with respect, dignity, and honor and to recognize their sovereignty, culture, history, protocol, and desire for self-determination when I am working in Indian country.

I hope you now understand the big picture and the paradigm shift that must take place in your thinking about Native Americans. Jim Saint Arnold expressed to me why this is so:

We have heard your words before and have been burned by believing you. You need to show us how your words are different.[45]

Tribal leaders may tell you over and over how they have been historically subjected to many lies and injustices. If you choose to simply dismiss these historical accounts presented by tribal leaders, I assure you there will be consequences. It only reinforces the perception by tribal leaders that you don't really care about what the tribe has been through—that you don't think their history is important, nor are you sensitive to a tribal leader's desire for you to understand. As I have said before, many tribal members relate to these historical accounts as if they happened yesterday—not decades or centuries ago. Memories are long and the stories of what happened to their great-grandparents continue to be passed from generation to generation.

---

[45] St. Arnold, Jim. 2010. Personal communication with author. April 6.

You will hear me repeat many times the importance of consulting with tribal leaders about numerous topics. History is a good place to start—asking tribal leaders to share with you the specific history for their tribe. You are taking the first step on the way to becoming successful in Indian country. After all, our textbook is history, and if we listen and understand the history, the road to the future will be paved with trust, friendship, and success!

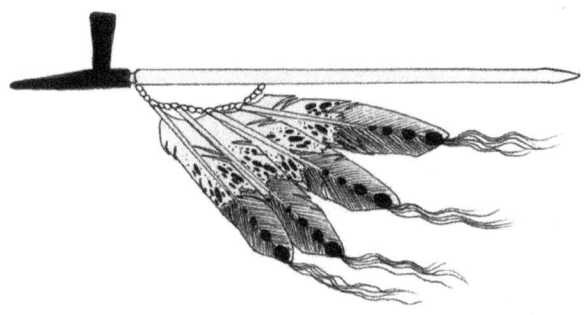

PART TWO

TRUST: THE FOUNDATION OF A GOOD RELATIONSHIP

There are many elements to a successful relationship: good communication, learning to respect one another's boundaries and differences, as well as similarities. When you are working in Indian country, you are developing a relationship with a tribe. It requires all of the courtesies and goodwill you can offer to anyone with whom you enter into a relationship. It is no lie to say that your relationship with the tribes with whom you work is hampered by the failures of others in the past that chose not to take the time to develop that relationship. But as I said in part one, what has happened in the past can only be rectified by what happens in the future. If you are charged, either personally or professionally, to work with an American Indian tribe, it is up to you to make the overtures of trust.

Part two is long, far longer than the other two sections of this book. It comprises the core of all the lessons I have learned over the years, and if you follow the Communication Protocols I list and pay attention to the Platinum Rules I offer, you have a much better chance of developing a rich relationship with a tribe based on respect and trust. You will then be able to reap all the benefits that come with that kind of relationship.

4

How Communication Can Break Down

Communication is the basis of how we understand each other. When two people are communicating well, they are sharing ideas, learning from one another, and they are willing to care for and trust each other. The capacity to communicate effectively is the heart and essence of any relationship. When communication is working, there is harmony.

One would think that with our advanced technologies we could eliminate the need to improve our communication abilities. However, the medium we use to communicate messages, whether orally, in writing, or electronically, has little to do with the clarity of the message itself. The sad fact is, when communication breaks down it can get downright ugly. When communication has gone sour, there is discord. When you are working in Indian country, it is vital that you be able to communicate openly with those you're working with, but in order to communicate well, it is important to know that human factors such as cultural norms, our knowledge levels, our feelings and perceptions, as well as our attitudes and fears, can get in the way of good communication, and no amount of advanced technology will rectify that.

I begin part two with a discussion of how communication can break down because, in effect, it is still a part of the paradigm shift that must take place. Before you can communicate effectively, you must understand that there are human factors, filters which we're often not aware of, that we use to evaluate, judge, and finally, to draw conclusions about others. These filters become barriers to effective communication, and we must overcome them first in order to move forward productively.

Raymond's Story

Not too long ago, a "letter to the editor," was published in my hometown newspaper. It illustrates the idea of filters perfectly. Here it is:

Routine flight provides lessons from the heart

I am not a great traveler, especially when it requires the use of commercial airlines. While in the spirit of rebuilding American's confidence, I was pleased to see my recent flight booked full on a trip to California. I had my usual pre-flight anxieties.

As the 200-plus passengers were seated one-by-one, the cabin became heated far beyond comfortable, and the seats became cramped as usual.

As the final passengers slowly proceeded down the aisle, I made my usual judgmental assessment of who I did or did not want to take the remaining seat next to me. Not the fat one, I thought–or maybe the pretty girl. But surely not the punk.

He was Hispanic, dressed in stylish rap attire complete with his baseball hat on backward, baggy jogging pants, unlaced, oversized tennis shoes and several gold chains. I guessed him to be in his mid-thirties, although the sunken appearance around his eyes skewed my already skewed judgment.

The needle tracks on his arms were surely those of an IV drug user. The large scar on his throat was undoubtedly placed by one of his rival gang colleagues. As he reached for the overhead storage to place his bag, I thought, great. How did he even make it through security? And then he made his way down the row, yes–right next to me.

As the plane taxied toward the runway and the flight attendant recited her instructions, I leaned over to the window and plunged my face into the latest New England Journal of Medicine. The man was quite talkative to the passenger to his right. I thought, maybe he will just fall asleep and not bother me.

Then the inevitable happened. "Are you a doctor?" the man asked.

"Yup," I replied.

"Where are you headed?" he asked.

I told him I was attending a medical convention in San Diego. What would follow in an otherwise unlikely discussion was one of those things that will not go away for what I hope is a very long time.

His name was Raymond. Like me, he was forty years old. Like me, he had an infant son. But unlike me, Raymond was dying. He had end-stage throat cancer, which had taken a nasty course, filling up his lungs and lymph nodes.

He had been operated on for removal of the primary mass in his throat, leaving a scar 8 inches long. His arms were filled with catheter holes from months of chemotherapy. His body weight had dissipated from a previous two hundred pounds to a mere 140, leaving dark circles under his eyes.

He was en route to California to see his sister for what may be the last time.

We spent the next two hours talking about life, children, and hope. Raymond was a house painter and had his own business that he very much wanted to return to as soon as he was strong enough. He was quick to show me pictures of his son. I was embarrassed that I did not even carry any photos of my children to share with him.

Raymond was a spiritual man. His brother was a Catholic priest, and he was preparing himself for the life to come–although he was hopeful it would not come too soon. I explained to Raymond that, although it was outside my specialty, I had gained a great deal of experience with throat cancer as my father-in-law succumbed to the same disease.

We discussed the details of his disease, including the plethora of therapies, both medical and surgical, he had undergone. He was searching for other treatment options and was pleased to learn from me that all his options had not been exhausted.

I referred him to a doctor at the James Cancer Center in my hometown, Columbus, Ohio. This was the same specialist who treated my father-in-law after all others had given up on him.

Raymond was very excited about this information and promised he would make arrangements to travel to Ohio immediately. We talked about maintaining his strength, both physical and spiritual, which were vital to winning this unfair, uphill battle.

As the plane made its descent, Raymond repeatedly thanked me for my time and attention. He said he was truly blessed and that it was a miracle he was seated next to me. He was profoundly grateful for his new sense of hope.

As the plane landed and the passengers left, Raymond noticed an old man across the aisle from him was having trouble with his cane and [who] was unable to remove his bag from the overhead compartment. Raymond said, "It's OK, old-timer. I'll help you out."

The surprised man watched the rapper take his luggage for him, and at a brisk walk, Raymond departed from the plane in front of the old man. I know the old man wondered if he would ever see his luggage again, as did several of the passengers behind him.

I walked behind the old man, and as we exited the plane, I could only smile. For, there was a wheelchair, with his luggage, and a dying Hispanic man there to offer the old-timer assistance through the terminal.

I learned more in that two-hour flight than I have learned in a long time. As I walked past him, he offered one more, "Thank you, Doc."

I responded, "No, Raymond, Thank you."

Ted P. Vlahos, DVM
Sheridan, Wyoming[46]

Raymond's story shared by Dr. Vlahos' provides a very valuable lesson about how these subliminal filters distort reality. The story is peppered with Ted's conclusions about Raymond based on visual filters—his

---

[46] Dr. Ted Vlahos, 2001. Sheridan Press, *Guest Opinion – Routine flight provides lessons from the heart,* December 13. Used with permission.

ethnicity, rap attire, baseball cap on backwards, baggy pants, needle tracks, scars, and more. And it does not end when Raymond grabs the old man's bag saying, "It's okay old-timer. I'll help you out," guessing the older gentleman might be thinking he might never see his luggage again. Most importantly, Ted has revealed to us how we can learn and enrich our life by recognizing and putting aside these filters, only to discover a new unbiased way of thinking within ourselves.

So it goes when working in Indian country, you must put aside your misperceptions and stereotypes, your filters, about American Indian people. Yes, some of them may dress differently, may speak more slowly, and a handshake might not be as expected, and just as with many non-Indians, a person may be soft-spoken, shy or reserved. That doesn't mean that they are ignorant or unwilling to communicate. That judgment comes from our filters.

Filters affect and influence your ability to communicate. Let's look at a simple communication model to illustrate. You are either a "sender of information" or "receiver of information." When you talk or write you are sending information; when you listen or read you are receiving information. In either manner, you are sending or receiving information through a set of personal filters. These filters can easily become skewed and significantly impede your ability to communicate effectively, especially over cultural schisms. The consequences may result in condescending behavior, erroneous conclusions about someone's intent, reproachful body language, slips of the tongue, ambiguous messages, or breaches of cultural protocol. Your goal should be to clean your filters by not assuming they are correct. This will ensure the message is received objectively and the response you receive is positive.

In order to put aside the many stereotypes and erroneous perceptions that engender your filters about American Indian people it is important to name them. Unfortunately, many are borne from these same stereotypes and erroneous perceptions that became, consciously or unconsciously, etched in our minds about how American Indians act, behave, and live.

You also need to recognize that these perceptions go in both directions; American Indian people have stereotypes and misperceptions about people in government and business, too. It is as important to understand how American Indians feel about people in the non-Indian world as it is to know our own filters in order to recognize and identify the environment we are confronting.

So, let's look at a couple of questions. First, what are the perceptions and stereotypes we, as government and business leaders, may have about Indian people, and second, what are the perceptions and stereotypes Indian people may have about us, as government and business leaders?

Perceptions and Stereotypes Government and Business Leaders May Have About American Indian People

First, let's take a short quiz about American Indian people. Simply answer True, False, or Don't Know to each of the following statements:

1. American Indians receive payments from the Federal government just for being an Indian.

2. Gaming (casinos) has made American Indians rich.

3. American Indians do not pay taxes.

4. All American Indian tribes are essentially the same.

5. Tribal Sovereignty and treaties do not have any significance in today's political, social and environmental arena.

The quick answer to these statements is that all are "False." They are all myths that have been generated by centuries of misunderstanding and innuendo. Let's examine each to understand why.

Statement #1—*American Indians receive payments from the Federal government just for being an Indian.* This is one of the most misunderstood myths today. Historically, treaties approved by Congress authorized the Federal government to make payments to American Indian tribes as compensation for lands ceded in those treaties. However, most payments were for a limited period of time, five years for instance, and then the payments were terminated. Today, American Indian people do receive payments from the federal government, but just like everyone else in the form of tax returns, welfare payments, or unemployment checks. And, American Indian people do receive payments for revenues generated from activities on reservation lands held in trust by the federal government, such as from oil and gas, coal, and other natural resources. The federal government has a trust and fiduciary responsibility to American Indian tribes meaning they collect revenues earned on tribally-owned lands and hold them in trust for tribal members. The federal government then has the responsibility to distribute these earnings to the tribe or its members on an annual basis. It is much like stock earnings you receive in the form of profits, dividends, and interest. However, no American Indian person receives a check from the federal government just for having American Indian descent or heritage.

Statement #2—*Gaming (Casinos) has made American Indians rich.* Another myth perpetuated by the media today is that American Indian people are getting rich from gaming on tribal lands. If we look at this issue from an objective perspective we find that few tribes are making it big in gaming. Most are break-even business ventures, at best, due to the remote location of most tribes and their proximity to large cities. Those near large cities or tourist destinations tend to be the most successful. In addition, most states have compacts with tribes who have casinos, requiring a portion of the profits to be paid to the state in the form of royalties. The figure I have heard is that only about five percent of American Indian-owned casinos are extremely profitable at the levels we see in Las Vegas, Atlantic City, or Reno.

Statement #3—*American Indians do not pay taxes.* Another commonly held myth is that American Indian people do not pay taxes. American Indian people are subject to the same federal income taxes assessed on earned income regardless of where it is earned; on or off the reservation. However, there are differences with state income taxes. For example, in most states, income earned on the reservation is not subject to state income tax. Income earned off the reservation is subject to state income tax. Property taxes are not assessed on tribal lands on the reservation but are assessed for those individuals living off the reservation or on deeded lands within the reservation. Sales tax is paid by American Indian people for purchases off the reservation (where applicable) and may or may not be assessed for purchases on the reservation. The area of taxation is a legal can of worms that varies widely across the country, but the point is that American Indian people do pay taxes. They are subject to the same tax liabilities and shelters as everyone else depending on where and how the income is earned.

Statement #4—*All American Indian tribes are essentially the same.* First, this is perhaps the most egregiously racist idea of them all. It's the same as saying all Asians are the same or all Blacks or Latinos are the same. In the case of the American Indian, this culturally-perpetuated myth probably comes from a lack of understanding of American Indian history. American Indian tribes are as diverse as the states in our country. To say that Wyomingites are culturally the same as New Yorkers will generate a tirade of differences articulated by those living in one place or the other. In Wyoming we have counties, in Louisiana we have parishes; in Montana our legislative sessions are once a year, in California our legislative sessions continue throughout the year; in Nevada gaming is legal, in other states it's prohibited; in the South the language dialect is different from that in the North; and on and on.

We pride ourselves in the culture and heritage where we are raised and live and sometimes envy those who live in other places. The same can be said of American Indian tribes in our country. Alaskan natives are as culturally distinct as the Seminoles in Florida. Southern tribes in New Mexico and Arizona have been historically influenced by the Spanish culture, whereas northern tribes have been historically influenced by the French Canadians. Some tribes are very affluent and others live with high levels of poverty and so forth. We must recognize that tribes are as distinct and diverse as any other culture.

Statement #5—*Treaties and tribal sovereignty do not have any significance in today's political, social, and environmental arena.* Again, this is a false perception based upon a poor understanding of the role of treaties and sovereignty in American Indian history and culture. The treaties negotiated in the 1800's have the same legal standing as those negotiated with other countries in the world. Treaties outline *retained* rights (hunting, fishing, and gathering), compensation for ceded lands, reservation boundaries, and other factors. Retained rights are those rights tribes had well before the first foreigner set foot in this country.

The law on sovereignty in the United States is quite complex and beyond the scope of this writing. However, you need to be aware of the basic premise behind tribal sovereignty. Simply stated, tribal sovereignty is pre-existing and inherent to that of the United States and was not given to tribes by the federal government. Treaties were negotiated between two sovereigns—the tribal government and the United States government. One term that is useful in describing tribal sovereignty is that tribes are a "domestic dependent nation" within a nation (the United States). I highly recommend you read Charles Wilkinson's book *Indian Tribes as Sovereign Governments*[47] to gain a thorough understanding of tribal sovereignty.

The upshot to all of this is simple: if you approach anyone in the tribe with any of these stereotypes in mind, you are setting yourself up for a communication breakdown. People know when you are talking to them through a filter. It would be the same if you were a little over-weight, for example, and the person talking to you thinks "Who is this guy? He can't even keep himself fit. How is he going to work with me?" In any communication situation, good communication only happens when both parties are comfortably able to look at each other as human beings, not a bunch of stereotypes. If you are going to have any kind of relationship at all, you have to recognize which filters you're operating from and simply decide to be rid of them. The same holds true for the person sitting across from you.

Perceptions and Stereotypes American Indian People May Have About Government and Business Leaders

As I said before, perceptions are a two-way street. Indian people do have biases, misconceptions, and stereotypes about non-Indian government and business leaders. In my interviews I often ask how

---

[47] Wilkinson, Charles and The American Indian Resource Institute 2004, *Indian Tribes as Sovereign Governments*, Second Edition. American Indian Lawyer Training Program, Inc., Oakland, California.

tribal leaders perceive government and business leaders. I have found that most perceptions American Indian people have about non-Indians are based on both historical and current experiences—those of their ancestors as well as those experienced by the individual. Here are some of the comments I have heard:

Comment #1—*I find it difficult to work with white people because all my experiences have been bad.* Such a feeling is borne in negative experiences an individual has had with government and business leaders. It might have been the result of broken commitments, a forceful approach, or bureaucratic behavior. The individual's communication filter becomes skewed as a result of these experiences, so when you first meet with that tribal representative, the first thought entering that person's mind might be, "What does this person want from us? Is this just another outsider trying to take advantage of our tribe?" You can't even get past this thought because of the suspicions and perceptions, and even disdain, the person has for anyone working in government and business.

Comment #2—*You're just another white man who has broken treaties and promises made to American Indians.* This perception has historical roots as well as experiences of today. So many of the treaties were never adhered to and the commitments in them never materialized. For example, an Indian agent in the 1800's may have negotiated payment for ceded lands in a treaty; Congress approved the treaty but never appropriated the funds promised. Or, hunting, fishing, and gathering rights on ancestral lands were retained in a treaty but tribal members were not allowed to continue exercising those rights because of governmental policy prohibiting such uses. Another big issue is, "Our great-grandfathers negotiated with the U.S. Government to retain our ancestral lands but they were taken away when gold was discovered." On the private business sector side, we might hear, "So-and-so discovered oil on our reservation and destroyed our land and sacred sites, and we never received the payments promised." The list goes on and on, and because of the way history is preserved in the American Indian community, these experiences are recounted from generation to generation.

Comment #3—*You're just another white man who is going to tell us what's good for us.* I have said this before. You wouldn't like it if someone approached you and said, "This is what you're going to do because it's good for you." No matter how well-intentioned you are, if you approach a tribe in such a manner, you're simply mimicking the typical approach of many previous government and business leaders towards tribes. They came forward saying, "We have this great program for you and it will accomplish all these wonderful things." Unfortunately experience has shown that many of these programs did not work and may have flown in the face of traditional or cultural norms of a particular tribe. Your intent might be honorable but the wrong approach can leave you empty-handed based on how you present the information. Tribal responses typically take the form of "What do you know about what's good for us—you don't know anything!"

Now, you might tell yourself, "This isn't fair, I don't fit any of those categories and have never done anything to earn these labels!" And this is probably true for most of us. So why do we have to face these realities? For the same reason American Indians have to face the same realities of the labels placed on them over the last two hundred years.

No matter what filter you're up against, yours or the person's sitting across from you, it is up to you to take responsibility to move beyond that filter. Don't ever get nasty or mean about it. You must certainly never become condescending. It is a simple matter of saying, "I'm sorry, I had a misunderstanding," and then showing that other person that you aren't like the stereotype.

Whenever anyone bumps up against filters, it becomes a teachable moment for all of us to get past it and into some real and good communication. Above all, we can and must do our part in making the first move to change the thinking about how we perceive one another. This is where trust and relationship building begins.

Overcoming Stereotypes and Misperceptions

The Sacred Circle provided me an opportunity to see how communication filters get in the way of effective communications. When we started the process, I heard many opinions of what each entity thought of the other as well as how they perceived one another's intentions. I heard from the non-Indian community expressing feelings that the tribe's intentions were to close the site to everyone except American Indian people, that non-Indian people would not be able to visit the site, and American Indian people were conducting a land grab. On the other side of the coin, I heard tribal leaders express feelings that the non-Indian community wanted to develop the site into a tourist trap, that they were only concerned about economic development, and that they didn't care about the important cultural or historical values of the site. I knew that we had to face that problem head-on or it was all going to fall apart again. We worked to create an opportunity for each entity to share their feelings, thoughts, and opinions about the Sacred Circle. In that meeting, something marvelous happened; each discovered that their perception of the others' intentions was wrong. Their filters painted a picture in their minds that was totally contrary to the others true thoughts and feelings.

After much introspection, both American Indian and non-Indian people agreed that the Sacred Circle was a very "special place," although for different reasons. Both entities found common ground and neither wanted to see it destroyed or ruined, the sacred and spiritual values diminished, or use exclusively limited to one side. Once the communication filters were purged of stereotypes, misunderstandings, and suspicion, the question became, "How can we work together to protect and preserve the Sacred Circle?" rather than "Should the Sacred Circle be protected and preserved?" The difference between those two questions is stark—and as I said at the end of part one, it's a question you should brand in your mind: "How can we work together?" In the case of the Sacred Circle, agreeing on this basic premise led to collaborative discussions that, in the end, resulted in a long-term management plan emphasizing public education in American Indian cultural and spiritual values without promoting the site and attracting additional visitors.

Now here's a point to ponder. If you answered "Don't Know" to any question in the quiz above, you might as well place it in the "True" column. This is because when you check "Don't Know" you are essentially saying it might be true, and your communication cues (verbal inflection and body language) could display those biases. Your filters can be just as skewed with an "I don't know if it's true or not" assumption as those you definitely perceive as being correct.

There are many other stereotypes and misperceptions about American Indians and many of us are reluctant to face the reality that these labels exist. As an exercise in my tribal relations workshops, I ask participants to share the stereotypes they hear about American Indian people. I know it's uncomfortable for many folks, but it's a necessary exercise to dispel these distasteful labels. Here's the list that consistently comes up in every workshop. American Indians are impoverished, thieves, drunks, lazy, and live off the government. They all live together, all are related; they won't look you in the eye and won't move off the reservation. Unfortunately, many of these have origins dating back hundreds of years. And even more unfortunate is that these labels are no truer than what any other sector of society faces anywhere around the globe. Yes, there is a percentage of the American Indian population who fall into these categories, just as there is in the population of Spokane, Washington or Washington, D.C. But we don't label all the people in Spokane or Washington, D.C. the same. It is simply not fair or just to label the entire American Indian population as such either.

There are also other stereotypes and cultural misunderstandings, thoughts that can get in the way of effective communication when working in Indian country, if for no other reason than you have two very distinct cultures bumping up against each other. Because these often impede good communication, I am going to look at them individually. They include cultural norms and differences, knowledge levels, feelings and perceptions, attitudes, and fears.

Cultural Norms and Differences

Cultural communication norms amongst American Indian tribes vary widely across the country. Again, not all American Indian tribes are the same or operate the same. For example, you might encounter tribal council meetings where tribal members are dressed in suits, are strict with time, and protocol is very formal. On the other hand, another tribal council operates in a more relaxed environment where dress is casual, time is lenient, and the protocol is informal. To operate and be successful you must learn and understand the local circumstances and protocol for the tribe you will be working with. Such an approach allows you to format your presentation to fit the local situation and enhances your likelihood of success.

However, violating cultural norms when working with American Indian Tribes can be a significant barrier to effective communication. We must be aware of these norms and differences and respect and honor them. Butch Blazer clarifies how these cultural differences may cause misunderstandings:

> I've been working with tribes my whole career and I'm told time and time again from various tribal elders that the non-Indian world thinks in a linear way and Indian people think in a very circular connected way where all things are connected. And, it's extremely important to them—that's just the way they believe. So, those differences in philosophy and thinking are going to create some problems when you try to bring the Indian and non-Indian worlds together ... It's that mutual understanding of each other that has allowed that [understanding] to occur in a very positive way in New Mexico.[48]

Cultural differences relating to communication norms are illustrated in the table below and were provided to me by Curley Youpee, Cultural Director on the Fort Peck Indian Reservation in Montana. One caveat though, there is a danger when providing comparisons. It is easy to generalize to the point that we categorize and/or stereotype all American Indian or non-Indian people one way or the other. You must realize that not everyone fits into either category one hundred percent. I have seen American Indian people who fit very well into the right column and non-Indians who fit into the left column. But the comparisons give you a basis for understanding how communications may break down due to cultural differences and norms.

---

[48] Blazer, Arthur "Butch." 2004. Interview by author. Video recording. July 14. New Mexico State Foresters Office, Santa Fe.

American Indian	Anglo-American
Slower, Softer Speech	Louder, Faster Speech
Avoids Speaker/Listener	Addresses Listener Directly
Little or No Eye Contact	In The Face, Often By Name
Interjects Less	Interrupts Frequently
Less "Encouraging Signs"	Much Verbal Encouragement
(Nodding, Uh Huh)	(Clapping, Nodding)
Delayed Response to Auditory Message	Immediate Response to Auditory Message
Nonverbal Communication Prized	Verbal Skills Highly Prized

Let's use an example of how these cultural differences may impede your ability to communicate effectively. You are meeting with a number of tribal elders about a project. An elder speaks up, talks very softly, slowly, and methodically with many pauses. He recounts a story full of historical descriptions of past abuses to his tribe. He goes on and on. There is little eye contact with the audience. You can't understand what any of this has to do with the topic at hand. Anxiously, you find an opportunity, jump in, interrupt, and with a quick tongue make a point; "Yes, but I have considered blah, blah, blah!" You wait for a response and there is no verbal or physical acknowledgement. You hate the silence and fill it with more verbal content. The meeting shuts down and no one speaks. You conclude that the tribe is not interested in your program.

Upon further examination you find that you have violated a number of communication protocols in the American Indian culture that encompass those of many different tribes. First, one never interrupts, as this is culturally inappropriate, especially toward elders. Second, when you speak rapidly the interest level begins to wane, with the view of you becoming that you're just another fast-talking government official or business person whose intentions are questionable. Third, you jumped in and did not allow adequate time for a response when the elder finished. And finally, you observed no verbal or physical cues that gave you an indication of which way the tribal representatives were leaning.

Further analysis will also reveal how your communication filters led to misperceptions and erroneous conclusions about your discussion with the tribal representatives. You presumed, based on your own cultural communication norms that the elder probably didn't understand the discussion because he was going in a direction that appeared to have no significance to the content of the discussion. You presumed that when he stopped for a brief moment to gather his thoughts that he was finished with his statement. You presumed that when you spoke it would be understood and accepted. You presumed that no response and no verbal and physical cues meant the tribal representatives were not interested.

The end result is simple; your presumptions were totally incorrect. If you had listened to the elder, you could have gained many insights about what the tribe's real issues were, since many times insights are conveyed through stories and anecdotes. These stories and anecdotes are often used to make a point, and sometimes a humorous story is used to break the tension in an emotionally charged environment. If you had waited rather than jumping in to offer your perspectives, you would have shown and displayed respect to the elder. If you had exhibited patience you might have realized that silence and the lack of verbal and physical cues might mean the tribal representative was thinking about a response. He might have been processing thoughts in his native language and was in the process of converting his thoughts to English—which just takes more time. I elaborate more on this in the next chapter.

I must emphasize again, though, that not all individuals and tribes function this way and you need to educate yourself on the communication protocol of the individual tribe you are working with. However, this discussion does illustrate how communications can break down when you do not understand cultural norms or when you operate with skewed communication filters.

Knowledge Level

Presuming you are knowledgeable about a particular topic, you can easily communicate above the level of the receiver leading to confusion and frustration. Likewise, if you perceive the receiver is not knowledgeable about a particular topic and oversimplify the message you can leave out pertinent information. Both scenarios can lead to a breakdown in communication. I have seen many people "talk down" or be condescending to people in the American Indian community with the assumption they are not knowledgeable about many topics, an assumption that can be fatal when building relationships. Never assume you are more knowledgeable about a subject, especially as it pertains to American Indian history, protocol, and culture.

Feelings and Perceptions

The feelings you have and perceptions you form are most likely based on your core values and past experiences about the topic or even the person with whom you are communicating. In most cases you will put an unconscious "spin" on the topic based on these values and experiences, either favorable or unfavorable. For example, say you harbor the erroneous stereotype that I talked about earlier, that American Indian people get payments from the federal government just for being an Indian. Many people have developed feelings and opinions on a topic based upon how they were raised and their past experiences, so let's presume that you have this assumption imprinted into your core values based on your upbringing. If you have this perception and are visiting a tribe that asked for your assistance in economic development, this attitude will most likely be reflected in your delivery during discussions. Your inner thoughts might be, "Why do American Indians need more money when they get paid by the government?" or "How can this tribal person talk about poverty when they all get paid by the government?" If you had educated yourself more on this topic you would find where the origin of this idea was and that your thinking and/or information was false. (Please refer to the section on "Perceptions and Stereotypes Government and Business People May Have About American Indian People" where I elaborated on this subject in detail.)

Again, you need to be careful about any feelings or conceptions you might have that are based on false data or stereotypes, on gossip (what someone has related to you verbally), or upon isolated, misunderstood incidents.

Attitudes

Your attitudes at a particular time can influence the way you send or receive information. These attitudes may be influenced by how you slept the night before, stresses you may be having at home or at the office, your physical well-being, and more. You may appear enthused about a topic one day and, if you become preoccupied with other situations or issues that have surfaced in the interim, only lukewarm the next day. Your actions may be warm and fuzzy one day and sharp and crisp the next, all because of your attitude at the time. Your attitude and the imprint it leaves on the other person you are attempting to communicate with can be lasting. Many tribal leaders have told me that one needs to have a passion for the issue to be effective and successful when working with a tribe. If you don't have passion, the tribe may have little interest in what you have to offer or propose. Passion is displayed in your attitudes! So, you must monitor your attitudes, put aside those issues that preoccupy and derail your positive attitude, and focus on the person, group, and topic at hand.

Experiences

Your personal and professional experiences with tribes play heavily on your ability to communicate effectively. For example, if you were verbally attacked at the last meeting you had with a tribe, your next effort to communicate may not reflect a very positive or open attitude. However, on the opposite extreme, if you were invited to a tribal pow-wow and the experience was positive—you were escorted around, introduced to people and learned so much—now your attitude might show that you can't wait to sit down with these folks and get some great things accomplished with your newfound friends. Your past experiences do influence the way you communicate and you must be in tune with these feelings and aware of how they may impede or help future communications. Also, keep in mind that so-called negative actions or behaviors you may have experienced with one individual in a tribe are not necessarily condoned by others in that tribal community.

Fears

Fears are often shaped by two factors: 1) past experiences and 2) the unknown. I have discussed past experiences, and they have the same influence in shaping your fears. Fear of the unknown is different because it stems from not knowing what to expect, or you conjure an end result in your mind that may be negative. Fears can also be shaped by the cultural differences you experience when working with tribes because you don't know how to act or what to do.

I can remember attending a traditional burial ceremony for a Northern Cheyenne friend. There were only a handful of non-Indians present out of more than a hundred people attending. At first it was intimidating because my colleagues and I didn't know what to expect. Then a close Northern Cheyenne friend took us under his wing and made us comfortable by explaining what was going on and including us in the ceremony. The fear was gone and we could participate in the ceremony and concentrate on why we were there—to remember and celebrate the life of our friend.

You must focus on educating yourself about tribes to dispel these fears and challenge yourself to face and walk through them. In most cases, your fears are unjustified, and building relationships are an important part of overcoming and conquering these fears. (I delve into this subject more in chapter 6.)

Communication Begins the Trust Process

Because of all the past history and the filters and barriers you must overcome, finding a way to communicate can be difficult. In an adversarial communication environment, the question that begs to be answered is, "How in the world can two entities, tribal and government or business, ever develop trust and build an effective working relationship when stereotyping and misperceptions run rampant?" The short answer is relatively simple: be cognizant of your own and others' communication filters that you judge or may be judged by. Recognizing and understanding why these biases exist enables you to face and confront them, handle them, and work towards building trust and strong working relationships. When you do successfully overcome this first hurdle, you start bridging the cultural divide that has widened and deepened as a result of these biases. Most importantly, it provides you opportunities to employ the communication principles described in the next chapter to effectively build trust and working relationships with American Indian tribes.

5

Ten Communication Protocols for Working in Indian Country

Developing trust in any relationship takes time. Recognizing and handling preconceived ideas about each other is only the first step. When you are working in Indian country, there are definite protocols, in other words, ways to practice good communication. They are culturally-based, and the ten I give you here are those that have consistently surfaced as I have worked with American Indian tribes. As such, they are generic in nature and *must* be customized to fit the individual protocols of specific tribes. In addition, you may find a wide variation in any one protocol between traditional and contemporary American Indians. For example, an elder may lean more toward a traditional method of communication and a young adult may lean more towards a contemporary communication practice. But you must remember that there is wide variation and as one friend of mine shared with me, "In my experience, the most effective and successful Indian leaders are those that walk in both worlds." As I have said many times before and will say again, you need to consult with local tribal representatives on how these protocols may or may not apply to them. Most importantly, the tribal representative will assist you in navigating through the cultural communication protocols that are necessary to achieving success with that tribe. However, these ten communication protocols (analogous to the leadership activities presented earlier) will afford you a starting point to build trust and valuable working relationships with American Indian tribes. The format of each protocol is meant to help you navigate that terrain. I explain what each one is and then give you helpful suggestions on how to work with that protocol. They are in no particular order of importance as they are all equally essential to successful communication.

Protocol #1—"The Moccasin Telegraph" or Modern Day Networking

Non-Indians are often amazed at how quickly information can travel within Native American communities, even in isolated, remote, and non-wired areas. This lightning fast "internet" of information-gathering and sharing by word-of-mouth is known in Indian country as the Moccasin Telegraph (in Alaska they call it the Mukluk Telegraph).

Montana Tribal Tourism Alliance

The "Moccasin Telegraph" is slang for Indian communication between tribes or individuals some distance apart. It is a phrase I hear often in the Indian community as a means of sharing important information. Albert White Hat, Sante Gleska University, related the following story of how the "Moccasin Telegraph" operated historically:

It was interesting, because the stories I've heard, is that as soon as they [white people] hit the eastern shores, the island, word got to us in a very short time of their arrival. There's a major network system. They, families, camped ... all camp in different locations. But they camp within ... a day's walk or run. If you measure that maybe about seven or eight miles apart ... so if anything happens a runner makes that contact.[49]

Albert's point is that the tribes in the Great Plains knew of Europeans landing on the east coast in a matter of months. The distance from Plymouth Rock, Massachusetts, to Rapid City, South Dakota, is 1,932 miles. Calculating ten miles per day as Albert states, this would mean that word of Pilgrims landing on Plymouth Rock reached the Sioux Nation in South Dakota in a little over six months.

While that's an interesting historical conjecture, the concept of the "Moccasin Telegraph" as a communication protocol is what is important here. It helps us understand how our community of interest can expand

---

[49] White Hat, Albert. 1998. Interview by author. Video recording. February 12. Sante Gleska University, Rosebud, South Dakota. © National Historic Trails Center, Casper, Wyoming. Used with permission.

very rapidly across Indian country. You might have a program or project that you feel a certain tribe might be interested in so you approach that tribe. Next, you start getting calls from other tribes asking why they were not included and others wanting to participate. You say to yourself, "I was only working with one tribe and now I have many others interested which exceeds my budget and the time I have to devote to the program."

What you need to realize is that there is a close network between American Indian tribes and organizations across the country sharing information about programs, projects, regulations, legislation, policies, and other important issues. If your program or project has implications regionally or nationally many other tribes may want to participate or become involved.

Another factor to keep in mind is the relocation policy of the 1800's I discussed previously. This policy displaced many tribes from their homelands sometimes thousands of miles away. Again, I use the Cherokee as an example. As a result of voluntary and forced removal there came to be three federally recognized Cherokee communities: the Cherokee Nation and the United Keetoowah Band of Cherokee, both in Oklahoma, and the Eastern Band of Cherokee in North Carolina. Now if you have a project or program that affects the Eastern Band of Cherokee you might get a call from the Cherokee Nation or United Keetoowah Band of Cherokee in Oklahoma. You will find there is a close network between the Cherokee Nation, the United Keetoowah Band of Cherokee, and the Eastern Band of Cherokee. This tight network between the three tribes ensures the protection of one another's interests.

Again, the point is that you need to make certain all interests are covered in your communications and be open to others who might have an interest. You need to do your homework to cover all bases in all your communications, and you need to not only be aware of the "Moccasin Telegraph," you need to respect its power.

One final thought. I would never use the phrase "Moccasin Telegraph" to request that information be shared amongst other tribes or individuals, particularly if I did not know the tribal representative very well. Some in the American Indian community may consider it derogatory when used by non-Indians or consider it as patronizing. You don't want to get started off on the wrong foot.

Protocol #2–Indian Speeches—A Cultural Communication Medium

… do not interrupt our elders when they are talking.

Cante Ethanhan Owaglake,
Speaking From The Heart, Customs and Norms for the Standing Rock Sioux Tribe
Standing Rock Tourism Alliance

We had a meeting on the Sacred Circle a number of years ago. It was one of the first scheduled meetings with tribal leaders and the non-Indian community to begin dialogue on developing a long-term historic preservation plan. In our contemporary way, we had a typical agenda: opening comments, introductions, and break-out groups with a defined timeframe for each agenda item. The meeting started with the introductions and from there the agenda went south on us. All the tribal leaders had something to say and it took ten to twenty minutes for each of them to say it. They talked about the exploitation of sacred sites, broken treaties, lost land, government abuses, and everything we had done wrong. It was at this meeting that I was called the "Custer of the World," accused of genocide, and breaking treaties. It was like each tribal representative was giving a sermon, releasing years of pent-up hostilities, anger, and frustrations. By lunchtime our agenda was nowhere near where we thought it should have been.

What we were not aware of is a traditional American Indian way of doing business by allowing everyone to express their feelings and opinions about the topic at hand before getting down to business. I call them "speeches," for lack of a better term, but you could also describe them as orations, homilies, lectures, or even sermons. That is the best way to describe what was happening in our meeting. Speech after speech after speech—everyone joined in to speak, despite our well planned agenda and schedule. I learned a lot from that first meeting and have since learned how to manage a meeting when this event takes place.

It is important that you understand what is happening here. Traditionally, tribal leaders speak about issues without timeframes or agendas. Leaders, particularly elders, talk and talk with messages embedded in their speeches. Marguerite Teller, from the Paiute Tribe of Utah shared with me:

> Yes, they do and you let them say it and it might take twenty, thirty, or forty minutes, but ... they say it. Sometimes ... especially in our area, the generations are so wide and things have changed and we just don't live or do things the way they did like fifty, forty years ago. It's hard, but you still have to respect them [and] hear what they have to say ... [50]

I have been told that sometimes an elder might tell a humorous story that doesn't appear to be on topic to break the tension if emotions run high. Or, a story might be told that takes a wide circle away from the topic and comes back making an important point. We never know what these speeches might contain but they almost always come back to the topic of discussion and have many lessons embedded. The late Poncho Bigby, a tribal planner from the Fort Belknap Indian Community in northern Montana explains it well:

> They'll [elders] have a tendency to jump around ... there's always an ultimate message when they jump around. So, you just bear with them out of respect and allow them to make the presentation in their own time and in their own way. They may start out with a story, whether it's a fictional story or whether it's a story from their own personal experiences or a story about an incident. Generally, they like to start out with a story to set the tone. There's many times when a person that follows this way can walk into a room and immediately sense the tenure and the tension level in the room. So, they'll find an appropriate story. If the tension level is very high they may come up with a very humorous story to make people laugh, to get them relaxed, but if it's not as high he may set a more moderate story. Or, if things are all

---

[50] Teller, Marguarite. 2001. Interview by author. Video recording. August 27. Paiute Tribe of Utah Tribal Office, Cedar City.

smooth he may come up with a story that tells a message that has to do with what the topic is.[51]

In his book *"A Little Bit of Wisdom—Conversations with a Nez Perce Elder"* Horace Axtell relates the following:

We don't have no set time to finish. If we need to carry it for a whole morning or afternoon, we do it. There's no time limit. When an Indian speaks there should not be a time limit. A long time ago I used to hear the old people talk and they just talked and talked. Nobody got up and told them to stop. There was respect for the old ways and the old people.[52]

The format of these speeches may vary but here are a few common denominators that you might expect:

- Meetings will often begin with many speeches, particularly if your topic is of importance.

- It is not uncommon for speeches to run ten to twenty minutes and include both historical and current issues.

- Subsequent meetings will often start again with speeches. Individuals have had time to think about the last meeting or other related issues.

- Speeches may include attacks against people and/or the system with references to "Custer of the World," genocide, and breaking treaties.

- Speeches may have history embedded in them so no one forgets, as we as westerners so often do.

- Speeches may contain issues about American Indian rights and abuses that may not even relate to the issues on the table.

- New players will often want to speak to express their opinions.

- Numerous people may enter into the foray of speeches, eating away time scheduled for topics on your agenda.

---

[51] Bigby, Poncho. 2002. Interview by author. Video recording. April 11. Fort Belknap Indian Community Tribal Office, Harlem, Montana.

[52] Horace P. Axtell and Margo Aragon, excerpts from *A Little Bit of Wisdom: Conversations With a Nez Perce Elder.* Copyright © 1997 by Margo Aragon. Reprinted with the permission of Confluence Press.

So, what do you do when your meeting is dominated by speeches focusing on broken treaties, broken promises, and the injustices of the past? Solo Greene, Nez Perce Education Specialist, suggests the following:

> *One of the things, instead of disagreeing with some of these people that stand up and exhort themselves about the pains and the hurts and bring up the past is not to deny them or blow it off. But, one of the best ways to handle it is to acknowledge it. Let them know that you know that there has been injustices; the treaties were broken, the promises were broken, and as a non-native and a government official you're here to help those things out, to get over those hurdles, to get through those obstacles which has been hindering your people, which is my people. And, that you acknowledge it and that you're sorry that it has happened, but as an individual there's nothing you can do that will change the past. You didn't have control over those people and what happened has unfortunately happened, but we're here to come together to kind of correct that, to work together as people. And, really, that's how you are going to do it, to acknowledge those people and say, "I know, I'm sorry it happened, but today we're here … " and present why you are here. Always stay with your agenda, go back to the purpose of why you are there. If you get side-tracked, if you allow these people to release all their pain, their hurt, their loss, you'll be there for a long time without getting your point across. But, always go back to your agenda. Always go back to the purpose of why you are there. But, acknowledge them, let them know that you do know something happened and it was wrong, but we can make things better, we can make things better, together we can make things better.[53]*

As I said in chapter three, it is vital that you do not dismiss the charges. What happened was wrong, but in the end there is nothing that you can do to fix the past—in the past. You can work to make a better future for all parties involved. That is what Solo is getting at in his last statement. Here is what I recommend if you find yourself in that position:

---

[53] Greene, Solo. 2007. Interview by author. Video recording. May 22. Nez Perce Tribal Office, Lapwai, Idaho.

- First, if speeches are pointed at you, don't take them personally and become defensive. I did this once and it was like pouring gasoline on a fire, fueling the pent-up emotions and literally inflaming the situation. I eventually learned that attacks are usually against the system you represent and all the historical issues that are linked with the particular issue you are addressing. This is true, of course, unless you have personally done or said something that significantly breeched the trust of the tribal leaders you are working with.

- I have been told by numerous tribal leaders that sometimes these attacks are a test to size you up and evaluate how you respond. Sometimes you are walking a thin line. Whose side are you on? Do you have the resolve to listen? What are you made of? How will you react? If you interrupt, become defensive, and lecture back you will be measured as being aggressive and just another official that doesn't understand how to do business in Indian country. If you listen intently you will be measured as being open to opinions and exhibiting a willingness to collaborate.

- Turn to active listening and use this as an opportunity to learn. There is much to be learned from these speeches if one listens intently, such as cultural implications, historical accounts, others' efforts and failings, and maybe some suggestions on your approach.

- Never interrupt! Remember Horace Axtell's advice that one must respect the old ways. In addition, interrupting is disrespectful in any culture; however, we need to understand there might be more severe cultural implications, such as shutting people down and having them walk away, when working in Indian country.

- In most instances you are not required to respond to these speeches. Most speakers are more interested in you listening rather than hearing more of what those in the non-Indian community have to say. Remember, tribal leaders have heard the non-Indian position for centuries and are well versed in the content.

- When addressing venting and attacks ask, "Where do *we* go from here?" "What is the next step *we* should take?" "How can *we* work together on this?" The use of *"we"* in the questions is paramount.

The purpose is to engage the parties in a manner that displays your openness to operating in a collaborative environment versus one that puts you at the center. If you phrase your questions in the *"I"* mode, I assure you tribal leaders will be more than willing to tell you what to do! Too often in the past, government and business leaders focus on the *"me"* rather than the *"we,"* leading to the perception that you are the sole authority and annulling any respect of the tribes' sovereign status. You are simply mimicking an historical approach that has not worked effectively in Indian country.

- Do not use individual feedback loops. Many of us have been to communications training where we learned to use feedback loops. The principle is that when one speaks we listen and parrot back what was said to the speaker. The speaker then says, "Yes, you heard me," or "No, this is what I said." Using this technique during a meeting with tribal leaders when emotions are running high is designed for failure. I assure you that if emotions are running high and you try to parrot back what was said after a fifteen-minute speech you will never get it right. Again, listen, acknowledge, and respectfully bring the group back to the agenda.

- While I wouldn't use "feedback loop" techniques, at the end of a series of speeches you should summarize what you heard, indicating that you really listened. We'll talk more about listening in the next section. For now, know that in the past government and business leaders approached tribes telling them what was best for them and ignoring what they had to say. So, it's important that you send a message that you sincerely listened. This is a critical point to building a lasting relationship and trust with tribal leaders.

- Look at speeches as a "personal public involvement" process where you can acquire important information. Much of the information you will need is embedded in these orations. As I mentioned previously, you will need to listen intently to find the messages and information that are being conveyed. It might be tempting to say "I've heard this before" and appear disinterested, but we need to keep in mind that each individual is conveying a message, sometimes building on what previous speakers have stated. So, your attention is paramount.

- Finally, survive the process. It might be a test or sizing-up exercise to determine if you are really interested in working with tribal officials. If you "tune out," I assure you that you will never earn the trust and develop the relationship required to work effectively with American Indian Tribes.

Once trust and relationships are built, the protocol of speech-making subsides and dialogue focuses more on a collaborative process. Since speeches occur mostly at the initial phase of the relationship-building process, your reaction and handling of this process will determine your future success or failure.

Protocol #3–Listening and Responding Protocols

Listen. Be Patient. Sometimes your enthusiasm, your needs and your commitment to your ideas prevents you from hearing or being an active listener.

Points of Protocol for Working with Tribes,
Confederated Tribes of the Umatilla Indian Reservation
January 2008

Most of us pride ourselves in our ability to "listen." However, what does "listening" really mean? How does an American Indian official, as a sender of information, really know that he or she was really heard by you? How you listened and responded will be the core skill you will be judged on.

My past associate, Velma Real Bird, shares the cultural implication that, in her tribe, the listener respects the words of the speaker by allowing him or her to finish thoughts, statements, and beliefs without being interrupted. The listener is sensitive to body language and avoids non-verbal cues such as looking disinterested, turning away, or being distracted. The listener understands that words are chosen wisely, as careless words may result in poor decisions. Therefore, the communication may be somewhat slower than what we in the non-Indian community are used to. The listener exercises patience and never interjects, interrupts or attempts to finish a thought or sentence for the speaker. We must bear in mind always that you will be measured by how well you listen and respond within the American Indian cultural environment and honor the fact that "Words are Sacred."

Aaron Miles from the Nez Perce Tribe in Idaho explains how tribal leaders evaluate if you are really listening to what is being said:

If you are a listener and emphatically hear what these leaders are saying, they'll respect you. But, if you have the attitude of "in one ear and out the other ear," they'll recognize that. They want somebody coming in really thinking of the tribe ... as a valued partner and not somebody that's going to be used. And, that's why it's [the communication process] so slow because they want to know if you're seriously listening or not and if you are truly valuing the tribe as opposed to somebody who's using the tribe.[54]

We all need to clean out our communication filters and welcome the cultural differences of how meetings are conducted, including the protocol of listening to speeches.

There are a number of principles you need to keep in mind when listening and responding to tribal leaders. Many are culturally significant, and when you honor those principles you continue to build trust and lasting relationships.

- Once again, do not interrupt as this is considered disrespectful in the American Indian culture and should be in any culture, for that matter.

- Use active listening; look at the speaker as you would anyone else to display interest. However, don't stare as some forms of eye contact are considered aggressive behavior in several American Indian cultures.

- Avoid side conversations. I remember meetings on the Sacred Circle when a colleague would turn and whisper in my ear a comment about what was being said by a tribal leader. This is distracting and you lose the continuity of what is being said by the speaker, particularly when a speech may go on for fifteen minutes. Encourage your colleagues to hold off if they have something to say when a tribal leader is speaking. Tell them you will discuss it later at a break or a time when you can do so without disturbing the proceedings or be distracted by them.

- Do not leave the room when a tribal leader is speaking. I have seen tribal leaders intentionally leave the room to show that they did not agree with or respect the person speaking. It is a cultural practice; rather than verbally interrupting and openly disagreeing, they walk out of the room to send the message. So, know who you are listening

---

[54] Miles, Aaron. 2007. Interview by author. Video recording. May 22. Nez Perce Tribal Office, Lapwai, Idaho.

to and their level of authority to speak, because walking out, even to use the restroom, get a cup of coffee, or answer your cell phone may send a negative message.

- To show you really listened, talk from your heart, not as a bureaucrat. Many times when we parrot the company line we get tangled up in bureaucracy and acronyms. Tribal leaders want you to be authentic, to be yourself. Tribal leaders can see through the transparency of whom you represent versus who you are.

- The statement or response you make after listening to a tribal leader about an issue will live with you throughout the process. Tribal leaders will evaluate you on what you say, any commitments you make, and how willing you are to carry out those commitments. If you are in a position where you are not sure what direction to take, avoid closed answers like "yes" or "no" unless you are making a definitive decision or commitment. If you do make a decision or commitment never forget it. As mentioned earlier, choose your words carefully.

There are times you might feel unnecessary distractions are preventing tribal leaders from listening to you, such as when there might be Indian children running around your meeting. I have been to numerous meetings where tribal leaders brought their children or grandchildren. This is not uncommon in Indian life as daycare may be limited or there are obligations as an extended family member. I have been told that this is a normal way of life. Indian people grew up this way, and they are still there intently listening to you. So, don't feel you are not being heard or listened to. Again, it's a cultural thing you might encounter, so don't take it personally.

Listening takes work, meaning that you have to really concentrate on what is being said and avoid the temptation of being distracted. Historically, officials in the non-Indian community obviously didn't feel listening was important. Rather, they were intent on telling tribes what was best for them, such as "We have a new place for you in Oklahoma, Indian country," "We want this piece or that piece of land for settlement and we will pay you handsomely for it," or "You need to quit your nomadic ways and settle down on a piece of land and become a farmer."

Today, with self-determination, things are different. Tribes want, and routinely demand, that they be heard to ensure their future destiny is not a repeat of the past. They want and demand respect as a sovereign government. So, when you talk to a tribal leader, it's just the same as if you were listening to the governor of your state. You can significantly advance the principle of trust and relationships through sincere and thoughtful listening.

Protocol #4–Asking Questions

Most tribes have had at least two-hundred years of someone trying to sell us goods we don't want. Know what you are seeking and recognize that whatever "it" is, it is subject to negotiation.

Points of Protocol for Working with Tribes,
Confederated Tribes of the Umatilla Indian Reservation
January 2008

Here's the scenario. You have a great program or project you want to present to a tribe. So, you approach the tribal leader(s) and say, "I have this great program or project for you and here are all the great things it will do for your tribe." You get no response, no reaction, and leave frustrated. Your communication filters tell you they were not interested when in reality it was your approach that was wrong.

Let's look at what happened here. First, many times in the past two hundred years government and business leaders have told tribes "what was good for them" with the final result ending up being nothing more than broken promises or a path with hidden agendas. Second, you do not know what is culturally appropriate for a tribe unless you are from that tribe and know the cultural protocols. And finally, you may not be aware of the tribe's agenda and priorities and come across as being "too pushy."

Ben Speak Thunder, past tribal chair of the Fort Belknap Indian Community, relates the following story about a government official making a presentation to their tribal council:

I'll never forget the day when ... this individual came in from the state ... and he says "Hello, how are you doing. I'm here from the government and how can I help you?" And that really brought the roof down and it was really humorous. The individual really embarrassed himself. I'm sure his intentions were good, but I guess those types of things to me are really the wrong approach.[55]

---

[55] Speak Thunder, Ben. 2002. Interview by author. Video recording. April 11. Fort Belknap Indian Community Tribal Office, Harlem, Montana.

The tribal council's response to this government official's approach is so predictable. The question, "I'm from the government and how can I help you?" evokes those past examples of failed government assistance to tribes and triggers immediate cynicism. What an important lesson for all of us to keep in mind when working with tribes.

In another situation some years back, I was attending a meeting between a state transportation official and a TERO (Tribal Employment Rights Office) official. The TERO official made a comment about hiring tribal members on state road construction contracts and asked the state official what they were going to do to enhance those opportunities. After I counseled the state official on "asking questions" verses "making statements" he said, "What do you think we should do?" The TERO official was taken aback and said, "This is the first time anyone from your organization has asked me what I thought." It made an incredible difference in the direction of the dialogue and was a key element in the trust and relationship-building process. More importantly, it displayed that the state official was sincerely interested in the TERO official's opinions and put the word "respect" into action.

A state aeronautics official came to me during one of my workshops and told me he had approached a tribe informing them he had a million dollars to build an airport on their tribal lands and it would be a great deal for them. It would assist in economic development, bring them closer to the real world, and enhance their infrastructure. He told me the tribal officials sat in silence except for a few that lectured him on, "What did he know what was good for the tribe?" He said he even had an additional million dollars for the next year if they would build the airport. He said he felt like they ran him off.

I asked him to put himself in their shoes and think of it this way: How many government officials have come to the tribe in the past century telling them what was good for them only to see their culture and sovereignty eroded and their lifestyle compromised? I told him to look back in history and think about how a nomadic or semi-nomadic society was confined to reservations, how a hunting and gathering lifestyle was changed to a farming lifestyle, how some treaties were negotiated on good faith only to be terminated by Acts of Congress, and how a nature-based spiritual society was condemned for practicing their traditional ceremonies, all with the intent of civilizing the American Indian. Each and every one of these measures was implemented on the basis of what someone else considered "good for the American Indian community."

I told him to consider changing his approach, one of asking a question rather than telling the tribe what was good for them. Approach the tribe in the following manner, "I have a million dollars to build an airport on tribal lands. Would you share with me how this may or may not be beneficial to your tribe?" This approach is simple but critical, and it can make the difference between success and failure of your programs or projects. The receptivity of the tribe is going to be based upon your knowledge of tribal issues, the relationship you have with the tribe, the level of trust you have earned with that tribe, and your approach.

Jim St. Arnold, an Ojibwa friend of mine in Michigan, told me exactly how we should ask questions when presenting a program or proposal to a tribe or tribal leader:

> I tell people not to come in with this attitude of, "I'm here to help you and what can I do for you?" And, that goes on quite a bit. Go in there quietly, go in there and say "This is what I have, this is what I can do, what would you like?" And, you will accomplish more with that type of attitude than if you say, "Well, here, I know what you want, I know what is good for you, here it is." The community, the tribal leaders, will [say], "You don't know anything!" and they'll turn around and walk away from you. You'll be sitting there [thinking] I have this great thing for them, why won't they take it? It may be great from your point of view, but it's not necessarily great from my point of view. And, you need to come in there and say, "Okay, this is what I have. How can we work together?" That's the key. How can we work together? My father used to say, "Talk to me, don't talk at me" because if you are talking at me you are not listening to what I'm saying. You need to

talk to me. And, that's what a lot of people need to understand when they work with tribes.[56]

So, if there is one thing you can do to align your approach with tribal protocol this is it—don't tell, ask!

---

[56] St. Arnold, Jim. 2003. Interview by author. Video recording. January 6. Great Lakes Indian Fish and Wildlife Commission Office, Odanah, Wisconsin.

Protocol #5—Delayed Responses

Learn that each community or tribe has its own timeline for getting things done. It may not be the same as your timeline. Adjust. Start earlier. Keep going back. Do follow-up. Share your target dates and be willing to change them.

Points of Protocol for Working with Tribes,
Confederated Tribes of the Umatilla Indian Reservation
January 2008

You meet with a tribe and do everything right when presenting your proposal. And, upon finishing your presentation, you get blank stares, no positive body language, and essentially no response. Many times we interpret these reactions as, "I guess the tribe is not interested in my proposal" or, "They just don't comprehend what I'm proposing." Nothing could be farther from the truth. To get the true answer, you need to understand the concept of "delayed responses."

Although a cultural norm with many American Indian people, most of us can't handle long pauses or delayed responses in dialogue. Our tendency is to jump in and help the person finish his statement. Gerri Grady, an Eastern Cherokee tribal official, related the following story to me about her experiences with delayed responses from her father:

My father, I take him things sometimes because I trust him. If I have[a] political issue, say it's with the tribal council and I'm questioning an action they did, I take it to Father and say, "Today at council I saw so-and-so." And, he'll stop carving and sit back, look way off, and he'll think on it. Sometimes he never says anything, sometimes a day or two later I'll say, "Father, did you ever, you know, what do you think of that?" … You can't ask him today on an issue like that to give you an opinion unless he really, really has a strong opinion on it. Then he'll give it to you, but if it's something that's a little bit, he wants to think on it and chew over it for a couple of days. Mother was the same way. If I had an issue and brought it to her it might be the next day.[57]

---

[57] Grady, Gerri. 2003. Interview by author. Video recording. January 12. Eastern Band of Cherokee Indians Tribal Office, Cherokee, North Carolina.

Gerri offers us some good advice as she concludes:

> *They have to have time to think it over. I wish, I kind of wish, other people would do the same thing because I'm very bad for making snap decisions ... and then end up paying the price for it later. So, you know, we need to follow that example a little bit more I think and chew it over a little bit more than making snap decisions that might not be in your best interest.*[58]

The problem is, in our cultural norm, we expect immediate verbal and physical cues during dialogue and if we do not get them we may draw erroneous conclusions about our encounters. We must, therefore, clean our communication filters and avoid drawing conclusions based on our cultural expectations to effectively communicate with American Indians.

Another factor to consider with delayed responses is many traditional American Indians consider English as a second language, the first being their native language. I have a very traditional American Indian friend who speaks very slowly and many times our conversations include much silence. Since we, in the non-Indian community, generally hate silence in our conversations, we will do anything to fill the void of silence with more talk, most likely interrupting the speaker. What is happening here is that many traditional people listen to us in English as a receiver of information and mentally translate the information into their native language. Then, they convert the thought back into English with a verbal response.

To reinforce this concept, Velma Real Bird and I were conducting a workshop at Southwestern Oklahoma State University in Weatherford a number of years ago. Velma shared with the students that Crow was her first language and English is actually her second language. However, she is very fluent in both. As we were discussing this topic an American Indian participant asked her, "Do you dream in Crow?" Her answer was yes. It becomes obvious that those who live their native language and are not fluent in their second language (English) may have difficulty bridging the translation process between languages, hence the delays in communication.

---

[58] Ibid.

Think of it this way. You learn a new language yet you are not fluent in speaking that language. When using that new language you must think of each word and place those words in an understandable sentence. This takes time and you would obviously want the person you are communicating with to be respectful and patient and avoid interrupting and filling in your pauses with their thoughts. So again, be patient and allow the person time to formulate his or her thoughts and communicate them verbally before presuming that it is time for you to interject and fill the "dead air."

Another reason for delayed responses from a tribe is that, in many cases, the tribal government that we directly interact with is what I call a shell government. Although my intent is not to negate their status, authority, or sovereignty, there might be other tribal organizations, such as elder, spiritual, or past government leader societies that the tribal government leaders must consult with before making a decision. This process takes time and is particularly important for government officials to know who have "Thirty Day Comment Periods" or business entities who are making business proposals. We send out a document to a tribe and request their comments in thirty days. However, we do not hear from the tribe within the thirty days and presume they are not interested. This can be a dangerous conclusion. What you might not realize is that it may take sixty days to complete the process of consulting with these embedded organizations within the tribe. So, give the tribes the time they need by consulting earlier in the process and, again, be patient.

The bottom line is that we, in the non-Indian community, suffer from impatience when we do not get immediate responses from a tribe. There are consequences when we fail to honor these cultural value differences. We become labeled as being pushy and insensitive. Take your time, value the cultural differences, and you will validate your intentions to tribal leaders that you are sincere about building trust and relationships.

Protocol #6–Communicating in the Meeting Environment

Each community or tribe has its own definition of success. It may differ from yours. We are rebuilding nations. Your priorities may not be ours, but they may intersect on a mutually beneficial project.

Points of Protocol for Working with Tribes,
Confederated Tribes of the Umatilla Indian Reservation
January 2008

Meetings, especially formal meetings, are an environment where a lot of "official" business takes place and are central hubs of communication. The meeting may be between two people or several—the more complex the situation, the more people involved. Now add in cultural differences on how those meetings will be conducted, such as timing, location, rules, protocols and behaviors and a lot can go wrong, but much can go right if done properly.

I have found that in many cases meetings between government and business officials and tribal officials fail simply due to a lack of cultural understanding. Business may be conducted differently in the tribe you're working with, and, as always, you need to be aware of and understand those differences. In fact, many of the communication factors presented previously come together in meetings. Let's look at why meetings between non-Indians and American Indians can be a test of your fortitude. We begin with the premise that there is little or no relationship between the government/business official and tribal official.

First, early stages of meetings may be contentious and chaotic depending on the subject matter. A subject generating a highly-charged atmosphere, such as issues on consultation, sacred sites, sovereignty, treaty rights, spiritual values, or lands will be more contentious or chaotic than more benign issues, such as cooperation and coordination, economic development, business relations, or job fairs. However, I have seen these benign issues become contentious when other factors come into play, particularly when they are linked to the more highly-charged issues. Regardless of the issue, people will need to speak freely about their feelings and ensure that they are heard. I believe two events are taking place: 1) the government or business official is being sized up and evaluated and 2) positions about issues are being put on the table. Agendas will tend to go awry if they are not carefully crafted.

This leads to the second point, that meetings often appear to be extremely slow and that nothing is getting accomplished. What we in the non-Indian world do not understand is that a lot is getting done, and we just can't see it because we are programmed to see only tangible results. There may be many hidden processes going on that we cannot see, such as exploring and clarifying values, understanding positions on issues, relationship and trust-building, and much more, as well as being tested and sized-up by tribal leaders. This all takes time and we need to exercise patience and let the process work. So what if meetings are slower, take more time and appear chaotic? The benefit in the long-term will outweigh the time taken to realize the end result.

The third point is that the same expectations may not be shared by all those present at the meeting. It happens all the time when we walk in with an agenda and have expectations for ourselves but fail to seek out and honor the expectations and perceptions of others. This is particularly true when other cultural norms are overlooked, as is often the case in the American Indian cultures. We clearly see our expectations but fail to see the expectations of others.

In many situations we may try to shortcut efforts to ferret out other's expectations of process, protocol, content, or time, in order to "save time." The investment of time is more than worth the effort if we spend more of it aligning the expectations of those involved in our collaborative endeavors. And, most importantly, it shows respect in honoring the diversity of cultures present at your meetings.

It becomes very apparent that many, if not most, tribal leaders value the process of building relationships before conducting business. So, what do you do? Here are some tips:

- As I have pointed out in the history section, before a meeting, arrange for an informal visit with key leaders just to get to know one another even if it's only a little bit. I cannot stress enough the importance of this one action. If you do not have a relationship with a particular tribal leader it will pay handsomely to slow down the process and evaluate the need for taking the time to "just get to know each other." You may have to go slow to go faster in the future.

- Begin the process early. This simply means that you do not contact the tribe a mere two weeks before a decision is needed on a project or proposal. If you expect to be in a position to work effectively with a tribe, you need to reach out early and often. This is where an ongoing relationship is valuable, both personally and professionally.

- Listen and be open to protocol. You can learn a lot about cultural protocol if you open your ears and listen. Much of our resistance to embracing other cultural norms is housed within us personally and not cast in legal procedures. Again, honoring the protocol of other cultures demonstrates respect.

- Prepare to be flexible and be open to adjustments. When you lock yourself into a schedule or way of doing business, you are setting yourself up for disappointment. Not only that, but when you are resistant to being flexible you can be cast as being exactly that— inflexible. Then you wonder why no one shows up at your next meeting!

- Be patient. Things always get better and you will never be disappointed in the end result if you allow the process to work.

Finally, the best advice is offered by Russ Townsend, Tribal Historic Preservation Officer for the Eastern Cherokee Tribe in North Carolina.

I think the more time you can take to get to know the Native American culture you are dealing with the better off you are. And I think tribal people; certainly around here ... feel a lot more confident when they don't deal with business right away. I think that if you are able to have an informal trip down where you want to go to the museum, and you want to see the surrounding landscape, and visit with people, go over to one of the local restaurants for lunch and just see what people are talking about. I think that's respected and you can come back two weeks later and get down to business.[59]

---

[59] Townsend, Russ. 2003. Interview by author. Video recording. January 13. Eastern Band of Cherokee Indians Tribal Office, Cherokee, North Carolina.

Protocol #7–Communicating Through Authority and Decisions

Relationships are built on points of agreement. Make lists; document what you agree to/on. Live up to agreements, every day. If collaborating, offer review, edit, and approval well before the product deadline.

Points of Protocol for Working with Tribes,
Confederated Tribes of the Umatilla Indian Reservation
January 2008

We often ignore the fact that the authority we carry with our position in government and business and the decisions we make are communication elements in themselves We can either abuse that authority or use it wisely, and the idea of "authority" is especially tricky in the American Indian community because it was so often abused in the past.

Authority can be defined as the "right bestowed on us" within or for an organization to speak on behalf of, to make decisions, to negotiate, or to issue orders and directions. Decision-making, on the other hand, is the act of implementing that authority in written or verbal form to finalize an action or direction. In government it might be a decision on a project involving a sacred site, a policy decision on relationships, or a regulation on process. In the corporate world, it might be a decision on a right-of-way for digital cable, moving a business to a reservation or expanding a coal mine. Although these decisions are made internally within an organization, the organization does not de facto have the authority to implement them. That will require consultation with the tribal government whether the decision is on tribal, ceded, or traditional land or regarding policies that may affect tribes. Authority in these situations is diffuse and it is critical that parties identify authority figures early on.

When we meet with someone or an organization, we do so with a certain amount of authority. First, we have the authority to meet that person or group, otherwise we wouldn't be there. But the extent of that authority from that point on can be muddy. In other words, do you have the authority to speak for your organization? Do you have the authority to make agreements? Do you have the authority to make decisions? Do you have the authority to set direction?

Now, let's presume you are meeting with the tribal chair of a sovereign nation, an American Indian tribe. The tribal chair normally has a broad scope of authority to speak for the tribe. He can negotiate, in other words, make decisions and agreements on behalf of the tribal organization. Your authority, on the other hand, limits you to negotiating but not making a final decision or agreement. You will have to go back to your boss for the final decision.

In the discussion you finally get to the point where the tribal chair says, "We can agree on this."

But you say, "Yes, but I'll have to get final approval from my boss or Washington, D.C."

The tribal chair will wonder, "Why am I negotiating with you if you don't have the authority to make a final decision?"

This happens all too often in Indian country, and tribes become reluctant to work with just anyone in our organizations. The cause is most certainly that we assign an archeologist or lower-level staff to be a tribal liaison for our organization. Ivan Posey, chairman of the Eastern Shoshone Tribe in Wyoming, once told me, "Don't send your archeologist. We are not cultural resources!"[60] We fail to remember that tribes are sovereign entities and they deserve the same respect we would offer a corporate CEO, Governor of a state, Cabinet Secretary in the White House, Senator, or Congressman. When we meet with a tribal official that has the authority to speak for his or her government, we must respect that and offer someone from our organization that has the same level of authority. By sending someone with a lower level of authority to speak with a tribal chair we are sending a message that the

---

[60] Posey, Ivan. 2001. Interview by author. Video recording. February 4. Eastern Shoshone Tribal Office, Fort Washakie, Wyoming.

tribal chair is not as important as the person in our organization with the same level of authority.

So, your options are many. First, send the CEO or highest government official with the necessary authority to meet with the tribal official. This will take time and require dedication on behalf of your organization. You will have to ensure you are committed to allocating the time to make this work and realize that it could be a lengthy process taking possibly many months or even years. The benefit is that decisions and agreements can be made throughout the process without internal reviews and approvals.

Second, you might delegate the authority to a person in your organization to speak for the decision-maker and make agreements and decisions with the tribe. In this case you must trust your subordinates and stand behind whatever they agree to with the tribe. The worst thing that can happen is you delegate the authority to negotiate with the tribe, they work out an agreement, and you veto it. Going back to the tribe and saying, "I guess we can't do this" is the worst scenario that can happen. The tribes will be thinking, again, "Why did you waste my time sending someone who cannot speak and make decisions for your organization?"

And finally, if the negotiation process is expected to be long and protracted and you cannot dedicate the time, use a meeting with the tribal authority to decide on a method of delegating the process to lower-level staff in both organizations. These lower-level staff can flesh out details and provide a draft product to you and the tribal authority for review and final approval.

Bruce Sun Child, Chippewa-Cree, shared with me the following account that is a good lesson for all of us in the non-Indian world:

That's the biggest stumbling block we have … trying to work with the government and getting something negotiated, done, and signed. I think it would be easier to work with a private entity because that private entity has somebody up there that's at the top of the line that makes decisions. And you can negotiate with the people and get that decision made. I'll give you an example. I was given the authority on this water rights negotiation that we've been working on. It's been a long process but I got involved in it about three years ago when I became chairman of water resources. I give a lot of credit to the people that work in water resources. I'll give you an instance, there was an agreement I signed, we had a signing ceremony, we had cameras, we had photographers ... I signed it and they didn't sign it until six months later. And, after eighteen solicitors, you know the buck stops here, when you are working with the tribal government, the buck stops here. But, the buck apparently doesn't stop anywhere there—it just keeps rolling up the hill and rolling back down and you never get a firm commitment from anybody. And, that's the biggest stumbling block I see.[61]

There are many guidelines one has to consider when exercising authority and decision-making when working with tribes.

- Demonstrate that you have the authority to speak, negotiate, and make decisions for your organization. Too many times government and business officials go to tribes portraying that they have the authority to work with a given tribe and end up having the rug pulled out from under them. They go back to the tribe with a, "We can't do this" response. Outline at the beginning what authority you have and when negotiations or decisions might have to be elevated to a higher level. You might consider having your boss draft a letter with your authorities outlined and provide that to the tribal officials so there are no surprises down the road.

- Exercise your authority cautiously! Remember you are working with a sovereign government and you must respect that principle. Making the statement, "Here's what we are going to do," without proper tribal consultation is a path to destroying any potential relationship and trust with a tribe.

- Keep in mind that people will seek out the highest possible level of authority in your organization. This is a natural tendency to expedite the negotiation or planning process. Always protect your

---

[61] Sun Child, Bruce. 2002. Interview by author. Video recording. May 6. Chippewa-Cree Rocky Boys Indian Reservation Tribal Council Office, Box Elder, Montana.

authority and never allow someone at a higher level to intervene. When working on the Sacred Circle, my authority allowed me to make any and all decisions leading to a Historical Preservation Plan. However, many tribal members wanted my boss or even someone from Washington, D.C. to attend in lieu of me. I articulated many times over that I had the necessary authorities and my boss was not going to attend any of the meetings. Had my boss attended and become involved, the negotiating parties would have said to me, "Why are we dealing with you, where is your boss?"

- Use simple process and content decisions to build trust and relationships. A process decision is one that is not really substantive to the project or program you are working on but rather focuses on procedural mechanisms, such as a commitment to meet, a willingness to collaborate and consult, or a philosophical definition of your agency's policy on a subject. A content decision, on the other hand, is a decision that is substantive in nature, such as an action that directly affects the project, program, and the tribe. Your goal should be to send a message through these types of decisions that you are serious about working with a tribe.

The safest approach is to use process decisions for your organization that displays a clear willingness to work with the tribe. For example, you might make a declaration to the tribe that, "We are committed to sitting down with the tribe, entering into the consultation process, and begin collaborating" for a particular project or program.

Content decisions, on the other hand, are a little trickier and riskier. If you make a unilateral content decision, even a simple one, you may be doing so without tribal consultation. This basically violates the principles I am attempting to teach you—that of consulting and collaborating with tribes before decisions are made.

Let me share with you a story that illustrates how both process and content decisions work and how content decisions can potentially go wrong. It happened during the first large meeting, called by the tribes, between us and all the other entities involved with the

Sacred Circle. We were facing an enormous amount of hostility and skepticism. Relationships between tribes and government officials were practically non-existent. When the agenda arrived in the mail, we were scheduled for the first two hours, and then others were scheduled to tell us all the things our agency was doing wrong. We felt we had to make an impact and that we were serious about moving forward in the planning process with the tribes. So we spent hours upon hours strategically planning our approach. One of the strategies we decided on was to make some simple process decisions to display that we were serious and committed.

When our time came the first person in our organization talked about us as people; we had careers, families, interests, and were real people, not just bureaucrats. The second person talked about putting aside the draft environmental impact statement that had been prepared for the Sacred Circle saying, "We heard you and obviously no one is happy about it and we need to start over" (another process decision). Finally, as the authority figure for our organization, it was my turn. I told those in attendance that I had made three simple decisions: 1) that I was going to close the area one-quarter mile around the Sacred Circle to snowmobiling and signed the closure order right there (a content decision) ; 2) that I was going to close the area one-quarter mile around the Sacred Circle to camping and signed the closure order right there (another content decision); and 3) that we were going to consider the Sacred Circle a Traditional Cultural Site, not an archeological site (a process decision).

The response took us by surprise as we didn't realize the impact we had made with these four simple decisions. First, a tribal leader got up and said, "This is a federal government we have never seen before and we don't know how to respond and I have to touch you to see if you are real!" Then, the subsequent presentations and the meeting itself were suspended until the next day so all could gather their thoughts. When we returned the next morning the tribal officials had drafted a letter, as if written from me to the tribes, stating I would acknowledge them as "Consulting Parties" in the future planning process for the Sacred Circle. This was perfectly acceptable and where we wanted to go with the process. My only caveat was that we wanted the local county involved as a "Consulting Party" also to represent the interests of the non-Indian community. There was no objection; the letter was rewritten and signed.

I thought the use of simple decisions in this example was the foundation of a long-lasting trust and relationship building process that led to a successful collaborative outcome years later. To us this was all amazing stuff, that is, until Jack Trope, Executive Director for the Association on American Indian Affairs and counsel for many tribes on sacred site issues, shared with me the tribal interpretation of what I had done. His insights are very valuable because they help to illustrate the difference between process and content decisions:

> *My recollection of this event is a little different than yours, Larry, having been on the other side of the process. As I recall, when the [tribes were] discussing your decisions that night, they were ambivalent about what was happening because (even though they agreed with the substance) the content decisions had been made unilaterally without consultation. The proposal about becoming a "consulting party" was in some respects a response to, and not a result of, those decisions. I would not want your readers to think that making decisions on matters of great tribal interest (even simple ones such as the closure to camping and snowmobiles) without prior tribal consultation is a particularly good strategy, except in unusual circumstances …*

In other words, we were successful at that meeting because of our process decisions, but we really could have messed things up on the content decisions. It's also another good lesson about how we perceive reality based on our communication filters, depending on which side of the fence we are on.

For years, I thought we had been wildly successful that day, but come to find out we were really walking on thin ice—we made enough right decisions, though, to move the process forward. Most important, Jack later shared with me what worked so well. It was that the *message* we conveyed (a willingness to work with the tribes) came through the process decisions. The content decisions could have caused us to fail because we did not make them in consultation with the tribes. It is vital that you differentiate between process and content decisions and communicate a willingness to work with the tribe or tribes at every point along the process.

- Do not make decisions on-the-spot unless you are absolutely positive that is the direction you want to go. You have the right to think, caucus, consult, and mull over any proposed decision. The problem here is that if you are pressured to make a decision on-the-spot and make that decision, you are now committed to that direction. And, if you think later, "We really shouldn't do that," it's too late. You will be cast as just another official who breaks commitments and adds to the list of "broken promises" made to tribes. A better approach is to say, "I am willing to consider … " and allow yourself the time to make that consideration after evaluating all the pros and cons. Always think through various courses of action and their consequences to your organization and the tribes.

- Canvass tribal leaders on what you are thinking about regarding a particular decision. Meet with them individually, share your thoughts, get their feedback, and seriously consider their comments. However, be sure to take the time to show equal consideration to all tribes involved.

- Ask questions freely of tribal leaders about a direction you are considering. You might ask questions about tribal, social, cultural, historical, and off-reservation implications. Questioning will help you see the impacts of your action and show respect to the tribes by displaying that you are sincerely seeking their contributions. A government official once told me that people wanted to see their "fingerprints" on a decision. This is an excellent concept and when you question tribes about their concerns and considerations you must be sure that they are addressed in writing in the final decision so they can see how they affected your thinking and the decision. In other words, they want to see their "fingerprints" on your decision.

This truly reinforces the fact that you really listened and shows respect for the time and effort tribal leaders invested in offering substantive comment.

- Finally, always back up your decisions with good rationale: laws, regulations, policies, fiscal constraints, and so forth. As an aside, it is important that you educate tribal leaders on the decision space you have to work within. If you begin a collaborative planning process and don't articulate the limits of your authority, you are opening the process to any and all options regardless of fiscal, legal, or ethical constraints. With the Sacred Circle, we could have entertained many options regardless of cost and might have had proposals into the millions of dollars. It was important to say at the beginning that we had only $100,000, so options must be within that budget. Another constraint I always conveyed was that "I will not break the law" indicating that all options must be within the legal limitations I had to work within. If you don't outline your decision space initially you might put yourself in the position, again, of breaking commitments. The response from the tribes might be, "Well, you didn't say anything about this so why are we wasting the time talking about it?" The danger of a collaborative environment is that not all parties understand we all have a limited decision space defined by legal, fiscal, and ethical parameters. It is up to you to educate those involved to move the process along smoothly. So, from the beginning, always outline your decision space and the limitations that go with it.

On a final note I would like to spend a little time discussing gender issues. I'm often asked at my workshops if women, regardless of their level of authority, can be effective working with tribal leaders who are in most cases, but not always, men. The short answer is yes. Non-Indian women in government and the corporate world are and can be very effective working with tribal leaders. In most cases, the characteristics I see in women who are successful working with tribal leaders are patience, being at ease, and sociability. As you are seeing, these are very important characteristics when working with tribal leaders regardless of gender. So, apart from the authority women may have, their effectiveness in working with tribal leaders is on par or better than men. There are, however, gender issues about spirituality and ceremonies you need to be aware of. I address these issues in detail under Platinum Rule #6—Acknowledging Prayer and Spirituality.

Protocol #8–Body Language

Respect our people who believe that direct eye contact is disrespectful by most elders and leaders of the communities. The people of Standing Rock lower their eyes as a form of respect.

Cante Ethanhan Owaglake,
Speaking From The Heart, Customs and Norms for the Standing Rock Sioux Tribe
Standing Rock Tourism Alliance

We learn overtly and subtly in our mainstream culture that body language sends messages as we communicate. In western culture, we value eye contact, a firm handshake, and acknowledgement of a message through nodding and other expressions. We also read these expressions and form opinions about the person with whom we are communicating.

Let's evaluate a couple of these expressions. When we talk to someone, we expect eye contact. We are programmed in our society to conclude that when someone avoids eye contact by looking down or away, the person we are communicating with may be dishonest, not interested in what we are saying, distracted by other events, or is being disrespectful. Our judgments are reaffirmed by the lack of other gestures we expect to see, such as nodding, smiling, or a hand movement for emphasis. We don't consider that the behavior may have other causative origins such as cultural norms we do not understand.

A firm handshake is expected in the business world. Anything short of a firm handshake suggests to us that the person may be weak (wimpy), not interested in us, or uncomfortable in the situation. Again, we may not be aware of cultural implications of such behavior and draw erroneous conclusions.

In the American Indian culture both of the examples presented previously about eye contact and handshakes can send us erroneous messages and plug our communication filters. Many traditional American Indian people will not look a person in the eye when speaking, as this is considered disrespectful. Instead, they will look down or to the side. Direct eye contact can be misconstrued as being aggressive. Children are taught this from an early age and it becomes their pattern of behavior. Consider the young American Indian child in school for the first time. The teacher says, "Look at me when I talk to you!" which violates how that child was raised in his Indian family. As the child grows into adulthood honoring traditional Indian behaviors, such as the lack of direct eye contact, he or she can be labeled as aloof, inattentive, or rude by Anglo observers.

The handshake may also have cultural differences about which we draw conclusions. Many traditional American Indians consider a firm handshake as aggressive behavior, or in other cases the handshake itself is reserved for friendship. I interviewed a tribal member from the Fort Belknap Indian Community in Montana a couple of years ago, and Poncho told me that he reserves his handshakes for friends. If he doesn't know you how can he be your friend? So, when you offer your firm handshake and receive a limp hand in return, it might be a message as conveyed by Poncho of "I really don't want to do this but if you force yourself on me I'll give you a limp hand hoping you get the message."[62] I have a friend who is a tribal leader in Oregon. When I approach to greet him he will turn aside and not face me directly, obviously avoiding the handshake. But he will be cordial, friendly and talkative. What I don't do is chase him around the room demanding a handshake that many of us might feel is necessary. Respect the desires of the individual and the cultural norms he or she is operating under.

How might various elements of body language be misinterpreted? A summary of cultural differences relating to body language might look like this:

---

[62] Bigby, Poncho. 2002. Interview by author. Video recording. April 11. Fort Belknap Indian Community Tribal Office, Harlem, Montana.

Behavioral Cue	Anglo American Behavior	American Indian Behavior	Miscues
Eye Contact	Direct eye contact—a lack of eye contact indicates mistrust or suspicion	Sometimes little or no eye contact—direct eye contact might be considered disrespectful or aggressive behavior	We dismiss the person as being uninterested, not trustworthy, or suspicious of their motives if their eye contact is not direct
Physical Acknowledgment	Nodding of the head, hand gestures, smiling all indicate listening and interest	Little nodding of the head, no hand gestures or smiling—not considered necessary	We judge that the person is not interested or listening if there is no physical acknowledgment
Handshake	Expected greeting, firm indicates strength	Reserved for friendship—strong handshake may indicate aggression, may avoid	We judge that the person may be weak (wimpy) or not interested in us if the handshake is not firm
Pointing	Used to emphasize a point, person, or object	Pointing can be considered an act of aggression	We judge that the person is not interested or listening
Temperament	Assertive and anxious indicates interest, passion	Patient, passive and quiet—otherwise might be considered pushy or aggressive	We judge that the person is not interested or not listening if they are inexpressive

Our filters about body language don't allow us to consider other factors, such as culture, when first impressions are so swift and lasting. We need to step back and ask ourselves one important question: "Are *my* filters about *my* cultural norms missing the target and getting in the way of effectively communicating with this person?"

So, how do we in the non-Indian community respond to these value differences in body language? First, and most important, do not judge body language, but instead deeply explore your own values and ask, "Are there cultural values and behaviors here that I do not understand?" Second, be yourself. If you look at a person when talking, then continue doing so. Trying to mimic other cultural behaviors makes you look cumbersome and artificial. Just be sensitive to staring and crushing handshakes that we all read as aggressive. Third, as my past associate Velma Real Bird shared with me, American Indians know and understand the non-Indian culture and how you are going to act. They know that you look people in the eye when speaking. They know the standard greeting is a handshake. They know people use hand expressions to make a point. So, as she tells me, "Be you. We know what to expect and how you are supposed to act!"

Protocol #9–Humor in Communications

Respect our humor—teasing, joking, and laughing are a part of our culture.

Cante Ethanhan Owaglake,
Speaking From The Heart, Customs and Norms for the Standing Rock Sioux Tribe
Standing Rock Tourism Alliance

I was at a meeting a few years ago visiting with some friends at a break. Out of the corner of my eye I saw a group of Northern Cheyenne friends of mine I hadn't seen in a while. They were laughing and looking at me talking in their native language. I went over, greeted them and asked, "What's so funny?" They told me "Oh, we were just talking about how our white man friend is here and going to set us straight and keep us in line," and they all broke out laughing again. This is a perfect example of what we refer to as "Indian Humor." It's different and has some cultural foundations.

Horace Axtell, in his book *A Little Bit of Wisdom—Conversations with a Nez Perce Elder*, illustrates the cultural implications of teasing:

The reason I tease you is because I want you to be able to take this kind of teasing. Throughout your life you're going to be teased in many different ways. You'll be teased by wrongdoings. Maybe you'll be teased by women. Maybe by different things that will make you angry. I made you angry. Now you've got to make yourself strong so you can take all this. Because, it's just like a trial—a test—to see how you can withstand all these things that nag at you.[63]

In your professional relationship with tribes, humor and teasing are good signs. They are a sign that you have built a relationship and friendship worthy of humor and that trust has been built. Believe me, if you do not have a good relationship and foundation of trust, tribal leaders will not afford you the compliment of making you the brunt of a joke. It's also like

---

[63] Horace P. Axtell and Margo Aragon, excerpts from *A Little Bit of Wisdom: Conversations With a Nez Perce Elder*. Copyright © 1997 by Margo Aragon. Reprinted with the permission of Confluence Press.

a test, as Horace Axtell explains, to see how you will respond or react. It is a measure of you and what you are made of. It is a measure of how well you take teasing. It is a measure of the depth of the relationship you have built and whether you can be trusted. It is a measure of the friendship you have developed.

We need to think of humor in the non-Indian cultural environment. When we meet someone for the first or second time we normally do not tease that person. But, after we get to know that person we feel more comfortable and might display some humor via a subtle situation. This is really not much different than what we might find in the American Indian value system, but the point of the joke or humor is in a different direction—at you personally as a friend. Rather than take it personally, we need to look at it as a positive sign of acceptance and friendship.

When we look at the characteristics of Indian humor we can see some definite value differences. In Indian humor, the humor is via people and situations where one takes on self-humiliation. Indian humor comes across at the expense of the other person, the one being teased. In other words, the joke is on you. The humor, however, is not intended to be disrespectful, so we must learn to laugh at ourselves and the situation.

A final point we need to keep in mind is that, in the non-Indian culture, we develop relationships more rapidly and humor is accepted earlier in the relationship. This is typically not so in the American Indian value system when dealing with non-Indians. The time to develop the relationship and trust where teasing and humor are accepted is much longer. Remember, there is a sizing-up process tribal members go through to assess your worthiness, and humor is a good sign that you have passed the test.

Protocol #10–Dress Communicates

Respect our people by dressing in a proper manner—unkempt appearance, short skirts, or shorts at ceremonies, feasts and other tribal events is considered disrespectful.

Cante Ethanhan Owaglake,
Speaking From The Heart, Customs and Norms for the Standing Rock Sioux Tribe
Standing Rock Tourism Alliance

A number of years ago I was visiting with a friend that worked for a major telecommunications company I'll call XYZ Telecom.

I asked Deb, "How is your company's working relationship with the Tribe?"

She responded, "Oh, we get along great; we have a great working relationship."

Later I was visiting informally with the tribal chairman and asked him about the working relationship with XYZ Telecom.

He responded, "Boy, Larry, they just don't get it. They come in here with their New York lawyers dressed in three-piece suits. They just don't know how to do business with tribes."

Later I ran into Deb again and shared what I had learned.

She exclaimed, "We don't send any New York lawyers dressed in three-piece suites to the tribe! We go there ourselves." Then after a pause she stated, "Oh, my boss, he always dresses in a three-piece suit, even when he visits the reservation."

It's obvious to see what was happening here. Many tribes reside in relatively remote areas of the country and dress rather casually. When someone walks in dressed in a suit the impression is that they are from a big city or even look like an attorney. The point being that they don't fit in with the attire locals are accustomed to. So, when the locals see someone dressed in a three-piece suit their communication filters tell them this person is from the big city and probably a lawyer.

This story illustrates how tribal officials' filters, as well as our own, can become plugged, and thus we can draw erroneous conclusions based on what we each see. This is despite our good intentions.

I told Deb to tell her boss to quit wearing three-piece suits if they wanted to have a genuine relationship with that particular tribe.

When working in Indian country, you will experience a wide diversity of dress by tribal officials; from business casual to Indian formal to three-piece business suits. It's much the same as I have experienced with local government officials across the country. I have visited with county commissioners in remote counties of Montana dressed in jeans and cowboy shirts and those in large cities dressed in three-piece suits. So, it is extremely important that you consult with someone in the tribe to determine the appropriate dress when working with a tribe. Another means would be to visit the tribe when the council is in session and observe their dress. Your objective is to match—neither under- nor over-dress—for your audience.

One exception is what I call "Indian formal" dress. A tribal official once invited me to make a presentation at his committee meeting in the Pacific Northwest. I asked Antone, "What is the dress for this occasion?" He replied, "Formal, very formal." So, taking his advice I showed up wearing a dress shirt, slacks, tie, and coat. When I arrived I noticed I was way over-dressed and became concerned that I had missed something in the communication. Most people there, Indian and non-Indian, were dressed in what I would call "business casual." Then I met Antone for breakfast and noticed he was wearing a pair of pressed black pants, a decorated shirt without a tie, a vest with beaded decorations, and his hair was in braids with native decorations. That's when I discovered that there is a difference between what I define as formal and what Indian people might culturally define as formal, or what might be called "Indian formal." Even though I had gone through the process of attempting to communicate clearly about the dress code, one can see how my different definition of "formal" permitted me to jump to a flawed conclusion. In the end, it was relatively easy to adjust my attire by simply removing my tie to fit in with the crowd.

This leads to another point about dress; don't try to mimic the dress of Indian people by wearing attire, decorations, or jewelry you purchased at a local gift shop. Many tribal leaders have asked me to convey to government officials and business leaders that it can be insulting and patronizing for you to try to mimic Indian dress. Their advice is leave the turquoise bracelet or beaded necklace at home and dress as you normally would to fit the occasion.

And, as with any situation, there are exceptions. I was once given a beautiful beaded belt buckle as a gift by Hamen, a tribal official. A few weeks later I was attending a meeting of tribal officials and took my own advice and did not wear anything that resembled Indian dress. I met Hamen at the meeting after he had given me the belt buckle, and his first remark was, "Why aren't you wearing the belt buckle I gave you?" I told him, which was true, that I was so honored to receive the belt buckle that I had it mounted in a framed case to display in my office. Had I worn the belt buckle it would have obviously pleased him, but it might have offended other tribal leaders in attendance since they did not have a clue the belt buckle was a gift. Had I been at a meeting at the reservation where Hamen worked, I might have worn the belt buckle as an honor to him. As you can see, the issue of dress requires sensitivity to the specifics one faces in a diversity of situations. So, use good common sense and when in doubt, ask.

Finally, many government employees have uniforms issued to them. Think about the purpose of a uniform. It can be a means to communicate authority, identification, power, and/or standing. When meeting a police officer, the uniform obviously identifies the person as someone with authority and power, the authority to enforce law and order and the power to elicit a certain set of behaviors from you. You may feel subordinate when someone has this power of authority over you just because he or she is wearing a uniform and badge. In essence, it says you are not equal to that person. So it goes with tribal leaders if you show up at a meeting wearing your agency uniform. My advice is, don't wear a uniform when meeting with tribal leaders! Uniforms display a level of importance, authority, and standing, and your objective should be to create an environment where you are all on an equal level. That's what a government-to-government or a business-to-government relationship is all about—respecting the fact that Indian tribes are sovereign nations and you are communicating directly with their governments.

As an illustration, I once attended a meeting between a federal agency and a tribe. The federal officials all wore uniforms except one; he was dressed rather casually. To compound matters, the room was set with a stage up front where all the federal officials sat looking down at the tribal members below. This set-up did not create a respectful government-to-government environment, as the tribal government officials appeared to be subordinate. Clearly, the government official that received the most communication and respect was the one casually dressed who mingled with the tribal leaders. And, by the way, he did not sit on the stage with his colleagues.

Again, there are exceptions, and if you are performing in an official law-enforcement role then a uniform is appropriate.

It is so easy to take how we dress for granted and fail to consider the potential implications of how others read us. The above examples are a testament to how this can happen. It is obvious that dress communicates! By simply thinking beforehand how we present ourselves, we can make a huge difference in how we are perceived by tribal leaders. The result, of course, is achieving a positive relationship between you and tribal leaders.

Putting It Into Perspective

Communication protocols are meant to help make the communication situation more "user friendly" so that real communication can happen. When communication is open, ideas are flowing, and when that happens, trust is built. So what does all this mean to you as a government official or as a businessman or woman? Being sensitive to these communication protocols, and implementing them where appropriate, will make a significant difference in the time it will take to achieve your collaborative goal. I say collaborative because whatever "business" you want to transact with a tribe involves a process of understanding and considering the needs of the tribe and integrating them with your needs. This can only be accomplished through a strong communication channel that honors and respects the cultural differences we face. There are other factors that will help you achieve success in you mission, whatever that may be. And while I can never guarantee your success, I do know that if you have done your level best to honor the cultural differences between you and the tribe you're working with, your chances of achieving your goals are much, much greater.

6

Respect: The Foundation of Trust

Respect is the foundation of building trust. That holds true no matter what the situation. It is obvious that without respect one cannot expect to be effective or successful in building trust or those valuable relationships needed to accomplish work—any work. This is particularly true with American Indian tribes because respect is central to so much of what they believe, far more than in our Euro-centric, non-Indian world. We can learn much from American Indians about respect, which we can use in all aspects of our lives.

I cannot stress this point deeply enough. In the American Indian way of life respect is embedded in the culture, deeply rooted as a social norm. Respect is displayed repeatedly in much of what I have been talking about all along: in behavior towards elders, in communication by not interrupting, or through body language where direct eye contact or pointing may be considered aggressive and disrespectful. In order to grasp the depth of respect in the American Indian culture, I consulted a couple of American Indian experts on the subject. Jim St. Arnold, my Ojibwa friend from Michigan, relates that respect is all-encompassing and goes beyond interactions with people. He says:

For example, when you harvest a deer for food and clothing you give thanks to that deer for allowing itself to be taken by you—it is a gift. You respect that gift. Most everything in life is a gift and when you start disrespecting these gifts you start taking them for granted and eventually those gifts will not be given to you. The same goes for interactions amongst people. For instance, respecting an elder goes beyond them personally and includes what they have to offer in terms of wisdom, teaching, and material items. When you dishonor that respect towards an elder, you lose more than just the elder, but all the gifts they have to give you in life. It's like a circle, you give respect and you receive respect in a perpetual cycle. This is what is ingrained into American Indian society over eons and defines who they are.[64]

In business, although our goal is to successfully accomplish work, projects, or programs, the truth of the matter is the value of a strong relationship outweighs the work produced and the relationship only happens when there is respect, respect in the American Indian sense. Projects and programs come and go, but strong personal relationships live with a person throughout his or her life. Again, this is true in any interaction, not just with those in the American Indian community.

The first step to building trust is to practice good communication skills and honor cultural differences in communication situations. But there are other factors that come into play, all cultural, when you start building a relationship based on trust and respect in the American Indian community, and that is what this chapter is all about.

The Platinum Rule

We have all heard the Golden Rule, "Do unto others as you would have them do unto you." But, we are going a little further in our thinking and applying the Platinum Rule which says, "Do unto others as they would have you do unto them." There is a stark difference in these two rules. One assumes that everyone wants to be treated as we want to be treated; the other assumes we treat people as they want to be treated. This simple concept is significant when attempting to build trust and

---

[64] St. Arnold, Jim. 2010. Personal communication with author. April 5.

relationships with American Indian Tribes. If we apply the Platinum Rule we are honoring culture. We are applying the principles of mutual respect, and that is the only kind of respect that is worth all your care and attention.

Jim St. Arnold, again, shares what mutual respect looks like:

One of the things that needs to be done … is a level of mutual respect. As a tribal member you want and expect me to respect you … as a tribal member I want and expect you to respect me … as a tribal government that has certain needs, certain desires, certain things I may need. And, that respect has to go both ways. One of the things I have seen in my years as a tribal member and tribal leader … is certain people do not have that respect and aren't interested in giving it. They demand it but when it comes to returning it they do not want to do it and it becomes a wall.[65]

At the beginning of my workshops I always ask participants to think of one to three words that describe an effective working relationship with American Indian Tribes. The number one answer that comes up is *respect*. After the exercise I always ask, "How would I show you that I respect you? In other words, how would I put the word 'respect' into action?"

When we analyze the word respect—we find there are two very important words used to define respect: esteem and deference.[66] Esteem is "to feel or show admiration and deference toward somebody or something." Deference is "putting another person's interest first" or "submitting to the judgment, opinion, or wishes of another person." As we take this a step further, the phrase "in deference to," means "out of respect or courtesy to somebody or something." The other significant word defining respect is, "thoughtfulness" or "treating people in a kind and considerate way, especially by anticipating their wants or needs."

---

[65] St. Arnold, Jim. 2003. Interview by author. Video recording. January 6. Great Lakes Indian Fish and Wildlife Commission Office, Odanah, Wisconsin.

[66] Encarta® World English Dictionary [North American Edition] © & (P) 2009 Microsoft Corporation. http://encarta.msn.com/encnet/features/dictionary/DictionaryResults.aspx?lextype=3&search=respect

In the Indian way we have come around full circle and are back to the Platinum Rule—treating others as they wish to be treated. If we truly practice respect when we work in Indian country, not only can we anticipate their wants and needs, but we can learn culturally what important protocols are essential to *them*.

Oh, and do you want to know the answer to our exercise of how to put the word "respect" into action? It always comes back to, "Treating others as they want to be treated." It is, again, embodied in the Platinum Rule. With American Indian Tribes, the Platinum Rule means honoring the cultural protocol that you might be asked to follow when working in Indian country.

Revisiting Current History

In chapter 3 we touched upon how history affects the ability to build a relationship based on trust. Unfortunately, there are still examples of actions by government and business leaders today that continue to erode trust and make relationship building difficult. These can include breaking commitments, displaying personal biases, failing to consult when legally required, appearing to be pre-decisional, exercising poor judgment, losing control of actions and reactions, and more. The following account was shared with me by John Pretty On Top, Crow Tribe, about how trust continues to become eroded today:

For instance, the area Valley of the Shields, which is just south of Fromberg, near Warren, there's an area, it's a basin, that I call a pharmacy of medicinal plants. In that area there are some rock walls that have paintings of shields ... and they are well preserved. About six years ago, the [government] contacted our tribe when I was cultural director ... and we explored that area. We located all these sacred areas and plants and we came to find out there was possible oil drilling exploration that was to go on there. They told us there was a bid out and they wanted to make sure there would be nobody protesting against it. We went up there, inventoried everything, wrote letters of recommendation, and advised them they shouldn't do this because it's such a small area and to preserve it would be more feasible than to build roads all over it. Well, we found out they let contracts out on this area fifteen years ago, were approved, and ready to drill. They came that late and there was no way we could stop it because contracts were signed already.[67]

It is unfortunate that these instances, related by John, persist today and continue to erode our trust and relationship-building efforts. And, it is not only unfortunate for the agency directly involved, but for all others in the government and corporate world that have a desire to work with tribes. The lack of trust extends well beyond those directly involved. American Indian leaders, just as we individuals, get their communication filters plugged when they have a bad experience illustrated by one of the actions described above, and subsequently stereotype an entire class of people, such as government officials or people in the banking industry. John Pretty On Top, again, relates to me how this happens:

It could be you personally or it could be the service you work with. There might be some time when others in that service came and did something ... There's times the Crows go up to that mountain for tee-pee poles ... Sometimes these Crows will go beyond the area [established by the federal agency] because it's picked out so bad there's no good straight ones [left]. Then the ranger comes over and things start—they get mad and they not only get mad at the ranger, but they get mad at the service because that was one time part of our land and we still claim it ... Those are the things that reflect on anybody that's up there in uniform.[68]

Tribal leaders related another story to me about a comment a federal official made regarding the Sacred Circle. Agency officials and tribal consultants were reviewing a timber sale when one of the elders asked about the effects of the timber sale on the Sacred Circle. A federal official responded, "Oh, that pile of rocks? We can take a bulldozer and push it over the cliff!" That statement spawned a life of its own. Even years after I began working on the project, tribal leaders still reminded us

---

[67] Pretty On Top, John. 2001. Interview by author. Video recording. April 4. Crow Tribe Senior Center, Lodgegrass, Montana.
[68] Ibid

that someone from our organization made that derogatory statement. It was almost like we had said it ourselves. So, keep in mind that others, past or present, can damage the trust and relationship-building process despite your most honorable intentions. You have to earn trust again and rebuild those critical personal relationships.

But fortunately, the American Indians' long historical memory can work both ways. I have cited example after example of the negative side of it, but it can have a positive effect as well. In his book "Conversations with a Nez Perce Elder," Horace Axtell tells us exactly what our trust and relationship-building efforts should look like:

> One time the City of Asotin, Washington, was digging a pipeline. They were redoing their city water system. They were digging pretty deep and come across some remains. Two of them. So they stopped right there and they called the tribe. I have to commend these people from Asotin. The Tribe got ahold of me and took my singers—my Long House people—out there. We placed the remains, buried them and took care of them in the right way. And the city was so nice about it. It was so beautiful that they felt that way.[69]

This is the best of all possible worlds, and it illustrates what I said in the previous chapter—in order to rectify the past, we must work to create a future that has trust and respect in it. As you can see, the respect shown for the discovered remains led to a high level of trust and a relationship that will be invaluable to those in the City of Asotin and the Nez Perce Tribe well into the future.

So, how do I treat American Indians as they want to be treated? That's the heart of what follows. There are twelve Platinum Rules (again, leadership activities) that are culturally important to American Indian Tribes. Learn them, apply them, and you will shed the bureaucratic image, overcome fear and intimidation, understand time and exhibit patience, become a student of American Indian culture and history, build social relationships, and honor prayers and gift-giving. When you

---

[69] Horace P. Axtell and Margo Aragon, excerpts from *A Little Bit of Wisdom: Conversations With a Nez Perce Elder*. Copyright © 1997 by Margo Aragon. Reprinted with the permission of Confluence Press.

guarantee confidentiality on sensitive issues and are willing to be tested, you will see progress and be able to assist tribes with your resources. Then you will be able to celebrate success.

Please keep in mind that what follows is long but broken up into chapter-like chunks so that you are not overwhelmed with the information. Read it carefully and apply the lessons presented, and you will go a long way towards not only creating success for your own project but engendering goodwill for the future. Let's begin our journey to learning those "Twelve Platinum Rules."

Platinum Rule #1–Shed the Bureaucratic Image

Be direct, be straight, and tell the truth.

Points of Protocol for Working with Tribes,
Confederated Tribes of the Umatilla Indian Reservation
January 2008

No one likes a bureaucrat, if you think about it. Bureaucracies connote large, authoritative but faceless entities that don't care about the individual. Many of you work for government or corporate bureaus, but that doesn't mean that you have to look like a bureaucrat. Eddie Tullis, past chairman of the Poarch Band of Creek Indians in Alabama, offers this to help us all understand how the bureaucratic image is interpreted:

If you look at it in the worst sense of the word, to me, if I'm going to say what my kind of extreme negative point of a bureaucrat is, it's some person that comes in here, always [has] on a coat and tie regardless of what the weather condition, always [has] a briefcase with them, and most of the time [has] an attorney with them so they make sure they say everything proper ... and to me that's a real negative perspective of it because that [doesn't] serve them or us. You know you sweat down in a hurry in our country here if you come here with a coat and tie on and try and lug a briefcase around full of paper and everything else. And you waste a lot of time getting past those perceived notions because while apparently most politicians come here and think, "I'm here from the government and here to provide service," whereas the people that are here say, "Well, here's someone coming to check on me." [70]

As is evident by Eddie's account, our bureaucratic behaviors are dictated by our organizational culture; how we dress, the words we use, acronyms common to our profession, the way we greet a person, or how we conduct business. Many American Indian leaders will tell you, "I have to know you before I can trust you and I have to trust you before we

---

[70] Tullis, Eddie. 2004. Interview by author. Video recording. July 24. Poarch Band of Creek Indians Tribal Office, Atmore, Alabama.

can do business." That means the relationship comes first and business second. In the non-Indian world, I can sit down with someone from another organization and begin doing business almost immediately, or at least after a little small talk. But the American Indian way of doing business is different and is often dictated by historical distractions of government and corporate behaviors. As a result, we must slow down and focus on shedding that bureaucratic image.

So, let's explore what differentiates "bureaucratic" versus "personal" behavior. I have asked many tribal leaders to explain the characteristics of these two behaviors and have summarized the results in the table below.

	Bureaucratic Behaviors	Personal Behaviors
Relating to Relationships	<ul><li>Formal</li><li>Cool</li><li>Cautious</li><li>Big Words</li><li>Acronyms</li></ul>	<ul><li>Genuine</li><li>Authentic</li><li>Personal</li><li>Passionate</li><li>Open</li></ul>
Relating to Trust	<ul><li>"Can't Do It" Attitude</li><li>Responds with "No"</li><li>Breaks Commitments</li><li>Hard Line</li><li>Only One Way—My Way</li><li>Always Business</li></ul>	<ul><li>"Can Do" Attitude</li><li>Seeks Solutions Within Decision Space</li><li>Keeps Commitments</li><li>Educates</li><li>Social</li></ul>

We do not need to go into each of these behaviors in depth as they are rather self-explanatory. However, being genuine and authentic are two characteristics highly valued by tribal leaders. My past associate, Velma Real Bird, defined authenticity to participants at our workshops. She told our audience, "Don't try to mimic or imitate American Indians, do what's comfortable for you, but don't be afraid to step outside your own comfort zone if invited. Most importantly, be authentic—be yourself!"

We need to keep in mind that in those first meetings with tribal leaders you may be evaluated, sized-up, and tested (more on this later). Their goal is to see what you are made of, your values, your sincerity, and if you can be trusted. Remember, many government officials and business leaders have come to the tribe before you and history has made tribal leaders cautious and sometimes skeptical. I assure you that if you come in pushy, using big words, talk a lot and not listen, your stay will be brief and get you very little response.

In your initial meetings, the key behaviors that I believe will help you become successful are being genuine, authentic, personal, and passionate. Many times tribal leaders have asked me to attend one of their meetings "just to meet me" before any discussion or commitment is initiated on my proposal. In these instances, I usually bring a gift (more on this later, too) to thank the tribe for their time and engage in small talk. I am prepared to answer questions and follow the lead of the tribal leaders in the discussion. Most importantly, I am myself—genuine, authentic, personal, and I display a passion for tribal issues. And, I do a lot of listening. Only at the end of the discussion will I ask if we can schedule another meeting to discuss specifics of what I might have to offer. Many times these informal meetings can be accomplished with one or two individuals over lunch or coffee. In most cases these tribal representatives will be more than willing to provide advice about working with the tribal government or even offer to support your program or project when presented to the full council later on.

Marguerite Teller from the Paiute Tribe of Utah sums it up most appropriately:

> First ... Indian people, if they don't know you, they are going to just observe and ask some questions. But, if you come off too pushy ... you come in there and just want to take over or ... put this program into place ... you're not going to get a reaction. You're going to get the reaction like, "Whoa I don't think we want to work with him." [71]

---

[71] Teller, Marguarite. 2001. Interview by author. Video recording. August 27. Paiute Tribe of Utah Tribal Office, Cedar City.

Platinum Rule #2—Overcome Fear and Intimidation

fear (fēr) n, an uneasy feeling that something may happen contrary to one's hopes. v. To be apprehensive; to suspect[72]

Most of us have experienced emotions relating to fear and intimidation, that uneasy feeling that something may happen contrary to our expectations. Being apprehensive relates to having reservations or feeling threatened or frightened. These feelings can come from what we have experienced in the past, something someone might have told us, being in an unfamiliar situation, or benign ignorance about a situation. Fear and intimidation are two very real emotions people may feel when first attempting to work with American Indian tribes. You are stepping outside the comfort of your own cultural norms and entering into a world that can be unfamiliar and mysterious. These are emotions I have experienced many times, particularly in the early stages of building relationships with tribal individuals.

I recall a meeting in Denver a number of years ago regarding the Sacred Circle. It was very early in the collaborative process and we knew very few of the tribal representatives attending. I can still see Luke today, silhouetted against a large glass window with the sun shining in behind him. He was wearing his trademark baseball cap pulled down low on his forehead, his dark-shaded reflective sunglasses, a traditional Northern Cheyenne jacket, and he was staring right at me—at least that's what I felt. I couldn't get over the feeling that he obviously did not like what I was saying or who I represented.

At a break, Luke came over to me and confronted me with some very direct questions, obviously testing and probing my intent. He was direct without any personal or small talk. I was experiencing these very real emotions of fear and intimidation! Why? Simply because I did not know this individual who looked very menacing, intimidating, and threatening and because he was very direct in his communication, asking some uncharacteristically pointed questions. I was not familiar with this

---

[72] Webster's Dictionary and Thesaurus, Copyright © 1997 V. Nichols.

environment, was out of my comfort zone, did not understand what was going on, and he wouldn't take off those damned reflective sunglasses! After a couple of years I got to know Luke personally and found he had a heart of gold, and he became a very good friend. I learned that Luke was a leader with the Northern Cheyenne Crazy Dog Society whose role was to serve as protector of the tribe and its members. And he had a role to play—that of being threatening, intimidating, and menacing!

So, I want to help you erase these emotions of fear and intimidation. The more you understand what is happening, the more effective you will be in building trust and strong relationships with tribal leaders. These emotions can get in the way if they become manifested into actions or behaviors such as defensiveness, challenges, confrontations, or even meekness. Let's explore why we should be concerned about these emotions.

First, we may have perceptions about Indian people because of the way they act, dress, communicate or where they live, such as on a reservation. As I noted before, these stereotypes plug our "communication filters" and blur our objectivity. We begin to judge intentions, motives, or actions and become suspicious or feel threatened (part of the definition of fear). During this process we lose our authenticity and become someone we are not. I have seen people act on these emotions and become defensive because they did not understand what was going on. In defense, they would make verbal comments that sometimes verged on being insulting. And, in the process they would erase any progress they might have made in their discussions. Many times I had to pull these people aside and explain what was going on and that they could not let fear and intimidation rule their behavior.

Second, as I pointed out in the chapter on "communication filters," many people have biases about American Indians. When the biases are based on prejudice and cannot be overcome, they can instill in us fear and intimidation that can affect our behavior. If you, or anyone on your team, have biases, assumptions, stereotypes, or prejudices about American Indians that cannot be overcome, I strongly suggest you or they relinquish the role in attempting to work with the tribes. One cannot hide these attitudes as they will eventually be reflected, at least subtly, in one's presence, statements, and decisions. Ray Gachupin, Past Lieutenant Governor of the Pueblo of Jemez in New Mexico makes the same point very diplomatically:

> I think that when people, the government, are looking at assigning their people they need to look at the geography … And, if there's an individual that feels "I just don't think I can work with the Indian tribes" it's got to be put on the table. There's nothing wrong with being honest about it. There's nothing wrong with saying "I don't understand them, I'm intimidated by them, [and] I don't think I can work with them." At least they are being honest and maybe they don't need to be [t]here. Or, maybe an individual that has an open mind that's willing to come in and say, "I do want a chance to work with them [the tribe] and I do know they have a culture. It's a very strong culture…" And, they have to be pretty open-minded. They have to be sensitive to their [the tribe's] needs and to their [the tribe's] cultural identity. So, that's very critical for any individual to succeed in geography or an area where they are going to be dealing with native people.[73]

Finally, fear and intimidation go both ways. Many tribal leaders have told me they face these same emotions when working with non-Indian entities. They face overt racism, inequity, discrimination, and profiling. A woman from a Montana Indian reservation shared with me her apprehension about going into a local town on the outskirts of the reservation. She described how she would be ignored when going into a restaurant or followed around in a department store. I hear many stories of Indian people being followed around in department stores because of the stereotype that they are going to steal something. And, stereotypes become reinforced when an individual from a reservation gets arrested for drugs or drunkenness. Aaron Miles, of the Nez Perce Tribe in Idaho, puts it this way:

> I think the most common perceptions … of us as a group of people … is that we're poverty-stricken, and of course there's a lot of things

---

[73] Gachupin, Ray. 2006. Interview by author. Video recording. July 14. Pueblo of Jemez Office, Jemez Pueblo, New Mexico.

associated with poverty—drugs and alcohol, domestic violence, abuse in the family ... It's no fun having to talk about those things, but I think they should be talked about. It's not right for anybody else to come in and point out your problems knowing that you know what your problems are. It doesn't help when somebody comes in and kicks you when you are already down. When something happens in the community, and it's really bad and in the front page of the paper or the news, we have to face it as a tribe. One individual, a non-Indian, does the same thing, gets busted for drugs ... doesn't have to face that. Not all the white people in the ... valley have to face, you know, we don't point the finger back and say, "You guys are all bad people because of that."[74]

The significance of Aaron's statement is this. Many American Indian tribes have their own social issues and problems. The injustice is not that the one individual should face the consequences of drugs, alcohol, or abuse, but the entire tribe may pay the price of that one individual's actions or behavior. Therefore, many tribal members face emotions of fear and intimidation due to non-Indian perceptions that were learned from many years of segregation, stereotyping, and just being different culturally.

So, how do we overcome our own fears and feelings of intimidation when visiting a tribe?

First, be yourself. Be personable, be authentic, and above all be genuine. At this point, don't let emotions overcome your natural self.

Second, become a student of American Indian culture and history. The more you know, the more comfortable you become.

Third, walk in an American Indian's shoes. Visit the reservation and participate in social events and experience the culture.

Fourth, respect the American Indian culture by showing deference to cultural protocol and norms.

---

[74] Miles, Aaron. 2007. Interview by author. Video recording. May 22. Nez Perce Tribal Office, Lapwai, Idaho.

Fifth, develop friendships with American Indian people to facilitate understanding and enhance your comfort level.

And, finally, create a safe, thoughtful, courteous, and respectful environment when meeting with tribal leaders. Remember, fear and intimidation go both ways.

In chapter 4, I told you that my colleagues and I had attended a Cheyenne burial ceremony and about the fear and intimidation I experienced. The Northern Cheyenne who had passed away was my good friend Luke, the leader of the Northern Cheyenne Crazy Dog Society. A few years after we met, he received a severe electrical shock while working on a construction project in Busby, Montana. His brother, Steve, shared with me that Luke felt okay after the accident and went home. He was in a sweat lodge that evening and after the fourth prayer his heart stopped. He was only thirty-eight. Steve called me and some others who worked closely with Luke and asked if we could attend his traditional burial. He explained that the ceremonies last for three days before the traditional burial and hoped we could attend. That evening we drove to the Northern Cheyenne Reservation, arriving after dark.

The ranch house sat in a narrow canyon dotted with ponderosa pine. Rock outcroppings lined the ridges above the canyon highlighted by a full moon rising in the east. A teepee stood illuminated by lanterns near a large bonfire where many Northern Cheyenne people milled around talking and singing. As we pulled into the driveway and parked, a young man came out of the dark and asked tersely, "What are you doing here?" We explained that we were invited by Steve and looking for him. The young man said, "Follow me!" As we walked up the long driveway we approached the ranch house and the young man told us to wait on the porch.

Another man came out and said, "What are they doing here?" The younger one explained we were here to see Steve and he told us again to wait. Being that it was dark and we were in an unfamiliar situation and the terseness of the men, we had a feeling of intimidation and apprehension—that feeling of "What *am* I doing here?"

A few minutes later Steve came to the door, smiled, welcomed us, embraced us, and said, "Let's go see Luke." We no longer felt intimidated. Our fear vanished within those very few seconds. He continued to stay with us on and off throughout the night explaining and educating us on the cultural protocols relating to a traditional Northern Cheyenne burial.

The point is we are always going to have fears and become intimidated when placed in an environment out of our comfort zone. This is particularly true when we experience a situation that is culturally different from what we are used to. But, if you take the time to nurture relationships that spawn close friendships, the fear and intimidation issues evaporate readily. Yes, we will always have the nagging feelings of apprehension and nervousness, but they can be diminished by those priceless personal relationships.

Platinum Rule #3—Exhibit Patience with Time Issues

Respect our concept of time. Everyone arrives when they get there to a meeting.

Cante Ethanhan Owaglake,
Speaking From The Heart, Customs and Norms for the Standing Rock Sioux Tribe
Standing Rock Tourism Alliance

When working with American Indians, no two words generate more anger or humor than "Indian Time!" In my interviews with tribal leaders I always ask them to tell me about Indian Time. About half will say, "It's a most derogatory term," and the other half will say, "I live it." So, whether we agree or disagree on the concept of Indian Time, there are cultural issues with time we need to understand.

One of the many benefits of my work on relationship building with American Indian tribes across the country is that I continue to learn about other cultures. I was conducting a workshop in Thermopolis, Wyoming a few years ago and one participant was an attorney who practiced international law. He had traveled extensively around the world. When we were discussing Indian Time he made a comment that stuck with me. He stated that from a global perspective, we in North America are in the minority when it comes to time. Most continents operate on a more relaxed system of time than we do—what we might call Indian Time.

I was at a meeting on the Sacred Circle with another federal agency and numerous tribal organizations a number of years ago. James worked for the Federal Aviation Administration and is African-American. Our meeting was scheduled to begin around 9:00 a.m., at which time people started drifting in, drinking coffee and visiting. When we finally got started about 10:00 a.m., James leaned over to me and whispered, "These people (referring to American Indians) operate on CPT." I looked at him and said, "What in the world is CPT?" He said, "Colored People Time!" We both chuckled, but I learned another lesson; that time is definitely a cultural issue that encompasses numerous races and cultures.

Indian Time, in reality, is a stereotype, and while many chuckle, others think of it as a slur. The important point here is that not all American Indian people operate on what we call Indian Time. I have been to meetings with tribal leaders where time was critical, and you had to be prepared and on time. I have been to tribal council meetings that were informal and time was much more relaxed. I have numerous friends and acquaintances in the non-Indian community that are chronically late. I think about the times I have traveled to Washington, D.C. to visit with Congressional leaders or to a state capitol to visit with a Governor. I don't believe any of these people were ever on time. In fact, I remember waiting sometimes hours to meet with these government officials. The lesson is that we cannot stereotype any one class of people about time. We must adjust accordingly to each individual and situation.

Perry Mathews, the man with whom I first visited the Sacred Circle, gave me a very important perspective on Indian Time. When we were working together he took it out of the dichotomy of good-versus-bad. He explained that Indian Time is a concept that focuses on the end product being more important than the time it takes to get there. After thinking about Perry's comment it made a lot of sense to me, especially when you factor in cultural aspects that take additional time, such as the need to socialize before conducting business or being evaluated and sized-up before a tribal leader is willing to do business with you. It demonstrates that, in the American Indian culture, relationships are built first and business comes second.

Thus Indian Time could encompass the all important socializing that must take place before "business" can happen. A teacher from the Salish Tribe on the Flathead Reservation in Montana told participants at one of my workshops how business is done in their community. He said people get together, drink coffee and visit, and when business is ready to be conducted it will happen. Socializing is an important component prior to doing business. You do not rush into doing business.

However, Russ Townsend, Eastern Band of Cherokee, stated that when they have an appointment with their Chief at say, one o'clock, they don't show up ten minutes before because that could put undue pressure on the Chief. They are very prompt, arriving right at the appointed time, and they don't spend time visiting.

Solo Green, Nez Perce Tribe in Idaho, explains the philosophy of time very well:

Indian time, if you are thinking of it in that sense, is a good thing, a good thing because with native people time is not really of [the] essence. People should have as much time as they need to express themselves or to get a point across. A lot of times in today's world we're so programmed—we're too institutionalized, we're too busy, we're too active—it's a fast world today, a fast-paced world today and we don't give people the time that they need. Just like today, you mentioned an hour and for me if we're going to do it right, what if [it] takes longer than an hour? I'm not going to cut it off; we're going to keep going. That's how important it is and when we set up meetings and times with people we have to understand that. That sometimes it's going to take longer than we projected. But we need to make sure both sides are heard, all sides are heard. Because if I set up a meeting and I only go there to share my part of it I'm being unfair, because what if someone else has something to say?[75]

These examples show us that time is a "cultural value" that is as diverse as there are cultures. You can't fight, fast forward, or accelerate time when a particular culture chooses to operate on their individual traditional protocols. Patience and understanding are the keys. The following suggestions will assist you in bridging the cultural difference when dealing with time.

First, plan on more time to accomplish a project. With American Indian tribes it may mean arranging social meetings before business meetings. It may mean attending a ceremony, such as a Powwow or celebration, and coming back later to do business. It means taking the time to get to know the people before conducting business.

Second, use the time you may spend waiting for a meeting to begin to build trust and develop relationships. In other words, take pleasure

---

[75] Greene, Solo. 2007. Interview by author. Video recording. May 22. Nez Perce Tribal Office, Lapwai, Idaho.

in the time socializing and drinking a cup of coffee with a tribal leader while waiting for the meeting to begin.

Third, use the time to learn about a specific tribe. If your meeting has been delayed an hour or so, go to the cultural center or ask for a tour of the reservation. Introduce yourself to people in other departments and learn about their programs that might be related to your interests. In other words, don't waste your time fuming about when the meeting should have started; rather use it wisely to learn more about the tribe you are going to be working with.

Fourth, always find comfort in the fact that a quality outcome will almost always offset the time it takes to accomplish your goal. I have never been disappointed in the outcome even though my idea of the path to the end result was much different than what actually emerged. I remember I had an appointment with a tribal leader for some interviews in northern Montana. I drove about seven hours to get there and told the secretary I had an appointment with such and such leader. She said, "He's in Billings this week."

I responded "I was just through there three hours ago and could have met him there."

Fortunately, she chose to ignore my impatience and instead offered, "Would you like to meet with our tribal chairman?"

I said, of course, "That would be great!" So, I met with the chairman for about an hour and the end result was better than I ever expected. I recorded some great interviews with the chairman and others that I use in my workshops repeatedly. As I said before, the path I had in my mind was not the path I ended up taking, but the result was better than I could ever have hoped for.

When scheduling meetings with tribal leaders many people become frustrated regarding time issues. The following offers some hints to being more successful. As an added note, these suggestions were given to me by tribal leaders that experience the same time issues as you.

One of the most successful actions I have found, to date, is to use a priority-driven rather than a time-driven agenda. In other words, don't set specific times on your agenda; instead use a beginning and ending time only. I was working with a federal agency a number of years ago that scheduled a meeting with four tribes over a sacred site. The day before the meeting I met with officials from the agency to review the agenda. They had a traditional business agenda with start time, welcome, introductions, and list of topics with timeframes for each item. This sacred site issue was extremely sensitive to the tribes, and I told the agency officials that I didn't think this agenda would work, that the issue was too sensitive, and the meeting would probably begin with many speeches and continue throughout the day. I told them, with a time-driven agenda, they would have a tendency to cut people off in order to get back on their timeframe or become frustrated because they weren't getting to the topics they needed to discuss.

I suggested we revert to a priority-driven agenda that began with each person introducing themselves and answering one question, "Why is this site so important to you?" Then, we could use the remaining time to begin addressing issues important to the agency. As it turned out, it took the entire first day to go through the thirty or so introductions and answer that one question. Some took only a couple of minutes while others spoke freely for fifteen to twenty minutes. The next day we were able to address a number of the topics the agency needed answers to.

There are some important points about time that we can learn from this example: First, taking the time to allow tribal participants to offer opinions, feelings, and thoughts, puts that word respect into action. This process mimics the traditional American Indian way of doing business. On sensitive issues, such as a sacred site, this process of expressing opinions, thoughts, and feelings is going to happen despite your agenda.

Second, allowing participants to express their opinions, feelings, and thoughts helps achieve better understanding of the issues and results in better solutions.

Third, the time invested by asking that one question, "Why is this site so important to you?" saved more time in the long run and allowed the group to move on to the business of specifically addressing the issues both the agency and tribal leaders desired. In other words, understanding traditional protocol will save you time in the end.

A Choctaw tribal leader told me that he had the same problem of getting people to meetings on time. Terry Cole shared with me a technique he uses that works well. He schedules a social event the evening before the meeting, such as a reception with appetizers or even a meal and some kind of entertainment. This could be traditional dancers, story tellers, or a speaker (such as the tribal chief, governor, or chairman). People show up at the reception to socialize, then travel is not an issue when beginning the meeting the next morning.

Russ Townsend, from the Eastern Band of Cherokee, taught me how to put together an agenda to facilitate meetings beginning on time. He suggested scheduling the meeting to begin at 9:00 a.m. with coffee and pastries and time to socialize for an hour or so. Then, schedule the meeting to formally begin at 10:00 a.m. with an invocation and opening comments.

We must also realize that tribal leaders are extremely busy and have limited time. We need to appreciate that fact. The typical response from government and business leaders is, "Well, I'm very busy, too!" Let me contrast your "busy-ness" with a tribal leader's "busy-ness": First, within your organization you have programs to manage, budgets to compile, people to supervise, supervisors to answer to, and others to coordinate with. Basically, the constituencies you serve are limited to your organization or business focus. Tribal leaders do all the same things you do. Yet on the other hand, because of sovereignty, they are on the top of their organization where the so-called "buck" stops. The constituencies served are very broad, ranging from a tribal member looking for a job, to testifying before a congressional committee. The issues tribal leaders address on a daily basis might include social, health, education, law enforcement, telecommunications, housing, employment, natural resources, gaming, economic development, elder and child care, culture, transportation, and internal politics. In many cases, tribal leaders address these issues with a very limited staff compared to what we enjoy in federal, state, or local government or in the corporate world.

In addition, there are scores of government agencies and businesses which wish, or are required, to provide some program or service to tribes. For example, most federal and state governments have a policy requiring each agency to develop some kind of government-to-government relationship with their local Indian tribes. Multiply this by the myriad of government agencies in the area where the tribe resides, and you can easily see how the demands on their time become compounded. Therefore, you are competing with many others for the extremely limited time tribal leaders have available in any given day.

Finally, one common thread you see in these suggestions is that time is scheduled for socializing. Again, that goes back to the traditional way of doing business in many American Indian communities and displays respect. We must remember that age-old advice that patience is a virtue. So, use your time wisely and make the most of enriching your life by getting to know people, learning, and enjoying the journey. Anger, frustration, and impatience over time issues will do nothing more than tarnish that journey.

Platinum Rule #4–The Tribe is Your Client (or Customer)

Respect—earn it every day. Do your homework; learn about your potential partner. Usually the burden of educating new partners about us is left to us. Remember fundamental human courtesies and be aware that Native people have been dehumanized (in museums, literature, movies, and policies) for centuries.

Points of Protocol for Working with Tribes,
Confederated Tribes of the Umatilla Indian Reservation
January 2008

In the chapter on history, I advised you to learn the specific history of the tribe with whom you're working. This platinum rule is an extension of that idea, for within the history of any given tribe, you're not only going to learn the culture, but the ways in which they conduct their government and operate their businesses.

Whenever we approach a tribe to form a partnership, provide services, or sell our wares, we need to realize that they become our customer. We need to learn about the history, culture, and protocol before making that first approach. It may mean understanding the tribe's geography, both historical and recent, their heritage, the operation, structure, and protocols of their government, the way people live, and much more.

I use the following quote by Ivan Posey, Chairman of the Eastern Shoshone Business Council in Wyoming, as an introductory slide in my workshops:

> *… governments or agencies just don't know us. The biggest letdown of government agencies … they haven't educated themselves about us enough. We're lawyers, and foresters, and doctors, and teachers … in the present realm. That's one of the biggest letdowns—non-education [about] us.*[76]

Many times I have been asked the question from individuals in the non-Indian community, "Why are we in government and business

---

[76] Posey, Ivan. 2001. Interview by author. Video recording. February 4. Eastern Shoshone Tribal Office, Fort Washakie, Wyoming.

the ones expected to learn about American Indian history, culture, and protocol? Why can't tribes just operate like everyone else?" The answer is not simple, but a complex array of reasoning, one we need to understand. My first answer comes from Ivan again:

> *Right now we're still trying to adapt to running governments that [weren't] specifically ours ... from the societies, the clans, but in terms of having a chairman, elected councilmen, those types of things are basically a new form of government to us.*[77]

He continued to share with me that, in the past fifty years, many tribes have come a long way in adapting to these new forms of government. Others continue to operate under their traditional government styles and choose not to operate with what we might call "contemporary forms" of government. Because tribes are sovereign entities under the treaties, they have the right to form and operate their governments as they choose, just like state governments.

The second point is that because our society is a diversity of cultures, many of those cultures tend to lose, forget, or ignore their own heritage. Very few people in the United States speak the language of their heritage, be it Italian, German, Polish, French, Farsi, Swahili, etc. However, many in the American Indian community focus strongly on, and practice, their traditional culture to retain and revitalize it. That is why you see, on many reservations, traditional language programs in schools, traditional dances and ceremonies, traditional foods, and forms of government that might seem different to us. Many in the American Indian community continue to live and practice their traditional heritage for fear of compromising or losing it further.

Finally, if we broaden our perspective, we see that across our great country nothing is the same. For instance, the State of California has a government that operates with essentially a full-time legislature, much like our federal congress. But the State of Wyoming operates with a legislature that meets once a year for a couple of months, and every other year is a budget session. We can contrast many other situations also. Why

---

[77] Posey, Ivan. 2001. Interview by author. Video recording. February 4. Eastern Shoshone Tribal Office, Fort Washakie, Wyoming.

doesn't Washington State University operate like Harvard? Why doesn't the USDA Forest Service operate like the National Park Service? Why are gaming and gambling allowed by the State of Nevada and not by the State of Kentucky? Why does the State of Montana have an income tax and the State of Wyoming doesn't? Why doesn't Ford Motor Company operate like General Motors? Based on this diversity of choice, it is obvious there is no one "right way" to do things, and they all operate on the basis of their traditions, cultures, heritage, and the will of the people. All these entities have the right to choose how they function as long as their choice falls within the limits of the Constitution of the United States and other applicable legislation. When we tell ourselves that an individual, culture, or particular group of people should conform to our perceived notion of what we consider right or normal, we are disrespecting their right of choice. So, why don't American Indian tribes operate and function like everyone else? Because they have the right of choice like every other government and private entity in our country!

Now that we understand why it is important to appreciate the differences that tribes operate and function under, we can focus on how we can effectively learn about these other cultures and protocols. Eddie Tullis, Poarch Band of Creek Indians, shared with me the importance of learning about tribes:

> *Those people that come along and say, "I've got a million dollars to build an airport," and I say, "Well the first thing, does it have to be on a reservation?" And they say, "Oh yeah, it has to be on a reservation." Well you don't need to spend ... time with me if you're telling me [it has] to be on a reservation. I don't care how much money you have because I [don't have a] reservation to put it on. There's no use in me taking up my time and my staff's time trying to decide ... If we could make those runways in a circle we might fit it on here. You've got to understand your customer and you've got to understand the reservation and all before you really start doing that ... A lot of that is getting to know your customer, getting to establish that relationship.[78]*

---

[78] Tullis, Eddie. 2004. Interview by author. Video recording. July 24. Poarch Band of Creek Indians Tribal Office, Atmore, Alabama.

I've never looked at it that way but Eddie is correct. In any business transaction, "you've got to understand your customer," and customers want to know that you have done your homework. You take the time to learn a corporation's business culture. This is basic business stuff and we need to extend that same consideration and courtesy to any tribe. Just like with any other customer, we need to learn the things that put that all-encompassing word respect into action to make the best use of the tribe's time and resources.

Here are a few resources you can use to become better informed about tribes and their operations:

- Visit a tribe and/or reservation before coming to do business. I have found that tribes are very open to arranging tours or just showing you around. Learn about their programs, natural areas, housing, community center, senior center, transportation system, and anything else that might interest you.

- Most tribes have a cultural center that houses and preserves their history and traditions. Arrange for a visit and you can learn about their history, traditions, treaties, significant individuals, dress, ceremonies, and more.

- Books are a great resource; however I encourage you to ask a tribal leader or the director of their cultural center for a recommended book about their tribe. There are many books available on American Indians and not all are credible. Tribes usually have a favorite that represents their history and culture accurately.

- Visit the official Website of a tribe and I put emphasis on "official." If you Google "Cherokee Nation" you will get 1,530,000 results. Because of the ease of placing information on the Internet it contains a lot of misinformation. That is why I suggest only using the official Websites of tribes as they have control of what information is placed there and authenticate the accuracy of that information. Most tribes provide information on history and culture, a list of tribal government leaders, their treaties, programs they manage, enterprises, and contacts. Also, tribal Websites are a good start for learning the basics about a specific tribe. Many tribes in the West have tribal colleges and their Websites are a good source of information also.

- Participating in tribal events, such as Powwows, fairs, and other celebrations is a great way to learn about tribal traditions. In addition, your presence will most likely be noticed and display your interest in the tribe. Russ Townsend, Eastern Band of Cherokee, related to me the importance of attending these events:

The more you can do those kinds of things [attending tribal events] the more you can immerse yourself into the culture, the more you will be embraced by the culture. When we do have officials come up unrequested and uninvited on non-business-related trips because they want to bring their kids to the museum or come to the fall festival—that is good for them because they are learning about the culture and what makes it tick. But, it also sets us at ease because we realize if you are willing to take part in this society that you are probably not going to do anything untoward, you're not going to be overtly destructive or deceitful if you're willing to be part of that society. And we have government officials ... who are all willing to just show up because they like it and they like the people and that comes across the way they meet people and greet people and it carries [over to] when we get to go and have business with them.[79]

Many tribes publish a listing of their tribal events on their Website and in brochures. The information is readily available.

- Ceremonies, on the other hand, are typically by invitation only. If you hear of a ceremony being conducted by a tribe, do not assume it is open to the public. Ceremonies can be sweats, prayer services, traditional burials, pipe ceremonies, Sundances, or other sacred or spiritual events. If asked to attend a ceremony, you should always accept the invitation and consider it an honor to be invited. Attending these special events is a learning opportunity that extends deep into the culture—something that you will never experience unless you willingly participate. Jim St. Arnold shared with me the following:

---

[79] Townsend, Russ. 2003. Interview by author. Video recording. January 13. Eastern Band of Cherokee Indians Tribal Office, Cherokee, North Carolina.

Inviting you to a funeral is not only an honor for you but an honor to them that you came. Because if they had invited you and you had said, "No, you have other things to do," there is a good chance you would not have been invited back because they were offering you something they do not do all the time, they were offering you their friendship; they were offering you their respect. And, by accepting that, you are returning that respect. So, it's not only an honor for you to be there, but it's an honor for them to have you come, too.[80]

- Another learning tool we often take for granted is that of just being inquisitive, not being afraid to ask questions. In this world of being politically correct, we're often afraid that we might ask a wrong question or culturally insult someone. This is where friendship and strong personal relationships come into play. I was having dinner one evening with Steve, a Northern Cheyenne friend of mine. Steve and I had been working on the Sacred Circle for many years and developed what I would call a close relationship, but I was always curious why his last name was Brady, being not in any way a traditional Northern Cheyenne name. I said, "Steve, we've known each other for years; you speak the Cheyenne language fluently, you look Cheyenne, you dress in your native attire, you are very traditional, but how did you get the name Brady?" Now that was a very inquisitive question, and it took some guts for me to ask—but I had a good relationship with Steve and I wanted to know.

Steve shared with me that in the late 1800's one of his great grandfathers was being registered in the census, as all American Indians were, and the agent asked him his name. Steve's grandfather could not speak English so gave his name in the native Cheyenne language, which translates today as Braided Hair. After going back and forth, the frustrated agent said, "You are now Brady!" and enrolled him in the census under that name. I later learned that many American Indians had names assigned to them arbitrarily and you will even find Jeffersons, Lincolns, Washingtons, and many others. But, if it

---

[80] St. Arnold, Jim. 2003. Interview by author. Video recording. January 6. Great Lakes Indian Fish and Wildlife Commission Office, Odanah, Wisconsin.

hadn't been for that close relationship Steve and I shared, I would never have learned what I did.

In my workshops I always get asked, "What is the proper reference for American Indians in our country—Native American, American Indian, Native, Indigenous, or even Native American Indian?" This is a great question for you to ask in a one-on-one setting in your quest for learning with tribal leaders. My answer is, "It depends on whom you are talking to, as each tribe or individual might have their own preference." However, the safest way is to refer to a specific people by their tribal name. For example, rather than ask, "What do Indian people think about ... ?" or "What do Native Americans think about ... ?" ask "What would the Ojibwa people think about ... ?"

Another common question is, "When does one become an elder in a tribe?" The answer again varies amongst tribes. A tribal leader from the Paiute Tribe of Utah shared with me that an elder can be someone in their forties or fifties since many of the older people had passed away and few remained in the older age brackets. Another individual shared with me that you are considered an elder, "When a child brings you a plate of food." Again, this is a great question to ask when learning the culture of your new-found acquaintances.

I suggest that when you want to be inquisitive, keep your questions to a few. Don't bombard the person with a bunch of questions, rather ask a few pertinent questions and spend a lot of time listening. As always, listening is the key to learning and shows respect.

In your eagerness to learn, remember that you are not an expert, so never come across as one. Velma Real Bird informed participants in our workshops that she becomes concerned when a non-Indian, who has studied American Indian culture, tells her how Crow people should dress or that her beading (taught by her grandmothers) is not traditionally correct. You would be much better off asking, "I've read about Crow beading and was wondering if what I read is an accurate representation of how it is done?" Those of us in the non-Indian community can rarely be a true expert because we do not live and experience the culture on a daily basis.

I will provide a final caveat by using an example before closing this section on learning about your customer and tribal customs. I scheduled a meeting with a number of tribal elders on the San Juan Pueblo in New Mexico. I had a contact with the Pueblo who arranged the meeting, laid the groundwork, shared with me their cultural protocol, and introduced me to the elders. I had done everything culturally proper to prepare for the meeting. I brought gifts and spent time socializing with the elders over a meal. As I met with one of the elders, I explained my intentions to learn more about the Pueblo and asked, "Would you share with me a little about your culture?" I received absolutely no response. I asked again, and rephrased it, "I would like to learn a little about your Pueblo's history or culture and could you share with me some of it?" He responded, "Ah, history yes, culture no!" The lesson of course, is that some tribes are extremely reluctant to share information about their specific culture. However, other tribes are very open to sharing information about their culture and willing, in many cases, to allow you to experience it. So, in our quest for learning, we must respect the desire of an individual tribe regarding what they are willing to share. If you see that a tribe or individual is reluctant to share information about their culture, don't push it! Rather, shift the focus of your learning to the topic of history which is a much safer topic.

As said before, your willingness to learn about your customer and tribal customs will go a long way in building those all-important relationships. As you learn about tribes you will be better prepared to address issues in your work and personal life that might affect American Indians. Don't be afraid to demonstrate your knowledge by asking questions to further your learning and understanding, but again, you are not an expert, you have never walked in an American Indian's shoes. Continue to be a student of American Indian culture and history. It will unquestionably enhance your abilities to build strong relationships with tribal leaders and enrich you personally many times over.

Platinum Rule #5–Cultivate Social Relationships

Respect our people by spending time with small talk before you start asking questions.

Cante Ethanhan Owaglake,
Speaking From The Heart, Customs and Norms for the Standing Rock Sioux Tribe
Standing Rock Tourism Alliance

I have mentioned the importance of social relationships many times. This platinum rule delves into how we can actually develop and nurture those social relationships. My experiences have shown me that most of the encounters I have with tribal leaders often begin with a social contact. It might be as simple as chatting over a cup of coffee or engaging in small talk. But the process is critical, as it becomes a time when you are being sized-up to determine who you are, your honesty and openness, and your level of seriousness about working with the tribe. Much of this, as mentioned earlier, comes from the historical events that eroded trust between tribes and governments. In many American Indian communities, social relationships are the foundation of building trust and business relationships, and in many cases, must be accomplished before business is conducted. However, once trust is established through social contacts, the working relationship accelerates to the point where goals and objectives can be jointly achieved. Solo Greene, Nez Perce Tribe in Idaho, puts it this way:

> When you build those social relationships it strengthens our ties [and] our ties go a little bit further. It stretches us, but it also strengthens us because if something were to happen to me, whether financial, physical, or whatever it is, I have that tie with you. I can rely on you. And, I have faith and trust. My friend, he has my back. If I fall down he's going to pick me up, he's going to brush me off, he's going to help me back up. So, once you have those social relationships like that and we build them the right way, they're going to be really helpful down the

line. Because we're going to know we can trust each other, we can rely on each other. That's what it's all about, that's how important they are.[81]

I often share with clients that trust is built between the tribal leader and you as an individual, not between organizations. In a situation where social and business contacts are merged, the relationship becomes strong and business can be accomplished readily. One must keep in mind, again, that the relationship is personal, with business almost a secondary element. If you should leave your organization, the trust you built with tribal representatives will not automatically transfer to the next individual taking over your responsibilities. The new person will have to build that social and trusting relationship all over again. Simply put, trust is between individuals, not organizations. So, a caveat is to have more than one individual in your organization working with a tribe when building trust and relationships. Then, if one of you leaves your organization through reassignment, retirement, or resignation there is another person to carry on the relationship and business with the tribe. It avoids having to start from scratch again.

There are many side benefits to social relationships one must be aware of as they relate to the American Indian community. For example, it's much easier to address issues and work jointly on programs when a social relationship is developed. Our communication is not hindered by constantly wondering what the hidden agenda is or if this person is being straight with me. All those unknowns hopefully are revealed during the building of a social relationship, and business can be conducted in a more open environment. As I have pointed out before, the investment of time to build a social relationship will significantly offset the lost time of actually conducting business. After a social relationship is built, business can be accomplished much more efficiently and expeditiously.

Another valuable side benefit is that, in an emotionally heated discussion, the person you have built that social relationship with will avoid blaming or attacking you personally. For example, in the many meetings I have attended, heated discussions often lead to tribal leaders saying

---

[81] Greene, Solo. 2007. Interview by author. Video recording. May 22. Nez Perce Tribal Office, Lapwai, Idaho.

things directed personally at a government or business official. It might be in the form of, "You have broken all the promises you made to us in the years we have been working on the Sacred Circle," or "You have not been forthright with us and we have a hard time believing what you say." Notice the focus on "you" in these examples. In most cases, you were not the one personally responsible for these past actions, but the organization or someone in the past was. In the same situation where a strong social and personal relationship has been developed, the antagonistic behavior will be deflected from you personally to the system or organization you represent. The statements, rather, might sound like, "Your company has not been forthright and we have a hard time believing what they will do next." You still have the trust and social relationships you built on your side as an individual, and have the opportunity to continue your work in a positive atmosphere with the tribe.

Another positive benefit of social relationships is that you build alliances with tribal members that will protect the progress you made working together. At one of the last meetings we had on the Sacred Circle, we were passing out draft documents of a management plan for the site to tribal leaders when a reporter from the Associated Press literally grabbed a copy. I told him that the document was a draft and not available for public distribution as the tribes had not had a chance to review it. We were in a formal consultation process with the tribes that legally prohibited public distribution of the document until the tribes had had a chance to review it. The purpose was to ensure that no confidential information relating to sacred sites, practices, or archeological information was mistakenly divulged to the public. I also reminded him that much of this information was protected by federal statute. The reporter proceeded to tell me that his First Amendment Rights were being violated as it was a public document, and he demanded to keep the copy he took. I told him that he could send us a Freedom of Information Request for the document and we would then sanitize it of any confidential information tribal officials felt should not be divulged. The reporter stated that this was a public meeting, that there were government officials present and again demanded to keep the copy he took from us.

My friend, the late Luke Brady, finally stood up in his trademark baseball cap and reflective sun glasses and said, "My name is Luke Brady and I am the Headsman for the Crazy Dog Society of the Northern Cheyenne." He raised his hand over the meeting participants and said, "Our role is to protect our tribe and its people, and if you don't give that document back to him as he requested, I'm going to come over and break your arm to get it!" The reporter promptly pushed the document to me and said he still disagreed. Luke went over, shook the reporter's hand, and said "Thank you."

The point of this account is that in the past, before we had a strong social relationship with the tribal members, we would have most likely not been included in Luke's role as protector. We would have probably been required to address the issue with the reporter by ourselves. But, over the years, we developed that critical relationship with tribal representatives in our many meetings and social encounters and built a strong bond of trust amongst ourselves. Luke now included us government officials under the umbrella of protection for the work we had so excruciatingly accomplished together. Simply put, Luke was protecting the progress we had made together over all those years.

So, how does one build a social relationship with members of a tribe? Not much differently than with anyone else. It is simply a matter of dedicating the time and priority to do it. First, identify someone with whom you want to work in a tribe and invite them to lunch or coffee on what I call neutral turf. Offices and government buildings are not beneficial to building social relationships. It's difficult to get to know someone when you are visiting across a desk. In fact, a desk represents authority and creates an unequal atmosphere implying that the one sitting behind it has power over the one in front of it. Your objective in developing a social relationship is to get to know the individual at a personal level—so prepare to get a little personal. You need to share information about yourself, your family. You don't have to "bare all," but you do want to be open as well as express a sincere interest in getting to know the person sitting across from you. As I have mentioned many times, meeting a tribal member over a meal or in a relaxed atmosphere is culturally significant for many tribes. Remember the Platinum Rule—treat someone the way they wish to be treated.

Next, invite the tribal representatives to share their interests by asking simple questions. We often want to jump into business, but I encourage you to restrain yourself and focus your discussion on topics such as their family, job, and career, tribal customs, history, traditions, and so forth. As with anyone, the visit will become more relaxed and you will begin to build a bond that over time will lead to a strong, trusting relationship.

Opportunities to initiate social relationships are often missed or ignored during meetings. A situation I often see during meetings is when a break is called. We take fifteen minutes to use the restroom and get something to eat and drink. Then we all congregate at different places in the room visiting with people we know and are comfortable with. I say resist this temptation to visit solely with your own kind; instead, go over to the tribal representatives, introduce yourself if you don't know them, and engage in non-business conversation. This is a great way to build a social relationship. It's also a time when you can offer to meet another time for lunch or over coffee to further pursue that vital relationship.

As mentioned earlier, food is often culturally significant and meeting over a meal can be important. When organizing a meeting, I suggest you have lunch brought in to the participants. It doesn't have to be fancy; pizza, "sub" sandwiches, or even ordering off a menu will do. When the food gets there, remember to go over and sit with one or more of the tribal representatives. Engage in non-business conversation, use the time to get to know them, and allow them to get to know you. All these simple contacts we might take for granted are critical in the trust and relationship-building process with tribal leaders. And most importantly, use these informal visits to spawn future visits.

Thomas Jefferson, a man of many diverse talents, ideas, and friends, said it most eloquently: "I have never considered a difference of opinion in politics, in religion, in philosophy, as cause for withdrawing from a friend."[82] While it is true he owned slaves, his point is well taken in the

---

[82] University of Virginia Library, The Jeffersonian Cyclopedia, *A Comprehensive Collection of the Views of Thomas Jefferson*, Quotation 3283, FRIENDSHIP, Enduring, http://etext.lib.virginia.edu/jefferson/quotations/foley/

context that one can have many differences yet maintain a friendship. So it goes working with tribal leaders; you will have differences in values, culture, traditions, religion, politics, policy, philosophy, and more. But, once you have sown that social relationship, you will forever cultivate and nurture the friendship.

Platinum Rule #6–Acknowledge Prayers and Spirituality

Respect our people and stand when we give the meal prayer or pray for the people.

Cante Ethanhan Owaglake,
Speaking From The Heart, Customs and Norms for the Standing Rock Sioux Tribe
Standing Rock Tourism Alliance

As I have told you, my first meeting in the early 1990's on the Sacred Circle began with a typical agenda: welcome, introduction, and then a discussion of issues. Shortly after the welcoming address I remember the late Francis Brown, the man who told me when we first met that we would handle all our issues in court and one of the first American Indians to extend his friendship to me, stood up at the meeting and said, "We haven't had a prayer yet!" This is where I began my journey of learning about the importance of prayer in the American Indian tradition. I do not profess to be an expert in American Indian spirituality, but I understand the basics enough to know that offering and honoring the wishes of tribal leaders to open a meeting with a prayer shows that you respect tradition and culture.

Many in the non-Indian community may have difficulty blending spiritual issues with business. I have learned that this spirituality, in many cases, is a blend of traditional and Christian values. This is due in part to the missionaries sent out in the 1800's to convert American Indians to what they considered "a more civilized culture." In addition, I was soon taught that in many tribes there is no word in their native language for what we label as "religion." Rather, spirituality, in a traditional sense, can be described as a spiritual or sacred belief without the breakdown of what we know as denominations, such as Lutheran or Catholic, Methodist or Muslim.

Velma Real Bird used to tell participants at our workshops that American Indian life historically was tough. One never knew what one would face any given day, but one always faced the potential for death or injury. You could be shot by an enemy, trampled by a herd of buffalo, frozen to death on a cold winter day, or succumb to deadly diseases brought from foreign travelers. So, one might pray many times each day to the Creator for strength to endure whatever misfortune might happen on that given day or during that particular event.

After attending many tribal events, from council meetings to festivals to conferences to ceremonies, I soon learned that, most always, they begin and end with a prayer. John Pretty On Top explains the importance of prayers this way:

When there's that gathering, when there's business, when there's something important, they want permission from the Creator before they start and with his blessing everything will be successful ... and it has to be done in [our] language because that's how we express ourselves. And, a lot of them will say if you bear with me I will say my prayer in my own language. That's from his heart, from his mind and from his mouth and it has to be that language.[83]

And so it goes with meetings between government, business, and tribal officials; there is the desire and wish to carry on the tradition of prayer to begin and end an event. I cannot overstate the importance of acknowledging this traditional and cultural practice, and you should welcome and embrace the desire for tribal leaders to begin your meetings with a few spiritual words.

There is one more very important point about this protocol on prayer. The prayer is usually given by an elder or spiritual person selected by the tribal officials in their native tongue. I recall a workshop I held in Thermopolis, Wyoming, a few years back. I asked Burton Hutchinson, Chairman of the Northern Arapaho Business Council, if he would like to begin our workshop with a prayer, as we had numerous tribal representatives present. I also wanted to illustrate to participants the process as an experiential learning demonstration. Burton said, "I'm not the eldest, Eugene is." I asked him if he would like to ask Eugene to offer a prayer. So, Burton approached Eugene and they were whispering and pointing to Star, an Eastern Shoshone elder. Finally, Eugene stated that

---

[83] Pretty On Top, John. 2001. Interview by author. Video recording. April 4. Crow Tribe Senior Center, Lodgegrass, Montana.

Star was the eldest and should give the prayer. Burton then approached Star and asked him if he would like to offer the prayer. Star agreed, came to the front of the room and offered a prayer in his native language. Even between tribes one can see that there is high regard for ensuring the proper individual is selected to offer the prayer.

In most cases, the person offering the prayer will tell all the people at the meeting what they are going to pray for in English. The late Poncho Bigby, Fort Belknap Indian Community, explained it this way:

> *It's a way to ask him [the Creator] to help those that are at that meeting and then at the same time ask the Creator to bestow blessing on those who are sick, who are unable to make it for various reasons, or are having trouble. So it's a way to not only set the tone of the meeting but to also ask the Creator for help not only for those who are there but those unable to make it who are sick and who may be in the Service.* [84]

Matthew Gachupin, Sr., past First Lieutenant Governor for the Pueblo of Jemez in New Mexico, adds:

> *The opening prayers usually deal with why we are there and also to ask the spirits, the spirit world, to help us with the meeting and to get a better understanding from our level ... and for our return that we have a good travel ... and get back to our destination. And to help us with understanding whoever's involved; Anglos [and] other parties involved. To get a better understanding of why we are there [and] to resolve the issues we are talking about ... and to leave in good faith and understanding.* [85]

How does a government official or business leader honor American Indian traditions by wanting to include a prayer at an event? The process is fairly simple, but critical, and takes a little coordination. First, if a prayer has not been planned in a meeting agenda, you merely approach a tribal leader and ask, "Would you be interested in beginning the meeting with a prayer?" much like I did with Burton. However, don't put

---

[84] Bigby, Poncho. 2002. Interview by author. Video recording. April 11. Fort Belknap Indian Community Tribal Office, Harlem, Montana.

[85] Gachupin, Matthew. 2006. Interview by author. Video recording. July 14. Pueblo of Jemez Office, Jemez Pueblo, New Mexico.

yourself in the position of canvassing the room and trying to identify the eldest or a spiritual leader—that is not your role. You do not know who might be the eldest or who is truly considered a spiritual leader. If a number of tribes are present, gather the leaders together before the meeting and make the same request. They will figure out the correct protocol for the person who should provide the opening and ending prayers for your event.

The most respectful approach is to give the tribe a call and ask if they would like to begin and end the event with a prayer. This should be done when you are planning your event agenda, well before the meeting. The tribal leader will then make arrangements and you can simply place it on the agenda as "Opening Prayer" and "Ending Prayer." This again demonstrates respect for the American Indian culture and facilitates trust and relationship building.

One final note on prayers: it is customary to provide a gift for the person offering the prayer and compensation for his or her travel if that person is not a part of your event. The next section on gift giving will provide you with ideas on how to do this.

Sacred ceremonies are another part of spirituality you may be invited to participate in once trust is built between you and a given tribal individual. These ceremonies, as I mentioned earlier, are usually by invitation only and may include sweats, burials, dances, or prayers. If you are ever invited, you should willingly accept the offer as it is an honor to you. Don't be shy or think you won't know what's going on. I have never been left alone to figure out what was taking place—there was always someone guiding and explaining what was happening. Indian people realize this is new to you and that you might be uncomfortable, so just follow the lead of your mentor or instructions given by the spiritual leader and value the experience.

You need to be sensitive to the fact that there might be gender issues when attending sacred ceremonies. I'll be blunt—the gender "issue" involves menstrual cycles. This is not a negative factor at all. First, a woman's ability to bring life into the world is considered a *great power.* The menstrual cycle is thus considered very powerful as well. Historically, when on their menstrual cycle, women were often isolated and taken great care of out of respect for their power. This is why women, when menstruating, may not be able to attend a ceremony. This great energy and power can interfere with spiritual leaders and the ceremony itself.

Let me share a story to emphasize this point. The late John Tarnese, an Eastern Shoshone friend and teacher of mine, called and offered to come to one of our houses to hold a sacred prayer ceremony. We readily accepted and a half dozen of us arrived at the agreed-to time. John and his wife, Vergene, took time to explain how the ceremony was to be performed and offered one caveat—any woman on her menstrual cycle should excuse herself and not participate. No one left. So, John began the ceremony and after about forty-five minutes he abruptly stopped saying, "Something is interfering with my prayers. I can't connect and communicate my prayers to the spirits." Vergene also noticed and said, "Something is wrong here. John just can't get into it." When the ceremony ended, one of the women came up and said, "I'm sorry! I'm on my period and I really didn't think it would make any difference." Needless to say, she felt terrible and embarrassed. The moral to the story is clear. When invited and participating in a sacred ceremony, respect the wishes and instruction of the spiritual leader. You cannot predict the effects of what you do not know!

Platinum Rule #7–The Spirit of Gift Giving

Respect our elders and leaders when asking for information by offering a small gift like tobacco (tobacco is considered sacred), or food, before you ask questions.

Cante Ethanhan Owaglake,
Speaking From The Heart, Customs and Norms for the Standing Rock Sioux Tribe
Standing Rock Tourism Alliance

Gift giving has a special meaning in the American Indian culture, and presenting gifts is a legitimate practice which government and business officials can perform. Gifts provided by a government official or business leader demonstrate that you, again, respect the American Indian culture and are willing to reach out and treat them as they wish to be treated culturally. And, gift-giving goes both ways. Many times government officials or business leaders may be honored with a gift from a tribal representative for something they have done. I, myself, have received many gifts from tribal representatives attending our workshops. These gifts are given in appreciation for the work I do in furthering relationship building between government and business officials and American Indian tribes. To refuse a gift can be considered improper in a cultural sense. Jim St. Arnold shared with me:

> *[Gift giving] is appropriate. What is inappropriate is if [you] are offered gifts and refuse them; that is not proper. Even if [you] take the gift and give it to someone else later on ... And I won't speak for other cultures, but among the Ojibwa I was taught that gift-giving, I should point out, is a very important part of our ceremonies. I was taught it's our way of showing respect; it's our way of honoring, our way of thanking the person for being there.*[86]

Gift-giving goes back centuries as a practice performed by most American Indian tribes across the country. Velma Real Bird shared with workshop participants that gift-giving is a way to honor an individual

---

[86] St. Arnold, Jim. 2003. Interview by author. Video recording. January 6. Great Lakes Indian Fish and Wildlife Commission Office, Odanah, Wisconsin.

for doing something special, such as offering a prayer, participating in an interview, helping with a project, recognizing an accomplishment, or, in many of my cases, providing cultural information. Gift-giving also symbolizes the desire for greater accomplishments and a positive outcome in the future.

James Bird, past Tribal Historic Preservation Officer for the Eastern Cherokee Tribe in North Carolina, explains it this way:

When you come to someone, you want something; you don't come empty-handed. You make an offering and this shows respect because you are in our house so you brought something in return. If you are asking for our opinions, if you are asking for our assistance, it's a good thing to come with something to show you have respect. I think it also helps Indian people understand that you are being honest about your purpose and the role you are playing on behalf of your agency.[87]

Robert Thrower, Tribal Historic Preservation Officer for the Poarch Band of Creeks in Alabama adds:

I greatly respect people when I see them come in and give, particularly to our leaders and our elders, and give them some tobacco. It doesn't really matter to me what it is if they make that gesture of giving. It's an affirmation of our culture to me ... it goes back to sharing in the old days. I'll tell you it breaks the ice, especially in a new setting, and facilitates a more open exchange of things because that person at least thought ahead of time ... and it's an act of respect.[88]

However, the giving of gifts should not be routine, but reserved as a special "thank you" for providing assistance, meeting with you, providing information, or honoring an individual. In addition, gifts need not be elaborate and can be something as simple as providing coffee and food for a meeting or event. I will discuss your options for providing gifts a little later in this section.

---

[87] Bird, James. 2003. Interview with author. Video recording. January 13. Eastern Band of Cherokee Indians Tribal Office, Cherokee, North Carolina.

[88] Thrower, Robert. 2004. Interview by author. Video recording. July 24. Poarch Band of Creek Indians Tribal Office, Atmore, Alabama.

Many government officials and business leaders will say that they cannot accept gifts because of ethics rules. I need to put this into perspective and will convince you that it is both ethically and legally appropriate to accept a gift from a tribe or tribal representative. First, we must always remember that we are working with a sovereign entity—the tribal government. As an analogy, the president often travels abroad and receives gifts from foreign leaders. These gifts are cataloged and become the property of the United States government. When working with tribes you are working in a government-to-government, business-to-tribal government, or business-to-tribal business relationship. Second, most federal, state and local government and corporate ethics rules allow officials to keep gifts at a lesser value, somewhere in the neighborhood of twenty-five dollars. The amount varies between agencies and corporations. So, if you receive a coffee cup with the tribe's logo inscribed on it as a gift, in most cases you can keep it personally. But, what if the tribe gives you an expensive gift? Again, you accept the gift graciously, now on behalf of your organization, and take the gift back to your office. You then place the gift in a display case or hang it on the wall in your conference room with a plaque showing who and why the gift was given. The gift becomes the property of your organization.

A federal official shared with me that she was given a very expensive Pendleton Blanket from a tribe for the work they had accomplished together. Obviously, the tribe was greatly appreciative of the work she had done and wanted to honor her. She accepted the blanket and took it back to her office where her supervisor told her, "We can't accept gifts and now we have to give it back to the tribe." Again, this is considered inappropriate and unnecessary if one is open and truly understands the ethics rules governing receiving gifts. First, the blanket was given from a sovereign entity, the tribal government, to, in this case, a federal government agency. Second, the blanket could have been received on behalf of her organization. And, finally, the gift could have been respectfully displayed in the organization's office. If the government employee had taken the gift home and kept it personally, she would obviously have violated ethics rules. I highly recommend that officials in both government and business consult with their local ethics officials in their organization regarding giving and receiving gifts. Keep in mind that some tribes have ethics rules about accepting gifts, also. Consult with your tribal contact and ask what is appropriate.

There is a caveat that one should be aware of when presenting gifts to a tribe. If you are working with one individual then it is appropriate to offer that person a gift. But, what if you are working with a number of tribal representatives? The protocol here is to provide a number of different gifts and present them to the tribal leader. He or she will then distribute the gifts to the other tribal representatives in a manner consistent with the value of their work. You do not know what goes on behind the scenes as far as amount and value of the work. For example, when we completed our work on the Sacred Circle, we presented the tribal leader with a number of traditional gifts: Sweetgrass braids, blankets, tobacco, colored cloth, and other items. The tribal leader then distributed the gifts to others. We knew who the leader was but did not know the value and amount of work that went on behind the scenes.

Now that we understand the importance and protocol of gift giving, what can you do to facilitate this practice to exhibit respect and to honor tribal representatives? There are many options for you, and gifts received from tribal representatives are a good indicator of what is appropriate. Therefore, gifts can be categorized four different ways:

First, we have gifts that are related to ceremonies such as tobacco, Sweetgrass, cedar and sage bundles, and other items. All are readily available at shops and stores that specialize in American Indian traditional items. They are used in prayer ceremonies in various ways. These herbs are considered sacred and the smoke is used to carry prayers to the Creator or ask for intercession much like incense is used in churches. Or it is used in purification ceremonies where one washes oneself with the smoke.

I have been told that tobacco is at the top of the list, but one needs to use caution when offering tobacco as a gift because it is considered very sacred. I say this based on an experience I had with the Blackfeet Tribe in northern Montana. I was meeting with three individuals and presented each of them with a box of Prince Albert, a common form of tobacco used by tribal members. The first individual took the box and thanked me for the gift. The second individual took the box, put it in his pocket and didn't utter a word. The third, Fish, looked at me and said, "I don't smoke!" I told him it was a gift in appreciation for him spending time with me. He stated, "I use natural tobacco like kinnikinnick, sage, and cedar." I looked at Fish and said, "Fish, you got me. I don't know what to do!" He laughed and said, "Larry, I'm just trying to teach you a lesson. Some will consider you a wannabe when you give tobacco and consider it offensive or patronizing. It is much safer if you give coffee mugs, pens, and those sorts of items rather than tobacco." I told him "I have Sweetgrass," and he said, "That's perfect and much safer." Fish taught me a good lesson. I still give tobacco as a gift, but much more cautiously than before.

Many times when I have given tobacco as a gift, it is received with no acknowledgment. The receiver takes it and puts it in his or her pocket and continues on with other conversation. I asked a lady from the Blackfeet Nation, Darnell, about this protocol and what the meaning of it was. She told me that when the tobacco is received that means it was accepted as a gift; no verbal acknowledgement is necessary. If the gift was not taken, as in the case with Fish, the gift is refused. Knowing these small signals will help you understand how the process works and avoid any confusion you might have.

Other sacred herbs, such as Sweetgrass, cedar, and sage have always been readily accepted. I once gave a Sweetgrass braid to a Paiute lady from Utah in appreciation for allowing me to interview her for my workshops. She accepted the Sweetgrass braid and said, "Now that I have accepted this from you I have to tell you the truth." I thought, that would be nice, but the lesson teaches us the influence and importance of certain gifts.

The second category of gifts is traditional American Indian objects, such as blankets, jewelry, decorated feathers, belt buckles, pottery, fetishes, and figurines. As an example, I have received hand-made carvings, decorated feathers, beaded belt buckles, beaded necklaces, miniature drums and teepees, and pictures as gifts. These items are typically hand-crafted by local artists and have special meaning, and many were made by the individual themselves. Blankets, Pendleton specifically, have special meaning. The late Poncho Bigby, Fort Belknap Indian Community, told me the symbolism of blankets:

> *In the days of the buffalo the gift usually consisted of something they could use. Maybe some food or a weapon of some type, or maybe a buffalo robe, or a parfleche or horse or something like that. But in today's society, we don't need those things and we don't use those things anymore. The thing that has replaced them is the blanket as a symbol of the meaning of the buffalo robe. It not only keeps you warm, but it shelters you from the cold and it envelops you in a sense of well being. So, it's a symbolic gesture on the part of those being honored by their presence.* [89]

Gifts in this category are well-received and safe so long as they are not cheap imitations. Make sure they are not made in China or Taiwan. Most tribes have local gift shops that sell items crafted by local artists. Purchasing these items from local businesses on the reservation or affiliated with the tribe demonstrates you are sincere and willing to support their local economy. Consult with your local tribal contact regarding where one can acquire these types of gifts.

The third category of gifts is food items. I have always known that food is an important focal point in many tribal events, but I never considered the importance of food as a gift. At many of our meetings on the Sacred Circle we brought pastries, coffee, and sometimes lunch to the meetings. Sometimes we purchased the food items and other times provided home-baked items. Looking back, I now realize this was integral to the trust and relationship-building process as it served two purposes: The food was considered a gift from us and it allowed time to visit during breaks or lunch to talk about subjects other than business. And, it allowed us time to get to know each other on a personal basis. James Bird, Eastern Band of Cherokee, explains the importance of food this way:

---

[89] Bigby, Poncho. 2002. Interview by author. Video recording. April 11. Fort Belknap Indian Community Tribal Office, Harlem, Montana.

Food, whenever someone comes to [our] house, they will ask if you are hungry or want something to eat. If you are going to convene a session it's always a good idea to have some sort of refreshments available for your guests. When we travel to your house, when you are convening and you ask somebody to attend, as a minimum you have donuts and coffee.[90]

A few years ago, I was working with a representative from the San Juan Pueblo in New Mexico. He arranged a meeting for me with elders from the Pueblo to learn a little about their history and protocol. He said we would have lunch at the senior center with the elders and after lunch I could visit with them individually. I asked him if it would be appropriate to bring a gift to the elders and what it should be. He told me "Yes! We'll go get some fresh fruit and put it in some baskets." So, we met the morning before lunch and went to the local grocery store where we found some nice baskets and fresh fruit—watermelons, peaches, cherries, oranges, apples, and more. He then introduced me to the elders and told them I had brought them a gift of fresh fruit and to help themselves. The elders rushed to the table and helped themselves to the fruit and thanked me in appreciation for the gift. The point of this example is that with the Pueblo representative's help, my meeting with the elders was very successful. He helped establish a level of trust by assisting me with the appropriate protocol for their particular traditions and culture.

I have heard many times, and experienced it myself, that government officials cannot buy food from government funds. This is true in many cases and in our meetings on the Sacred Circle, we purchased the food items from our personal resources. However, when you think about this, one should realize that a gift offered in a personal manner has more meaning; it comes from the heart and not as an obligation.

The fourth and final category of gifts is those items your organization provides as incentives, awards, or for marketing purposes. These might include pens, lapel pins, coffee mugs, ice scrapers, tote bags, calculators,

---

[90] Bird, James. 2003. Interview with author. Video recording. January 13. Eastern Band of Cherokee Indians Tribal Office, Cherokee, North Carolina.

and other items with your organization's logo embossed on them. These items are normally readily available in your organization and greatly appreciated by tribal representatives. And they are safe as previously explained by Fish from the Blackfeet Nation.

The key is, it's not important what you give but whether you give. And, equally important is how you give: from the heart versus as an obligation. Mic Isham from the Lac Courte Oreilles Band of Lake Superior Chippewa in Wisconsin sums up the practice of gift giving appropriately:

> *I always say tobacco and a gift is very important. It's like the ice breaker and it shows that you are not thumbing your nose at our culture. After that, it's about being together, eating together, and joking together until you get a comfortable feeling with each other and that's the best way to work something out with the tribe ... When Cheri came with some tobacco and a gift, right away I thought, "she's sincere," as my first impression.*[91]

And finally, Solo Greene makes an excellent conclusion: "It really isn't the gift that counts the most, it's the feeling you get from your heart, [that] this person means good."[92]

---

[91] Isham, Mic. 2003. Interview by author. January 17. Lac Courte Oreilles Casino, Lodge, and Convention Center, Hayward, Wisconsin.

[92] Greene, Solo. 2007. Interview by author. Video recording. May 22. Nez Perce Tribal Office, Lapwai, Idaho.

Platinum Rule #8–Respect Confidentiality

Respect our decision not to answer some of your questions. We have things in our culture we would like to keep to ourselves.

Cante Ethanhan Owaglake,
Speaking From The Heart, Customs and Norms for the Standing Rock Sioux Tribe
Standing Rock Tourism Alliance

As I have said numerous times, many tribal representatives are reluctant to be open if they don't know you or trust you. Once you gain their trust, they may share cultural or sensitive tribal information to assist you in understanding and being more effective in working with them. However, the important point I want to make with this Platinum Rule is that any information provided in this environment is intended, in most cases, to be confidential. What is unfortunate is that tribes have historically provided information only to have it exploited for commercial use or even used against them. Bobby Gonzalez, from the Caddo Nation in Oklahoma, shares how this continues today:

There's always been some sort of agency official or historian, or book writer, or some archeologist or someone, that came to our tribe, or other tribes, and say [sic], "This is what we are doing here." And, then they take that information from the elders in the tribe and turn around and use it for whatever they want to use it for and the person that did that interview never said anything ... that breaks that trust.[93]

It is no wonder tribal representatives are hesitant to divulge such information unless they are sure the person they are sharing it with can be truly trusted. The best way to wipe away all the trust and relationships you have built is to divulge this information in the public arena. Let's look at an example:

At a meeting some time ago on the Sacred Circle an elder approached me, tapped me on the shoulder, and asked me to come out into the hall outside the meeting. Many tribal and non-tribal representatives were in

---

[93] Gonzalez, Bobby. 2006. Interview by author. Video recording. January 11. Caddo Nation Historical Preservation Office, Binger, Oklahoma.

attendance at the meeting. He shared with me some sensitive information about the importance of sacred sites and practices. He qualified his offering of this very important information by saying he couldn't talk about this in an open meeting because the information was very private. However, he wanted to make me aware of it to assist me in making a better decision. I thanked him for trusting me with this information and was quite honored that he shared it. I also told him that I would honor his request and keep it private. That meant not writing the information down in notes, broadcasting it at the meeting, or sharing it with anyone, even my colleagues.

In government, the problem lies with the Freedom of Information Act. Under this act documents, communications, records, and other written instruments are available to the public if requested. Certain items are exempt, such as archeological information. If you are working on a project and write down some confidential or private information a tribal representative shared with you, it could become available in the public domain as it may be considered part of the record. The best advice is not to write down the information. Tuck it in the back of your mind, and use it mentally in your analysis.

When a tribal representative shares such information with you, don't sit there and take notes. Consider it the same as if a close friend was sharing information with you about their business or personal life. You don't take notes then, so afford the same courtesy to tribal representatives when they confide in you information that is valuable in your decision-making process. Listen closely. Consider it an honor and a sign of great respect, much like the friend sharing his or her feelings with you.

Platinum Rule #9–Survive When You Are "Put To the Test"

That's part of the trust-building process. So, if you are at a federal agency trying to build up relationships with Native American Tribes, you want to welcome those kinds of tests.[94]

Russ Townsend
Tribal Historic Preservation Officer
Eastern Cherokee

I ask this question in many of my interviews with tribal leaders, "Do you test government officials and business leaders?" The question was borne from my experiences with tribes when I was tested to see if I could be trusted, if I listened, or if I would keep my commitments. The concept of testing people outside the tribe originates in history as a result of the many broken commitments made by government and business. Bruce Sun Child, Chippewa-Cree, puts it this way:

That comes from many years of mistrust and we're always apprehensive … when there's something going on. I guess subconsciously we do test to see if your commitments are there, and if those processes that are going to be done are in the best interest of everybody. It just comes from a lot of years of mistrust.[95]

So, one can see even today that you may have to prove yourself by being tested. This is where patience is truly a virtue and being authentic and genuine is so important. The benefits of being tested are invaluable. A state employee from South Dakota shared with me her experience of being tested:

At the meeting, I was tested, tested again, and then ultimately personally invited to visit several tribes. (Each chairman even shook my hand.) My colleagues were quite offended by the "testing" that I went through, but thanks to the training, I knew that was common and had

---

[94] Townsend, Russ. 2003. Interview by author. Video recording. January 13. Eastern Band of Cherokee Indians Tribal Office, Cherokee, North Carolina.

[95] Sun Child, Bruce. 2002. Interview with author. Video recording. May 6. Chippewa-Cree Rocky Boys Indian Reservation Tribal Council Office, Box Elder, Montana.

actually expected it. Since I wasn't offended and could keep my own filters in check, it really helped my project and the relationships to progress. If I hadn't attended the training, I would have been offended … and we wouldn't have made the progress that we did.[96]

This testament illustrates the importance of going into meetings with an open mind. The testing process is not intended to be offensive, but merely to ensure you are worthy of being trusted and that the time invested with you is worthwhile.

Testing might come in many different ways. On the Sacred Circle we were tested many times to determine if the commitments we made were, in reality, going to be kept. I remember one situation where we committed to the tribes that we would close the Sacred Circle to the public for special private ceremonies for up to three days. Several ceremonies can last many days. Soon after, we received a request for a ceremony that was to last for three days. They requested the Sacred Circle be closed to the public over the Fourth of July weekend, one of the busiest times of the year for visitors to the site. We knew that this was a test to see if we would really keep our commitment. The Fourth of July is not really significant to northern tribes like the summer solstice or autumnal equinox. But it didn't matter. We carried through with our commitment and subsequently "passed" the test.

Testing may also come in the form of challenging verbiage, such as terse statements, direct questions, or even caustic comments during a meeting. This is to see how you will react. Will you become defensive? Will you become meek? Will you be respectful in light of challenging questions? And, many times you may not even know you are being tested in these situations.

Again, Russ Townsend, Eastern Band of Cherokee, shares a situation about how an official might be tested:

I do know that unofficially, when we have consultants, Native American consultants that we bring in, they will construct tests. They can ask some pretty outlandish things … I know that we had some elders ask the Forest Service to protect a non-important piece of land

---

[96] Personal Communication from state employee July 24, 2008.

as if it was important to ascertain whether they could really protect an important piece of land. But, they weren't willing to point out the important piece of land and why it was important until they knew that the Forest Service was going to shoot straight with them ... [97]

So, how does one address this concept of being tested? How does one react or behave while being tested? There are some simple rules that apply and are the foundation of earning trust:

- Only make commitments you are willing to keep.
- Make sure you have the authority and resources to carry out your commitments.
- "Walk the talk" and make sure you do what you say you're going to do to the letter.
- Thoroughly understand the limitations of your commitments and ensure tribal leaders also understand those limitations.
- Do not take liberties to make changes to a commitment without consulting the tribal representatives. You cannot speak or think for them on the impacts of these changes.
- Be yourself—authentic and genuine.
- Don't become defensive and interrupt but be respectful and listen.

Although these appear to be common-sense rules, one would be surprised at how many times they are violated and obliterate any chance of building trust with tribal representatives.

So, how do you know if you pass or fail a test? For starters, you will most likely not receive any acknowledgement that you "passed" a test. The tip-off will be in the behavior of tribal leaders as illustrated above by the state employee from South Dakota. If you recall, the tribal leaders shook April's hand and invited her out to visit their tribe.

Back in the section on communication protocols, I told the story of what happened during one of the early meetings on the Sacred Circle. The previous meetings had not gone well, and we knew something was

---

[97] Townsend, Russ. 2003. Interview by author. Video recording. January 13. Eastern Band of Cherokee Indians Tribal Office, Cherokee, North Carolina.

up because we were scheduled first, with many other tribal representatives and organizations scheduled after us to tell us what we were doing wrong. At the meeting, we took a different approach. We made sure that the people in attendance recognized us as people, not as bureaucrats, that they knew we knew we had messed up and were willing to start over, and that we were willing to follow through with our commitments. We knew we passed the test because the representatives shut down the meeting to regroup and the one representative had to come up to touch us to see if we were real. It's a moment that tickles me still and one I am still very proud of—we all like to pass tests after all.

Failure, on the other hand, will generally result in verbal reprimands about how government or business has taken advantage of tribes and can't be trusted to keep commitments. If you interrupt someone, you might be reprimanded for how government or business officials talk down to tribal leaders. But, remember, failure is often in the eyes of the beholder and you may have simply made an innocent mistake. If that happens, simply apologize and move on.

If you fail a test, what do you do then? It's rather simple, just admit it and apologize. Arguing will not move you in a positive direction. You will probably have to prove yourself over again, but most importantly never give up. And, this may even be a test in itself. If you get angry, hold a grudge, walk away, or give up you will never move forward. I have seen many government officials and business leaders say, "I don't have to take this," and walk away. What you are doing if you do that is playing the victim card, severing your ties forever, and doing an injustice to yourself and the tribe. You are also holding onto the past as opposed to helping us all move beyond it and into a more productive, respectful future.

Platinum Rule #10–Show Progress

Sometimes it's difficult to see progress when you walk a mile one inch at a time.[98]

People like to see the fruits of their labor. Working with tribes is no exception and goes both ways. Tribes might become frustrated with their perception of the lack of progress. You might become frustrated with what you perceive as a painfully slow pace. Either way, both parties working on a project must understand realistic expectations and why there might be a difference in how one defines progress. This is particularly true when accounting for the need of many tribes to build relationships as a first action. It is difficult, unless you really focus, to quantify the investment of time and progress when relationship, trust, social, and cultural factors come into play. It's a delicate balance, because demonstrating progress, even in simple terms, keeps people engaged in the process.

In this part, I hope to put into perspective for you what progress looks like and attempt to align your expectations with reality. Such a discussion as this takes into account almost everything presented previously, from lessons in history, to communication protocols, to trust and relationship building.

First, let's take a generic peek at what progress is. Progress in the simplest form is to move forward or advance towards a goal. Furthermore, we often measure or weigh progress against time. In other words, we have an expectation of meeting specific goals or objectives in a certain time period. If this timeframe is interrupted by factors we do not understand, such as cultural factors, we might become frustrated and walk away from the process blaming the inefficient use of time in achieving goals and objectives. Simply put, the perceived lack of progress may result in parties walking away from the process. A good example is the cultural aspect of relationship building on the part of many tribes before conducting business. If one does not understand the

---

[98] Keown, Larry D. 1996. HPP Signing Ceremony Speech.

cultural value of relationship building, one may define the time used as wasted. In contrast, tribal representatives consider the investment of time in relationship building to be a prerequisite for doing business. This misalignment of expectations has the potential to derail the project you are working on with a tribe.

When working on the Sacred Circle it took about three years before what we defined as progress was really made. Looking back, I now understand the value of those three years to tribal members. Those three years were consumed building relationships and trust and educating everyone on what we were about to pursue. However, in the second three years, progress, as we defined it, moved rapidly. Someone without the patience to understand the protocol might have said, "Enough! We aren't getting anywhere so let's just give up!"

I previously discussed at length the concept of "time and patience." It applies here in the discussion of progress, for patience is a virtue. A representative from a Pueblo in New Mexico, shared with me:

> ... go in a little at a time, take one step at a time. You don't want to take a giant leap ... because you are going to miss all this information, all this knowledge you just jumped over ... And you missed the knowledge from this step to this step. With the little step you are gathering knowledge, knowledge you can go forward with.[99]

This knowledge can be gained by listening, being inquisitive, learning, and just taking the time to allow the process to move forward. Progress may come in small steps. It can be slow or even seem to be not moving, but if you are listening and learning and taking the time to build good relationships, progress will be happening.

To put progress into perspective when working with tribes, let's look at three levels of progress measured against time.

The first, and slowest, stage begins when you may not know anyone within the tribe, do not have a solid contact, nor any relationships built. Progress may be extremely slow as phone calls may not be returned, appointments may not be kept or may be postponed, or you may be

---

[99] Interview with Pueblo official. July 13, 2004.

passed off to others in the tribe. When you do get the opportunity to meet someone, you will go into the listening mode and there will be little in the way of commitments and you will probably be tested in some way. Many, including myself, sometimes give up at this stage when the investment of time and effort appears to be nonproductive. It's a matter of accepting the fact that the tribe simply may not be interested in your program or project or the time is just not right. Sometimes it is most effective to move on and approach the tribe at a later time.

You enter the second stage when the ice has been broken and you have been successful in solidifying a tribal contact. At this point, some relationships have been built but may be immature. You can expect your appointments to be kept, phone calls returned, and social encounters become an important part of your contacts. You may work together on simple projects and reach simple agreements on technical and complex programs or projects. Many of these agreements might be in the form of processes you jointly agree to pursue, such as meeting once a month, sharing assignments, exchanging information, and so forth. Testing may be ongoing and your commitment to working with the tribe may be evaluated in some form. At this point, the trust and relationship-building process is continuing and strengthening with simple accomplishments and socializing to a greater or lesser extent.

Finally, when a personal and working relationship has matured, you will be achieving many goals and objectives with the tribe. Socializing, humor, and productive work are all indicators that a strong relationship exists and trust has been proven. At this stage you can expect tribal representatives to possibly share confidential cultural information, work with you on cooperative agreements, jointly prepare management and strategic plans, jointly implement projects as partners, and even complete complex projects in shorter timeframes. Coming to this point is the result of long hard work on the part of both you and the tribal representative(s). You honor and respect the culture, listen, provide assistance, show a willingness to learn, keep an open mind, and put into practice many of the strategies presented previously.

Sometimes, as I said in the epigraph to this rule, it's difficult to see progress when you are walking a mile one inch at a time. That's how I described progress on the Sacred Circle. We met quarterly on Friday, Saturday, and Sunday for six years. In between meetings, much work was accomplished but sometimes steps had to be repeated. So, how do you keep your perspective on progress when doubts start to appear or your supervisor is asking what, if anything, is really being accomplished? A chronology is a useful tool. Keeping track of highlights, decision points, agreements, and accomplishments, however small they may appear, helps keep your perspective in focus. When added together over time, they will indicate significant progress. It helps to look at the process as a journey and learning experience and not simply a checklist to be completed.

Platinum Rule #11—Provide Assistance to Tribes

Solve problems together. Define a way to do it together.

Points of Protocol for Working with Tribes,
Confederated Tribes of the Umatilla Indian Reservation
January 2008

We all need help. Think about this. Any time an outside organization can and is willing to provide assistance to you, you might not only be very grateful, you may be more willing to do business in the future with that entity. A tribe is no different, and providing assistance to a tribe helps build significant trust. Many tribal representatives have shared with me how much they appreciated an organization providing data or analysis that they did not have the resources to gather or achieve. To further understand this, many tribes do not have the resources or skills to gather data, analyze data, or develop plans and programs. Although many do, those tribes that do not will hold individuals from outside organizations in high regard for providing such assistance.

Eddie Tullis, Poarch Band of Creeks Indians, explains the importance of providing these types of services to tribes:

I'm a firm believer that tribes know what's best for them. But I am absolutely convinced that there are people outside the tribe that can provide a real positive service by helping us apply some of their training and education ... at how we will arrive at what's best for us. They may not be able to tell me what is best for me, but they may have a system or they may have some training that will help me draw out of the tribal member what really is best ... I never eliminate [the] contribution that people can make to me to find out what is best for my people here because there are systems out there and training that has been developed that will help us do that.[100]

Let's examine some examples of what a government or business organization can provide for tribes in the form of technical assistance.

---

[100] Tullis, Eddie. 2004. Interview by author. Video recording. July 24. Poarch Band of Creek Indians Tribal Office, Atmore, Alabama.

Those in economic development can provide data and strategic planning to assist a tribe with improving its economy and business climate. A natural resource department can provide geographical information system data or other inventories to assist a tribe in sustaining, maintaining, and producing water, timber, or forage for grazing, or help with insect and disease control or energy development. Someone in health-services can provide data, analysis, and education for disease prevention, such as diabetes, heart disease, or cancer. And, someone in social sciences can provide services in child care, elder care, education, or job training. However, one must keep in mind what Eddie Tullis said earlier—it must be to assist the tribe in helping them get where they want to go—not merely in a direction you or your organization want them to go. This means having a thorough understanding of a tribe's culture, history, values, social structure, and desires. Tribes have a desire for self-determination, just like anyone else. They want to pursue their dreams and their vision of the future, not the dreams and vision of someone who doesn't understand their culture, history, values, social structure and desires. The role from someone on the outside, you or your organization, is to assist the tribe by providing skills, training, and resources to support them in achieving their dreams and their visions of the future.

I discussed gift-giving extensively in Platinum Rule # 7 but I need to spend a little time on how this concept interconnects with providing assistance to tribes. In many cases, providing assistance to a tribe is considered a gift from you to the tribe. Aaron Miles, Nez Perce Tribe in Idaho, illustrates how simple this concept can be: " ... for a governmental official to come in and sometimes give coffee cups or whatever or sometimes it's just words of wisdom. Those things are important."[101]

I have seen this interconnection happen many times in the form of volunteering technical assistance, assisting in preparing a grant, or providing ideas and incentives for economic development. The options are endless for those in government and business to provide such services.

---

[101] Miles, Aaron. 2007. Interview by author. Video recording. May 22. Nez Perce Tribal Office, Lapwai, Idaho.

Just remember, your role is to offer and share, not dictate, what is best for the tribal organization.

Again, Eddie Tullis, shares some important final thoughts on providing assistance to tribes.

> *I'm just real tickled that we've got people that understand that the awareness of culture is part of our historical understanding and we need to be conscious of it. It's another good point where people can really provide a service to people that I'll guarantee you down the road sometimes they'll look back and say, "God, I'm proud of the fact that I helped the Poarch Creeks get started on something that I now see producing and improving the quality of life of those people." Because, if people have a good spiritual [and] cultural understanding of their history they'll certainly improve the quality of life of those people and ... it can be real rewarding ...* [102]

[102] Tullis, Eddie. 2004. Interview by author. Video recording. July 24. Poarch Band of Creek Indians Tribal Office, Atmore, Alabama.

Platinum Rule #12–Celebrate Successes

Thank people and organizations. Some cultures believe that you should give thanks seven times. Doing so helps focus on the good repeatedly.

Points of Protocol for Working withTribes,
Confederated Tribes of the Umatilla Indian Reservation
January 2008

One day Velma Real Bird and I were reworking our workshop and I suggested we delete the section on "Celebrating Success" as a time-saver. I knew celebrating success was important, as my own experiences on the Sacred Circle suggested, but it was a logical topic to cut in comparison to others. She responded rather unenthusiastically to my suggestion making the point that there are so few successes between government or businesses and tribes working together that when achievements do take place they should be celebrated. Being on the non-Indian side of the equation, I wasn't attentive, until then, to the importance that many tribes place on celebrating success. So, in deference to Velma, we kept this topic in our workshops and even strengthened the weight of it in our presentation.

There are many ways, from the simple to the complex, for you to celebrate your accomplishments when working with tribes. Not all have to be pomp and circumstance, but might be as simple as bestowing small gifts. The range of options to celebrate successes can be from taking the tribal representative(s) to lunch, ordering a celebration cake, presenting an award, writing a letter of appreciation and presenting it to the tribal council, publishing your accomplishment in a newsletter or magazine, or holding a signing ceremony.

When we completed the Historic Preservation Plan for the Sacred Circle, all the parties involved over the past six years decided we should hold a signing ceremony. We agreed that the tribes would offer a Morning Prayer session, the local community would host a barbeque lunch, and the Forest Service would organize the actual signing ceremony. In addition, the tribes would provide traditional music and dancers. In mid-morning, busloads of tribal elders began showing up and I commented to one tribal leader about this. He told me that many of the elders considered this celebration equivalent to a treaty signing and that it was very important to them.

When everyone had arrived, the tribal leaders began the prayer ceremony around a buffalo robe-and-skull altar. Following a number of prayers in their native language, a ceremonial pipe was passed to all who wanted to smoke. Then a pail of water with a ladle was passed around for each to drink. After the prayer ceremony we all gathered for a lunch prepared by volunteers from the local community and then retreated to a large tent for the actual signing of the document. We had numerous special pens made up for each signatory which they kept as a gift. Each leader, both Indian and non-Indian, gave a short presentation and signed the document. Tribal drummers, singers, and dancers performed in celebration of the event. All those attending received a small ceremonial leather pouch containing tobacco for adults or candy for kids as a gift. In all, about two hundred people attended and everyone considered it a great success.

The signing of the Historic Preservation Plan was a significant event and we all decided it was worthy of a large celebration. As I mentioned earlier, not all celebrations need to be as grand as what we did for the Sacred Circle. However, celebrating successes in even the simplest way shows respect and appreciation for the work done and honors the end product.

The Upshot of the Platinum Rules

I want you to know something very important. American Indian leaders sharing their knowledge and traditional customs have allowed me to fashion these Platinum Rules. It goes back to the fundamental of respect that I opened this very long chapter with. Respect for elders in a tribal community is not only a respect for their age but for their wisdom. What I have learned over the years from tribal elders and friends is invaluable to all aspects of my life, for I have found that not only do they work in Indian/non-Indian relationships, they are useful in any business or personal relationship.

We can all learn so much from their shared words of wisdom. We can enrich our lives even more by practicing them in our everyday interactions with all people. Sometimes these rules can seem overwhelming, but if we look at them as a journey, a learning experience, they become simply a part of how we relate to others, Indian and non-Indian alike. If we learn to respect each other with the deep respect American Indians hold for each other and the world around us, think about how much nicer—and easier—life will be.

There really is no better way to sum up this discussion than with advice from a tribal leader himself. Eddie Tullis concludes:

> *Keep an open mind, keep an open mind because I firmly believe there's something for everyone to learn from dealing with the Indian people. If you come in … you've got to be a specialist, you've got to know your business, but keep an open mind because Indian people may be able to teach you a better method of using your education or they may be able to teach you something that will provide benefits for you from now on.[103]*

---

[103] Tullis, Eddie. 2004. Interview by author. Video recording. July 24. Poarch Band of Creek Indians Tribal Office, Atmore, Alabama.

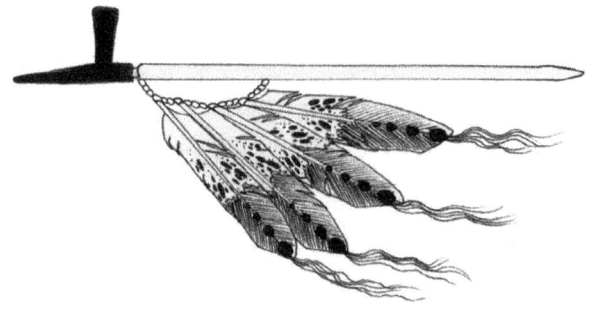

— PART THREE —

THE BUSINESS ENVIRONMENT

The aim of an argument or discussion should not be victory, but progress.[104]

—Joseph Joubert

Building trust and respect is the foundation to accomplishing anything in Indian country. Without them you will never be able to move to a successful completion of your project. However, there are some important procedural points that I have not yet covered, points that take into account all that has come before. In a way, they're the "how to" of the whole subject, for part three is how to successfully set up and execute in the business environment.

---

[104] Joseph Joubert. BrainyQuote.com, Xplore Inc, 2010. http://www.brainyquote.com/quotes/quotes/j/josephjoub157297.html.

7

How to Plan and Run a Successful Program in Indian Country

The business environment can be defined as those factors and processes that characterize the framework of how business is conducted in Indian country. These are factors and processes that are subtle, but can affect the quality of your interaction. In a business environment in the non-Indian world, we might take them for granted, but I assure you they are significant when working in Indian country. They are as simple as how a meeting is recorded or how to plan a meeting to more complex processes such as managing conflict or facilitating group maturity.

What is presented in previous chapters is what I was taught by tribal leaders and elders. What you find in this chapter is what I have learned on my own or in consultation with colleagues working with me on numerous projects in Indian country. And, most importantly it augments the principles presented earlier. I believe it is valuable information and worthy of your time to enhance your likelihood of success. It consists of planning your approach, executing successful meetings, and handling some of the peripheral elements that could hinder you if you're not aware of them.

Business Element #1–Pre-planning Strategies

I believe one of the most worthwhile endeavors you can undertake is pre-planning your approach to working with a tribe. I say worthwhile, because the benefits to you and the tribe far outweigh the time you might invest in such an exercise. Pre-planning a strategic approach means analyzing the situation as it exists today and projecting what needs to be done in the future to achieve success. Compare it to a wilderness adventure. In that scenario, you have two options: Be dropped off in the middle of the wilderness and you'll navigate your way through it the best you can, or take the time to plan the adventure beforehand. Just dropping you off will result, at best, in many dead-end hikes, but you also run the risk of unknowingly wandering into dangerous terrain. Without some planning, you will most likely have an overall bad experience and if you're lucky, you'll come out of it with no personal injury. However, if you plan your trip beforehand, the result will most likely be a positive experience with you achieving your goals, whether they are sightseeing, solitude, fishing, camping, or just getting away from the stresses of the job. Pre-planning your approach with tribes is just as important as planning that wilderness adventure.

Consider this point—many believe they can just walk into a tribal office or schedule a meeting and start doing business, just like being dropped off in the middle of the wilderness. While this may be a successful approach in the non-Indian world, the potential for it to backfire on you in Indian country is very high. It sometimes works with tribes, but more often than not, something will happen that derails your approach—from blank stares and unreturned phone calls to out-and-out conflict.

Pre-planning a strategic approach minimizes the unknowns that might surprise you and maximizes the likelihood of success. As I said before, it is a very worthwhile exercise and investment of your time. What it means is getting up on the "balcony" and examining the business environment as it exists today in Indian country as well as envisioning how it might look in the future, which would be beneficial to both you and the tribe. This exercise forces you to focus on and address many unknowns.

The process of developing your strategic approach is relatively simple and follows typical goal- and objective-setting protocols we use regularly in our organizations. However, you must always keep in mind there are the all-important cultural considerations that are often overlooked in this process and which must be recognized and included when working in Indian country. I have included a sampling of these cultural considerations in the process narrative that follows.

The process of pre-planning your strategy to work in Indian country is a matter of exploring and examining a series of questions. These questions compel you to reflect on what the business environment looks like today, what it should look like tomorrow and how you will get there. Engaging an outside expert in tribal relations can be beneficial in facilitating this process.

The questions that define the Business Environment in Indian country fall into eight areas: your issues, goals, and objectives; the community of interest; current attitudes; cultural considerations; timeframes and priorities; decisions, authorities, and legal considerations; "what if" scenarios and testing; and help and assistance. Let's look at each of these question areas individually.

What are the issues and what are your goals and objectives?

The issues generated by your organization may be much different than issues generated by a tribe. For example, let's say you have an objective to resolve issues on hunting, fishing, and gathering rights with a particular tribe. You perceive the issues as those of properly using these natural resources and managing populations for other users. On the other hand, tribes may view the issues very differently, as that of rights issues outlined in treaties. So, when it's time to get down to business it becomes difficult to communicate clearly when one side is talking apples and the other oranges. Therefore, it's important to thoroughly understand what's behind the issues in order to ensure all entities are on the same page and to facilitate fruitful dialogue. This is why it is helpful to know what the specific issues are and who initiated them.

As an example, one issue we addressed on the Sacred Circle was that of ceremonial use of the site. Our focus on the issue was rather narrow, that of the Sacred Circle itself. But, the tribes defined ceremonial use much more broadly—that of important areas physically separate from, but linked to, the Sacred Circle. One elder described to me a sacred trail his tribe used that began a few miles from the site. Practitioners would begin their spiritual journey along this trail, praying along the way, and ultimately ending at the Sacred Circle. As you can see, the way we define issues in the non-Indian world can be rather narrow and lead us down the wrong path if we do not understand and acknowledge the cultural interests of tribes.

Now, as far as goals and objectives are concerned, we need to define our focus of why we want to work with a tribe. We use the issues to formulate our goals and objectives and ensure tribal concerns are included as well. This needs to be clear in your mind and conveyed clearly to tribal representatives. Let me use a hypothetical example. Let's say you head an economic development organization and are planning a meeting with a tribe. You have a general goal to talk about "working better together on economic development opportunities with the tribe." Here's the problem: The tribe may read this any number of ways—do you have a specific opportunity you are going to present? Is there a problem with a program already in place? Are you looking to take advantage of tribal enterprises? Or, the question might merely be, "Who are you and what is your organization about?"

In order to maximize the efficiency of your time and the tribe's time you need to be more specific, such as "Our goal is to strengthen the relationship with the tribe to facilitate ongoing communication for a future partnership in economic development." Remember the old adage, "How do you eat an elephant?" The answer, of course, is, "One bite at a time." So, let's break down that broad goal into specific objectives that are clear. Specifically, your objectives are to: 1) get to know the tribal leaders and initiate a relationship, 2) learn about the tribes economic development programs and issues they are facing, 3) share with the tribe who you are and the services you can offer as well as find out if there are benefits to the tribes, and 4) seek opportunities for partnering with the tribe on economic development grants. You can see the pattern here from what I have presented previously. First, you are initiating a relationship. Second you begin learning about tribal needs and issues. Third, you are asking the tribe, not telling them, about the benefits. And fourth, if all comes together, you can now begin doing business with the tribe. This may all take place over a period of time ranging from weeks to months. What this all means is that if you don't fully understand the objective of why you are meeting with a tribe, then how can you expect the tribe to readily join or partner with you? So, again, formulate your goals and objectives based on the issues and convey them clearly to tribal officials.

Some questions you might ask to ferret out the issues and construct mutually beneficial goals and objectives include: How would I define the problem or opportunity? What are the issues that drive the problem or opportunity? How does the tribe perceive the problem or opportunity? How does the tribe define the issues? How can we formulate goals and objectives that are beneficial to both the tribe and our organization?

What are the current attitudes in Indian country about our project or program?

The purpose of this question is to help you avoid being surprised about any negative attitudes lurking in the business environment which you may not be aware of. Upon researching this question you might find that someone in the past has left a bad taste in the mouths of tribal leaders or another organization failed to follow through on commitments to the tribe. In any event, tribal leaders may be reluctant to work with another government agency or business based on their past experience. Knowing this information might tell you that work needs to be done, initially, on credibility-building and showing how you are different from your predecessors or another organization. Sub-questions you might explore include:

What is the current climate about the issue(s)—sensitive, something new, an opportunity? Is there distress over the issue(s) inside and/or outside our organization? Have past actions from your organization or another organization contributed to the distress? If so, what and who are they? Are you being proactive or reactive? If reactive, can you turn it into a proactive position? What is the level of trust on the issue(s)? What relationships exist? What must you do to build credibility, trust and relationships?

Who is, and how broad is, the community of interest?

Back in chapter 5, I discussed "The Moccasin Telegraph or Modern Day Networking" to illustrate how news of your project or program can rapidly spread throughout Indian country. So, when pre-planning your approach it is incumbent upon you to answer some basic questions, such as who else might be interested in what you are addressing: tribes, agencies, and businesses? What other agencies or organizations need to be involved—tribes, agencies, and businesses? What tribal entities need to be involved—government, societies, coalitions, organizations, etc.? These questions provide you with an idea of the breadth of interest in your project or program and ensure all interested parties at least have the opportunity to participate. In addition, once you contact the appropriate tribal officials, they may be helpful in identifying other interested parties you may not be aware of.

What cultural considerations must we take into account?

As I have said many times before, we must be aware of and respectful of the cultures, customs, and traditions of the tribal people we meet. It is one of the first steps in earning trust necessary to move forward successfully. The best question you can ask yourself is, "What are the cultures, customs, and traditions of the tribal people you will meet?" You might explore some other pertinent questions, such as: Do you understand the tribe's culture, customs, and traditions? What can you do to display respect for those cultures, customs, and traditions? Are there any ethics questions you need to be aware of when honoring cultural practices? Are you willing to honor and allow cultural practices to occur if a tribe requests them? Is there someone from the tribe who can teach you and assist you in navigating through the traditional cultural protocols of that particular tribe?

These questions help you focus on your learning needs; they help you incorporate culture and tradition in your collaborative effort, which exhibits respect to the tribe.

Are the timeframes and priorities for our organization and the tribe ready to come to fruition?

Your answer to this question gets to the heart of a very important point—are you and the tribe willing to devote the time to prioritize the project or program on the table? If one side or the other's interest wanes or they are not willing to devote the necessary time to work on it, you will find it impossible to see progress. Also, in some cases a tribe just might not be interested in what you have to offer. Or they may not have the time to devote to your task. So, before embarking on a project or program with a tribe you might ask yourself some basic questions, such as, do *you* have the time and resources to initiate this effort? If not, can you make it a priority? How much time, realistically do you expect it to take? Are you willing to invest the time even if it takes longer than expected? Is the issue(s) a priority to the tribe(s)? Is the timing ripe to address the issue(s) with the tribe(s)?

What authorities and legal considerations must be taken into account?

As I discussed in detail in chapter 5, Protocol # 7, "Communicating Through Authority and Decisions," having an understanding in your organization about who can make decisions when meeting with tribes is paramount. I encourage you to go back and re-read Protocol # 7 and answer the following questions: Who in your organization has the decision-making authority on this issue(s)? Is there a higher level in your organization you will have to consult with on decisions? Do you have the authority to address the issue(s)? Are there legal or regulatory constraints you need to recognize, and if so, do they affect your decision space? Are there legal processes you must undertake, for example, consultation? Are there treaties, sovereignty, or rights issues involved? Are there legal precedents, court cases, or laws on the issue(s)? Is the tribe aware of these legal or regulatory sideboards? Once these questions are answered, you can now decide who in your organization should take the lead, what the scope of their authority will be, and the limitations of their decisions and commitments.

Will you be tested and what is the worst that can happen?

This question prepares you for any number of outcomes if you are tested on trust, commitment, or integrity concerns. You need to prepare yourself if you are tested on how you might respond to direct statements, pressure to make a decision, or even personal attacks. Ask yourself, what kind of "trust tests" can you expect? How will you respond to these tests? What can you do to make sure you pass these tests? What could go wrong? What's the worst that could happen with your response? What's the best that could happen with your response? In the event you are tested by tribal officials, these questions prepare you with responses and reactions that are constructive and not detrimental to the process as a whole.

Where can you find help and assistance to work effectively with the tribe?

Many times in this book I have counseled you to seek assistance from a tribal representative to help you navigate through the maze of cultural and tribal protocol. To help you achieve that end, here are some questions you might explore: Has this issue been addressed successfully elsewhere? Is there an experienced person with whom you can consult? Is there someone in another agency or business who can give you advice and council? Do you have tribal contacts that can assist and council you? Is there a network in the tribe(s) you might tap into for help and assistance? Are there other networks you can tap into—local, regional, or national? What learning do you need to undertake before approaching the tribe(s)?

So, how do you make all this information useful? First, if you can't answer many of the questions presented, this is an indication that more time needs to be invested in the learning process. Or, if many of the questions cannot be answered readily, it would behoove you to bring in someone who has experience working with the tribes and allow them to assist you in formulating your strategy. Use the answers to the questions to build an action plan on how you will approach and interact with the tribe to initiate interest in your project or program. This action plan should include: 1) a description of the situation (issues, problems, or opportunities) as they appear today, 2) how you would like the situation to look tomorrow (your goals), 3) what needs to be accomplished to change the situation (your objectives), 4) who will be assigned the tasks, and 5) realistic timeframes. Your goal is to plot a strategic path that will guide your organization through the process of building trust, developing relationships, and accomplishing your objectives.

Once you have gone through this exercise you will have a better handle on the task at hand. It will maximize the efficient use of time for your organization and the tribe. It will provide a clear path to follow and allow for adjustments along the way. And, finally, it will significantly increase your probability of success in working with the tribe.

Business Element #2—Planning Meetings with Tribal Representatives

Okay, now that I have gone through the pre-planning process it's time to begin thinking about how you will conduct your meeting with a tribe or tribes. I have already addressed communication protocol in meetings in chapter 5. Here I want to sum up how to take all that and use it to plan a productive meeting.

First, let me summarize the assumptions that may come into play that define the meeting environment. Recognizing these assumptions will make it easier to navigate through the cultural protocols that are necessary for you to have a successful meeting with tribal leaders. They are:

- There may be cultural differences in the way meetings are conducted. Honoring these cultural differences builds trust and cultivates the relationship.

- There may be differences in philosophy as it relates to time. Plan on flexibility to account for this. As mentioned before, the end product is more important than the time it might take to get there. Simply put, be patient.

- Socializing may be a prerequisite to conducting business. Provide opportunities to socialize and capitalize on them to build trust and develop relationships.

- Meetings may begin and end with a prayer, particularly if your meeting is attended by elders or traditional people. Remember to consult with a tribal leader about who should offer the prayer and what kind of gift would be appropriate.

- If many tribes are present you may not have a single point of authority. You may have representatives from tribal governments, cultural organizations, societies, or coalitions and inter-tribal organizations. Remember, each tribe is unique and each has its own government and cultural protocol that must be respected.

- Tribal officials may need time to present their issues, opinions, and positions. Plan on this happening. Do not force or push your agenda during a meeting. Allow everyone to be heard, as it will happen despite your wishes to move forward.

- Meetings may become or appear to be fragmented. Do not become frustrated. Over time you will see accomplishments. As mentioned earlier, prepare yourself to walk a mile one inch at a time.

These assumptions may or may not all happen, depending on the tribe you are working with. However, it is my experience that many of these assumptions are realistic and you must be prepared to face them. So, with that said, let's begin preparing your meeting.

Who do I invite?

An effective leader convenes and mobilizes people to accomplish work. This means identifying the community of interest which is, basically, those who are or may be interested in an issue you are addressing or the program you are proposing. I have seen many people become selfish with their relationships with a tribe and exclude others who might benefit from a program or contribute to resolving an issue. Unfortunately these people have a very narrow view of those who should be participating (both within and outside a tribe). The value of being inclusive benefits the final outcome by building alliances, encouraging open thinking, and producing a far superior product. You will also have the satisfaction of seeing people work through issues in a positive environment. Excluding key players can be costly in reaching consensus on an issue.

There are two questions you need to explore. First, which government or private entities should be involved in discussions? And second, are there other tribal entities that should be invited into the discussion, such as cultural groups, tribal governments, staff, tribal organizations or even other tribes? As a case in point, our discussions on the Sacred Circle included five federal agencies, one state agency, one county government, one local government, about seventeen tribes in addition to non-profit organizations and half-a-dozen private entities. All these parties were not present at each and every meeting but did participate at one time or another.

At the end of our planning effort for the long-term management plan, only one private entity walked away unsatisfied. In fact, that entity refused to join in the meetings with tribes despite briefings and numerous invitations to participate. They eventually challenged the process in court and the judge ruled that our collaborative efforts were fair and sound.

So how do I figure out who to invite to these meetings? First, develop a meeting list and, I repeat, be inclusive rather than exclusive. Use tribal contacts to develop the participant list and even include the tribe in your planning efforts. If you are addressing a big issue, ensure that all interested tribal governments, bands, organizations, societies, and others are included. Do not assume one tribe or band represents all others. It is helpful to develop a network of tribal contacts to assist you in getting the word out about your meeting. Also, consider inviting other government or business entities that might have an interest in the issue(s). Keep attendance from your organization to a few and always speak with one voice to avoid confusion and misunderstandings.

Build a successful meeting agenda.

I've discussed agendas and timeframes at length and the information is worth repeating. Develop your agenda in cooperation with the tribe(s) and pare it down to a few issues. In some cases, two-day meetings may be more efficient than one-day meetings. The rationale is that if you hold a one-day meeting, you may expend the allotted time with speeches and other discussions. In contrast, two-day meetings allow more time for socializing, general discussion, and addressing more topics in your agenda. Use a priority-driven agenda rather than specific time limits for topics. Be sure to solicit topics from the tribe(s) as they will have items they want to discuss also. And, finally, avoid holding meetings during ceremony, Powwow, fair, and other festival seasons, as you may end up with limited attendance.

There are many cases where tribal officials will be unable or unwilling to meet for an extended period of time. You may only have an opportunity to make a presentation at a tribal council meeting or a short meeting with tribal officials. In those cases, pre-meetings with tribal staff are invaluable. These people will assist you in preparing your presentation and navigating through their specific tribal protocol.

Choose a neutral location for the meeting.

Your meeting location can also make a difference in setting the tone of the meeting. Neutral locations are best, such as hotel conference rooms. However, be sure to arrange for a room large enough to accommodate invited tribal officials plus at least an equal number of guests. If you are planning on regular meetings over time with numerous tribes, rotate the location to minimize travel for each tribe. Also, allow tribes to host or offer future meeting locations on or near their reservation. This allows tribal leaders who are very busy to attend at some point or showcase a project or program on the reservation.

Build in time for socializing.

I have said enough on this subject for you to know its importance. This is how I have handled socializing during meetings—carefully plan breaks to facilitate socializing. Plan on thirty minute breaks every couple of hours. These breaks provide time for socializing, caucusing, private discussion, and organizing thoughts. Finally, always have refreshments available during breaks, as food is often a focal point.

Arranging the meeting room.

Finally, arranging your meeting room is paramount to success. To make sure your room is laid out for all to be on an equal footing, for example, avoid having a head table or a stage. In smaller meetings (as opposed to a conference-type setting), speakers typically talk from their chairs, not from a podium. The arrangement should facilitate groups sitting together to allow the sharing of information and caucusing. Two rows of chairs around the tables allow room for guests that may choose to sit with a particular party. An ideal layout is where tables are set out in a circular, square, or U-shaped pattern so no one is perceived as sitting at a head table. One end can be used for a flip chart, computer, screen, or presentations.

Business Element #3—Conducting Meetings with Indian Tribes

There is no doubt that conducting or self-facilitating a meeting with tribal officials can generate a myriad of challenges, such as framing issues, managing chaos and conflict, orchestrating progress, dealing with the media, and much more. In previous discussions I have addressed many of the elements concerning meetings with tribal leaders. These discussions are scattered throughout the sections on communications and trust and relationship building. Here, I provide some organization and guidelines on how to make the most of your meeting with tribal leaders.

About facilitation.

I often have potential clients approach me asking if I facilitate meetings between government agencies or businesses and tribes. My answer is an emphatic no! I know this will not sit well with those that make a living doing facilitation, but there is a reason. If I stand up and facilitate communications between you and a tribe, I become the focal point, the one asking questions, reviewing agreements, and managing conflicts. In this scenario, who becomes the respected individual for being successful? Me, the facilitator! Trust is built between the tribal representative and facilitator and not the government or business leader. So, when the meeting is over and everyone leaves, the government or business leader has not benefited from my efforts as facilitator at all.

In lieu of facilitating, I will coach you to become comfortable, confident and passionate, objective and non-judgmental, fair and unbiased, inquisitive, a builder of respect, a seeker of common ground, studious, willing to listen and learn, and teach you how to survive being a target for venting. I will sit next to you and suggest things to say, actions to take, and provide advice on how to continue moving forward. But I will not do it for you! The focus must be on you as a leader, so that you will reap the benefits of building the relationship and trust with the tribe.

Therefore, I firmly believe through experience, that a leader must learn to self-facilitate meetings with tribal officials. Relationship and trust-building must focus on the leader, not the facilitator. You must leave the meeting with the spotlight on your good deeds, not those of a facilitator.

Frame issues to encourage collaboration.

An effective leader knows how to frame issues when working with tribes. He knows persistence, patience, packaging a proposal and presentation. He knows that if no relationship has been established with a tribe, he must work on building that relationship first. Framing issues to make them important to a tribe is much easier if you have the confidence of the tribal leaders built on a foundation of trust and a strong relationship.

I've seen it happen time and again. A government or business leader has a program or issue to discuss with a tribe. He or she organizes a meeting with a tribal leader and gets a less-than-receptive response. This is most likely because the question or issue was not clear, a foundation of trust or cooperation did not exist, or the tribe just wasn't ready. It's the equivalent of trying to push a rope uphill. Your crisis, issue, or proposal is most likely not important to a tribe until you make it so. If you have no trust or relationship, your intentions might be questioned. Now, you must frame the issue to make it as important to the tribes as it is to you.

Think of your presentation in this context; "I have an issue that needs addressing" versus "We have an issue that needs addressing." The challenge is to frame the issue on how we are both affected and must work together. If you have a problem, the tribe will think, "That's too bad." If we have a problem (and you can effectively frame it that way) then the tribe thinks, "How can we work together on this issue?" If you and the tribe have a good working relationship built on trust, the "we" becomes automatic. The tribe knows that your intentions are honorable, you can be trusted, and they will exhibit a willingness to work with you. This is what framing issues is all about.

Group Maturity and the Holding Environment.

These are two important concepts in the business environment when working with tribes. Let us first explore the definition of each.

- Group Maturity—The capability of a group to discuss and address issues in a collaborative environment. Maturity is based on trust and relationships and the group's ability to facilitate agreements, manage conflict, and become resilient to set backs.

- Holding Environment—A placeholder for issues and topics the group is not able to address because of embryonic group maturity, lack of trust, or superficial relationships.

These concepts come into play when tough complex issues surface early in discussions, the dynamics of the working group have not matured enough to address issues, or trust is lacking. The idea is to develop a "holding environment" or placeholder for issues, not eliminate them from future dialogue.

It is useful to illustrate how these two concepts come into play. Let us presume you are at your third meeting with a tribe discussing a cluster housing project. The past two meetings have ended without any progress as tribal representatives disagree with government regulations about who can live in them, cost sharing, architectural design, extended families, and location. Tribal representatives comment that you do not understand the cultural and traditional characteristics of the family environment on the reservation, and had the government honored their treaty, they wouldn't be in this position in the first place. Your third meeting ends as the previous two, without any progress.

As we analyze this scenario we can see that because of little or no trust and the lack of a working relationship, it becomes difficult to address issues across cultural divides. In addition, there is mis-understanding on both sides about the cultural needs of the tribe and the program itself. It becomes obvious that "group maturity" is lacking, in other words, the group does not have the ability to work effectively together to arrive at consensus or agreement.

Based on this conclusion, it would be wise to place the topic in a "holding environment" and not discuss the details at this time. You might address the group by stating, "I believe that we need to build our trust and working relationship with each other and learn more about this issue before we deal with it in detail." The consensus or agreement process is put on hold. Rather, the group invests its time in learning and educating themselves more about the program details and the traditional and cultural norms of the tribal/family environment relating to housing. This is accomplished through presentations, experiential learning, experimentation (trying something on a temporary basis), field trips, and/or listening to outside opinions (both tribal and non-tribal). The benefit is that "group maturity" develops and grows as learning takes place. Eventually, the group will be more efficient in working together, trust will be built, understanding will be enhanced, and the group will arrive at a collaborative conclusion that all will be pleased with.

In our rush to achieve results, these two concepts (group maturity and the holding environment) will slow us down yet produce productive work. As mentioned previously, they exemplify the concept of "Going slow to go fast!" which brings us to our next topic, pacing work.

Pacing work.

Pacing work is another matter. Pacing work means how fast you desire to move on an issue or program. It asks the question, "Do I need an answer tomorrow, next week, next month, or next year?" Put yourself in a tribal leader's shoes. You and your ancestor's past experiences with governments and businesses have created a mindset of mistrust and suspicion. Or, the issue or program may not be a priority for the tribe at this time. Therefore, pushing an agenda too hard or too fast may arouse caution and suspicion from tribal leaders based on their past experiences or their priorities. You simply become labeled as pushy and tribal officials become hesitant to work with you.

Remember I asked earlier how do you eat an elephant? Right—one bite at a time. The same philosophy applies to working with many tribes—you must break down your large issues into manageable chunks. As an example, in our collaboration on the Sacred Circle we had huge issues to address. One in particular was how large an area we needed to manage and protect in order to maintain the integrity of the site. This issue could involve hundreds to thousands of acres. The problem was our relationship (government and tribal) had not matured enough to even talk about this issue in a civil manner. Suspicion and mistrust (on all sides) remained the dominant emotion and was often verbalized. So to start, we chose a non-threatening smaller issue—trash cans. Should we have trash cans at the site or away from the site? We all agreed—away from the site! One small success, but one giant leap, and after many years of building on other small successes, we eventually built the trust necessary to address the larger, more complex issue of how many acres were needed to protect the Sacred Circle. We paced our work based on group maturity and what we could mutually agree on at the time. In addition, small successes kept people at the table and maintained interest.

So, finally, the lesson when working with tribes is this: you can generally only go as fast as the relationship allows. With little or no effective relationship, progress on an issue will be slow, but as relationships blossom, progress will accelerate. This is what pacing work is all about. Again, the lesson is to build the relationship first and take care of business second.

Maintaining harmony in the dialogue.
Tribal leaders have means of self-facilitating meetings where typically everyone gets a chance to speak regardless of status. However, that does not mean everyone will stay around and listen. As a result, meetings may seem fragmented, off-beat, and even chaotic. Your role is to apply a "light-handed" facilitation approach. You might feel you are in a "Catch 22" because of what you might have learned about conventional meeting facilitation with regard to managing

time, an agenda, or someone speaking too long. But let me assure you that exercising a heavy-handed facilitation approach, such as cutting an elder off when he or she is speaking for what seems a long time, will generate problems and violate cultural rules of respect. So, what do you do? Find natural breaks in the dialogue and use those to move from one discussion point to another. Yes, it is difficult, but by truly listening and tracking the dialogue you can identify those natural breaks. Many times, long unscheduled dialogue can be avoided by opening a meeting and allowing participants to introduce themselves and share their thoughts on a particular point or issue.

If you become lost in the dialogue, again find a natural break and pose a question, such as, "Do we need a break or a caucus?" or "How do we want to approach the issues to move ahead?" or "I've lost track, where do we want to go from here?" Keep in mind that your ability to maintain order in a meeting is directly proportional to your level of patience. If you choose to intervene you take the risk of further exacerbating the situation. So, again, use a light-handed approach and exercise a lot of patience.

Make sense out of chaos.

I'm sure you have attended meetings and listened to effective leaders who have the skill to summarize a group's dialogue and make sense out of a chaotic discussion. They sort through the dialogue and single out the pertinent points, areas of disagreement, positions and interests, and areas of common ground.

When working with tribes, this is a critical skill because much of the dialogue can depart from the subject matter on the table to other issues. I've seen meetings between a government agency and tribe where the subject was roads and highways, but one tribal leader wanted to talk about alcoholism on the reservation and how it was destroying their people. That is where the discussion went for half an hour. The worst offense you, as a government or business leader, can commit is to interrupt the individual and try to force the discussion back to where you want it. This is particularly true when you are addressing an emotional subject such as tribal rights, sovereignty, or cultural topics. Discussions often have a tendency to depart from what is on the table. You might hear about the historical abuses to Indian people, discrimination, how land was taken away, how non-Indian people cannot be trusted, broken treaties, something someone else did, and on and on. It is likely that many tribal members may contribute to these departures. An effective leader will take advantage of the situation, listen, learn, and incorporate the subject in his or her summary. There are lessons and messages in the dialogue you need to absorb and summarize at the end of the discussion. This is sorting though chaos.

With all due respect, this is easier said than done, especially when you might be the target of some unpleasant venting. However, your ability to make sense out of the chaos is an affirmative signal that you really listened, and will thus advance the trust-building process. Specific approaches for addressing these situations are discussed at length in chapter 5, "Communication Protocols." As pointed out previously, "Think with your head and listen with your heart."

Manage conflict.

I have seen conflict between government and business leaders and Indian tribes range from simple verbal disagreements to physical altercations. I remember a time in discussions on the Sacred Circle where a verbal disagreement between two individuals escalated into a situation where both had their hands around each other's throat.

Emotions, based on strong values, can easily lead to a situation that manifests into actions—verbal or physical. This is conflict! Particularly with tribal issues, emotions can often run high due to mistrust, poor relations, local historical circumstances, or past actions. Fortunately, in most cases, a leader is only required to step in and address verbal disagreements, as they rarely escalate into physical altercations.

We often perceive conflict as a negative but, effectively managed, it can result in stronger relationships, especially for the leader who has built a high level of respect because of his or her ability to pull opposing parties together to achieve positive results.

Effective leaders continuously monitor the levels of distress, identify issues that may trigger conflict, diagnose conflicts (value or interest driven), and break down conflicts into workable issues. Most importantly, effective leaders remain impartial, fair, objective, and unbiased. You, as a leader, will attain more respect when you are perceived as having these attributes. The consequences of being perceived as not possessing these attributes will result in a continuous stalemate and continuing conflict.

Effective leaders also know when, and when not, to intervene and how to manage conflicts between groups and individuals. They garner respect by remaining neutral, clarifying issues, facilitating venting, finding common ground, placing issues in a "holding environment," and sometimes assisting groups and individuals to simply agree to disagree.

Conflicts are inevitable in meetings. A number of interpersonal conflicts can arise when meeting with tribes. They include:

- Indian to Indian
- Indian to non-Indian
- Non-Indian to non-Indian

Here are some appropriate responses for each type of conflict:

Type of Conflict	What You Can't Do	What You Can Do
Indian to Indian or Tribe to Tribe	<ul><li>Intervene</li><li>Take sides</li><li>Take control</li></ul>	<ul><li>Nothing, wait it out! Do not become involved in disputes between tribal individuals or tribes</li></ul>
Indian vs. Non-Indian	<ul><li>Take sides–you must remain neutral</li><li>Lecture the parties</li></ul>	<ul><li>Call for a break</li><li>Council the non-Indian parties that are involved in the dispute</li><li>Protect the progress of the group</li></ul>
Non-Indian vs. Non-Indian	<ul><li>Take sides–you must remain neutral</li><li>Lecture the parties</li></ul>	<ul><li>Call for a break</li><li>Council parties involved in the dispute</li><li>Protect group progress</li></ul>

The bottom line on conflict is not to get drawn into the conflict yourself, but serve as a neutral moderator. Always address conflicts at a sidebar or caucus. Tribal leaders have ways to address conflicts between themselves, so never put yourself personally in the middle of such a conflict. Again, there may be cultural implications you do not understand. The best approach is to allow the time necessary for the dispute to resolve itself through a break or time to caucus.

The value of caucusing.

A caucus is a side-bar conversation to discuss issues, decisions, positions, and interests in a private setting outside of a meeting. It is beneficial to both the tribe and your organization to allow time for a caucus when a meeting might become chaotic, heated, or ambling in no particular direction. Caucusing is also beneficial to you and your organization and allows you time to regroup, reorganize, and gather thoughts and ideas.

Caucusing can be considered a traditional American Indian protocol used by tribes in negotiating treaties. In the past, oftentimes tribal leaders would meet with government officials in treaty negotiations and adjourn to consult with elders, spiritual leaders, and others not present at the meeting. Or, at other times, there might be multiple tribes that need to meet independently from government officials to discuss treaty options.

When calling a caucus you simply tell the meeting participants that it might be beneficial for all to take a break and discuss the issue for thirty minutes or so and then reconvene. If a tribe calls for a break to discuss issues in private, they are requesting a caucus and you should honor the request. Regardless of who calls for a caucus or the reason for a caucus, the benefits far outweigh the time invested.

Remembering what's happened—plowing old ground.

As new participants emerge in the process and dialogue, a lot of old ground can get re-plowed and sometimes old conflicts resurface. It's inevitable that new participants will come on board midway into the process. These people have a desire to provide input and fresh thoughts, yet they may not know what has already happened. Therefore, you must keep a mental diary of decisions, agreements, and issues that have been addressed. Your objective is to keep the group moving forward and not regress into an environment of conflict, especially over old issues you have resolved. If the new participant begins with a speech that covers ground you have previously addressed, let them finish; remember we don't interrupt. Acknowledge the points the person made, the progress you have made in the past, and move on. Do not ignore the person or cut them off saying, "We've already covered this and we need to move forward." Remember, this person may be a tribal leader from another tribe that has not been engaged in your past discussions and needs to express his or her tribal concerns and positions. Use the same principles of showing respect you would to those that have been engaged throughout the process.

Running out of time in a meeting.

Many times, because of the apparent chaotic nature of some meetings, you may need to get a topic on the table and addressed before adjourning. As I've said many times, never interrupt a discussion to force your topic or issue, but rather find a natural break and pose a question, such as, "We have been discussing many important issues, and here is one topic I must get on the table before we adjourn. It is critical to all of us because ..." Another strategy to use is during a break approach the tribal leader and articulate the need to get your topic or issue on the table. You may learn that the issue has been simply overlooked, the issue is not ripe, or the right people may not be present. In any event, as discussed previously, don't be pushy, but finesse the discussion so the issue falls naturally on the table and it will be more readily received. If the time is not ripe for a particular issue to be addressed you may have to do more homework, reframe the issue, or approach the tribe(s) individually to determine if the issue is even ripe for consideration.

Political intervention.

One significant element I have learned over time is that tribal representatives tend to have political contacts at higher levels than we enjoy in government or business. A number of years ago I was in Washington, D.C., and had some time to attend a senate committee meeting on the Sand Creek Massacre site in Colorado. As I entered the committee meeting room I ran into a Cheyenne friend of mine. He told me he was testifying before the Senate committee considering the bill and would be visiting the White House and the President the next day. This is not an uncommon occurrence and one should be aware of these high-level political contacts. It is possible that tribal leaders might seek relief from these higher level political contacts if they cannot find satisfactory results with your efforts, particularly if the subject is sensitive.

You will need to think strategically on how you will address political inquiries, whether from a Congressman, Department Secretary, or Governor. First, think about who a tribal individual, government, or faction might approach politically to help address your issue. In other words, keep your ears open. Develop relationships with those politicians and keep them informed of the group's progress. Frequent updates, with a chronology to their staff, are a great approach. Your objective is to ensure political figures are not surprised, so keep them informed. An ideal approach is to use briefings and bring the tribal representative with you to make a joint presentation. This shows that you are both engaged in the process, that you value their contributions, and you are using a collaborative approach.

Managing the media.

Particularly in government, meetings are often open to the public, and as a result journalists from newspapers or television stations may have a desire to attend. This is predominantly true when the issue is sensitive and creates a lot of debate and dialogue. One thing I have learned is that many journalists love to watch an issue being debated and spin it into a headline. Although I have worked with a few journalists who were truly objective, this is the exception rather than the rule. What's unfortunate is that I have seen many journalists pit one side against another in their stories when in actuality high-quality dialogue was taking place. A typical approach is that the journalist will listen to the dialogue and then separately interview the parties involved. When the article is published you wonder if you were at the same meeting!

So how do you avoid being the big news, and what approaches can you use to manage the media? First, do not get sucked into a debate by a journalist using inflammatory questions like, "The tribe said in the meeting that your organization hasn't been responsive to their needs in the past. How would you respond to that?" When in fact you might have been constructively discussing with the tribe how your organization can be more responsive to their needs in the future. And, a tactic that journalists often use is to interview a tribal representative, then you, and then the tribal representative again. When the article is published you are the one cast in a negative light. It goes like this:

Journalist to tribal representative: "How has the agency failed in the past to be responsive to your tribal needs?"

Response from tribal representative: "Well, in the past we were not consulted on our specific needs and the program was implemented anyway. It's obvious that the agency ignored cultural protocol and created a program we cannot live with."

Journalist to you: "The tribal representative said you are ignoring their needs. How would you respond to that?"

Your response: "Well, we have our regulations and rules to follow and sent the tribe a letter outlining the program. Since we didn't hear from them we assumed, erroneously, they were not interested or had no comments on the program. We have learned, since that time that we need to be more proactive when programs are proposed and meet with the tribes directly to hear their concerns and issues."

Journalist back to tribal representative: "The agency official said you didn't respond to their requests for comments and they assumed you weren't interested in their program. How would you respond to that?"

Response from tribal representative: "How would they know? They never consulted with us. The government has a responsibility to consult on these programs and we didn't receive any letters. This is just a continuation of the past, breaking treaties and agreements and not following through with their (government's) responsibilities to tribes!"

You can see how important information is left out of the questions between each entity to create a sensational story about your agency being unresponsive to tribal needs. Now, here's how the headline will read, "TRIBES ACCUSE AGENCY OF IGNORING NEEDS." And furthermore, the article will portray you in a negative light when in fact your intentions were honorable, trying to amend past errors in failing to properly consult with the tribe. I assure you also that the last line in the article will be a quote from the tribal representative stating, "This is just a continuation of the past, breaking treaties and agreements and not following through with their (government's) responsibilities to tribes!" Again, guess who looks bad in the entire article—you!

What's most unfortunate in this entire scenario is that you began your discussions with the tribe in a positive light and the tribe was very appreciative of your efforts. The journalist put the entire scenario in a negative light just to make a good headline for him or her and sell newspapers.

Again, don't fall for this tactic by journalists. Instead, focus on the progress of the group and hold the moral high ground. Use responses like, "We are trying to do what is right by meeting with the tribe to build a positive relationship for the future," or "Our most important accomplishment is we are able to sit down and have positive discussions with the tribe on these important issues," or "We are having some serious dialogue and making progress in a positive way." These are true statements and focus on the positive intentions you are pursuing with the tribe.

In order to avoid these situations, I highly recommended that you entertain discussions with the tribe on media involvement and discuss how you and the tribe will respond to a journalist's inquiry. Yes, tribal officials have the right to talk about the lack of proper consultation in the past, but they also need to recognize your positive and honorable efforts for the future. The key is to be able to weather intervention by a journalist in light of the positive progress you are making. The trust and relationship you have with a tribe will determine how this plays out.

I would also suggest developing a relationship with the reporters who are covering your "beat." Those who know the background of your project, and you personally, hopefully, will have a more objective approach than those who are out to merely get a by-line.

Assigning work between meetings.

In our contemporary business environment it is not uncommon to "staff out" work, in other words, assign work to participants to be completed outside the meeting environment. The purpose is to address unanswered questions, formulate options, or conduct research. When working with tribes they may or may not have the resources to conduct work outside your meeting environment. Particularly if multiple tribes are present, the option of staffing out work could be precluded due to travel constraints, time, workloads, or lack of staffing resources. Keep in mind that sometimes it is best for the entire group to take the time to work on an issue, rather than one entity, as work that is staffed out has a tendency to reflect that organization's interests or positions.

Once you have developed trust and an effective working relationship and have proven your objectivity, tribes will most likely empower you to conduct staff work outside the meeting environment. You should consider this an honor as you have arrived at a point that the tribe(s) has the trust and confidence that you will be objective and representative of their interests. The value of your listening skills pays off at this point, as tribal leaders are confident their interests are represented in all work conducted outside the meeting environment.

Recording meetings.

I have been to tribal council meetings that were recorded on local television much like city-council meetings. I have been to meetings where a tape recorder was set up in the center of the room. And I have been to meetings where someone merely recorded the discussion by taking notes. The reason tribes may want to record meetings electronically, if they choose to, is to capture your dialogue. It goes back, again, to history where government and business officials and leaders made statements or commitments that were not carried through. The mistrust that continues today puts tribes in a position to ensure they heard you correctly and that you follow through with your commitments.

Assigning someone to take notes is very appropriate and should be clearly articulated to all participants at the meeting. I do not recommend that you record the meeting on an electronic device, as much of the dialogue may not apply to the pertinent point of discussion, and electronic devices may hinder and be intimidating to those that wish to speak freely. However, if a tribe chooses to electronically record your meeting then I would honor that request, but not rely on those recordings as your record of the meeting.

The importance of meeting notes are threefold: 1) to address important points made by tribal leaders, 2) to address important points made by you, and, 3) to document decisions. First, documenting important points made by tribal representatives is vital. I previously discussed how tribal leaders need to see their "fingerprints" on a decision. Only by documenting their comments can we ensure they see this happening whether verbally or in writing. If a decision is documented in writing and you addressed the tribal leader's concerns, you are showing respect. This demonstrates that you really listened and attended to his or her comments.

Second, you and your organization may require a record of the dialogue in meetings with tribal leaders. I believe that notes are an important component of your business to ensure the dialogue is accurately recorded. It is beneficial to review your organization's notes with all participants at the end of the meeting to ensure everyone agrees on their accuracy.

And finally, decisions need to be documented exactly as you expressed them in order to facilitate understanding by all present. Remember that your perception of what you are saying as a speaker and that of any receiver can be filtered and become distorted. It is incumbent upon you to ensure the decision is documented exactly as you intend it and that the participants understand it that way.

As you personally exercise your leadership role, you should not, and cannot, be occupied by taking notes. Yes, brief notes taken by you of salient points you want to address or recall are important. These brief notes help you recall vital points when summarizing a discussion and honor that person by reiterating what they put forward. Again, this shows respect and demonstrates that you really listened. Never forget, your predominant role should be to listen and focus your attention on the speaker.

Wrap-up

My hope is that these thoughts and tips will assist you in orchestrating a successful collaborative environment with tribal leaders. They are ideas and concepts we often benignly forget or take for granted when conducting business with American Indian tribes. However, we must always remember that we may be operating in a unique business environment in conjunction with unique cultural dynamics. Taking the time to appreciate cultural differences, thinking beforehand about your approach, and deciding how you will conduct business is paramount to being successful in Indian country. If I have helped motivate you to at least consider these thoughts, ideas and concepts in the business environment, then I have been successful. That is my hope, because the benefits go beyond just you and the tribe. You set an example for others and give them confidence that anyone can be successful in Indian country by respecting and implementing these few simple concepts.

Epilogue

Working in Indian country can be one of the most humbling, and even at times frustrating experiences, but I have also found that it is some of the most rewarding work I've ever done. I have learned how to negotiate across very wide cultural chasms, and I have made many good friends along the way. Most importantly, as many people who attend my workshops will tell you, these principles taught to us by tribal elders and leaders from around the country transcend Indian country. My workshop participants tell me that they find the principles I teach them are applicable when working with individuals in their own organization, with other organizations, and even with their families.

I began this book with the idea that in order to work successfully in Indian country, you have to experience a paradigm shift and learn to lead from your heart—not from your head. In its simplicity, leading from your heart means that you learn to first care for the people you're working with. It means that you learn to trust them, and they, you. It means that you work to find a common ground of respect from which to move forward. Both should become common qualities we exhibit to all individuals we work and live with on a routine basis.

In my long years of association with American Indian tribes, I never cease to be amazed at how deep those two principles—trust and respect—run in their cultures. Unfortunately they worked against them in many cases when outsiders began moving through and occupying their traditional lands. Indian people were welcoming, tolerant, provided assistance, and in many cases, were responsible for those outsiders' survival. But, as we all know, trust and respect were not reciprocated, and many times the trust American Indians offered was taken advantage of, often forcing tribes into a defensive or offensive posture that continues today.

That trust was broken in the past is a fact. But it is to the future that we all must look. Only by rebuilding trust between governments and businesses and tribes can relationships between us become restored. I firmly believe it can be accomplished by the trust and relationship-building principles presented in this book.

But why take my word for it? Solo Greene, Nez Perce Tribe, describes the link between trust and relationship building and how it can become contagious:

> *If you have that relationship ... and if you have trust, and if you have loyalty and you build off that honesty and those kinds of things ... you're going to expand. It's going to be a reflection, not only of you; it's also going to be a reflection on the Nez Perce Tribe. If we can do it other people are going to see that and other people are going to want that. I really believe that's what it's all about—being a reflection.*[105]

Your success, your ability to work in Indian country will depend, of course, on your willingness and ability to put into practice the lessons I have learned from tribal leaders and that I have now presented to you. And, it is vital to remember that these practices are not mine, but those articulated by tribal leaders themselves. I merely have had the honor of sharing them from the perspective of someone in your shoes. It is now up to you to take them forward. I hope that you will be able to contribute to the expansion of trust and loyalty Solo talks about, for the reflection of which he speaks is a reflection of all of us.

---

[105] Greene, Solo. 2007. Interview by author. Video recording. May 22. Nez Perce Tribal Office, Lapwai, Idaho.

About the Author

Larry Keown received his undergraduate degree from the University of Montana and graduate degree from the University of Idaho in Forestry and Natural Resources Management. He began his career with the USDA Forest Service in 1975 holding numerous technical, management, and leadership positions. In 1998, Larry founded LDK Associates, LLC, a company dedicated to providing educational and consulting services to government and businesses in the area of tribal-government-corporate relations. His clients have included federal, state and local governments, businesses, chambers of commerce, weed and pest districts, economic development districts, school districts, and American Indian tribes.

Larry has extensive experience assisting government agencies and corporate entities that desire or are required to collaborate and consult with tribes on a diversity of issues, such as sacred sites, economic development, energy development, interpretative exhibits, telecommunications, transportation, education, leadership, and trust and relationship building. In addition, he has assisted tribes in economic development, grant preparation, working with government and corporate entities, sacred sites, tribal community assessments, and more. Larry began offering workshops on tribal relations in 2000, training thousands of government and corporate leaders and managers. After seven years of collecting vital information on tribal relations he completed his first book *Working in Indian Country*. He can be reached at www.WorkinginIndianCountry.com.